C. Daniel Prather, Ph.D., A.A.E., CAM

Airport Management

Aviation Supplies & Academics, Inc.
Newcastle, Washington

Airport Management
by C. Daniel Prather, Ph.D., A.A.E., CAM

Aviation Supplies & Academics, Inc.
7005 132nd Place SE
Newcastle, Washington 98059-3153
asa@asa2fly.com | www.asa2fly.com

See the ASA website at **www.asa2fly.com/reader/airptmgt** for the "Reader Resources" page containing additional information and updates relating to this book.

Resources for instructors using this textbook in their courses are available at **www.asa2fly.com/instructor/airptmgt**.

ASA-AIRPT-MGT
ISBN 978-1-61954-209-9

Printed in the United States of America
2019 2018 2017 2016 2015 9 8 7 6 5 4 3 2 1

Photography © C. Daniel Prather unless otherwise noted.
Cover photos: Bottom image courtesy of Louisville Regional Airport Authority.
Top image ©iStock.com/jxfzsy.
The airport photo used as a background for the chapter beginnings is courtesy of Hillsborough County Aviation Authority.

Library of Congress Cataloging-in-Publication Data:
Prather, C. Daniel
Airport management / by C. Daniel Prather, Ph.D., A.A.E., CAM.
pages cm
Includes index.
"ASA-AIRPT-MGT."
ISBN 978-1-61954-209-9 (trade paper) – ISBN 1-61954-209-9 (trade paper)
1. Airports–United States—Management–Textbooks. I. Title.
TL725.3.M2P73 2015
387.7'36068–dc23

2014041887

Contents

Foreword xi
Acknowledgments xiv
About the Author xvi
Introduction 1

CHAPTER 1 **Historical Overview** **6**
- Introduction 9
- The Beginning of an Industry 10
- World War I 14
- Post World War I 15
- World War II 19
- Post World War II 20
- Pre-Deregulation 21
- Deregulation 24
- Post-Deregulation 24
- 9/11 33
- Post 9/11 33
- Contemporary and Future Period 40
- Concluding Thoughts 41
- Chapter Summary 42
- Review Questions 45
- Scenarios 46
- References and Resources for Further Study 46

CHAPTER 2 **Structure of Airports** **50**
- Introduction 53
- Categories of Airports 53
- Ownership of Airports 63
- Organizational Structure 75
- Major Airport Departments 78
- Airport Training Programs 89
- Career Advancement 90
- Concluding Thoughts 92
- Chapter Summary 93
- Review Questions 94
- Scenarios 95
- References and Resources for Further Study 96

CHAPTER 3 **Air Traffic, Capacity, and Delay** 98

Introduction 101
ATC System Overview 101
Signage and Markings 121
Radio Communications 130
Federal Contract Tower Program 134
NextGen 135
Airfield Capacity 137
Airfield Delay 143
Demand Management 145
Concluding Thoughts 149
Chapter Summary 149
Review Questions 151
Scenarios 152
References and Resources for Further Study 153

CHAPTER 4 **Planning** 154

Introduction 157
NPIAS 157
Regional Aviation System Plans 159
State Aviation System Plans 159
Metropolitan Aviation System Plans 160
Airport Master Plans and Airport Layout Plans 161
Strategic Plans 171
Business Plans 175
Aviation Activity Forecasts 176
Concluding Thoughts 182
Chapter Summary 183
Review Questions 185
Scenarios 186
References and Resources for Further Study 187

CHAPTER 5 **Design and Construction** 188

Introduction 191
Construction Standards 191
Design Standards 200
Airspace and Approach Standards 221
Selection Process 226
International Practice 229
Concluding Thoughts 229
Chapter Summary 230
Review Questions 233
Scenarios 234
References and Resources for Further Study 235

CHAPTER 6 **Environmental** **236**
Environmental Regulations 239
Environmental Management System 239
Compliance and Enforcement 240
Impacts 241
Noise 243
Compatible Land Use 251
Zoning 252
Easements 253
Water Quality 254
Air Quality 259
Hazardous Waste 261
Sustainable Environmental Stewardship 265
Concluding Thoughts 268
Chapter Summary 268
Review Questions 271
Scenarios 272
References and Resources for Further Study 273

CHAPTER 7 **Operations** **274**
Introduction 277
Title 14 CFR Part 139 277
Airport Communications 306
Wildlife Hazard Management 308
New Generation Aircraft 312
Concluding Thoughts 314
Chapter Summary 314
Review Questions 317
Scenarios 318
References and Resources for Further Study 319

CHAPTER 8 **Maintenance** **320**
Introduction 323
Inspections 323
Preventive Maintenance 323
Maintenance Equipment 324
Recordkeeping 324
Airside Maintenance 325
Landside Maintenance 337
Concluding Thoughts 340
Chapter Summary 341
Review Questions 343
Scenarios 344
References and Resources for Further Study 345

CHAPTER 9 **Safety and Security** 346

Safety 349
Security 367
Concluding Thoughts 383
Chapter Summary 384
Review Questions 387
Scenarios 388
References and Resources for Further Study 389

CHAPTER 10 **Marketing** 390

Purpose of Marketing 393
Marketing Basics 394
Developing a Marketing Plan 395
Variables 408
Implementing the Plan 410
Characteristics of an Effective Marketing Plan 411
Air Service Development 412
Concluding Thoughts 417
Chapter Summary 417
Review Questions 419
Scenarios 420
References and Resources for Further Study 421

CHAPTER 11 **Governmental, Legal, and Public Relations** 422

Governmental Relations 425
Industry Relations 444
Public Relations 448
Concluding Thoughts 452
Chapter Summary 453
Review Questions 457
Scenarios 458
References and Resources for Further Study 459

CHAPTER 12 **Properties, Contracts, and Commercial Development** 460

Agreements 463
Interacting with Tenants 478
Commercial Development 479
Disadvantaged Business Enterprise 483
Information Systems 483
Concluding Thoughts 484
Chapter Summary 485
Review Questions 487
Scenarios 488
References and Resources for Further Study 489

CHAPTER 13 **Financial Management** 490
Budgeting Overview 493
Budget Development 493
Revenues 498
Expenses 508
Financial Statements 509
Establishing Fees, Rates and Charges 524
Risk Management 526
Concluding Thoughts 528
Chapter Summary 529
Review Questions 531
Scenarios 532
References and Resources for Further Study 533

CHAPTER 14 **Funding and Financial Impacts** 534
Introduction 537
Sources of Capital Development Funding 537
Economic Impact of Airports 549
Impacts of Airline Bankruptcies on Airports 549
Performance Management and Benchmarking 551
Concluding Thoughts 553
Chapter Summary 553
Review Questions 555
Scenarios 556
References and Resources for Further Study 557

CHAPTER 15 **Future Challenges and Opportunities** 558
Introduction 561
Airline Bankruptcies and Mergers 561
New Large Aircraft 562
Capital Development Funding 563
Unfunded Federal Mandates 564
Passenger Leakage 565
Customer Service 566
Sustainability Initiatives 567
Airside Congestion 568
Unmanned Aircraft Systems 569
Concluding Thoughts 570
Chapter Summary 571
Review Questions 572
Scenarios 573
References and Resources for Further Study 573

APPENDIX A **Case Studies** 574
APPENDIX B **Grant Assurances** 602
Index 625

Foreword

I consider it an honor to be asked to write the foreword for *Airport Management*. This textbook's author, Dr. C. Daniel Prather, A.A.E., CAM, has been my mentor since I entered this dynamic and fast-paced community of airports. Dr. Prather has extensive airport experience from his tenure as an Assistant Director of Operations at Tampa International Airport, and is now a key player in education program development and in the training of hundreds of airport professionals nationally and internationally. He is an accredited member of the American Association of Airport Executives (AAAE), and recently developed and implemented the first aviation program at California Baptist University in Riverside, California.

Dr. Prather's objective in all of his educational development and presentations is to provide airport professionals with practical, industry-focused information. You will find this as the baseline throughout all chapters of *Airport Management*. This textbook covers the exciting areas that other airport professionals and I are involved with on a daily basis, including airport planning, design, and construction; air traffic and capacity delay; environmental issues; regulatory compliance; airport operations and maintenance; safety and security; and much more. The chapter scenarios and case studies are designed to allow readers to apply knowledge gained in the text to solving real-world airport challenges.

Some of the more specific topics on the minds of airport professionals include the integration of the National Incident Management System (NIMS), Incident Command System (ICS) into airport emergency plans, and the training and exercise of personnel for use during incidents and events; operational safety on airports during construction, as most airports are always in some phase of construction; addressing FAA Runway Safety Action Team (RSAT) action items; implementation of safety management systems (SMS); measurable metrics; and airport sustainability, just to name a few.

I personally began my aviation career in the United States Marine Corps as an avionics technician on CH-46E Sea Knight helicopters, and quickly progressed through the enlisted ranks as well as becoming a qualified Aerial Observer/Door Gunner, Quality Assurance Inspector, and working on other helicopter and fixed-wing aircraft platforms. While traveling and serving in the United States Marine Corps, I was fortunate to have the opportunity to complete my undergraduate degree from Southern Illinois University, Carbondale, where I got my first taste of aviation industry business management from an academic perspective.

At the end of my second enlistment in the United States Marine Corps, my family and I decided to take the leap from the military and I began my civilian aviation career as an Airport Operations—Communications Center Dispatcher at Tampa International Airport in Tampa, Florida. This position was ideal for someone new to an airport. I was able to experience the full spectrum of daily operations at an airport, ranging from response coordination to small incidents such as broken plumbing pipes in a terminal, to higher-level incidents such as security breaches, people jumping from parking structures to commit suicide, and aircraft alerts. Since that first position as a dispatcher, I have again been very fortunate to hold several positions within airport operations departments at Tampa International Airport (TPA), Burbank Bob Hope Airport (BUR), and now at Los Angeles International Airport (LAX). I have held positions ranging from my initial position as a dispatcher, to Airside and Landside Operations Manager, to my current position as a Chief of Operations I at LAX.

My current job responsibilities include working some shifts as the Airport Duty Manager, and serving as the LAX Department Operations Center (DOC) Director during large-scale events. In this position, I was on duty for the Asiana Airlines Flight 214 accident at San Francisco Airport in which we received multiple flight diversions; utility disruptions affecting multiple terminals and other facilities; and one of the most challenging incidents our airport has experienced in the past ten years involving an active shooter at Terminal 3 in which three of our nine terminals were evacuated, and Terminal 3 remained closed for 28 hours.

If this is your first exposure to the airport community, airports are often referred to as "cities within cities." Airports have several components, regulations, and political pressures similar to a city. Depending on the size of an airport, it may have components similar to a city, such as a municipal fire station or its own fire department; a police, security, and/or public safety department; emergency medical personnel; administrative and financial services; and a maintenance department similar to city public works. Unlike a city, however, hazards at airports can pose unique challenges since the operation of aircraft traffic, vehicle traffic, pedestrian traffic, baggage, and cargo throughput must continue to flow, or be restored promptly, to sustain commerce and e-commerce.

In addition, airports have multiple federal agencies, private entities, contractors, and airport personnel that all operate within the same few acres of airport property to provide safe and secure services to the traveling public. In addition to these departments and divisions that are similar to those of a city, airports will also have an airport operations department. The personnel in this department conduct inspections of the airside, terminals, and landside to identify and report any irregular conditions that impact operations, and coordinate the response by emergency services, maintenance personnel, and others to resolve these issues. Airport operations, along with public safety, agency, and stakeholder partners, also responds to emergencies such as aircraft accidents, security breaches, structure fires, hazmat spills, property damage incidents, utility disruptions, etc., with the primary objective of coordinating the flow of the airport's operation around the incident, and then becoming the incident commander during the recovery phase of an accident or incident.

The best phrases, words, and guidance that I have learned from fellow employees and leaders in airports include: exciting, high consequence, and political; operations revolve around local, state, and federal regulatory compliance; airports must partner, train, and build solid relationships with stakeholders and mutual aid responders to ensure efficient response plans and procedures have a common operational picture; the only thing constant at an airport is change; your customers include the traveling public, airport tenants, contractors, and your own airport employees; and the most critical asset at an airport are the employees that keep it operating, so keep them involved.

In conclusion, you will find this textbook and the aviation professionals you meet to be valuable resources as you progress through your career. Anyone who intends to work and succeed in this exciting and challenging field must master a thorough understanding of the rules, regulations, and standards that affect airports, and be able to apply critical thinking skills to continue to progress. *Airport Management* will prove to be an excellent resource for current and future airport professionals.

Richard N. Steele, C. M., MCA
Chief of Operations I
Los Angeles International Airport (LAX)
Los Angeles World Airports (LAWA)

Acknowledgments

The development of this book would not have been possible without the significant level of support provided by colleagues in the industry. My experiences have been enriched because of others. I would like to thank Mr. Robert Burr, Mr. Grant Young, and Mr. Ed Cooley for believing in me. These gentlemen provided me with ten outstanding years of experience in airport operations at Tampa International Airport (TPA). Ms. Marilyn Gauthier, a coworker at TPA, was a friend from day one and continues to be to this day. I would also like to thank collegiate aviation faculty everywhere who are members of the University Aviation Association (UAA), as well as Mrs. Carolyn Williamson, former UAA Executive Director. Collegiate aviation faculty are a small group of devoted professionals, and I have learned from and with them extensively over the years. These professionals have supported me in many ways as I transitioned from the airport industry to being a faculty member at a collegiate aviation program. I especially benefitted from the annual UAA Fall Education Conferences and the *Collegiate Aviation Review*. I would like to particularly thank Dr. Julie Speakes for providing me an opportunity to teach online as an adjunct faculty member in the Delta State University Master of Commercial Aviation degree program and being a close friend. Dr. Alexander Wells graciously provided me the first opportunity to author a book, by asking me to revise his *General Aviation Marketing and Management* textbook. Mr. Dave Boelio and Ms. Nicole Sgueglia both encouraged me to write this *Airport Management* text, while Mr. Fred Boyns and Ms. Jackie Spanitz enthusiastically asked me to write this text for ASA.

I would like to thank Dr. Paul Craig for giving me my first position as a faculty member at Middle Tennessee State University. California Baptist University (CBU) President Dr. Ronald Ellis, former Provost Dr. Jonathan Parker, and College of Arts and Sciences Dean Dr. Gayne Anacker believed in me and trusted that I was the right person to develop the nation's newest collegiate aviation program at their fine institution. I am humbled by this opportunity and would like to express my heartfelt gratitude for their tremendous support. This has been by far the greatest professional challenge and thrill of my life. Mrs. Kim Roper and Mrs. Maria LeBlanc have been instrumental in my success at CBU, as have our wonderful team of faculty and flight instructors.

I would also like to thank the staff of the American Association of Airport Executives, specifically Mr. James Johnson, A.A.E. (now retired), Ms. Starla Bryant, Mr. Kevin Miller, C.M., ACE (now with the Boca Raton Airport Authority) and Mr. Scott Boeser, C.M., ACE for trusting me to revise the Airport Certified Employee (ACE)—Operations modules and subsequently train airport professionals across the country in Part 139. I would also like to thank

Mr. Jay Evans and Mrs. Sarah Wolf of the National Business Aviation Association for allowing me the opportunity to serve on the Professional Development Program (PDP) Review Committee and provide professional training to business aviation professionals nationwide. I would also like to thank Ms. Anne Nevel of the Helicopter Association International for allowing me the opportunity to provide professional training to helicopter aviation professionals nationwide.

My past and current students have provided me significant insight and allowed me the opportunity to improve my teaching abilities. I am proud of each and every one of you who have graduated and are now making significant contributions to the industry. Your success keeps me motivated.

I am indebted to the following individuals who have provided me the greatest direct support in the development of this text, through their research, photographs and case studies:

Mr. Jordan Biegler, A.A.E.
Mr. Lee Brown, C.M., ACE
Ms. Patricia Burke
Mr. Brett Fay, C.M.
Ms. Diana Fernandez, ACE
Ms. Robin Gardner, C.M., ACE
Mr. Peter Lubbers, ACE
Mr. Adam Lunn, C.M., ACE
Mr. Kevin Miller, C.M., ACE
Ms. Lacey Schimming
Ms. Amanda Snodgrass
Mr. Richard Steele, C.M.
Ms. Laura Walker

Additionally, I must recognize Mr. David Nicewinter (TPA) and Mr. John Padgett (Nashville International Airport), both of whom spent a number of hours with me allowing me to tour their respective airfields to obtain photos.

I would like to express my love and gratitude to my family, who supported me throughout this project. My wife, Grace, my daughter, Savannah, and my son, Layton, are the joys of my life and I would not be the man I am today if not for you guys. Thanks for being such an awesome family.

My dad, Mr. Louis Prather, and my mom, Dr. Barbara Corry, provided me the opportunity to take flying lessons with Mr. Langley Nelson at Hawkins Field in Jackson, Mississippi, while I was still in high school. These lessons fueled my passion for the aviation industry, which led me to Delta State University for a Bachelor of Commercial Aviation degree, Southern Illinois University for a Master of Public Administration degree, and ultimately to Tampa International Airport, which allowed me the experiences necessary to be able to write this textbook. Thanks Mom and Dad!

Finally, my Lord and Savior Jesus Christ daily provides me the strength and wisdom to accomplish and succeed to bring Him glory. My life verse is found in Philippians 4:13, "I can do all things through Christ who strengthens me." This book would not be possible without the breath He alone provides me.

About the Author

Serving as Assistant Director of Operations at Tampa International Airport (TPA) from 1998 to 2006, and Associate Professor of Aerospace at Middle Tennessee State University (MTSU) from 2006 to 2012, Dr. C. Daniel Prather, A.A.E., CAM, has been serving as professor and founding chair of the Department of Aviation Science at California Baptist University (CBU) since July 2012. In this position, Dr. Prather has been responsible for developing curriculum and recruiting students and faculty to the nation's newest collegiate aviation program.

Active with the University Aviation Association (UAA), the American Association of Airport Executives (AAAE), and the National Business Aviation Association (NBAA), Dr. Prather is an Accredited Airport Executive through AAAE, a Certified Aviation Manager through the NBAA, and an instrument-rated private pilot. He is also an active aviation industry consultant, often busy on projects with the Airport Cooperative Research Program (ACRP) of the Transportation Research Board (TRB). He holds a Doctor of Philosophy degree from the University of Nebraska at Lincoln, a Master of Public Administration degree from Southern Illinois University at Carbondale, and a Bachelor of Commercial Aviation degree from Delta State University.

In addition to this textbook, Dr. Prather is author of *General Aviation Marketing and Management: Operating, Marketing and Managing an FBO.* He is also the designated Airport Certified Employee (ACE) – Operations trainer for AAAE, and a leadership trainer for NBAA and the Helicopter Association International (HAI).

Not counting his one year as a flight coordinator intern at FedEx Express while in college, or flight training he undertook while in high school, Dr. Prather entered the aviation industry in 1996 and has never looked back. Visit Dr. Prather at www.dprather.com.

Introduction

As a collegiate aviation professor with ten years of airport managerial experience, I have always endeavored to teach courses in airport management from a practical, real-world perspective. However, the available textbooks on this topic are lacking in practical application. For me, this was not significant, because I could easily supplement the text I was using with real-world examples from my ten years of experience at Tampa International Airport. However, I began to meet other faculty members across the country who were being asked to teach courses in airport management, but had no professional airport industry experience from which to draw when teaching these courses. As a result, students in these courses learned less practical application than is necessary to be prepared for positions in the airport industry.

It was this realization that led me to begin writing this practical book on airport management. Of course, I soon learned that writing a book was a tremendous undertaking. Writing this book soon became a labor of love that required a significant investment. While working on the manuscript each day, I thought of all the current students who would become airport professionals in the future. This book has been written for your benefit. My goal has been to provide practical insight into the airport management business, and I trust this first edition will accomplish that.

The book has been designed to cover all areas of airports, to give a future airport manager a thorough understanding of the many aspects of the airport business. Key terms are identified at the beginning of each chapter and set in bold within the text. Features throughout the chapters shine the spotlight on specific airlines, airports, and other entities. Each chapter ends with scenarios designed to allow readers to apply knowledge gained from studying the chapter to solving real-world airport issues. The book also includes comprehensive case studies that allow readers to dive even deeper into the topics. Helpful review questions are provided for each chapter to prompt reflection and focus attention on the most important concepts. As these questions are meant to stimulate thought, discussion with your instructor, and classroom conversation, specific answers are not provided. Additional resources and information related to airport management can be found on the Reader Resources webpage for this book at www.asa2fly.com/reader/airptmgt.

Chapter 1, Historical Overview, presents a historical perspective of both the airport and airline industry, including important pieces of legislation that played an integral role in the safe development of both. The funding of airports is also discussed to allow the reader to better understand the role of federal funding in airport development. This chapter is important to the reader to gain a full understanding of the airport industry; we must understand from where we came to better prepare for future challenges.

Chapter 2, Structure of Airports, presents the organizational structure of airports, including types and the nature of ownership. It covers the major departments common at larger airports, as well as available airport training and career opportunities. This chapter is important in understanding the breadth of airports in this country, including how they are organized and owned.

Chapter 3, Air Traffic, Capacity and Delay, introduces the capacity and delay issue that airports must confront. In addition, it presents classes and types of airspace; NAVAIDs; airport lighting, signage, and markings; radio communications; the federal contract tower program; and NextGen. This chapter is full of information that introduces readers to the airspace in which airports are located, as well as the facilities and equipment in place to provide guidance to pilots and ground vehicle operators on the airfield.

Chapter 4, Planning, presents the need for airport planning, from the national level to the local airport-specific level. Airports are always planning for the future, and specific processes are in place to carry out this planning. To effectively plan, however, forecasting must take place, and this chapter covers the types and uses of forecasting in airport planning. This chapter is important for the reader in understanding the nature of and need for airport planning to prepare for future demand.

Chapter 5, Design and Construction, is a lengthy chapter that explains the nature of design and construction, from pre-bid to project completion. Airport construction projects can require many months or even years from start to finish, and there are specific procedures to be followed in designing a project, selecting a contractor, and maintaining safety on the airfield during construction. This is especially true of projects funded by the FAA. This chapter is important for the reader in understanding the design and construction side of airport management, which can oftentimes appear too technical for non-engineers. However, even the smallest airports have need for the occasional construction project, which makes the information in this chapter important to understand.

Chapter 6, Environmental, presents the many environmental impacts of an airport, and the regulations and requirements necessary to ensure environmental compliance. This chapter addresses noise, compatible land use, zoning, easements, water quality, air quality, and hazardous materials. For airports to be good neighbors and operate within regulations, it is imperative that airport management understand various environmental impacts and implement procedures to ensure environmental compliance (from both the airport and all tenants). Sustainable environmental stewardship is the ultimate goal, and this chapter is important in leading readers to that goal.

Chapter 7, Operations, focuses on the actual operation of the airport with a specific emphasis on airfield operations. Specifically, 14 CFR Part 139, Airport Certification, provides the foundation for this chapter. This is the regulation to which air carrier airports must comply to maintain an airport operating certificate and is, as a result, an important regulation to understand. Topics addressed in this chapter include snow and ice control, emergency response, aircraft rescue and firefighting, wildlife, and NOTAMs. This chapter is important for all future airport professionals because of the extreme importance placed on Part 139 compliance at air carrier airports. Lack of Part 139 compliance could result in the airport losing its operating certificate (in extreme cases), which would prohibit air carrier operations at that airport.

Chapter 8, Maintenance, is to some degree the flip side of Chapter 7. Operations personnel rely heavily on support of maintenance personnel to maintain the airfield in peak condition and within Part 139 requirements. Specifically, this chapter addresses airport pavements and airside and landside maintenance, including the use of contracted maintenance providers. This chapter is important for readers to understand because maintenance is integral to maintaining a safe and efficient airport.

Chapter 9, Safety and Security, addresses the need to ensure a safe and secure airport. This chapter addresses the protection of the public, employees and tenants; fire hazards; driving on the movement area; safety management systems; emergency preparedness; aircraft accidents and incidents; media relations; security; etc. This chapter is valuable for the reader in understanding the role of safety and security in maintaining a top-notch airport.

Chapter 10, Marketing, focuses on the importance of effectively marketing airports to ensure a competitive position to minimize the leakage of passengers and ensure positive publicity in the community. Topics include the basics of marketing; goals and objectives; SWOT analysis; promotional mix; marketing plans; and air service development. This chapter is important for the reader in understanding the role of marketing in airport management, which includes much more than securing additional air service or building a website.

Chapter 11, Governmental, Legal, and Public Relations, presents a valuable overview of the politically active climate in which airports always operate, and covers national, state, and local governmental relations. This chapter examines the manner in which FAA regulations and advisory circulars are revised, and describes Robert's Rules of Order to enable the reader to understand formal procedures typically in use during city council meetings, airport board meetings, and other formal meetings. Regulatory agencies and industry trade associations are also presented within the chapter. This chapter is important for the reader to gain an understanding of the political nature of airports and the concepts to be adhered to in managing an airport facility in this environment. The politically naïve airport manager (with no knowledge of the concepts presented in this chapter) will likely encounter more of a challenge on the job than is necessary.

Chapter 12, Properties, Contracts, and Commercial Development, is the first of the "money" chapters. Without an understanding of airport property, the nature of contracts, and the common ways in which to develop airport property to increase revenues (and create jobs), an airport will effectively lose money annually from lost opportunities in the form of commercial development of property. The chapter presents aeronautical lease agreements, airline operating agreements, land lease agreements, rate-making methodologies, concessionaires, FBOs, minimum standards, rules and regulations, MOUs/LOAs, self-fueling, etc. This chapter is important for the reader in understanding the myriad of ways in which airports earn revenue through various tenants, vendors, and others and the legal agreements that must be in place to define these relationships.

Chapter 13, Financial Management, is the second of the "money" chapters and presents operating and capital budgets, including budgeting techniques; financial ratios; fees, rates, and charges; and risk management. This chapter is important for the reader in understanding how to budget properly and manage the budget to track revenues and expenditures, as well as assets and liabilities. Although the chapter presents common financial management terminology, airports have unique budgeting requirements that airport managers must fully understand. Otherwise, the knowledge gained in chapter 12, even if applied properly, will be less successful.

Chapter 14, Funding and Financial Impacts, continues the "money" discussion with a focus on capital development funding, including matching funds, bonds, PFCs, internally generated funds, state and local sources, and AIP. This chapter covers grant assurances, which airports must comply with once federal funds are accepted, as well as methods to determine the economic impact of airports, the impact of airline bankruptcies, and benchmarking. This chapter is important for the reader in understanding the methods available to airports in funding large capital projects, as well as the role airports play in the economy.

Chapter 15, Future Challenges and Opportunities, wraps up the book by presenting the expected challenges airports will face in the future, as well as the opportunities that may be grasped. Specifically, airline bankruptcies and mergers, new large aircraft (such as the A380), capital development funding, unfunded federal mandates, passenger leakage, customer service, sustainable initiatives, airside congestion, and unmanned aircraft systems are presented. This chapter provides a few last thoughts on future challenges to be faced by airport managers.

Tampa International Airport, with main terminal complex and satellite terminals connected by automated people movers shown. (Hillsborough County Aviation Authority)

Chapter 1

Historical Overview

Key Terms

14 CFR Part 139, Certification of Airports
AIP Temporary Extension Act
Air Cargo Deregulation Act of 1976
Air Commerce Act of 1926
Airline Deregulation Act of 1978
Airport and Airway Development Act of 1970
Airport and Airway Improvement Act of 1982
Airport and Airway Revenue Act of 1970
Airport and Airway Safety and Capacity Expansion Act of 1987
Airport and Airway Safety, Capacity, Noise Improvement, and Intermodal Transportation Act of 1992
Airport and Airway Trust Fund
Airport Development Aid Program (ADAP)
Airport Improvement Program (AIP)
Airways Modernization Act
Americans with Disabilities Act of 1990
Aviation and Transportation Security Act (ATSA) of 2001
Aviation Investment and Reform Act for the 21st Century (AIR-21)
Aviation Safety and Capacity Expansion Act of 1990
Aviation Safety and Noise Abatement Act of 1979
Aviation Security Improvement Act of 1990
cargo revenue ton miles
Civil Aeronautics Act of 1938
Civil Aeronautics Administration (CAA)
Civil Aeronautics Authority (CAA)
Civil Aeronautics Board (CAB)
Civil Works Administration (CWA)
Clean Air Act
continuing resolution
Contract Air Mail Act of 1925
Contract Air Mail (CAM) routes
Department of Transportation Act of 1966
Development of Landing Areas for National Defense (DLAND)
Emergency Relief Appropriation Act of 1935

Objectives

Upon completion of this chapter, you should:

- Understand the historical events and important pieces of legislation affecting the development of airlines.
- Understand the historical events and important pieces of legislation affecting the development of airports.
- Understand the historical funding of airport development.
- Understand the pre- and post-deregulation periods.
- Understand the significance of the events of 9/11 on the aviation industry.
- Be able to discuss contemporary issues and future challenges confronting the airport industry.

Essential Air Service (EAS)
Federal Aid to Airports Program
Federal Airport Act of 1946
Federal Aviation Act of 1958
Federal Aviation Administration Authorization Act of 1994
Federal Aviation Agency (FAA)
Federal Aviation Reauthorization Act of 1996
Federal Emergency Relief Administration (FERA)
Federal Water Pollution Control Act
general aviation (GA) airports
Homeland Security Act of 2002
hub and spoke
Implementing Recommendations of the 9/11 Commission Act of 2007
Kelly Act
load factors
low-cost airlines
Military Airport Program (MAP)
National Airport Plan
National Civil Aviation Review Commission
National Commission on Terrorist Attacks Upon the United States
National Transportation Safety Board (NTSB)
oligopolistic
omnibus spending bill
passenger facility charge (PFC)
Planning Grant Program (PGP)
revenue passenger miles
Security Guidelines for General Aviation Airports
spending bill
State Block Grant Program
Transportation Security Administration (TSA)
Vision 100—Century of Aviation Reauthorization Act of 2003
Works Progress Administration (WPA)
World War I
World War II

In Chapter 1

Introduction 9
The Beginning of an Industry 10
World War I 14
Post World War I 15
World War II 19
Post World War II 20
Pre-Deregulation 21
Deregulation 24
Post-Deregulation 24
9/11 33
Post 9/11 33
Contemporary and Future Period 40
Concluding Thoughts 41
Chapter Summary 42
Review Questions 45
Scenarios 46
References and Resources for Further Study 46

FEATURES

The Role of Federal Express in the Air Cargo Industry **25**

Federal Express played an integral role in establishing the air cargo industry and the subsequent deregulation of that industry.

The Rise and Fall of People's Express **27**

A low-cost airline that attained great success, but eventually went out of business due to competition from other airlines during the deregulated era.

Introduction

Airports are an integral part of the aviation industry. In this industry, billions of passengers and billions of tons of cargo have been moved from point to point since it began, which could not have occurred without airports. The industry is a little more than 100 years old and yet responsible for more than $1 trillion per year in economic activity and almost 10 million jobs. Consider the U.S. airlines (Figure 1-1). Although down from a ten-year high of 769.6 million enplaned passengers in 2007, U.S. airlines enplaned 720.5 million passengers, which equates to 798 billion **revenue passenger miles**, in 2010. Additionally, airlines generated more than 27 billion **cargo revenue ton miles** and generated more than 10 million departures during the year (Air Transport Association, 2011).

Each of these departures, passengers, and pounds of cargo were accommodated at an airport. Whether large or small, public or private, airports serve as an interface between ground and air transportation (Figure 1-2). As an industry, they directly serve the needs of pilots, passengers, and meeters and greeters, and provide employment to hundreds of thousands of employees nationwide. Indirectly, they serve the communities in which they are located by providing facilities to support emergency medical transport, law enforcement services, and the movement of goods and services. Even **general aviation** (GA) **airports** provide beneficial economic impacts to the local community. Airports in the United States have a significant impact on local, state, regional, and national economies. As part of an industry that provides 10 million jobs, $396 billion in wages, and an impact of $1.3 trillion to the economy, airports clearly play a crucial role in the aviation industry (Federal Aviation Administration, n.d.). In sum, airports serve a unique and substantial need throughout the world, and have an interesting history in the United States—the birthplace of aviation.

Figure 1-1. Number of enplaned passengers, U.S. airlines, 2000–2010

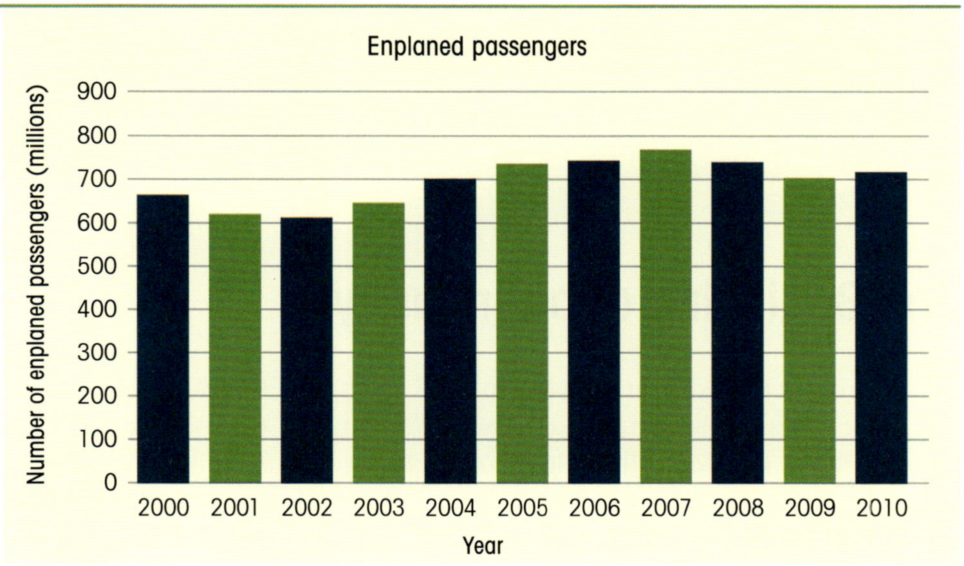

Figure 1-2. Airports are transportation lifelines, often serving airline passengers and cargo carriers, flight training and general aviation pilots, with beneficial economic impacts felt locally, regionally, and nationally.

(jlye/Bigstock.com)

The Beginning of an Industry

The history of the aviation industry in the United States began on December 17, 1903. It was on this day that Orville Wright first flew the now-famous Wright Flyer I in a controlled flight lasting 12 seconds (see Figure 1-3). However, aviation did not immediately succeed. After these first flights at Kitty Hawk, North Carolina, the Wright brothers faced quite a challenge in promoting their aircraft to a willing buyer. In fact, five years passed before they were able to convince the U.S. government to test a much improved version.

Figure 1-3. The first flight of Orville Wright (1871–1948) at Kill Devil Hills, Kitty Hawk, North Carolina, on December 17, 1903 (120 feet in 12 seconds). His brother Wilbur Wright (1867–1912) is standing on the right.

(Wikimedia Commons; see credit on page 623)

Although the four flights flown by the Wright brothers on that day marked the beginning of controlled, powered, and sustained heavier-than-air human flight, the first scheduled commercial airline flight using heavier-than-air aircraft did not occur until eleven years later, when on January 1, 1914, Tony Jannus piloted the Benoist XIV flying boat biplane across Tampa Bay (Florida) on an historic 23-minute flight (see Figure 1-4). This inaugural flight also carried the mayor of St. Petersburg, Florida—Mr. Abram C. Pheil. At a fare of five dollars per passenger, this was the first time in history that tickets were sold to the general public for point-to-point scheduled air travel. Known as the St. Petersburg-Tampa Airboat Line, the airline offered service six days per week with two roundtrip flights daily until ceasing service on March 31, 1914, which was five weeks after the termination of a three-month contract that had been signed with the St. Petersburg Board of Trade. This service greatly improved travel between the two cities, as travel by steamship took 2 hours, rail between 4 and 12 hours, and automobile around 20 hours (Bluffield, 2010).

Figure 1-4. The historic departure of Jannus and Pheil.

(Wikimedia Commons; see credit on page 623)

Although the early days of aviation did not start and end at airports as we know them, these airfields did serve as the first airports. Whether in the form of a grassy field, sand dune, body of water, or other flat place, these first airfields served the unique needs of the early aviators. As more aircraft were built and the aviation industry began growing, the need for landing areas grew.

Providing dedicated airfields was seen as the best solution to this need. One way in which to do this was to develop dirt-only fields (see Figure 1-5). This option improved aircraft performance on takeoff roll, due to an elimination of the drag produced by grass. As can be imagined, however, these dirt landing sites were only usable in dry conditions. Muddy landing sites were, in fact, worse than the old grass landing sites. Often, race tracks, golf courses, or fairgrounds doubled as landing sites.

A significant boost in the quality of airfields came about with the addition of concrete landing areas. Portland cement, which had been invented in 1824 by English inventor Joseph Aspdin, was the preferred material. However, macadam or cinders were also used. Macadam was a type of road construction pioneered by Scotsman John Loudon McAdam around 1820. Single-sized aggregate layers of stone with a coating of binder as a cementing agent were mixed in an open-structured macadam. Cinder, on the other hand, is a small type of volcanic rock that has many uses, including material for road construction and decorative rock for landscaping, especially in the southwest U.S.

Possibly the first use of the term "airport" was by a Brazilian airship inventor, Mr. Alberto Santos-Dumont. According to the April 11, 1902 edition of *The New York Times*, Mr. Santos-Dumont explained his expectation that the city of New York would be "the principal 'airport' of the world in less than a score of years" (*The New York Times*, 1902). However, the nation's first municipal airport was built in 1908 in Albany, New York. Located on a former polo field, the airport was moved to Westerlo Island after one year due to the unsuitability of the former polo field. Deemed an ideal location, Westerloo Island had long, level stretches of land bordering the Hudson River. During its early years, the airport welcomed such famous aviators as Glenn Curtis, Charles Lindbergh, Amelia Earhart, and James Doolittle. The mayor of Albany at the time, Mr. John Boyd Thacher II, once said, "A city without the foresight to build an airport for the new traffic may soon be left behind in the race for

Figure 1-5.
Early landing strip.

(©iStock.com/andipantz)

competition." So, in 1928, a new modern airport was built. The new airport originally consisted of 249 acres and contained two brick hangars and a brick administration building. As part of airport construction, three runways were built—the first was 2,200 feet long, the second 2,350 feet long, and the third measured 2,500 feet long. Two of the runways were paved with macadam and one with cinders. By 1930, Albany was known as the "aerial crossroads of the great Northeast." Although the airport was closed for a brief period by the Civil Aeronautics Administration (CAA), it remains in operation to this day, overseen by the Albany County Airport Authority (Hakes, n.d.).

Although Albany Airport was initially funded by the City of Albany, its operation and upkeep during the first eight years was financed through a special fund established by the Albany Chamber of Commerce. Even in those early years, airports required financial resources for maintenance and operation. Airport maintenance during this time involved grading to maintain the level runway, mowing grass, and keeping the runway free of obstructions. In January 1939, however, the newly formed **Civil Aeronautics Authority (CAA)** closed the new airport to commercial flights declaring it unsuitable for use. This action was taken by the CAA following a long dispute between the city and federal officials over who should be responsible for paying for needed improvements to the airport. Mayor Thacher believed the city should not have to pay for improvements that would benefit national defense and commerce. The CAA disagreed and as a result, eventually closed the field to all air traffic. The city then initiated a **Works Progress Administration (WPA)** project to make the necessary improvements at the airport, resulting in the CAA allowing daylight operations to begin once again in December 1940. On January 21, 1942, the CAA, recognizing the improvements to the airport, allowed the airport to reopen for nighttime use. Except for wartime restriction, the airport has had uninterrupted flight service since that time (Hakes, n.d.).

The College Park Airport in Maryland was established by Wilbur Wright in 1909, one year after the Albany Airport. It claims the distinction of being the "World's Oldest Continually Operating Airport." It is indeed an airport with a long history. In 1909, after the U.S government agreed to purchase a Wright Flyer, the aircraft was officially accepted by the U.S government. However, the contract required the Wrights to teach two army officers to fly the plane. A field in the small town of College Park, Maryland, was selected for this flight instruction and the College Park airfield was established. Operating strictly as a general aviation facility, in 1977 the airport was added to the National Register of Historic Places (College Park Aviation Museum, n.d.).

Even so, very few airports were built during these early years of aviation. Rather than focus on areas at which to land aircraft, efforts were focused on improving the design of aircraft. In fact, by 1912, only 20 landing facilities were thought to exist in the U.S. Although this seems like a small number, this network of landing facilities was sufficient to meet the needs of aviation at that time. It is interesting to note that all of these landing facilities, including Albany and College Park, grew from fields or country clubs. They had not been designed as airports, per se (Mola, n.d.).

World War I

However, the environment soon changed as **World War I** (WWI) began in 1914, triggered by the assassination on June 28 of Archduke Franz Ferdinand of Austria, the heir to the throne of Austria-Hungary. Thousands of aircraft were subsequently produced to serve in WWI, most of which were produced and utilized in France, Germany, and England (Figure 1-6). Of course, hundreds of pilots were needed to fly these aircraft and numerous landing facilities were needed to accommodate their operation. Although the U.S. Army had established three military airfields by the time WWI began, an additional 67 military airfields were established during the war to meet this need. These airfields provided facilities for fueling, maintenance, and aircraft parking. At the time, the military envisioned returning these airfields to grassland upon the war's conclusion.

By the end of WWI in 1918, the U.S. Army listed no less than 980 official landing fields. However, many of these fields were unsuitable for regular aircraft operations. For instance, pilots may have had to avoid flags, sand traps, and water hazards while landing on a golf course. Additionally, racetracks were generally sufficient for landing aircraft, but too short to allow for takeoffs. Some, however, worked quite well—including dry lakebeds in Nevada or long stretches of country roads. During this time, "aerial garages" were being built to accommodate aircraft storage and maintenance needs. These forerunners to contemporary hangars and maintenance shops were oftentimes built out of whatever materials were on hand, including the packing crates used for new aircraft delivery (Mola, n.d.).

Figure 1-6. Aviation in use during World War I.

(©iStock.com/igs942)

Post World War I

Upon the conclusion of WWI, there were a large number of aircraft and skilled pilots that desired to utilize their talents. Conveniently, in 1918, the U.S. Congress appropriated $100,000 for the first regularly scheduled airmail service. This route, between Washington, DC, and New York, was to be flown roundtrip once daily by U.S. Army Service pilots (Figure 1-7). Major Reuben H. Fleet was picked by Army Colonel E.A. Deeds to manage the first regular airmail flights. Although Assistant Postmaster General Otto Praeger and Fleet disagreed about landing fields, pilots, and the date airmail service would begin, the inaugural airmail flight occurred on schedule on May 15, 1918.

Interestingly, the two pilots selected for these inaugural airmail flights were not chosen for their experience or abilities; rather, they were the sons of politically important men. Lt. George Boyle was to fly from the Potomac Park Polo Grounds in Washington, DC, to a relay handover point in Philadelphia. Simultaneously, Lt. James Edgerton was to fly from Hazelhurst Field on Long Island, New York, to the same relay handover point in Philadelphia. Lt. Boyle's flight was a failure. He was inexperienced, encountered low visibility due to thick fog, flew a poorly equipped airplane in the form of an open cockpit Curtiss Jenny, and followed the wrong railroad tracks to Philadelphia. He quickly became lost, flying for only 24 miles before landing in a field and flipping over. Although he was not injured, the mail he was carrying (3,300 letters weighing 140 pounds) had to be offloaded and placed on a train to Philadelphia. Lt. Edgerton's flight, however, was a success, leading the newspapers to declare this inaugural airmail service a success (Mola, n.d.).

Figure 1-7. Early days of airmail in the United States.

(Wikimedia Commons; see credit on page 623)

Two months later, pilot Leon Smith refused to fly his route of New York to Washington, DC, due to rain, clouds, and 200 feet visibility. Praeger ordered him to make the trip regardless of the weather. Smith and his fellow pilot, E. Hamilton "Ham" Lee refused to fly in those weather conditions. As a result, they were both fired, which then led to a strike by all pilots in the airmail system. After three days of talks, it was agreed that field managers would make a flight check in bad weather. If the field managers were not pilots, they would sit in the mail bin in front of the pilot to visually verify the weather. Flights would then continue only if the field manager gave the go-ahead (U.S. Centennial of Flight Commission, n.d.[c]).

Over the following three months, pilots flying these airmail routes were heartily challenged. With only a simple magnetic compass and maps with no elevations or landmarks, these pilots were pressured to maintain a six day per week schedule regardless of weather. In less than three months, the army had made 270 flights and carried 40,500 pounds of mail. Although several pilots had been injured, none had been killed. However, the Post Office felt that the army had not sufficiently met the schedule and had been uncooperative. As a result, the army contract was cancelled and the Post Office began carrying the mail on August 12, 1918 (Mola, n.d.).

As the airmail system grew, so did the country's airports. Indeed, many communities began constructing airports to allow them a connection to the rest of the world. Early airfields built by the Post Office typically had a 2,000-foot by 2,000-foot square to allow for takeoffs and landings in any direction. Landing surfaces were generally of gravel or cinders, as they allowed for adequate drainage. Airfields generally ranged in size from 70 to 100 acres and consisted of a hangar, storage of gasoline and oil, a wind indicator, a telephone connection, and a location marker. By the end of 1920, there were 145 airports owned and operated by municipalities. Clearly, a national network of airports was being established (Mola, n.d.).

The first permanent, hard-surfaced runway in the United States, at 1,600 feet long, is thought to have been constructed at Newark, New Jersey, in 1928. Some airports were being developed by airlines. For instance, Pan American Airways, flying a Miami–Key West–Havana route twice daily, constructed the first U.S. land-based international airport: Pan American Field.

Yet as airmail began crossing the country successfully in the mid-1920s, the owners of various railroads expressed their frustration with the government's sponsorship of the airmail system. They felt that railroad profits were being negatively impacted due to the carriage of mail by air. Congressman Clyde Kelly of Pennsylvania, chairman of the House Post Office Committee, was a friend of the railroad industry and on February 2, 1925, sponsored H.R. 7064: the Contract Air Mail Bill, which, upon enactment, became the **Contract Air Mail Act of 1925**, also known as the **Kelly Act**. The act elevated airmail to another level by allowing the postmaster general to contract for domestic airmail service with commercial air carriers. It also set airmail rates and the level of cash subsidies to be paid to companies that carried the mail. The Act was successful in expanding airmail service without undue burden on the taxpayers. Routes created as part of the Act were known as **Contract Air Mail routes** or **CAM routes** (see Figure 1-8). Initial routes were flown between cities such as New York and Boston, Detroit and Cleveland, and Atlanta and Jacksonville. Eventually, a transcontinental route was established. In essence, this Act effectively established the commercial aviation industry. Indeed, several airlines that existed well into the twentieth century (such as Trans World Airlines, Northwest Airlines, and United Airlines) were formed during this time (U.S. Centennial of Flight Commission, n.d.[a]).

To financially support the airmail service, 80 percent of the airmail stamp revenues received by the Post Office were to be paid to the airmail carriers. The number of stamps needed depended on the weight of the mail and the number of zones the mail had to cross.[1] Due to the structure of the system, air-

[1] The country had been divided into three air zones on July 1, 1924.

Figure 1-8.
CAM routes.

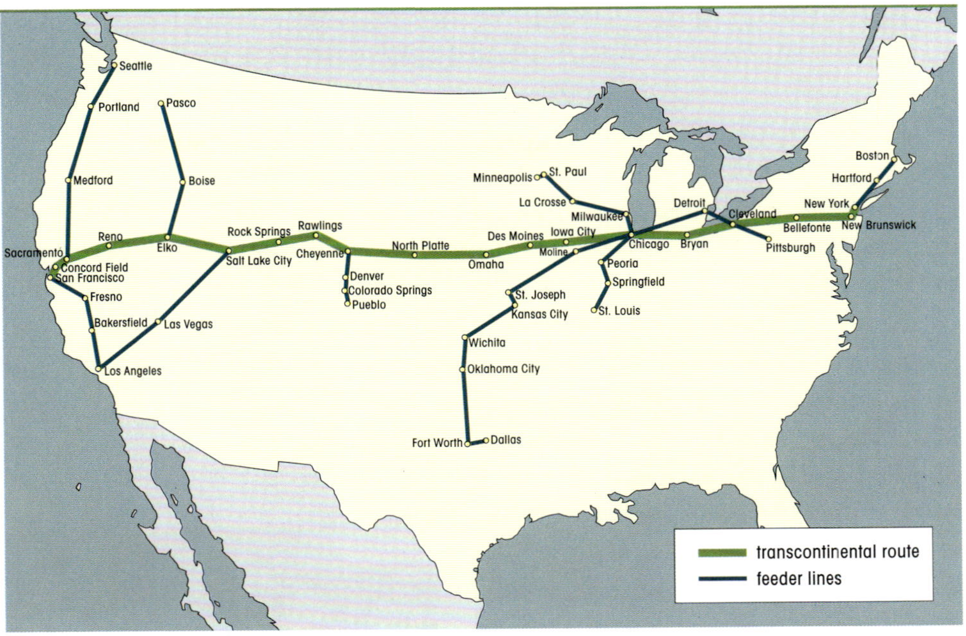

mail operators realized that carrying smaller, but heavier, pieces of mail would result in greater revenues. Additionally, since they received the same amount of money regardless of the miles flown within a zone, they preferred shorter trips. Postmaster General Harry New, in an effort to encourage passenger service, encouraged operators to buy larger aircraft and engage the passenger.[2] Beginning in October 1925, New awarded eight airmail routes to seven airmail carriers.

In these early years of the aviation industry, the industry remained without regulations and as a result, there were many accidents. To enhance safety and increase public confidence in the industry, on May 20, 1926, the **Air Commerce Act of 1926** became law. This new law, considered the "cornerstone of the Federal Government's regulation of civil aviation," was designed to promote the development, and ensure the stability, of commercial aviation (Preston, n.d.). To achieve this, the Act created an Aeronautics Branch assigned to the United States Department of Commerce, and vested that entity with the fundamental regulatory powers needed to ensure civil air safety. The Secretary of Commerce was responsible for fostering air commerce, issuing and enforcing air traffic rules, licensing pilots, certificating aircraft, establishing airways, operating and maintaining aids to air navigation, and investigating aviation accidents and incidents. Initially, the Department of Commerce focused on safety rulemaking and the certification of pilots and aircraft. In time, they began further developing the nation's system of lighted airways, as well as improving and introducing radio beacons. The first head of the Aeronautics Branch was William P. MacCracken, Jr., who, interestingly, received the nation's first pilot license on April 6, 1927 (U.S. Centennial of Flight Commission, n.d.[a]; Preston, n.d.).

2 To generate revenues from passenger service rather than the Post Office.

In 1934, an administrative order of the Secretary of Commerce effectively renamed the Aeronautics Branch as the Bureau of Air Commerce. Two divisions, air navigation and air regulation, made up the Bureau of Air Commerce. In one of its first acts, the Bureau encouraged a group of airlines to establish the first air traffic control centers (Newark, New Jersey; Cleveland, Ohio; and Chicago, Illinois) to provide enroute air traffic control. In 1936, the Bureau took over these centers. These early air traffic controllers used nothing more than maps, blackboards, and mental calculations to control aircraft (see Figure 1-9).

Although progress was being made in the regulation of air traffic, pilots, aircraft and airways, this was not the case for airports. In fact, the Air Commerce Act specifically prohibited the use of federal funding for building or maintaining airports. However, the political landscape changed with the stock market crash in October 1929. In response to this period known as the Great Depression, the federal government began a massive spending effort in civil works projects to stimulate the economy and employ the unemployed. As part of this, an exception to the prohibition on federal funding of airport projects was made. This allowed the **Civil Works Administration (CWA)**, and later the **Federal Emergency Relief Administration (FERA)**, to spend approximately $11.5 million by spring 1934 for 943 airport projects in small cities, resulting in 585 new airports (U.S. Centennial of Flight Commission, n.d.[b]).

Figure 1-9. Early air traffic control in the U.S.

(FAA)

The following year, the WPA was established and funded by Congress with passage of the **Emergency Relief Appropriation Act of 1935** on April 8, 1935. The WPA was the largest of the "New Deal" programs put in place by President Franklin D. Roosevelt to put millions back to work and help Americans weather the Great Depression. The WPA employed millions to carry out public works projects, including the construction of public buildings, roads, and airports. Total WPA expenditures from 1936 to 1939 totaled nearly $7 billion, although only about half of the expense for materials and equipment for an airport project were provided by the federal government. The other half was contributed by the airport sponsor. During its eight-year history, the WPA built 651,087 miles of highways, roads, and streets; and constructed, repaired, or improved 124,031 bridges, 125,110 public buildings, 8,192 parks, and 853 airport landing areas (Indiana University, n.d.).

While the Department of Commerce made great strides in improving aviation safety, several high profile accidents created doubt as to the department's oversight responsibilities. In 1931, popular University of Notre Dame football coach Knute Rockne was killed in an aircraft accident. Four years later, U.S. Senator Bronson Cutting of New Mexico died in an aircraft accident. Thus, the public cry for greater federal oversight of aviation safety made this a top priority for Congress.

As a result, the **Civil Aeronautics Act of 1938** was signed into law. With this act, the civil aviation role of the Department of Commerce was transferred to a new independent agency—the Civil Aeronautics Authority (CAA). Now all functions and regulation of air transportation were under one authority. In addition, the Act created the Administrator of Aviation and the Air Safety Board. The CAA was mainly focused on the economic regulation of air carriers. In essence, the federal government now had the authority to regulate airline fares and airline routes. This form of regulation was important for the young airline industry and would continue for some 40 years, prior to the deregulation of the airline industry. The Administrator of Aviation was responsible for implementing the safety policies promulgated by the CAA, as well as addressing the construction, operation, and maintenance of the airway system. The role of the Air Safety Board was to investigate aviation accidents (Preston, n.d.).

By 1940, it was necessary to reorganize these agencies. Thus, the Reorganization Act was signed by President Franklin Roosevelt. The Act divided the CAA into two agencies. First, the **Civil Aeronautics Board (CAB)**, which evolved from the CAA, was responsible for safety rulemaking, accident investigation, and economic regulation of the airlines. Second, the **Civil Aeronautics Administration (CAA)** became responsible for air traffic control, airman and aircraft certification, safety enforcement, and airway development. Although both organizations were part of the Department of Commerce, the CAB functioned independently of the Secretary.

World War II

Under Section 303 of the Civil Aeronautics Act, federal funding of airport construction was authorized as "reasonably necessary for use in air commerce or in the interest of national defense" (U.S. Centennial of Flight Commission, n.d.[b]). This "interest of national defense" was recognized by the administrator in September 1939, with the invasion of Poland by Nazi Germany. As a result, Congress authorized the appropriation of $40 million for the **Development of Landing Areas for National Defense (DLAND)**. Under this program during **World War II**, the Secretaries of War and Commerce and the Secretary of the Navy authorized expenditures for airports. These airports were constructed if governmental units provided the land and agreed to operate and maintain the facility. Additionally, in 1940, due to an expansion of the Army Air Corps, many more airports were needed than had been appropriated under DLAND. In the end, a total of 986 airports were built nationwide under DLAND. (U.S. Centennial of Flight Commission, n.d.[b]; Murdock, 1997).

In total, during the 1939–1945 period of WWII, the federal government, through the CAA, expended more than $353 million for the construction and repair of military landing areas in the continental United States. At the same time, the CAA expended $9.5 million for the development of civil airports. Once the war was over, more than 500 airports that had been constructed for the war effort were declared surplus and handed over to various municipalities and states for civil use. For this to occur, however, the new airport sponsor agreed to make the airport available to the public without discrimination and to the government in the event of a national emergency (U.S. Centennial of Flight Commission, n.d.[b])

Post World War II

In 1944, the CAA submitted a **National Airport Plan** (NAP) that had the effect of generating congressional interest in postwar needs. This Plan contained recommendations for airport construction, improvement, maintenance and operation. Two years later, in 1946, Congress passed the **Federal Airport Act of 1946**. The Act provided, through the **Federal Aid to Airports Program**, $500 million in grants for airport projects paid over seven years. The maximum federal grant for a project would equal half of the project's costs. The remaining half of a project's costs would need to be provided by the airport sponsor, either through bond financing or other means. To be eligible for this funding, an airport would need to be included in the newly established National Airport Plan. Additionally, all projects had to meet CAA standards for location, layout, grading, drainage, paving, and lighting. Further, all tax money collected by local governments for aviation facilities or fuel had to be expended for airport operations and maintenance (U.S. Centennial of Flight Commission, n.d.[b]).

As the initial seven-year period of funding provided by the Federal Airport Act neared its end, the Act was extended in 1950 to last until 1958. During this period, only runways and taxiways were eligible for federal money. If a sponsor needed a new terminal building or equipment, they would have to secure the funds. Five years into this second period of funding, on August 3, 1955, Public Law 84-211 was signed by President Dwight Eisenhower. This law included a new four-year program that committed $63 million of federal funds annually. At the end of this four-year period, another bill continued the money for two more years, and then additional amounts were appropriated annually until 1970 (U.S. Centennial of Flight Commission, n.d.[b]).

The 1950s was a period of prosperity for the United States. For example, consider the year 1958: the 55 scheduled U.S. airlines served 703 cities with 1,900 aircraft in service and 103,700 daily seats, flew 49,075,000 passengers, employed 146,000 people, and carried 501,591,000 ton miles of freight. At the same time, however, the 1956–1958 time period was rather dark for the aviation industry. On June 30, 1956, a TWA Super Constellation and a United DC-7 collided at 21,000 feet over the Grand Canyon, killing all 128 people on board both aircraft. The collision occurred while the aircraft were flying under visual flight rules in uncongested airspace. It became apparent that even with regulations and funding, aviation safety remained an issue (ATA, 1959).

As a result, on August 14, 1957, the **Airways Modernization Act** was signed into law. This act was based on the recommendations contained in the "Aviation Facilities Planning" report prepared by President Eisenhower's special assistant for aviation facilities planning, Mr. Edward P. Curtis. His report warned of "a crisis in the making" as a result of the current airspace management system and the growing pressures on that system. The main goal of the act was to modernize the air traffic control system and navigation facilities to meet the present and future needs of both civil and military aviation. Mr. Elwood R. Quesada's appointment as chair of the Airways Modernization Board was approved by the U.S. Senate on August 16, 1957.

Less than a year later, however, on May 20, 1958, a Capital Airlines Vickers Viscount aircraft collided in midair with an Air National Guard Lockheed T-33 over Brunswick, Maryland, killing all eleven on board the Capital Airlines Flight and one of the two crewmembers of the T-33. Oklahoma Senator A. S. "Mike" Monroney introduced a bill to create an independent Federal Aviation Agency to provide for the safe and efficient use of national airspace.[3] On August 23, 1958, this bill was signed into law. The **Federal Aviation Act of 1958**, which repealed the Air Commerce Act of 1926, created the new **Federal Aviation Agency (FAA)**. In essence, safety rulemaking was no longer a responsibility of the CAB. The FAA would assume safety rulemaking and the responsibility for developing and maintaining a common civil-military system of air navigation and air traffic control. The Agency's first administrator, Elwood "Pete" Quesada, had served as President Dwight Eisenhower's principal advisor on civil aeronautics. Once appointed, Quesada took great efforts to improve airline safety (Preston, n.d.).

Pre-Deregulation

On January 12, 1966, in an annual message to Congress on the State of the Union, President Lyndon Johnson asked Congress for help to "modernize and streamline the Federal Government by creating a new Cabinet level Department of Transportation and reorganizing several existing agencies" (Johnson, 1966). Congress listened and on October 15 of that year approved the **Department of Transportation Act of 1966**. This Act created the Department of Transportation (DOT), which began operations on April 1, 1967. The mission of the DOT is to, "Serve the United States by ensuring a fast, safe, efficient, accessible and convenient transportation system that meets our vital national interests

---

3 The FAA Mike Monroney Aeronautical Center in Oklahoma City, Oklahoma, houses the Logistics Center, the FAA Academy, the FAA Leadership and Learning Institute, the Enterprise Services Center, Information Technology Services, Media Solutions Division, and Office of Acquisition Services.

and enhances the quality of life of the American people, today and into the future" (Department of Transportation, 2007). Under the DOT Act, the Federal Aviation Agency was renamed the Federal Aviation Administration (FAA) and placed within the DOT along with several transportation-related organizations. The FAA Administrator then began reporting directly to the Secretary of Transportation. Additionally, the CAB's accident investigation responsibilities were transferred to a new **National Transportation Safety Board (NTSB)**. The NTSB was also responsible for hearing any appeals regarding the suspension, modification, or revocation of any certificate of license issued by the DOT secretary or FAA Administrator (Preston, n.d.).

By the late 1960s, demand for aviation had almost exceeded the capacity of the system. The flying public experienced substantial flight delays, congestion in both terminal buildings and parking areas, and the resulting frustrations of air travel. Then on February 9, 1969, the "jumbo jet" Boeing 747 had its first flight. With a double-deck configuration and four engines, the original 747 was two-and-a-half times the size of the Boeing 707 (Figure 1-10). With the ability to carry hundreds of passengers, the introduction of this large passenger aircraft made it clear that improvements in the nation's airports and airways were necessary. During the following decade, estimates for needed airport capital improvements were in the billions of dollars.[4] It became clear that the Federal Airport Act of 1946 would be unable to meet the financial demands of the industry.

Figure 1-10. Boeing 747.

(Wikimedia Commons; see credit on page 623)

As a result, on May 21, 1970, President Nixon signed a two-title law into effect: Title I, the **Airport and Airway Development Act of 1970**, and Title II, the **Airport and Airway Revenue Act of 1970**. These were intended to replace the Federal Airport Act of 1946. Title I of the Act provided for, among

[4] 1970 to 1980.

other things, $250 million annually for the "acquisition, establishment, and improvement of air navigational facilities" and security equipment for the next ten years (U.S. Centennial of Flight Commission, n.d.[b]). It also provided authority for the FAA to establish minimum standards for airports and issue operating certificates to commercial-service airports that met these standards.[5] Title I accomplished this via the **Planning Grant Program (PGP)** and the **Airport Development Aid Program (ADAP)**. The PGP provided up to $25 million annually for airport planning purposes, including master plans and system plans. ADAP provided $250 million annually for air carrier and reliever airports and $30 million annually for GA airports.

Title II of the Act created the **Airport and Airway Trust Fund,**[6] which was financed by an eight-percent tax on domestic passenger fares, a three-dollar surcharge on passenger tickets originating in the United States, a tax of seven cents per gallon on gasoline and jet fuel, a five-percent tax on airfreight waybills, and an annual registration fee and charge per pound for aircraft. The trust fund concept created a steady source of revenue for the continued development of airports and airways, which meant that the aviation system now would not have to compete with other needs for general treasury funds (U.S. Centennial of Flight Commission, n.d.[b]).

Of the $3.9 billion in development undertaken during the first eight years of ADAP, $2.7 billion were federal funds and $1.2 billion were state and local funds. This surpassed the $1.2 billion spent by the federal government during the entire twenty-four-year history of the Federal Aid to Airports Program. About half of ADAP funds were used to increase airport safety, while the other half were used to increased airport capacity (FAA, 1980).

Due to the original five-year lifespan of the two grant-in-aid programs, amendments were necessary to continue funding the programs. On July 12, 1976, President Gerald Ford signed amendments to the law that increased the taxes levied. Additionally, snow removal equipment, noise mitigation strategies, and the purchase of land to meet environmental needs were considered eligible for federal funding.[7] Additionally, federal money could now meet 90 percent of project costs for certain airport projects. This amendment, as well as subsequent ones, also raised the amount of money available to airports.

5 Thus, airports being served by commercial air carriers using aircraft with 30 seats or more were required to obtain an operating certificate from the FAA. 14 CFR Part 139 eventually grew from this authority.

6 Commonly referred to as the "aviation trust fund."

7 Noise mitigation strategies included equipment to reduce aircraft noise, physical barriers and landscaping.

Deregulation

Although the airline industry had been economically regulated since the establishment of the CAB in 1939, that period of regulation came to an end, ironically enough, with the passage of new legislation in the form of the **Air Cargo Deregulation Act of 1976** and the **Airline Deregulation Act of 1978**. The deregulation of both cargo carriers and passenger carriers was not a decision made overnight, however. During the 1970s, the general political climate favored less involvement in private industries. When President Jimmy Carter appointed economist and former professor Alfred Kahn, a vocal supporter of deregulation, to head the CAB, the stage was set for deregulation.

Yet another force for deregulation was occurring overseas. In 1977, Freddie Laker, a British entrepreneur who owned Laker Airways, created the Skytrain service, which offered extraordinarily low fares for transatlantic flights. These low-priced flights occurred during the same time there was a boom in low-cost domestic flights in the United States as the CAB eased limitations on charter flights. The major carriers responded by proposing their own lower fares. Although they had to seek CAB approval, American Airlines was one airline able to gain that approval for their Super Saver fares. At the same time, however, deregulation of the airline industry had its opponents. Mainly, the major airlines were fiercely opposed to the bill. The airlines in opposition feared free competition, its impacts on the industry, and negative consequences to their bottom line. Additionally, labor unions were opposed because they feared nonunion employees. Many safety proponents were also opposed, as they felt that safety would be sacrificed. However, the support of the public was strong enough to enable passage of these acts. The Airline Deregulation Act appeased the major airlines by offering generous subsidies and it pleased workers by offering high unemployment benefits if they lost their jobs as a result. It also allowed for a six year phase-out of the CAB[8] (American Association of Airport Executives, 2005; Kahn, 1993).

Post-Deregulation

As a result of the deregulation of both the air cargo industry and air carriers, the industry was permanently altered. First, air cargo carriers were now free to raise or lower rates, serve any markets they chose, and own and operate trucks in support of their operation to pick up and deliver goods.[9] Additionally, airlines could now enter the market at will. Beginning in 1981, airlines also had the freedom to expand their routes. Beginning in 1982, airlines were completely free to set airfares. By 1984, the CAB had been abolished, as it was no longer necessary in an economically deregulated industry.

---

8 The sunset of the CAB would not occur until December 31, 1984.

9 As long as the movement of goods was related to an air cargo operation.

The Role of Federal Express in the Air Cargo Industry

Federal Express was one cargo carrier that lobbied heavily for deregulation of the air cargo industry. Having been incorporated in June 1971 and begun operations on April 17, 1973, founder Frederick W. Smith was aware of the benefits that deregulation would bring to his company and the air cargo industry. With deregulation, Federal Express was allowed to use larger aircraft (such as Boeing 727s and McDonnell-Douglas DC-10s) and grow rapidly from its humble beginning with 14 small aircraft serving 25 U.S. cities. Today, FedEx Express has the world's largest all-cargo aircraft fleet, including Boeing 777s, MD-11s, Airbus A-300s, and A-310s (Figure 1-11). The company's aircraft have a total daily lift capacity of more than 30 million pounds. In a 24-hour period, the fleet travels nearly 500,000 miles while its couriers log 2.5 million miles a day—the equivalent of 100 trips around the earth (FedEx, 2011).

Figure 1-11. FedEx Express aircraft.
(Wikimedia Commons; see credit on page 623)

In a free market, where airlines had the freedom to set airfares and enter and leave markets at will, some negative consequences were likely to occur. For instance, in this profit-driven industry, airlines began to pull out of less profitable markets. This, of course, resulted in loss of commercial airline service for many communities. Anticipating this, the Airline Deregulation Act contained a provision known as the **Essential Air Service (EAS)** program, which provided subsidies to encourage carriers to remain in less-profitable, smaller markets. The EAS program was put into place to guarantee that small communities that had been served by air carriers before deregulation would continue to be served after deregulation. Even today, approximately 100 rural communities across the country, outside of Alaska, enjoy the benefits of the EAS program via commuter airline service that they would not otherwise have. The state of Alaska has approximately 45 EAS airports (Department of Transportation, 2010).

Yet another consequence of deregulation was the formation of the **hub and spoke** route structure. Although this was mostly adopted by the larger air carriers, it had a significant impact on the aviation industry—an impact that continues to be felt today. In essence, with a hub and spoke route structure, an airline bases their operations in one or more major cities, such as Delta Airlines in Atlanta or American Airlines in Dallas/Fort Worth. From these cities, the airlines develop routes (spokes) that serve numerous destinations (see Figure 1-12). For this route structure to be most effective, the airlines schedule banks of arrivals into a hub, with time for passengers to transfer aircraft, and then a bank of departures to take these passengers to their final destination. With this, airlines utilizing the hub and spoke network could provide a large number of roundtrip flights from their hub cities, as well as maximize aircraft productivity

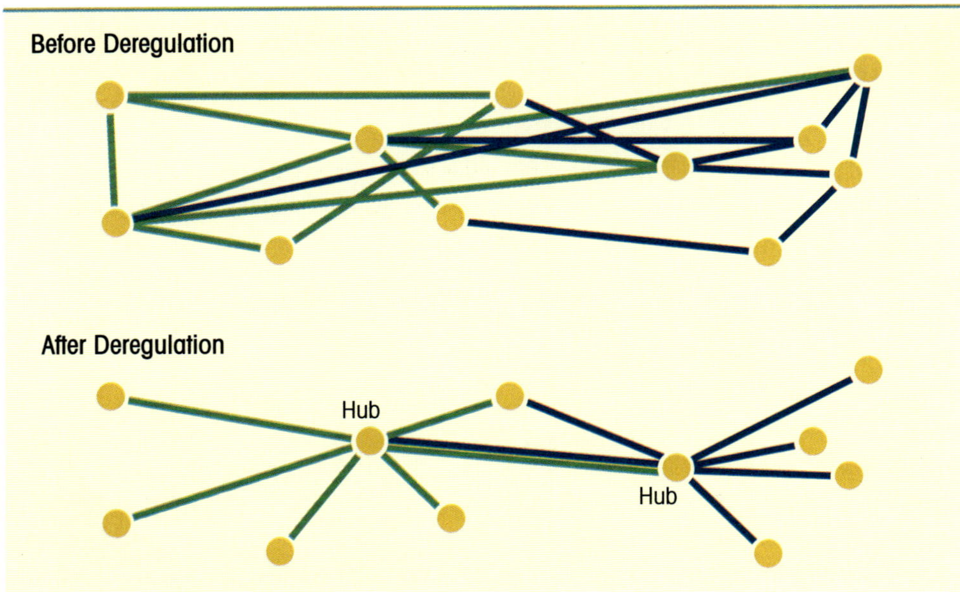

Figure 1-12. Hub and spoke network.

and enhance **load factors**. Of course, passengers typically would have to endure at least one stop, often with a change in aircraft, to get to their final destination. The passengers greatly benefitting from the hub and spoke network are those living in hub cities. These passengers have hundreds of non-stop destinations from which to choose. Even those living in smaller outlying cities benefit by having access to numerous destinations, including international, with one stop.

Deregulation also opened up the industry and allowed the entrance of new start-up airlines. This was significant, as an **oligopolistic** industry (as the airline industry is characterized) has significant barriers to entry. While that is still true in terms of investment required (aircraft, personnel, equipment), by at least allowing airlines who could acquire the necessary capital to enter a market, the industry opened up. These new start-up airlines were not bound by the demands of the larger established airlines. They typically had much lower cost structures than the established airlines, because they were established during the period of deregulation, rather than the period of regulation (as were the established airlines). With lower wage rates and overhead, they could offer lower fares and yet still operate with a surplus due to their lower cost structures. Thus, **low-cost airlines** were born.

With freedom to expand into new markets, both regional and major airlines initiated service to new markets with gusto. Airlines began competing aggressively for passengers. This competition dramatically reduced airfares, while allowing airline operating revenues to increase to a new high in 1979. That same year was also the peak year for passengers up to that point: an unprecedented 317 million passengers flew on U.S. airlines, with system-wide load factors averaging 63 percent (ATA, 1980).

Alas, the successes of the late 1970s were not to last. Rising fuel costs, an economic recession and overcapacity began to bring about changes in the industry. Within only two years of record-breaking numbers, the airlines recorded a net operating loss of $421 million in 1981, while carrying only 286 million

The Rise and Fall of People's Express

One new start-up airline with a low cost structure and enabled by airline deregulation was People's Express, established by Donald Burr. As an innovative entrepreneur, Burr initiated low salaries, a lower number of managers, job rotation, and employee stock ownership. People's Express initiated charges, for items such as meals and checked baggage, that many passengers are familiar with today. Competing with public transportation, such as buses, the airline had dramatically low fares. The business model was a success, and People's Express reached $1 billion in revenues by 1985 (Figure 1-13). The larger, more established airlines paid attention to the success of People's Express, and decided to compete with lower fares and better service. The larger airlines also allowed more convenient ticketing options to passengers through their relationships with travel agents. Within a year of reaching its peak in 1986, and with increasing financial losses and passenger dissatisfaction, People's Express was sold. (Siddiqi, n.d.)

Figure 1-13. People's Express aircraft.

(Wikimedia Commons; see credit on page 623)

passengers. Additionally, members of the Professional Air Traffic Controllers Organization (PATCO), seeking better working conditions, better pay, and a 32-hour workweek, went on a nationwide strike on August 3, 1981. In so doing, the union violated a law that prohibited strikes by government unions. President Ronald Regan declared the strike "a peril to national safety" and ordered striking employees back to work. With only 1,300 of the 13,000 controllers returning to work, President Reagan, in an August 3 press conference, stated that "They are in violation of the law and if they do not report for work within 48 hours they have forfeited their jobs and will be terminated" (Reagan, 1981). On August 5, 1981, following refusal by PATCO workers to return to work, Reagan fired the 11,345 striking air traffic controllers who had ignored the order, and banned them from federal service for life (although this ban was rescinded by President Bill Clinton in 1993).

Airline bankruptcies and industry consolidation were common. Braniff, for example, began operations in 1930 and grew into one of the most profitable airlines in the United States. However, due to rising fuel costs, aggressive expansion, and fierce competition, the airline had collapsed completely by 1982. Although the airline had operated from 1984 to 1989 under new ownership, its demise indicated significant problems with the industry. Airlines such as Continental and Eastern also declared bankruptcy by 1989. Pan American, arguably the most important international carrier for the United States and one that was now forced to compete with low fare entrants such as Laker and People's Express, was bankrupt by 1991. The number of major carriers in the

United States was reduced from six in 1978 (United, American, Delta, Eastern, TWA, and Pan Am) to three by 1991 (United, American, and Delta). This was a significant time for the airline industry in which its face was rapidly changing (ATA, 1982).

Although deregulation did produce negative consequences for the industry, it also produced some positive consequences, particularly for passengers. Inflation-adjusted airfares have decreased 44.9 percent between 1978 and 2008. It is estimated that when prices are adjusted for changes in quality and amenities, passengers save $19.4 billion annually from deregulation. Airfares have continued to fall in the decades since deregulation and when adjusted for inflation, have fallen 25 percent since 1991. According to the Brookings Institution, airfares are 22 percent lower than they would have been had regulation continued. Deregulation also produced fertile grounds for new entrants, and allowed smaller airlines to take over short-haul routes that were not profitable for the larger carriers. Travelers now have more convenient travel options with greater flight frequency and more non-stop flights. In sum, it appears that new entrant airlines and passengers gained the most from deregulation (Morrison and Clifford, 2000; Smith and Cox, 2008).

Although the airline industry was deregulated economically, new pieces of legislation affecting airport noise, funding, safety, security and other areas continued to be signed into law. One such piece of legislation, the **Aviation Safety and Noise Abatement Act of 1979**, provided the FAA authority to issue regulations on "air noise compatibility planning" and to make funds available for airport projects as part of an approved noise compatibility program. The Act also required the Secretary of Transportation to establish federal standards for measuring and assessing noise impacts on residences near airports (Airport Noise Law, 2010).

In 1980, the Airport and Airway Development Act expired. With airports needing a continuing source of funds for capital improvements, the **Airport and Airway Improvement Act of 1982** was signed into law. This act not only reestablished the Airport and Airway Trust Fund, but also established a new airport funding program known as the **Airport Improvement Program (AIP)**. Similar in concept to ADAP, the AIP not only funded land acquisition and the construction of runways, taxiways, and public areas of terminal buildings, but also funded the acquisition of friction measuring equipment, safety-related equipment, automated weather observing systems, and airport planning and noise studies. The Act also reorganized the NAP as the National Plan of Integrated Airport Systems (NPIAS). As part of this reorganization, various hub categories were created based on passenger enplanements. Commercial service airports were categorized as large hub, medium hub, small hub, and nonhub. The amount of funding was then determined on the basis of an airport's category (AAAE, 2005).

During the nine-year period 1971 to 1980, the Airport and Airway Trust Fund received approximately $13.1 billion in revenues. However, only $4.1 billion was expensed through ADAP grants. With the expiration of the Airport and Airway Development Act in 1980 and prior to the passage of the Airport and Airway Improvement Act of 1982, trust fund revenues received were deposited into the General Fund and the Highway Trust Fund. Approximately $900 million was appropriated by Congress for airport improvement during these two years.

The Airport and Airway Improvement Act was amended several times during the 1980s, which (a) allowed for discretionary grants to be issued for unused apportioned funds and (b) increased AIP funding authorizations. Then in 1987, the **Airport and Airway Safety and Capacity Expansion Act of 1987** authorized the AIP for another five years, carrying it into 1992. This Act authorized $1.7 billion each fiscal year through 1990 and an increase to $1.8 billion for FY1991 and FY1992. This 1987 Act also introduced two new concepts. The first, known as a letter of intent (LOI), allowed for multi-year funding of large-scale capacity projects at primary or reliever airports. This allowed airports planning multi-year projects to be assured of multi-year funding. With an LOI, reimbursement is made according to a given schedule as funds become available from Congress during each year of the LOI. The second concept involved the Disadvantaged Business Enterprise (DBE) Program. The Act set forth the requirement that 10 percent of AIP funds were to be used for DBEs. These small businesses are owned and controlled by socially and economically disadvantaged individuals.

Although federal funding of airports totaled billions of dollars annually, the need for funds was always greater than the supply. In an effort to supplement federal funding, airport passenger charges were proposed. Although airlines opposed this concept (and in fact, most still do today), Secretary of Transportation Samuel R. Skinner was able to convince Congress in 1990 to allow airports to impose a **passenger facility charge (PFC)** of $3.00 per passenger. Airport organizations, such as the American Association of Airport Executives (AAAE), were strongly in favor of the PFC. In November of that year, Congress agreed and passed the **Aviation Safety and Capacity Expansion Act of 1990** (AAAE, 2005).

Specific guidelines governed the PFC program. These guidelines were as follows:

- The airport sponsor may only apply to collect PFCs in whole dollar amounts of $1, $2, or $3 per enplaned passenger.
- PFCs will be collected by air carriers, and remitted back to the airport sponsor on a regular basis minus an administrative fee.
- PFCs are limited to no more than two charges on each leg of a roundtrip at airports at which passengers enplaned an aircraft.
- PFC revenue must be expended at the designated airport controlled by the same body that imposes the fee.
- PFC revenues may only be used to pay all or part of the allowable cost of an FAA approved project or pay debt service and financing costs associated with bond issuance.
- PFC revenue must be spent for the project on which the PFC application was approved.

- PFC projects must preserve or enhance safety, security, or capacity of the national air transportation system; reduce noise or mitigate noise impacts resulting from an airport; or present opportunities to enhance competition between or among air carriers.
- PFC funds can be combined with federal grant funds (such as AIP) to accomplish an approved project.
- PFC revenues can be used to meet the non-federal share of the cost of projects funded under the federal airport grant program.
- To address a concern expressed by those opposed to PFCs, the legislation requires large and medium hub airports collecting a PFC to have their AIP funding reduced.

(FAA, 2010b; FAA, 2001)

As of January 1, 2014, 387 airports were approved to collect PFCs. This includes 29 large hub airports, 35 medium hub airports, 69 small hub airports, 187 nonhub airports, and 39 non-primary commercial service airports. A total of 347 airports were approved to collect PFCs at the $4.50 level. Actual collections from calendar years 1992 to 2012 were $38.2 billion (see Figure 1-14). A full 100 percent of this amount has been paid by users of the system. This is a substantial amount of airport funding that most likely would not have been made available to airports had PFCs not been approved in the 1990 legislation (FAA, 2010c).

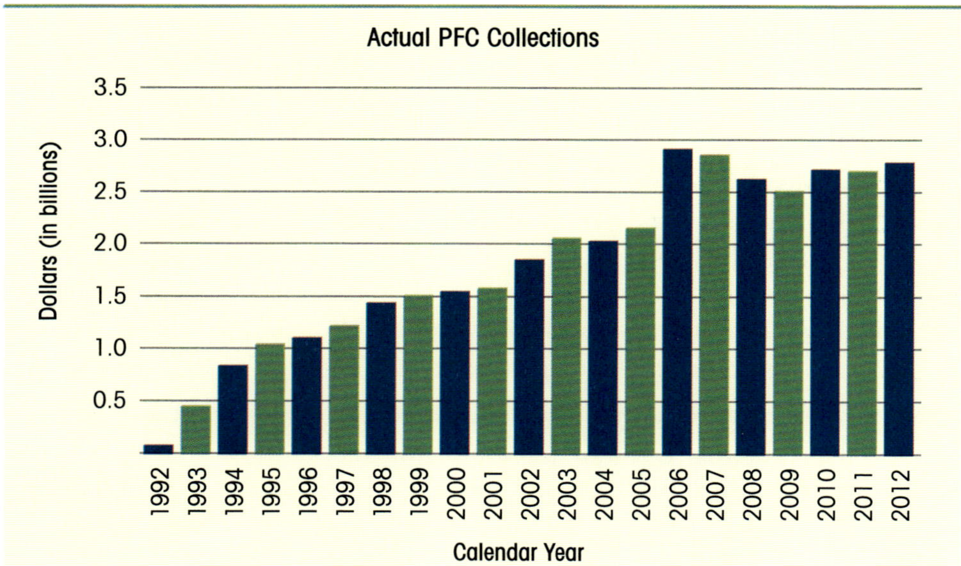

Figure 1-14. Actual passenger facility charge collection amounts.

In addition to authorizing the collection of PFCs, the Aviation Safety and Capacity Expansion Act also addressed aircraft noise by requiring the phaseout of Stage 2 aircraft by the end of the decade. (See Chapter 6 for more information.) The Act established Stage 3 as the new national standard for aircraft noise levels.[10] Additionally, the **Military Airport Program (MAP)** was authorized. This program allows AIP funding, via a special MAP set-aside of AIP discretionary funds, for either capacity or conversion-related projects at current and former military airports. Generally, MAP-funded projects include building or rehabilitating parking lots, fuel farms, hangars, utility systems, access roads, and cargo buildings. A maximum of 12 airports were initially allowed to participate in the MAP. As of 2011, a total of 15 airports may participate in the program at any one time, including one general aviation airport. Airports may be selected to receive funding for up to five years and may reapply. Since 1990, the FAA has provided MAP funds totaling $587 million. Interestingly, many of these MAP-funded projects are not eligible for AIP funding, but with unique eligibility rules for converting military airports to civilian or joint-use, these projects can be funded through the MAP set-aside. (AAAE, 2005; FAA, 2010a).

Although airport funding now had a more secure future in the form of AIP and PFCs, aviation security remained turbulent. In fact, 1987 and 1988 proved deadly in this regard. On December 7, 1987, a disgruntled former employee of Pacific Southwest Airlines, David Burke, used his unsurrendered USAir credentials to board a flight in Los Angeles with a loaded .44 magnum revolver. This was the same flight his former supervisor took daily commuting from his home in San Francisco to his workplace at Los Angeles International Airport. While en route to the aircraft's San Francisco destination, Mr. Burke killed his former supervisor as well as the flight crew and crashed the aircraft, killing a total of 43 people. The following year, on December 21, 1988, Pan American Airlines flight 103 departed London's Heathrow Airport and while en route to New York, the aircraft disintegrated over Lockerbie, Scotland, killing all 259 on board and 11 on the ground. The cause of the accident was terrorism. A bomb comprised of plastic explosive had been disguised inside a radio cassette player that was inside a piece of unaccompanied checked luggage. In an effort to address these issues and prevent future such attacks, President George H. Bush established the President's Commission on Aviation Security and Terrorism (Rumerman, n.d.).

The Commission focused on the ability of the present aviation security system to prevent security threats in the future. Findings of the Commission were rather sobering. The final report stated:

> The Commission found an aviation security system that was sorely lacking. As implemented, principally by the Federal Aviation Administration, it had failed to keep pace with the changing times. At a time when bombings already had become the preferred method for terrorists, the security program was still aimed largely at preventing hijackings.
> (Commission on Aviation Security and Terrorism, 1990)

[10] For subsonic transport-category large airplanes and subsonic jet airplanes, applying for type certification on or after January 1, 2006, Stage 4 compliance is required.

As a result of this "sorely lacking" aviation security system, on November 16, 1990, George H. Bush signed the **Aviation Security Improvement Act of 1990** into law. President Bush stated:

> In signing this legislation, I am doing more than signing a bill into law. This Act reflects the workings of the American democracy, an effort by private citizens, the Congress, and the executive branch to join in the common cause against international terrorism. H.R. 5732 is an expression of our national unity and determination to continue our fight against international terrorists and to help prevent another tragedy like Pan Am 103.
> (Bush, 1990, para. 5)

In particular, the Act required the FAA to place a renewed emphasis on explosives detection research and development.

In 1992, the **Airport and Airway Safety, Capacity, Noise Improvement, and Intermodal Transportation Act of 1992** brought about some changes in AIP funding. First, it specifically authorized a $2.1 billion extension of the AIP through 1993. The Act additionally expanded the projects authorized under the MAP program; provided for the relocation of air traffic control towers and NAVAIDs if their location interfered with AIP-funded projects; funded land, paving, drainage, aircraft deicing equipment, and aircraft deicing areas; and required compliance with various laws such as the **Americans with Disabilities Act of 1990**, the **Clean Air Act**, and the **Federal Water Pollution Control Act**. The number of states authorized to participate in the **State Block Grant Program**, which provided a block of AIP funds to a state to then distribute to airports within their state, was increased from three to seven, and the program was extended through 1996.

Various acts extended the AIP in subsequent years, including the **AIP Temporary Extension Act**, which extended the AIP to the end of June 1994; the **Federal Aviation Administration Authorization Act of 1994**, which extended AIP funding through the end of September 1996; and the **Federal Aviation Reauthorization Act of 1996**. During the eight-month period prior to the signing of the 1996 Act, the trust fund was gradually reduced as Congress authorized spending of trust fund money for the operations and maintenance of the FAA. With the passage of the 1996 Act, however, aviation taxes were reinstituted, but the trust fund authorization again lapsed on January 1, 1997. To resolve this issue, the Act directed the FAA to work with an independent organization to assess FAA funding requirements through 2002.

To comply with this mandate, the **National Civil Aviation Review Commission** was established, with Norman Mineta, a former U.S. representative, as chairman. The purpose of the Commission was to evaluate the long-term financing needs of the FAA and make recommendations for funding. The 1996 Act also authorized the FAA to certificate airports served by aircraft with 10 or more passenger seats. Airports served by aircraft with more than 30 passenger seats were already certificated by 14 CFR Part 139. The 1996 Act also revised the manner in which primary and cargo entitlements, state apportionment, and discretionary set asides are calculated. Pilot programs were also authorized in the areas of privatization of airports, innovative financing, and pavement maintenance. Lastly, the State Block Grant Program was finally made permanent, and the number of states authorized to participate was increased from seven to nine.

In an effort to ensure a stable funding source for AIP and avoid the year-to-year reauthorizations or lapses in funding that had become common, Senator Wendell H. Ford (Kentucky) led the charge that ensured the passage of the **Aviation Investment and Reform Act for the 21st Century (AIR 21)**. This Act, signed into law on April 5, 2000, authorized the AIP for fiscal years 2000 to 2003 and increased funding levels to about $3.1 billion annually. Additionally, the cap on the PFC was increased from $3.00 to $4.50. However, if a large or medium hub airport desired to implement the $4.50 PFC, they would need to demonstrate the manner by which the proposed project would make a significant contribution to improve safety or security, increase competition, reduce congestion or minimize the impact of noise. If an airport were approved to implement the $4.50 PFC, the airport would forgo 75 percent of AIP entitlements.

9/11

Just over one year later, one of the most significant events in civil aviation history occurred. On September 11, 2001, two commercial aircraft that had been hijacked by a group of terrorists were intentionally flown into the twin towers of the World Trade Center in New York City. Almost simultaneously, a third hijacked aircraft crashed into the Pentagon and a fourth slammed into a Pennsylvania field (Figure 1-15). These coordinated terrorist attacks, carried out by members of the Islamic extremist group, Al-Qaeda, resulted in extensive death and destruction. In fact, more than 3,000 people were killed in the attacks in New York City and Washington, DC, including 400 police officers and firefighters. Further, the New York City skyline was catastrophically altered (History.com, 2011).[11]

Post 9/11

In response to the terrorist attacks, and acting swiftly to address aviation security concerns in the United States, Congress drafted the **Aviation and Transportation Security Act (ATSA) of 2001**. President George W. Bush signed the Act into law on November 19, 2001, during a signing ceremony at Ronald Reagan Washington National Airport. This law created the **Transportation Security Administration (TSA)**, a new organization within the Department of Transportation. The TSA was charged with all federal security

[11] Chapter 9 presents a more in-depth discussion of aviation security.

Figure 1-15. Images from the 9/11 attacks: destruction at the World Trade Center and Pentagon, and recovery efforts.

(Wikimedia Commons; see credit on page 623)

responsibilities in all modes of transportation. Specifically, all aviation security functions formerly handled by the FAA were transferred to the TSA. The ATSA also spelled out specific deadlines to enable the industry to transition to a more secure environment:

- November 19, 2001: New federal background checks required for all airport and airline employees to gain access to security sensitive areas.
- January 18, 2002: Requirement for 100 percent of checked baggage at U.S. airports to be screened using explosive detection equipment, passenger bag matching, manual searches, or canine units.
- February 17, 2002: Official transfer of all civil aviation security responsibilities from FAA to TSA.
- November 21, 2002: Requirement for TSA screeners to screen all passengers and carry-on baggage at the nation's 429 largest commercial air carrier airports.
- December 31, 2002: Requirement for TSA screeners to screen, with certified explosive detection equipment, 100 percent of checked baggage at the nation's 429 largest commercial air carrier airports.

(Aviation Transportation and Security Act, 2001; "Actions by Deadline," 2001)

Meeting these ambitious deadlines required a great deal of investment in both equipment and human resources. Specifically, the TSA invested more than $5 billion in hiring more than 50,000 screeners and administrative staff, and acquiring security screening equipment. To fund these expenses, the Act authorized a $2.50 per flight segment surcharge on air carrier passenger tickets, with a maximum $10 charge per roundtrip flight.

One year later in November 2002, President George W. Bush signed the **Homeland Security Act of 2002** into law. The Homeland Security Act consolidated 22 federal agencies into the newly established Department of Homeland Security (DHS). This was a tremendous reorganizing of the federal government and affected the Transportation Security Administration, the U.S. Customs Service, and the enforcement functions of the Immigration and Naturalization Service. Additionally, the **National Commission on Terrorist Attacks Upon the United States**, also known as the 9/11 Commission, was created. This independent, bipartisan commission was created to prepare a full and complete account of the circumstances surrounding the September 11, 2001, terrorist attacks, as well as recommendations to guard against future attacks. On July 22, 2004, the Commission released its 585-page report (Price and Forrest, 2010; National Commission on Terrorist Attacks Upon the United States, 2004).

In the latter part of 2003, and in honor of the Wright Brothers' first flight in 1903, the **Vision 100—Century of Aviation Reauthorization Act of 2003** was signed into law. This law reauthorized the Airport Improvement Program for 2004 to 2007, with funding levels between $3.4 and $3.7 billion.

By reauthorizing AIP for another multi-year period, airports were provided a more stable funding source and could plan long-term capital improvements.

Although the 9/11 Commission Report had been issued on July 22, 2004, a bill implementing the recommendations of the 9/11 Commission was not signed into law until August 3, 2007. On this day, President George W. Bush signed into law the **Implementing Recommendations of the 9/11 Commission Act of 2007**. The Act provided for a number of grants, improved communication, and enhanced security infrastructure for all areas. Regarding aviation, Title XVI had the following 18 sections:

- Section 1601—Establishes the Checkpoint Screening Security Fund, to be funded by a uniform fee on air passengers, the amounts of which shall be available for the purchase, deployment, installation, research, and development of equipment to improve the ability of security personnel at screening checkpoints to detect explosives.
- Section 1602—Requires the Secretary of the DHS to establish a system to screen 100% of cargo transported on passenger aircraft, phased in over a three-year period.
- Section 1603—Extends funding for aviation security improvements. Requires the Secretary to submit a cost-sharing study for projects to install in-line baggage screening equipment.
- Section 1604—Requires (current law authorizes) the Under Secretary for Border and Transportation Security of DHS to make grants to airport sponsors for specified airport security improvement projects, with priority to small hub and nonhub airports.
- Section 1605—Directs the Secretary to submit to Congress a plan that describes the system to be used by DHS to compare passenger information to the Automatic Selectee and No Fly Lists utilizing the consolidated and integrated Terrorist Watchlist, as well as a timeline for testing and implementing the system.
- Section 1606—Directs the Secretary to establish a timely and fair process for individuals who believe they have been delayed or prohibited from boarding a commercial aircraft because they were wrongly identified as a threat, including an Office of Appeals and Redress to oversee the process.
- Section 1607—Directs the Secretary to prepare a strategic plan, with full plan implementation within one year, to promote the optimal utilization and deployment of explosive detection equipment at airports to screen individuals and their personal property.
- Section 1608—Amends the Aviation and Transportation Security Act to extend funding for research and development of aviation security technology.
- Section 1609—Requires the TSA Administrator, before January 1, 2008, to evaluate the results of the blast-resistant cargo container pilot program; and develop and implement a program to acquire, maintain, and replace blast-resistant cargo containers, pay for the program, and make such containers available to air carriers by July 1, 2008, for use on a risk-managed basis.

- Section 1610—Directs the Secretary to expedite research and development for technology that can disrupt or prevent an explosive device from being introduced onto a passenger plane or from damaging a passenger plane while in flight or on the ground; and establish a grant program to fund pilot projects to deploy such technology and test technology to expedite the recovery, development, and analysis of information to determine the cause of aircraft accidents.
- Section 1611—Directs the Administrator to provide advanced training to transportation security officers for the development of specialized security skills, including behavior observation and analysis, explosives detection, and document examination.
- Section 1612—Provides that any statutory limitation on the number of employees in TSA, before or after its transfer to DHS from DOT, does not apply after FY2007. Directs the Secretary to recruit and hire such TSA personnel as necessary to provide appropriate levels of aviation security and to reduce the average aviation security-related delay experienced by airline passengers to less than 10 minutes.
- Section 1613—Directs the Administrator to conduct a pilot program to identify technologies to improve security at airport exit lanes.
- Section 1614—Directs the Administrator to report on the status of its efforts to institute a sterile area access system that will enhance security by properly identifying authorized airline flight deck and cabin crew members at screening checkpoints and granting them expedited access; and begin full implementation of the system no later than one year after transmitting the report.
- Section 1615—Directs the Secretary to establish a national registered armed law enforcement program for law enforcement officers needing to be armed when traveling by air.
- Section 1616—Prohibits the FAA Administrator from certifying any foreign repair station if specified conditions are not met. Reduces the period in which a security review and audit of such stations must be accomplished.
- Section 1617—Directs the TSA Administrator to develop a standardized threat and vulnerability assessment program for general aviation airports; implement a program to perform such assessments on a risk-assessment basis; complete a study of the feasibility of a program, based on a risk-managed approach, to provide grants to general aviation airport operators for projects to upgrade security; and develop a risk-based system under which foreign-registered general aviation aircraft are required to submit passenger information at the same time as advance notification requirements for Customs and Border Protection (CBP) before entering U.S. airspace and under which such information is checked against appropriate databases maintained by TSA.
- Section 1618—Extends aviation security funding through FY2011.

(Congressional Research Service, 2007)

On December 12, 2003, President Bush signed a four-year FAA reauthorization bill into law. The four-year measure contains more than $14 billion for airport construction projects, funding to help small communities retain and attract commercial air service, and funding to reimburse airports for their increased security costs (AAAE, 2004a).

On February 10, 2004, the FAA released the long-awaited final rule on **14 CFR Part 139, Certification of Airports** (Figure 1-16). The Notice of Proposed Rulemaking for this revision was issued in June 2000. There were numerous changes in the regulation, including:

- Changes the applicability of the rule from airports serving scheduled or unscheduled operations with aircraft of more than 30 passengers to airports serving scheduled passenger-carrying operations with aircraft of more than nine passengers and unscheduled of more than 30 passengers.
- Establishes four classes of airports.
- Removes the term limited certificate airport.
- Establishes that to obtain a certificate the airport must have air service.
- Changes the exemption process.
- Provides greater detail as to what needs to be in the airport certification manual for the different classes of airports.
- Includes more recordkeeping standards for training of personnel.
- Provides greater clarity for Aircraft Rescue and Firefighting (ARFF) operational requirements.
- Outlines emergency plan requirements for small airports.
- Adds new requirements to airports' wildlife hazard management plans. (AAAE, 2004b)

Figure 1-16. An airport operations vehicle in use to ensure this airport's compliance with 14 CFR Part 139 and other requirements.

Figure 1-17. Airport perimeter fencing, one component contributing to security at this airport.

On May 17, 2004, the TSA released Information Publication A-001, **Security Guidelines for General Aviation Airports**. Although these guidelines are intended to provide the GA community with federally endorsed security enhancements and methods for implementing them, the document does not have any regulatory language or suggest that any recommendations or guidelines be considered a mandatory requirement. The guidelines contain the Airport Characteristics Measurement Tool that helps to define unique security needs for differing airports, as well as suggested security improvements (Figure 1-17). It is designed to be self-administered by airport operators, allowing them to assess an airport's security characteristics and determine which enhancements are most appropriate (AAAE, 2004c).

Although major pieces of legislation receive more press, funding of departments and federal agencies is often completed through the signing of spending bills. The president may sign into law fiscal year **spending bills** which continue funding for one department, such as the Department of Homeland Security or Department of Transportation. One example of this form of funding is the October 18, 2004, signing of the fiscal year 2005 spending bill for the Department of Homeland Security. This bill contained a number of provisions, one of which was $295 million for explosives detection system (EDS) installation at airports. Another form of funding is an **omnibus spending bill**. These bills, once signed into law by the president, provide funding for a number of federal departments. An example of this form of funding is the fiscal year 2005 omnibus spending bill signed into law by President Bush on December 8 to fund the federal government, which included $3.5 billion for AIP. Occasionally, the House of Representatives and Senate cannot agree on funding, and a temporary funding bill, known as a **continuing resolution**, has to be signed to allow for continued funding of the federal government. This may be a one-month or three-month extension, for example. One such continuing resolution was signed by the president in October 2008. This was necessary to ensure continued operation of the federal government as a new fiscal year began on October 1. A continuing resolution only buys some time for House and Senate negotiators to reconcile differences between the House and Senate versions of a funding bill. Multi-year FAA reauthorization bills are important for airports, especially when planning capital investment based on AIP funding levels. (AAAE, 2004d; AAAE, 2004e; AAAE, 2008).

Contemporary and Future Period

Although the aviation industry has indeed matured and experienced significant growth since the Wright Brothers' first flight in 1903, the Air Transport Association reports that the U.S. airline industry experienced net losses of $23.2 billion from 2001 through 2003. Interestingly, the low-cost carriers largely remained profitable during this period. Clearly, the effects of September 11 and the complete shutdown of the nation's air transportation system for a three-day period immediately following the attacks played a substantial role in the enormous losses experienced by U.S. airlines from 2001 to 2003. Unfortunately for the airline industry, the events of 9/11 could not have come at a worse time. The industry was already experiencing net operating losses for many reasons, including the mild recession, severe acute respiratory syndrome (SARS), and the increase in services by low-cost carriers, as well as the decline in business fares relied on by legacy carriers. Additionally, rising fuel prices, ever-present issues with labor-management relations, concerns with terrorism, and unfunded security mandates also weighed on the industry (ATA, 2011; Smith and Cox, 2008).

The effects of 9/11 and the airline industry's woes also negatively impacted the airport industry. Airports have been faced with airline bankruptcies, airline mergers, and reduced capacity, many times resulting in loss of service and reduced revenues for the airport. As a result, some airports have been faced with abandoned facilities, such as maintenance hangars, and have accordingly reduced staff and developed contingency plans to meet the dynamics of the airline industry.

Even with these challenges, today's aviation industry in the United States is strong. Approximately 590,000 active pilots, 232,000 general aviation aircraft, and 4,520 air carrier jets utilize 19,734 landing areas consisting of 5,179 public-use (open to the public) and 14,555 private use (closed to the public) facilities. This includes 13,477 airports, 5,576 heliports, 495 seaplane bases, 35 glider ports, 13 balloon ports, and 138 ultralight parks. Although student pilot starts have declined in recent years, the new Light Sport Pilot Certificate and efforts by organizations such as the Aircraft Owners and Pilots Association have had positive effects on the industry (FAA, 2010d).

Although the future is difficult to forecast, one can be fairly certain of issues of future importance for the airport industry. One such issue will involve the continued debate on proposed higher PFC amounts. Although the highest PFC amount was increased from $3 to $4.50 in the year 2000, the purchasing power of the dollar has degraded since that time. Additionally, according to Charles Barclay, former AAAE President, construction costs have risen by more than 53 percent since that time. As a result, a $3 PFC is worth approximately $1.53 today, and a $4.50 PFC is worth about $2.51. According to current AAAE President, Todd Hauptli, "At a time when there is enormous pressure to reduce federal spending, modernizing the local Passenger Facility Charge (PFC) is the best way to deliver additional resources to airports and make our infrastructure more competitive. Last adjusted in 2000, a modernized PFC would help airports of all sizes." (Laing, 2015). Therefore, airports will continue to press for higher PFCs, while airlines are expected to fight back. This, even as the airlines collected a total of $3.5 billion in baggage fees (2.1 percent of total operating revenue) and $3.0 billion from reservation change fees (1.8 percent of total operating revenue) in 2014 (AAAE, 2010; Laing, 2015; Bureau of Transportation Statistics, 2015).

In addition to PFCs, AIP funding levels will likely be a continued issue of importance in the future. It seems that each president and Congress are at odds with the amount of AIP funding that should be made available for infrastructure improvements. Of course, airports typically press for more AIP funding, especially with the maximum of $4.50 for PFCs. Additionally, airport security will likely remain an important issue. The TSA continues to evolve passenger screening methods, as well as airport security requirements. Due to the new security environment in which airports operate post-9/11, airport security will remain a focus in the future.

Concluding Thoughts

Clearly, a historical overview of the aviation industry is both necessary and helpful in understanding from where the industry came and in considering its future. At only a little more than 100 years old, the industry has made great strides. While much of this progress is attributable to the men and women passionate about the industry, much is also attributed to the governmental regulations that have provided the foundation, standards, and funding necessary to ensure the industry's growth and stability. As discussed in this chapter, these regulations and funding sources have been integral to the industry and have provided airports, specifically, with the means necessary to meet the current and future demands of the aviation system.

Chapter Summary

- On December 17, 1903, Orville Wright flew the Wright Flyer I in the first controlled, powered, and sustained flight.
- The first scheduled commercial airline using heavier-than-air aircraft, the St. Petersburg-Tampa Airboat Line, first flew on January 1, 1914, with Tony Jannus as the pilot.
- The nation's first municipal airport was built in 1908 in Albany, New York.
- Airmail service began on May 15, 1918, with the inaugural flight.
- The Post Office began carrying airmail on August 12, 1918, after the army contract ended.
- The Contract Air Mail Act of 1925 (Kelly Act) allowed the postmaster general to contract for domestic airmail service with commercial air carriers. The routes established were known as Contract Air Mail routes, or CAM routes.
- The Air Commerce Act of 1926 was designed to promote the development, and ensure the stability, of commercial aviation. This act created an Aeronautics Branch within the Department of Commerce.
- In 1934, the Aeronautics Branch was renamed the Bureau of Air Commerce.
- In response to the Great Depression, the Civil Works Administration, later the Federal Emergency Relief Administration, spent approximately $11.5 million by spring 1934 for 934 airport projects in small cities, resulting in 585 new airports.
- From 1935 to 1943, the Works Progress Administration built 651,087 miles of highways, roads, and streets; and constructed, repaired, or improved 124,031 bridges, 125,110 public buildings, 8,192 parks, and 853 airport landing areas.
- The Civil Aeronautics Act of 1938 created the Civil Aeronautics Authority, the Administrator of Aviation, and the Air Safety Board.
- The 1940 Reorganization Act divided the Civil Aeronautics Authority into the Civil Aeronautics Board (CAB) and the Civil Aeronautics Administration (CAA). The CAB became responsible for safety rulemaking, accident investigation, and economic regulation of the airlines. The CAA became responsible for air traffic control, airman and aircraft certification, safety enforcement, and airway development.
- As a result of World War II, the Development of Landing Areas for National Defense (DLAND) allowed the Secretaries of War and Commerce and the Secretary of the Navy to authorize expenditures for airports. In total, DLAND provided aid for a total 986 airports nationwide.
- The National Airport Plan, submitted to Congress in 1944, contained recommendations for airport construction, improvement, maintenance, and operation.

- The Federal Airport Act of 1946 provided, through the Federal Aid to Airports Program, $500 million in grants for airport projects paid over seven years.
- The Airways Modernization Act of 1957 was passed to modernize the air traffic control system and navigation facilities.
- The Federal Aviation Act of 1958, which repealed the Air Commerce Act of 1926, created the new Federal Aviation Agency (FAA). This Act transferred safety rulemaking from the CAB to the FAA. The FAA would also assume responsibility for developing and maintaining a common civil-military system of air navigation and air traffic control.
- The Department of Transportation Act of 1966 created the Department of Transportation, which housed the newly renamed Federal Aviation Administration, and the independent National Transportation Safety Board.
- The Airport and Airway Revenue Act of 1970 created the Airport and Airway Trust Fund, which would create a steady source of revenue for the continued development of airports and airways.
- The Air Cargo Deregulation Act of 1976 allowed air cargo carriers the freedom to raise or lower rates, serve any markets they chose, and own and operate trucks in support of their operation to pick up and deliver goods.
- The Airline Deregulation Act of 1978 allowed airlines the freedom to enter and exit markets at will, expand routes, and set airfares.
- The Essential Air Service program provides subsidies to encourage air carriers to remain in less-profitable, smaller markets.
- Consequences of airline deregulation include the hub and spoke route structure, loss of airline service in some markets, new start-up airlines, lower airfares, consolidation, and airline bankruptcies.
- The Aviation Safety and Noise Abatement Act of 1979 allowed the FAA to issue regulations on "air noise compatibility planning" and to make funds available to airports as part of an approved noise compatibility program.
- The Airport and Airway Improvement Act of 1982 established the Airport Improvement Program (AIP), which funded land acquisition; construction of runways, taxiways, and public areas of terminal buildings; as well as friction measuring equipment, safety-related equipment, automated weather observing systems, and airport planning and noise studies.
- The Airport and Airway Safety and Capacity Expansion Act of 1987 authorized AIP from 1987 to 1992.
- The Aviation Safety and Capacity Expansion Act of 1990 allowed authorized airports the ability to assess a passenger facility charge (PFC) in the amount of $1, $2, or $3 per enplaned passenger. The Act also authorized the Military Airport Program (MAP), which allows AIP funding for either capacity- or conversion-related projects at current and former military airfields.

- The Aviation Security Improvement Act of 1990 required the FAA to place a renewed emphasis on explosives detection research and development.
- The Airport and Airway Safety, Capacity, Noise Improvement, and Intermodal Transportation Act of 1992 was a significant act that benefitted airports in several ways. In addition to extending AIP through 1993 and increasing the number of states eligible to participate in the State Block Grant Program, it also expanded the MAP program and provided funding for relocation of air traffic control towers and new aircraft deicing facilities. Compliance with various laws, such as the Clean Air Act, was also required.
- The Federal Aviation Reauthorization Act of 1996 authorized the FAA to certificate airports served by aircraft with 10 or more passenger seats. The Act also created pilot programs in the areas of airport privatization, innovative financing, and pavement maintenance. The State Block Grant Program was also made permanent.
- The Aviation Investment and Reform Act for the 21st Century (AIR-21), signed into law in 2000, authorized the AIP for three more years and increased the cap on PFCs to $4.50.
- The Aviation and Transportation Security Act of 2001 was signed into law in response to the terrorist attacks on September 11, 2001. It created the Transportation Security Administration, a new organization within the DOT. The Act transferred all aviation security functions from the FAA to the TSA and spelled out a number of security-related deadlines.
- The Homeland Security Act of 2002 consolidated 22 federal agencies, including the TSA, into the newly established Department of Homeland Security and established the National Commission on Terrorist Attacks Upon the United States. Known as the 9/11 Commission, this independent, bipartisan commission was created to prepare a full and complete account of the circumstances surrounding the 9/11 terrorist attacks, as well as recommendations to guard against future attacks.
- The Vision 100—Century of Aviation Reauthorization Act of 2003 reauthorized the AIP from 2004 to 2007, with funding levels of between $3.4 and $3.7 billion.
- The Implementing Recommendations of the 9/11 Commission Act of 2007 provided a number of grants, improved communication, and enhanced security infrastructure for all areas.
- 14 CFR Part 139, Certification of Airports, was revised in 2004 and included numerous changes, such as establishing four classes of airports.
- The TSA Security Guidelines for General Aviation Airports, released in 2004, provides practical guidance for GA airports in enhancing their security posture.

Review Questions ↘

1. What was the significance of December 17, 1903?
2. What was the name of the first scheduled commercial airline using heavier-than-air aircraft?
3. What impact did WWI have on the development of aviation?
4. Explain why the Post Office cancelled the first contract to carry mail by air after only three months.
5. Explain the significance of the Contract Air Mail Act of 1925.
6. Explain the significance of the Air Commerce Act of 1926.
7. Explain the importance of the Civil Aeronautics Act of 1938.
8. What impact did WWII have on the development of aviation?
9. What was significant about the Federal Airport Act of 1946 in terms of funding for airports?
10. Explain the significance of the Federal Aviation Act of 1958.
11. Explain the significance of the Department of Transportation Act of 1966.
12. What was the purpose of the Airport and Airway Revenue Act of 1970?
13. Explain the significance (including the impacts) of the Airline Deregulation Act of 1978.
14. Who has benefitted the most from airline deregulation?
15. What is the purpose of the Essential Air Service program?
16. What is a hub and spoke route structure?
17. Explain the Airport Improvement Program (AIP).
18. What was the purpose of the National Civil Aviation Review Commission?
19. What was the purpose of the Homeland Security Act of 2002?
20. What was the purpose of the National Commission on Terrorist Attacks Upon the United States?
21. Explain the purpose of "Security Guidelines for General Aviation Airports."
22. Describe the events of September 11, 2001.

Scenarios ↘

1. Consider the role of WWI and WWII on the development of aviation in the U.S. In what way did these two wars advance the designs of aircraft, impact the growth of airports, and produce numerous skilled pilots? Do you feel the aviation industry would be as advanced and well developed as it is today without these two wars serving as a stimulus? Explain.
2. Consider the pieces of legislation discussed in this chapter. Which one piece of legislation do you feel most benefited the development of airports? Explain.
3. What if you had been selected as the first administrator of the Federal Aviation Agency? What three issues would be on your "to do" list?
4. Consider the role of commercial service airports after the events of 9/11. In what ways could they continue to meet the needs of the traveling public, while enhancing security and meeting the economic challenges to come?
5. Look back on the past 100 years of aviation in the United States. Consider the significant advances made, and in light of these advances, what do you foresee for the next 100 years? Be willing to think outside the box, as all great visionaries do.

References and Resources for Further Study

"Actions by Deadline." 2001. Retrieved from http://media.nara.gov/dc-metro/rg-237/74 19198-9-11-faa/5.%20Miscellaneous/(e)%20Other/5%20AWA%20274%20Report %20Aviation%20and%20Transportation%20Security%20Act%20Actions.pdf

Airport Noise Law. 2010. Retrieved from http://airportnoiselaw.org/acts.html

Air Transport Association (ATA). 1959. "Facts and Figures," 20th ed. Retrieved from http://airlines.org/about-us/history/

———. 1980. "The Annual Report of the U.S. Scheduled Airline Industry." Retrieved from http://airlines.org/about-us/history/

———. 1982. "The Annual Report of the U.S. Scheduled Airline Industry." Retrieved from http://airlines.org/about-us/history/

———. 2011. "We Connect the World: 2011 Economic Report." Retrieved from http://airlines.org/about-us/history/

American Association of Airport Executives (AAAE). 2004a, January 1. "Bush signs FAA reauthorization bill." *Airport Report.* Vol. XLVIII, No. 24.

———. 2004b, February 15. "FAA Releases Final Part 139 Rule." *Airport Report.* Vol. XLIX, No. 4.

———. 2004c, June 1. "TSA Issues GA Security Guidelines." *Airport Report.* Vol. XLIX, No. 11.

———. 2004d, November 1. "President Signs DHS Spending Bill." *Airport Report.* Vol. XLIX, No. 21.

———. 2004e, December 15. "Fiscal Year 2005 Spending Bill Cleared." *Airport Report.* Vol. XLIX, No. 24.

———. 2005. "Body of Knowledge Module 1. History, the Regulation of Air Transportation, Airports, and the Federal Aviation Administration." Washington, DC: AAAE.

———. 2008, October 1. "President Signs FAA Authority Extension Bill." *Airport Report.* Vol. LIII, No. 19.

———. 2009. Press release, "AAAE's Barclay Outlines Airport Priorities Before Key Senate Committee." Retrieved from http://www.aaae.org/news_publications/aaae_press_releases/viewRelease.cfm?p=3B7F3C6E-918A-6EC6-53E975E74716A34D

———. 2010, May 5. Press release, "AAAE Questions Airline Opposition to PFCs Given Industry's Growing Embrace of Fees." Retrieved from http://www.aaae.org/news_publications/aaae_press_releases/viewRelease.cfm?p=8F8049D1-F3F1-2451-4D317FE736353EE3

Aviation Transportation and Security Act. 2001. Pub. L. No. 107-71, 115 Stat. 597. Retrieved from http://www.tsa.gov/sites/default/files/assets/pdf/aviation_and_transportation_security_act_atsa_public_law_107_1771.pdf

Bluffield, B. 2010, June. "St. Petersburg-Tampa Airboat Line: World's First Scheduled Airline." Airways. Retrieved from http://www.tonyjannusaward.com/wp-content/uploads/2010/04/Airways-article-on-Tony-Jannus-and-First-Commercial-Flight.pdf

Bureau of Transportation Statistics. 2015. "2014 Airline Financial Data." BTS Press Release No. BTS 22-15. Retrieved from http://www.rita.dot.gov/bts/press_releases/bts022_15

Bush, G. 1990. "Statement on Signing the Aviation Security Improvement Act of 1990." Retrieved from http://www.presidency.ucsb.edu/ws/index.php?pid=19048#axzz1HhzYkbNf

College Park Aviation Museum. n.d. "Founding of the College Park Airport." Retrieved from http://www.collegeparkaviationmuseum.com/About_Us/History/Founding_of_the_College_Park_Airport.htm

Commission on Aviation Security and Terrorism. "Findings and Recommendations of the Commission on Aviation Security and Terrorism." 1990. Retrieved from http://www.globalsecurity.org/security/library/congress/1990_cr/s900511-terror.htm

Congressional Research Service. 2007. "Summary—Implementing Recommendations of the 9/11 Commission Act of 2007." Retrieved from http://www.govtrack.us/congress/bill.xpd?bill=h110-1&tab=summary

Department of Transportation. n.d. "Mission and history." Retrieved from http://www.dot.gov/mission/about-us

———. 2010, January. "Subsidized EAS Report." Retrieved from http://www.dot.gov/office-policy/aviation-policy/essential-air-service-reports

Federal Aviation Administration (FAA). n.d. "NextGen 101" video. Retrieved from http://www.faa.gov/nextgen/

———. 1980. "A Review of the Airport Development Aid Program (ADAP) and Assessment of Future Program Needs." Retrieved from http://oai.dtic.mil/oai/oai?verb=getRecord&metadataPrefix=html&identifier=ADA082637

———. 2001. "Passenger Facility Charge." FAA Order 5500.1. Retrieved from http://www.faa.gov/documentLibrary/media/Order/PFC_55001.pdf

———. 2010a. "Fact Sheet—2010 Military Airport Program Selections." Retrieved from http://www.faa.gov/airports/aip/military_airport_program/

———. 2010b. "PFC Overview." Retrieved from http://www.faa.gov/airports/central/pfc/pfc_overview/

———. 2010c. "Passenger Facility Charge (PFC) Program." Retrieved from http://www.faa.gov/airports/pfc/

———. 2010d. "2011–2015 National Plan of Integrated Airport Systems."

———. 2012. "Key Passenger Facility Charge Statistics." Retrieved from http://www.faa.gov/airports/pfc/monthly_reports/media/stats.pdf

FedEx. 2011. "FedEx History." Retrieved from http://about.fedex.designcdt.com/our_company/company_information/fedex_history

Hakes, C. D. n.d. "Albany Airport History." Retrieved from http://www.albanyairport.com/alb_history.php

History.com. "9/11 attacks." 2011. Retrieved from http://www.history.com/topics/9-11-attacks

Indiana University. n.d. "More About the WPA." Retrieved from http://www.indiana.edu/~liblilly/wpa/wpa_info.html

Johnson, L. B. 1966, January 12. "Annual Message to the Congress on the State of the Union." Retrieved from http://www.lbjlib.utexas.edu/johnson/archives.hom/speeches.hom/660112.asp

Kahn, A. E. 1993. "Airline Deregulation." *The Concise Encyclopedia of Economics.* Library of Economics and Liberty. Retrieved from http://www.econlib.org/library/Enc1/AirlineDeregulation.html

Laing, K. 2015. "Airlines, airports clash over passenger fees." Retrieved from http://thehill.com/policy/transportation/239923-airlines-airports-clash-over-plane-ticket-fees

Mola, R. n.d. "The Earliest Airports." U.S. Centennial of Flight Commission. Retrieved from http://www.centennialofflight.net/essay/Government_Role/earliest_airports/POL9.htm

Morrison, S. A., and W. Clifford. 2000. "The Remaining Role for Government Policy in the Deregulated Airline Industry." In Sam Peltzman and Clifford Winston, eds., *Deregulation of Network Industries: What's Next?* Washington, D.C.: AEI Brookings Joint Center for Regulatory Studies.

Murdock, S. 1997. "The Use in 1995 of World War II Army Airfields in the United States." Retrieved from http://www.airforcebase.net/aaf/grphtml.html

National Commission on Terrorist Attacks Upon the United States. 2004. "The 9/11 Commission Report." Retrieved from http://govinfo.library.unt.edu/911/report/index.htm

Preston, E. n.d. "The Federal Aviation Administration and its Predecessor Agencies." U.S. Centennial of Flight Commission. Retrieved from http://www.centennialofflight.net/essay/Government_Role/FAA_History/POL8.htm

Price, J., and J. Forrest. 2010. Finance and Administration. Body of Knowledge modules. Washington, DC: American Association of Airport Executives.

Reagan, R. 1981, August 3. "Remarks and a Question-and-Answer Session with Reporters on the Air Traffic Controller Strike." Retrieved from http://www.reagan.utexas.edu/archives/speeches/1981/80381a.htm

Rumerman, J. n.d. "Aviation Security." U.S. Centennial of Flight Commission. Retrieved from http://www.centennialofflight.net/essay/Government_Role/security/POL18.htm

Siddiqi, A. n.d. U.S. Centennial of Flight Commission. "Deregulation and its Consequences." Retrieved from http://www.centennialofflight.net/essay/Commercial_Aviation/Dereg/Tran8.htm

Smith, F. L. and B. Cox. 2008. "Airline Deregulation." *The Concise Encyclopedia of Economics.* Library of Economics and Liberty. Retrieved from http://www.econlib.org/library/Enc/AirlineDeregulation.html

The New York Times. "Santos-Dumont Arrives." 1902. http://query.nytimes.com/mem/archive-free/pdf?_r=2&res=9807E4D91230E733A25752C1A9629C946397D6CF

U.S. Centennial of Flight Commission. n.d.(a) "Airmail. The Airmail Act of 1925 through 1929." Retrieved from http://www.centennialofflight.net/essay/Government_Role/1925-29_airmail/POL5.htm

———. n.d.(b) "Government Funding of Airports." Retrieved from http://www.centennialofflight.net/essay/Government_Role/govt_funding/POL11.htm

———. n.d.(c) "The Post Office Flies the Mail." Retrieved from http://www.centennialofflight.net/essay/Government_Role/1918-1924/POL3.htm

Chapter 2

Structure of Airports

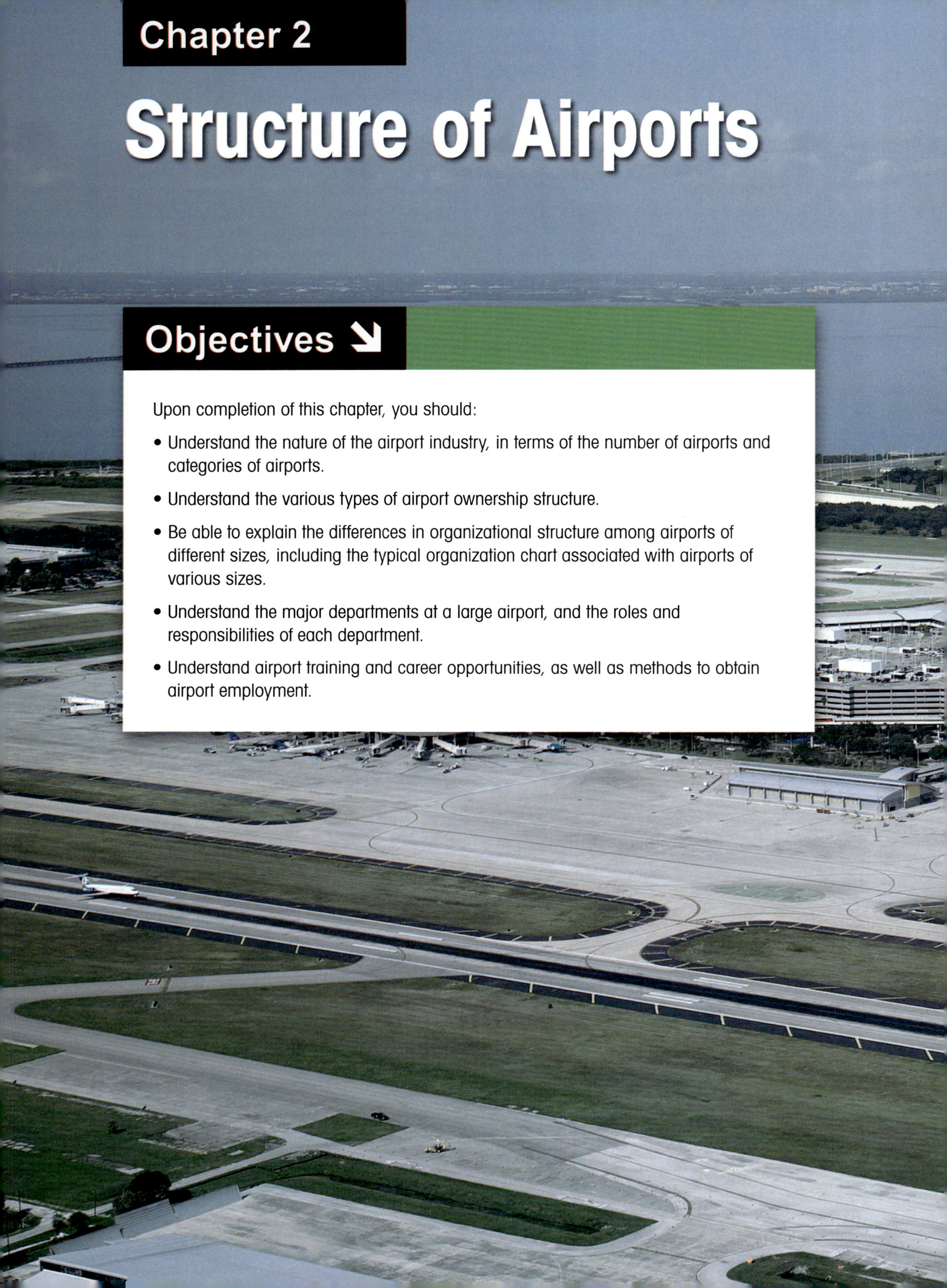

Objectives

Upon completion of this chapter, you should:

- Understand the nature of the airport industry, in terms of the number of airports and categories of airports.
- Understand the various types of airport ownership structure.
- Be able to explain the differences in organizational structure among airports of different sizes, including the typical organization chart associated with airports of various sizes.
- Understand the major departments at a large airport, and the roles and responsibilities of each department.
- Understand airport training and career opportunities, as well as methods to obtain airport employment.

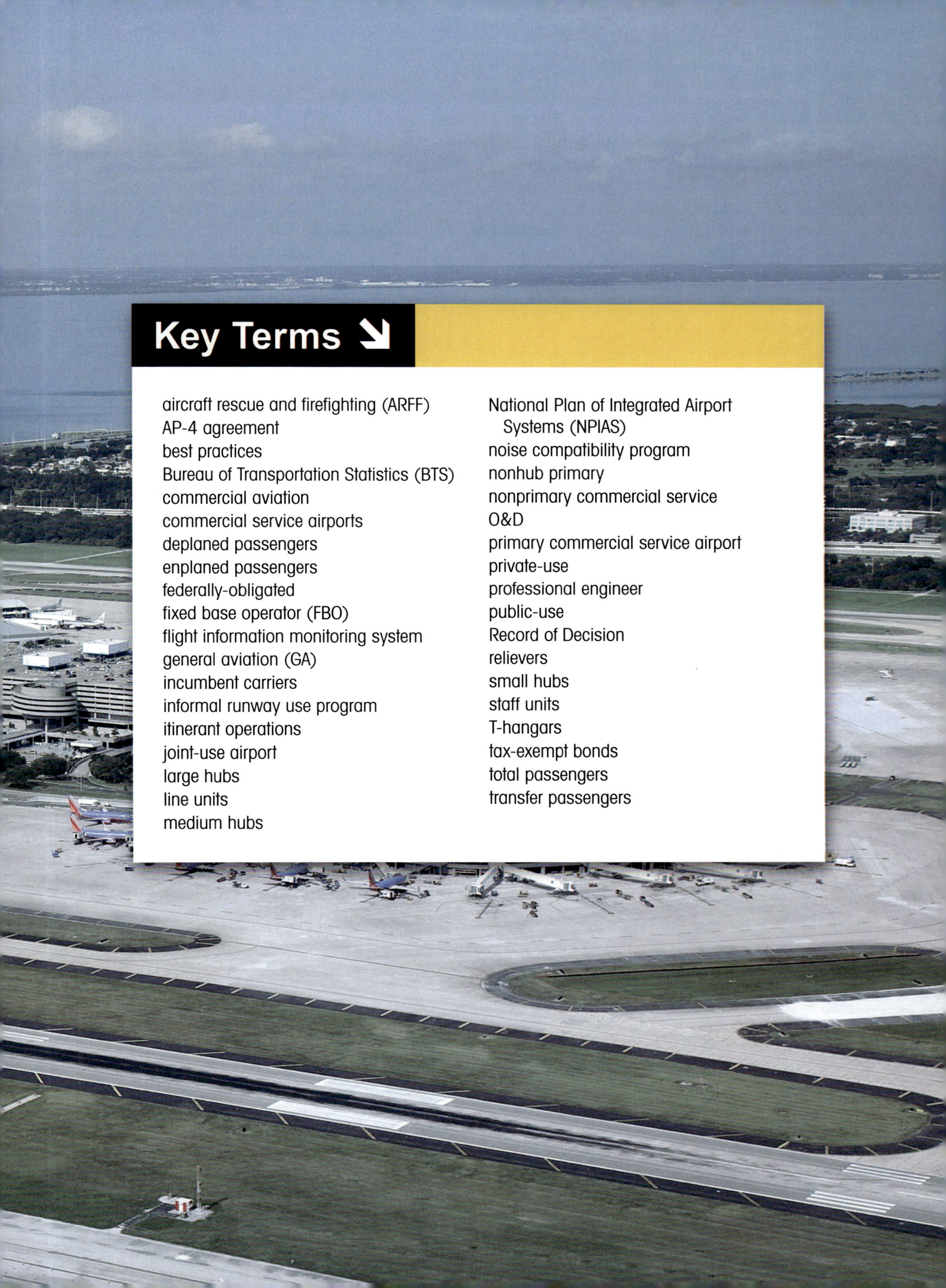

Key Terms

- aircraft rescue and firefighting (ARFF)
- AP-4 agreement
- best practices
- Bureau of Transportation Statistics (BTS)
- commercial aviation
- commercial service airports
- deplaned passengers
- enplaned passengers
- federally-obligated
- fixed base operator (FBO)
- flight information monitoring system
- general aviation (GA)
- incumbent carriers
- informal runway use program
- itinerant operations
- joint-use airport
- large hubs
- line units
- medium hubs
- National Plan of Integrated Airport Systems (NPIAS)
- noise compatibility program
- nonhub primary
- nonprimary commercial service
- O&D
- primary commercial service airport
- private-use
- professional engineer
- public-use
- Record of Decision
- relievers
- small hubs
- staff units
- T-hangars
- tax-exempt bonds
- total passengers
- transfer passengers

In Chapter 2

Introduction **53**

Categories of Airports **53**

- Commercial Service Airports 54
- Reliever 59
- General Aviation Airports 60
- Joint Use 61

Ownership of Airports **63**

- Private 63
- Public-Private Partnership 64
- Local Government 65
- State Government 66
- National/Federal Government 67
- Authorities or Commissions 69
- Advisory Boards 72
- Privatization 72

Organizational Structure **75**

Major Airport Departments **78**

- Air Service Development & Int'l Commerce 78
- Human Resources 78
- Governmental and Legal Affairs 79
- Public Information and Community Relations 80
- Performance Management and Internal Audit 80
- Planning and Development 81
- Operations 84
- Public Safety 85
- Properties and Contracts Administration 85
- Maintenance 86
- Marketing 86
- Information Technology 87
- Finance 88
- Customer Service 88

Airport Training Programs **89**

Career Advancement **90**

- Advertising of Airport Vacancies 90
- Methods to Obtain Employment 91

Concluding Thoughts **92**

Chapter Summary **93**

Review Questions **94**

Scenarios **95**

References & Resources for Further Study .. **96**

FEATURES

Joint Use Airport **62**

Joint civil/military use of Marine Corps Air Station Yuma and Yuma International Airport.

Multi-Use Airport **62**

A multi-use facility, Austin-Bergstrom International Airport is a commercial service airport with general aviation, the State Aircraft Pooling Board, and the Texas Army National Guard.

Privately-Owned, Public-Use Commercial Service Airport **63**

Branson Airport is a privately-owned, public-use commercial service airport.

State of Hawaii Airport System **67**

The Hawaii Airports Division operates and maintains 15 airports located throughout the state.

The Massachusetts Port Authority **71**

The role and mission of the Massachusetts Port Authority

Introduction

The United States accounts for a substantial portion of the entire world's aviation activity. Specifically, **commercial aviation** in this country represents 40 percent of all commercial aviation worldwide. Additionally, the country's **general aviation (GA)** activity represents 50 percent of the worldwide GA activity. Clearly, the country needs a substantial network of airports to support this high level of activity. In fact, this need is filled by almost 20,000 airports currently in operation throughout the United States (see Figure 2-1). Of this tremendous number, however, only about 5,000 are open to the public. Therefore, almost three-quarters of the total U.S. airports are closed to the public. Additionally, approximately 1,000 of these 5,179 airports are privately owned. This differentiation is important, as these differences affect federal funding, compliance, and use by commercial air carriers (FAA, 2010b).

Figure 2-1. U.S. airports by ownership and use.

(FAA: NPIAS)

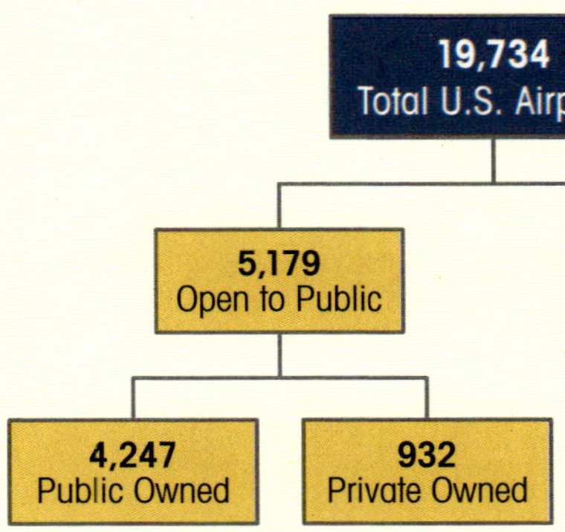

Categories of Airports

To keep track of the huge number of airports in the United States, a system for organizing them had to be developed. U.S. airports are categorized based on their purpose and size. Commercial service airports are further categorized based on the number of **enplaned passengers**. Enplaned passengers are those passengers boarding an aircraft. This includes passengers originating, as well as those transferring to another aircraft. Each time a passenger boards an aircraft, it is counted as an enplaned passenger. These categories are important, as a large degree of funding is determined by the category of the airport. Figure 2-2 shows the breakdown of all airports included in the **National Plan of Integrated Airport Systems (NPIAS)**, which represents 65 percent of the nation's public-use airports. The NPIAS identifies nearly 3,400 existing and proposed airports that are significant to national air transportation and thus eligible to receive federal grants under the Airport Improvement Program (AIP). However, there are 1,799 airports open to the public that are not included in the NPIAS.

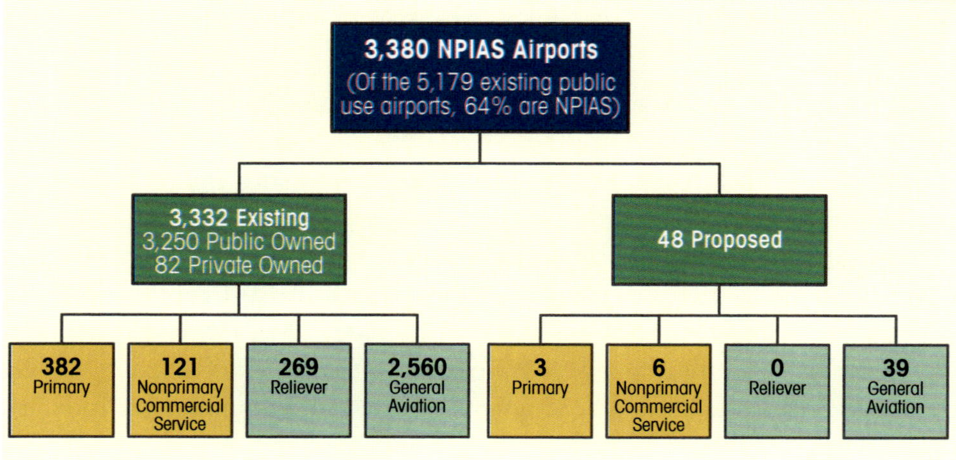

Figure 2-2. Number of NPIAS airports by use.

(FAA: NPIAS)

Additionally, there are 932 privately-owned, public-use airports that are not included because they are located at inadequate sites, are redundant to publicly owned airports, or have too little activity to meet NPIAS criteria. There are 867 publicly owned, public-use airports that are not included because they do not meet the minimum criteria for the NPIAS of ten based aircraft, or they are within 20 miles of a NPIAS airport, are located at inadequate sites, cannot be expanded and improved to provide safe and efficient airport facilities, or do not have adequate justification showing a significant national interest (FAA, 2010b).

COMMERCIAL SERVICE AIRPORTS

Airports with scheduled airline service are known as **commercial service airports** (see Figure 2-3). Clearly, some commercial service airports are very large, such as Hartsfield-Jackson Atlanta International Airport which has five runways and served over 96 million passengers in 2014. At the other end of the spectrum are single-runway airports such as the Gogebic-Iron County Airport in Ironwood, Michigan, which served approximately 3,500 passengers in 2014. Regardless of the size, as long as the airport is a public airport receiving scheduled passenger service and having a minimum of 2,500 annual enplaned passengers, it is categorized as commercial service. According to the 2009–2013 NPIAS and as shown in Figure 2-2, there were 503 commercial service airports in the U.S. as of 2008 (382 primary plus 121 commercial-service). Of these 503, only 382 airports had more than 10,000 annual passenger enplanements, thus meeting the threshold to be qualified as a **primary commercial service airport**.

Confusion often results when discussing total passengers and enplaned passengers. Enplaned passengers are those boarding an aircraft and **deplaned passengers** are those leaving the aircraft. Airports typically advertise their **total passenger** numbers, which would include both enplaned and deplaned passengers. In other words, total passengers represent every passenger at an airport,

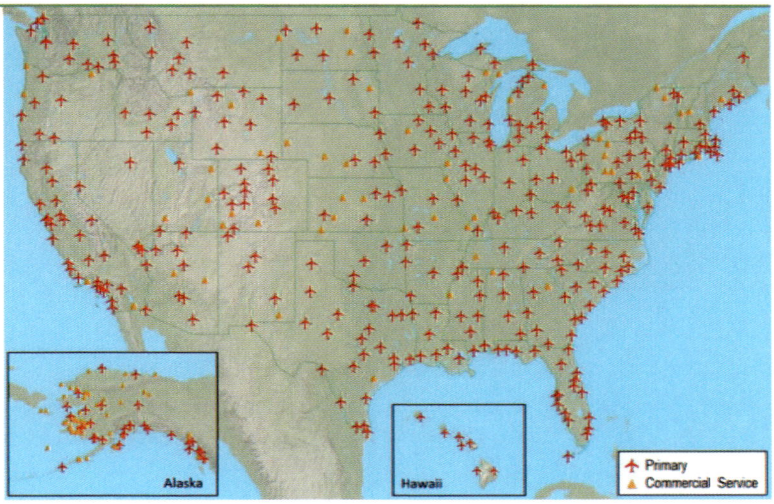

Figure 2-3. Commercial service airports.

(FAA: NPIAS)

generally measured on a monthly and annual basis—whether this passenger was departing or arriving. However, when categorizing airports, the focus is on enplaned passengers. As a result, the number of enplaned passengers is typically half of total passengers. Or stated alternatively, one could multiply the number of enplaned passengers by two to get a rough idea of total passengers. For instance, Hartsfield-Jackson Atlanta International Airport had 41.4 million enplanements in calendar year (CY) 2006. Yet the airport's 2006 Annual Report begins by stating, "It was another record-setting year in 2006 for Hartsfield-Jackson Atlanta International Airport, which was once again named the world's busiest, with more than 85 million passengers." (Hartsfield-Jackson International Airport, 2006)

Large Hubs

The largest of the commercial service airports are known as **large hubs** (see Figure 2-4). To be categorized as a large hub airport, the airport must serve at least one percent of total U.S. passenger enplanements; based on 739 million enplanements nationwide in CY13, this would amount to 7.39 million. This number changes every year; thus, the numerical threshold for being categorized as a large hub changes each year. If all U.S. passenger enplanements are added up for the 12-month period, any airport serving at least one percent of that total would be categorized as a large hub. Keep in mind that the hub category does not refer to airline hubs.[1] In fact, an airport could be categorized as a large hub airport and yet have no airline hub located there (FAA, 2010b).

It does not matter if these passengers originate in the local community (as would be the case at a mostly **O&D** [origin and destination] airport such as Orlando International) or are **transfer passengers** connecting from one flight to another (as would be the case at a mostly hub airport such as Atlanta). Due to the sheer size of these large hub airports, there are only 30 in the United States. In sum, they account for almost 70 percent of total U.S. passenger

[1] As in hub and spoke route structure.

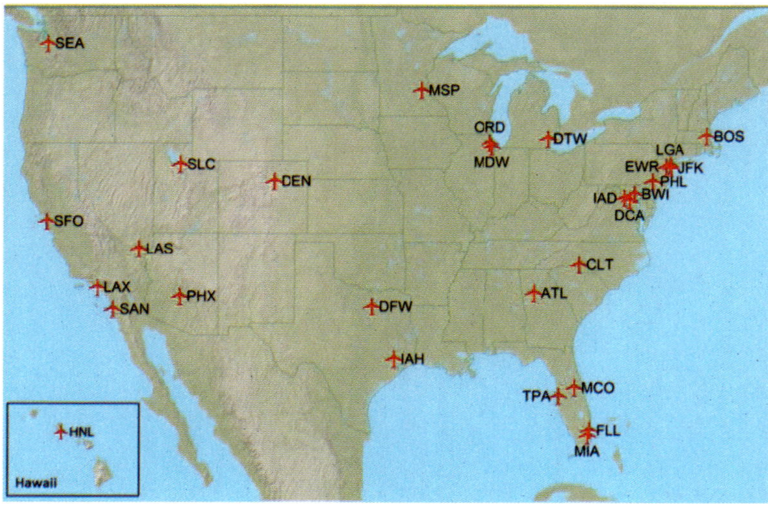

Figure 2-4. Large hub airports in the United States.

(FAA: NPIAS)

enplanements. This means that 7 out of 10 passengers flying commercially in this country either begin or continue their journey at one of the 30 large hub airports (FAA, 2010b).

Medium Hubs

Airports categorized as **medium hubs** must serve between 0.25 percent and 1 percent of total U.S. passenger enplanements; based on 739 million enplanements nationwide in CY13, this would amount to 1.84 million to 7.39 million. The 37 medium hub airports in the United States typically account for 20 percent of all passenger enplanements (Figure 2-5). It is important to note that even though they are considered commercial service airports, medium hub airports (and smaller) also typically have a substantial amount of GA activity, in addition to commercial airline activity. In fact, two medium hubs in the United States (Dallas Love Field—DAL, and John Wayne Airport/Orange County—SNA) have an average of over 600 based aircraft. This is quite amazing considering that these airports are also projecting enplanements in 2013

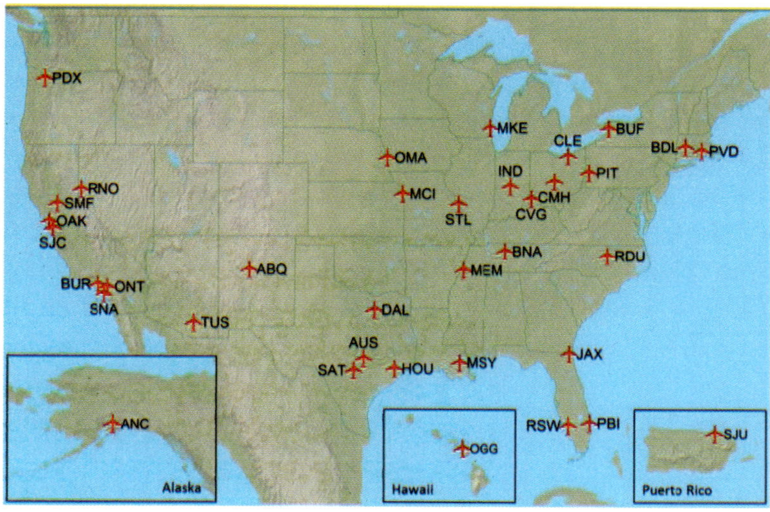

Figure 2-5. Medium hub airports in the United States.

(FAA: NPIAS)

to total 4.2 million and 5.3 million, respectively. The remaining medium hub airports average a much lower 129 based aircraft. Still, it is clear that both commercial airline activity and general aviation activity can coexist to a certain degree at an airport (FAA, 2010b).

Small Hubs

Airports that are not as busy as medium hubs are categorized as **small hubs.** Specifically, small hubs are those airports enplaning 0.05 percent to 0.25 percent of all passenger enplanements; based on 739 million enplanements nationwide in CY13, this would amount to 369,000 to 1.84 million. There are currently 72 small hub airports in the United States that collectively account for 8 percent of all passenger enplanements (see Figure 2-6). Small hub airports, which typically are not congested and don't have any significant air traffic delays, also accommodate a large degree of general aviation activity. Although small hubs average 134 based aircraft, there are some airports, such as Long Beach Airport, with many more based aircraft and a substantial amount of general aviation activity. For instance, Long Beach Airport in California had 435 aircraft in 2013 (FAA, 2010b).

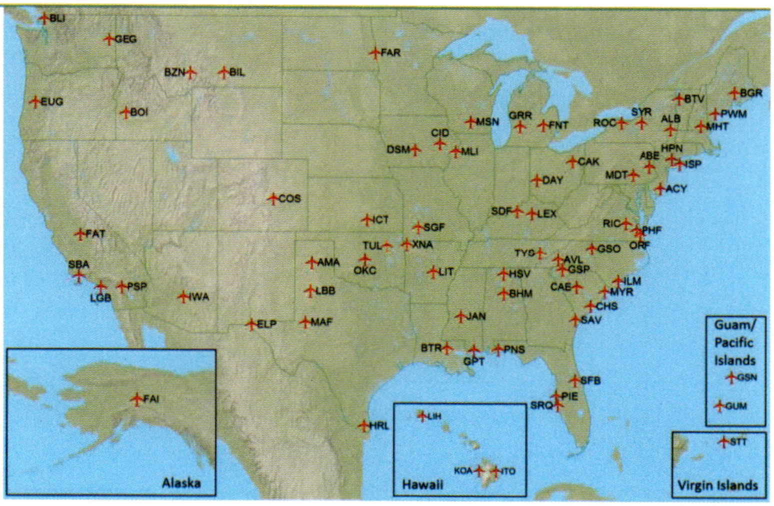

Figure 2-6. Small hub airports in the United States.

(FAA: NPIAS)

Nonhub Primary

There are some commercial service airports that are not categorized as hub airports, and yet still maintain their commercial service status. The first of these categories is **nonhub primary** (see Figure 2-7). Commercial service airports that enplane less than 0.05 percent of all commercial passenger enplanements and have at least 10,000 annual enplanements are categorized as nonhub primary airports. Although these airports collectively account for only 3 percent of all enplanements in the United States, they number 244. Generally, as the airport size decreases, the number of airports of a particular size increases. The United States has many more small airports than larger airports and that holds

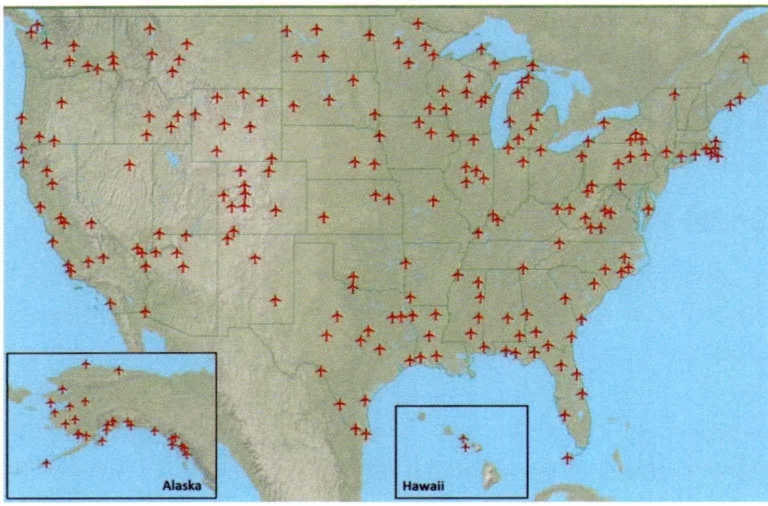

Figure 2-7. Nonhub primary airports in the United States.

(FAA: NPIAS)

true with this category. Additionally, nonhub primary airports are extensively utilized by general aviation pilots, accounting for almost 11 percent of all U.S. based aircraft (FAA, 2010b).

Nonprimary Commercial Service

The final category of commercial service airports is known as **nonprimary commercial service**. These are the smallest commercial service airports with at least 2,500 annual passenger enplanements, but no more than 10,000. Although these airports account for only 0.1 percent of all enplanements, there are 139 airports in this category (see Figure 2-8). There are fewer airports in this category than in the nonhub primary category, but this is due to the narrow definition for this category of airport. It can be difficult to have commercial service and enplane fewer than 10,000 passengers per year. In effect, an airport in this category would likely have commuter service by only one carrier and would be enplaning less than 833 passengers per month, on average. On the one hand, this can be difficult to accomplish. In reality, these are mostly general

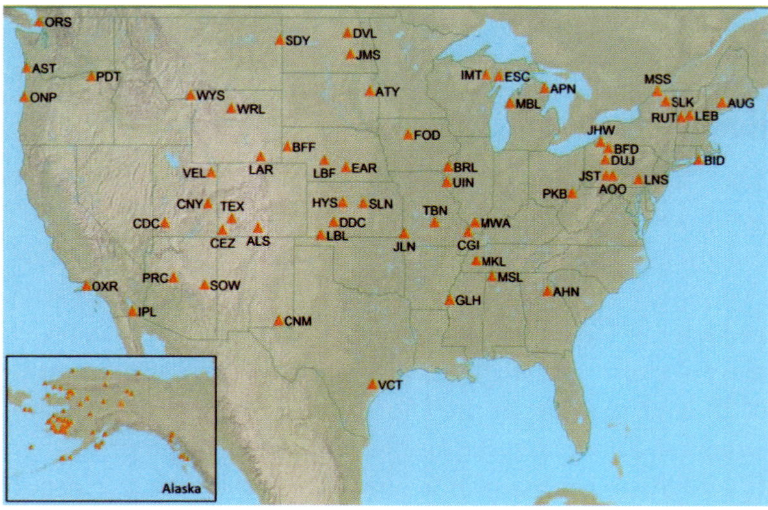

Figure 2-8. Nonprimary commercial service airports in the United States.

(FAA: NPIAS)

aviation airports that also have a small amount of commercial airline service, possibly through the Essential Air Service Program (FAA, 2010b).

RELIEVER

Although a review of the commercial service categories just discussed makes it apparent that commercial aviation and general aviation can coexist at an airport, GA activity, especially in the form of small aircraft and flight-training activities, is generally not very compatible with the larger commercial service airports. This is due to several factors, including mix of aircraft (and subsequent approach speeds and wake turbulence), Class B and C airspace requirements for aircraft equipment and pilot qualifications, the large volume of commercial aircraft operations, and the lack of familiarity among some GA pilots with complex airfield layouts and procedures at these large commercial service airports. Some airports even prohibit touch-and-gos or other flight-training activities due to the conflict these would create with large commercial service aircraft present in high numbers.

In recognition of this, and to encourage the development of high-capacity general aviation airports in major metropolitan areas, the FAA has designated certain airports as **relievers**. These airports are attractive alternatives for GA pilots desiring access to a major metropolitan area, but also desiring to stay out of the busy, and possibly congested, commercial service airport. To be categorized as a reliever, the airport must have 100 or more based aircraft or 25,000 annual **itinerant operations**. Itinerant operations are those operations that are not local, meaning they are conducted by aircraft not based at the airport. The United States currently has 270 reliever airports with an average of 230 based aircraft (see Figure 2-9). This represents almost 30 percent of the country's GA fleet (FAA, 2010b).

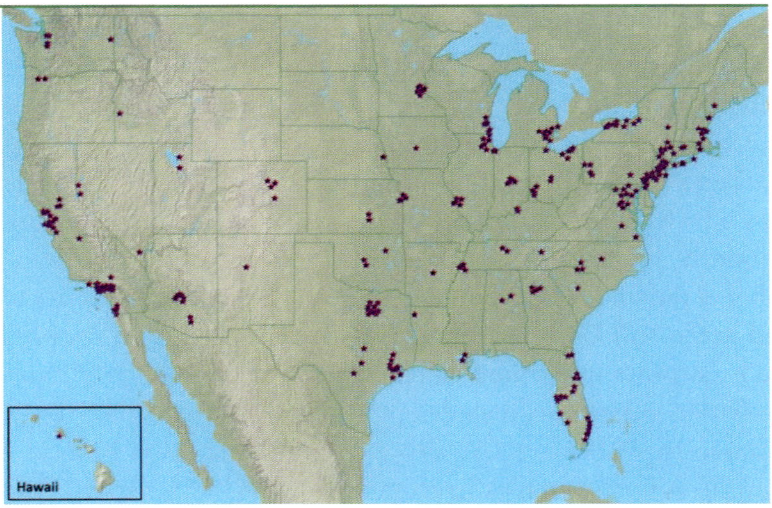

Figure 2-9. Reliever airports in the United States.

(FAA: NPIAS)

GENERAL AVIATION AIRPORTS

There is a plethora of airports in this country without commercial airline service (or with less than 2,500 annual passenger enplanements). General aviation is the category into which these airports fall (see Figure 2-10). The U.S. has some very active GA airports. For instance, Van Nuys Airport, located in the heart of the San Fernando Valley, ranks as the world's busiest general aviation airport. It averages nearly 400,000 takeoffs and landings annually. Interestingly, this airport is busier than many commercial service airports, in terms of number of operations. At the same time, there are also some very sleepy airports with no based aircraft. For instance, the majority of airports in Alaska have no based aircraft. Quite a few others have only a handful of based aircraft. Of course, with no based aircraft, these airports serve only itinerant operations (Van Nuys Los Angeles World Airports, 2011; FAA, 2010b).

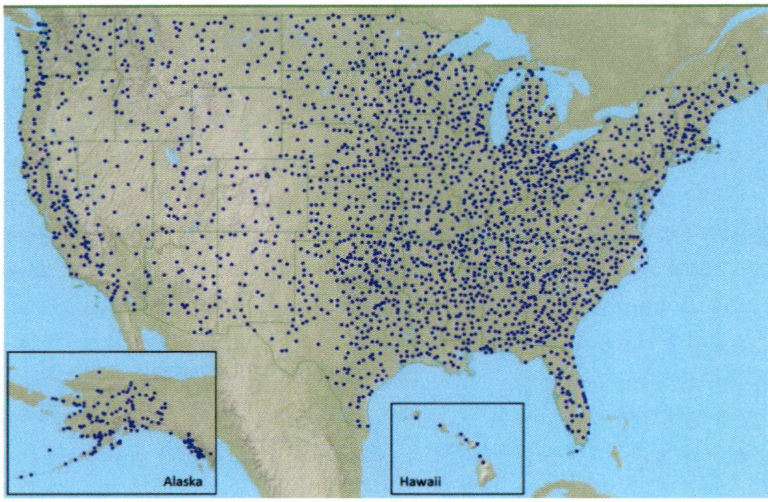

Figure 2-10. General aviation airports in the United States.

(FAA: NPIAS)

The NPIAS, however, is not a complete document. It does not identify all airport capital development needs nationwide. The NPIAS is designed to "identify for Congress and the public those airports included in the national system, the role they serve, and the amounts and types of airport development eligible for federal funding under the Airport Improvement Program (AIP) over the next five years" (FAA, 2010b, p. 1). Only 65 percent of the 5,179 public-use airports throughout the United States are included in the NPIAS. This means that a large number of public-use airports (almost 1,800) are not included in the NPIAS. As stated in the NPIAS, "All primary and commercial service airports, all general aviation airports designated as reliever airports by the FAA, and selected general aviation airports are included in the plan" (NPIAS, 2009, p. 1).

To be included in the NPIAS, a GA airport must have at least 10 locally based aircraft and be at least 20 miles from the nearest NPIAS airport. The more than 2,500 GA airports included in the NPIAS tend to be distributed on a one-per-county basis in rural areas and typically located near the county seat.

These airports have an average of 35 based aircraft and account for 41 percent of the U.S. GA fleet. Of particular importance, these airports are the nearest source of air transportation for almost 20 percent of the U.S. population (FAA, 2010b).

JOINT USE

Although not specifically included in the NPIAS, there are also joint-use airports in this country. According to the **Bureau of Transportation Statistics (BTS)** Dictionary (available on the BTS website), a **joint-use airport** is a "military installation at which the Department of Defense permits some degree of civil aviation use" (Bureau of Transportation Statistics, n.d.). Stated another way, a joint-use facility is established by agreement to allow use of a military runway for a public airport. The degrees of civil aviation use include either all civil aviation under a joint-use agreement, or limited use. Strictly military airports do not qualify for primary or commercial service status. Table 2-1 presents the joint-use airports in the United States as of October 2012.

Table 2-1. U.S. joint-use airports as of 2012.

Air Force	
AF Plant 42, Palmdale, CA	Kelly/Lackland AFB, San Antonio, TX
Barter Island LRRS, Barter Island, AK	March ARB, Riverside, CA
Charleston AFB, Charleston, SC	Pt. Lay LRRS, Point Lay, AK
Dover AFB, Dover, DE	Scott AFB (Mid America), Belleville, IL
Eglin AFB, Valparaiso, FL	Sheppard AFB, Wichita Falls, TX
Grissom AFB, Peru, IN	Westover ARB, Chicopee, MA
Army	
Blackstone AAF (Ft. Pickett), VA	Grayling AAF (Camp Grayling), MI
Camp Guernsey AAF, Guernsey, WY	Libby AAF (Ft. Huachuca), Sierra Vista, AZ
Dillingham AAF, Waialua, HI	Sherman AAF (Ft. Leavenworth), KS
Forney AAF (Fort Leonard Wood), MO	Sparta/Fort McCoy (Sparta), WI
Robert Gray AAF, Ft. Hood/Killeen, TX	Wright AAF (Fort Stewart) Midcoast Rgnl, Ft Stewart/Hinesville, GA
Navy	
MCAS Yuma, Yuma, AZ	

Joint-Use Airport

One example of a joint-use airport that is currently owned by the U.S. Department of Defense is Yuma (Arizona) International Airport. The Marine Corps Air Station Yuma and the Yuma County Airport Authority have entered into a joint-use operating agreement to allow both civilian and military activity on the same airport. The agreement "formalizes the coexistence of two independent, but mutually operating parties legitimately sharing a single common airfield since 1956." Specifically, the agreement establishes procedures and outlines responsibilities for the joint civil/military use of Marine Corps Air Station Yuma and Yuma International Airport. The actual agreement is available for viewing on www.yumaairport.com.

(Yuma International Airport 2009)

Multi-Use Airport

An example of a former U.S. Department of Defense facility now owned by a municipality and used as a multi-use airport (as contrasted to a joint-use airport) is in Austin, Texas. In 1990, the Base Realignment and Closure Commission notified the City of Austin, Texas that Bergstrom Air Force Base, after nearly 50 years of service, would be decommissioned and the land would be returned to the City. Timing could not have been better for the City of Austin, which had been exploring alternative sites for building a new commercial service airport to replace land-locked Robert Mueller Municipal Airport, which was not prepared to handle the future needs of the city and had 30,000 residents living in noise impact areas. The base was only eight miles from the capitol, was large enough to meet the community's growing needs, and had runways and other facilities already in place. As an added incentive, the surrounding area was sparsely populated, which meant that relatively few residents and businesses would be affected by noise. As a result, the City initiated an airport master plan to study Bergstrom's feasibility as a civilian airport. The results proved the feasibility of the project, and the Austin City Council unanimously approved the proposal. The voters then overwhelmingly approved it in 1993. With a $585 million budget, one-fourth funded by the FAA, a second, 9,000-foot runway was added to complement the existing 12,250-foot runway, a new terminal was constructed, both surface and garage parking were added, and a new cargo facility was built. Interestingly, cargo carriers began operating at the new Austin-Bergstrom International Airport on June 30, 1997, two years before passenger operations began on May 23, 1999. A multi-use facility, Austin-Bergstrom International Airport hosts general aviation, the State Aircraft Pooling Board, and the Texas Army National Guard, as well as 10.7 million annual passengers in 2014.

(Austin-Bergstrom International Airport, 2005)

Ownership of Airports

The ownership of airports in the United States is quite varied. Indeed, just as airports range in size from very large commercial service airports to unattended landing strips, there is wide variation in how these airports are structured in terms of ownership. Even so, specific types of airport ownership structures exist that all airports must fall into.

PRIVATE

According to the NPIAS, there are over 14,000 airports in the United States that are closed to the public. These are termed **private-use** airports. Typically, these private-use airports are also privately owned. However, there are also privately-owned airports that are open to the public, also known as **public-use**. The NPIAS lists almost 1,000 of these. Privately-owned airports are owned by either a private individual or company. How this is accomplished varies. Many times, a private individual may build a runway on their land and open a private-use airpark. Other times, a for-profit company may build an airport with private funds and open a public-use airport. The main determinant is that no public funding was made available in building the airport, and as such, it can either remain private or be open for public-use.

Privately-Owned, Public-Use, Commercial Service Airport

Although most airports in the United States are privately owned, building an airport with private funds (rather than federal grants) is not something to be undertaken lightly. One modern-day example is the Branson Airport, which opened in May 2009. This airport was built for $140 million, composed of $26.5 million in private equity and $114 million in revenue bonds. Located on a 922-acre site in Taney County, Missouri, the airport is considered the first privately financed and operated commercial airport in the United States. It is owned and operated by Branson Airport, LLC. Thus, this airport is a privately-owned, public-use airport.

As a privately-owned, public-use, commercial service airport, Branson Airport, LCC operates with a unique business approach to managing an airport. As a private enterprise, Branson Airport has flexibility not typically afforded to **federally-obligated** airports, meaning those airports that have accepted federal funds. For example, according to their website, Branson Airport "is able to offer exclusivity to airlines and vendors and develop unconventional revenue streams, such as offering naming rights and other sponsorship opportunities."

(Branson Airport, 2011)

PUBLIC-PRIVATE PARTNERSHIP

Yet another option in the ownership of airports is that of a public-private partnership. In this instance, the ownership is somewhat of a hybrid with a certain degree of both public and private ownership characteristics. In a public-private partnership, several options are available, not all of which fall under "ownership." First, an airport capital project could be partially funded or financed by a private firm. For instance, an airline could fund the construction of a new maintenance hangar from which the airline would operate. Another option is for an airport to enter into an agreement with a private firm for the joint operation of the airport. For example, the Orlando Sanford International Airport (SFB), although operated, maintained, and developed by the Sanford Airport Authority, is operated through a public-private partnership between the Sanford Airport Authority and TBI Airport Management, Inc. TBI Airport Management, Inc. has been contracted by the Sanford Airport Authority to manage both the international and domestic terminals, develop additional air service, and provide ground handling and cargo services. As stated by the airport, "This public/private partnership has created an environment with valuable service benefits for SFB customers and passengers" (Orlando Sanford International Airport, n.d.).

In fact, most of the world's airports, even though owned by local, regional, or national governments, are leased to private corporations that oversee the airports' operation. For example, BAA Limited operates seven of the commercial service airports in the United Kingdom, as well as several other airports outside of the UK. Germany's Frankfurt Airport is managed by the quasi-private firm Fraport. A third option, which is quite common at most U.S. commercial service airports, allows the airport to enter into an agreement with a private firm to operate concessions, ground handling, fueling, or other services at the airport. The airport may also enter into an agreement with a private firm to operate the **fixed base operator (FBO)**, which provides services to aircraft, typically in the form of fuel, maintenance, and other services (Figure 2-11). While smaller airports may operate the FBO, the parking lot, and aircraft **T-hangars**, the large, commercial service airports typically look to the private sector for assistance with managing the many services available at these airports. Whether it is automobile parking, rental car services, the FBO, fueling, or ground handling, there are firms in the private sector with experience and expertise useful to managing these activities. Airports recognize this and willingly pay for the services of these providers experienced in managing these services. This arrangement typically allows the airport to have one-third to one-half less employees than if all these services were handled in-house by employees (Prather, 2009).

Figure 2-11. A fixed base operator, which under agreement with the airport provides fuel, maintenance, and other services to aircraft.

LOCAL GOVERNMENT

The predominate form of public airport ownership in the United States is that of local government ownership. This is also referred to as municipal ownership. Indeed, there are variations of this concept, as local government may include city, county, multiple cities or counties, or parishes in the state of Louisiana. Regardless of the variation, this form of ownership allows a local government to own and operate an airport within its jurisdiction.

One of the main reasons why local government is the predominate form of public airport ownership is the 1946 Federal Airport Act. One intent of this Act was to transfer airfields built before World War II to state or local government entities. In other words, the military was transferring ownership of these assets and the federal government, in an agreement known as an **AP-4 agreement**, required the new owners to "assure" the federal government that the airport would continue to be operated and maintained as needed. Generally, with their financial resources and stability, a municipality could provide the best assurance that the airport would remain in operation and maintained as needed. Thus, numerous local governments became the owner and operator of airports throughout the United States. And while most AP-4 agreements have been superseded by AIP grants and their associated grant assurances, the local government form of ownership continues in popularity today.

Of course, there are pros and cons to the ownership of airports by local government. It usually works well for small airports that may need the support (financial and otherwise) of the municipality. These smaller airports may not be self-sustaining and the financial assistance of the municipality to fund both operating budgets and capital budgets is oftentimes a necessity. Additionally, the municipality has the power to tax and issue government bonds to fund the airport's operation and capital development.

On the other hand, with a municipally-owned airport, the airport manager must report to the city or county administrator just as, for example, the director of building and codes, director of city schools, director of planning and engineering, director of parks and recreation, and director of solid waste must. With this structure, the airport director is one of many voices all competing for the same finite resources. What makes the airport more important than the parks and recreation department, for instance? Depending on the views of the city or county administrator, the airport may be viewed as much less important. As a result, particularly with the local government form of airport ownership, it is incumbent upon the airport manager to impress upon local government officials the benefits (economic and otherwise) of the airport to the local community. Even so, during periods of financial constraint on the municipality, the airport will likely suffer the same budget reductions common to all municipal departments and services. Worse, the airport may be seen as a liability and a way to reduce expenses if it were closed and sold to a developer. Unfortunately, this last situation is quite common in this country.

STATE GOVERNMENT

Yet another option of airport ownership is that of state government ownership. In some states, such as Hawaii, all public-use airports are owned and operated by the state. In other states, such as Idaho, a large number of public-use airports are owned and operated by the state. For example, the state of Idaho has 30 state owned and operated airports. At the same time, the state has airports with other ownership structures, such as the Boise Airport, which is a division of the City of Boise Department of Aviation and Public Transportation and is overseen by a seven-member airport commission. Yet in other states, such as Arizona, only a handful of airports are owned and operated by the state. In Arizona specifically, the state owns and operates only one airport—the Grand Canyon National Park Airport (Arizona Department of Transportation, n.d.).

Generally, state ownership of airports is not too common in the United States, although it does occur more regularly in the western states. In any event, state ownership presents a unique set of challenges for states. As the state DOT is typically located in the capital city, and if no regional offices exist, how are airports to be managed on a daily basis by someone sitting in an office several hundred miles away? Unless the airport is rarely used, this is not a good solution. Thus, the state may assign a full-time state employee to the airport to serve as the airport manager, or may contract with a private firm to provide these services. If an FBO is present on the field, the FBO manager possibly could serve in this capacity. Regardless of who fills the position, the state-operated airport must compete with all of the other state-operated airports and state services and facilities for the funding of operations and maintenance, as well as capital development. It can be argued that although a state aviation department has a good grasp on the aviation infrastructure needs of the state and the manner in which airports comprise the entire state system, the state may not

State of Hawaii Airport System

In Hawaii, the State of Hawaii Department of Transportation's Airports Division has jurisdiction over and control of all State of Hawaii airports as well as air navigation facilities, and general supervision of aeronautics within the state. The Hawaii Airports Division operates and maintains 15 airports located throughout the state. An airports administrator is responsible for day-to-day operations of the division, including the four district offices that manage the day-to-day operations of the airports under their control. The mission of the Airports Division is to develop, manage and maintain a safe and efficient global air transportation organization.

(State of Hawaii, 2011)

be as knowledgeable regarding local airport issues and community concerns as would be possible by having a local airport manager on-site.

The State of Oregon is unique in that it has airports that fall under most of the ownership categories previously discussed. As shown in Table 2-2, airports in Oregon fall into one of eight distinct categories. The most popular of these categories is city ownership, with 30 airports throughout the state falling in this category. The next most common category is state owership, with the state owning and operating no fewer than 28 airports.

NATIONAL/FEDERAL GOVERNMENT

Although it's an option for ownership of U.S. airports, the national or federal government ownership structure is most popular at airports outside the United States. However, prior to June 7, 1987, Dulles International and Reagan National Airports were owned and operated by the FAA in the U.S. Department of Transportation. On June 7, 1987, Washington Dulles International and Washington National Airports were transferred to the Metropolitan Washington Airports Authority under a 50-year lease authorized by the Metropolitan Washington Airports Act of 1986. All property was transferred to the Airports Authority and the federal government holds title to the lease (Metropolitan Washington Airports Authority, 2011).

Currently, a large number of military airports, and some airports operated by the U.S. Department of the Interior, remain under federal government ownership and operation. For instance, Furnace Creek and Stovepipe Wells Airports in Death Valley National Park are operated by the Department of the Interior. Likewise, there are 440 military bases in the continental United States, but not all of these are considered military airports.

Table 2-2. Ownership categories of airports in the state of Oregon.

OREGON AIRPORTS BY TYPE OF OWNERSHIP	
City	
Albany Municipal	Lakeside
Arlington Municipal	Madras City - County
Ashland Municipal - Sumner Parker Field	Malin
Baker City Municipal	McMinnville Municipal
Bend Municipal	Miller Memorial Airpark
Burns Municipal	Monument Municipal
Columbia Gorge / The Dalles	Myrtle Creek Municipal
Corvallis Municipal	Newport Municipal
Creswell Hobby Field	Ontario Municipal
Eastern Oregon Regional @ Pendleton	Portland Downtown Heliport
Enterprise Municipal	Redmond Municipal—Roberts Field
Eugene Mahlon Sweet Field	Roseburg Regional
Florence Municipal	Salem McNary Field
Hermiston Municipal	Seaside Municipal
Klamath Falls / Kingsley Field	Vernonia Airfield
County	
Curry Coast Airpark	Lake County
Grant Couny Regional / Ogilvie Field	Lexington
Grants Pass	Paisley
Illinois Valley	Prineville
LaGrande / Union County	Rogue Valley International—Medford
Federal	
Memaloose (USFS)	
Silver Lake (USFS)	
Airport District	
Southwest Oregon Regional	
Other	
Christmas Valley	
Port	
Astoria Regional	Portland International
Boardman	Powers
Gold Beach Municipal	Scappoose Industrial Airpark
Hillsboro	Tillamook
Ken Jernstedt Airfield	Troutdale

Private	
Beaver Marsh	Sandy River
Chehalem Airpark	Sisters Eagle Air
Country Squire Airpark	Skyport
Davis	Sportsman Airpark
George Felt	Stark's Twin Oaks Airpark
Lake Billy Chinook	Sunriver
Lake Woahink Seaplane Base	Valley View
Lenhardt Airpark	
State	
Alkali Lake State	Mulino State
Aurora State	Nehalem Bay State
Bandon State	Oakridge State
Cape Blanco State	Owyhee Reservoir State
Cascade Locks State	Pacific City State
Chiloquin State	Pinehurst State
Condon State	Prospect State
Cottage Grove State	Rome State
Crescent Lake State	Santiam Junction State
Independence State	Siletz Bay State
Joseph State	Toketee State
Lebanon State	Toledo State
McDermitt State	Wakonda Beach State
McKenzie Bridge State	Wasco State

(oregon.gov)

AUTHORITIES OR COMMISSIONS

Although the local government ownership structure is the predominate form of airport ownership, especially among smaller airports, there has been a movement in recent decades toward authority ownership. There are several reasons for the increasing popularity of authorities:

1. By having a governing board that is specifically focused on airport matters, greater concentration on airport issues is possible, and as a result, less time is spent on non-airport issues. Further, an airport authority board is composed of members interested in the success of the airport and with specific expertise on airport issues. On the other hand, with a city-owned and operated airport, the city council must discuss issues and set policy on a number of municipal services, such as parks and recreation, public safety, education, and airports.
2. More efficient operation and enhanced economies of scale are obtained when several political jurisdictions, each with separate airport responsibilities,

choose to combine these responsibilities under one governing board. In essence, if two public-use airports exist in two contiguous counties, it may be in both counties' interest to create one airport authority with board representation from each county to manage the two airports. There are many airport authorities with responsibility for more than one public-use airport. Similarly, governing boards can have representation from several political jurisdictions. As an example, the Tri-Cities Airport Commission, charged with the operation of Tri-Cities Regional Airport located in Blountville, Tennessee, is governed by a 12-person commission appointed by the airport's owners: the Cities of Kingsport, Bristol, Johnson City, TN and Bristol, VA; and Washington and Sullivan Counties, TN (Tri-Cities Regional Airport, n.d.).

3. An authority can provide experienced decision makers located on airport who are able to operate the airport with less political interference than might be the case with a municipally-owned and operated airport. For instance, at a municipal airport, the airport manager answers to the city or county manager, mayor, or other (oftentimes) political appointee. However, the executive director of an authority reports directly to the authority board.

(AAAE, 2005)

An authority is generally in the form of either an airport authority or port authority. Airport authorities are specific to an airport (or airports), whereas port authorities also operate shipping terminals, railroads, seaports, and irrigation facilities. The Port Authority of New York & New Jersey, Massport, Port of Seattle, and Port of Portland are all examples of port authorities that also own and operate airports.

There are typical terms and provisions in place for autonomous airport or port authorities. Using Massport as an example, these provisions are outlined below:

1. The authority acts as the owner, manager, and operator of the facilities under its control, including all related property and services. As discussed above, the authority may also have responsibility for other transportation facilities and services. In Massport's case, airports including Boston Logan International, Hanscom Field, and Worcester Regional, as well as a container port, cruiseport, autoport, and other secondary facilities, are all owned and operated by Massport.
2. The authority is governed by a board of directors appointed by the state or local government (many times, the governor). Board members typically volunteer their time and expertise and normally receive no compensation. In the case of Massport, the authority is governed by a seven-member board, with members appointed by the governor. Governors are elected to four-year terms in Massachusetts. Thus, a governor elected to one four-year term will normally obtain a board with a majority of members appointed by him or her only during the last year of his or her tenure. The intent of this provision is to minimize the political forces on the Massport board and ensure some level of continuity and stability in its policies.

The Massachusetts Port Authority

The mission of the Massachusetts Port Authority, Massport, is to "promote economic growth and vitality throughout Massachusetts and New England by operating many of the region's largest transportation facilities safely, securely and efficiently while being mindful of the environment and our neighboring communities." The authority is self-supporting and receives no state tax revenues to support its operations or facilities. A recent economic impact report estimated that Massport contributes $8.7 billion per year in total economic impact.

(Massport, 2011)

3. The authority operates on a not-for-profit basis and is exempt from taxes. Although this provision is not necessarily different than municipally-owned and operated airports, the unique aspect of authorities allows them to make "voluntary contributions" to its shareholders, typically the state or local government. In Massport's instance, part of the operating surplus it generates is allocated to providing financial assistance to a number of Boston-area cities and townships. Note that while this act of "voluntary contributions" may occur with port authorities, it is prohibited by airport authorities that are federally obligated. This creates a condition of revenue diversion, in which airport revenues are diverted to some non-airport use. Revenue diversion is prohibited by the DOT/FAA.
4. The authority, as a legal entity, is permitted to acquire land and property at fair market value, and may undertake construction projects and other enhancements to its property and facilities. Clearly, Massport has acquired a great deal of land and property and commences various capital improvement projects to maintain and expand its facilities.
5. The authority may issue **tax-exempt bonds** secured by future airport revenues (known as revenue bonds) to fund capital improvements. Although bonds and other airport funding mechanisms are presented in-depth in Chapter 14, it should be noted that tax-exempt bonds, while also available to municipally-owned and operated airports, allow the authority to issue bonds at lower interest rates. This has the effect of reducing the cost to borrow money. In essence, an investor in a high tax bracket may be willing to accept a lower interest rate on their bond investment if the interest will be tax-free.
6. Just as with all federally-obligated airports, the authority must strive toward economic self-sufficiency. This concept includes the ability to fund capital improvements from its own revenues. In reality, many of the nation's smaller airports have difficulty obtaining self-sufficiency. For an airport offering only fuel, fuel sales alone make it difficult to cover all operating expenses, let alone fund any capital improvements. Authorities, however,

are typically managing commercial service airports at which it is easier to achieve economic self-sufficiency. User charges may be adjusted to achieve this objective.

7. A final provision common to authorities provides for all of the authority's property to be returned to the shareholders (state or local government) at some future time if the authority is ever dissolved. It is rare for an authority to dissolve; nonetheless, this provision may be present. In Massport's case, the property would be returned to the Commonwealth of Massachusetts.

(DeNeufville and Odoni, 2003)

ADVISORY BOARDS

Although not truly an ownership form, airport advisory boards do play an important role in the affairs of many local airports. Typically, the airport manager is hired by the city council, board of county commissioners, or the city or county administrator directly. The airport manager is oftentimes expected to be an expert in airport operations, capital development, land-use planning, community concerns, etc. To provide additional input to the airport manager to facilitate the decision-making process, a municipality may establish an airport advisory board. These boards are just that—advisory in nature. They do not promulgate rules or polices, but the board will generally provide an alternative view, while bringing up community concerns, to the airport manager. This advising may be seen by the airport manager as very helpful—or as a hindrance. The view often depends upon the board's perceived role in advising. Some advisory boards feel they should direct the work of the airport manager, which of course can make life difficult for the airport manager, when the manager is in fact expecting only advisement on various issues. Board members should be from diverse backgrounds, preferably with either experience in, or a connection to, aviation. However, it should be noted that all too often, this is not the case.

PRIVATIZATION

Although airports quite often privatize certain functions and services, as discussed in the previous section entitled "public-private partnership," the outright privatizing of an entire airport is a rare act in the United States—and for good reason. FAA grant assurances, which are the "strings attached" to federal AIP grants, prohibit revenue diversion, the sale of land acquired with federal funds to private interests, and other acts related to privatization.

However, in response to increasing interest about the benefits of airport privatization, an Airport Privatization Pilot Program was included in the 1996 FAA Reauthorization Act. The Airport Privatization Pilot Program, which began in September 1997, allowed only a select number of participants—one large hub airport, one general aviation airport, and three airports from small, medium, or nonhub categories. The GA airport could be sold or leased, while airports served by air carriers could only be leased to private investors. To make an airport attractive to the private investor, the FAA had to alter the rules (grant assurances) discussed previously. These alterations include the following:

- The public airport sponsor may receive an exemption to use the lease or sale proceeds for non-airport purposes. Generally, all proceeds from the lease or sale of airport land must be used for the capital or operating costs of the airport. This exemption requires the approval of 65 percent of the air carriers at the airport (by number of carriers and by landed weight).
- The public sponsor can also be exempted from an obligation to repay federal grants.
- The public sponsor can also be exempted from returning property acquired with federal assistance upon the lease or sale of the airport (FAA, 2010a).

There are, however, conditions which must be satisfied in order to grant these exemptions. First, the private operator must prove it will comply with the public operator's grant obligations, including the obligation to ensure continued access to the airport on reasonable terms. Second, the private operator must provide assurance that it will operate the airport safely, maintaining and improving the airport, providing security, mitigating noise and environmental impacts, and adhering to any current collective bargaining agreements with employees at the airport. Third, the public operator must provide a plan for continued operation of the airport if the private operator declares bankruptcy or otherwise defaults (FAA, 2010a).

Submitting an application to be considered for the FAA Airport Privatization Pilot Program can be a rather lengthy process. According to the FAA, the process contains the following steps:

- The public sponsor may submit a preliminary application for FAA review and approval. It must contain summary narratives identifying the objectives of the privatization initiative, a description of the process and timetables for selecting a private operator, current airport financial statements, and a copy of the request for proposal. The FAA has 30 days to review the preliminary application.
- When the FAA approves the preliminary application, the applicant is guaranteed one of the five slots in the program, subject to FAA approval of the final application.
- The airport sponsor may select a private operator, negotiate an agreement, and submit a final application to the FAA. There is no timeline for the FAA to complete its review of the final application.
- After the FAA reviews and approves the final application and lease, it publishes a notice in the *Federal Register* for a 60-day public review and comment period.

- The FAA completes its review, prepares its Findings and **Record of Decision** (ROD), and addresses the public comments in the ROD.
- The FAA publishes its ROD and, if approved, observes the legal settlement and transfer of the airport from public owner and sponsor to the new private operator and sponsor.

(FAA, 2010a)

Even though the Privatization Pilot Program began in 1997, only a handful of airports have expressed an interest in the program. Only 10 airports have applied, and only two airports remained in the program in some form or another as of April 2015. Seven applications had either been withdrawn or were terminated.

Interestingly, air carrier airports that are privatized under this program may receive Airport Improvement Program (AIP) entitlement and discretionary grants, collect passenger facility charges, and charge reasonable fees. However, unless 65 percent of air carriers at the airport approve, the private operator may not increase air carrier rates and charges at a rate that exceeds the consumer price index. This should dispel any fears that the private operator will raise rates and charges excessively because of their for-profit motive. Private operators of general aviation airports are able to receive AIP discretionary grants.

One may wonder why a municipality would want to privatize their airport. First, privatizing an airport will likely open up sources of private capital which can fund airport improvements and capital development. For cash-strapped municipalities, this can be an enticing alternative. Additionally, some municipalities may feel that a private operator can manage the airport more efficiently and with greater cost-effectiveness. While these proposed benefits are not necessarily a popular view, as indicated by the lack of interest in the airport privatization pilot program, there are those who (a) believe in the initiative and efficiency characteristic of private industry and (b) value those aspects more than the typical government model. Additionally, a private operator may be able to decrease airfares, introduce lower-cost parking, enhance frequency of flights, and introduce high-speed rail or other transportation options. It should be noted that almost all commercial service airports in the United States privatize concessions (including food, beverage, and retail), parking management, ground handling, fuel handling, and many other services. Thus, municipalities and airport boards are quite familiar with the enhanced efficiencies associated with the private sector. If it were not the case, all of these services would be handled in-house by airport employees.

Similarly, what would motivate a potential investor to buy or enter into a long-term lease of an airport? First, there is incentive in being able to operate the airport as a proprietor. Airports are being developed in many areas to enhance revenues, and a private operator will likely endeavor toward greater revenues through a variety of offerings. Second, the private operator will improve air service through attractive incentives for airlines. Advances could also be made in minimizing passenger leakage to surrounding, competing airports. A lack of governmental bureaucracy could indeed lead to greater efficiencies, which in turn would lead to greater profit margins for the private operator.

To be fair, there are also potential disadvantages of privatization. Disadvantages may include:

- The loss of municipal assets to private investors
- Threat of increased costs for airport users
- Lack of compliance with safety standards and federal regulations
- Higher employee turnover, as a result of elimination of positions and longer working hours stemming from a for-profit focus and pursuit of efficiencies

The degree of future interest in the FAA Airport Privatization Pilot Program is uncertain. There will likely always be an interest in privatization among airports, although it seems that privatizing certain services at airports is much more popular in the U.S. than the outright sale or long-term lease of an entire airport to private investors.

Organizational Structure

Although the airport ownership model will also affect the organizational structure, there are similarities within categories. The size of the airport also affects that organizational structure. At the smallest of airports, there may not even be a full-time airport manager. Oftentimes, due to either lack of financial resources or lack of importance placed on the airport by the municipality, municipal officials may either manage the airport as part of their duties, or place that responsibility on another position within the municipal government.[2] For instance, the director of public works may also be responsible for managing the operations and capital development of the airport. Figure 2-12 visually conveys this concept.

Commonly, however, there is an airport manager, and at larger airports, hundreds of additional employees. Although the actual organizational structure of airports varies, there are some common departments, or areas, that

Figure 2-12. Municipal organization chart.

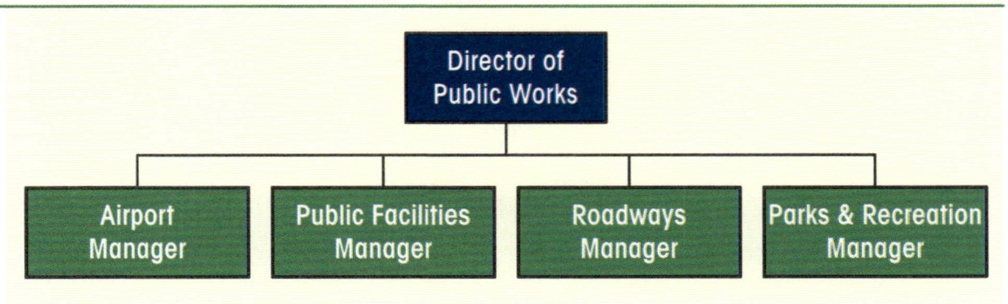

2 "Municipal officials" such as the county or city administrator.

may be viewed visually in an organization chart. It is important to distinguish between **staff** (or supporting) **units** and **line** (or operating) **units** within the organizational chart. Staff units provide support to the airport director and report directly to this chief executive. Line units are responsible for carrying out the day-to-day activities of the airport. In comparing line and staff units, one can quickly determine that the majority of the airport's employees work in line units. With employees numbering in the hundreds or thousands, the line units carry out the direction produced by the staff units. While there may be only several staff units with a small number of employees, staff units are often very influential and represent the airport's senior management team.

A small GA airport typically has a very simple organizational structure. In fact, it typically has only line units. It should be noted that staff units (such as human resources, legal, and finance) appear in the municipality's organization chart, but typically not in the GA airport organization chart. As seen in Figure 2-13, the GA airport organization chart may consist of only a few employees. In reality, this may be all that is needed. With a small terminal building and few operations, the maintenance employees typically mow grass, maintain pavement markings and lighting, and handle any building maintenance needs, including janitorial. Some GA airports only have one employee—the airport manager.

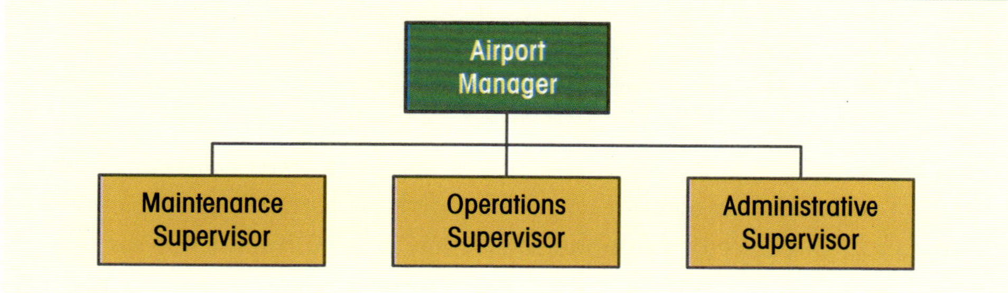

Figure 2-13. General aviation airport organization chart.

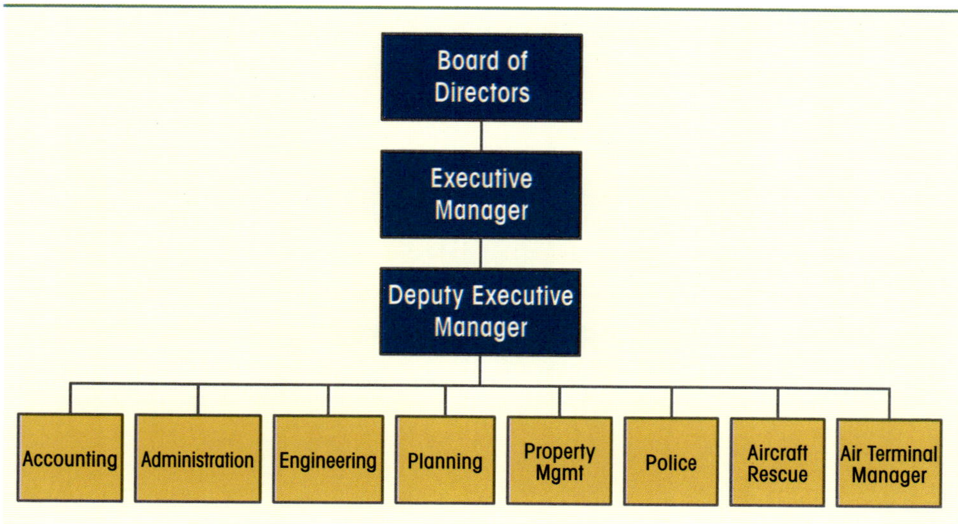

Figure 2-14. Small hub airport organization chart.

Figure 2-14 shows an organization chart for a small hub airport. Although it varies, a small hub airport will typically employ 50–150 employees among the departments shown on the organization chart.

The large hub airport may have 400–600 employees or more. These are the largest airports in the country and enplane tens of millions of passengers per year. As shown in Figure 2-15, large hub airports have numerous departments with multiple levels. The staff units are visible on each side reporting directly to the executive director. The line units have directors reporting to a senior director, who then reports to the executive director or possibly a deputy executive director.

Figure 2-15. Large hub airport organization chart (average 400–600 employees or more).

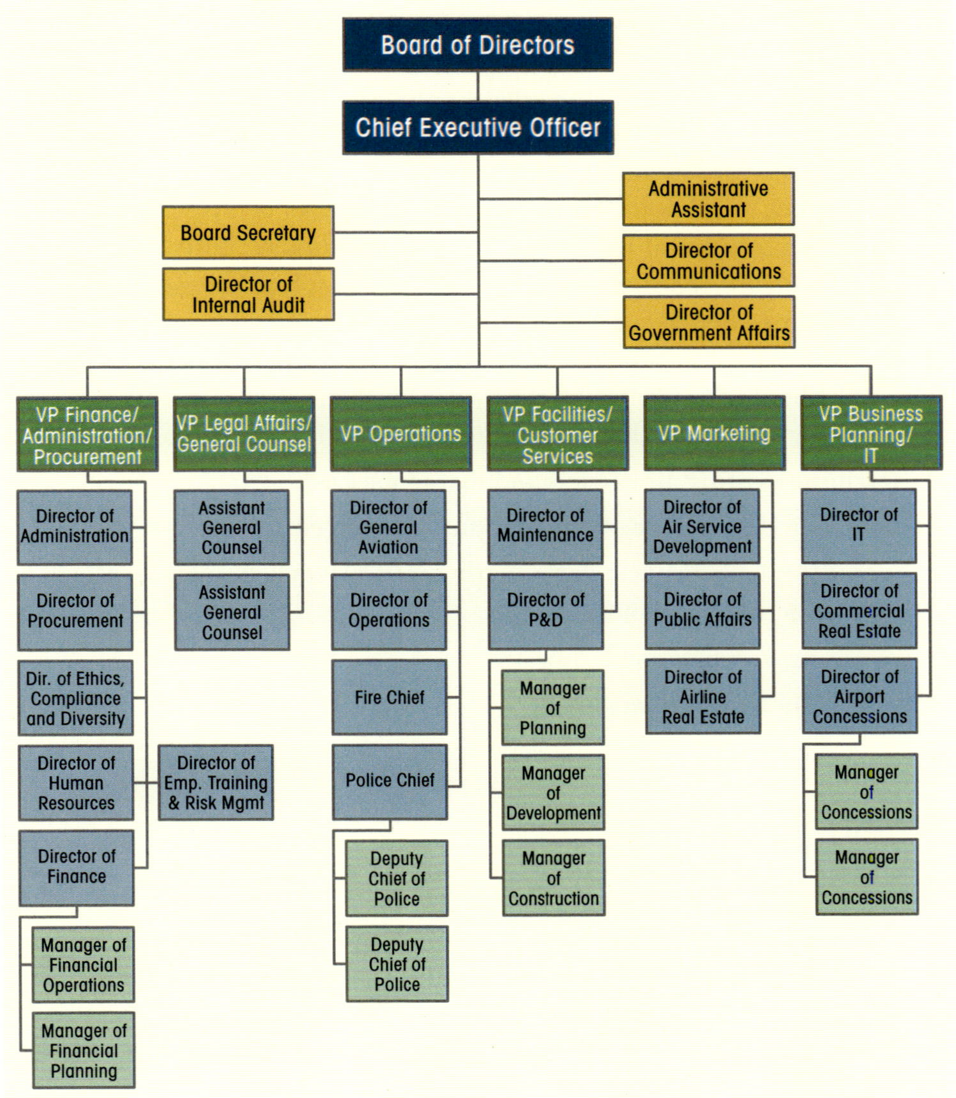

Major Airport Departments

To fully understand the nature of airports, it's necessary to develop an understanding of the major departments at an airport. Although much is said about the airport manager or executive director, much of the real work at an airport is accomplished by employees of the many airport departments.[3]

AIR SERVICE DEVELOPMENT AND INTERNATIONAL COMMERCE

Many airports, even those with few passengers, have either an in-house employee (whether full or part-time) or consultant retained for the purpose of developing air service and international commerce, including cargo. During the 2007–2009 recession, many of the nation's airports lost air service as airlines cut capacity and consolidated routes and service to cope with the downturn in travel. However, airports are not pleased with reduced or complete loss of airline service; in fact, communities generally demand additional airline service with correspondingly lower airfares. Thus, rather than simply suffer the effects of the recession in terms of reduced airline service, airports ramped up efforts to retain the service that was in place, and recruit either new carriers or increased service from **incumbent carriers**. To effectively do this, some airports hired a full-time director of air service development. This individual is typically responsible for:

- Retaining existing air carriers and markets served
- Increasing the number of non-stop markets served
- Recruiting new airlines, particularly low-cost carriers such as Allegiant, Frontier, JetBlue, or Southwest
- Increasing international airline service
- Enhancing air cargo service

HUMAN RESOURCES

All airports must have resources, in the form of humans, to function. In other words, airports do not run themselves. Grass must be cut, lighting must be repaired, buildings must be maintained, and decisions must be made. Thus, human resources are a very integral component of airports. Typically, the functions associated with acquiring, training, and managing human resources is handled by a human resources department. Even with small GA airports, this function is handled by the city or county's human resources department.

[3] True, general aviation airports may only have an airport manager and several maintenance employees. This section, however, refers to those large hub commercial service airports with hundreds of employees working in very specific areas.

Larger airports, especially those operated by an airport authority, have their own human resources department specifically dedicated to the human resource needs of the airport. A director of human resources is typically responsible for:

- Developing and ensuring the adherence to all personnel policies and laws governing employees and work environments
- Developing a budget for personnel, including salaries and benefits
- Recruiting, hiring, and terminating employees
- Processing separation of employees from service
- Managing all employee benefits, including insurance, retirement, and other benefits
- Assisting supervisors and department directors with employee grievances, counseling, and other work-related issues
- Developing training programs for all employees, including new employee orientation

GOVERNMENTAL AND LEGAL AFFAIRS

The proactive airport director will keep a close eye on matters in the nation's capital, as well as in the statehouse and in city hall. Numerous regulations, policies, and orders, as well as matters affecting airlines, have a direct impact on the airport. At the same time, however, it can be quite time-consuming to stay abreast of all federal, state, and local issues affecting airports and the airline industry. And while trade associations, such as the American Association of Airport Executives (AAAE), have staff in governmental affairs, these individuals typically only keep association members informed of issues and actions being taken at the national level. Thus, larger airports generally have at least one employee in the governmental and legal affairs department to stay abreast of issues at the state and local level, as well as the federal level. This person is also typically an attorney and referred to as general counsel. A director of governmental and legal affairs is generally responsible for:

- Maintaining contacts with national, state and local officials to stay abreast of issues being proposed that will impact their airport
- Briefing airport management of issues of national, state, and local importance that may impact their airport, or the airport or airline industries
- Providing legal research and opinion to management
- Drafting language for lease agreements, contracts, and other legally binding documents to minimize airport liability
- Assuming the role of airport attorney when formal complaints, grievances or lawsuits are filed against the airport
- Coordinating initiatives pertaining to airport property management, commercial development and parking management, and all legal services

PUBLIC INFORMATION AND COMMUNITY RELATIONS

Airports must always be aware of their public perception, as many citizens can be quite vocal in their complaints of airport policies or management decisions. Indeed, airports will have press, whether that press is positive or negative. Thus, airports must be proactive in maintaining a positive public image and generating positive press. Large airports have personnel employed in this area, typically managed by a director of public information and community relations. This person is responsible for:

- Preparing and distributing press releases
- Coordinating community hearings on various issues
- Handling interviews with news media
- Providing tours to interested citizens, school groups, and members of civic organizations
- Coordinating updates to the airport's website with the airport webmaster
- Coordinating grand openings, ribbon-cuttings, groundbreaking ceremonies, and introduction of new services, such as new airline service

PERFORMANCE MANAGEMENT AND INTERNAL AUDIT

Benchmarking is a term that many airports are familiar with today. This concept requires that an airport compare itself in various areas of operational performance with peer airports to determine how well it "measures up." Additionally, many times airports endeavor to adopt industry **best practices**. These two activities alone can be time-consuming and require an individual skilled at program evaluation and performance management. Oftentimes this individual also directs a team of internal auditors to audit not only the airport's way of doing business, but various tenants as well. For instance, FBOs are required to submit revenues (in the form of fuel flowage fees, terminal building rents, hangar receipts, etc.) to the airport on a monthly basis. To be certain that an FBO is accurately reporting these amounts, the airport may audit their activities and records. A director of performance management and internal audit is typically responsible for:

- Setting goals and objectives for the airport, in coordination with department directors and the airport director
- Measuring the attainment of goals and objectives
- Benchmarking peer airports, in areas such as costs per enplaned passenger, concession revenue, and rates and charges
- Conducting internal audits of all tenants, including concessionaires, airlines, FBOs, and others
- Measuring the performance of the airport in many key areas and developing innovative methods to gauge the business proficiency of the airport

PLANNING AND DEVELOPMENT

The department of planning and development plays an important role in the capital development of an airport and, in fact, consists of many complimentary areas of specialty. Although some airports contract many of these services out to consultants and to planning and engineering firms, the larger airports typically have a full in-house staff to represent the airport's interest in these areas. By conducting these services in-house, the airport maintains greater control.

Design Services

Although some airports contract out all design services required for projects, other airports choose to hire the staff to perform this in-house. Airports are very project-focused, as they continually make progress on their capital improvement plan. Some projects are completed in-house by maintenance staff, such as building a ramp into a temporary building, constructing a roof overhang, or installing an additional sidewalk. Most projects, however, are so large that they require an outside contractor to perform the work. Extending a taxiway, building a new terminal, or renovating all concession areas requires a contractor with sufficient subcontractors and personnel to successfully complete the project. Whether designing for an in-house project or for one that will be bid out to a contractor, the design services department plays an important role in designing a project and the required specifications. This department typically consists of only a few individuals, with each generally holding the title of **professional engineer** (PE). The director of design services is typically responsible for:

- Designing a project, including the associated project specifications that will become part of the bid package
- Developing all drawings to be used by either in-house staff or outside contractors in completing the project
- Working with in-house staff or outside contractors on a weekly basis to ensure the project is being completed as designed
- Serving as staff engineer in troubleshooting project issues and approving of change orders and alterations to projects
- Maintaining all as-built drawings
- Developing estimated costs for a project to allow staff to effectively rank bids for new projects

Planning and Environmental Programs

With aggressive capital improvement programs at airports, it is beneficial to have a department with an outlook on the future. The planning and environmental programs department will coordinate updates to the airport's master plan, as well as ensuring compliance with all environmental laws, regulations, and policies. The director of planning and environmental programs typically will:

- Ensure that on-airport developments are consistent with applicable FAA advisory circulars, regulations and grant assurances
- Through project management and in-house coordination, ensure that the primary guides for future airport development—namely the master plan, airport layout plan, and land use plan—are updated every 5 to 6 years, and that they are consistent with the primary implementation document for future airport development (the strategic business plan)
- Ensure that necessary environmental studies, permits and mitigation program(s) are implemented in a timely manner to avoid delays in airport-wide capacity enhancement projects
- Ensure that the federal, state and metropolitan capital projects programs are consistent with the airport's strategic business plan's capital improvement program
- Ensure that county and city comprehensive plans include the most current forecasts and requirements of the airport's master plan with particular focus on maintaining compatible land uses surrounding the airport
- Through the use of the airport's height zoning regulations and coordination with the city and county zoning offices, ensure that land uses in the influence areas of the airport are compatible with aircraft operations and maintain the utility, present and future, for the airport
- Ensure that the public and the federal, state, metropolitan and local transportation, planning, environmental and zoning agencies are kept abreast of future airport development projects and capacity needs
- Coordinate and provide guidance in the implementation of the airport's administrative procedures for procuring professional services
- Ensure that the FAA-approved **noise compatibility program** in the 14 CFR Part 150 Study is implemented and monitored for compliance utilizing a **flight information monitoring system** managed by a noise officer who investigates deviations to the **informal runway use program**, coordinates compliance with air traffic control and airlines, and facilitates citizens' awareness of the noise compatibility program. A noise compatibility program is developed to formalize airport efforts to minimize noise in the surrounding area. Effects are minimized by installing a flight information monitoring system to track flight arrival and departure paths, as well as developing an informal runway use program, which requires pilots to utilize certain runways and approach/departure corridors to minimize noise impacts on the surrounding communities.

Development and Program Services

Due to the extensive capital development programs at larger airports, there is a great need for program management at the capital development level. The director of development and program services will typically:

- Develop contract and agreements
- Develop requests for qualifications (RFQ) and requests for proposals (RFP)
- Coordinate advertisements, pre-bid conferences and pre-proposal conferences
- Conduct bid openings
- Prepare presentation of contracts to the airport board
- Oversee all contract payments
- Provide monthly project cash flow requirements
- Maintain master project schedules
- Manage project budget and schedule performance and benchmarking
- Prepare operation, maintenance and equipment budgets
- Prepare annual capital improvement program budget
- Prepare and manage change orders/amendments
- Provide independent project cost estimating
- Provide records management for all project documentation
- Prepare and manage all state and FAA grants
- Maintain capital improvement program database
- Coordinate and manage all audits associated with projects
- Provide all administrative support for planning and development

Construction

Airports, especially commercial service airports, always seem to be experiencing growing pains. Regardless of the season, it seems as if a construction project is always in progress. Maybe it is a restroom renovation, or a taxiway extension, or a new cell phone lot or expanded curbside. In any event, construction is a fact of life for airports. Thus, having an in-house construction department to manage this activity can be very beneficial. A director of construction is typically responsible for:

- Coordinating construction related to the airport's capital improvement program
- Preparing RFQs, RFPs, and bid specifications
- Meeting regularly with contractors to initiate change orders, and ensure progress leading to project completion that is on time and on budget
- Processing invoices for contractor payouts
- Project staging
- Verifying work in place and ensuring quality control by regularly inspecting all ongoing projects
- Managing all project change orders
- Coordinating with the operations department to ensure the continued operation of facilities during projects to minimize disruption.

OPERATIONS

Aircraft operations are integral to an airport. Clearly, without aircraft, there is no need for an airport. Thus, whether at a very small GA airport with only three operations per day or at a larger commercial service airport with several hundred per day, aircraft operations drive the revenues and are the impetus for an airport's growth. Due to the importance of aircraft operations, as well as passenger movements, and the number of regulations that must be adhered to in this regard, larger airports typically have an operations department. This department may incorporate general aviation or GA may be within its own department. The director of operations is typically responsible for:

- Maintaining compliance with 14 CFR Part 139
- Managing aircraft operations
- Managing the airfield
- Managing aircraft deicing and snow removal operations
- Reporting conditions via the NOTAM system
- Performing self-inspections
- Ensuring a safe and secure airport, including both airside and landside
- Representing airport management in all emergency situations
- Resolving passenger and community concerns

In its responsibility to ensure a secure operation, the operations department oftentimes employs an airport security coordinator. This position is typically responsible for:

- Establishing policies and procedures for airport operator security operations in compliance with established security directives
- Documenting all policies and procedures in a Transportation Security Administration (TSA) approved airport security program
- Conducting multiple varying comprehensive assessments and investigations of the airport
- Representing airport management in coordinating airport continuity of operations disaster management plans with air carrier management, other tenants, and emergency relief organizations
- Establishing and maintaining an access control system for the airport operators, capable of immediate termination of access upon demand by the TSA or other law enforcement agency
- Establishing and maintaining an airport closed-circuit television video surveillance system with monitoring capability by the TSA of the passenger screening checkpoints and baggage handling
- Implementing projects and programs to support restricting access to commercial aircraft and/or the airport to only personnel with a documented work-related need to be in proximity to airline operations

PUBLIC SAFETY

Oftentimes, due to the number and skill level of personnel required, the **aircraft rescue and firefighting (ARFF)** personnel and police at an airport will be housed in a separate department. ARFF and police may also be found in the operations department, as they are closely related. Some airports have a senior director of operations and public safety, which oversees the director of operations and the director of public safety. In any event, the director of public safety may be a police chief or fire chief or both, and is typically responsible for:

- Maintaining a safe and secure operation 24 hours per day, 365 days per year
- Ensuring that personnel respond to all emergencies, whether related to aircraft or individuals
- Ensuring that personnel respond to all security incidents, whether related to aircraft or individuals
- Complying with 49 CFR Part 1542 in regards to security and Part 139 in regards to ARFF
- Developing an effective first aid program within the terminal(s)
- Training personnel to maintain currency

PROPERTIES AND CONTRACTS ADMINISTRATION

Large airports have thousands of acres of land with many aeronautical uses and non-aeronautical uses of that property. As a result, this includes many tenants, buildings, and facilities. To manage the use of these facilities and protect the interests of the airport, there are various letters of agreement (LOA), memorandums of understanding (MOU), leases, use agreements, and contracts of all sorts. Airports typically have a properties department responsible for negotiating leases and use agreements, setting rates and charges, and overseeing all contracts and agreements. The director of properties and contracts administration is typically responsible for:

- Setting fees, rates, and charges in coordination with the finance department
- Negotiating terms of new agreements and extensions of existing agreements
- Ensuring the airport's interests are protected by inserting "hold harmless" language in all agreements in coordination with the governmental and legal affairs department
- Managing various programs associated with airport properties

MAINTENANCE

Airports have a tremendous responsibility for maintaining not only the airfield (including runways, taxiways, safety areas, and ramp areas), but also the landside (including terminal buildings, curbside and other access points, loading bridges, baggage sorting systems, heating ventilation and air conditioning [HVAC] systems, security control systems, people mover systems, and more). At busy airports, it seems that maintenance needs never end. A loading bridge breaks down, an automated door quits working, the air conditioning is too hot, etc. In this regard, the maintenance department is always focused on three types of maintenance: preventive maintenance, routine requests, and urgent requests. Preventive maintenance can be handled during scheduled hours. However, maintenance requests are rarely anticipated and many must be addressed immediately. As a result, maintenance departments are often one of the airport departments requiring 24/7 staffing, especially at the larger airports.

The director of maintenance is typically responsible for:

- Negotiating and managing all maintenance contracts
- Overseeing multiple employee groups, including airfield, landside, etc.
- Managing the operation of the airport's wastewater treatment, alternative power generation, standby generators, and other sources of power
- Managing the operation of access control, fire alarms, elevators and escalators, and people movers
- Managing landscaping on the public side, including plantings within buildings
- Managing the maintenance of airfield pavement, lighting, markings, and signage

MARKETING

Marketing, a field about which entire textbooks are written, is an important component of the success of any airport. Although the local general aviation airport may only perform marketing by having an airport entrance sign and a few brochures printed to place inside the terminal building, larger airports spend a great deal annually to promote their airport, minimize leakage, and ensure a positive image. Marketing may take the form of billboard advertisements, radio spots, television commercials, social networking presence, and much more. In fact, larger airports have entire departments dedicated to marketing the airport's facilities and airline service. The director of marketing is typically responsible for:

- Developing a marketing plan to promote the airport and its many services
- Promoting the airport by utilizing multiple forms of media
- Positive community outreach
- Interacting with customers via social media

- Developing a theme and coordinating the layout of the airport's annual report
- Coordinating an Art in the Airport Program
- Managing all advertising in the airport

INFORMATION TECHNOLOGY

The world has truly opened up in the past decade with the evolution of information technology (IT). This evolution has benefitted companies throughout the world, including airports. The majority of airport employees have a personal computer and printer at their desk, which allows them to work on projects in a number of applications and print documents of extremely high quality from their workstation. Many airports are now offering employees an intranet site that allows secure access to company documents and policies. Some airport-specific IT uses include geographic information systems (GIS), noise monitoring technology, flight tracking software, and gate reservation systems.

Additionally, the internet allows airports to develop a commanding web presence. Specifically, airports are promoting airfares, air service, actual times of arrivals and departures, facilities, and services on their website. Further, with social networking sites such as Twitter and Facebook, airports are developing a loyal following and are able to daily interact, albeit virtually, with their customers. Several airports have even developed applications (apps) to allow passengers and others to check flights, see terminal maps, check the status of parking garages, etc. In addition to email, web, and a multitude of software applications to benefit employees, IT has improved the handling of baggage, detection of lightning, processing of passengers and their baggage, ticketing, gate utilization, and informing passengers and meeters and greeters of flight arrival and departure times.

The director of information technology is typically responsible for:

- Developing and maintaining a modern website
- Deploying computers, printers, and other technology for the benefit of airport employees
- Providing input to the design services department regarding IT requirements for all airport projects
- Managing an IT help desk and work order system for IT requests
- Building an IT infrastructure for the benefit of the airport, tenants, and passengers
- Ensuring proper integration of project-related IT with airport IT infrastructure
- Maintaining all airport IT infrastructure, including a replacement program for PCs

FINANCE

Even the smallest of airports incur expenses and realize revenues. At many GA airports, the airport manager is required to pay invoices and record revenues, in essence serving as the bookkeeper or accountant. However, as the size of an airport increases, so do expenses and revenues and the time necessary to maintain accurate records. For instance, large commercial service airports have parking revenues in the millions of dollars, million-dollar bond issues, and million-dollar AIP grants. Due to these large dollar amounts and the effort required to manage the airport's finances, these airports have a dedicated finance department.

The director of finance is typically responsible for:

- Managing all accounts payable and accounts receivable
- Coordinating bond issues and bond re-financing
- Submitting PFC applications, as well as AIP and state funding requests
- Accounting for and managing all PFC revenue
- Accounting for and managing all AIP and state grants
- Developing budgets for operations and maintenance, as well as capital improvement
- Coordinating the payment of all personnel salaries and benefits with the department of human resources
- Accounting for all revenues from rates and charges, including those collected from various tenants
- Managing petty cash and all financial investments

CUSTOMER SERVICE

A somewhat new area of specialty at airports is that of customer service. Airports have always been aware of the need for providing high levels of customer service, but only in the past few years has customer service seemingly been taken to the next level at airports. Airports are providing greater choices in concessions, play areas for children, business centers, Wi-Fi, valet parking, cell phone lots, and many other customer-service offerings. As a result, airports now have departments of customer service with an associated director or manager of customer service. The typical responsibilities of this person include:

- Managing a customer service outreach program
- Managing the volunteer information or airport ambassador program
- Regularly gauging the level of customer satisfaction with various airport services and facilities
- Enhancing the level of service being offered at the airport by developing innovative service offerings and working with management to implement these new services

- Developing and implementing a customer service training program for airport employees and tenants
- Leading the delivery of an integrated customer experience and ensuring the successful development and implementation of projects that enhance and expand the quality of current customer experience offerings while ensuring that departments operate in a cost-effective environment

Airport Training Programs

All airports have personnel that need to be trained. Whether this training is in customer service, airfield maintenance, or accounting, an airport that values not only initial training but also recurrent or continuing training is an airport that values human resources and sees benefits to employing well-trained employees.

In general terms, airport training programs are one of two types: either in-house training or external training. In-house training, while oftentimes allowing an airport great flexibility and creativity, can be either cost-effective or cost-ineffective. For the larger airport with hundreds of employees, in-house training makes a great deal of sense. In this environment, training takes place daily, whether in the form of new employee orientation, Security Identification Display Area (SIDA) training, or customer service training. Typically, the larger airport will employ a training manager or possibly even an entire training department with up to a dozen or so employees. These individuals are computer savvy and can design computer-based training to effectively engage learners on a daily basis. They are also well-versed in adult training methods and have superb presentation skills. Lastly, the training department employees keep strict records of all training that takes place.

On the other hand, the small GA airport with only a handful of employees cannot justify an in-house training department. The airport manager may, however, appoint someone in charge of training new employees (typically in line service and/or airfield maintenance). Small airports typically rely more on the second type of airport training program—external training.

External training can take many forms, but one nationwide source of airport training is offered by AAAE. This organization holds training sessions, workshops, and conferences on a monthly basis throughout the year. AAAE does an outstanding job of offering training in many different areas, including operations, security, customer service, environmental, and financial. One training program that benefits operations employees is the Basic Airport Safety and Operations Specialist (ASOS) workshop and its sister, the Advanced ASOS workshop. Additionally, organizations such as Airports Council International (ACI) and the Federal Aviation Administration offer various workshops and events that benefit airport employees. State airport manager associations and state departments of transportation/aeronautics also generally hold at least one annual conference which contains various sessions on airport-specific issues.

In addition to simply attending a training session and receiving a certificate of completion, airport employees can be handsomely recognized for their training achievements by pursuing various forms of certification. For instance, AAAE offers the Certified Member (C.M.) program and the Accredited Airport Executive (A.A.E) program. While these designations are challenging to achieve, the airport employee obtaining the C.M. or A.A.E. is recognized throughout the industry as having an outstanding level of knowledge about all aspects of airports. For airport employees not necessarily interested in obtaining the C.M. or A.A.E., the AAAE Airport Certified Employee (ACE) program allows an employee to become recognized as an expert in a specialty area. Currently, the ACE program has five areas of specialty: Operations, Communications, Airfield Lighting Maintenance, Security, and Trusted Agent. Many airports, recognizing the value of such training distinctions, financially support the airport employee in their pursuit.

Career Advancement

Individuals in many industries have a goal of advancing in their careers, and airport employees are no different. In fact, just as an individual employed as an airport operations specialist may be on the lookout for opportunities to become an operations supervisor or assistant director of operations at their current or a different airport, current airport managers may also be looking for opportunities at larger airports or in different geographic locations.

ADVERTISING OF AIRPORT VACANCIES

Airports may advertise vacancies in a number of ways. Typically, airports (especially municipally-owned airports) must at least advertise any employment opportunities in a local source, such as the city newspaper. Oftentimes, by purchasing an employment ad in the newspaper, the ad also appears virtually on the newspaper's website. However, for those searching for airport positions, unless they live in the local area it may be difficult to become aware of positions posted only in local newspapers. Additionally, airports have discovered that newspaper advertisements typically result in less-qualified candidates who are simply looking for work anywhere in the local area. Thus, to address these shortcomings of newspaper ads, airports may also advertise on sites such as monster.com and careerbuilder.com. This approach allows individuals nationwide to become aware of a position, yet may also result in applicants with little airport experience (Figure 2-16).

One of the most useful approaches to advertising airport vacancies is to target the audience of current airport personnel. To effectively do this, airports may advertise vacant positions on the AAAE Career Center or the Airport Employment Opportunities section of the Airports Council International

Figure 2-16. The job search.

(©iStock.com/wdstock)

(ACI) website. Both of these sites are free for those searching for positions, although employers pay a reasonable fee to post an advertisement. Any position posted on these sites may be seen by anyone searching the sites, which includes airport personnel nationwide as well as college students, recent graduates, and others interested in airport positions. Posting a vacancy on such a specialized job board provides the best "bang for the buck" for airports. Indeed, executive search firms hired by an airport often utilize the AAAE and/or ACI site to advertise the opportunity.

One last method to advertise airport vacancies is the tried-and-true "word of mouth" method. Although some job searchers do not believe in the value of this method, and thus do not take advantage of it, it clearly does pay to know individuals in hiring positions. Whether referred to as networking, "schmoozing," or simply introducing yourself, getting to know those individuals currently working in the field in which you wish to gain employment or advance your career is a worthy exercise. Many times someone has become aware of a vacancy simply as a result of shaking hands or speaking to someone at a conference.

METHODS TO OBTAIN EMPLOYMENT

Although methods used to obtain employment in the airport industry closely relate to where vacancies are advertised, certain methods can be used to obtain employment. First, before graduating college, it is very beneficial to contact the airport manager or department director at the local airport and request an informational interview. In practical terms, this involves meeting with the individual to ask a few questions and find out how they entered the industry. In practical terms, a resume should be brought to this meeting and after asking questions to find out about the individual's career history, the resume can be presented for feedback on how it may be improved. This places the resume in front of a high-level decision maker, yet without any pretense. This method has produced internship opportunities, entry-level employment, and advance notice of airport vacancies for those who have taken the time to implement it.

Airport internships are yet another method useful for gaining airport employment. In fact, this may be the only way for someone to gain airport experience, at least initially. Whether for the summer or the entire year, and whether paid or unpaid, if at all possible, airport internships should be given serious consideration by the job seeker, especially those still in college. Airport internships have opened doors to permanent full-time employment for many interns over the years. If nothing else, having some airport experience on a resume greatly enhances the success of a job search.

Even with informational interviews and internships, the main method used to obtain airport employment is to formally apply for a permanent position. This can be done simply by emailing a resume, completing an online employment application, or completing a hard copy employment application and mailing it in. The method used depends on the employer, and the applicant must be careful to follow all directions presented by the employer. If the employer requests that a resume and cover letter be emailed by January 31, then the applicant should do this—nothing more, nothing less. The airport business is built around RFPs, RFQs, specifications, rules and regulations, grant assurances... the list goes on and on. Thus, the hiring airport expects applicants to follow directions precisely. Airport management reasons that if an applicant cannot follow simple directions during the application process, they'll likely have difficulty following directions and paying attention to detail on the job.

Concluding Thoughts

There is a great variety of airports throughout the United States. Whether categorized by NPIAS category, type of ownership, organizational structure, or the departments that exist within the airport's organizational structure, many variations exist. Indeed, it has been said that if you've seen one airport, you've seen one airport. This chapter has highlighted these many variations and revealed the diverse nature of the dynamic airport industry.

Chapter Summary

- The five categories of commercial service airports (large hub, medium hub, small hub, nonhub primary, and nonprimary commercial service) are determined by the number of annual enplaned passengers and the degree to which this number accounts for the total U.S. passenger enplanements on a percentage basis.
- Reliever airports are classified by the FAA and are so designated due to their role in reducing demand by GA aircraft at commercial service airports.
- The GA airport category contains the most airports and although many of these are quite small, some GA airports are busier in terms of number of operations than many commercial service airports.
- Joint-use airports are military installations at which the Department of Defense permits some degree of civil use.
- Airports may be privately or publicly owned and available for private or public use.
- Airport advisory boards do not promulgate rules or policies, but do advise the airport manager by providing an alternative view and bringing up community concerns.
- Although a small GA airport may have only one employee—the airport manager—larger commercial service airports may have employees numbering in the hundreds or even thousands.
- Although it varies by airport, larger airports generally have numerous departments which allow employees with specific skills and expertise to focus in distinct areas, such as air service development and international commerce, human resources, governmental and legal affairs, public information and community relations, performance management and internal audit, planning and development, operations, public safety, properties and contracts administration, maintenance, marketing, information technology, finance, and customer service.
- Airports generally offer either in-house training or external training, or both, to their employees.
- There are a number of methods used by airports to advertise position vacancies, and word-of-mouth remains effective even with the technological options available today.
- Informational interviewing and internships are effective methods used to enter the airport profession.

Review Questions

1. How many total airports are there in the U.S., and what is the breakdown of public and private use versus public and private ownership?
2. What are the criteria for an airport to be included in the National Plan of Integrated Airport Systems (NPIAS)?
3. What condition must be met for an airport to be categorized as a large hub airport?
4. What condition must be met for an airport to be categorized as a medium hub airport?
5. What condition must be met for an airport to be categorized as a small hub airport?
6. What condition must be met for an airport to be categorized as a nonhub primary?
7. What condition must be met for an airport to be categorized as a nonprimary commercial service?
8. What is the role of a reliever airport in the nation's air transportation system?
9. What condition must be met for an airport to be categorized as a general aviation airport?
10. Explain the differences between private-use and public-use, as well as privately-owned and publicly-owned airports.
11. What is the predominate form of airport ownership in the United States?
12. What are the reasons for the increasing popularity of airport authorities?
13. Explain the role of the airport advisory board and the challenges this may present to the airport manager.
14. Explain the FAA Airport Privatization Pilot Program.
15. Why would a municipality pursue airport privatization?
16. Describe the typical organization chart of a municipality with no airport manager.
17. Describe the typical organization chart of a GA airport.
18. Describe the typical organization chart of a small hub airport.
19. Describe the typical organization chart of a large hub airport.
20. Explain the roles and responsibilities of the following airport departments:
    a. Air service development and international commerce
    b. Human resources
    c. Governmental and legal affairs
    d. Public information and community relations
    e. Performance management and internal audit
    f. Planning and development
    g. Operations
    h. Public safety
    i. Properties and contracts administration
    j. Maintenance
    k. Marketing
    l. Information technology
    m. Finance
    n. Customer service

Scenarios

1. The City of Oak Bluff and the governor of the state feel it is time for a new airport in the Oak Bluff area. The City Council proposes a small GA airport with one runway and one FBO on the field. As you currently own an airport consulting firm, the City of Oak Bluff has contracted with your firm to provide expert guidance on the creation of this new airport. First, they have asked you how the airport ownership should be structured (i.e., city, county, authority, etc.). Additionally, they are seeking input into the organizational structure of the airport, which will have an estimated eight employees. Please provide them with an organization chart to visually convey your recommended structure.

2. As the executive director of an aviation authority with responsibility for both a large hub airport and GA airport, you are surprised to hear that the airport authority board is considering privatizing the GA airport under authority control. Their intention is to sell the airport to a private investor through the FAA Airport Privatization Pilot Program. This would raise funds to support the large hub airport's capital improvement program. However, as executive director, the board is asking for your advice on this proposal. What are the pros and cons to privatization? What do you recommend and why?

3. You are currently the director of public works for a small city, which has a small GA airport. In this city structure, there is no airport manager. In fact, the director of public works manages the airport, roads and streets, and solid waste. The new city manager is considering hiring an airport manager dedicated to managing the airport and growing the facilities. He has asked for your opinion on this and has made it clear that if the city decides to hire an airport manager, you will first be considered for the position.

4. As a newly hired director of human resources, you have been asked to create position announcements for the following positions: (a) operations manager, (b) director of finance, and (c) director of maintenance. Utilize the internet to explore currently available airport job opportunities and write position announcements to be advertised online for these three vacant positions.

5. As airport manager of a small, non-primary commercial service airport with 50,000 flight operations per year and an FBO, consider the typical airport departments one would see at an airport. Which departments presented in this chapter would you desire to have staffed for your airport? Considering a reduced budget, what innovative methods would you consider to ensure the responsibilities of these departments are carried out for your airport, even if all departments are not represented?

References and Resources for Further Study

American Association of Airport Executives. 2005. Body of Knowledge Module 1. "History, the Regulation of Air Transportation, Airports, and the Federal Aviation Administration." Washington, DC: AAAE.

Arizona Department of Transportation. n.d. "Grand Canyon Airport." Retrieved from http://www.grandcanyonairport.org/

Austin-Bergstrom International Airport. 2005. "Austin's Aviation History, Awards, and Accomplishments." Retrieved from http://www.ci.austin.tx.us/austinairport/default.htm

Branson Airport. 2011. "About Branson Airport." Retrieved from http://flybranson.com/about.php

Bureau of Transportation Statistics. n.d. "Dictionary." Retrieved from www.bts.gov/dictionary/index.xml

De Neufville, R. and A. Odoni. 2003. Airport Systems: Planning Design and Management. New York: McGraw Hill.

Federal Aviation Administration. 2010a. "FAA News." Retrieved from http://www.faa.gov/news/fact_sheets/news_story.cfm?newsId=14174

———. 2010b. National Plan of Integrated Airport Systems (NPIAS) 2011–2015. Retrieved from http://www.faa.gov/airports/planning_capacity/npias/reports/historical/

———. 2011. "Airport Privatization Pilot Program." Retrieved from http://www.faa.gov/airports/airport_compliance/privatization/

———. 2012. "Joint Civilian/Military (Joint-Use) Airports." Retrieved from http://www.faa.gov/airports/aip/military_airport_program/index.cfm?sect=joint

Hartsfield-Jackson International Airport. 2006. "2006 Annual Report: Focused on the Future." Retrieved from http://www.atlanta-airport.com/docs/Financial/2006_Annual_Report.pdf

Massport. 2011. "History." Retrieved from http://www.massport.com/massport/about-massport/Pages/AboutMassport.aspx

Metropolitan Washington Airports Authority. 2011. "About the Authority: History." Retrieved from http://www.metwashairports.com/263.htm

Orlando Sanford International Airport. n.d. "Airport organization." Retrieved from http://www.orlandosanfordairport.com/organization.asp

Prather, C.D. 2009. *General Aviation Marketing and Management: Operating, Marketing, and Managing an FBO.* Malabar, FL: Krieger.

State of Hawaii. 2011. "State Airport System." Retrieved from http://hawaii.gov/ogg/airport-information/state-airport-system

State of Oregon. n.d. "Oregon Airports by Type of Ownership." Retrieved from http://www.oregon.gov/Aviation/docs/aplistbyown.pdf

Tri-Cities Regional Airport. n.d. "Airport Authority." Retrieved from http://www.triflight.com/about-tri/airport-commission/

Van Nuys Los Angeles World Airports. 2011. "Airport Information." Retrieved from http://www.lawa.org/welcome_VNY.aspx?id=92

Yuma International Airport. 2009. "Joint-Use Operating Agreement." Retrieved from http://www.yumainternationalairport.com/yuma/airportreflibrary.nsf/4ee27e9b609182af0725723b0018389f/36b643751ee6e071072575ac002e9ecd?OpenDocument

Chapter 3

Air Traffic, Capacity, and Delay

Objectives

Upon completion of this chapter, you should:

- Understand the role of the air traffic control system, including its history.
- Be able to explain the various classes of U.S. airspace.
- Understand various NAVAIDs.
- Understand airfield lighting.
- Understand airfield signage and markings.
- Understand proper radio communication.
- Understand the Federal Contract Tower program.
- Understand NextGen.
- Understand aspects of capacity and delay.
- Understand components of demand management.

Key Terms

air operations area (AOA)
airport surface detection equipment (ASDE)
airport surveillance radar (ASR)
air traffic control
Air Traffic Control System Command Center
alert area
approach lights
automatic direction finder (ADF)
available landing distance (ALD)
boundary signs
CAT I ILS
CAT II ILS
CAT III ILS
Class A airspace
Class B airspace
Class C airspace
Class D airspace
Class E airspace
Class G airspace
clearance bars

Key Terms

clearance delivery
common traffic advisory frequency (CTAF)
congestion pricing
contact approach
controlled firing area
crossbar lights
declared capacity
demand management
destination signs
direction signs
Federal Contract Tower Program
global positioning system (GPS)
ground-based augmentation system (GBAS)
ground control
high-intensity runway lights (HIRL)
information signs
instrument approach
instrument landing system (ILS)
instrument meteorological conditions (IMC)
land and hold short lighting
land and hold short operations (LAHSO)
localizer (LOC)
localizer directional aid (LDA)
location signs
low-intensity runway lights (LIRL)
mandatory instruction signs
marker beacons
maximum takeoff weight (MTOW)
maximum throughput capacity
medium-intensity runway lights (MIRL)
microwave landing system (MLS)
military operations areas (MOA)
National Airspace System Plan
navigational aids (NAVAIDs)
Next Generation (NextGen)
non-directional beacon (NDB)
non-precision instrument approach
obstruction light
practical hourly capacity (PHCAP)
precision approach path indicator (PAPI)
precision instrument approach
prohibited areas
radio detection and ranging (RADAR)
ramp control
restricted areas
rotating beacon
runway centerline lighting
runway distance remaining signs
runway end identifier lights
runway end lights
runway guard lights
runway occupancy time (ROT)
runway visual range (RVR)
sequence flashing lights
simplified directional facility (SDF)
slot
stop bars
stopway edge lights
sustained capacity
tactical air navigation (TACAN)
taxiway centerline lights
taxiway edge lights
taxiway edge reflectors
taxiway ending marker
threshold end lights
touchdown zone lights
tower
vehicle roadway signs
very high frequency omnidirectional range (VOR)
visual approach
visual approach slope indicator (VASI)
visual meteorological conditions
warning area
wide area augmentation system (WAAS)

In Chapter 3

Introduction **101**

ATC System Overview **101**
- History 101
- Classes of Airspace 104
- NAVAIDs 107
- Lighting 113

Signage and Markings **121**

Radio Communications **130**
- Movement Areas 132
- Non-Movement Areas 133

Federal Contract Tower Program **134**

NextGen **135**

Airfield Capacity **137**
- Measures of Capacity 137
- Factors Affecting Capacity 139

Airfield Delay **143**
- Acceptable Levels of Delay 144
- Causes of Delay 144

Demand Management **145**
- Administrative Approaches 145
- Economic Approaches 146
- Hybrid Approaches 147
- Ideal Demand Management System 148

Concluding Thoughts **149**

Chapter Summary **149**

Review Questions **151**

Scenarios **152**

References and Resources for Further Study **153**

FEATURES

Tampa International Airport Informal Runway Use Program 143

By adopting an informal runway use program, the airport and airport users cooperate in reducing noise impacts to surrounding communities.

Introduction

The efficiency of the nation's air transportation system depends, to a large degree, on the efficiency of the air traffic control system. Whether this system operates with the ability to fully accommodate all users with minimal delay depends upon many factors, such as weather, airport and airspace characteristics, and aircraft mix. Nonetheless, there are specific areas that, if properly addressed by both airports and the FAA, can lead to a more efficient system. This chapter addresses those areas, as well as techniques to minimize delay and manage demand.

ATC System Overview

The **air traffic control** (ATC) system in the United States is made up of many components. These components are interrelated and interact to ensure a safe and efficient national airspace system. Today's modern ATC system, however, had very humble beginnings.

HISTORY

The history of the air traffic control system actually begins in Europe. Although there were aircraft being flown in the United States, so few aircraft were in the skies that ground-based control of aircraft was not needed. In Europe, however, aircraft were flying between countries and a standardized system was called for. Thus, in 1919, the International Commission for Air Navigation (ICAN) was created to develop "General Rules for Air Traffic." The United States was not party to ICAN, but later developed U.S. air traffic rules after the passage of the Air Commerce Act of 1926 directed the Department of Commerce to "establish air traffic rules for the navigation, protection, and identification of aircraft." (U.S. Centennial of Flight Commission, n.d.)

Although these basic air traffic rules were initially effective, it soon became clear that more control over aircraft would be needed to prevent collisions between aircraft. Some airport operators began using ground-based, visual signals involving "air traffic controllers" standing on the field waving flags to communicate with pilots. Archie League was one of the system's first flagmen, beginning in the late 1920s at the airfield in St. Louis, Missouri. As has been the case with aviation, even this system would soon become outdated (U.S. Centennial of Flight Commission, n.d.).

As more aircraft were being equipped with radio communication, the flagmen were soon replaced by airport traffic control towers. In 1930, the first of these radio-equipped towers began operating at Cleveland Municipal Airport. Only two years later, virtually the entire fleet of airline aircraft had been equipped for radio-telephone communication. By 1935, approximately 20 radio control towers were in operation throughout the United States. Up to this point, the control of air traffic was focused on airport areas. Yet the safety and control of aircraft en route was also becoming a concern. As a result, in 1935, the major airlines using the Chicago, Cleveland, and Newark airports decided to coordinate the handling of aircraft between these cities. In December of that year, the first airway traffic control center opened at Newark, New Jersey. The following year, additional centers opened at Chicago and Cleveland (U.S. Centennial of Flight Commission, n.d.).

During these early days, aircraft were tracked by controllers using maps, blackboards, and small boat-shaped weights that became known as "shrimp boats" (Figure 3-1). Conrollers had no direct radio link with aircraft, but stayed in touch with airline dispatchers, airway radio operators, and airport traffic controllers via the telephone to stay abreast of aircraft position and progress on their route of flight (U.S. Centennial of Flight Commission, n.d.).

By the summer of 1936, the federal government assumed the responsibility for enroute air traffic control. However, airport towers continued to be operated by airports. This began to change in 1941 as the Civil Aeronautics Administration (CAA) began constructing and operating ATC towers. Once constructed, the CAA began operating these towers and was responsible for the operation of 115 towers by 1944. The CAA soon began taking over the operation of existing towers at airports as well (U.S. Centennial of Flight Commission, n.d.).

The first revolution to occur in air traffic control after WWII was the introduction of **radio detection and ranging (RADAR)**. By using radio waves to detect distant objects, radar technology allowed controllers the unique ability

Figure 3-1. Early days of controlling air traffic with shrimp boats.

(FAA)

to "see" the position of aircraft on an electronic display. This technology was first used by the CAA in an experimental fashion in 1946, but by 1952 the CAA implemented routine use of radar technology for approach and departure control. In 1956, the CAA placed a large order for long-range radars that were to be used in enroute ATC (U.S. Centennial of Flight Commission, n.d.).

In an effort to consolidate some airport traffic control towers at smaller airports, the CAA began combining them with airway communication stations in 1950. These communications stations were the forerunners of flight service stations. By 1958, the CAA operated 84 of these combined station-towers, the last of which closed in 1981 (U.S. Centennial of Flight Commission, n.d.).

Radar beacons, or aircraft transponders, were first tested by the FAA in 1960. Aircraft operating in certain "positive control" areas were required to have a transponder, be piloted using instruments, and remain in contact with controllers. With the aid of transponders and these additional rules, controllers were able to reduce the separation between aircraft by as much as half the standard distance (U.S. Centennial of Flight Commission, n.d.).

In 1964, in an effort to minimize the complex web of airways that existed at the time, the FAA developed two layers of airways: one from 1,000 to 18,000 feet above ground level and the second from 18,000 to 45,000 feet above ground level. It also standardized aircraft instrument settings and navigation checkpoints to reduce the workload of controllers (U.S. Centennial of Flight Commission, n.d.).

The next breakthrough in ATC advances occurred with the adoption of computer technology. Although experimental use of computer technology by the FAA had begun as early as 1956, the period of 1965–1975 was characterized by a deliberate effort to apply this technology throughout the ATC system. Specifically, the FAA developed complex computer systems designed to replace the "shrimp boats" used to track aircraft. The system allowed controllers to view aircraft identification and position formation on a simulated three-dimensional radar screen. The automation this provided allowed controllers to focus on providing separation services to aircraft (U.S. Centennial of Flight Commission, n.d.).

In 1970, the FAA, in an effort to minimize the consequences of system congestion, established a Central Flow Control Facility. By analyzing clusters of congestion at a national level, this facility allows the FAA to implement programs (such as ground delay programs) to temporarily reduce demand in certain regions or metropolitan areas. In essence, this allows the FAA the ability to adopt a proactive approach to managing demand with capacity in the national airspace system. In 1994, the FAA opened a new **Air Traffic Control System Command Center** outside Washington, DC, which is considered to be the largest and most sophisticated facility of its kind in the world (U.S. Centennial of Flight Commission, n.d.).

In 1982, the **National Airspace System Plan** was introduced by the FAA. This plan was characterized by modernization and included goals of modernizing flight service stations, the ATC system, and ground-to-air surveillance and communication. Additionally, computers and software were modernized, air route traffic control centers were consolidated, and the number of flight service stations was reduced. In addition, new Doppler radars and advanced transponders complemented automatic radio broadcasts of surface and flight conditions (U.S. Centennial of Flight Commission, n.d.).

In an effort to further modernize ATC, in 1988 the FAA selected IBM to develop a new multi-billion dollar Advanced Automation System for the nation's enroute centers. By 1993, little had been accomplished and IBM was behind schedule and over budget. In response, the FAA revaluated its needs and in 1994 selected new contractors. Although additional delays were experienced, in 1999, controllers first began using an early version of the Standard Terminal Automation Replacement System, which included new displays and capabilities for approach control facilities. During the following year, the FAA finished replacing all of the display systems, which provided more efficient workstations for en route controllers (U.S. Centennial of Flight Commission, n.d.).

CLASSES OF AIRSPACE

There are two categories of airspace in the United States: regulatory and nonregulatory. Within these two categories of airspace, there is controlled, uncontrolled, special use, and other airspace. Regulatory airspace includes Class A, Class B, Class C, Class D, Class E, restricted areas, and prohibited areas (Figure 3-2). Nonregulatory airspace includes Military operations areas (MOAs), Warning areas, Alert areas, and Controlled firing areas. Controlled airspace refers to airspace in which air traffic control services are provided to both IFR flights and VFR flights in accordance with the airspace classification. Uncontrolled airspace is airspace within which air traffic control service is not provided.

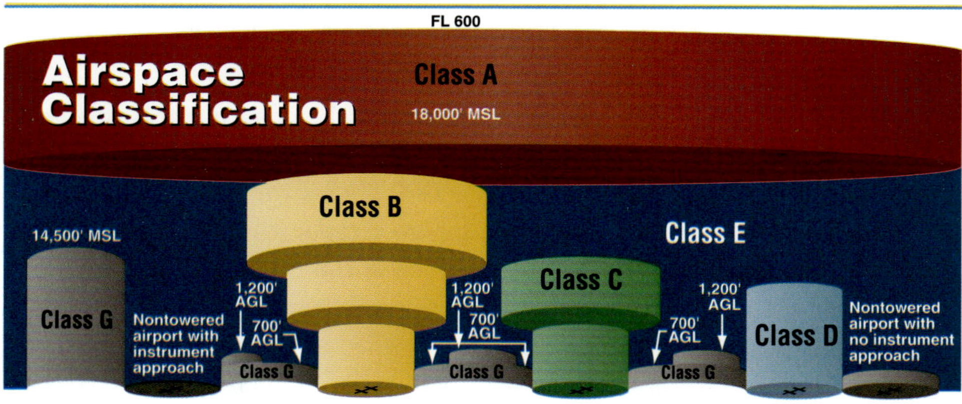

Figure 3-2. Classes of U.S. airspace.

(FAA *Pilot's Handbook of Aeronautical Knowledge*)

Controlled Airspace

Class A airspace is that airspace from 18,000 feet mean sea level (MSL) up to and including flight level (FL) 600, including the airspace overlying the waters within 12 nautical miles of the coast of the 48 contiguous states and Alaska. Unless otherwise authorized, each pilot operating aircraft in Class A airspace must operate under instrument flight rules (IFR) (FAA, 2011b).

Class B airspace is, generally, that airspace from the surface to 10,000 feet MSL surrounding the nation's busiest airports in terms of IFR operations or passenger enplanements. The configuration of each Class B airspace area is individually tailored and consists of a surface area and two or more layers, with some Class B airspace areas resembling upside-down wedding cakes. Each Class B airspace area is designed to contain all published instrument procedures once an aircraft enters the airspace. An ATC clearance is required for all aircraft to operate in the area, and all aircraft that are so cleared receive separation services within the airspace. The cloud clearance requirement for VFR operations is "clear of clouds" (FAA, 2011b).

Class C airspace is, generally, that airspace from the surface to 4,000 feet above the airport elevation surrounding those airports that have an operational control tower, are serviced by a radar approach control, and that have a certain number of IFR operations or passenger enplanements. Although the configuration of each Class C airspace area is individually tailored, the airspace usually consists of a surface area with a 5 nautical mile (NM) radius, and an outer circle with a 10 NM radius that extends from 1,200 feet to 4,000 feet above the airport elevation. Each pilot must establish two-way radio communications with the ATC facility providing air traffic services prior to entering the airspace and thereafter maintain those communications while within the airspace. This communication must begin within 20 miles of the Class C airport. Approach control frequencies are given in the *Airport/Facility Directory* (A/FD) and on sectional charts in magenta-bordered white boxes. VFR aircraft are only separated from IFR aircraft within the airspace (FAA, 2011b).

Class D airspace is, generally, that airspace from the surface to 2,500 feet above the airport elevation surrounding those airports that have an operational control tower. The configuration of each Class D airspace area is individually tailored and when instrument procedures are published, the airspace will normally be designed to contain the procedures. Arrival extensions for instrument approach procedures may be Class D or Class E airspace. Unless otherwise authorized, each pilot must establish two-way radio communications with the ATC facility providing air traffic services prior to entering the airspace and thereafter maintain those communications while in the airspace. No separation services are provided to VFR aircraft (FAA, 2011b).

Class E airspace is, generally, that controlled airspace not designated as Class A, Class B, Class C, or Class D. Class E airspace extends upward from either the surface or a designated altitude to the overlying or adjacent controlled airspace. When designated as a surface area, the airspace will be configured to contain all instrument procedures. Also in this class are federal airways, airspace beginning at either 700 or 1,200 feet AGL used to transition to or from the terminal or enroute environment, and enroute domestic and offshore airspace areas designated below 18,000 feet MSL. Unless designated at a lower altitude, Class E airspace begins at 14,500 MSL over the United States, including that airspace overlying the waters within 12 nautical miles of the coast of the 48 contiguous states and Alaska. Class E airspace does not include the airspace 18,000 MSL or above (FAA, 2011b).

Uncontrolled Airspace

Class G airspace is the only category of uncontrolled airspace. It includes that airspace not designated as Class A, Class B, Class C, Class D, or Class E. Although Class G airspace is uncontrolled and mainly the domain of VFR flights, pilots may operate on an IFR flight plan within Class G airspace for the purpose of arriving into or departing from an airport under IFR conditions with an instrument approach (FAA, 2011b).

Special Use Airspace

Special use airspace is that airspace where activities must be confined because of their nature, or where limitations are imposed on aircraft operations that are not a part of those activities, or possibly both. **Prohibited areas** contain airspace of defined dimensions identified by an area on the surface of the earth within which the flight of aircraft is prohibited. Such areas are established for security or other reasons associated with the national welfare. **Restricted areas** contain airspace identified by an area on the surface of the earth within which the flight of aircraft, while not wholly prohibited, is subject to restrictions. Activities within these areas must be confined because of their nature or limitations imposed upon aircraft operations that are not a part of those activities, or both. Restricted areas denote the existence of unusual, often invisible, hazards to aircraft such as artillery firing, aerial gunnery, or guided missiles. A **warning area** is airspace of defined dimensions, extending from three nautical miles outward from the coast of the United States that contains activity that may be hazardous to nonparticipating aircraft. **Military operations areas** (MOAs) consist of airspace of defined vertical and lateral limits established for the purpose of separating certain military training activities from IFR traffic. **Alert areas** are depicted on aeronautical charts to inform nonparticipating pilots of areas that may contain a high volume of pilot training or an unusual type of aerial activity. **Controlled firing areas** (CFAs) contain activities which, if not conducted in a controlled environment, could be hazardous to nonparticipating aircraft.

NAVAIDS

Any navigational approach made by an aircraft to an airport is conducted either with visual reference (**visual meteorological conditions**) or use of instruments (**instrument meteorological conditions**). A **visual approach** is an approach when either part or all of an instrument approach procedure is not completed (or was never initiated) and the approach is executed with visual reference to the terrain. This type of approach can be made anytime ATC approves it, when the destination airport meets visibility requirements of three statute miles or greater, and the cloud ceiling height is at least 1,000 feet above the ground level. A **contact approach** is a procedure that results from an instrument approach when the visibility is greater than one mile. In such cases, a pilot is cleared by ATC to make an instrument approach to land, and the pilot then uses visual reference to complete the approach when conditions allow. An **instrument approach** is an approach using horizontal and/or vertical guidance and is a procedure established by the FAA that outlines the routes and altitudes to be flown by an aircraft for safe flight from takeoff to landing. Instrument approaches can be either precision or non-precision. **Precision instrument approaches** provide both vertical and horizontal guidance, whereas **non-precision instrument approaches** provide only horizontal guidance.

To support these various types of approaches, **navigational aids (NAVAIDs)** are installed on or near airports. Many of these NAVAIDs can be used for both enroute and approach guidance. Although most are usable for non-precision approaches, some are also usable for precision approaches.

The most widely used precision NAVAID is the **instrument landing system (ILS)** (see Figure 3-3). This system provides both vertical and horizontal electronic guidance information to the pilot for purposes of aligning an aircraft with the centerline of a runway at the proper approach angle (typically 3 degrees). An ILS consists of a localizer beam (which provides horizontal guidance); a glide slope transmitter (which provides vertical guidance); an outer marker; a middle marker, and possibly an inner marker (providing distance information); an FAA-determined decision height (at which point a missed approach is executed if the runway environment is not in sight); and an approach lighting system (which allows the pilot to transition from instrument flight to visual flight). Functionally, aircraft guidance is provided by the localizer and glide slope, aircraft range information is provided by the marker beacons and distance measurement equipment (DME), and pilot visual information is provided by the approach and runway lighting systems (including touchdown, centerline, and runway light systems, as well as visual approach slope indicators [VASI] or precision approach path indicators [PAPI]).

The localizer antenna is usually located on the extended runway centerline outside the runway safety area between 1,000 to 2,000 feet beyond the end of the runway. The localizer equipment shelter is located at least 250 feet to either side of the antenna array and within 30 degrees of the extended longitudinal axis of the antenna array. The glideslope antenna may be located on either side of the runway, but is preferably located on the side providing the least

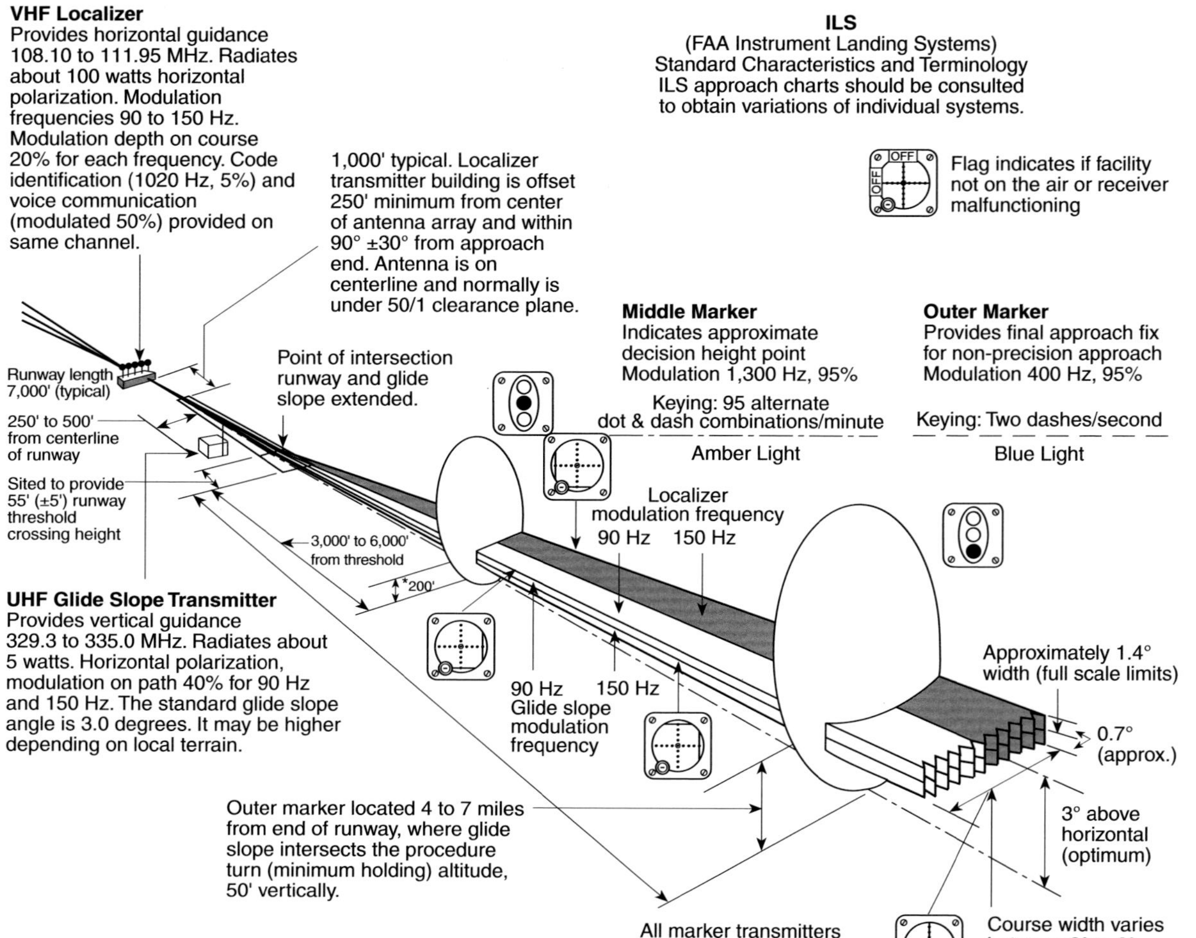

Rate of Descent Chart (feet per minute)

Speed (Knots)	Angle		
	2.5°	2.75°	3°
90	400	440	475
110	485	535	585
130	575	630	690
150	665	730	795
160	707	778	849

Compass locators, rated at 25 watts output 190 to 535 KHz, are installed at many outer and some middle markers. A 400 Hz or a 1020 Hz tone, modulating the carrier about 95% is keyed with the first two letters of the ILS identification on the outer locator and the last two letters on the middle locator. At some locations, simultaneous voice transmissions from the control tower are provided, with appropriate reduction in identification percentage.

* Figures marked with asterisk are typical. Actual figures vary with deviations in distances to markers, glide angles and localizer widths.

Figure 3-3. Instrument landing system (ILS).

(From the FAA *Aeronautical Information Manual*)

interference from buildings, power lines, vehicles, and aircraft. The glideslope equipment shelter is located 10 feet behind the antenna and a minimum of 400 feet from the runway centerline. **Marker beacons** associated with the ILS may include an outer marker (OM), middle marker (MM), and inner marker (IM). The OM beacon is located four to seven nautical miles from the runway threshold to mark the point at which the glideslope altitude is verified or at which the descent without glideslope begins. The MM beacon is located 2,000 to 6,000 feet from the runway threshold. It marks the approximate decision point of a CAT I ILS approach. Finally, the IM beacon may be used to locate the decision point of a CAT II or III ILS approach, normally 1,000 feet from the threshold. Inner marker beacons are not used for CAT I ILS approaches (FAA, 2014a).

A standard ILS Category **(CAT) I** approach consists of a localizer, glide slope, final approach fix (FAF) or compass locator, marker system (outer and middle), an approach light system, and runway marking and lighting. Runways equipped with an ILS **CAT II** approach also require an inner marker and have specific RVR requirements. Likewise, a **CAT III** approach requires an inner marker along with specific RVR requirements, and is the most stringent and expensive of ILS systems because of the equipment involved. However, the CAT III approach also allows landings during the poorest visibility. Within the CAT III approach category, there are sub-categories consisting of **CAT IIIA**, **IIIB**, and **IIIC** (see Table 3-1).

Table 3-1. ILS decision height and visibility requirements.

ILS Category	Decision Height	Visibility or RVR
I	200 feet	1/2 mile (2400 feet)
I (with centerline and TDZ lights and RVR)	200 feet	1800 feet
II	100 feet	1200 feet
IIIA	*	700 feet
IIIB	*	150 feet
IIIC	*	+

* Decision height not specified, only visibility limits apply
\+ Aircraft must have autoland capabilities and a qualified pilot

Runway visual range (RVR) equipment allows for measurement of horizontal visibility, although the exact number of RVRs required will depend on the runway approach category and physical runway length. ILS CAT I runways only require one touchdown RVR. CAT II runways with visibility minimums down to 1,600 feet require one touchdown RVR, while a CAT II runway with minimums below 1,600 RVR require touchdown and rollout RVRs. All CAT II runways require a touchdown RVR, with a rollout sensor also required for CAT II operations below 1,600 feet RVR. When the runway is in excess of 8,000 feet in length, a midpoint RVR sensor is also required in addition to the touchdown and rollout sensors for CAT II operations below RVR 1600.

CAT II runways greater than 8,000 feet in length, as well as CAT III runways with visibility minimums below 1,200 RVR, require touchdown, rollout, and midpoint RVRs. Touchdown RVRs are located 750 to 1,000 feet from the runway threshold, generally behind the MLS elevation antenna or ILS glideslope antenna. Midpoint RVRs are located within 250 feet of the center of the runway. Rollout RVRs are located 750 to 1,000 feet from the rollout end of the runway. Although older systems are composed of two separate parts (a projector and receiver), newer units are single-point and contain the projector and receiver on the same pole. Laterally, single-point units are located at least 400 feet from the runway centerline and 150 feet from a taxiway centerline. Older, dual-point units contain a transmissometer projector that is located 400 feet from the runway centerline and 150 feet from a taxiway centerline, and a receiver that is located 250 to 1,000 feet from the runway centerline (FAA, 2009; FAA, 2014a).

Although the localizer is part of the ILS, an airport may have a localizer-only approach. The **localizer (LOC** or LLZ) or **localizer directional aid (LDA)** projects a radio frequency beam down the runway from the departure end toward the approach end. The signal fans out narrowly along its path toward the centerline of the runway. This component provides lateral guidance, assisting the pilot in aligning the aircraft with the runway centerline. A localizer-only approach is considered a non-precision approach. The normal operation and use of a localizer result in what is known as a front course approach. On some localizer installations, the installed equipment and terrain allow for a reverse approach to the airport, or what is known as a non-precision localizer back course approach. Most of these approaches are being phased out of service. Newer localizers are more stable in their signal generation and do not normally generate a signal that can be used as a back course localizer approach.

A **non-directional beacon (NDB)** is used for air navigation primarily where bad terrain exists or if cost considerations dictate its use. Because NDBs are generally inexpensive and occupy little ground space, they can be situated almost anywhere (Figure 3-4). In fact, only a single short vertical antenna and normal electrical power are required for its operation. Non-directional refers to the type of radio signal transmitted. The transmitted signal is omnidirectional and can be received by an aircraft instrument known as an **automatic direction finder (ADF)** in the cockpit. In essence, the signal acts as a homing device for an aircraft.

Figure 3-4. Non-directional beacon.

(Wikimedia Commons; see credit on page 623)

NDBs are subject to environmental disturbances such as lightning, precipitation static, and interference from other radio stations, especially at night.

The **very high frequency omnidirectional range (VOR)**, which broadcasts 360-degree bearing information from the station using VHF signals, provides considerably greater accuracy and reliability than NDBs. VHF is used because it is not greatly affected by lightning static or reflection from terrain. The VOR located on an airport is typically a terminal VOR (TVOR). With this NAVAID, a distance of at least 500 feet from the centerline of any runway and 250 feet from the centerline of any taxiway should be maintained. Additionally, if an airport has intersecting runways, the TVOR should be located adjacent to the intersection to provide approach guidance to both runways. However, the TVOR antenna should be located at least 1,000 feet from any structures to avoid signal distortion. Metal fences should be at least 500 feet from the antenna (FAA, 2014a).

Tactical air navigation (TACAN) is the military's version of the VOR system. If VORs and TACANs are co-located within the same facility, it is known as a VORTAC (see Figure 3-5).

Figure 3-5. Very high frequency omnidirectional range (VOR) collocated with Tactical Air Navigation (TACAN), also known as VORTAC.

At those airports where siting or cost factors preclude installation of an ILS system, a **simplified directional facility (SDF)** may be installed to provide increased runway use during inclement weather. An SDF provides course information similar to a localizer, but it is less accurate, while also being more flexible given the surrounding environment. The approach techniques and procedures used in an SDF instrument approach are essentially the same as those employed in executing a standard localizer approach, except the SDF course may not be aligned with the runway and the course may be wider, resulting in less precision.

There was great effort during the 1970s and 1980s to develop an alternative instrument landing system that would resolve some of the problems experienced by the standard ILS. As a result, the **microwave landing system (MLS)** was developed. The MLS would alleviate standard ILS problems associated with terrain interference, long straight approaches into an airport, and growing radio frequency congestion. The MLS signal is fan-shaped and up to 60 degrees either side of the centerline (see Figure 3-6). The MLS signal provides continuous DME information to the pilot and allows for any number of multiple curved and segmented approaches to a runway. However, the FAA halted further development of MLS in 1994 with the recognition of GPS capability.

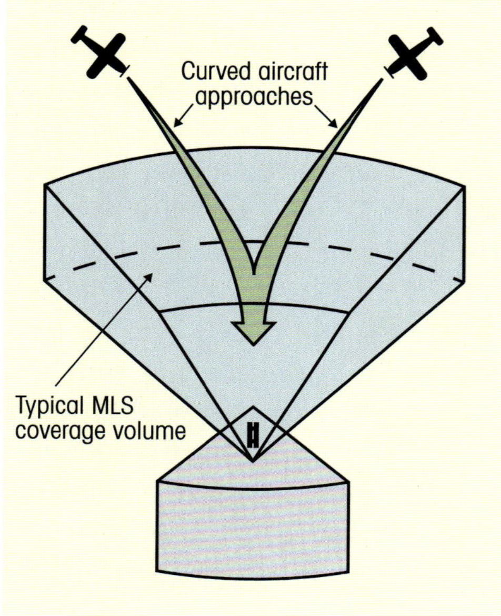

Figure 3-6. Typical approaches into a microwave landing system-based approach.

(Wikimedia Commons; see credit on page 623)

The most advanced NAVAID is the **global positioning system (GPS)**. GPS is a satellite-based navigation system designed to eventually replace most of the current ground-based navigational systems in the United States. GPS achieves better accuracy than most land-based systems in that it provides velocity information and is less susceptible to ground-derived interference or error. GPS is not without faults, however. It is dependent on line-of-sight availability and unless augmented with ground-based stations, can only be used for non-precision approaches. For instance, signals from four satellites are necessary to provide a three-dimensional position. The loss of even one satellite signal can affect the integrity of the approach (Figure 3-7).

To obtain the precision guidance necessary for instrument approaches, an augmentation signal on the ground is necessary to ensure that the GPS signal is accurate, reliable, and available to everyone using the approach or enroute signal. The **Wide Area Augmentation System (WAAS)** is designed to enhance the capabilities of GPS signals to allow the system to be used for precision approaches without the need for on-airport equipment. The installation of a ground-based reference station improves GPS accuracy to within 30 feet. The FAA has determined that approximately 24 ground-based stations are required in the United States to meet the requirements for safety of flight. When coupled with the existing 24 orbiting satellite stations, WAAS is expected to satisfy the Category I instrument approach needs of most U.S. airports.

Figure 3-7. Global positioning system satellite.

(Wikimedia Commons; see credit on page 623)

A **Ground-Based Augmentation System (GBAS)** places a ground-based transmitter in close proximity to, if not on, an airport. It performs the same function as the WAAS, which is to augment the satellite transmitters and to verify the satellite signals. However, it is of a lower power and range, as its purpose is to satisfy the need for accuracy and the number of transmitters for an aircraft to make a Category II or III approach to a runway.

LIGHTING

Airfield lighting systems may utilize incandescent lighting, tungsten-halogen lighting, fluorescent lighting, or light-emitting diodes (LEDs). The oldest lamp type in use, the longevity of incandescent lighting is primarily based upon the temperature generated. The higher the lumen output, the shorter the lifespan and hence the more frequent replacement requirement. Commonly called a "quartz lamp," tungsten-halogen bulbs produce a much hotter filament, and the quartz lens is better able to withstand the heat. However, the quartz bulb system is very sensitive to temperature variation and lens contamination. Fluorescent lamps generate light through low-pressure gas discharge. A ballast that is matched to the electrical requirements of the lamp is used to limit the current to the lamp electrodes. Florescent lamps are used for internal lighting of airfield signs. They are used only at airports where low ambient temperatures are not routinely experienced. Otherwise, incandescent or tungsten-halogen bulbs must be used, due to their heating characteristics. Lastly, a light-emitting diode (LED) has the benefits of a brighter emitting light, a longer lamp life, and lower power consumption. A drawback to LED lamps is that they do not generate heat to melt snow or ice accumulation. For this reason, LED installations may require supplemental heater coils in colder areas. LED technology is becoming more common at airports.

According to FAA Advisory Circular (AC) 150/5340-30, *Design and Installation Details for Airport Visual Aids*, airfield lighting can be grouped into the following categories:

1. Runway and taxiway edge lighting systems
2. Runway centerline and touchdown lighting systems
3. Taxiway lighting systems
4. Land and hold short lighting systems
5. Miscellaneous airfield aids
6. Approach lighting

(FAA, 2011a)

Runway edge lights define the edge of the runway (see Figure 3-8). Runway edge lighting systems may be **low-intensity runway lights (LIRL), medium-intensity runway lights (MIRL)**, or **high-intensity runway lights (HIRL)**. LIRL runway edge lights emit white light. MIRL and HIRL runway edge lights emit white light, except in the caution zone, which is the last 2,000 feet of runway or one-half the runway length, whichever is less. In the caution zone, yellow lights are substituted for white lights in the direction facing the instrument approach threshold, with white lights in the opposite direction. Further, MIRL and HIRL have varying lighting intensities, or "steps," depending on intensity of lighting required (FAA, 2011a).

Figure 3-8.
Runway edge lights.

Threshold and **runway end lights** are installed in combination and emit green light outward from the runway toward the approach and red light toward the runway to mark the ends of the runway (see Figure 3-9). The green lights indicate the landing threshold to landing aircraft and the red lights indicate the end of the runway to both landing and departing aircraft (FAA, 2011a).

Stopway edge lights are unidirectional red lights oriented toward the takeoff direction of the runway. They are placed along its full length in two parallel rows that are equidistant from the runway centerline and coincident with the rows of runway edge lights (FAA, 2011a).

Figure 3-9.
Threshold end lights.

(Brett Fay, Lakeland Linder Regional Airport.)

Taxiway edge lights define the edge of the taxiway and are blue in color (see Figure 3-10). The standard taxiway edge lighting system for airports is MITL—medium-intensity taxiway lights (FAA, 2011a).

Figure 3-10.
Taxiway edge lights.

(Brett Fay, Lakeland Linder Regional Airport.)

Taxiway edge reflectors may be installed (a) in lieu of taxiway edge lights or (b) to enhance taxiway edge lights (see Figure 3-11). Reflectors are permitted in lieu of edge lights where a centerline system is installed. 14 CFR §139.311 actually requires airports

Figure 3-11. Taxiway edge reflectors.

(Adam Lunn, Lakeland Linder Regional Airport.)

to have one taxiway lighting system installed, which can consist of centerline lights, centerline reflectors, edge lights, or edge reflectors (FAA, 2011a).

Runway centerline lighting is required for CAT II and CAT III runways and for CAT I runways used for landing operations below 2,400 feet RVR. Runway centerline lights are required on runways used for takeoff operations below 1,600 feet RVR. The last 3,000-foot portion of the runway centerline lighting system is color coded to warn pilots of the impending runway end. Alternating red and white lights are installed, starting with red, as seen from 3,000 feet to 1,000 feet from the runway end, and red lights are installed in the last 1,000-foot portion (FAA, 2011a).

Touchdown zone lights consist of two rows of transverse light bars located symmetrically about the runway centerline. Each light bar consists of three unidirectional lights facing the landing threshold. The touchdown zone lights extend to 3,000 feet, or one-half the runway length for runways less than 6,000 feet, from the threshold with the first light bars located 100 feet from the threshold (FAA, 2011a).

Taxiway centerline lights provide taxi guidance between the runway and apron areas (see Figure 3-12). A taxiway centerline lighting system consists of unidirectional or bidirectional in-pavement lights installed parallel to the centerline of the taxiway. Taxiway centerline lights are green, with the exception of lead-off lights,[1] lead-on lights,[2] and taxiway centerline lights that cross a runway[3] (FAA, 2011a).

Runway guard lights (RGL) provide a visual indication to pilots and ground vehicle operators approaching the runway holding position that they are about to enter an active runway (see Figure 3-13). They can be elevated or in-pavement (FAA, 2011a).

Stop bars provide a distinctive "stop" signal to a pilot or ground vehicle operator approaching a runway, in the form of a row of unidirectional in-pavement red lights and an elevated red light on each side of the taxiway. In low-visibility conditions, controlled stop bars are used to permit access to the active runway. Uncontrolled stop bars protect the active runway at taxiway/runway intersections that are not part of the low-visibility taxi route (FAA, 2011a).

---

1 Alternating green and yellow lights are installed from the runway centerline (beginning with a green light) to one centerline light position beyond the runway hold or ILS/MLS critical area hold position, ending with a yellow light.

2 Color-coded with the same yellow/green color pattern as lead-off lights.

3 Color-coded yellow/green, ending with a bidirectional yellow/green light fixture one centerline light position beyond the runway holding position painted marking or ILS/MLS critical area holding position painted marking.

Figure 3-12. Taxiway centerline lights.

(Wikimedia Commons; see credit on page 623)

Clearance bars are designed to (a) advise pilots and vehicle drivers that they are approaching a hold point (other than a runway holding position), and (b) advise pilots and vehicle drivers that they are approaching an intersecting taxiway. Clearance bars consist of a row of three in-pavement yellow lights to indicate a low visibility hold point (FAA, 2011a).

Figure 3-13. Elevated runway guard lights.

Land and hold short lighting systems are installed to indicate the location of hold-short points on runways approved for **land and hold short operations (LAHSO)**. LAHSO is an air traffic control procedure that requires pilots to land and hold short of a point (typically an intersecting runway being used), allowing the airport to balance the needs for increased airport capacity and system efficiency, consistent with safety. The pilot-in-command should determine if the aircraft can safely land and stop within the **available landing distance (ALD)**, a distance published in the *Airport/Facility Directory* (A/FD). If unable, the pilot-in-command should not accept a LAHSO clearance. To provide a visual of the LAHSO point, the land and hold short lighting system consists of a row of six or seven in-pavement unidirectional pulsing white lights installed across the runway at the hold-short point (see Figure 3-14) (FAA, 2011a).

Figure 3-14. Land and hold short lighting.

(Brett Fay, Lakeland Linder Regional Airport.)

Airport **rotating beacons** are designed to indicate the location of a lighted airport; as such, the rotating beacon is an integral part of an airfield lighting system (see Figure 3-15). All airport rotating beacons project a beam of light in two directions, 180 degrees apart. For civil land airports only, the beacon flashes an alternating white (clear) and green light at 24–30 flashes per minute. Beacons should be installed within 5,000 feet of a runway and in an area that will not (a) create light interference for pilots or controllers and (b) obstruct the projection of the rotating beacon light beam. Generally, rotating beacons are located on airport property (FAA, 2011a; FAA, 2014).

Obstruction lights are installed on all obstructions that present a hazard to air traffic, warning pilots of the presence of an obstruction during hours of darkness and during periods of limited daytime visibility (see Figure 3-16). An obstruction's height, size, shape, and the area in which it is located determine the position of lights on the obstruction and the number of lights required to

Figure 3-15. (left) Rotating beacon.

Figure 3-16. (right) Obstruction lights.

adequately light the obstruction to assure visibility of such lighting from an aircraft at any angle of approach (FAA, 2011a).

In addition to various types of airfield lighting, approach lighting systems are utilized to allow the pilot to transition from instrument flying within the cockpit to visually locating the runway outside the cockpit (Figure 3-17). Approach lighting systems are oriented on the extended runway centerline, and extend from the runway threshold toward the approach. All approach lighting systems require a space 400 feet wide extending 200 feet beyond the outermost light of the approach lighting system. According to FAA categorization, the following are common approach lighting system configurations:

1. High intensity approach lighting system with sequenced flashing lights (ALSF-2)—A high intensity ALS that is 2,400 feet in length with sequenced flashing lights. Required for CAT II and III precision approaches.
2. Medium intensity approach lighting system with runway alignment indicator lights (MALSR)—A medium intensity ALS that is 2,400 feet in length with runway alignment indicator lights (RAILS). Approved for CAT I approaches, the MALS portion is 1,400 feet in length, while the RAIL portion extends outward an additional 1,000 feet.
3. Medium intensity approach lighting system (MALS)—A medium intensity ALS that is 1,400 feet in length. It enhances nonprecision instrument and night visual approaches.
4. Medium intensity approach lighting system with sequence flashing lights (MALSF)—A medium intensity ALS that is identical to MALS, with the exception of sequenced flashing lights that are added to the outer three light bars. The purpose of the sequenced flashing lights is to improve recognition of the ALS by pilots when there is light pollution/distraction in the local airport vicinity.

Figure 3-17. Approach lighting system.

(hkratky/Bigstock.com)

5. Omnidirectional approach lighting systems (ODALS)—Typically installed on a nonprecision instrument runway that is difficult to identify due to light pollution in the local airport vicinity. It consists of seven lights, with five of these seven serving as sequence flashing omnidirectional lights. These five lights are located on the extended runway centerline beginning 300 feet from the runway threshold and spaced at 300-foot intervals. The remaining two lights are installed on either side of the runway threshold. ODALS require a 400-foot-wide area that extends 1,700 feet from the threshold.

(FAA, 2014a)

Depending upon the system, the approach lighting system may consist of the following components:

1. Sequence flashing lights
2. Approach lights
3. Crossbar lights
4. Runway end identifier lights (REIL)
5. Visual approach slope indicators (VASI)
6. Precision approach path indicators (PAPI)

Sequence flashing lights are a series of five lights that extend past the 1,000-foot mark of the approach lights. Flashing in sequence and in one direction, they are commonly referred to as "the rabbit" because they lead the aircraft toward the runway, just as a mechanical rabbit leads greyhounds around a race track (FAA, 2011a).

The **approach lights** are a series of lights uniformly extending from the threshold out to a point where the pilot can make a timely transition from instrument to visual reference. Approach lighting varies based on the operational requirements of a particular approach. Their purpose is to allow the pilot to visually verify the runway environment in low visibility conditions, which is made easier by extending approach lighting closer to the pilot on approach (FAA 2011a).

White **crossbar lights** are a series of lights positioned perpendicular on both sides of the primary approach lights. They are used by a pilot as a visual aid for leveling the aircraft's wings. They also provide information on distance to the runway, since they are positioned at fixed distances from the threshold (FAA, 2011a).

Additionally, **runway end identifier lights (REIL)** aid in early identification of the runway and runway end. These lights, in the form of two flashing lights located near the end of the runway, are mostly used at airports located in areas with significant light pollution.

Visual approach slope indicators (VASI) provide a visual approach path on proper glide slope to the runway (Figure 3-18). These lights are visible from 3–5 miles during the day and up to 20 miles or more at night. The visual glide path of the VASI provides safe obstruction clearance within plus or minus 10 degrees of the extended runway centerline and up to 4 nautical miles from the runway threshold. They come in different arrays of 2- or 3-bar systems that have 2, 4, 6, 12, or 24 lights each. The most common VASI type is a 2-bar, 4-light unit (FAA, 2011a).

Precision approach path indicators (PAPI) serve the same purpose of VASI but are generally more standard. They are installed in a single row of either two or four light units (Figure 3-19). These lights are visible from about 5 miles during the day and up to 20 miles at night. The visual glide path of the PAPI typically provides safe obstruction clearance within plus or minus 10 degrees of the extended runway centerline and to 4 nautical miles from the runway threshold.

Figure 3-18. Visual approach slope indicator (VASI).

Figure 3-19. Precision approach path indicator (PAPI).

(Nan Phanitsuda Sophonpanasak, Denver International Airport)

Signage and Markings

Appropriate and proper signage on the airfield is critical to ensuring safety of aircraft and ground vehicles. In addition to markings, signs are used to identify boundaries of runway approach areas, ILS critical areas, runway safety areas or obstacle-free zones, as well as no entry areas, deicing pads, ground run-up enclosures, and other areas. The FAA, through various advisory circulars, provides guidance on the sizes, styles, classes, and modes of signs, as well as detailed inscriptions for sign faces on a grid pattern and spacing requirements between characters. Specifically, each sign should contain a message element, a sign face (including the legend and sign panel), proportionality, readability, and the sign border, margin, and/or edge. Signs are constructed to withstand exposure to sunlight, rain, and wind loads.

Although the specific signage required at an airport may vary, the following types are typical:

- **Mandatory instruction signs** (white inscription with a black outline on a red background)—Require ATC clearance at a controlled airport before proceeding. At an uncontrolled airport, proceed only with caution and appropriate precautions. These signs denote taxiway/runway intersections, runway/runway intersections, instrument landing system (ILS) critical areas, precision obstacle free zone (POFZ) boundaries, runway approach areas, CAT II/III operations areas, military landing zones, and no entry areas (Figure 3-20).
- **Location signs** (yellow inscription with a yellow border on a black background; the yellow border is set in from inner edge of the sign to yield a continuous black margin)—These signs identify the taxiway or runway upon which the aircraft or vehicle is located (Figure 3-21).

Figure 3-20. Mandatory instruction sign.

Figure 3-21. Location sign.

- **Boundary signs** (black inscription on a yellow background)—These signs identify the location of the boundary of the runway safety area (RSA)/obstacle free zones (OFZ) or ILS critical area for a pilot or vehicle operator exiting the runway (Figure 3-22).
- **Direction signs** (black inscription on a yellow background; always contains arrows)—These signs indicate directions of taxiways leading out of an intersection. The signs may also be used to indicate a taxiway exit from a runway (Figure 3-23).
- **Destination signs** (black inscription on a yellow background; always contain an arrow)—These signs indicate the general direction to a remote location, such as APRON, FULE, TERM(inal), CIVIL, MIL(itary), PAX (passenger handling), CARGO, INTL (international area), FBO, and GRE (ground run-up enclosure) (Figure 3-24).
- **Taxiway ending marker**—These signs indicate that a taxiway does not continue beyond an intersection (Figure 3-25).

Figure 3-22. Boundary sign.

(Brett Fay, Lakeland Linder Regional Airport.)

Figure 3-23. Direction sign.

Figure 3-24. Destination sign.

Figure 3-25. Taxiway ending marker.

- **Information signs** (black inscription on a yellow background)—These signs are installed on the airside of an airport and provide information other than mandatory holding positions, taxiway guidance, and runway distance remaining signs (Figure 3-26).
- **Vehicle roadway signs**—These are signs located on the airfield and are intended solely for vehicle operators (Figure 3-27).
- **Runway distance remaining signs** (white numeral inscription on a black background)—Runway distance remaining signs are used to provide the length of runway distance remaining in thousands of feet to pilots during takeoff and landing operations (Figure 3-28).

Airports are required to develop airport signage plans noting the location of each sign on the airfield. These plans must be submitted to the FAA and require FAA approval.

Figure 3-26. Information sign.

Figure 3-27. Vehicle roadway sign.

Figure 3-28. Runway distance remaining sign.

In addition to appropriate signage, airports are required to install various markings. Like signage, the purpose of markings is to relay information to pilots and operators of ground vehicles.

Runway markings include:

- *Runway landing designator marking*—This marking consists of a number of one or two digits (and possibly a letter) and is used to identify a runway end (Figure 3-29).
- *Runway centerline marking*—This marking identifies the center of a runway, providing centerline alignment guidance to pilots and ground vehicle operators. Stripes are white and 120 feet in length with gaps 80 feet in length (Figure 3-30).
- *Runway threshold marking*—Consisting of a 10 foot white threshold bar and a number of longitudinal stripes, this marking closely identifies the actual beginning point of the runway used for landing. The number of stripes varies, based on the runway width. A 150-foot wide runway, for example, has 12 symmetrical stripes, 6 on each side of the runway centerline (Figure 3-31).
- *Runway aiming point marking*—This marking provides a visual aiming point for landing operations. It is in the form of two white rectangular markings, one on each side of the runway centerline, located approximately 1,000 feet from the runway threshold (Figure 3-32).
- *Runway touchdown zone marking*—Used to identify the touchdown zone on a precision instrument runway, this marking consists of symmetrically arranged pairs of rectangular bars in groups of one, two, and three along the runway centerline (Figure 3-33).
- *Runway edge marking*—Designed to provide enhanced visual contrast between the runway edge and the surrounding terrain or runway shoulders, this marking also delineates the width of suitable paved area for runway operations. This marking consists of two parallel stripes, one placed along each edge of the usable runway with the outer edge of each stripe approximately on the edge of the paved usable runway (Figure 3-34).
- *Runway displaced threshold marking*—A runway may have a displaced threshold, requiring the placement of a displaced threshold marking. This marking includes a runway threshold bar and arrowheads with and without arrow shafts. The threshold bar marking delineates the beginning section of the runway available for landing from the unusable section on the approach side of the displaced threshold, while white arrowheads with and without arrow shafts provide centerline guidance for pilots during approaches, take-offs, and landing rollouts from the opposite direction (Figure 3-35).

Figure 3-29. Runway landing designator marking.
(iofoto.com/Bigstock.com)

Figure 3-30. Runway centerline marking.

Figure 3-31. Runway threshold marking.

Figure 3-32. Runway aiming point marking.
(iofoto.com/Bigstock.com)

Figure 3-33. Runway touchdown zone marking.
(shutterrudder/Bigstock.com)

Figure 3-34. Runway edge marking.

Figure 3-35. Runway displaced threshold marking.
(©iStock.com/DraganSaponjic)

- *Chevron markings*—This marking, yellow in color, identifies paved blast pads, stopways, and EMAS (engineered materials arresting systems) in relation to the end of the runway (Figure 3-36).
- *Runway shoulder marking*—This marking is used, when needed, as a supplement to further delineate a paved runway shoulder that pilots have mistaken or are likely to mistake as usable runway. This marking is used only in conjunction with the runway edge marking (Figure 3-37).

Figure 3-36. Chevron markings.

Figure 3-37. Runway shoulder marking.
(Diana Fernandez, San Diego International Airport)

In addition to runways, taxiways also provide guidance and direction information to pilots and operators of ground vehicles. This is done primarily through markings. Taxiway markings include:

1. *Holding position markings*—This marking is designed to prevent aircraft and vehicles from entering into critical areas associated with a runway safety area and from entering into critical areas associated with navigational aids, or to control traffic at the intersection of taxiways. There are six operational situations (cases) in which three different holding position marking schemes may be used. The most common application is used for an aircraft that will need to hold short prior to entering an active runway (Figure 3-38).
2. *Taxiway centerline markings*—Designed to provide pilots and ground vehicle operators continuous visual guidance along a designated path, this marking—unlike the runway centerline marking—has no gaps, except in certain situations. To reinforce situational awareness before entering a runway, taxiway centerlines are enhanced for 150 feet prior to a runway holding position marking on those taxiways that directly enter a runway. This enhancement creates a triple-wide marking, with a row of dashed yellow markings on each side of the standard taxiway centerline marking. (Figure 3-39).
3. *Taxiway edge marking*—This marking can be either a dual continuous or dashed marking and is used along a taxi route to alert pilots where the demarcation line exists between usable pavement for taxi operations and

unusable pavement. The dashed taxiway edge marking is used on pavement that permits pilots to cross over this surface marking (Figure 3-40).

4. *Surface painted holding position signs*—This surface painted sign provides supplemental visual cues that alert pilots and vehicle drivers of an upcoming holding position location and the associated runway designator as another method to minimize the potential for a runway incursion. This surface sign painted is identical to the mandatory sign located adjacent to each taxiway entering a runway. It has a red background with white numbers (and letters if required to indicate the runway designation) (Figure 3-41).
5. *Taxiway shoulder marking*—Although optional, this marking indicates the non-usable paved shoulders. The taxiway shoulder marking is yellow, with straight lines painted perpendicular to the taxiway on the paved shoulder. (Figure 3-42).

Figure 3-38. Holding position marking.

Figure 3-39. Taxiway centerline markings.

Figure 3-40. Taxiway edge marking.

Figure 3-41. Surface painted holding position signs.

Figure 3-42. Taxiway shoulder marking.

6. *Surface painted taxiway direction signs*—The surface painted taxiway direction sign is used with an arrow to provide directional guidance at an intersection (Figure 3-43).
7. *Surface painted taxiway location signs*—This surface painted sign identifies the taxiway upon which the aircraft is located. This marking is used to supplement other signs located along the taxiway system (Figure 3-44).
8. *Surface painted gate destination signs*—This surface painted sign is used to assist pilots in locating their assigned terminal gate, especially useful for low-visibility operations.
9. *Surface painted apron entrance point sign*—This surface painted sign is used to assist pilots in locating their position along the edges of a large, continuous apron serving the terminal gates. The marking is especially useful for identifying both the entrances and exits in and along the terminal complex.
10. *Geographic position marking*—This marking is used repeatedly along a designated taxi route to serve as an indicator of a location or spot so that pilots can confirm holding points or report their location while taxiing during periods of low-visibility operations. It is generally used along low-visibility taxi routes associated with a surface movement guidance and control system (SMGCS) plan. It is known as a pink spot and is the only airfield marking with pink paint. It is circular and outlined by a white border and a black border, with black number/letter designation (Figure 3-45).
11. *Ramp control markings*—This optional marking is used to facilitate the local ramp tower or the FAA airport traffic control tower in the movement of aircraft and vehicles to designated areas of ramps, aprons, and other paved areas between non-movement areas and the movement area. These markings may be either circular or triangle-shaped and consist of a black inscription on a yellow background.

Other markings include:

1. *Vehicle roadway markings*—These consist of (a) roadway edge lines to delineate each edge of the roadway, (b) a dashed line to separate lanes within the edges of the roadway, and, where appropriate, (c) a roadway stop line (bar) (Figure 3-46).
2. *Very high frequency omnidirectional range (VOR) receiver checkpoint marking*—The VOR receiver checkpoint marking is used by pilots to check their aircraft instruments with navigational aid signals. It consists of a painted circle with a painted directional arrow that is aligned toward the azimuth of the VOR facility.
3. *Non-movement area boundary marking*—This marking is used to delineate the movement areas under direct control by the airport traffic control tower from the non-movement areas that are not under their control. It is a marking important for everyone with driving privileges at the airport to properly

Figure 3-43. Surface painted taxiway direction sign.

(Lee Brown, Fort Lauderdale-Hollywood International Airport)

Figure 3-44. Surface painted taxiway location sign.

Figure 3-45. Geographic position marking.

(Nan Phanitsuda Sophonpanasak, Denver International Airport)

Figure 3-46. Vehicle roadway markings.

identify. In essence, it appears as a smaller marking very similar to the mandatory holding position marking. With one solid yellow marking and one dashed yellow marking, the solid line is always on the non-movement side, signifying that permission must be received prior to crossing over the marking. (Figure 3-47).

4. *Runway and taxiway closure markings*—For runways and taxiways that are permanently closed, the lighting circuits are disconnected. For closed runways, all markings for runway thresholds, runway designations, touchdown aiming points, and touchdown zones are obliterated. Only solid yellow "X" markings are painted to indicate closed pavement. For runways that closed only temporarily, lighted X markings are typically used. These hydraulically raised lighted Xs are powered by a generator and provide significantly enhanced visibility of the closure marking both in day and night situations. Lights can be steady or flashing (Figure 3-48).

Figure 3-47. Non-movement area boundary marking.

Figure 3-48. Lighted X used for temporary runway closures.

(Nan Phanitsuda Sophonpanasak, Denver International Airport)

Radio Communications

In aviation, effective communication is critical. To ensure safety, this communication must occur in both controlled and uncontrolled airspace. This communication generally involves ATC, and involves both pilots and ground vehicle operators. First, aircraft communicate with ATC at controlled airports. At uncontrolled airports, pilots communicate with each other via the **common traffic advisory frequency (CTAF)**. Likewise, drivers of vehicles (such as ARFF, operations, or maintenance) communicate with ATC at controlled airports and with aircraft at uncontrolled airports via the CTAF.

Whether contact is initiated by a pilot or driver of a vehicle, proper radio communication requires the person to identify who is being contacted, who is contacting, location, and intention. For instance, "Tampa Ground [who is being contacted], this is Airport 8 [who is contacting] on the west ramp [location], requesting permission to start airfield inspection [intention]." Generally, a newly hired airport operations employee will find radio communication much easier if they already have experience (such as may have been acquired while pursuing a private pilot certificate). If not, it can be quite intimidating to both learn the airfield layout at a major international airport and properly communicate with ATC. It takes patience and plenty of practice.

At controlled airports, either **ground control** or **tower** can be contacted (although other frequencies may exist, such as **clearance delivery** or **ramp control**) (Figure 3-49). If aircraft are located on a ramp that is controlled by ramp control (typically by company), the first contact by the pilot, when ready for pushback, is to ramp control. This is generally after contact has been made to clearance delivery for departure/route clearance. Upon contacting ramp control, the pilot simply requests clearance for pushback. Often, the response is, "Pushback at your discretion, advise when ready for taxi." If located on a ramp that does not have a ramp tower, this contact is made to ATC ground control, and the response is typically identical.

Once the aircraft is pushed back by the tug and disconnected, the pilot contacts ramp control or ground control and requests permission to taxi: "Tampa Ground, Cactus 432 pushed back from gate 14 and ready for taxi." In response, ramp or ground control provides taxi clearance: "Cactus 432, Roger, taxi to runway 36R via Juliet and Charlie." Sometimes the taxi instructions can be quite complex, such as, "Cactus 432, Roger, taxi to 36R via Victor, Alpha, Alpha 12, and Charlie. Hold short of 28." It is imperative that a pilot have an airport diagram in the cockpit to refer to while navigating the airport ground environment. Once holding short of the runway, the pilot switches over to the tower frequency. "Tampa Tower, Cactus 432 holding short of 36R." Often, this contact takes an informal tone and may be, "Tower, Cactus 432 Ready to go." In any event, the pilot does not cross the mandatory holding position marking until instructed by the tower. Takeoff clearance may come in one or two steps. Tower may reply, "Cactus 432, cleared for takeoff Runway 36R." At which point, the pilot taxis the aircraft onto the runway and begins the takeoff roll. However, tower may respond, "Cactus 432, line up and wait." This instruction used to be "Taxi into position and hold." In either case, the aircraft departs and is instructed to contact departure control once airborne.

Figure 3-49. Air traffic control tower.

For ground vehicles, such as an airport operations vehicle preparing to begin the daily self-inspection, the driver contacts either ramp control or ground control via radio. Generally, the driver would simply explain who they are, where they are located, and their plan to begin the daily self-inspection. "Hawkins Ground, Airport 8 on the west ramp to begin airfield inspection." In response, ground control may give specific directions or general directions. Generally, a response may be, "Airport 8, Hawkins Ground, proceed as requested and give way to all aircraft." Or, the response may be more specific, such as, "Airport 8, Hawkins Ground, cleared onto taxiway Charlie, remain clear of all runways and contact for further clearance." During a night airfield inspection, when aircraft traffic is non-existent, ground control may say, "Airport 8, Hawkins Ground, cleared onto all runways and taxiways, notify once complete." Or an informal airport-wide clearance may be, "Airport 8, the airport's yours. Advise when clear." Typically, ground control is the main frequency for the driver of a vehicle on the movement area.

However, if a runway needs to be accessed, tower control may need to be contacted (depending on the agreement the airport has with ATC). "Hawkins Tower, Airport 8 at Tango One for runway inspection." If traffic allows, tower may respond, "Airport 8, Hawkins Tower, cleared onto runway 16." If an aircraft is inbound or one is waiting for departures, tower may instruct the driver to "expedite." This would require the vehicle to travel as quickly as possible down the runway. However, this raises another question. Can a driver conduct a proper runway inspection at 60 miles per hour? Most likely, the answer is no. Therefore, to conduct the inspection at a slower, more thorough, pace, the driver may need to exit the runway several times and then request clearance to continue the inspection once the traffic has cleared.

Radar is used by ATCT at many airports to track aircraft and vehicles on the ground. Airports equipped with **airport surface detection equipment (ASDE)** enjoy a safe ground-operating environment even during periods of reduced visibility. The preferred location for the ASDE antenna is on top of the ATCT. Alternatively, it may be placed on a stand-alone tower that is located within 6,000 feet of the ATCT. To track aircraft in the air, ATCT uses the **airport surveillance radar (ASR)**. The ASR antenna scans a 360 degree, 60-mile radius around the airport to identify aircraft for the benefit of ATC. It is used by approach and departure control as well as air traffic control towers to identify and surveil aircraft entering or leaving the airport environment. Although the location of the ASR varies among airports, it should be located in close proximity to the ATCT control room and at least 1,500 feet from any building or object that might cause signal reflections and at least one-half mile from other electronic equipment (FAA, 2014a).

MOVEMENT AREAS

Areas on the **air operations area (AOA)** that are under the control of ATC are considered movement areas. These areas typically include runways and taxiways (Figure 3-50). To access these areas, the aircraft or vehicle must be in contact with ATC and receive ATC clearance prior to entering the movement area. Additionally, certain equipment is required. For instance, an airport operations vehicle should be equipped with a yellow flashing light mounted on the uppermost part of the vehicle and an aeronautical radio, while movement area training is required of the driver and a call-sign is required of the vehicle. Movement areas are delineated from non-movement areas by a movement/non-movement area boundary marking.

NON-MOVEMENT AREAS

Areas on the AOA that are not under the control of ATC are considered non-movement areas. These areas typically include terminal area aprons or ramps, FBO ramps, maintenance and corporate hangar ramps, and taxilanes (Figure 3-51). The non-movement area is always delineated from the movement area by a movement/non-movement area boundary marking. Vehicles and aircraft can be operated in non-movement areas without ATC authorization. For example, a tug may drive up to the movement/non-movement area boundary marking on the FBO ramp without needing movement area training, an aeronautical radio, a yellow flashing light, and authorization from ATC.

At some airports, such as Memphis International and Atlanta-Jackson Hartsfield International, portions of the ramp are under the control of a ramp tower—typically staffed by airline personnel or contract personnel (such as TBI Airport Management). This is mainly to coordinate the movement of aircraft in these non-movement areas and prior to aircraft contacting ATC. Even with traffic coordination by a ramp tower, the area could still be considered a non-movement area.

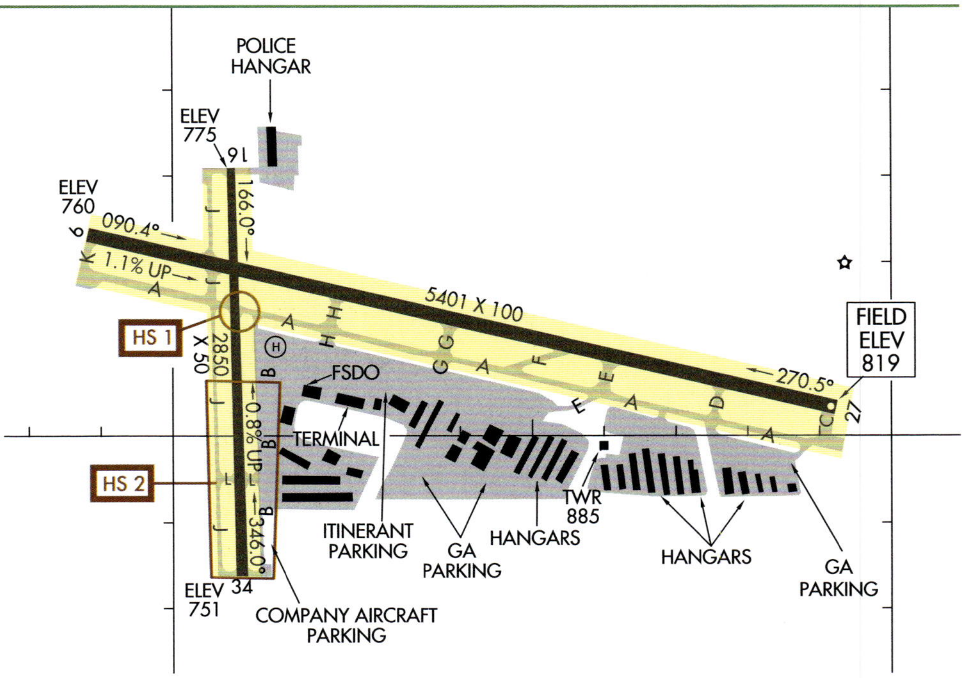

Figure 3-50. Movement areas (shown in yellow).

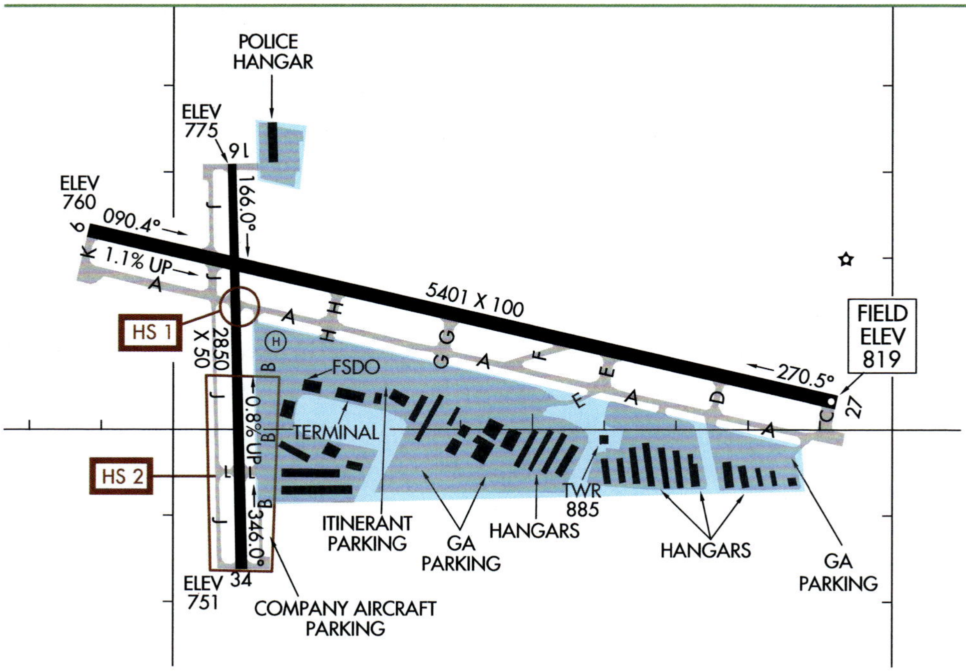

Figure 3-51. Non-movement areas (shown in blue).

(Figures 3-50 and 3-51: Excerpted from FAA AeroNav airport diagram for Riverside Municipal Airport.)

Federal Contract Tower Program

In 1982, the FAA began the **Federal Contract Tower Program**, which allows some smaller, VFR airports to have a control tower. The three main advantages of the program, as noted by the AAAE-affiliated U.S. Contract Tower Association, are enhanced safety, improved ATC services, and significant VFR ATC cost savings to the FAA. Indeed, the success of the program lies in the contracting out of ATC services to the private sector. According to a 2012 Office of Inspector General Audit Report, the average contract tower costs about \$1.5 million less to operate than a comparable FAA tower. Clearly, the cost savings alone justify the program. Currently, 252 smaller airports in 46 states participate in the program. Together these 252 towers handle approximately 28 percent of all ATCT aircraft operations in the United States, but only account for about 14 percent of FAA's overall budget allotted to ATCT tower operations. Sixteen of the 252 contract towers share costs of tower operation with the FAA (FAA, 2012).

According to the U.S. Contract Tower Association, the program has received positive endorsements from all stakeholders, including the Federal Aviation Administration (FAA), the National Transportation Safety Board (NTSB), the Department of Transportation (DOT) Inspector General (IG), airport management, Congress, and users of the aviation system. It should be noted that FAA contract towers are continually overseen and monitored by the FAA. Further, all contract controllers must be certified by the agency. This public-private partnership is a success story and has been lauded by various members of Congress and the FAA as an example of a public-private partnership providing an important service to aviation users with minimal financial burden on taxpayers. As of January 2013, a total of 251 airports had a contract tower under this program (Jones, 2013).

NextGen

NextGen is the abbreviation used to refer to the FAA's **Next Generation** Air Transportation System. NextGen is defined by the FAA as "a comprehensive and ongoing transformation of our national airspace system," characterized by a continuous rollout of improvements and updates. NextGen was formulated to proactively address the following future challenges:

- Increase capacity while assuring safety.
- Reduce environmental impacts and maintain aviation's contributions to the economy.
- Accommodate a greater mix of aircraft types.

According to the FAA, the following six programs are either providing critical NextGen capabilities or providing the foundation upon which critical NextGen capabilities will be built:

- Automatic Dependent Surveillance–Broadcast (ADS-B)
- Data Communications (Data Comm)
- En Route Automation Modernization (ERAM)
- Terminal Automation Modernization and Replacement (TAMR)
- NAS Voice System (NVS)
- System Wide Information Management (SWIM)

(FAA, 2014c)

The essence of NextGen involves transitioning from a radar-based system to one based on satellite technology (Figure 3-52). As explained by the FAA, "NextGen is all about getting the right information to the right person at the right time with fewer delays, greater capacity, reduced environmental impacts, and safe as always" (FAA, n.d.). NextGen is not a single system that is "turned on," however, but rather an incremental implementation of new technologies and flight procedures that will make the overall flow of air traffic more efficient and stable.

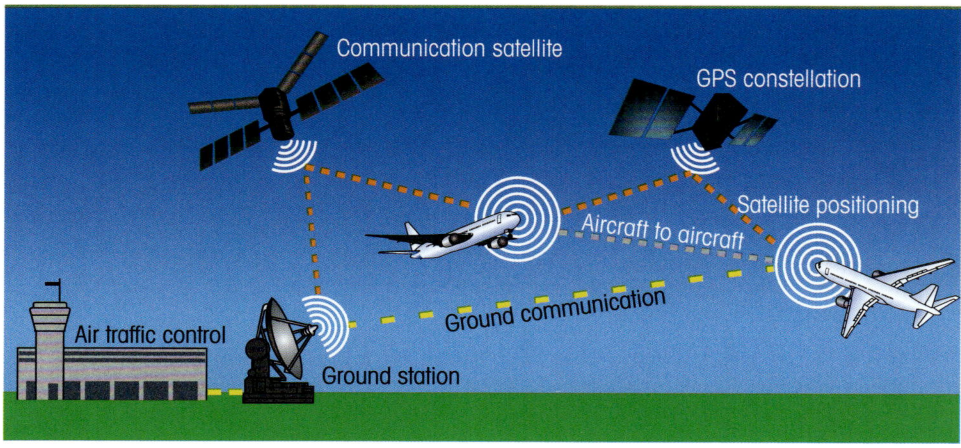

Figure 3-52. NextGen.

The FAA highlights benefits in the following areas:

Benefits to Airspace:

- More aircraft able to fly closer together on more direct routes.
- Controllers and pilots able to make more informed decisions with access to real-time weather conditions.
- National security enhanced by giving FAA and the military more effective means of monitoring airspace.

Benefits to Airports:

- Increased flight deck and airport safety with moving maps of aircraft and vehicles on the airfield.
- Better use of airfield capacity with reduced separation of aircraft.
- Reduced congestion and delays in metropolitan areas with multiple airports via automated departure procedures and taxi instructions.
- Increased airport design flexibility with reduced spacing between parallel runways.

Benefits to the Environment:

- Reduced use of petroleum-based fuels.
- Reduced carbon emissions and noise, with continuous descent arrivals.

The FAA estimates that by 2018, considering the benefits of NextGen and the growth in flights, that delays will be reduced by 21 percent, CO_2 emissions reduced by 14 million tons, and fuel usage reduced by 1.4 billion gallons. Although there have been delays in moving toward NextGen, the financial investment in NextGen by the federal government between 2013 and 2030 is estimated at $29 billion, generating an estimated $133 billion in benefits (FAA, 2014b).

Airfield Capacity

One of the determining factors that clearly plays a role in the success of any airport is the capacity of the airfield. Although the majority of airports in the United States are not challenged in this area, there are also many (mostly in the commercial service category) that regularly see demand approach and even exceed capacity, especially during certain times of the day (Figure 3-53). The capacity of an airfield is, therefore, integral in allowing that airport to meet demand for air traffic.

The concentration of aircraft arrivals and departures at an airport can create congestion and result in delay. Delay is an indicator that activity levels are approaching or exceeding capacity levels. The impacts of delays can be measured in many ways, and include direct costs (such as increased fuel use and crew time), indirect costs (such as the extra travel time for passengers and missed connections, resulting in delays on other airlines and their passengers), and increased air emissions (FAA, 2010).

Airfield capacity can be explained using an interstate as an example. If the capacity (i.e., number of lanes) is not sufficient to accommodate the demand (i.e., rush hour traffic), congestion and, subsequently, delays will result. Similarly, if an airport does not have the runway, taxiway, and gate capacity to accommodate the number of aircraft operations scheduled for that airport during a specific period of time, demand will exceed capacity, resulting in congestion and delays.

Figure 3-53. Airfield congestion.

(Wikimedia Commons; see credit on page 623)

MEASURES OF CAPACITY

Although several measures of runway capacity are in use, each is designed to estimate the number of aircraft operations (arrivals and/or departures) that can be accommodated on the runway system during some specified time period. It is important to note, however, that runway capacity is not static. It changes depending on the circumstances involved, and there are many factors (to be discussed next) that affect capacity. Thus, when discussing runway capacity, it is important to remember that numbers typically refer to the average number (or stated another way, the expected number) of movements that can be performed in a given time period.

Maximum Throughput Capacity

Considered the most fundamental and least subjective measure of runway capacity, the **maximum throughput capacity** is defined as the expected number of movements (or operations) that can be performed in one hour on a runway system without violating air traffic rules. It assumes continuous aircraft demand. In essence, how many aircraft operations can the runway system handle when the system is maxed out? Also known as saturation capacity, this measure of capacity requires various conditions—such as separation requirements, aircraft mix, mix of movements, and allocation of movements among runways—to be defined. One significant disadvantage of this measure is that it does not take into account any service criteria. In other words, the measure only specifies the number of aircraft movements that can be processed on average per hour, if the runway system is utilized at its maximum potential and considering continuous aircraft demand. Delays, whether they are several minutes or several hours, are not a concern with this measure (de Neufville and Odoni, 2003).

Practical Hourly Capacity

The **practical hourly capacity (PHCAP)** is a measure of capacity that has been in use by the FAA since the 1960s. PHCAP is defined as the expected number of movements that can be performed in one hour with some average delay per movement (typically defined as 4 minutes). This measure differs from maximum throughput capacity because it defines a level of service (average delay of four minutes per movement). The runway system is considered at capacity when that delay threshold is exceeded. Generally, the PHCAP of a runway system is approximately 80 to 90 percent of its maximum throughput capacity. Of course, at most major airports today, delays often greatly exceed 4 minutes per movement. As a result, these airports are operating at a level of service that is much lower than what was considered acceptable in 1960 (de Neufville and Odoni, 2003).

Sustained Capacity

Sustained capacity is a measure of runway capacity defined as the number of movements per hour that can be reasonably sustained over a period of several hours. The term "reasonably sustained" refers to the air traffic control system, including the workload of controllers. Although it is preferable for the air traffic system to operate at full potential all the time, this is not realistic. Indeed, such a level of full potential and maximum efficiency can often only be sustained for periods of one to several hours. As a result, sustained capacity only considers what can be sustained over this period of several hours. As a rule of thumb, the sustained capacity is equal to approximately 90 percent of maximum throughput capacity when runway configurations with high maximum throughput capacity are in use. Likewise, the sustained capacity is equal to approximately 100 percent of maximum throughput capacity with configurations with low maximum throughput capacity (de Neufville and Odoni, 2003).

Declared Capacity

A final measure of runway capacity is known as **declared capacity**. This measure is defined as the number of aircraft movements that can be accommodated per hour at a reasonable level of service. Even though this measure is mostly relied upon at airports outside the United States (especially in connection with schedule coordination and slot allocation), there is no standard definition of declared capacity, nor a standard methodology for setting it. Although declared capacity may be determined by the capacities of the terminals or gate areas (which may be more constraining than the capacity of the runway system), it is typically equal to approximately 85 to 90 percent of the maximum throughput capacity (de Neufville and Odoni, 2003).

FACTORS AFFECTING CAPACITY

The capacity of an airfield is very dynamic, often varying throughout the day. This variation is caused by a number of factors that interact in an oftentimes complex manner. Although airport management may be able to control some aspects of airfield capacity, other factors, such as weather and airspace characteristics, are impossible to control. This section details many of the factors affecting the capacity of airports.

Number and Geometric Layout of Runways

One of the most important factors affecting the capacity of an airfield is the number and geometric layout of runways. Simply having a certain number of runways is not enough; these runways must be in use. Therefore, the number of "simultaneously active runways" must be considered. The runway configuration in use is also important. Although an airport may have two parallel runways, is each used for both arrivals and departures, or is one dedicated to arrivals while the other is dedicated to departures? What about the types of aircraft? This allocation of types of aircraft and movements may change throughout the day, for reasons such as noise, weather, operational needs, etc. For example, Boston/Logan International Airport can operate in about 40 different configurations, although it only has five runways. Finally, the separation between parallel runways and the runway intersections will determine the degree of dependence among runways. Independent runways are preferred, but not always a reality. Although an airport can greatly enhance capacity by constructing a new runway, this is an expensive option that requires available land and political support (de Neufville and Odoni, 2003).

Separation Requirements

To ensure safety within the airspace system, the FAA has developed certain separation standards that apply to aircraft flying under instrument flight rules (IFR). These separation requirements, however, effectively determine the maximum number of aircraft that can safely operate in a given amount of airspace or a runway system at one time. In the United States, aircraft belong to one of the following classes, according to their **maximum takeoff weight (MTOW)**:

- MTOW greater than 255,000 pounds: Class H—Heavy
- MTOW between 41,000 pounds and 255,000 pounds: Class L—Large
- MTOW less than 41,000 pounds: Class S—Small
- Boeing 757—due to strong and unique wake vortices that were the factor in several accidents

Based on the class, there are minimum separation standards that must be maintained at all times between two aircraft operating successively. The distance (in nautical miles) that must be maintained will vary based on whether a single runway or parallel runways are in use. Additionally, the sequencing of movements will affect the separation requirements. Specifically, sequencing can include arrival followed by arrival, arrival followed by departure, departure followed by departure, and/or departure followed by arrival (de Neufville and Odoni, 2003).

Visibility, Cloud Ceiling, Precipitation, Winds

Of all weather conditions that most affect airfield capacity, cloud ceiling and visibility have the most impact. As stated in 14 CFR §91.155, no person may operate an aircraft under VFR when the flight visibility is less, or at a distance from clouds that is less, than shown in Table 3-2. Generally, capacity improves as the weather improves. Under visual meteorological conditions (VMC), ATC often requests that pilots maintain visual separation from preceding aircraft during final phases of flight, which greatly increases capacity per runway compared to what can be achieved under IFR.

Winds also affect airfield capacity in a number of ways. A runway can be used only when crosswinds are within certain limits and tailwinds do not exceed 5 or 6 knots. This means, of course, that the specific runway configuration in use is often dictated by prevailing winds. At some airports, prevailing winds can greatly reduce capacity. Consider Boston/Logan International Airport. When winds are strong out of the northwest, only runway 33L is available for arriving turbojet aircraft because runway 33R is only 2,557 feet long. In these conditions, arrivals into Boston/Logan may be delayed up to two hours. At airports with winds less than 5 knots (calm or light and variable), the airfield configuration in use is at the discretion of ATC (de Neufville and Odoni, 2003).

Aircraft Mix

The mix of aircraft types will also influence runway capacity. For instance, consider a mix of 50 percent each of heavy and small aircraft arriving into a single runway. This nonhomogeneous mix of aircraft will require increased separation standards and will negatively impact the capacity of that runway. If, however, a relatively homogenous mix of aircraft is the norm, capacity will improve and the work of air traffic controllers will be simplified.

Table 3-2. Flight rules related to ceiling and visibility.

<table>
<tr><th colspan="3">Airspace</th><th>Flight Visibility</th><th>Distance from Clouds</th></tr>
<tr><td colspan="3">Class A</td><td>Not applicable</td><td>Not applicable.</td></tr>
<tr><td colspan="3">Class B</td><td>3 statute miles</td><td>Clear of clouds.</td></tr>
<tr><td colspan="3" rowspan="3">Class C</td><td rowspan="3">3 statute miles</td><td>500 feet below.</td></tr>
<tr><td>1,000 feet above.</td></tr>
<tr><td>2,000 feet horizontal.</td></tr>
<tr><td colspan="3" rowspan="3">Class D</td><td rowspan="3">3 statute miles</td><td>500 feet below.</td></tr>
<tr><td>1,000 feet above.</td></tr>
<tr><td>2,000 feet horizontal.</td></tr>
<tr><td rowspan="6">Class E</td><td colspan="2" rowspan="3">Less than 10,000 feet MSL</td><td rowspan="3">3 statute miles</td><td>500 feet below.</td></tr>
<tr><td>1,000 feet above.</td></tr>
<tr><td>2,000 feet horizontal</td></tr>
<tr><td colspan="2" rowspan="3">At or above 10,000 feet MSL</td><td rowspan="3">5 statute miles</td><td>1,000 feet below.</td></tr>
<tr><td>1,000 feet above.</td></tr>
<tr><td>1 statute mile horizontal.</td></tr>
<tr><td rowspan="13">Class G</td><td rowspan="4">1,200 feet or less above the surface (regardless of MSL altitude)</td><td>Day*</td><td>1 statute mile</td><td>Clear of clouds.</td></tr>
<tr><td rowspan="3">Night*</td><td rowspan="3">3 statute miles</td><td>500 feet below.</td></tr>
<tr><td>1,000 feet above.</td></tr>
<tr><td>2,000 feet horizontal.</td></tr>
<tr><td rowspan="6">More than 1,200 feet above the surface but less than 10,000 feet MSL</td><td rowspan="3">Day</td><td rowspan="3">1 statute mile</td><td>500 feet below.</td></tr>
<tr><td>1,000 feet above.</td></tr>
<tr><td>2,000 feet horizontal.</td></tr>
<tr><td rowspan="3">Night</td><td rowspan="3">3 statute miles</td><td>500 feet below.</td></tr>
<tr><td>1,000 feet above.</td></tr>
<tr><td>2,000 feet horizontal.</td></tr>
<tr><td colspan="2" rowspan="3">More than 1,200 feet above the surface and at or above 10,000 feet MSL</td><td rowspan="3">5 statute miles</td><td>1,000 feet below.</td></tr>
<tr><td>1,000 feet above.</td></tr>
<tr><td>1 statute mile horizontal.</td></tr>
</table>

*except as provided in §91.155(b)

Sequencing of Movements

Yet another factor that influences airfield capacity is the sequencing of movements on a runway. This specifically refers to the mix of arrivals and departures, particularly when a runway is used for both operations. Generally, the capacity of a runway used only for departures is higher than the capacity of a runway used only for arrivals, given the same mix of aircraft. In reality, airports tend to see clusters of arrivals or departures, depending on the time of day. Even with a steady stream of arrivals, ATC may "squeeze" in one or more departures between arrivals, especially when there is a significant separation between arriving aircraft, as would occur with a small aircraft landing behind a heavy aircraft. At Los Angeles International Airport, for example, the outboard parallel runways (7R-25L and 6L-24R) are generally used for arrivals, while the inboard parallel runways (7L-25R and 6R-24L) are used for departures.

Taxiway Exits

The presence and location of taxiway exits also affect runway capacity. The longer an aircraft stays on the runway, the less capacity that runway has over a given time period. Therefore, it is important for well-placed taxiway exits to be part of any runway. **Runway occupancy time (ROT)** is defined as the time between when an aircraft touches down on the runway until it is clear of that runway. Most important to reducing runway occupancy time is the appropriate use of high-speed exits. Rather than the 90-degree angle of a typical exit, the 30-degree high-speed exit allows an aircraft to exit a runway at a speed faster than that required for a 90-degree exit. However, constructing a high-speed exit requires more land and engineering and construction expense. Generally, however, a runway will need no more than two or three high-speed exits for a single direction of runway operation.

Air Traffic Control System

To ensure efficient use of an airfield resulting in greater capacity, properly trained air traffic controllers must operate within an efficient and functional ATC system. For example, with an ATC system that provides accurate position information on aircraft to skilled controllers, tight separations between successive aircraft on final approach can be achieved. The role of the ATC system to maximize airfield capacity should continue to improve with the implementation of NextGen. Indeed, NextGen is designed to accommodate the growing number of users expected in the air transportation system of tomorrow with continued safety and reduced delays.

Noise and Other Environmental Considerations

Of the various environmental considerations that affect airports and airport capacity, noise tends to be the most significant. Many airports have noise-restricted runways spelled out in a noise abatement program. Noise curfews and

Tampa International Airport Informal Runway Use Program

The informal runway use program at Tampa International Airport is a voluntary program that seeks pilot cooperation to minimize the impact of aircraft noise (specifically from turbojet aircraft) in the surrounding community. The program is in the form of a Letter to Airmen, which is an agreement between the airport and ATCT. In general, the program is based on a priority runway use assignment for turbojet aircraft operations dependent on the direction of the prevailing wind, weather, and operational constraint. Specifically, from 6:00 a.m. to midnight, if on a south operation, runway 19R for departures is preferred. If on a north operation, runway 1L for arrivals is preferred. During the evening hours of midnight to 6:00 a.m., if traffic, wind, weather, and field conditions permit, runway 19R will be used for turbojet departures and 1L for turbojet arrivals. Additionally, after departure, south operations will be assigned a heading of 200 if departing runway 19R and a heading of 210 if departing runway 19L. Although noise complaints are still recorded, this program has significantly reduced noise-affected areas of Tampa and generally created better community relations for the airport.

aircraft stage restrictions may also be in force. As such, air traffic controllers use noise criteria in determining which runway configurations to use, affecting airport capacity. Noise-related restrictions, therefore, negatively impact airfield capacity by reducing the frequency with which various high-capacity configurations can be used.

Airfield Delay

When airfield capacity is insufficient to meet aircraft demand, airfield delay results, and these delays can be significant. Rather than being rare, flight delays at the nation's major airports are quite common. A great deal of effort is expended in measuring airfield delay and enacting solutions to minimize delay at the nation's airports. Currently, we know that delays:

- May be present even when the demand rate is lower than capacity
- Depend in a nonlinear way on changes in demand and/or capacity, becoming very sensitive to even very small changes when demand is very close to or greater than capacity
- Display a complex dynamic behavior over any time span when the runway system is heavily utilized

(de Neufville and Odoni, 2003, p. 435)

Delay is measured and tracked in different ways. For example, the U.S. Department of Transportation tracks the on-time performance of airlines and the reasons for flights arriving after their scheduled arrival times. Air traffic controllers track instances in which aircraft are delayed 15 minutes or more in a given flight segment. The FAA then uses this information to monitor the day-to-day operation of the air traffic control system. Airport planners typically use the average delay per aircraft operation as a measure of congestion. This statistic can be forecast and translated into a dollar cost of delay (FAA, 2010).

ACCEPTABLE LEVELS OF DELAY

It is often impossible to eliminate all delays; therefore, airports and aircraft operators have generally considered a certain average level of delay to be acceptable. Although this level varies among stakeholders, acceptable delay is a judgment involving several factors. First, stakeholders must realize that some level of delay is unavoidable due to factors (such as weather) that simply cannot be controlled. Next, the demand for service is often quite random and affected by many different stakeholders (such as when airlines choose to schedule arrivals and departures). It should also be recognized that some delays would be too costly to eliminate (such as constructing an additional runway). Finally, due to the previously mentioned random nature of demand, there will typically be some aircraft experiencing delay that has been deemed acceptable (AAAE, 2005).

Based on these considerations, what is an acceptable average level of delay? Although this will vary by airport, and even throughout a 24-hour period, delays generally average from 4–6 minutes per operation at the point when practical capacity is reached. If average delays are greater than 9 minutes per operation, the airport would be considered severely congested. There is no defined acceptable level of delay, although the U.S. Department of Transportation specifically records delays of 15 minutes or greater.

CAUSES OF DELAY

Aircraft experience delays due to a number of factors. These factors, some of which are controllable, can be grouped into airfield characteristics, airspace characteristics, air traffic control, meteorological conditions, and demand characteristics. These same factors affect capacity (as previously discussed), but as capacity is reached and demand begins to exceed capacity, delays result (AAAE, 2005).

According to the U.S. DOT, in February 2015, air carriers reported that 6.88 percent of their flights were delayed by aviation system delays, 7.76 percent by late-arriving aircraft, 6.44 percent by factors within the airline's control (such as maintenance or crew problems), 1.07 percent by extreme weather, and 0.03 percent for security reasons. Weather was a factor in both the extreme-weather category and the aviation-system category. This included delays due to the re-routing of flights by the FAA in consultation with the carriers involved. Weather is also a factor in delays attributed to late-arriving aircraft, although airlines do not report specific causes in that category. According to the FAA, 66 percent of aircraft delays are due to weather at a cost of over $2 billion to airlines in one 18-month period, which adds up to over $9 billion in lost productivity during that period (FAA, n.d.).

Demand Management

As most airports are unable to increase capacity (in the form of new runways, for instance) to accommodate demand, managing the demand is a valid alternative. **Demand management** is defined as any set of administrative or economic measures designed to constrain the demand for access to an airport, or modify the characteristics of such demand. Although demand management is quite common at almost every busy commercial service airport outside the United States, demand management methods are not as popular at U.S. airports. This may change in the future as airports try to accommodate an estimated 50 percent increase in aircraft traffic by 2025. The FAA does, however, employ a tactical form of demand management on a daily basis through its Air Traffic Control System Command Center. At this location, the FAA employs a collaborative decision-making process with airlines to determine how best to meter, re-route, or ground hold aircraft to better meet existing airport capacity in major metropolitan areas considering weather, special events, etc. (de Neufville and Odoni, 2003).

ADMINISTRATIVE APPROACHES

Administrative approaches to managing demand at airports are designed to restrict aircraft or discourage demand with purely managerial approaches. In essence, these approaches do not rely on economic incentives or disincentives to adjust demand. The two most common administrative approaches are slots and schedule coordination (de Neufville and Odoni, 2003).

Slots

The most common aspect of administrative approaches is the **slot**. A slot is defined as an interval of time which is reserved for the arrival or departure of a specific flight. Each slot is allocated, by various means, to an air carrier or other operator for a specific time period. If an airport can accommodate 60 arrivals or departures during a one-hour period, 60 slots will be made available for users. For example, Airline X has been assigned the 1105 time slot for arrival of Flight 887 at Airport ABC during winter 2012. The slot does not require Airline X to land exactly at 1105, but that is the scheduled arrival time of Flight 887 during winter 2012.

In developing a slot-based system, criteria must be developed to fairly allocate slots to users. Some examples of criteria are:

- Higher priority is assigned to flights operating for an extended length of time.
- Higher priority is assigned to scheduled flights operating on a daily basis.
- Higher priority is assigned to flights serving certain locations or new markets.
- Higher priority is assigned to new entrants.

In the United States, the High Density Traffic Airports Rule, also known as the High Density Rule (14 CFR Part 93, subpart K), was enacted in 1968 to reduce delays at five congested airports: John F. Kennedy International Airport (JFK), LaGuardia, O'Hare International Airport (O'Hare), Ronald Reagan Washington National Airport (Reagan National) and Newark International Airport (Newark). The regulation limits the number of instrument flight rule (IFR) operations at each airport during certain hours of the day. It also provides for the allocation to carriers of operational authority, in the form of a "slot" for each IFR takeoff or landing during a specific 30- or 60-minute period. The restrictions at Newark were lifted in the early 1970s. In 2000, the Wendell H. Ford Aviation Investment and Reform Act for the 21st Century (AIR-21) was signed into law and called for slots to be phased out at O'Hare as of July 1, 2002, and at LaGuardia and JFK on January 1, 2007. Air carriers meeting certain criteria were allowed to obtain exemptions (referred to as exemption slots) from the requirements (FAA, 2002).

Schedule Coordination

The most widely used approach to administrative slot allocation is the International Air Transport Association (IATA) schedule coordination approach. Airports are categorized as Level 1 (noncoordinated), Level 2 (coordinated), or Level 3 (fully coordinated). In essence, Level 1 airports have adequate capacity to meet aircraft demands. Level 2 airports have demand approaching capacity and require a schedule facilitator. Level 3 airports are quite congested, requiring the appointment of a schedule coordinator. All slot requests at Level 3 airports must be approved by the schedule coordinator. Schedule coordination takes place at Schedule Coordination Conferences held twice each year by IATA (de Neufville and Odoni, 2003).

ECONOMIC APPROACHES

The economic approaches to demand management utilize some form of **congestion pricing** to alter demand. The economic approaches can be used as a sole method of demand management, or used in conjunction with administrative approaches. Regardless, without attaching a price to delay, it is often difficult to effectively manage aircraft demand at airports (de Neufville and Odoni, 2003).

Landing Fee Surcharge

With a landing fee surcharge, users pay a higher weight-based landing fee during peak periods. For example, all aircraft landing between 0700 and 0800 must pay a surcharge of $300 in addition to the standard weight-based landing fee. Airlines choosing to land during time periods not subject to a landing fee surcharge will save money in landing fees (de Neufville and Odoni, 2003).

Flat Fee

A flat fee may also be imposed upon users operating during peak periods. A decision must be made as to whether this fee is entirely or partly independent of the aircraft's weight. For example, all aircraft landing between 0700 and 0800 may be required to pay a landing fee of $475, regardless of weight. Similarly, aircraft weighing under 50 tons may be required to pay a fee of $250, while aircraft weighing over 50 tons may be required pay $550 (de Neufville and Odoni, 2003).

Multiplier

A multiplier may be added to the weight-based landing fee charged during peak periods. As an example, with a multiplier of 1.20, an aircraft normally charged $400 would be required to pay $480 (1.20 x $400) during peak periods (de Neufville and Odoni, 2003).

Minimum Landing Fee

To be certain that all aircraft pay a specified minimum amount while operating during peak periods, an airport may specify a minimum landing fee. This prevents aircraft from paying a lesser amount than would be determined adequate, considering the delay cost of operating during a peak period. For example, if a minimum landing fee of $200 is established for the 0700–0800 time period, an aircraft that would have normally paid only $100 would be required to pay a $200 landing fee if operating during this time period (de Neufville and Odoni, 2003).

HYBRID APPROACHES

Hybrid approaches to demand management combine administrative and economic methods. With a hybrid approach, a slot system is developed, and economic methods such as congesting pricing, slot markets, and slot auctions are adopted to determine the final allocation of slots among users (de Neufville and Odoni, 2003).

Slot Plus Congestion Pricing

With slot plus congestion pricing, the number of available slots is determined and a schedule of landing fees is developed. A schedule coordinator is used to allocate slots, based on requests from prospective users. With this approach, users must consider the cost to access the airport at different times when requesting slots (de Neufville and Odoni, 2003).

Buying and Selling Slots

Yet another hybrid approach treats slots as a market-driven commodity. Once slots have been allocated to users, they become the property of their holders and can be leased, bought, and sold. One advantage to this market-driven approach is that the market determines the price that will lead to equilibrium, which is a point of stability at which too many or too few users will not be driven away (de Neufville and Odoni, 2003).

Slot Auctions

A final hybrid approach involves slot auctions. Although this approach is advocated by numerous economists, it has not been widely adopted by airports. In essence, it requires prospective users to submit sealed bids for the slot(s) they wish to secure. After all bids are received, slots are awarded to the highest bidders in each time period. In practice, the price the winning bidders pay is equal to the lowest successful bid in each time period. In this way, two successful bidders will not, for example, pay different amounts for slots during the same time period (de Neufville and Odoni, 2003).

IDEAL DEMAND MANAGEMENT SYSTEM

Although there are many approaches, both administrative and economic, to manage demand at airports, an ideal demand management system will have certain attributes, regardless which approach is chosen. A system should:

- Promote economically efficient use of scarce airport capacity
- Maintain access to a congested airport for all users willing to pay the full economic cost of using the airport
- Not be perceived as unfair or discriminatory by any class of airport users
- Not serve as another way to regulate air transport
- Not provide opportunities for collusion among airlines and for anticompetitive practices
- Not result in any "windfall" revenues to airport operators or airport users
- Be transparent in its methodology and easy to administer

  (de Neufville and Odoni, 2003, p. 493)

Concluding Thoughts

Although the air traffic control system in the United States is not perfect, it provides numerous benefits for airports and the users of airports. With the gradual implementation of the many facets of NextGen, delays are expected to decline while existing capacity is maximized. Even so, airports have various strategies available to better manage demand and minimize delays at their facilities. It is likely that both NextGen and the proactive adoption of various demand strategies will be necessary to ensure an efficient air transportation system in the future.

Chapter Summary

- During the early days of air traffic control, aircraft were tracked by controllers using maps, blackboards, and small boat-shaped weights that became known as "shrimp boats."
- During these early days, controllers had no direct radio link with aircraft, but stayed in touch with airline dispatchers, airway radio operators, and airport traffic controllers via the telephone.
- The first revolution to occur in air traffic control after WWII was the introduction of radio detection and ranging (RADAR).
- The next breakthrough in ATC advances occurred with the adoption and application of computer technology during the 1960s and 1970s.
- Regulatory airspace includes Class A, Class B, Class C, Class D, Class E, restricted areas and prohibited areas.
- Nonregulatory airspace includes military operations areas (MOAs), warning areas, alert areas, and controlled firing areas.
- Any navigational approach made by an aircraft to an airport is conducted either with visual reference (visual meteorological conditions) or use of instruments (instrument meteorological conditions).
- To support these various types of approaches, navigational aids (NAVAIDs) are installed at airports. Many of these NAVAIDs can be used for both enroute and approach guidance.
- The VOR, which broadcasts 360-degree bearing information from the station, provides considerably greater accuracy and reliability than NDBs.
- The instrument landing system is the most common precision approach NAVAID and provides both alignment guidance (provided by the localizer) and descent guidance (provided by the glideslope).
- The most advanced NAVAID is the global positioning system (GPS).

- Runway visual range equipment allows for measurement of horizontal visibility, although the exact number of RVRs required will depend on the runway approach category and physical runway length.
- Airfield lighting systems may utilize incandescent lighting, tungsten-halogen lighting, fluorescent lighting, or light-emitting diodes (LED).
- In addition to various types of airfield lighting, approach lighting systems are utilized to allow the pilot to transition from instrument flying within the cockpit to visually locating the runway outside the cockpit.
- Approach lighting systems are oriented on the extended runway centerline, and extend from the runway threshold toward the approach. They include ALSF-2, MALSR, MALS, MALSF, and ODALS.
- Rotating beacons at airports, which assist pilots with identifying an airport at night or in instrument meteorological conditions, project beams of light spaced 180 degrees apart.
- In addition to markings, signs are used to identify boundaries of runway approach areas, ILS critical areas, runway safety areas or obstacle-free zones, as well as no entry areas, deicing pads, ground run-up enclosures, and other areas.
- The airport surveillance radar antenna scans a 360 degree, 60-mile radius around the airport to identify aircraft for the benefit of ATC.
- Airports equipped with airport surface detection equipment enjoy a safe ground-operating environment even during periods of reduced visibility.
- Areas on the air operations area (AOA) that are under the control of ATC are considered movement areas. These areas typically include runways and taxiways.
- NextGen is defined by the FAA as "a comprehensive and ongoing transformation of our national airspace system," characterized by a continuous rollout of improvements and updates.
- The capacity of an airfield is integral in allowing an airport to meet air traffic demand.
- As most airports are unable to increase capacity (in the form of new runways, for instance) to accommodate demand, managing the demand is a valid alternative.
- Although there are many approaches, both administrative and economic, to managing demand at airports, an ideal demand management system will have certain attributes, regardless of which approach is chosen.

Review Questions ↘

1. Explain the history of the U.S. air traffic control system.
2. Define Class A airspace.
3. Define Class B airspace.
4. Define Class C airspace.
5. Define Class D airspace.
6. Define Class E airspace.
7. Define Class G airspace.
8. What is the difference between precision instrument and non-precision instrument approaches?
9. What is a very high frequency omnidirectional range (VOR)?
10. What is a global positioning system (GPS)?
11. What are the four types of lighting that may be utilized in airfield lighting applications?
12. What are the various categories of airfield lighting?
13. What are the components of an approach lighting system?
14. What is the purpose of mandatory instruction signs?
15. List the types of runway markings.
16. List the types of taxiway markings.
17. Explain airport surface detection equipment.
18. Define the air operations area (AOA).
19. Explain the benefits of NextGen to airspace, airports, and the environment.
20. Explain the factors affecting airfield capacity.
21. Explain administrative and economic approaches to demand management.

Scenarios

1. As an airport manager of Oak Cliff Airport, you have been petitioning the FAA for some additional approaches to your runways. Although you have been seeking an ILS, the FAA has stated that they will not install an ILS at your airport, but a GPS approach is possible. What are your concerns about this? Will you support this in lieu of an ILS installation?
2. As the airport director of an airport that is severely congested, what are some available options to enhance capacity and reduce congestion at your airport?
3. With the numerous markings, signage, and lighting present on airports, it can be rather confusing for pilots. What are some ways an airport operator can reduce this confusion for pilots?
4. NextGen is designed to greatly introduce efficiencies into the national airspace system. As manager for a small GA airport, you question whether NextGen is producing any real benefits for your airport and your airport users. "It's just an air carrier thing," you recently heard one of your tenants say. What can you, as airport manager, do to ensure your airport and airport users benefit from NextGen? Are there other areas that are not currently part of NextGen but should be, in your mind?
5. In the past three weeks, your medium hub airport has experienced no less than three surface incidents. First, a tug crossed right in front of an aircraft taxiing into a gate, requiring the pilot to apply strong and immediate braking to avoid hitting the tug. Second, a catering truck flipped over while making a fast turn on the ramp. Third, a catering truck backed into an aircraft at the gate, causing significant damage to the right wing. The FAA is demanding action to address ramp safety. What will you do?

References and Resources for Further Study

American Association of Airport Executives. 2005. "Body of Knowledge Module 2. Planning, Construction and Environmental." Washington, DC: AAAE.

———. 2010. "U.S. Contract Tower Association Annual Report, 2010." Retrieved from http://www.contracttower.org/ctaannual/USCTAAR10.pdf

de Neufville, R. and A. Odoni. 2003. *Airport Systems: Planning Design and Management.* New York: McGraw Hill.

Federal Aviation Administration (FAA). n.d. NextGen 101 video. Retrieved from http://www.faa.gov/nextgen/

———. 2002. "High Density Airports; Notice of Adopted Lottery Allocation Procedures for Slot Exemptions at LaGuardia Airport." *Federal Register*, 67 FR 65826. Retrieved from http://federalregister.gov/a/02-27381

———. 2009. "Procedures for the Evaluation and Approval of Facilities for Special Authorization Category I Operations and All Category II and III Operations." FAA Order 8400.13D.

———. 2010. "2011–2015 National Plan of Integrated Airport Systems."

———. 2011a. *Design and Installation Details for Airport Visual Aids.* AC 150/5340-30. Washington, DC: FAA.

———. 2011b. *Pilot/Controller Glossary.* Retrieved from http://www.faa.gov/air_traffic/publications/atpubs/PCG/introduction.htm

———. 2012. "Contract Towers Continue to Provide Cost-effective and Safe Air Traffic Services, but Improved Oversight of the Program is Needed." Retrieved from https://www.oig.dot.gov/sites/default/files/FAA%20Federal%20Contract%20Tower%20Program%20Report%5E11-5-12.pdf

———. 2014a. *Airport Design.* AC 150/5300-13A. Washington, DC: FAA.

———. 2014b. "The Business Case for the Next Generation Air Transportation System, FY 2014." Retrieved from http://www.faa.gov/nextgen/media/BusinessCaseForNextGen-2014.pdf

———. 2014c. "Nextgen Implementation Plan." Retrieved from http://www.faa.gov/nextgen/library/media/nextgen_implementation_plan_2014.pdf

Jones, T. R. 2013. "FAA Contract Tower (FCT) Program Office Update." Retrieved from http://www.contracttower.org/FCT_Program_Office_Update_12413_Final.pdf

U.S. Centennial of Flight Commission. n.d. "Air Traffic Control." Retrieved from http://www.centennialofflight.net/essay/Government_Role/Air_traffic_control/POL15.htm

Chapter 4

Planning

Objectives ↘

Upon completion of this chapter, you should:

- Understand the role of the National Plan of Integrated Airport Systems (NPIAS).
- Understand the role of regional aviation system plans.
- Understand the role of state aviation system plans.
- Understand the role of airport master plans and airport layout plans.
- Understand the purpose of business plans.
- Understand the purpose of strategic plans.
- Be able to explain the forecasting steps.
- Understand the various types of forecasting used in aviation activity forecasting.
- Be able to explain the various uses of forecasts.

Key Terms

airport access plans
airport airspace drawing
Airport Capital Improvement Plan (ACIP)
airport layout plan (ALP)
airport master plan
airport property map
aviation activity forecasts
business plan
computer-aided design (CAD)
econometric model forecasting
facilities layout plan
geographic information systems (GIS)
inner portion of the approach surface drawing
market share forecasting
metropolitan aviation system plan
off-airport land use drawing
on-airport land use drawing
regional aviation system plan
regression analysis
runway departure surface drawing
simulation modeling
state aviation system plan
strategic plan
terminal area forecast (TAF)
terminal area plan
time series model forecasting
utility drawing

In Chapter 4

Introduction **157**

NPIAS **157**

Regional Aviation System Plans **159**

State Aviation System Plans **159**

Metropolitan Aviation System Plans **160**

Airport Master Plans and Airport Layout Plans **161**

Strategic Plans **171**

Business Plans **175**

Aviation Activity Forecasts **176**

- Steps in Forecasting 178
- Types of Forecasts 178
- Selection of Forecasting Method 180
- Uses of Forecasts 181

Concluding Thoughts **182**

Chapter Summary **183**

Review Questions **185**

Scenarios **186**

References and Resources for Further Study **187**

FEATURES

The New England Regional Airport System Plan **160**

A plan to utilize Boston Logan Airport and under-utilized regional airports could support air carrier service in the New England region.

Sample Mission, Vision, and Values Statements **172**

Examples from airports of these three statements, which are key elements in the strategic planning process.

SWOT Analysis **174**

The components of a SWOT Analysis.

Introduction

As Winston Churchill once said, "He who fails to plan is planning to fail."

All airports currently in operation were first planned, and with adequate investment, were then developed. This oversimplification introduces the foundational concepts of this chapter, which covers airport planning, including various types of plans at the national, regional, state, and local levels. The role of aviation activity forecasts in airport planning is also discussed.

In general terms, airport planning refers to the systematic process used to establish guidelines for the efficient development of airports that is consistent with local, state and national goals. The main objective in airport planning is to satisfy future demand in a financially feasible manner. Airport plans may be quite broad (such as the National Plan of Integrated Airport Systems) or very specific to the airport (such as an airport master plan).

NPIAS

At the highest level, airport planning occurs nationally. Since 1946, a national airport plan has been prepared at regular intervals. Today, that plan is the National Plan of Integrated Airport Systems (NPIAS). The general principles guiding federal involvement in airports has remained fairly uniform since the 1940s:

- Airports should be safe and efficient, located at optimum sites, and developed and maintained to appropriate standards.
- Airports should be affordable to both users and government, relying primarily on user fees and placing minimal burden on the general revenues of the local, state, and federal governments.
- Airports should be flexible and expandable, and able to meet increased demand and to accommodate new aircraft types.
- Airports should be permanent with assurance that they will remain open for aeronautical use over the long term.
- Airports should be compatible with surrounding communities, maintaining a balance between the needs of aviation and the requirements of residents in neighboring areas.
- Airports should be developed in concert with improvements to the air traffic control system and technological advancements.
- The airport system should support national objectives for defense, emergency readiness, and postal delivery.
- The airport system should be extensive, providing as many people as possible with convenient access to air transportation, typically by having most of the population within 20 miles of a NPIAS airport.

- The airport system should help air transportation contribute to a productive national economy and international competitiveness.

  (FAA, 2010, p. 3–4)

As discussed in Chapter 2, although the NPIAS contains nearly 3,400 existing and proposed airports, thousands of additional airports are not included in the NPIAS.[1] The FAA evaluates airports and decides which ones to include in the NPIAS based on:

1. Whether an airport is considered a public-use airport.
2. The number of enplanements the airport has or is forecast to have.
3. The number of based aircraft located at the airport.
4. Whether an airport receives U.S. Mail service.
5. Whether there is a component of the U.S. Military, Reserves or National Guard permanently based on or adjacent to the airport.
6. Special justification that would consider the isolation of the community being served, whether the airport serves the need of an Indian tribe, supports recreation areas, or is needed to develop or protect important national resources.

   (Central Region Airports Division, 2010)

Airports included in the NPIAS are eligible to receive federal grants under the Airport Improvement Program (AIP). Included in the NPIAS are estimates of the amount of AIP funding required by each airport to fund capital development projects that will either enable these airports to meet current design standards or add capacity to relieve congestion. These cost estimates are obtained primarily from state airport system plans and airport master plans. The inventory of airport development contained in the NPIAS is the basis for the FAA's **Airport Capital Improvement Plan (ACIP)**. The FAA formulates the ACIP based on the airport development needs identified by the NPIAS. Essentially, the ACIP is a subset of the NPIAS and highlights airport needs over a three-year funding cycle.

Through the NPIAS, which is updated every two years, the FAA provides Congress a five-year estimate of AIP-eligible development. As noted in the plan, the NPIAS should be used in evaluating investment priorities. However, it should be noted that the listing of any location, airport or item of development in the NPIAS does not obligate or commit the federal government to provide funds for that specific development. It also does not imply environmental approval of the proposed development. The NPIAS is categorized by state and available online via the FAA website (FAA, 2010).

In the 2011–2015 NPIAS, there is $52.2 billion in AIP-eligible infrastructure. This represents a record amount and a $2.6 billion increase from the 2009–2013 NPIAS. Approximately 57 percent of the $52.2 billion is intended

[1] Many of these additional airports are private.

to bring airports up to current design standards and rehabilitate existing infrastructure (mostly pavement and lighting systems). The remaining 43 percent is intended to accommodate growth in travel, including more passengers, cargo, and activity, and larger aircraft. The 503 airports serving scheduled air carriers represent 70 percent of the total development in the NPIAS, while GA airports represent 21 percent.

Regional Aviation System Plans

In addition to planning at the national level, planning for airports takes place at the regional level. Generally, a regional aviation system plan provides the foundation for a regional strategy to meet air transportation needs of an entire region, which may cover multiple states. Although not all states and metropolitan areas or regions will have such a plan, airports in regions with a plan adopt a cooperative approach to meeting the air service needs of an entire region, rather than trying to vigorously compete with one another. Often, a regional aviation system plan is developed by a consortium of airports to relieve congestion at a major commercial service airport.

Typically, a regional aviation system plan aims to develop and preserve a balanced system of airports designed to meet the aviation needs of the region. It is important to do this by considering the regional system of airports, airspace, public demand, and ground access. Each specific airport has a role to play in meeting the region's aviation needs, whether for GA activity or commercial activity (including passengers or cargo). By considering the role of these individual airports in the region, a comprehensive regional aviation system plan can be developed for a strategic and regional approach.

State Aviation System Plans

Just as planning takes place at the regional level, aviation system plans also exist at the state level. **State aviation systems plans** are, in fact, more common than regional plans. Each state has a state aviation agency, typically in the form of a state Department of Transportation. These state agencies generally develop a plan for the airports within their state. This allows for a coordinated air transportation system on a state-wide level. Specifically, by developing state plans, planners are able to better determine how to maximize the return on investment of public funds and identify what capital improvements would best serve the state's aviation needs.

Generally, state aviation system plans are long-term plans with a 10- to 20-year planning horizon. The plan will present an inventory of current airports (including their facilities, operations, based aircraft, form of ownership,

The New England Regional Airport System Plan

The New England Regional Airport System Plan is the result of an ongoing program of regional planning that began around 1990. This regional effort was initiated to address two concerns: (1) the increasing congestion at Boston Logan Airport and the inability to expand capacity, and (2) the awareness that under-utilized regional airports could support air carrier service in the New England region. In response to these concerns, three objectives were formulated:

1. Improve customer service.
2. Support the region's economy.
3. Provide an environmentally sound air service system.

To achieve these objectives, a coalition was formed consisting of the six New England state aviation agencies, all of the scheduled jet air carrier airports, and the New England Council. In developing the New England Regional Airport System Plan, this coalition conducted a New England Regional Air Service Study, held a "Fly New England" workshop with airline representatives, and implemented various phases of the New England Regional Airport System Plan. According to the Plan:

> **Looking ahead it is vital that, while each airport plans its own development program, we maintain at the same time a shared vision of how the New England Airport System can function in a way that provides optimal air transportation services to serve the region's future. (New England Airport Coalition, 2006)**

etc.) in the state. The plan will also generally highlight the economic benefits of airports in the state, as well as the capital development needs of these airports. The key with a state plan is that the needs of state airports are considered together, rather than separately, as would occur in a local plan.

Metropolitan Aviation System Plans

More specific than a regional or state plan, a **metropolitan aviation system plan** is typically developed for airports located in close proximity to each other within a major metropolitan area. Consider, for instance, Newark Liberty International Airport, LaGuardia Airport, and JFK International Airport in the New York City metropolitan area. Consider also Mineta San Jose International Airport, Oakland International Airport, and San Francisco International Airport in the San Francisco Bay area. These metropolitan airports are so closely linked (geographically and in terms of air service coverage), that a plan for these airports as an interconnected system may be developed.

Often, a metropolitan aviation system plan considers airport capacity, airspace, ground access, types of travelers, destinations served, etc. A metropolitan area may have several commercial service airports, but with unique purposes. Consider, for instance, the Washington, DC, area. Ronald Reagan National

Airport has three runways, but with the longest less than 7,000 feet, this airport handles mostly domestic flights. The airport is, however, located only three miles from Washington, DC, making it the closest commercial service airport to the nation's capital. Washington Dulles International Airport, on the other hand, has four runways ranging from 9,400 to 11,500 feet in length. Although it is located 20 miles west of Washington, DC, this airport handles a significant amount of international flights. By developing a metropolitan aviation system plan that incorporates these two airports (as well as others in the metropolitan area), the aviation needs of the nation's capital can be strategically met.

Airport Master Plans and Airport Layout Plans

For airports, the most important planning is carried out at the local level. This local-level planning is generally in the form of an **airport master plan**. An airport master plan is a comprehensive study of an airport, and typically presents the short-, medium-, and long-term development plans necessary to meet future aviation demand, generally planning for 20 years into the future. The preparation of an initial airport master plan is referred to as "master planning," while the revision of only parts of the existing document is referred to as "master plan updates." In essence, the master plan presents the airport's strategy for the future development of the airport. The main goal of a master plan is to present that strategy considering potential environmental and socioeconomic impacts. A successful master plan will meet the following objectives:

1. Document the issues that the proposed development will address.
2. Justify the proposed development through the technical, economic, and environmental investigation of concepts and alternatives.
3. Provide an effective graphic presentation of the development of the airport and anticipated land uses in the vicinity of the airport.
4. Establish a realistic schedule for the implementation of the development proposed in the plan, particularly the short-term capital improvement program.
5. Propose an achievable financial plan to support the implementation schedule.
6. Provide sufficient project definition and detail for subsequent environmental evaluations that may be required before the project is approved.
7. Present a plan that adequately addresses the issues and satisfies local, state, and federal regulations.
8. Document policies and future aeronautical demand to support municipal or local deliberations on spending, debt, land use controls, and other policies necessary to preserve the integrity of the airport and its surroundings.

9. Set the stage and establish the framework for a continuing planning process. Such a process should monitor key conditions and permit changes in plan recommendations as required.

   (FAA, 2007, p. 2)

Because of the specific nature of airport development, a master plan is specific to each airport. Although the level of detail will differ between plans, there are elements that are common to all master plan studies:

1. *Pre-planning*—This involves identifying the general need for the study, determining the type of study, selecting a consultant, developing the study design, negotiating consultant contracts, and applying for federal funding.
2. *Public involvement*—This includes timing, tools and techniques, identifying stakeholders, identifying key issues, and documenting key issues and public involvement.
3. *Environmental considerations*—This includes considering the environmental implications of various alternatives considered for the master plan.
4. *Existing conditions*—This requires an inventory and description of existing facilities, including the regional setting and land use, historical aviation activity, and airport financial resources.
5. *Aviation forecasts*—This involves forecasting future operations, passengers, and based aircraft. Specific forecasting techniques may include regression analysis, trend analysis, market share analysis, and smoothing. Forecast results are compared to FAA terminal area forecasts.
6. *Facility requirements*—Required to determine if additional facilities (including airfield, terminals, airspace, security, general aviation, cargo, support facilities, parking, ground access, and utilities) will be needed to meet future demand, based on forecasts. It is important to consider peak hour demand in addition to general demand levels to avoid having too little capacity in the future during peak demand times.
7. *Alternative development and evaluation*—Involves identifying and evaluating alternatives for meeting the needs of airport users, as well as the strategic vision of the airport considering many different factors of importance.
8. *Airport layout plans*—The ALP will graphically depict current and future airport facilities. This allows the main results of the master plan to be reflected graphically and reviewed quickly in relation to the existing airport boundary and facilities.
9. *Facilities implementation plan*—Provides guidance on how to implement the findings and recommendations of the planning effort.
10. *Financial feasibility analysis*—Identifies sources of funding (whether federal, state, third party, passenger facility charges, bonds, or local funds), financial feasibility, and benefit cost analysis (BCA).

   (FAA, 2007)

A completed master plan may include any of the following products:

1. *Technical report*—Includes results of the analyses conducted during the development of the master plan.
2. *Summary report*—Summarizes the typically lengthy master plan into a less lengthy version for the benefit of the public, and other stakeholders.
3. *Airport layout plan drawing set*—Graphically represents the development proposed in the master plan.
4. *Web page*—Useful for providing information about the master planning process (including community hearings) as well as the completed master plan to various stakeholders.
5. *Public information kit*—Useful for providing information to community associations, civic clubs, and other organizations with an active interest in the airport. This kit may include models, summary brochures, or electronic presentations.

(FAA, 2007)

Of the products included in the master plan, the ALP drawing set is quite beneficial because it provides a graphical representation of planned development presented in the master plan. This drawing set may include the following:

1. **Cover sheet**—A separate cover sheet, with approval signature blocks, airport location maps, and other pertinent information as required by the local FAA Airports office (see Figure 4-1).
2. **Airport layout plan** (required)—A drawing depicting the existing and future airport facilities (see Figure 4-2). The drawing should include required facility identifications, description labels, imaginary surfaces, runway protection zones, runway safety areas, and basic airport and runway data tables. It may be necessary to include the data tables on a separate sheet.
3. **Data sheet**—A separate sheet containing basic airport and runway data tables (see Figure 4-3).
4. **Facilities layout plan**—A drawing that depicts existing and future facilities, and only critical, non-overlapping clearance criteria, with minimal text. It is essentially a simplified ALP (see Figure 4-4).
5. **Terminal area plan**—This plan consists of one or more drawings that present a large-scale depiction of areas with significant terminal facility development. Such a drawing is typically an enlargement of a portion of the ALP (see Figure 4-5). At a commercial service airport, the drawing would include the passenger terminal area, but might also include general aviation facilities and cargo facilities.
6. **Airport airspace drawing** (required)—14 CFR Part 77, Safe, Efficient Use, and Preservation of the Navigable Airspace, defines this as a drawing depicting obstacle identification surfaces for the full extent of all airport development. It should also depict airspace obstructions for the portions of the surfaces excluded from the inner portion of the approach surface drawing (see Figure 4-6).

7. **Inner portion of the approach surface drawing** (required)—Drawings containing the plan and profile view of the inner portion of the approach surface to the runway and a tabular listing of all surface penetrations (see Figure 4-7). The drawing will depict the obstacle identification approach surfaces contained in Part 77, Safe, Efficient Use, and Preservation of the Navigable Airspace. The drawing may also depict other approach surfaces, including the threshold-siting surface, those surfaces associated with the United States Standard for Instrument Procedures (TERPS), or those required by the local FAA office or state agency. The extent of the approach surface and the number of airspace obstructions shown may restrict each sheet to only one runway end or approach.
8. **On-airport land use drawing**—A drawing depicting the land uses within the airport property boundary (see Figure 4-8).
9. **Off-airport land use drawing**—A drawing depicting land uses and zoning in the area around the airport. At a minimum, the drawing must contain land within the 65 Day-Night Sound Level (DNL) noise contour. DNL represents noise exposure events over a 24-hour period. To account for human sensitivity to noise between the hours of 10 p.m. and 7 a.m., noise events occurring during these hours receive a "penalty" when the DNL is calculated. Each nighttime event is measured as if ten daytime events occurred.[2] For general aviation airports or low-activity commercial service airports, where noise issues are less important, on-airport land use and off-airport land use drawings may be combined.
10. **Airport property map**—A drawing, commonly referred to as Exhibit A, depicting the airport property boundary, the various tracts of land that were acquired to develop the airport, and the method of acquisition (see Figure 4-9). This drawing is only required for those airports that have acquired land with federal funds or through an FAA-administered land transfer program; however, it may be useful to all airport sponsors. If any obligations were incurred as a result of obtaining property, or an interest therein, they should be noted. Obligations that stem from federal grants or an FAA-administered land transfer program, such as surplus property programs, should also be noted. The drawing should also depict easements beyond the airport boundary. The airport property map should be prepared in accordance with FAA Advisory Circular 150/5100-17, *Land Acquisition and Relocation Assistance for Airport Improvement Program Assisted Projects.*
11. **Runway departure surface drawing**—This drawing depicts the applicable departure surfaces as defined in Appendix 2 of FAA AC 150/5300-13, *Airport Design*. The surfaces are shown for runway end(s) designated primarily for instrument departures. The one-engine inoperative (OEI) obstacle identification surface (OIS) should be shown for departure runway end(s) supporting air carrier operations.

[2] Refer to chapter 6 for more information on aircraft noise.

12. **Utility drawing**—This drawing depicts the location and capacity of major utilities on the airport and in the surrounding area.
13. **Airport access plans**—If access to the airport is a significant issue, a separate airport access drawing should be created, depicting the major routes of various modes of transportation that serve the airport. Such a drawing could also include proposed improvements to the system.
14. Other plan(s)—Drawings that address a specific, unique need at the airport. The sponsor, FAA and other approving agencies must discuss and agree to include them.

(FAA, 2007, pp. 76–79)

FT. LAUDERDALE - HOLLYWOOD INTERNATIONAL AIRPORT

AIRPORT LAYOUT PLAN UPDATE

BCAD Project No.: BCAD RLI 20050422-0-AV-01EB

Broward County Board of Commissioners

Sue Gunzburger, Mayor
John E. Rodstrom, Jr., Vice-Mayor
Ilene Lieberman, Commissioner
Kristin Jacobs, Commissioner
Stacy Ritter, Commissioner
Chip LaMarca, Commissioner
Lois Wexler, Commissioner
Barbara Sharief, Commissioner
Dale V.C. Holness, Commissioner

Prepared for:
Broward County Aviation Department
Fort Lauderdale, Florida

SHEET INDEX

1. COVER SHEET
2. EXISTING AIRPORT CONDITIONS
3. FUTURE AIRPORT CONDITIONS
4. AIRPORT DATA SHEET

VICINITY MAP
NTS

MAY, 2011

LOCATION MAP
NTS

Figure 4-1. ALP drawing set cover sheet. (Lee Brown, Fort Lauderdale-Hollywood International Airport)

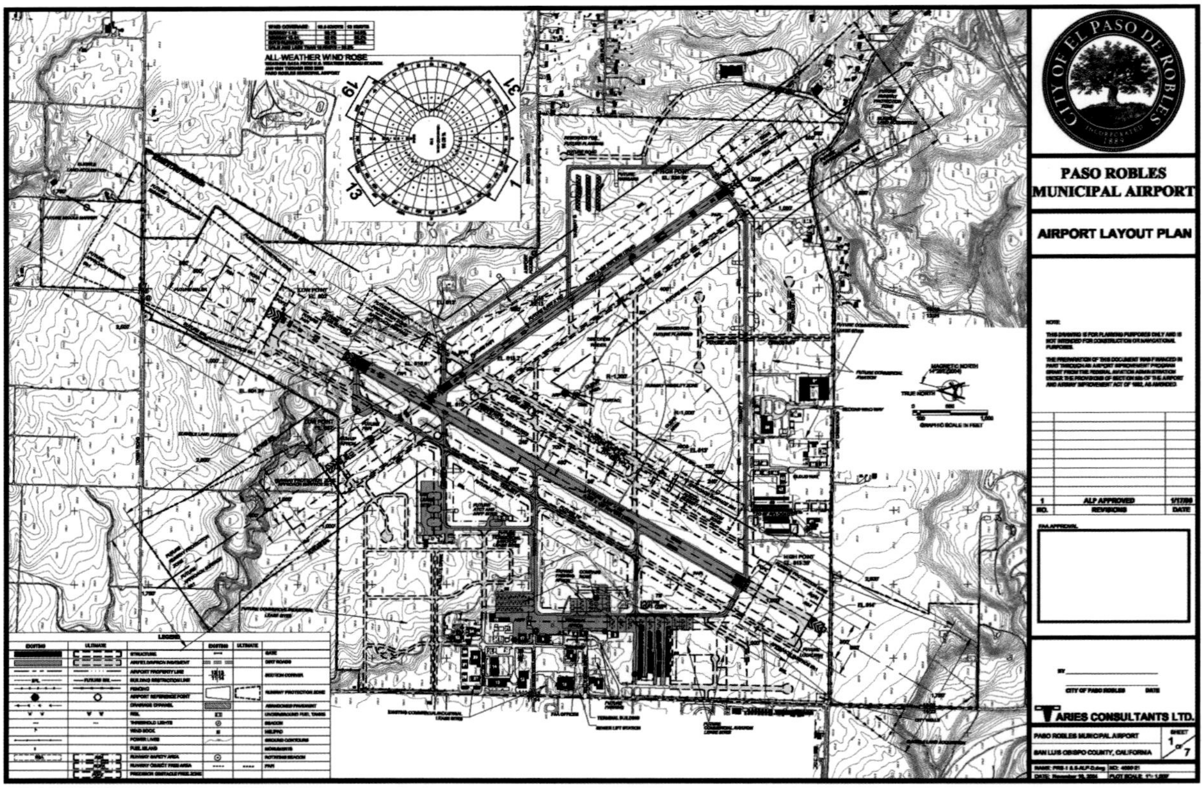

Figure 4-2. Airport layout plan drawing, Paso Robles Municipal Airport. (Paso Robles Municipal Airport)

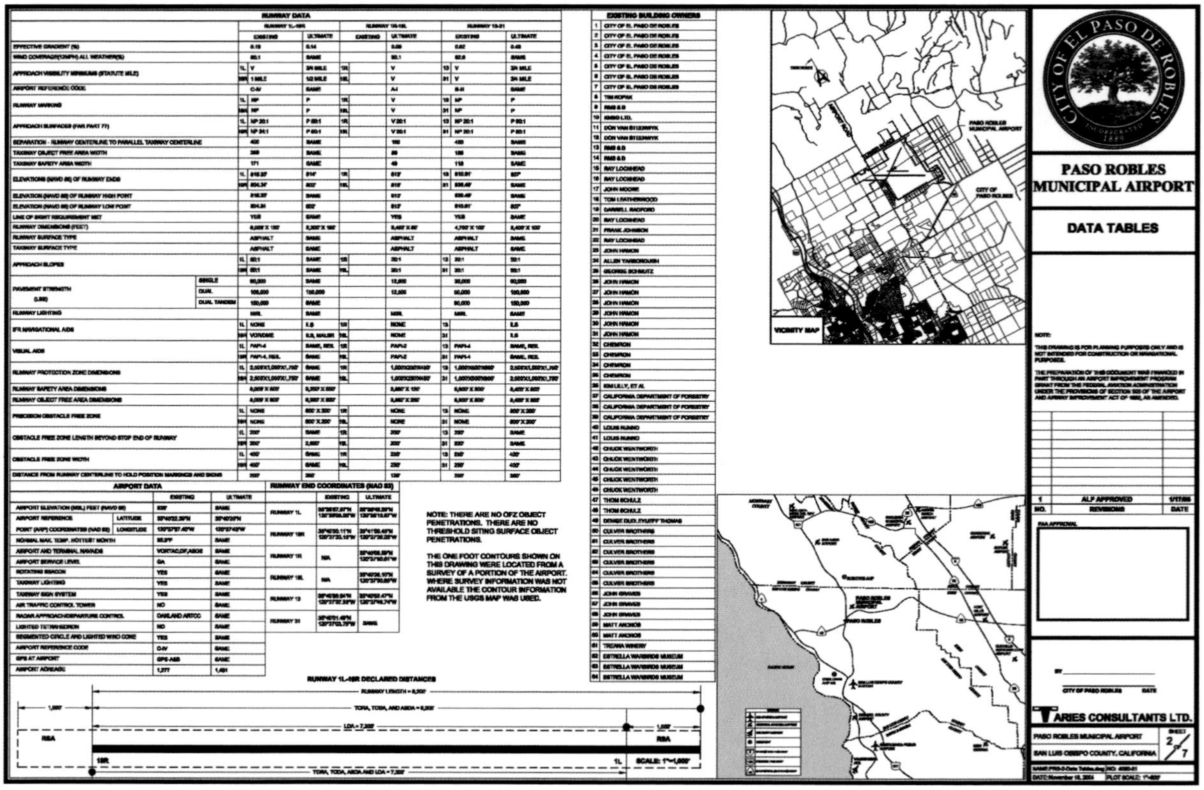

Figure 4-3. ALP drawing set data sheet, Paso Robles Municipal Airport. (Paso Robles Municipal Airport)

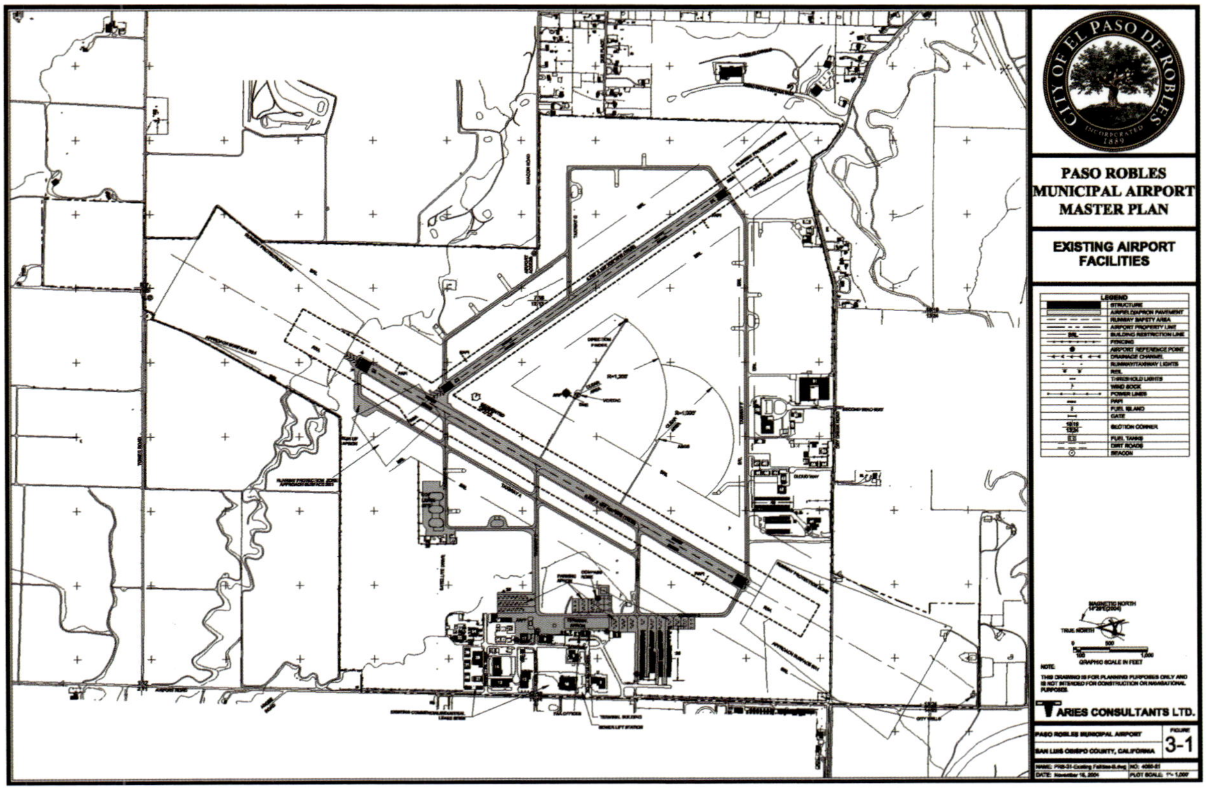

Figure 4-4. Facilities layout plan, Paso Robles Municipal Airport. (Paso Robles Municipal Airport)

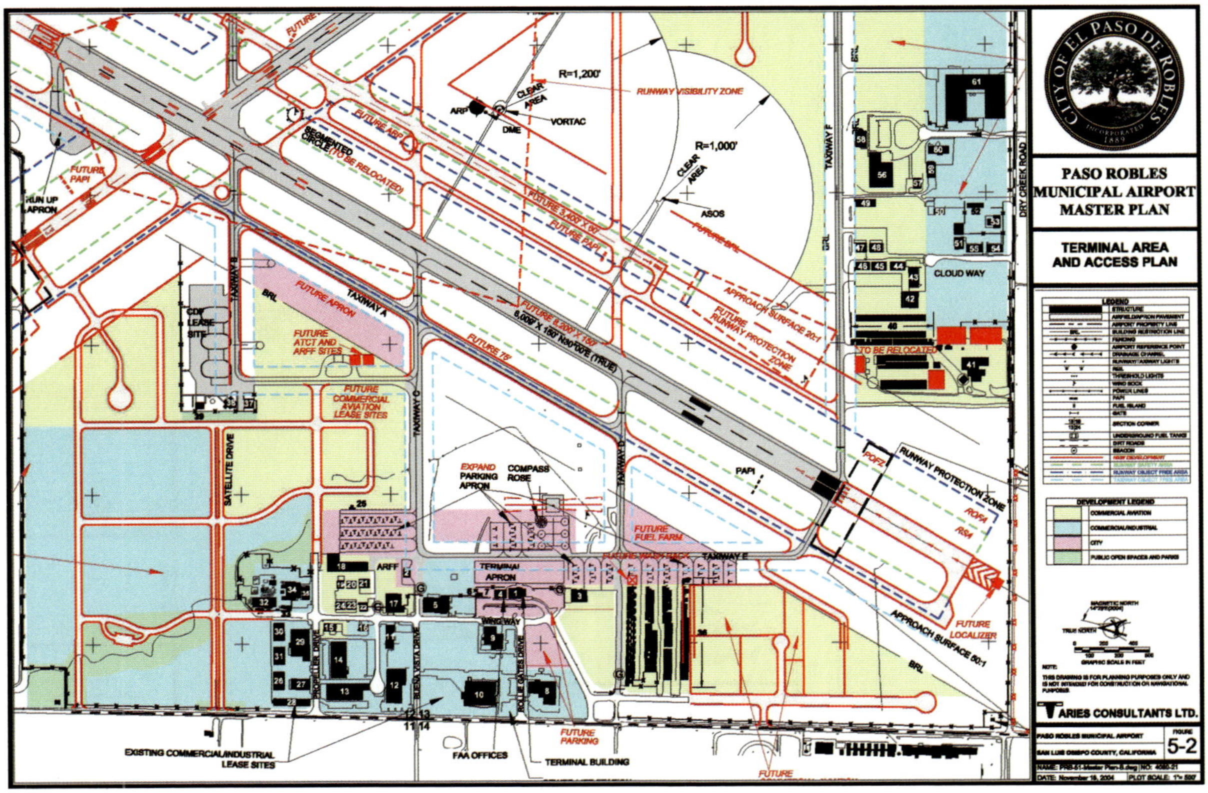

Figure 4-5. ALP drawing set—terminal area plan, Paso Robles Municipal Airport. (Paso Robles Municipal Airport)

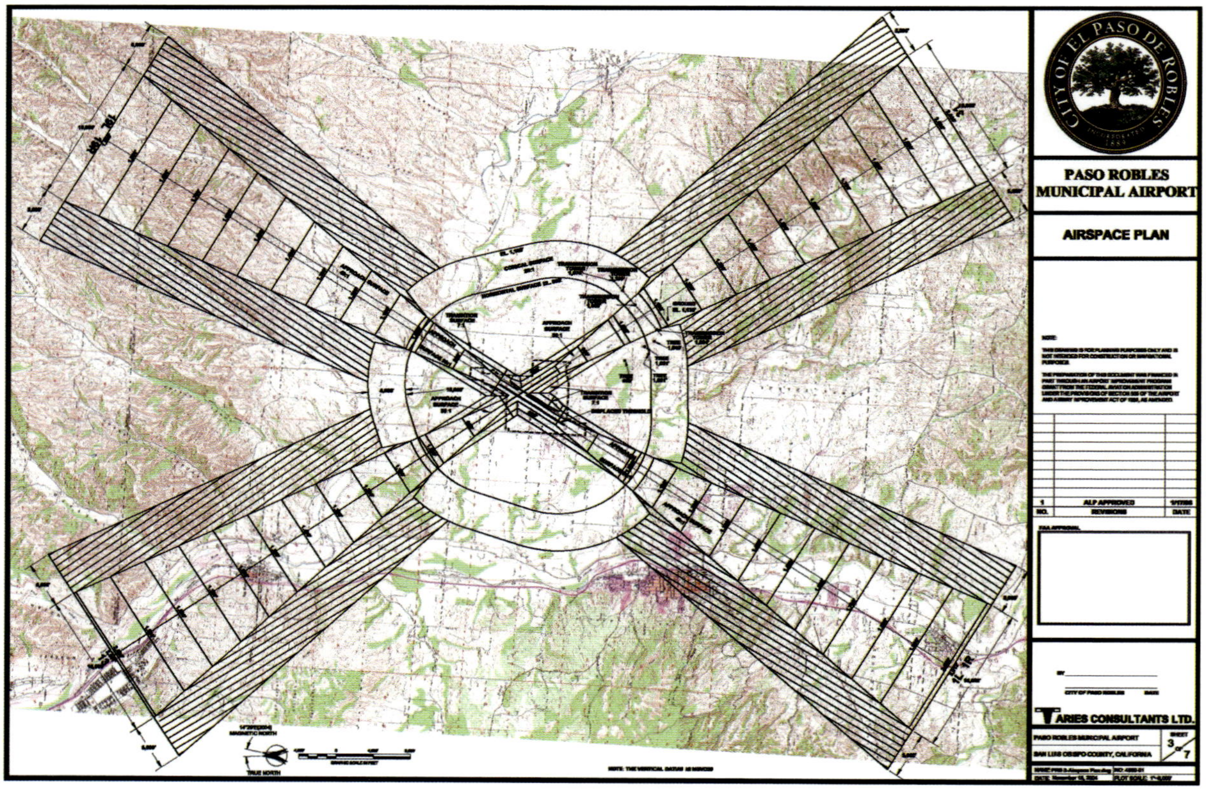

Figure 4-6. ALP drawing set—airport airspace drawing, Paso Robles Municipal Airport. (Paso Robles Municipal Airport)

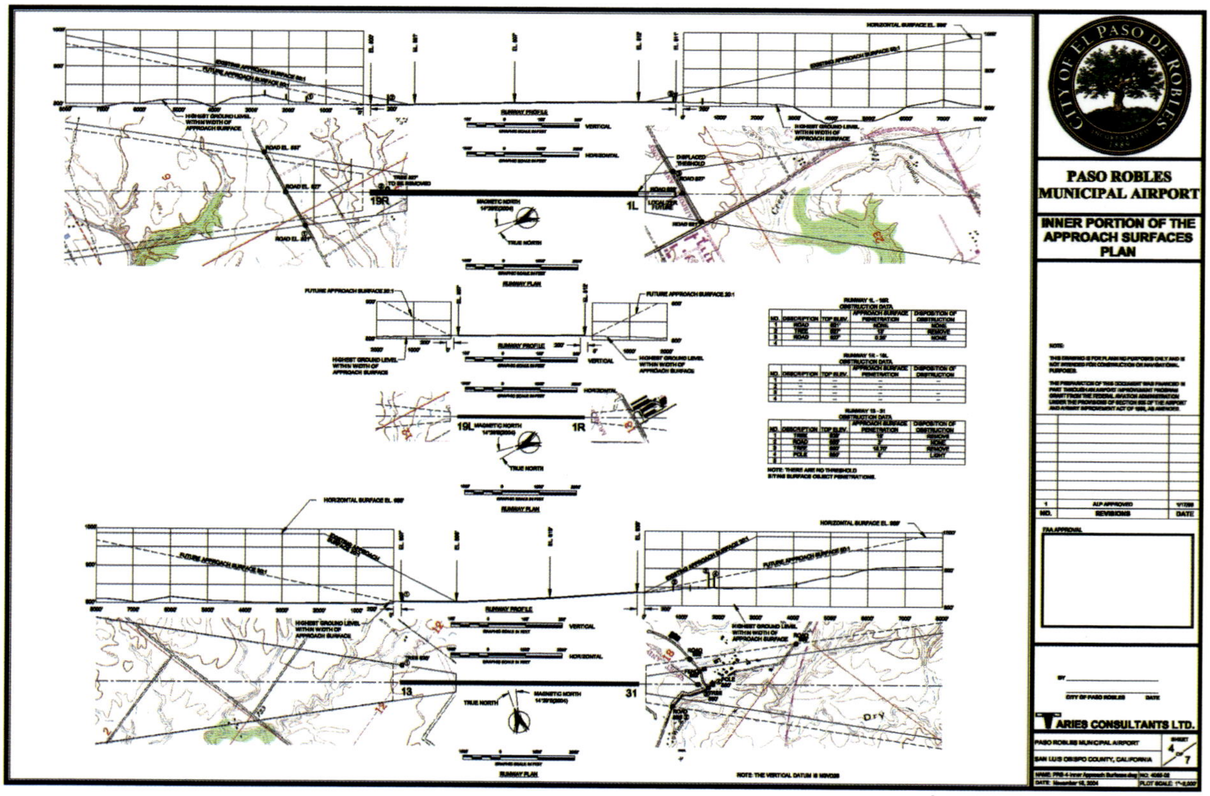

Figure 4-7. ALP drawing set—inner portion of the approach surface drawing, Paso Robles Municipal Airport.

(Paso Robles Municipal Airport)

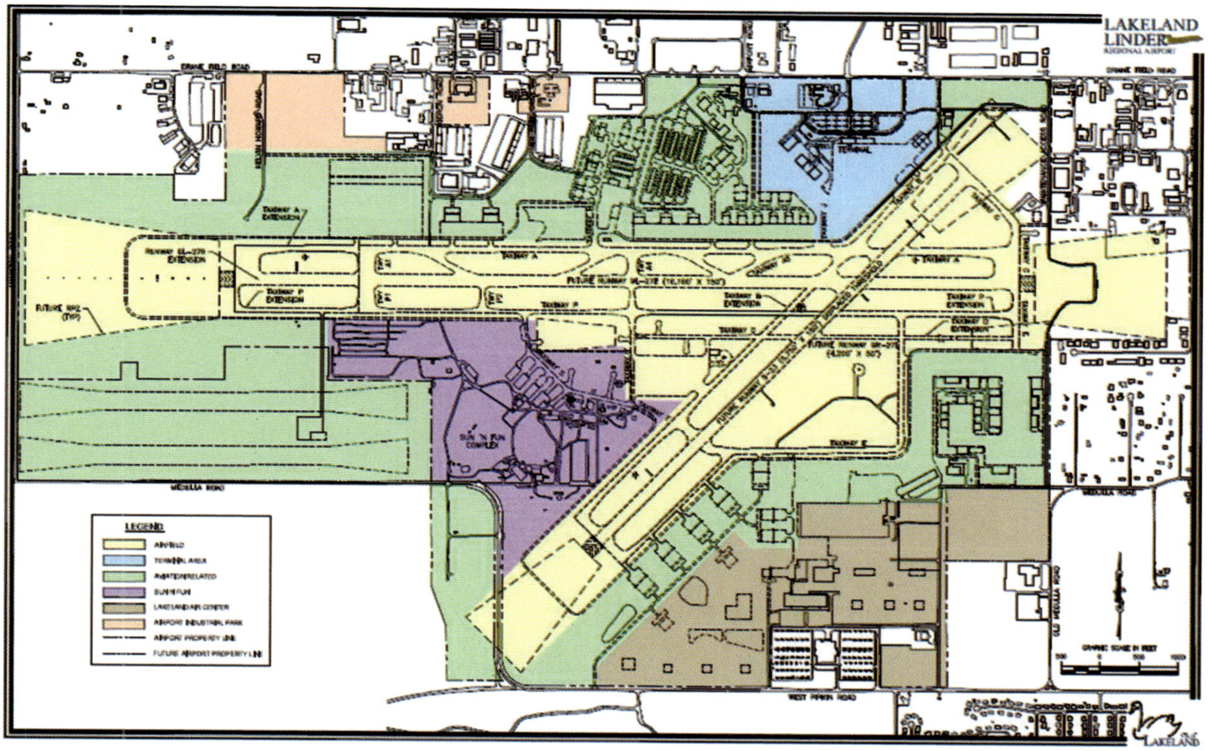

Figure 4-8. On-airport land use drawing, Lakeland Linder Regional Airport. (Lakeland Linder Regional Airport)

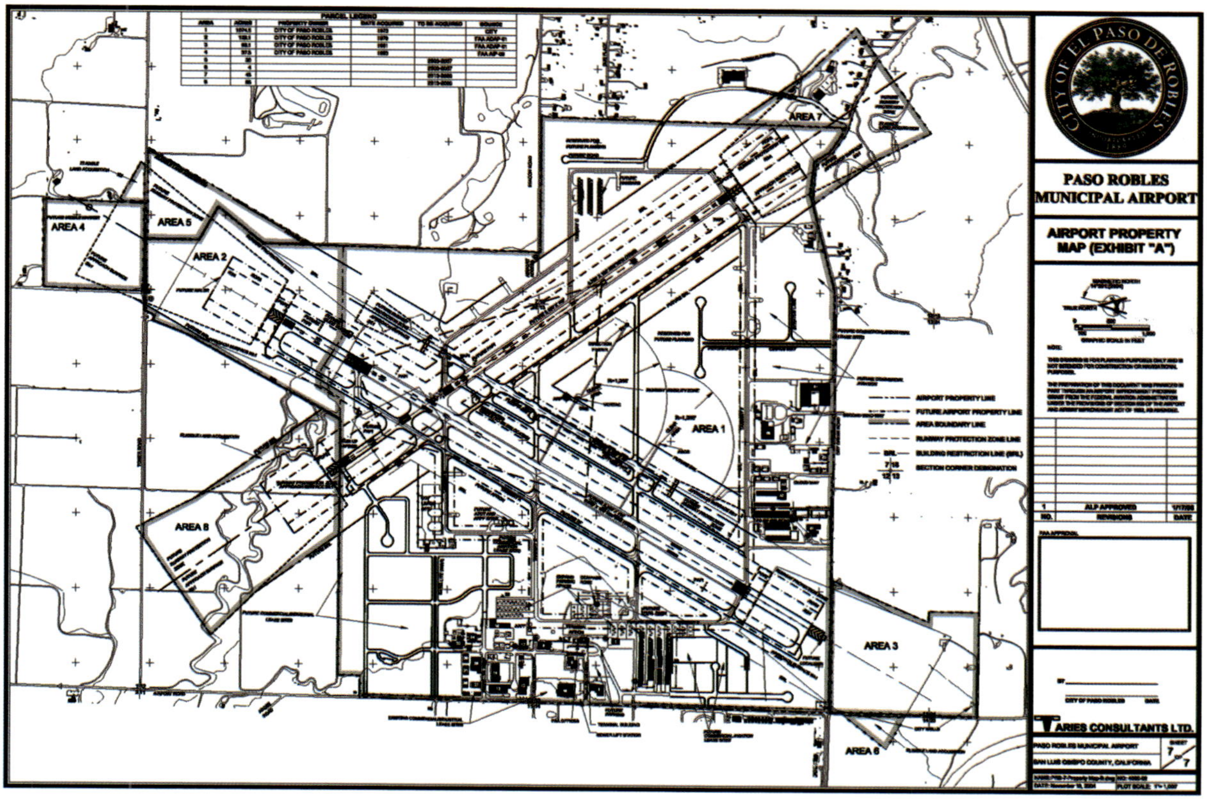

Figure 4-9. Airport property map drawing, Paso Robles Municipal Airport. (Paso Robles Municipal Airport)

The narrative accompanying the ALP drawing set should include:

1. Basic aeronautical forecasts
2. Basis for the proposed items of development
3. Rationale for unusual design features and/or modifications to FAA Airport Design Standards
4. Summary of the various stages of airport development and layout sketches of the major items of development in each stage

(FAA, 2007, p. 6)

Of these components of the drawing set, the airport layout plan is the most commonly referenced. This is because the ALP is a plan for an airport that shows:

1. Boundaries and proposed additions to all areas owned or controlled by the sponsor for airport purposes
2. The location and nature of existing and proposed airport facilities and structures
3. The location on the airport of existing and proposed non-aviation areas and improvements thereon

(Central Region Airports Division, 2010, pp. 500–503)

In essence, the ALP is a scaled drawing of existing and proposed land and facilities necessary for the operation and development of the airport. All airport development at federally obligated airports must be done in accordance with an FAA-approved ALP. Airports are required to keep this ALP current. According to the FAA, ALPs become "out of date" when they:

1. Do not adequately provide for future needs
2. Do not conform with current airport design standards
3. Do not accurately reflect existing features
4. Do not reflect airport and critical land use changes which may affect the navigable airspace or the ability of the airport to expand

(Central Region Airports Division, 2010, pp. 500–503)

Projects may require an ALP update before a grant is issued and an "as-built" ALP after the project is completed. Airports are aware of the need to maintain a current ALP, typically accomplished by revising a **computer-aided design (CAD)** file as necessary. Generally, the costs associated with the preparation of and updates to an ALP are eligible under an FAA planning grant (Central Region Airports Division, 2010).

With the integration of **geographic information systems (GIS)** at airports, the submission of ALPs is now via an electronic format—known as the eALP. The eALP is produced by a web-based application within the airport's GIS system that uses updated, precise airport data to generate eALPs. The benefits of the eALP are that it allows airports, consultants, and the FAA to (a) coordinate airport plans in a timelier manner and (b) share accurate airport data in an integrated environment. Since it is GIS-integrated, the eALP provides the capability to visualize purposed airport development reflected on the ALP (Central Region Airports Division, 2010).

Strategic Plans

Yet another type of plan specific to an airport is a **strategic plan**. These plans are not as much about facility planning as they are about staffing, financial resources, property development, customer service, and revenue generation. Although strategic planning is not an FAA requirement for airports, it is a recommended practice with numerous benefits. Indeed, organization benefits, operational/managerial benefits, community/stakeholder benefits, and economic benefits have all been identified. A strategic plan provides a roadmap to guide an airport from the present to a desired future. This is based on the assumption that business decisions made today will impact the future of the airport.

By developing a strategic plan (either in-house or via a consultant), an airport can be more strategic about its future. Often, an airport manager may not necessarily initiate the development of a strategic plan by name, but upon discussing the airport's needs with an airport consultant, it may become clear that developing a "niche" and determining "where we go from here," refers to the need for an airport strategic plan. With a well-developed strategic plan, goals will be stated and agreed upon, and action plans will be developed to enable management to work toward specific end results.

According to Ricondo and Associates, et al. (2009), the strategic planning process includes the following key elements:

1. Mission statement—A concise statement of the organization's purpose and reason for existence, developed from the perspective of an organization's customers. A mission statement is operational and focuses on the purpose of the organization, including its current activities.
2. Vision statement—A brief description of the goals of the organization and the ideal state that the organization aims to achieve in the future. A vision statement is future-oriented.
3. Values statements—Although optional, values statements describe the way an airport endeavors to conduct business, both internally and externally.
4. Strengths, weaknesses, opportunities, and threats (SWOT)—Involves an analysis of internal strengths and weaknesses and external opportunities and threats. This is often one of the most detailed and time-consuming phases of the strategic planning process.
5. Strategic issues that must be addressed over the course of the strategic plan.

6. Generic and grand strategies, long- and short-term objectives, and action plans—These provide a roadmap for realizing the airport's vision.
7. Key performance indicators—Allow an airport to evaluate the progress made toward achieving long- and short-term objectives.

Generally, the first step in developing a strategic plan for an airport involves a review of the existing airport facilities, including terminals, hangars, runways and taxiways, GA ramps, cargo areas, private/corporate hangar areas, support facilities (such as aircraft rescue firefighting and maintenance), parking areas, ground access, NAVAIDs, etc. Next, the airport's current administrative picture is reviewed, including finances, marketing plan, customer service initiatives, organizational hierarchy, personnel, mission and vision statements, goals and objectives, etc. During either of these first two steps, it is also beneficial to review past newspaper articles, press releases, and other public relations products to gain a feel for the community's perspective of the airport. Next, it is helpful to survey and/or interview current stakeholders, including airline station managers, based aircraft owners, transient GA pilots, airport board members, etc. Then a SWOT analysis should be performed. This will be very helpful in

Sample Mission, Vision, and Values Statements

Sample Mission Statement

To develop and operate for the public benefit an airport system which supports the economic development and cultural diversity of South Central Ontario and Canada, providing aviation facilities that achieve: the highest standards of safety and security; excellence in customer service, environmental stewardship and sustainability; and cost effectiveness and efficiency. This mission will be achieved through: developing a skilled and dedicated workforce; maximizing technology innovation; and excellence in corporate governance.

—Greater Toronto Airports Authority,
Lester B. Pearson International Airport,
Ontario, Canada

Sample Vision Statement

The Authority's vision is to exceed our customer's expectations by making the aviation system in Hillsborough County one of the most efficient, safe, secure, convenient, and cost competitive air transportation centers in the world.

—Hillsborough County Aviation Authority,
Tampa, Florida

Sample Values Statements

Manage responsibly all resources entrusted to us.

Value forward thinking and innovation.

Serve with honor and integrity.

Be responsible for our actions.

Provide friendly and efficient service.

Value the public's confidence and trust.

Value our community and corporate partnerships.

Value open and honest communication.

Work as a team

—Lebanon Municipal Airport,
Lebanon, New Hampshire

(Ricondo and Associates, 2009, pp. 53–56)

determining positive and negative aspects of the airport, as well as future threats to be aware of and opportunities to take advantage of. Finally, this should lead to specific strategic objectives that airport management can focus on to strengthen the airport in a very proactive and strategic manner. This may mean developing new mission and vision statements, or possibly a new organizational structure.

A well-developed strategic plan should provide airport management with short-term, medium-term, and long-term goals on which to focus. The following are some examples of the types of goals that these might include.

Short-term goals:

- Explore the possible restructuring of the airport authority to allow for staggered 2–3 year terms for members.
- Work to develop trust and accountability in local officials and members of the community by making all decisions in public and seeking counsel as appropriate.
- Evaluate the current agreement with Miller's Aircraft Sales, Inc. to determine whether or not the terms of the agreement should be renegotiated to allow the airport to receive fair market value for land/fuel. Conversely, the airport authority should seek FAA acceptance of the terms contained within the present agreement.
- Consider the present White Farms agreement and the effect that on-airport agricultural activity has on the safety of aircraft operations.
- Update the airport master plan.
- Develop a public relations plan.
- Strive to continually enhance customer service.

Medium-term goals:

- Pursue self-sufficiency through the establishment of new long-term leases/tenants.
- Consider revising the airport's organizational structure to allow for an executive director, director of operations, director of facilities, and administrative assistant, along with staff in the operations and facilities departments.
- Consider transitioning from an airport authority to city or county ownership/operation.
- Develop a marketing plan and marketing budget.
- Develop a proactive approach to community relations.
- Regularly conduct user surveys and remain aware of services being offered and facilities available at competing airports. It is important to stay ahead of the competition.
- Pursue installation of an instrument landing system (ILS).
- Maintain a clean, presentable facility at all times.
- Diversify revenues.

- Attain airport financial self-sufficiency.
- Forge new relationships with the local military base.
- Forge new relationships with the local university.
- Cater to, and attract more, GA traffic.
- Cater to, and attract more, corporate traffic.

Long-term goals:

- Pursue self-sufficiency through establishment of new long-term leases/tenants.
- Pursue diversification of leases.
- Develop a long-term marketing plan.
- Establish timeline/goals from the airport layout plan (ALP) for acquiring property to enable expansion and installation of ILS to increase the potential for future business and support of local industry.
- If the airport is successful in securing commercial airline service, the marketing plan should be revised to incorporate marketing to the community and advertising of the new airline service.

SWOT Analysis

Although the SWOT analysis is time-consuming, it is integral to developing an airport strategic plan. Areas to be considered as part of the strengths and weaknesses of the internal environment include:

- Management practices
- Human resources
- External relations
- Planning and development
- Operations, safety, and security
- Environmental
- Customer satisfaction
- Finance

Areas to be considered as part of the opportunities and threats of the external environment include:

- Macro-level economic environment
- Population and economic base
- Technological development and trends
- Regulatory changes
- Competition
- Airline industry
- Public support
- Catastrophic events

(Ricondo and Associates, 2010, pp. 63–65; 81–82)

Business Plans

In addition to a strategic plan, an airport may also have a business plan. Although some airports refer to their "strategic business plan," these two plans serve different purposes. While the strategic plan sets the direction for the airport in the medium- to long-term, the **business plan** identifies the short- to medium-term steps that should be implemented to enable the airport to achieve its desired future. Often, business plans are developed by a company before even opening for business to lure investors and obtain start-up capital. Regardless, it is beneficial for an airport to have a business plan, even if the airport has been in operation for years.

According to the Small Business Administration, a business plan should be considered a "working plan" in that changes can be made to the plan as the business evolves. Successful business plans contain the following elements:

1. Executive summary
2. Market analysis
3. Company description
4. Organization and management
5. Marketing and sales management
6. Service or product line
7. Funding request
8. Financials
9. Appendix

(SBA, n.d.)

Developing a business plan for an airport first requires conducting a market analysis to determine the degree of existing competition, including air carrier service, service for aircraft, parking facilities, ground access, terminal concessions, etc. This is completed from a competitive viewpoint. In other words, what does this airport have that another airport 100 miles away, for example, doesn't have? This is especially important in securing funding, especially for new organizations. The airport should then be fully described, as if explaining to someone unfamiliar with it everything it has to offer. This description should be comprehensive. Next, the airport's organizational structure, including senior management staff, should be spelled out. Then the airport's marking plan should be presented (possibly including the entire plan in an appendix). The service or product line of the airport should also be spelled out. For example, is this mostly a GA airport or a commercial service airport? Finally, the plan presents financials and any funding request (necessary if approaching a potential funding source, such as a commercial bank). In sum, the business plan presents a complete picture of the business, whereas a strategic plan provides strategic direction for the business.

Aviation Activity Forecasts

To successfully meet the demands of the future, airports (as well as regional and state aviation organizations) engage in forecasting future aviation activity. As stated by the FAA, "Forecasts of future levels of aviation activity are the basis for effective decisions in airport planning" (FAA, 2007). Indeed, without an indication of future demand, airports would be blind in attempting to meet that demand, possibly resulting in "overbuilding" or "underbuilding."

Generally, **aviation activity forecasts** are conducted as part of the master planning process. By definition, an airport master plan is future-focused, making the process of forecasting integral to that plan. Similar to master plans and ALPs, aviation activity forecasts undergo review at the national level. The FAA reviews aviation activity forecasts prepared in conjunction with airport master plans and environmental studies. These forecasts may then be adopted for inclusion in the FAA **terminal area forecast (TAF)** and the National Plan of Integrated Airport Systems (NPIAS). The TAF is the official FAA forecast of aviation activity for U.S. airports. It contains those airports listed in the NPIAS and is prepared for users, including air carrier, air taxi/commuter, general aviation, and military.

In any aviation activity forecasting, it is important to remember that certain causal relationships drive aviation activity. In essence, aviation activity levels are affected by the interaction of supply and demand. Specifically, according to the FAA, demographic variables and economic activity variables drive demand for aviation. Variables of cost, competition, and regulations influence supply (FAA, 2001). According to the FAA (2005), the following factors affect aviation activity:

- *Economic characteristics*—These include the economic characteristics of the local community, as well as national and regional economic activity, as these will affect the demand for air traffic. It also includes the types of companies and industries in the local area. Consider that manufacturing and service industries typically generate more aviation activity than resource industries such as mining, timber, or oil.
- *Demographic characteristics*—These include characteristics such as disposable income, leisure time, and recreational activity, as these will affect the demand for air traffic. Data shows that if an area has a high level of disposable income per capita, there will likely be a higher rate of demand for commercial airline service, as well as general aviation (GA) activity.
- *Geographic attributes*—These include the distances between populations and centers of commerce, as well as the physical characteristics of the area and the local climate.
- *Aviation-related factors*—These factors include airline mergers, airline bankruptcies, and new marketing (codeshare) agreements. General industry trends, such as the introduction of new low-fare service, the use of jet or newer types of aircraft, and the growth or decline of airline hubs, may

also impact aviation activity. Additionally, local actions, such as changes in user charges and airport access policies can greatly impact aviation activity.

- *Other factors*—These include various external factors that may impact the demand for aviation activity. Consider fuel prices, aviation taxes, and changes in the political landscape. These factors are difficult if not impossible to control, and yet may result in significant impacts on aviation activity.

In light of these factors, various demand elements are considered standard when conducting aviation activity forecasts. At a minimum, aircraft operations are considered, including identifying the critical aircraft that are currently utilizing and forecast to utilize the airport. Commercial service airports will also include passenger enplanements in their forecasts, while general aviation airports will include the number and type of based aircraft. The aviation demand elements to be forecast, according to the FAA (2007), are shown in Table 4-1.

Table 4-1. Aviation demand elements to consider when forecasting.

Required	Included Where Appropriate
Operations (annual)	

Itinerant
  Air Carrier
  Air Taxi and Commuter (Regional)
  General Aviation
  Military
Local
  General Aviation
  Military
	Domestic vs. International
	Annual Instrument Approaches
	IFR vs. VFR Operations
	Air Cargo Aircraft Operations
	  Touch and Go Operations (Training)
	Helicopter Operations
	  Average Load Factor
	  Fuel Use

Passengers (annual)	

Enplanements
  Air Carrier
  Commuter
Enplanements
  Originating
  Connecting
	Passenger and Cargo Data
	Domestic vs. International
	General Aviation Passengers
	Helicopter
	Air Taxi
	Other
	  Number of Student Pilots
	  Number of Hours Flown

Aircraft	
Based Aircraft Aircraft Mix Critical Aircraft	Average Seats/Aircraft

(FAA, 2007)

STEPS IN FORECASTING

To effectively forecast aviation activity, certain steps must be followed. According to the FAA (2001), these steps are:

1. Identify aviation activity parameters and measures to forecast.
2. Collect and review previous airport forecasts.
3. Gather data.
   a. Determine data requirements.
   b. Identify data sources.
   c. Collect and evaluate historical and forecast data.
4. Select forecast methods.
5. Apply forecast methods and evaluate results.
6. Summarize and document results.
7. Compare airport planning forecast results with the terminal area forecast (TAF).

Although the time and tools necessary to complete each step may vary depending upon the forecasting method utilized, the general steps listed above are typically adhered to.

TYPES OF FORECASTS

Depending on the forecasting method utilized, the process of forecasting can be quite simple or rather complex. The availability of data often determines which type of forecasting technique can be used. Regardless, according to FAA Order 5090.3C, "Field Formulation of the National Plan of Integrated Airport Systems (NPIAS)," forecasts should:

- be realistic;
- be based on the latest available data;
- reflect the current conditions at the airport;
- be supported by information in the study;
- provide an adequate justification for the airport planning and development. (FAA, 2000)

Based on this, forecasting methods can be grouped into the following four main categories:

- Market share forecasting
- Econometric model forecasting
- Time series model forecasting
- Simulation

Market Share Forecasting

Market share forecasting requires measuring current activity at an airport and relating this to a share of some other aggregate measure, which may be at the regional, state, or national level. The forecaster must assume that the share will remain constant, or possibly change in a known way. If done properly, airport activity can be forecasted to grow along with the estimated growth in the aggregate activity (Spitz and Golaszewski, 2007).

However, even with this assumption, the share may change over time. As a result, studies conducted with market share forecasting often include only the recent past and a small number of historical data points. The consequence of this approach is less meaningful forecasts, because the actual relationship between the airport activity and the aggregate measure is likely to change again during the forecast horizon. Even with this shortcoming, the use of the market share forecasting method is often justified when data is limited, such as the number of operations at non-towered airports. This method is also relied upon when past airport activity does not correlate well with other factors, and when more sophisticated methods may not yield results that are statistically reliable (Spitz and Golaszewski, 2007).

Econometric Model Forecasting

Often referred to as **regression analysis**, **econometric model forecasting** is a sophisticated forecasting technique. This method uses a mathematical equation that supposes a causal relationship between a dependent variable (referred to as *Y*) and a set of independent explanatory variables (referred to as *X*). For example, seasonal demand for air travel at a particular airport (in terms of passenger enplanements) may be posited to be a function of the seasonal tourism to that area (Spitz and Golaszewski, 2007).

$$Y = \alpha + \beta X + \varepsilon$$

where:
Y is the dependent variable,
X is the independent variable,
α is the constant term of the equation,
β is the coefficient describing how a change in X affects Y, and
ε is a random error term (with a mean value of zero).

With this formula, forecasts of *Y* may be made based on observed or assumed values of *X*.

As with any forecasting method, econometric models have drawbacks. First and foremost, the forecaster using this method must assume the dependent variable can be calculated as a linear function of a specific set of independent variables. However, if there is a changing or nonlinear relationship between the dependent and independent variables, this assumption would be wrong. Further, the wrong set of explanatory variables may be used. Known as "specification errors," the nature of these errors is often difficult to determine. It is wise for the forecaster considering this method to consult an econometrics textbook or expert for guidance (Spitz and Golaszewski, 2007).

Time Series Model Forecasting

The approach to forecasting known as **time series model forecasting** is simpler than econometric modeling, although specific statistical techniques can be applied that create a more sophisticated and complex forecasting model. This approach extrapolates (or forecasts) data into the future. In simple terms, time series forecasting projects the value of a variable into the future based on current or past trends. With this approach, data on only one variable is necessary, which equates to lower-cost forecasting. However, this approach is most accurate when

- a long series of historical data are available;
- no large changes in airport use or activity are expected; and
- forecasting over a relatively short time period in the future
  (Spitz and Golaszewski, 2007, p. 20).

As a result, time series forecasting is best utilized for short-term planning and annual budgeting. Additionally, since this technique does not consider external factors, it should not be used to examine alternative policies or environments. Nonetheless, this technique is very effective at projecting a relatively consistent variable into the future.

Simulation

Quite different than other forecasting techniques, **simulation modeling** methods are designed to create "high-fidelity estimates of the particular itinerary that passengers or aircraft may take across an airline network, how passengers may travel through a particular airport terminal, or how aircraft may traverse over an airport tarmac and runways" (Spitz and Golaszewski 2007, p. 21). In essence, simulation models are based on known movements of passengers and routing of aircraft. With this understanding, simulation modeling can aggregate results to reveal future demand, which then allows one to gauge whether the network or airport will be able to accommodate forecast traffic. It should be noted that the inputs for simulation models are generally those outputs produced from the other forecasting methods discussed (such as total enplanements or operations) (Spitz and Golaszewski, 2007, p. 21).

SELECTION OF FORECASTING METHOD

When selecting an appropriate forecasting method, two main questions should be asked. First, what is the purpose of the forecast and what historical data is available in relation to that? Second, what budgetary constraints must be dealt with? Although each situation will be different and the reasons for choosing a specific forecasting method may vary, answers to these two questions will generally lead the forecaster to choose one method over another. Generally, time series model forecasting is appropriate for short-term operational planning or budgeting, but only if the variable is consistent over time. In situations where consistency is less likely (such as seasonal effects that have varied historically), more sophisticated statistical techniques could be applied to time series modeling. Further, market share forecasting or econometric modeling is appropriate for medium- and long-term forecasts used to forecast (a) future capacity needs of landside or airside components, and (b) financial needs associated with expansion of capacity (Spitz and Golaszewski, 2007).

USES OF FORECASTS

Forecasts can be used for a variety of purposes, with short-, medium-, and long-term planning horizons. Forecasts generally reflect the demands for aviation services, the results of which are useful in making supply decisions, in terms of infrastructure, capacity, and revenues necessary to meet the projected demand. However, according to Spitz and Golaszewski (2007, p. 7), "*observed* airport aviation activity is driven not just by demand, but by the interaction between demand for and supply of aviation services." As a result, forecasts are integral to airports in making supply-side assessments regarding long-term airport planning and capacity needs, short-term operational planning, and financial planning (Spitz and Golaszewski, 2007).

Long-Term Airport Planning and Capacity Needs

First, forecasts can be useful in anticipating both airside and landside capacity needs. For instance, airside forecasts can be made to determine if runways and taxiways are sufficient to meet projected demand. Additionally, what additional air cargo facilities and FBO ramp space is necessary to meet forecast demand? On the landside, forecasts can be made to determine if and when expansion may be needed in terminals, concourses, parking, and airport access (Spitz and Golaszewski, 2007).

Short Term Operational Planning

Effective forecasts can be made to assist with decision-making regarding short-term operational needs. For instance, are the current number of airport personnel and FAA personnel sufficient to meet forecast activity? The effects of seasonal, daily, and hourly peaks can also be identified. Additionally, aircraft and passenger travel time and delays can be identified and considered in meeting future demands with existing capacity (Spitz and Golaszewski, 2007).

Financial Planning

As future demand is forecast and required expansion is identified, the funding necessary to support this expansion can also be forecast. As airports develop capital improvement plans (CIP), which represent multi-year airport development projects, a projection of costs is integral to the effectiveness of these plans. Such medium- to long-term financial planning allows for the development of AIP and PFC requests, a determination of the amount of bond issues, and the desired amount of other funding sources. Short-term financial planning also benefits from forecasting as airports develop annual budgets, as well as the monthly and yearly oversight of these. Indeed, multiple measures of aviation activity relate—either directly or indirectly—to airport revenues and expenses. For example, the number of aircraft operations will affect landing fee revenue, as well as fuel sales, per-use fees, and FBO sales. These same operations also increase expenses associated with airside personnel, airfield maintenance, utilities, etc. Additionally, passengers drive revenues and expenditures associated with concessions, parking facilities, etc. (Spitz and Golaszewski, 2007, p. 7).

Concluding Thoughts

On many levels, airport planning is integral to an aviation system as active as that in the United States. Without proper planning, future demands will not be adequately met. And, of course, this planning is dependent upon accurate and reliable forecasts. Although it is practically impossible to predict the future, airports and planners can examine the past, look for trends, and make certain assumptions about the future. In reality, we do that in our personal lives every day. We expect our automobile to behave as it did yesterday. We assume today that we have the same job we had yesterday. We predict that we'll earn the same income as we did last year. We even project our income tax refund and may even spend the refund money before we even receive it. Thus, just as we make forecasts in our personal lives, airports can, and should, make forecasts about future aviation activity to enable them to be fully prepared to meet the demands of the future.

Chapter Summary

- The National Plan of Integrated Airport Systems (NPIAS) is the current name of the national airport plan that has been carried out since 1946.
- Airports included in the NPIAS are eligible to receive federal grants under the Airport Improvement Program.
- Generally, a regional aviation system plan provides the foundation for a regional strategy to meet air transportation needs of an entire region.
- A state aviation system plan allows for a coordinated air transportation system on a state-wide level.
- A metropolitan aviation system plan is typically developed for airports located in close proximity to each other within a major metropolitan area.
- An airport master plan is a comprehensive study of an airport, and typically presents the short-, medium-, and long-term development plans necessary to meet future aviation demand.
- An airport layout plan (ALP) is a scaled drawing depicting existing and proposed land and airport facilities.
- A facilities layout plan drawing depicts existing and future facilities, and only critical, non-overlapping clearance criteria, with minimal text.
- A terminal area plan consists of one or more drawings that present a large-scale depiction of areas with significant terminal facility development.
- An airport airspace drawing depicts obstacle identification surfaces (14 CFR Part 77) for the full extent of all airport development.
- The inner portion of the approach surface drawing contains the plan and profile view of the inner portion of the approach surface to the runways and a tabular listing of all surface penetrations.
- The on-airport land use drawing depicts the land uses within the airport property boundary.
- The off-airport land use drawing depicts land uses and zoning in the area around the airport.
- The airport property map depicts the airport property boundary, the various tracts of land that were acquired to develop the airport, and the method of acquisition.
- The runway departure surface drawing depicts the applicable departure surfaces as defined in AC 150/5300-13.
- The utility drawing depicts the location and capacity of major utilities on the airport and in the surrounding area.
- The airport access plans, if necessary, depict the major routes of various modes of transportation that serve the airport.

- A strategic plan provides a roadmap to guide an airport from the present to a desired future, and may address staffing, financial resources, property development, customer service, and revenue generation.
- A business plan identifies the short- to medium-term steps that should be implemented to enable the airport to achieve its desired future.
- Forecasting steps include identifying aviation activity parameters and measures, collecting and reviewing previous forecasts, gathering data, selecting forecast methods, applying forecasting methods and evaluating results, summarizing and documenting results, and comparing airport planning forecast results with the terminal area forecast.
- Forecasting methods can be grouped into four main categories: market share forecasting, econometric model forecasting, time series model forecasting, and simulation.
- Market share forecasting requires measuring current activity at an airport and relating this to a share of some other aggregate measure, which may be at the regional, state, or national level.
- Econometric model forecasting uses a mathematical equation that supposes a causal relationship between a dependent variable and a set of independent explanatory variables.
- Time series model forecasting extrapolates data into the future based on current or past trends.
- Simulation modeling is based on known movements of passengers and routing of aircraft and can aggregate results to reveal future demand.
- Forecasts can be useful for anticipating both airside and landside capacity needs.

Review Questions

1. How many airports are included in the NPIAS?
2. Within what must airports be included to be eligible for federal grants under the Airport Improvement Program (AIP)?
3. What type of plan provides the foundation for a regional strategy to meet air transportation needs of an entire region?
4. What do state aviation system plans enable planners to do?
5. What is one example of a metropolitan area in the United States with several commercial service airports that are closely linked?
6. What are the products that are part of a completed master plan?
7. What are the fourteen components of the ALP drawing set?
8. Which statement contains a brief description of the goals of the organization and the ideal state that the organization aims to achieve in the future?
9. What is the difference between a strategic plan and a business plan?
10. Why do airports engage in forecasting future aviation activity?
11. Which factors affect aviation activity?
12. Which aviation demand elements are required when conducting aviation activity forecasts?
13. What are the steps to follow in forecasting aviation activity?
14. What five characteristics are necessary for an effective forecast?
15. What are the four main categories of forecasting methods?
16. Define market share forecasting.
17. Define time series modeling.
18. What two questions must be asked when selecting an appropriate forecasting method?
19. What are some examples of short-term operational needs that can be forecast?
20. What are some examples of financial planning needs that can be forecast?

Scenarios

1. As airport director of a large hub commercial service airport, you have been approached by the metropolitan planning organization in your area about participating in the development of a regional aviation system plan. This plan would include two other GA airports and one additional commercial service airport. How would you respond and why?
2. The city manager (to whom you report as airport manager of the local GA airport) has mentioned that the airport should be more strategic in the future. What do you think this means? How can you best do this? Would you attempt to provide this strategic focus yourself or rely on a consultant?
3. Recently hired to increase revenues, traffic, and passengers at a small commercial service airport, you would like to forecast revenues, traffic, and passengers based on current numbers with no improvements being implemented. How would you do this?
4. Select a local airport and conduct a SWOT analysis. This will likely require you to meet with the airport manager, select staff, and possibly a few tenants. Do your research. You cannot expect that everyone you speak to will have knowledge of all strengths, weaknesses, opportunities, and threats at the airport.
5. As the newly hired airport manager at a small GA airport, you become aware of a 20-year-old master plan. In short order, you decide a master plan update is long overdue. How do you begin this process? What steps would you expect to take to see this project through to completion?

References and Resources for Further Study

Central Region Airports Division (FAA). 2010. "AIP Sponsor Guide." Retrieved from http://www.faa.gov/airports/central/aip/sponsor_guide/media/0500.pdf

Federal Aviation Administration (FAA). 2000. "Field Formulation of the National Plan of Integrated Airport Systems (NPIAS)." FAA Order 5090.3C.

———. 2001. "Forecasting Aviation Activity by Airport." Retrieved from www.faa.gov/data_research/aviation_data_statistics/forecasting/media/af1.doc

———. 2007. *Airport Master Plans.* AC 150/5070-6B. Washington, DC: FAA.

———. 2010. "National Plan of Integrated Airport Systems, 2011–2015."

New England Airport Coalition. 2006. New England Regional Airport System Plan. http://www.faa.gov/airports/new_england/planning_capacity/airport_system_plan/media/nerasp_complete.pdf

Ricondo & Associates, Booz Allen Hamilton, George Mason University, and National Service Research. 2009. "ARCP Report 20. Strategic Planning in the Airport Industry." Washington, DC: Transportation Research Board.

Small Business Administration. n.d. Retrieved from http://www.sba.gov/writing-business-plan

Spitz, W. and R. Golaszewski. 2007. "ACRP Synthesis 2: Airport Aviation Activity Forecasting." Washington, DC: Transportation Research Board.

Chapter 5

Design and Construction

Objectives

Upon completion of this chapter, you should:

- Understand the purpose of predesign, prebid, and preconstruction conferences.
- Understand the components of a construction safety and phasing plan.
- Understand the responsibilities of the airport and contractor(s) in ensuring safety during construction.
- Be able to discuss the main components of the Airport Design advisory circular.
- Be able to determine runway design code.
- Understand the factors which affect the layout and configuration of runways.
- Understand when additional runways may be justified.
- Understand various runway separation criteria and object clearing criteria/areas.
- Understand taxiway design principles.
- Understand various taxiway characteristics.
- Be able to discuss the two types of pavement in use at airports.
- Understand the purpose and design considerations of runway and taxiway bridges.
- Understand the basic configurations of terminals.
- Be able to discuss the three major components of airport traffic and the issues associated with airport ground access.
- Understand common-use facilities.
- Understand the role of EMAS.
- Understand the purpose of 14 CFR Part 77 and the imaginary surfaces.
- Understand the purpose of TERPs.
- Understand the role of avigation easements.
- Understand the selection process, to include RFP, RFQ, the bid process, and contractor selection and negotiation.
- Be aware of ICAO requirements in the area of airport design.

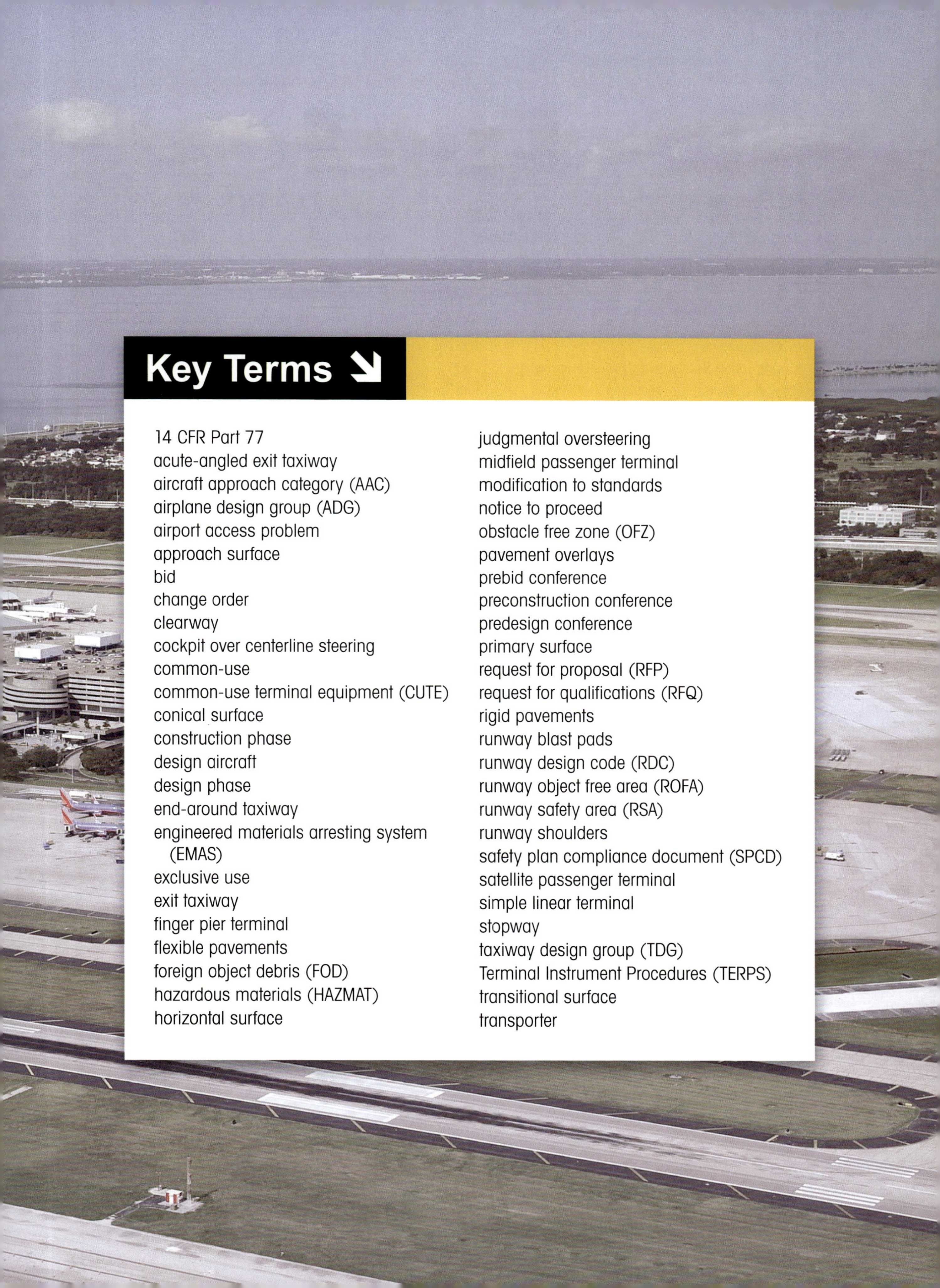

Key Terms

- 14 CFR Part 77
- acute-angled exit taxiway
- aircraft approach category (AAC)
- airplane design group (ADG)
- airport access problem
- approach surface
- bid
- change order
- clearway
- cockpit over centerline steering
- common-use
- common-use terminal equipment (CUTE)
- conical surface
- construction phase
- design aircraft
- design phase
- end-around taxiway
- engineered materials arresting system (EMAS)
- exclusive use
- exit taxiway
- finger pier terminal
- flexible pavements
- foreign object debris (FOD)
- hazardous materials (HAZMAT)
- horizontal surface
- judgmental oversteering
- midfield passenger terminal
- modification to standards
- notice to proceed
- obstacle free zone (OFZ)
- pavement overlays
- prebid conference
- preconstruction conference
- predesign conference
- primary surface
- request for proposal (RFP)
- request for qualifications (RFQ)
- rigid pavements
- runway blast pads
- runway design code (RDC)
- runway object free area (ROFA)
- runway safety area (RSA)
- runway shoulders
- safety plan compliance document (SPCD)
- satellite passenger terminal
- simple linear terminal
- stopway
- taxiway design group (TDG)
- Terminal Instrument Procedures (TERPS)
- transitional surface
- transporter

In Chapter 5

Introduction **191**

Construction Standards **191**

Predesign, Prebid, and Preconstruction Conferences 192

Construction Safety and Operational Plans........ 193

Airport Construction Activities........................... 198

Design Standards **200**

AC 5300-13 Airport Design............................. 200

Runway Layouts and Design 203

Taxiway Layouts 206

Gradient and Line of Sight 208

Pavement Design 209

Runway and Taxiway Bridges 210

Terminal Layouts 211

Ground Access.. 216

Common-Use Facilities 217

EMAS 220

Airspace and Approach Standards **221**

14 CFR Part 77—Objects Affecting Navigable Airspace 221

TERPS 226

Avigation Easements 226

Selection Process **226**

Specifications 226

RFP 227

RFQ 227

Bids 228

Contractor Selection...................................... 228

Contract Negotiation 228

International Practice **229**

Concluding Thoughts **229**

Chapter Summary **230**

Review Questions **233**

Scenarios **234**

References and Resources for Further Study **235**

FEATURES

End-Around Taxiway 208

The nation's first end-around taxiway at Hartsfield-Jackson Atlanta International Airport.

Common-Use Technology at Fresno Yosemite International Airport 218

The adoption of common-use technology has allowed virtual expansion without physical expansion of the terminal.

Introduction

Airports are developed according to specific design criteria set forth by the FAA. The specific criteria with which a specific airport must comply are based, in large part, on the design aircraft that will be utilizing the airport. This chapter provides insight into the design and construction of airports.

Construction Standards

Airports often have ongoing construction projects. Especially at larger commercial service airports, it seems that a construction project is always in progress. As a result, specific construction standards must be developed and adhered to. Typically, construction projects within the terminal area or on the landside of the airport are subject to different construction standards than those in place for projects on the AOA or airside of the airport. Regardless, construction standards are important to ensuring a safe project with minimal impact on airport activity (Figure 5-1).

The airport is responsible for all project engineering, including the preparation of plans and specifications, construction supervision, and inspection and testing for acceptability and quality of the work performed. If there is not sufficient or qualified airport staff to perform these services, it is in the best interest of the airport to retain a consulting engineering firm. The consultant will represent the airport's interest and assume overall responsibility for reporting on the acceptability and quality of the work. As with all contracted work, a written agreement will clearly define the role of the consultant.

Figure 5-1. Airport construction.

PREDESIGN, PREBID, AND PRECONSTRUCTION CONFERENCES

Prior to commencement of the construction project, various conferences or meetings are held. A **predesign conference**, coordinated by the airport or an authorized agent, is used to discuss design parameters, airport safety, routing of aircraft and equipment, sequencing of construction operations, environmental considerations, and civil rights requirements. This meeting is also the proper forum to resolve potential conflicts between construction activities and airport activities. Held soon after sufficient preliminary design work has been completed and prior to the preparation of the final plans and specifications, invited parties may include the airport's design engineer, airport staff, Air Transport Association (ATA) regional representatives, Air Line Pilots Association (ALPA) representatives, fixed base operators (FBOs), airline representatives, FAA airport certification inspectors, and representatives of the FAA Airports Regional Office (FAA, 2009).

A **prebid conference** may also be conducted, usually by the airport's engineer. Typically held for large projects or projects with unique features, the purpose of a prebid conference is to help clarify and explain construction methods, procedures, and safety measures required by the contract. Usually held at least 10 days before the bid opening date, this conference enables all potential contractors to be fully knowledgeable about the airport's expectations and requirements for the project to enable a successful bid to be developed. Participants normally include prospective bidders, subcontractors, and material suppliers. Generally, the FAA's participation in the prebid conference is neither expected nor required (FAA, 2009).

Finally, once a contractor has been selected and a contract has been negotiated, the **preconstruction conference** is held. This meeting is conducted soon after the contract has been awarded and before issuance of the **notice to proceed**. This important meeting is coordinated by the airport or an authorized agent, and provides an opportunity to discuss operational safety, testing, quality control, quality acceptance, security, safety, labor requirements, environmental factors, and other issues with the contractor and any subcontractors. All airport expectations are spelled out in this meeting. Attendees may include the airport's engineer; resident engineer; airport staff; testing laboratory representative; contractor and subcontractor(s); contractor's project superintendent; contractor's project clerk; various airport users, including airline representatives, fixed base operators, Air Line Pilots Association (ALPA) representative, Air Transport Association (ATA) regional representative, and military representative (joint-use airport); utility companies affected by the proposed construction; federal, state, or local agencies affected by the proposed construction; and representatives of the FAA Airports regional or field office (FAA, 2009).

CONSTRUCTION SAFETY AND OPERATIONAL PLANS

Although all airport construction projects present certain hazards, construction projects located on the airfield present greater risk simply due to the presence of aircraft, higher activity and noise levels, and unique operating environment (Figure 5-2). Therefore, it is important to develop a construction safety and phasing plan (CSPP) for all construction projects on the airfield.[1] According to FAA AC 150/5370-2F, *Operational Safety on Airports During Construction*, an effective CSPP is developed through the following steps:

1. Identify affected areas, to include construction haul routes, materials storage, etc.
2. Describe current operations, which involves identifying normal airport operations in each area affected during each phase of the project. Determining this baseline is important in measuring the impact of construction activities on airport activity.
3. Although current airport operations should be maintained if possible, it is important to allow for temporary changes to operations. Construction activities should be planned, through project phasing if necessary, to safely accommodate the most important operations. If this is not possible, temporary changes to operations may be necessary, to include temporary revisions to approach procedures, restricting certain aircraft to specific runways and taxiways, suspension of certain operations, and decreased weights for some aircraft due to shortened runways.

Figure 5-2. Safety during construction on the airfield, with barricades and area of removed pavement shown.

(Wikimedia Commons; see credit on page 624)

[1] A CSPP must be developed for each on-airfield construction project funded by the Airport Improvement Program (AIP) or the Passenger Facility Charge (PFC) program or located on an airport certificated under Part 139.

4. Once the level and type of aircraft operations to be maintained are identified, it is important to determine the measures required to safely conduct the planned operations during the construction.
5. Manage safety risk, to include appropriate safety risk management (SRM) documentation. It is important to coordinate with the appropriate FAA Airports Regional or District Office early in the development of the CSPP to determine the need for specific SRM documentation.[2]

   (FAA, 2011a, pp.1–2)

More specifically, the CSPP should contain the following components:

1. Coordination—Airport operators, or tenants conducting construction on their leased properties, should use predesign, prebid, and preconstruction conferences to introduce the subject of airport operational safety during construction.
   a. Contractor progress meetings
   b. Scope or schedule changes
   c. FAA Air Traffic Organization (ATO) coordination
2. Phasing—The sequence of construction may be phased to gain maximum efficiency while allowing for the required operations.
   a. Phase elements
   b. Construction safety drawings
3. Areas and operations affected by the construction activity—Runways and taxiways should remain in use by aircraft to the maximum extent possible without compromising safety.
   a. Identification of affected areas
   b. Mitigation of effects
4. Protection of navigation aids (NAVAIDs)—Prior to commencing construction activity, parking vehicles, or storing construction equipment and materials near a NAVAID, coordinate with the appropriate FAA Air Traffic Organization (ATO)/Technical Operations office to evaluate the effect of construction activity and the required distance and direction from the NAVAID. Construction activities, materials/equipment storage, and vehicle parking near electronic NAVAIDs require special consideration since they may interfere with signals essential to air navigation.
5. Contractor access—The CSPP must detail the areas to which the contractor must have access, and explain how contractor personnel will access those areas.
   a. Location of stockpiled construction materials
   b. Vehicle and pedestrian operations
6. Wildlife management—The CSPP and safety plan compliance documents (SPCD) must be in accordance with the airport operator's wildlife hazard

[2] See Chapter 9 for more information on SRM.

management plan, if applicable. Construction contractors must carefully control and continuously remove waste or loose materials that might attract wildlife.

a. Trash
b. Standing water
c. Tall grass and seeds
d. Poorly maintained fencing and gates
e. Disruption of existing wildlife habitat

7. **Foreign object debris (FOD)** management—Waste and loose materials, commonly referred to as FOD, are capable of causing damage to the aircraft fuselage, landing gears, propellers, and jet engines. Construction contractors must not leave or place FOD on or near active aircraft movement areas.
8. **Hazardous materials (HAZMAT)** management—Contractors operating construction vehicles and equipment on the airport must be prepared to expeditiously contain and clean up spills resulting from fuel or hydraulic fluid leaks. Transport and handling of other hazardous materials on an airport also requires special procedures.
9. Notification of construction activities—The CSPP and SPCD must detail procedures for the immediate notification of airport users and the FAA of any conditions adversely affecting the operational safety of the airport.

   a. Maintenance of a list of responsible representatives/points of contact
   b. Notices to Airmen (NOTAMs)
   c. Emergency notification procedures
   d. Coordination with ARFF personnel
   e. Notification to the FAA

10. Inspection requirements—regular inspections are important during construction activity.

    a. Daily (or more frequent) inspections
    b. Final inspections

11. Underground utilities—The CSPP and/or SPCD must include procedures for locating and protecting existing underground utilities, cables, wires, pipelines, and other underground facilities in excavation areas.
12. Penalties—The CSPP should detail penalty provisions for noncompliance with airport rules and regulations and the safety plans.
13. Special conditions—The CSPP must detail any special conditions that affect the operation of the airport and will require the activation of any special procedures (for example, low-visibility operations, snow removal, aircraft in distress, aircraft accident, security breach, vehicle/pedestrian deviation (VPD), and other activities requiring construction suspension/resumption).
14. Runway and taxiway visual aids—Includes marking, lighting, signs, and visual NAVAIDs. The CSPP must ensure that areas where aircraft will be

operating are clearly and visibly separated from construction areas, including closed runways.

15. NAVAIDs
    a. General
    b. Markings
    c. Lighting and visual NAVAIDs
    d. Signs
16. Marking and signs for access routes—The CSPP should indicate that pavement markings and signs for construction personnel will conform to AC 150/5340-18 and, to the extent practicable, with the Federal Highway Administration Manual on Uniform Traffic Control Devices (MUTCD) and/or state highway specifications.
17. Hazard marking and lighting—Hazardous areas must be properly marked and lighted.
    a. Purpose
    b. Equipment
18. Protection of runway and taxiway safety areas—Protection of these areas includes limitations on the location and height of equipment and stockpiled material. An FAA airspace study may be required. The CSPP should include drawings showing all safety areas, object free areas, obstacle free zones and approach departure surfaces affected by construction.
    a. Runway safety area (RSA)
    b. Runway object free area (ROFA)
    c. Taxiway safety area (TSA)
    d. Taxiway object free area (TOFA)
    e. Obstacle free zone (OFZ)
    f. Runway approach/departure surfaces
19. Other limitations on construction—The CSPP must specify any other limitations on construction.
    a. Prohibitions
    b. Restrictions

    (FAA, 2011a, pp. 9–11)

Additionally, the contractor selected to perform the construction project has a responsibility to develop a **safety plan compliance document (SPCD)**. This document will specifically detail how the contractor will comply with the CSPP. In essence, the SPCD is the contractor's specific plan in response to the CSPP. The details included in such a plan will be reviewed by the airport for approval prior to issuing a notice to proceed (FAA, 2011a).

Even though plans are beneficial, these plans must be practiced to ensure both a safe construction project and a safe airport operating environment. Indeed, everyone has a role in operational safety on airports during construction, including the airport operator, the airport's consultants, the construction contractor and subcontractors, airport users, airport tenants, ARFF personnel, air traffic personnel, FAA Airports Division personnel, and others. It is imperative that all of these parties effectively communicate prior to and during a construction project to ensure a safe operating environment (FAA, 2011a).

The airport is responsible for:

1. Developing a construction safety and phasing plan (CSPP).
2. Reviewing and approving the contractor's safety plan compliance document before issuing a notice to proceed.
3. Coordinating a preconstruction meeting with the construction contractor, consultant, airport employees, FAA personnel and, if appropriate, tenant sponsor and other tenants to review and discuss project safety prior to the commencement of construction activity.
4. Ensuring that contact information is accurate for each representative/point of contact identified in the CSPP and SPCD.
5. Holding weekly or, if necessary, daily safety meetings with all affected parties to coordinate activities.
6. Notifying users, ARFF personnel, and FAA personnel of construction and conditions that may adversely affect the operational safety of the airport via Notices to Airmen (NOTAMs).
7. Ensuring that construction personnel are aware of any applicable airport procedures and changes to those procedures that may affect their work.
8. Ensuring construction contractors and subcontractors undergo training required by the CSPP and SPCD.
9. Ensuring vehicle and pedestrian operations addressed in the CSPP and SPCD are coordinated with airport tenants, the airport traffic control tower (ATCT), and construction contractors.
10. At certificated airports, ensuring each CSPP and SPCD is consistent with 14 CFR Part 139.
11. Conducting regular inspections to ensure construction contractors and tenants are in compliance with the CSPP and SPCD.
12. Resolving safety and/or security deficiencies immediately.
13. Notifying appropriate parties when conditions exist that invoke provisions of the CSPP and SPCD (for example, implementation of low-visibility operations).
14. Ensuring prompt submittal of a Notice of Proposed Construction or Alteration (Form 7460-1).
15. Promptly notifying the FAA Airports Regional or District Office of any proposed changes to the CSPP prior to implementation of the change. Changes to the CSPP require review and approval by the airport operator and the FAA.

   (FAA, 2011a, pp. 3–4)

The contractor also has specific responsibilities. The contractor must:

1. Submit a safety plan compliance document, which describes the manner in which the contractor will comply with the requirements of the CSPP.
2. Have available at all times copies of the CSPP and SPCD for reference by the airport, subcontractors, and contractor employees.
3. Ensure that construction personnel are knowledgeable about safety procedures and regulations on the airport.
4. Identify in the SPCD the contractor's on-site employees responsible for monitoring compliance with the CSPP and SPCD during construction.
5. Conduct frequent inspections to ensure construction personnel comply with the CSPP and SPCD.
6. Prevent construction vehicles and personnel from entering active airport operating areas by providing flagging, barricading, temporary fencing, or escorts.
7. Ensure that Form 7460-1 is timely submitted for any tall equipment (cranes, concrete pumps, other equipment), stock piles, and haul routes, as required by 14 CFR Part 77.

(FAA, 2011a, pp. 4–5)

AIRPORT CONSTRUCTION ACTIVITIES

For all projects, the airport must provide engineering supervision and construction inspection by qualified personnel during all stages of the work. The FAA actually may require the airport to provide written verification that it has reviewed the qualifications of personnel who will be performing these functions (FAA, 2007a).

After the preliminary phase in which the project is conceived and initial planning takes place, the **design phase** begins. The design phase includes all activities required to develop a complete project design, to include development of plans and specifications. FAA Advisory Circular 150/5370-10, *Standards for Specifying Construction of Airports*, spells out general materials and methods used in the construction of airports (FAA, 2011b).

Next, the **construction phase** begins. The construction phase includes all activities required to complete the construction project. Typically, an engineering agreement would include periodic inspection of the work in progress, but the airport would provide a full-time inspector to oversee the project. Alternately, these full-time consulting services may be provided by the consulting engineer under a supplemental agreement. Regardless of whether inspection is performed by a resident engineer or an airport inspector, the following duties are generally expected of this individual (FAA, 2007a):

1. Checks activities to ensure compliance with the plans and specifications and informs the contractor of any work that is in noncompliance.

2. Ensures that all testing required by the specifications is performed.
3. Visits the testing laboratory to determine if it has the equipment and qualified personnel necessary to conduct the tests required by the specifications.
4. Ensures that tests are performed at the frequency stated in the specifications and observes tests.
5. Reviews test reports and certifications for conformance with the specifications.
6. Maintains a file of test reports and certifications.
7. Informs the contractor of deficiencies to allow corrections to be made and retesting performed prior to covering any substandard work with additional material.
8. Documents quantities of materials used on the project by actual measurements and computations.
9. Maintains a set of working drawings on the job site that can be used to prepare "as-built" drawings.
10. Reviews payment requests from the contractor.
11. On a daily basis, maintains record of:
    a. Date and weather conditions.
    b. Names of important visitors.
    c. Construction work in progress, and location.
    d. Size of contractor's work force and equipment in use.
    e. Number of hours worked per day for contractor and subcontractors.
    f. The substance of important conversations with the contractor about conduct, progress, changes, test results, interpretations of specifications, or other details.
12. Submits copies of FAA Form 5370-1, Construction Progress and Inspection Report, to the appropriate FAA Airports Division/District/Field Office upon request.

    (FAA, 2007a, pp. 2–3)

A **change order** may be initiated if changes are needed to a project once the contract has been signed. A change order is a written order to the contractor specifying changes to the plans, specifications, or proposal quantities and establishing the basis for payment and contract time adjustment, if any, for the work affected by the changes. Although change orders often result in increased project costs, they are quite common.

The airport may also temporarily suspend work as deemed necessary due to unsuitable weather or other conditions considered unfavorable for the work to continue, or if the contractor fails to perform any aspect of the contract. Additionally, if the contractor does not complete the project on time by the project deadline, liquidated damages may be deducted from any money due to the contractor. This is not in the form of a penalty, but rather as liquidation of a reasonable portion of damages, such as additional engineering services that may be required as a result of the delayed project completion.

Additionally, the contractor will be considered in default of the contract, leading to termination of the contract, for any of the following reasons—if the contractor:

1. Fails to begin the work under the contract within the time specified in the "Notice to Proceed"
2. Fails to perform the work or fails to provide sufficient workers, equipment or materials to assure completion of work in accordance with the terms of the contract
3. Performs the work unsuitably or neglects or refuses to remove materials or to perform anew such work as may be rejected as unacceptable and unsuitable
4. Discontinues the prosecution of the work
5. Fails to resume work which has been discontinued within a reasonable time after notice to do so
6. Becomes insolvent or is declared bankrupt, or commits any act of bankruptcy or insolvency
7. Allows any final judgment to stand against him unsatisfied for a period of 10 days
8. Makes an assignment for the benefit of creditors
9. For any other cause whatsoever, fails to carry on the work in an acceptable manner.

(FAA, 2011b, pp. 46–47)

Design Standards

AC 5300-13 AIRPORT DESIGN

FAA Advisory Circular (AC) 150/5300-13A, *Airport Design*, is the main AC that applies to the design of airports. This is clearly one of the most technical ACs in the Part 150—Airport series. This lengthy 322-page AC is divided into the following chapters:

1. Introduction
2. Design Process
3. Runway Design
4. Taxiway and Taxilane Design
5. Aprons
6. Navigation Aids and On-Airport Air Traffic Control Facilities
7. Airfield Bridges and Tunnels.

(FAA, 2014)

To know which specific design criteria apply to a specific airport, the **design aircraft** must first be determined. The design aircraft represents the most demanding aircraft (in terms of tail height, wingspan, approach speeds, width of aircraft main gear, and distance from the cockpit to the main gear) that is intended to be accommodated by the airport. Airports with multiple runways designate a design aircraft for each runway, which may or may not be the same aircraft type.

Technically, the design aircraft designation is actually driven by three parameters:

- Aircraft Approach Category (AAC)
- Airplane Design Group (ADG)
- Visibility minimums
- Taxiway Design Group (TDG)

The **Aircraft Approach Category (AAC)** relates to aircraft approach speed (operational characteristics) (see Table 5-1).

Table 5-1. Aircraft approach categories.

AAC	Approach Speed
A	Approach speed less than 91 knots
B	Approach speed 91 knots or more but less than 121 knots
C	Approach speed 121 knots or more but less than 141 knots
D	Approach speed 141 knots or more but less than 166 knots
E	Approach speed 166 knots or more

The **Airplane Design Group (ADG)** relates to either the aircraft wingspan or tail height (physical characteristics), whichever is most restrictive, of the largest aircraft expected to operate on the runway and taxiways (see Table 5-2).

Table 5-2. Airplane design groups.

ADG	Tail Height (in feet)	Wingspan (in feet)
I	Less than 20'	Less than 49'
II	20' to less than 30'	49' to less than 79'
III	30' to less than 45'	79' to less than 118'
IV	45' to less than 60'	118' to less than 171'
V	60' to less than 66'	171' to less than 214'
VI	66' to less than 80'	214' to less than 262'

The visibility minimums refers to visibility expressed by runway visual range (RVR) values. Visual runways do not have visibility minimums, indicated by VIS. See Table 5-3.

Table 5-3. Visibility minimums.

RVR (in feet)	Instrument Flight Visibility Category (in statute miles)
5000	Not lower than 1 mile
4000	Lower than 1 mile but not lower than 3/4 mile
2400	Lower than 3/4 mile but not lower than 1/2 mile
1600	Lower than 1/2 mile but not lower than 1/4 mile
1200	Lower than 1/4 mile

The **Taxiway Design Group (TDG)** relates to the undercarriage dimensions of the aircraft. Taxiway/taxilane width and fillet standards, and in some instances, runway to taxiway and taxiway/taxilane separation requirements, are determined by TDG. In application, the TDG will affect the taxiway width, taxiway edge safety margin, and taxiway should width, among other dimensions.

Generally, runway standards are related to aircraft approach speed, aircraft wingspan, and designated or planned approach visibility minimums. Runway to taxiway and taxiway/taxilane to taxiway/taxilane separation standards are related to ADG, TDG, and approach visibility minimums.

The selected AAC, ADG, and approach visibility minimums are combined to form the **runway design code (RDC)** of a particular runway. The RDC provides the information needed to determine certain design standards that apply in each situation. The RDC is a combination of the three components presented above, presented in an AAC-ADG-Vis fashion. For example, an airport's air carrier runway may have an RDC of C-IV-1200. The same airport's smaller runway used for general aviation activity may have an RDC of B-II-2400.

It should be noted that although AC 150/5300-13A presents the standards for airport design, an airport is allowed to request a "**modification to standards**." In essence, local conditions may require modification to airport design standards for a specific airport. The request for modification must show that the modification will provide an acceptable level of safety, economy, durability, and workmanship. An example would be a request to allow a Group VI aircraft (Airbus 380) to operate at a Group V airport (Figure 5-3). Although the FAA has granted a modification to standards for some airports in this same situation, not all requests are approved (FAA, 2014).

Figure 5-3. A380 taxiing.

(Nan Phanitsuda Sophonpanasak, Denver International Airport)

RUNWAY LAYOUTS AND DESIGN

Crucial to the efficiency and safety of any airport is the layout and configuration of runways. According to the FAA (1989, p. 9), "runway location and orientation are paramount to airport safety, efficiency, economics, and environmental impact." The layout and configuration of runways depends upon:

1. Wind
2. Airspace availability
3. Environmental factors
4. Obstructions to air navigation
5. Topography
6. Air traffic control tower visibility
7. Wildlife hazards

(FAA, 2014)

Although there are numerous single-runway airports (including GA and some commercial service), an additional runway may be justified in the following circumstances:

1. Operational demands—When traffic volume exceeds the runway's operational capability
2. Wind conditions—If an existing runway provides less than 95 percent wind coverage, a crosswind runway is recommended. This 95 percent wind coverage is based on the crosswind not exceeding 10.5 knots for ARC A-I and B-I, 13 knots for A-II and B-II, 16 knots for A-III, B-III, and C-I through D-III, and 20 knots for A-IV through D-VI. In essence, the most desirable

orientation of runways based on wind is the one which has the largest wind coverage and minimum crosswind components.

3. Environmental impacts—An additional runway may be necessary to divert air traffic from environmentally sensitive areas.

   (FAA, 2014)

Airports with more than one runway oftentimes have parallel runways. Separation criteria exist specifically for parallel runways. For simultaneous landings and takeoffs using visual flight rules, the minimum separation between centerlines of parallel runways is 700 feet. For Airplane Design Group V and VI runways, this minimum separation increases to 1,200 feet.[3] For approaches under instrument flight rules, the minimum separation standards between parallel runways increase significantly. Dual simultaneous instrument approaches normally require 4,300 feet separation between centerlines of parallel runways. It is possible that an airport may receive approval on a unique basis with only 3,000 feet separation between parallel runway centerlines, if the 4,300 feet is impractical; however, this would require special radar, monitoring equipment, etc. Triple simultaneous instrument approaches for airports below 1,000 feet elevation require parallel runway centerline separation of 5,000 feet. For departures, the standards are less strict. For simultaneous nonradar departures, a parallel runway centerline separation of at least 3,500 feet is required. Simultaneous radar departures require a parallel runway centerline separation of at least 2,500 feet. Generally, airports with terminal buildings constructed between parallel runways (such as Tampa International Airport) exceed these minimums. Additionally, these airports benefit users as taxiing across active runways is either minimized or possibly completely eliminated (FAA, 2014).

Separation criteria also exist between a runway and parallel taxiway or taxilane. These criteria are designed to satisfy the requirement that no part of an aircraft on a taxiway or taxilane centerline penetrate the runway safety area or the obstacle free zone (OFZ) and are specified in AC 150/5300-13A.

AC 150/5300-13A also contains various object clearing criteria. It is necessary for certain areas both on and near the airport to be clear of objects or restricted to certain objects that meet specific criteria. Areas that have specific object clearing criteria include the object free area, runway and taxiway safety areas, obstacle free zone, threshold, NAVAIDs, Part 77 obstructions, and runway protection zone (RPZ). The RPZ is specifically designed to enhance the protection of people and property on the ground, which is most effectively achieved with ownership and control over RPZs (FAA, 2012).

The specific criteria applied to the design of runways varies, based on the airplane design group and the needs of the airport. For instance, consider runway length. What is appropriate for one airport may not be appropriate for another airport. FAA Advisory Circular 150/5325-4, *Runway Length Requirements for*

[3] Runways with centerline spacings less than 2,500 feet are treated as a single runway by ATC when wake turbulence is a factor.

Airport Design, and aircraft flight manuals provide guidance on runway lengths. Likewise, runway widths vary (FAA, 2005b).

Runway shoulders provide resistance to blast erosion and accommodate the passage of maintenance and emergency equipment and the occasional passage of an airplane veering from the runway. **Runway blast pads** provide blast erosion protection beyond runway ends. The **runway safety area (RSA)** is centered on the runway centerline and graded to have no potentially hazardous ruts, humps, depressions, or other surface variations. It is also drained by grading or storm sewers to prevent water accumulation and capable, under dry conditions, of supporting snow removal equipment, aircraft rescue and firefighting equipment, and the occasional passage of aircraft without causing structural damage to the aircraft. The RSA must also be free of objects, except for objects that need to be located in the runway safety area because of their function. Objects higher than 3 inches above grade must be constructed on frangible mounts with the frangible point no higher than 3 inches above grade.

In addition, the **obstacle free zone (OFZ)** clearing standard precludes taxiing and parked airplanes and object penetrations, except for frangible visual NAVAIDs that need to be located in the OFZ because of their function. The runway OFZ and, when applicable, the precision OFZ, the inner-approach OFZ, and the inner-transitional OFZ comprise the obstacle free zone. The runway OFZ is a defined volume of airspace centered above the runway centerline. The inner-approach OFZ is a defined volume of airspace centered on the approach area. It applies only to runways with an approach lighting system. The inner-transitional OFZ is a defined volume of airspace along the sides of the runway OFZ and inner-approach OFZ. It applies only to runways with lower than 3/4-statute mile approach visibility minimums. The precision obstacle free zone (POFZ) is defined as a volume of airspace above an area beginning at the runway threshold, at the threshold elevation, and centered on the extended runway centerline, 200 feet long by 800 feet wide.

The **runway object free area (ROFA)** is centered on the runway centerline. The ROFA clearing standard requires clearing the ROFA of above-ground objects protruding above the runway safety area edge elevation. Except where precluded by other clearing standards, it is acceptable to place objects that need to be located in the ROFA for air navigation or aircraft ground maneuvering purposes and to taxi and hold aircraft in the ROFA. The **clearway** is a clearly defined area connected to and extending beyond the runway end available for completion of the takeoff operation of turbine-powered airplanes. A clearway increases the allowable airplane operating takeoff weight without increasing runway length. A **stopway** is an area beyond the takeoff runway, centered on the extended runway centerline, and designated by the airport owner for use in decelerating an airplane during an aborted takeoff. It must be at least as wide as the runway and able to support an airplane during an aborted takeoff without causing structural damage to the airplane (FAA, 2012).

TAXIWAY LAYOUTS

Typically, taxiways do not receive the same level of attention as runways. They do not endure the loads that runways do, nor are they part of the critical arrival and departure phases of flight. Yet, as runway traffic increases, the capacity of the taxiway system can become a limiting operational factor. The goal of the taxiway system is to provide for free movement of aircraft to and from the runways, terminals, cargo areas, hangars, GA areas, and remote parking areas. Well-designed taxiways enable aircraft to maintain a smooth flow with a minimum number of points requiring a change in the airplane's taxiing speed.

General taxiway design principles include to:

1. provide each runway with a parallel taxiway or the capability therefore;
2. build taxiways as direct as possible;
3. provide bypass capability or multiple access to runway ends;
4. minimize crossing runways;
5. provide ample curve and fillet radii;
6. provide airport traffic control tower line of sight; and
7. avoid traffic bottlenecks.

(FAA, 2014, p. 10)

Taxiways benefit from having stabilized or paved shoulders, as this reduces the possibility of blast erosion and engine ingestion problems associated with jet engines that overhang the edge of the taxiway pavement. Similar to runways, taxiways have safety areas that are designed to support snow removal equipment, aircraft rescue and firefighting equipment, and the occasional passage of aircraft without causing structural damage to the aircraft. Taxiways also have object free areas which prohibit vehicle service roads, parked airplanes, and above ground objects, except for objects that need to be located in the OFA for air navigation or aircraft ground maneuvering purposes (FAA, 2012).

Specifically, AC 150/5300-13A specifies that airports consider the **taxiway design group (TDG)** in the design of taxiways. The TDG is a classification of airplanes related to the undercarriage dimensions of aircraft. Specifically, this is based on outer-to-outer main gear width, as well as cockpit-to-main gear distance. Taxiway/taxilane width and fillet standards, and in some instances, runway-to-taxiway and taxiway/taxilane separation requirements, are determined by TDG.

Unique to taxiways, intersections require the pilot to negotiate a turn either by maintaining the cockpit over the taxiway centerline or by using judgmental oversteering. **Cockpit over centerline steering** is preferred, but this method requires more pavement at taxiway intersections (see Figure 5-4). This method allows the pilot to simply keep the aircraft nose gear on the taxiway centerline, assured that the main gear will not leave the pavement, even in turns. **Judgmental oversteering**, on the other hand, requires less pavement but is a

Figure 5-4. Cockpit over centerline steering, with the taxiway centerline on the curve for intersections with sufficient pavement width to avoid wide turns by aircraft. (FAA)

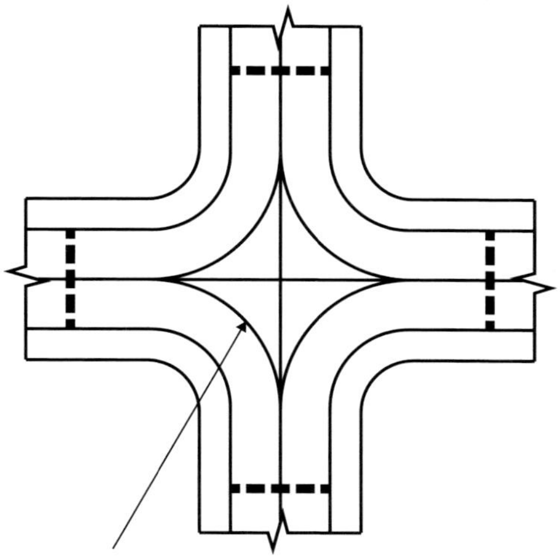

Figure 5-5. Judgmental oversteering, with the taxiway centerline not on the curve, indicating insufficient pavement width requiring a wider turn by aircraft to avoid main gear from leaving the pavement. (FAA)

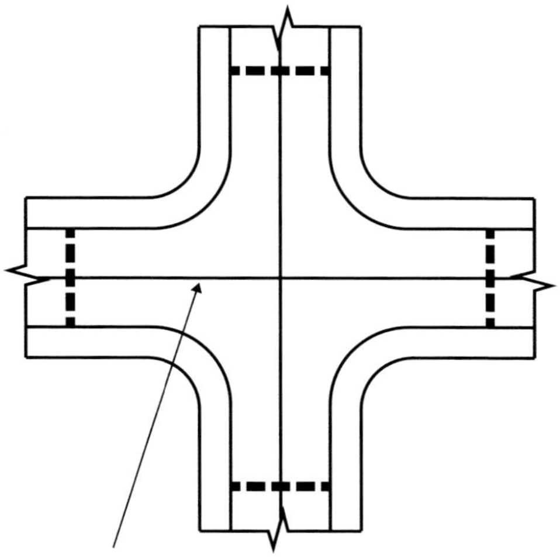

complex method, increasing the risk of an aircraft excursion from the pavement surface and considerably slowing down the flow of traffic (see Figure 5-5). Pilots must swing wide in turns (similar to tractor trailer rigs and their wide right turns) to avoid the main gear from leaving the pavement in turns (FAA, 2012).

Similar to entrance taxiways, **exit taxiways** are often designed at a right angle to the runway. However, during the process of slowing down an aircraft to exit the runway at a right-angle, the length of time an aircraft remains on the runway increases, thus effectively increasing runway occupancy time (ROT). When ROT increases, the capacity of the runway is actually reduced. Thus, many airports have developed "high-speed exit" taxiways, more appropriately referred to as **acute-angled exit taxiways**. The purpose of a high-speed exit is to reduce ROT, which enhances airport capacity. The high-speed exit requires at least 600 feet of separation between the runway and taxiway, as well as the installation of more pavement. The standard angle of a high-speed exit is 30 degrees (see Figure 5-6) (FAA, 2012).

Figure 5-6. High-speed taxiway exit.

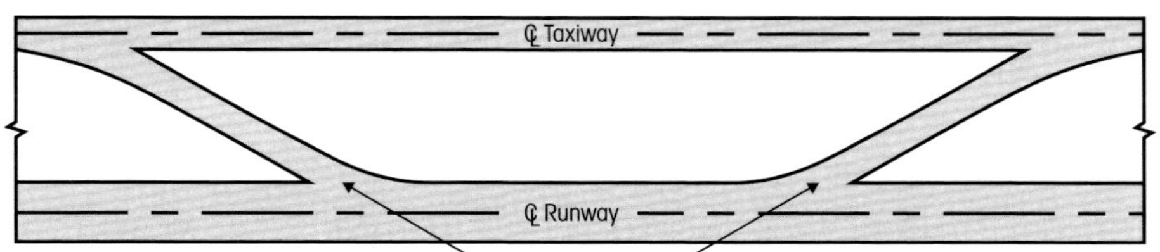

Another recent innovation in taxiway design is the **end-around taxiway**. These taxiways are designed to allow aircraft to safely move around the departure or approach end of a runway, and to do so without requiring ATC authorization and without incurring delays while waiting to cross an active runway. Although there are specific standards associated with the construction of an end-around taxiway (including the installation of a visual screen to prevent pilots of departing aircraft from mistaking an aircraft on an end-around taxiway as being on the active runway), the benefits in safety and reduced delays often justify these costs (FAA, 2014).

End-Around Taxiway

In 2007, Hartsfield-Jackson Atlanta International Airport was the first airport in the nation to construct an end-around taxiway. This new taxiway "V" allowed arriving aircraft landing on Runway 26R to taxi to the passenger terminal complex without having to cross Runway 26L, as was the case in the past. Aircraft can also depart on Runway 26L without incurring delays created by the Runway 26R arrivals crossing the runway. This end-around taxiway has resulted in an increased Runway 26L departure rate, which has increased the efficiency of the airfield and reduced the risk of runway incursions.

GRADIENT AND LINE OF SIGHT

AC 150/5300-13A presents criteria for surface gradient and line of sight. The maximum longitudinal (length of runway) gradient for aircraft approach categories A and B is ±2 percent. For C and D aircraft approach categories, the maximum longitudinal gradient is ±1.5 percent, although this grade may not exceed ±0.8 percent in the first and last quarter of the runway. For aircraft approach category C and D runways, transverse grade (across the runway width) limitations range from 1 to 1.5 percent for the runway width, to 1.5 to 5 percent on the shoulder, and 1.5 to 3 percent on the runway safety area. To ensure adequate line of sight along a runway, any two points five feet above the runway centerline should be mutually visible for the entire length of the runway. If, however, the runway has an associated full-length parallel taxiway, it is sufficient to provide an unobstructed line of sight from any point five feet above the runway centerline to any other point five feet above the runway centerline for one-half the runway length. Further, a clear line of sight between the ends of intersecting runways is recommended. For taxiways, no line-of-sight criteria exist. However, the sight distance along a runway from an intersecting taxiway should be sufficient to allow a taxiing aircraft to safely enter or cross the runway (FAA, 2014).

PAVEMENT DESIGN

There are two main types of airport pavements: flexible and rigid. **Rigid pavements** normally use Portland cement concrete (PCC) as the prime structural element. Depending on conditions, engineers may design the PCC pavement slab with plain, lightly reinforced, continuously reinforced, prestressed, or fibrous concrete. The PCC pavement slab usually lies on a compacted granular or treated subbase, which in turn is supported by a compacted subgrade (see Figure 5-7). The subbase provides uniform stable support and may provide subsurface drainage. The PCC pavement slab has considerable flexural strength and spreads the applied loads over a large area (FAA, 2007a).

Flexible pavements, on the other hand, support loads through bearing rather than flexural action. They comprise several layers of carefully selected materials designed to gradually distribute loads from the pavement surface to the layers underneath (see Figure 5-8). The design ensures the load transmitted to each successive layer does not exceed the layer's load-bearing capacity.

Figure 5-7. Typical rigid pavement structure.

(ACE Operations, AAAE)

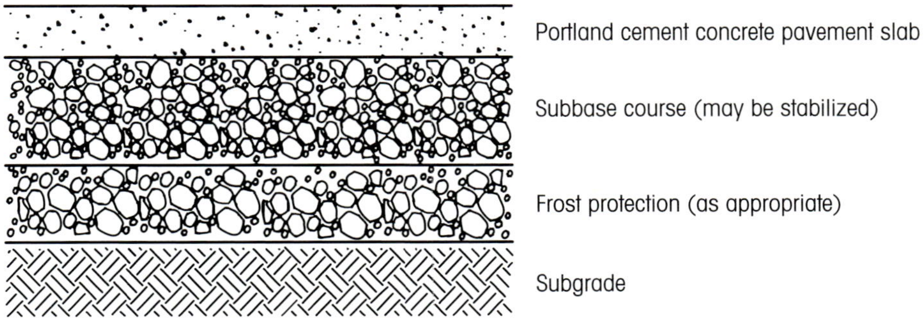

Figure 5-8. Typical flexible pavement structure.

(ACE Operations, AAAE)

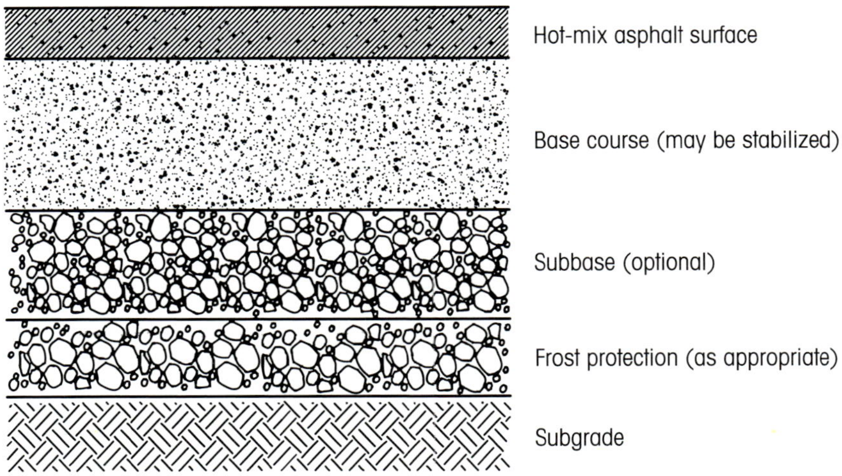

Airports may also utilize pavement overlays. Airport **pavement overlays** may correct deteriorating pavement surfaces, improve ride quality or surface drainage, maintain structural integrity, or increase pavement strength. Overlays are used when a pavement is damaged by overloading, requires strengthening to serve heavier aircraft, shows severe ponding because of uneven settling, or simply has served its design life and is worn out. Airport pavement overlays generally consist of either PCC or hot-mix asphalt (HMA) pavements, and the resulting pavement system may be classified as either rigid or flexible for load-support purposes (FAA, 2007a).

RUNWAY AND TAXIWAY BRIDGES

Airports are often presented with significant obstacles when constructing or extending a runway or taxiway. Occasionally, these obstacles are in the form of an existing roadway or railroad that cannot be closed or re-routed. One option to overcome such an obstacle is to construct a runway or taxiway bridge over the roadway or railroad (see Figure 5-9). It is important that taxiway bridges are installed on straight portions of taxiways and away from taxiway intersections or angled taxiway exits. The recommended width of the full-strength bridge structure is the width of the runway or taxiway plus safety area. Bridges should be capable of supporting both static and dynamic loads imposed by the heaviest aircraft expected to use the structure. Each bridge should have three equally-spaced obstruction lights on each side; chevrons spaced 25 feet apart on the shoulders; and taxiway centerline lights or centerline reflectors, taxiway edge lights or reflectors, and taxiway edge markings (FAA, 2014).

Figure 5-9. Taxiway bridge.

TERMINAL LAYOUTS

Without a passenger terminal, passengers would have no means to transfer from ground transportation to the aircraft. Therefore, a passenger terminal is crucial, even at small GA airports. In reality, airport passenger terminal buildings provide many services to meet the needs of passengers, tenants, meeters and greeters, and airport administration. These services include passenger check-in, baggage claim, security screening, international passenger processing, waiting areas, transfers between flights, and concessions (including food and beverage, retail, rental cars, etc.). Although a number of these services are common to all commercial-service airports, airports have unique characteristics regarding their service area, passengers, airlines, aircraft mix, and services. Therefore, a terminal layout that is appropriate for one airport may not be appropriate for another. Although there is no "one size fits all" terminal, there are specific terminal designs in use today (FAA, 2014).

The selection of a terminal building site depends on several factors. Obviously, the terminal, once constructed, should not interfere with any safety areas or 14 CFR Part 77 surfaces. Preferably, the ATCT should continue to have an unobstructed view of runways and taxiways. Otherwise, the ATCT will request any areas that are not visible to the ATCT tower cab to be designated non-movement areas. The airport's runway configuration also has a significant impact on the terminal site. The site should allow for ease of access by aircraft utilizing the main runways. Additionally, a terminal must be spaced sufficiently from an adjacent terminal to allow simultaneous pushback of aircraft from opposing gates.

There are five basic configurations of passenger terminal buildings in use today. They are:

- Simple linear terminal
- Finger piers
- Satellites with and without finger piers
- Midfield, either linear or X-shaped
- Transporter

(de Neufville and Odoni, 2003)

Linear with One Airside

At small airports with the need for only a few gates, a **simple linear terminal** is sufficient. With this configuration, aircraft are parked on one side of the terminal, while on the other side, parking for automobiles is provided (see Figure 5-10). This configuration is very convenient for passengers. Once parked and inside the terminal, passengers check in and then simply walk out the other side of the building to board the aircraft. The terminal may have loading bridges or simply require passengers to board an aircraft from stairs on the ramp. At larger airports, a linear terminal may be lengthened to accommodate dozens of gates

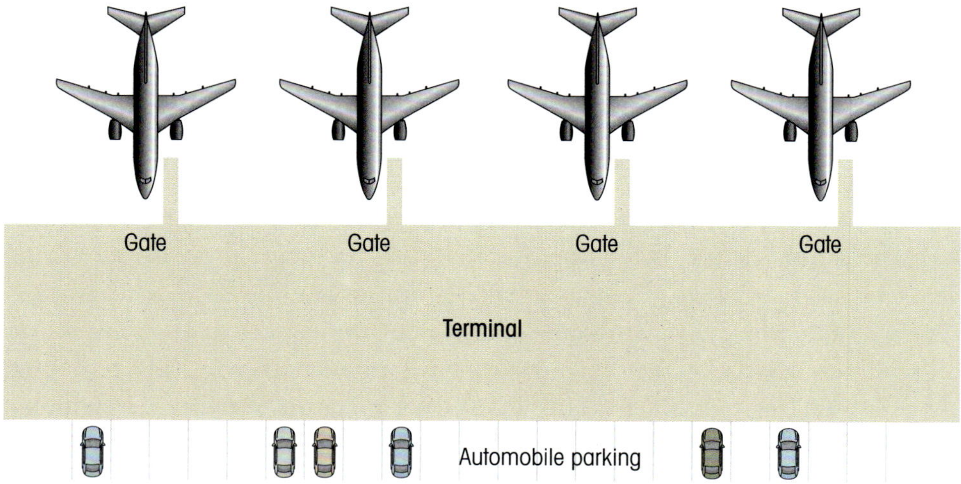

Figure 5-10.
Simple linear terminal.

with loading bridges. With this configuration, walking distances are increased as passengers must enter the terminal building through one of only several entrance points, process through a centrally located area, and then walk to the required gate. At some airports, the linear concept has been applied to a curved building to provide more architectural appeal (de Neufville and Odoni, 2003).

Finger Piers

Finger pier terminals are created by adding extensions to a linear terminal building. When viewed from the air, these terminal buildings resemble fingers attached to the palm of a hand (see Figure 5-11). One form of a finger pier places aircraft gates on both sides of the fingers extending from the linear core. This arrangement places more gates closer to the linear core and thus in a more convenient location for passengers than the gates located at the end of the finger pier. Another possible form of a finger pier widens the end of each finger to form a "T". In this arrangement, the crosspiece of the "T" normally serves as a small central core. Although there are some advantages with this arrangement (such as the possibility of shared waiting areas), by placing a significant number of aircraft and passengers away from the central part of the main terminal building, passenger walking distances are increased. First introduced during the 1950s, finger piers were the standard terminal configuration for several decades (de Neufville and Odoni, 2003).

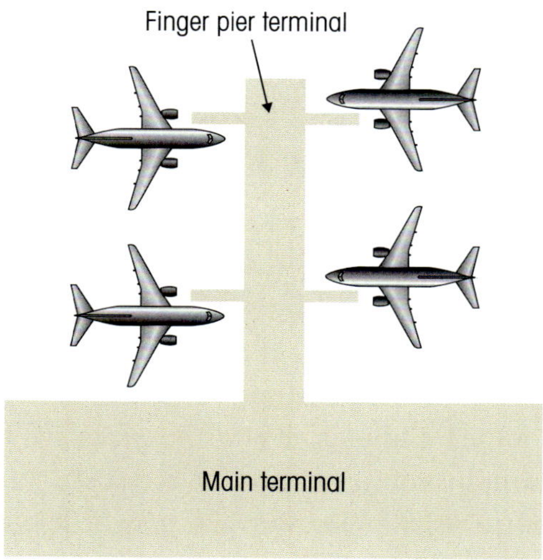

Figure 5-11.
Finger pier terminal.

Satellites with and without Finger Piers

Satellite passenger terminals concentrate aircraft gates at the end of either a finger pier (which may be above or below ground) or a people mover (which also may be above or below ground) (see Figure 5-12). If the satellite passenger terminal is at the end of a finger pier, it resembles a larger T-shaped finger pier. An advantage of satellite terminals that have an underground connection to the main terminal lies in the efficiency with which aircraft are able to freely maneuver around the entire satellite terminal. When the satellite terminal is connected to the main terminal via a people-mover system (as is the case at Orlando International Airport and Tampa International Airport), passenger walking distances are greatly minimized (de Neufville and Odoni, 2003).

Figure 5-12.
Satellite terminals.

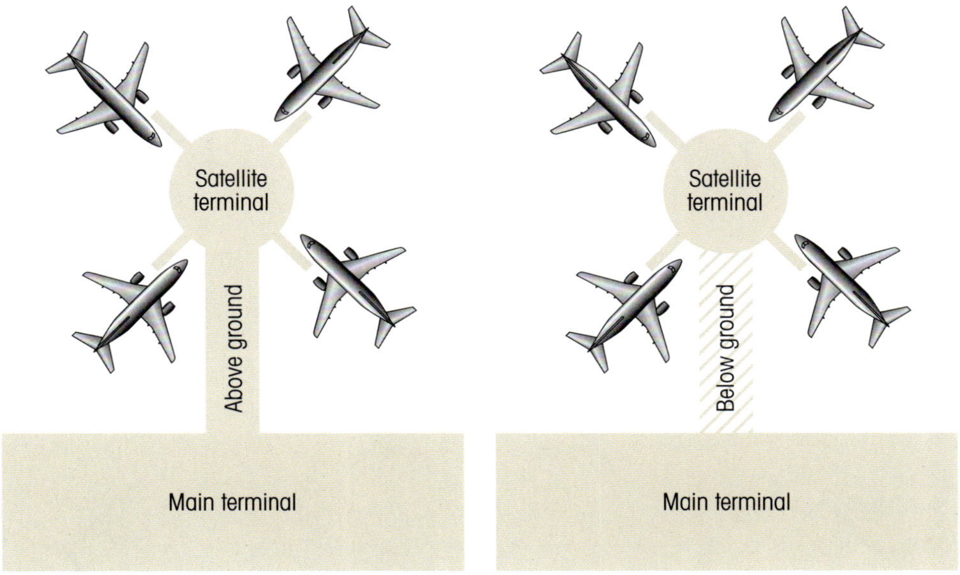

Midfield, Either Linear or X-shaped

Midfield passenger terminals are independent passenger buildings generally located far from the main passenger building which passengers initially access from the landside. A midfield terminal is a major terminal that may contain 50 or more aircraft gates. Midfield terminals are typically located between two parallel runways and separated from other terminal buildings by taxiways. Because of the distance that needs to be covered by passengers to access a midfield terminal, self-propelled people movers (in the form of shuttle cars, monorail, subway, moving walkways, etc.) are provided for passenger convenience (de Neufville and Odoni, 2003).

Midfield terminals can be of the linear design or the X-shaped design. Linear concourses are long buildings with aircraft gates on both sides of the building (see Figure 5-13). This configuration may be wider in the middle to accommodate a people-mover station, as well as concessions. Both Hartsfield-Jackson International Airport and Denver International Airport have linear midfield terminals. X-shaped midfield terminals (in use at Pittsburg International Airport, for instance) feature intersecting fingers that appear as an X-shape (see Figure 5-14). This design is useful when space is limited, as the same number of aircraft gates can be accommodated when, in essence, two shorter linear midfield terminals are intersected in an X-shape (de Neufville and Odoni, 2003).

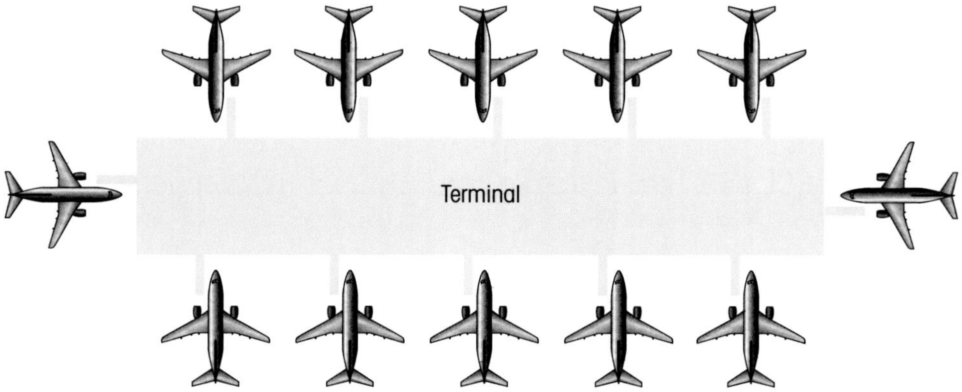

Figure 5-13. Linear midfield terminal.

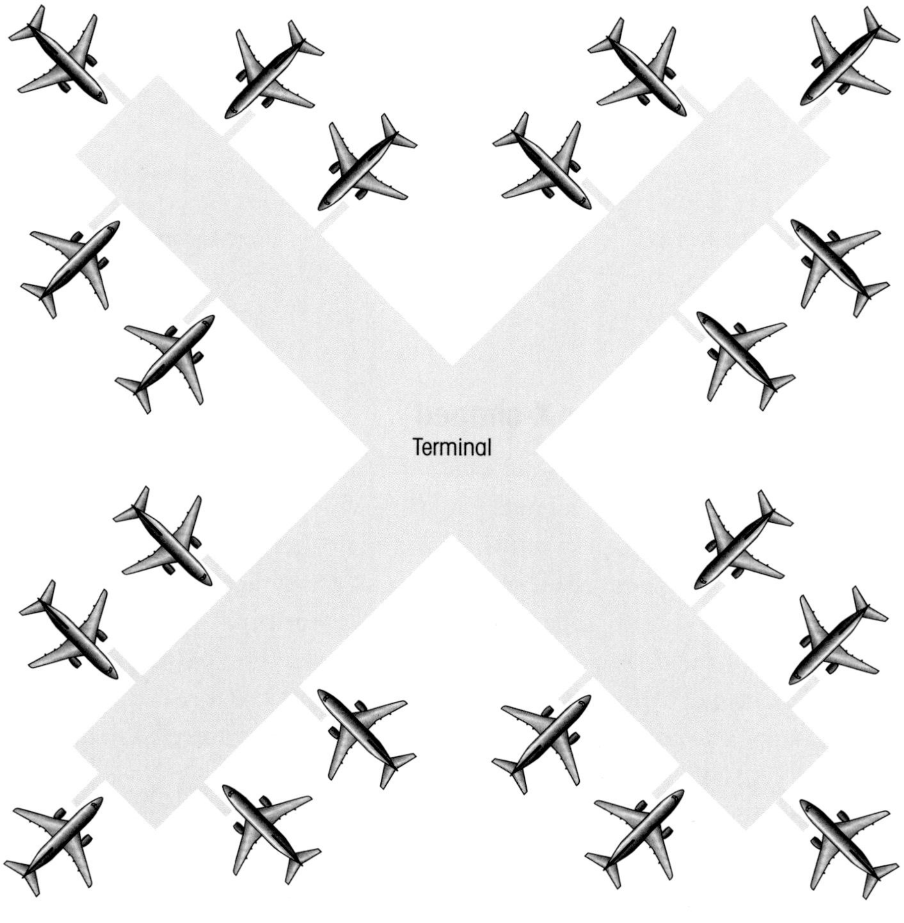

Figure 5-14. X-shaped midfield terminal.

Transporter

Rather than being a specific terminal configuration, **transporters** refers to the category of rubber-tired vehicles that move passengers between passenger buildings and aircraft (see Figure 5-15). Typically, these are buses with low platforms and wide aisles that allow easy access for passengers with baggage. Although many of these buses require passengers to walk up and down stairs leading to the aircraft, buses also exist that lift the entire unit up to aircraft height to allow passengers to walk directly from the aircraft to the bus and vice versa. These units with lifting capability are known as lift lounges and can carry 80 to 100 passengers in conditioned comfort safe from the elements. Regardless of whether lift lounges or more traditional buses are used, they can be expensive to acquire and operate/maintain, require skilled drivers capable of driving on the aprons, and place a small group of skilled drivers in a position to interrupt airport operations if they choose to strike due to unmet needs (de Neufville and Odoni, 2003).

The specific terminal configuration chosen will be driven by airport and tenant (airline) needs, which is greatly affected by passenger mix and the specific needs of the majority passenger groups. Although the needs of domestic passengers, international passengers, business passengers, and leisure passengers all deserve consideration in the design of a new terminal building, the group perhaps deserving the greatest consideration is transfer passengers. Transfer passengers need the ability to make fast, reliable, and easy-to-find connections between aircraft, which requires unique considerations in the terminal design process. Transfer passengers also have little need for check-in facilities, baggage claim areas, or ground transportation options. The distinct needs of transfer passengers should dominate the passenger terminal design process if transfer passengers make up 50 percent or more of the total passengers at an airport. Additional considerations include passenger walking distances, aircraft taxiing and maneuvering around terminal buildings, flexibility to support future growth, and economics (de Neufville and Odoni, 2003).

Figure 5-15. Parked transporters at Philadelphia International Airport.

GROUND ACCESS

Integral to the success of an airport, adequate and efficient ground access is beneficial to passengers, commercial ground operators, employees, vendors, tenants, and others accessing the airport. Formally, airport traffic has three major components:

- Originating and terminating passengers
- Employees
- Supply, delivery, and other commercial vehicles

  (de Neufville and Odoni, 2003)

Although it is often assumed that passengers make up the majority of airport traffic, each of these three groups in fact accounts for at least 20 percent of total trips to the airport. In essence, airport passengers represent only one component of the airport access problem. The general consensus is that only a small portion of traffic to and from an airport can be traced to any specific destination. Most of an airport's ground traffic spreads out over a wide area. In fact, only a small percentage of traffic can be traced back to the city center. Regardless, the trip to the airport can oftentimes be the most annoying part of the trip to/from the airport and has become known as the "**airport access problem**" (de Neufville and Odoni, 2003).

The irony of the airport access problem is that while the congestion caused by automobile traffic is problematic, resulting in increased automobile wait times and curbside congestion, the parking revenues generated by this traffic accounts for a substantial component of the revenue stream at commercial service airports, possibly accounting for \$50–100 million or more on an annual basis. Los Angeles World Airports, for example, earned \$84.3 million in auto parking revenues during FY2012. Thus, airports have learned to better manage the demand created by automobile traffic, whether representing passengers, employees, or supply/delivery vehicles. Many airports now offer the first 30–60 minutes free in short-term parking simply to move automobile traffic from the curbside to the garage. Others have constructed cell phone lots, which allow meeters and greeters the opportunity to stay abreast of flight arrival times in their automobiles, and then drive to the curbside for passenger pickup at the appropriate time. Actively managing the curb is also a priority at many airports. By placing a maximum on curbside dwell time, traffic specialists or police officers actively move vehicles from the curb to minimize congestion and increase the number of vehicles able to access the curb at any given time. Although this could be implemented at the ticket counter curbside, it is most utilized at baggage claim curbside areas, because the baggage claim curbside tends to have much higher curbside dwell time as meeters and greeters arrive early for arriving passengers and simply wait in their vehicles—effectively creating a short-term parking area at the curbside (de Neufville and Odoni, 2003; LAWA, 2012).

Although highways provide the dominant mode of airport access, mass transit may be adopted to partially solve the airport access problem. Whether this is in the form of intercity buses, subway, or high-speed rail, by bringing groups of passengers and employees to and from the airport in larger numbers, the number of trips by individual vehicles will be substantially reduced. For many individuals, however, automotive vehicles provide the best value for the money, especially when considering convenience. Therefore, even cities that have well-developed mass transit systems must consider the vehicular traffic aspect of the ground access problem. It is most effective for airports to consider a multi-pronged approach toward solving the ground access problems at airports. This may involve mass transit, active curbside management, and cell phone lots, among other solutions (de Neufville and Odoni, 2003).

COMMON-USE FACILITIES

Many airports must now consider how to meet the needs of various tenants, including airlines, within their existing terminal space. By adopting the **common-use** philosophy, airports can effectively increase airport capacity without constructing any additional gates, terminals, or check-in areas. Airports accomplish this by more effectively utilizing existing space. Although gaining in popularity, common-use remains a relatively innovative concept among U.S. airports (Belliotti, 2008).

In essence, common-use allows an airport to take space that was once used exclusively by a single airline and make that space available to multiple airlines, based on demand. Although there may still be a need for exclusive-use areas, by transitioning exclusive-use areas to common-use areas, the airport can actively manage capacity to meet demand, including providing sufficient space for flight diversions and charter operations (Belliotti, 2008).

The four degrees of common-use appear below:

1. Exclusive use
2. Mixed use
3. Preferential use
4. Common-use

(Belliotti, 2008, p. 8).

An airport adopting the **exclusive use** approach allows airlines to exclusively lease space, including gates, ticket counters, and baggage claim devices as well as office areas. This arrangement is preferred by airlines with substantial operations at an airport, as it allows for a high degree of airline control, allows for "branding" of space, and limits competitors. However, it often results in underutilized spaces and can deter new entrant airlines, especially if not enough space is available for a new carrier. Passengers generally prefer this approach as they can easily locate their airline of choice. Airports with this approach may require airlines to fully utilize their exclusive leased areas with the airport retaining the right to capture gates and other spaces not being fully utilized so as to make them available for other carriers (Belliotti, 2008).

Common-Use Technology at Fresno Yosemite International Airport

Fresno Yosemite International Airport in California needed to expand to meet growing passenger demand, but preferred to avoid the estimated $30 million required for a terminal expansion. Instead, the airport adopted common-use technology at a cost of only $3 million. This technology is greatly enhancing flexibility, allowing for more efficient utilization of existing terminal space. Specifically, the new technology will allow the airport the ability to place the nine airlines currently serving the airport into approximately half the physical terminal space, creating room for expansion without actually expanding the physical space in the terminal. The common-use technology includes the installation of the common-use system, a multi-user flight information display system (MUFIDS) and five years of technical support. Each airline agent will have the ability to log into any workstation with direct connection to the host system at the corporate headquarters. Each 2 of the 40 check-in positions will also share a 47-inch plasma screen on the wall, which will reflect that airline's logo to make it easy for passengers to find their preferred airline (Richards, 2008).

At the other end of the continuum is the common-use approach. With this approach, all usable airport space may be used by any airline serving that airport. There is no exclusive use space whatsoever. The main objective with common-use is to minimize the amount of time any airport resource is not used, thereby maximizing the full use of the airport. Common-use may be applied to aircraft gates, ticket counters, waiting/holding areas, ground handling, paging systems, access control, building systems, information displays, etc. The prevalent types of common-use technology include:

- Networking—both wired and wireless
- Passenger paging systems
- Telephone systems
- Multi-user flight information display systems (MUFIDS)
- Multi-user baggage information display systems (MUBIDS)
- Resource and gate management
- Common-use terminal equipment (CUTE)
- Common-use self-service kiosks (CUSS) (Figure 5-16)
- Local departure control system (LDCS)
- Airport operational database (AODB)
- Common-use baggage sorting systems
- Baggage reconciliation

(Belliotti, 2008)

Figure 5-16. Common-use self-service kiosk (CUSS).

Common-use terminal equipment allows for any airline to use the same computer terminal (see Figure 5-17). Common-use allows an airport to maximize efficient use of airport space, but it does require high upfront investment in the technology required to have common-use areas. Generally, this investment is recouped with long term per passenger savings and reduced need for staff and future facility expansion. Passengers can benefit from common-use approaches if dynamic signage is changed to note airline locations. Check-in kiosks that utilize common-use technology can be used by a passenger for any airline, rather than requiring passengers to only utilize kiosks associated with their specific airline. Even with these benefits, airlines may be hesitant to adopt common-use facilities due to branding concerns, less autonomy, and the need to train personnel on the technology of the new systems. Airlines will benefit, however, from space made available for emergency diversions and new service, as well as cost savings when underutilized spaces are released (Belliotti, 2008).

Somewhere in the middle of the continuum, mixed use and preferential use approaches provide hybrid concepts of both exclusive use and common-use. With mixed use, there are some forms of common-use, possibly in the form

Figure 5-17. Common-use terminal equipment (CUTE).

of MUFIDS and MUBIDS, but exclusive use arrangements are also in use. With preferential use, the airport has made substantial investments in common-use technology, but preferential use agreements allow majority airlines priority over certain space. Application of common-use technology is common at ticket counters and in gate management (Belliotti, 2008).

EMAS

Designed to minimize the hazards of aircraft overruns, the FAA requires safety areas beyond the runway end (typically 1,000 feet at commercial service airports), the dimensions of which have been incorporated into airport design standards. Not all airports have adequate runway end safety areas as required by FAA criteria. In fact, there are numerous runways nationwide, particularly those constructed prior to the adoption of current safety area standards, where natural obstacles, local development, and/or environmental constraints prevent the construction of a standard runway end safety area. Even so, runway safety area standards cannot be modified or waived by the FAA. Importantly, the FAA will not require an airport to reduce the length of a runway or declare its length to be less than the actual pavement length to meet runway safety area standards if there is an operational impact to the airport (FAA, 2005a).

To assist airports in this situation, the FAA, in partnership with industry, has developed **engineered materials arresting systems (EMAS)**. First installed in 1996, EMAS is composed of a bed of cellular cement material, designed to crush under the weight of an aircraft, which allows for predictable, controlled deceleration of an aircraft exiting the runway at 70 knots (see Figure 5-18). This is accomplished without imposing loads that exceed the aircraft's design limits, causing major structural damage to the aircraft, or imposing excessive forces on its occupants. To effectively do this, EMAS must be at least 600 feet in length (or the length of the standard runway safety area, whichever is less) between the runway threshold and the far end of the EMAS bed if the approach end of the runway has vertical guidance. It is installed at the end of a runway in the safety area and is designed to provide a level of safety that is typically equivalent to a full runway safety area built to the current FAA design standards. If an aircraft damages the EMAS bed, it must be repaired in a timely manner, with undamaged areas of the EMAS bed protected from further damage until repairs are made (FAA, 2005a).

Figure 5-18. Engineered materials arresting system installed within a runway end safety area. Chevrons are visible.

(Diana Fernandez, San Diego International Airport)

Airspace and Approach Standards

The FAA has developed criteria to protect airspace and approaches into airports. Pilots rely on these criteria to enable them to fly an approach into an airport according to the published procedures without fear of obstacles.

14 CFR PART 77—OBJECTS AFFECTING NAVIGABLE AIRSPACE

In order to provide for safe aircraft flight and the transition of aircraft from takeoff to landings, federal regulations have been promulgated to help protect the airspace and approaches to airports from the construction of towers, buildings, and other objects that would interfere with the use of the airspace. **14 CFR Part** 77 establishes procedures for reporting to the FAA proposed construction that may constitute potential obstructions or hazards to safe air navigation as determined by the criteria found in the regulations (see Figure 5-19). The criteria identify height notification requirements and imaginary surfaces that must be protected from obstructions.

As defined by the FAA, an object can be any natural growth, terrain, or permanent or temporary construction or alteration, including equipment or materials used, and apparatus of a permanent or temporary character. This definition includes items such as trees, construction cranes, well-drilling equipment, stockpiled material or earth, buildings, and parked vehicles.

Figure 5-19. Example of objects affecting navigable airspace that required notification to the FAA under Part 77 before being constructed.

Airports, construction contractors, and/or developers are required to provide notice to the FAA via Form 7460-1, Notice of Proposed Construction or Alteration. This notice is required when proposed construction or alteration falls within any of the following categories:

1. Is greater than 200 feet in height above ground level at its location
2. Is near a public use or military airport, heliport, or seaplane base[4]
3. Is a traverse way (highway, railroad or waterway) that exceeds standards
4. Is located on a public-use or military airport or heliport
5. Is requested by the FAA

If an object will be less than 200 feet above ground level (AGL) and more than 5 statute miles from a public-use airport, it is deemed to not be a hazard. However, any construction or alteration of structures 200 feet or more in height AGL, or at a height that penetrates any of the defined imaginary obstacle surfaces near a public-use airport, requires 45-day advance notice to the FAA.

[4] Depending upon the length of the longest runway, a proposed object is considered to be near a public-use airport if it is within 10,000 feet of an airport having runways less than 3,200 feet, or within 20,000 feet of an airport with a runway that is greater than 3,200 feet.

Part 77 defines various imaginary surfaces for the purpose of determining whether or not an object is an obstruction to air navigation (see Figure 5-20 and Table 5-4). These surfaces are identified as:

1. **Primary surface**—Centered on the runway centerline and extends 200 feet past the runway end. The width of this surface varies from 250 feet to 1,000 feet, depending on the type of approach to the runway. This is the only imaginary surface that exists solely at ground level.
2. **Transitional surface**—Starts at the edges of the primary surface, perpendicular to the runway centerline, and transitions to the horizontal surface. The slope of the transitional surface is 7:1.[5]
3. **Approach surface**—Starts 200 feet from the runway end at the edge of the primary surface and extends outward from the end of the primary surface. The approach slope can vary from 20:1 for a visual runway for a distance of 5,000 feet; to ratios 20:1, 34:1, and 50:1 for a non-precision runway, for a distance of 10,000 feet; or to 50:1 for a precision runway for the first 10,000 feet and 40:1 thereafter to 40,000 feet.
4. **Horizontal surface**—A level plane 150 feet above the runway elevation. The surface area is determined by connecting tangents of radii extended from the edges of the primary surface area at the runway ends. The length of the surface area of the radii is dependent upon the approach category for the runway. For utility or visual runways it is 5,000 feet and for all others it is 10,000 feet. The area is intended to accommodate the safe operation and maneuvering of aircraft that are performing circle-to-land or missed approaches.
5. **Conical surface**—Starts at the perimeter of the horizontal surface and continues upward at a slope ratio of 20:1 for a horizontal distance of 4,000 feet.

Table 5-4. Part 77 imaginary surface angles.

Ratio	Percent	Angle	Surface
7:1	14.3	8.1°	Transitional
20:1	5.0	2.9°	Conical, visual approach
34:1	2.9	1.7°	Non-precision approach
40:1	2.5	1.4°	Precision (outer)
50:1	2.0	1.1°	Precision

[5] Run:Rise

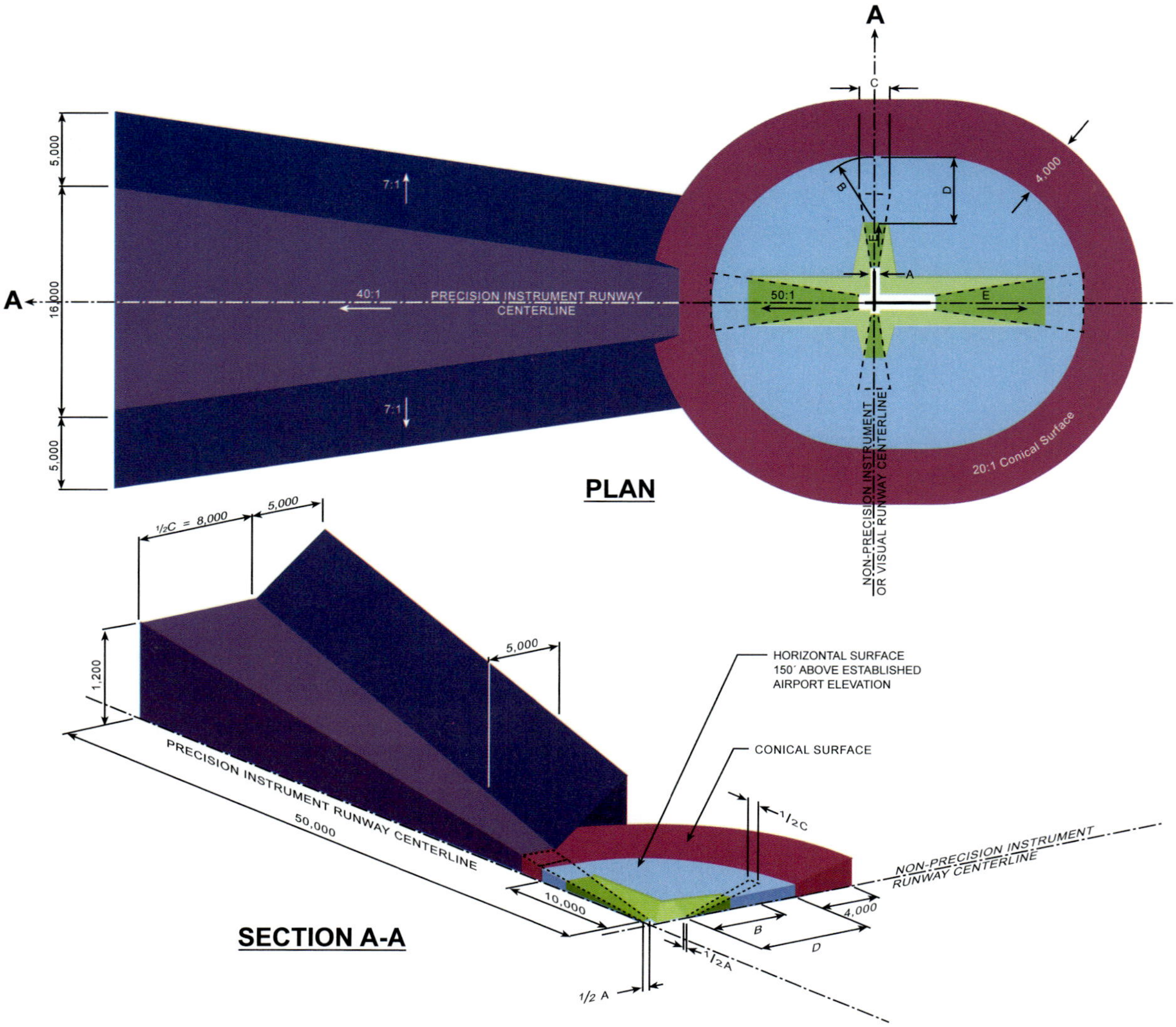

CIVIL AIRPORT IMAGINARY SURFACES

DIM.	ITEM	DIMENSIONAL STANDARDS (FEET)					
		VISUAL RUNWAY		NON-PRECISION INSTRUMENT RUNWAY			PRECISION INSTRUMENT RUNWAY
		UTILITY	LARGER THAN UTILITY	UTILITY	LARGER THAN UTILITY		
					X	Y	
A	WIDTH OF PRIMARY SURFACE AND APPROACH SURFACE WIDTH AT INNER END	250	500	500	500	1,000	1,000
B	RADIUS OF HORIZONTAL SURFACE	5,000	5,000	5,000	10,000	10,000	10,000
		VISUAL APPROACH		NON-PRECISION INSTRUMENT APPROACH			PRECISION INSTRUMENT APPROACH
		UTILITY	LARGER THAN UTILITY	UTILITY	LARGER THAN UTILITY		
					X	Y	
C	APPROACH SURFACE WIDTH AT END	1,250	1,500	2,000	3,500	4,000	16,000
D	APPROACH SURFACE LENGTH	5,000	5,000	5,000	10,000	10,000	*
E	APPROACH SLOPE	20:1	20:1	20:1	34:1	34:1	*

X - VISIBILITY MINIMUMS GREATER THAN 3/4 MILE
Y - VISIBILITY MINIMUMS AS LOW AS 3/4 MILE
* - PRECISION INSTRUMENT APPROACH SLOPE IS 50:1 FOR INNER 10,000 FEET AND 40:1 FOR AN ADDITIONAL 40,000 FEET

SURFACE SLOPE KEY

- HORIZONTAL SURFACE
- 20:1
- 7:1
- 7:1
- VARIES (SEE "E" VALUE IN TABLE)
- 40:1 (PRECISION INSTRUMENT RUNWAY ONLY)

AVIATION DIVISION
Washington State Department of Transportation

Figure 5-20. Part 77 imaginary surfaces.

(Carter Timmerman, Aviation Planner, WSDOT)

Upon receipt of any proposed construction via Form 7460-1, the FAA conducts a Part 77 study by analyzing the impact a proposed object would have on the airspace surrounding an airport. A Part 77 study concludes with one or more of six possibilities:

1. The obstruction to air navigation is a hazard to air navigation.
2. The object or activity on or in the vicinity of an airport is objectionable.
3. The need exists to alter, remove, mark, or light the object.
4. The airport layout plan is approved.
5. The proposed construction, enlargement, or modification to the airport would have an adverse effect on the safe and efficient use of navigable airspace.
6. A change in operational procedure is feasible or required.

When penetration to an approach surface exists, the airport operator must take one of five actions:

1. Remove or lower the object to acceptable threshold siting requirements.[6]
2. Displace the threshold, thereby shortening the landing distance.
3. Revise the glide path angle or threshold crossing height.
4. Raise the visibility minimums on the runway approach.
5. Restrict night operations.

It is important to understand that Part 77 does not provide the FAA with authority to prevent constructing or altering a structure, regardless of the results of the study. This authority to prevent construction or alteration is reserved for the states and resides with the local regional or municipal zoning authorities. For this reason, the FAA insists upon land use planning in and around airports to promote compatible land uses and to protect the FAA's investment in the airport and the airways. If a community does not protect its approaches under federal grant assurances, future federal AIP funding for the airport may be in jeopardy. Many airports have had to displace thresholds due to obstructions that were erected after the airport was built, indicating a lack of proper height zoning regulations at the local level.

Additionally, 14 CFR Part 157, Notice of Construction, Alteration, Activation, and Deactivation of Airports, requires those proposing to construct, activate, or deactivate an airport to provide notice to the FAA at least 30 days prior to the proposed alteration or deactivation. This notice requires a completed Form 7480-1, a layout sketch, and a location map. Additionally, 14 CFR Part 77, Safe, Efficient Use, and Preservation of the Navigable Airspace, requires notice to the FAA by those proposing any construction or alteration described in §77.13. Specifically, this includes any construction or alteration of structures more than 200 feet in height above ground level or at a height that will penetrate any of the imaginary surfaces defined in Part 77 (FAA, 2014).

6 May not be possible if proposed object is not under control of the airport.

TERPS

A stated objective of the airspace system is for instrument procedures to be provided at civil airports open to the public whenever a need is shown. Although a minimum number of potential instrument approaches is not specified, an instrument procedure must be beneficial to more than a single user or interest. It is the responsibility of the FAA to establish and approve instrument procedures for civil airports. Within the 495-page FAA Order 8260.3B, "United States Standard for **Terminal Instrument Procedures (TERPS)**," the criteria by which these instrument procedures are established and approved are found.

TERPS refers to the methods for use in designing instrument flight procedures. This includes procedures for instrument approaches—including straight-in and simultaneous precision approaches, and straight-in non-precision approaches—as well as departure procedures (FAA, 2007b).

AVIGATION EASEMENTS

Often, it is not feasible for airports to own all parcels of land in areas affected by aircraft noise. Therefore, it may be prudent for an airport to purchase avigation easements. With this type of easement, airports purchase the "right" for aircraft to overfly a particular property, thus avoiding future noise complaints and the liability associated with such complaints from the property owner.

Selection Process

For airport planning and design projects, construction projects, and other consulting work, airports must undergo a process to develop project specifications, advertise for the project, and select a contractor to perform the work.[7]

SPECIFICATIONS

Once an airport has a project in mind, the first step is to develop the specifications for that project. In other words, this is the stage during which the airport staff clearly develop the concept of the work to be performed by the contractor. The specifications become the written directions and requirements for completing the contract work, including standards for specifying materials or testing. The specifications are often very detailed, and become an essential part of the RFP, RFQ, or bid documents. Without specifications for the project (or equipment, as would be developed for an ARFF truck), a potential contractor would

[7] The contractor is the individual, partnership, firm, or corporation primarily liable for the acceptable performance of the work contracted.

not be able to adequately determine costs associated with the project, which would result in proposals or bids which are not very useful to the airport.

RFP

Once the project specifications have been developed, it is necessary to advertise for the work to be performed. The published advertisement will state the time and place for submitting sealed proposals; a description of the proposed work; instructions to bidders for obtaining proposal forms, plans, and specifications; proposal guaranty required; and the airport's right to reject any and all bids. Additionally, the airport may hold either a mandatory or optional prebid conference for interested bidders. This conference (or meeting) allows airport staff to explain more about the project and answer questions from potential bidders. A site visit is also usually included, allowing potential bidders the opportunity to see the project site and better understand the requirements of the work to be performed.

One manner in which this advertisement is carried out is via a **request for proposal (RFP)**. An airport will issue an RFP, which is a document that specifically spells out the work to be performed, the required format of the proposal, the date on which the proposal is due, and the criteria for selection. The RFP will clearly inform a potential contractor about all aspects of the project and will provide all information necessary for the potential contractor to effectively respond to the RFP by developing a proposal detailing their qualifications, how they intend to carry out the project, and possibly (if requested) the monetary amount they are willing to accept for completion of the project. Proposals generally must also include statements covering the bidder's past experience on similar work, a list of equipment that would be available for the work, a list of key personnel that would be available for the project, and evidence of financial strength. Further, each proposal may be required to include a certified check, or other acceptable collateral, in the amount specified in the proposal form. Such financial guaranties are returned once the contract is awarded.

RFQ

Similar in purpose to an RFP, a **request for qualifications (RFQ)** is an airport's way of seeking the most qualified contractor to carry out a task. If an RFQ is issued, the airport is requesting the qualifications of a potential contractor. This will include resumes of key personnel, company experience with similar projects, location of the company, etc. Generally, with an RFQ, no dollar amount is included in the potential contactor's statement of qualifications. Once the most qualified contractor is chosen, the airport and the contractor will then negotiate a dollar amount for the work to be performed.

BIDS

The **bid** process requests potential contractors or vendors/suppliers to bid a specific monetary amount to supply the piece of equipment requested (such as a new ARFF truck), perform the work requested (such as a terminal demolition), or provide the expertise requested (such as an updated master plan). Usually, the airport has a pre-calculated budget in mind, meaning it knows what to expect as a reasonable bid for the project, equipment, or expertise. Although jokes abound about projects being awarded to the "lowest bidder," it should be noted that award of contracts are made to the lowest, qualified bidder whose proposal conforms to the requirements as spelled out in the bid documents. Even so, if a bid is submitted at 50 percent below the expected cost, for instance, an airport will need to evaluate whether the potential contractor did not understand the specifications or if the contractor is willing to realize a loss simply to win the contract. In either case, red flags will be raised requiring further evaluation by airport staff prior to awarding the project. Additionally, bids can be considered non-responsive if the bid is not submitted by the deadline or does not meet any other requirements spelled out in the bid advertisement. To be fair, airports must hold all proposers to the published deadlines.

CONTRACTOR SELECTION

All proposals, qualifications, or bids received by the deadline are opened, and read, publicly at the time and place specified in the advertisement. Bidders, their authorized agents, and other interested persons are welcome to attend the opening. Proposals that have been withdrawn by the bidder or not received by the deadline are returned unopened to the bidder (FAA, 2011b).

CONTRACT NEGOTIATION

Once a contractor is successful in securing a project, the airport will enter into a contract with the contractor. A contract is the written agreement covering the work to be performed. The contract usually includes the advertisement; contract form; proposal; performance bond; payment bond; any required insurance certificates; specifications; plans, and any addenda issued to bidders. The contract time refers to the number of calendar days or working days allowed for completion of the project. Finally, the contractor will be given a written notice, or notice to proceed, to begin the actual contract work on a previously agreed-to date (FAA, 2011b).

International Practice

Airport design criteria on the international level is promulgated by the International Civil Aviation Organization (ICAO). As an agency of the United Nations, member states (countries) abide by the Standards and Recommended Practices (SARPs) issued by the ICAO. However, a member state may have its own national aviation agency (such as the FAA in the United States) that develops regulations and recommended practices specific to the airports in that country. ICAO Annex 14, Volume I, *Aerodrome Design and Operations*, is a 230+ page document that provides guidance in the following areas:

- Aerodrome data
- Physical characteristics
- Obstacle restriction and removal
- Visual aids for navigation
- Visual aids for denoting obstacles
- Visual aids for denoting restricted use areas
- Electrical systems
- Aerodrome operational services, equipment and installations
- Aerodrome maintenance

Concluding Thoughts

The proper design and construction of airports requires a significant level of technical knowledge. AC 150/5300-13A provides FAA guidance in the design of airports. Airports commonly rely on consultants for the design and construction of facilities. However, airport personnel must be knowledgeable in the areas of design and construction to ensure facilities are developed according to the master plan and the desires of the airport.

Chapter Summary

- A predesign conference, coordinated by the airport or an authorized agent, is used to discuss design parameters, airport safety, routing of aircraft and equipment, sequencing of construction operations, environmental considerations, and civil rights requirements.
- A prebid conference is to help clarify and explain construction methods, procedures, and safety measures required by the contract.
- A preconstruction conference is coordinated by the airport or an authorized agent, and provides an opportunity to discuss operational safety, testing, quality control, quality acceptance, security, safety, labor requirements, environmental factors, and other issues with the contractor and any subcontractors.
- It is important to develop a construction safety and phasing plan for all construction projects on the airfield due to the greater risks involved.
- The CSPP should address coordination, phasing, affected areas, protection of NAVAIDs, contractor access, wildlife management, foreign object debris, hazardous materials, notification, inspections, underground utilities, penalties, special conditions, runway and taxiway visual aids, NAVAIDs, marking and signs for access routes, hazard marking and lighting, protection of runway and taxiway safety areas, and additional limitations on construction.
- The safety plan compliance document details how the contractor will comply with the CSPP.
- The runway design code, formerly the airport reference code, is a coding system used to relate airport design criteria to the operational and physical characteristics of the airplanes intended to operate at the airport. It incorporates the aircraft approach category, airplane design group, and approach visibility minimums.
- A request for modification to standards must show that the modification will provide an acceptable level of safety, economy, durability, and workmanship.
- Runway location and orientation are paramount to airport safety, efficiency, economics, and environmental impact.
- The layout and configuration of runways depends on wind, airspace availability, environmental factors, obstructions to air navigation, topography, air traffic control tower visibility, and wildlife hazards.
- Runway shoulders provide resistance to blast erosion and accommodate the passage of maintenance and emergency equipment and the occasional passage of an airplane veering from the runway.
- Runway blast pads provide blast erosion protection beyond runway ends.

- The obstacle free zone clearing standard precludes taxiing and parked airplanes and object penetrations, except for frangible visual NAVAIDs that need to be located in the OFZ because of their function.
- The runway object free area is centered on the runway centerline and free of above-ground objects protruding above the runway safety area edge elevation.
- The clearway is a clearly defined area connected to and extending beyond the runway end available for completion of the takeoff operation of turbine-powered airplanes. A clearway increases the allowable airplane operating takeoff weight without increasing runway length.
- A stopway is an area beyond the takeoff runway, centered on the extended runway centerline, and designated by the airport owner for use in decelerating an airplane during an aborted takeoff.
- Taxiways have stabilized or paved shoulders, safety areas, and object free areas.
- Cockpit over centerline steering is preferred over judgmental oversteering on taxiway turns.
- There are two main types of pavement: flexible (typically asphalt) and rigid (typically Portland cement concrete).
- Airport pavement overlays may correct deteriorating pavement surfaces, improve ride quality or surface drainage, maintain structural integrity, or increase pavement strength.
- There are five basic configurations of passenger terminal buildings: simple linear terminal, finger piers, satellites with and without finger piers, midfield (either linear or X-shaped), and transporter.
- In a simple linear terminal, aircraft are parked on one side of the terminal, while automobiles are parked on the other side.
- Finger pier terminals are created by adding extensions to a linear terminal building.
- Satellite passenger terminals concentrate aircraft gates at the end of either a finger pier (which may be above or below ground) or a people mover (which may be above or below ground.
- Midfield passenger terminals are independent passenger buildings generally located far from the main passenger building and which passengers initially access from the landside. These are major terminals that may contain 50 or more aircraft gates.
- Transporters are not a specific terminal configuration, but rather a category of rubber-tired vehicles that move passengers between passenger buildings and aircraft.
- Airport traffic has three components: originating and terminating passengers; employees; and supply, delivery, and other commercial vehicles.

- By adopting the common-use philosophy, airports can effectively increase airport capacity without constructing any additional gates, terminals, or check-in areas.
- Common-use occurs on a continuum and includes exclusive use, mixed use, preferential use, and common-use.
- Common-use terminal equipment allows for any airline to use the same computer terminal.
- Engineering materials arresting systems (EMAS) is composed of a bed of cellular cement material, designed to crush under the weight of an aircraft, which allows for predictable, controlled deceleration of an aircraft exiting the runway at 70 knots.
- 14 CFR Part 77 establishes procedures for reporting to the FAA proposed construction that may constitute potential obstructions or hazards to safe air navigation as determined by the criteria found in the regulations. The criteria identify height notification requirements and imaginary surfaces that must be protected from obstructions.
- The primary surface is centered on the runway centerline and extends 200 feet past the runway end.
- The transitional surface starts at the edges of the primary surface, perpendicular to the runway centerline, and transition to the horizontal surface. The slope of the transitional surface is 7:1.
- The approach surface starts 200 feet from the runway end at the edge of the primary surface and extends outward from the end of the primary surface.
- The horizontal surface is a level plane 150 feet above the runway elevation.
- The conical surface starts at the perimeter of the horizontal surface and continues upward at a slope ratio of 20:1 for a horizontal distance of 4,000 feet.
- Terminal Instrument Procedures (TERPS) refers to the methods for use in designing instrument flight procedures.
- A request for proposal is a document that specifically spells out the work to be performed, the required format of the proposal, the date on which the proposal is due, and the criteria for selection.
- A request for qualifications, which is an airport's way of seeking the most qualified contractor to carry out a task, results in obtaining the qualifications of potential contractors.
- The bid process requests potential contractors or vendors/suppliers to bid a specific monetary amount to supply the piece of equipment requested, perform the work requested, or provide the expertise requested.

Review Questions

1. What components should be included in the construction safety and phasing plan?
2. Explain what occurs during the design phase of a project.
3. Explain what occurs during the construction phase of a project.
4. What is the runway design code?
5. For what purpose would an airport request a modification to standards?
6. The layout and configuration of runways depends on what factors?
7. Explain the two types of pavement.
8. Explain the simple linear passenger terminal building.
9. Explain the finger pier terminal.
10. Explain the satellite passenger terminal.
11. Explain the midfield passenger terminal.
12. Explain the purpose of transporters.
13. Explain the three major components of airport traffic.
14. What are the benefits to adopting common-use at airports?
15. Explain engineering materials arresting system.
16. Explain the imaginary surfaces of Part 77.
17. What is the purpose of a request for proposal?
18. What is the purpose of a request for qualifications?
19. Explain the bid process.

Scenarios

1. As director of operations at Johnson International Airport, you have been instructed by the senior director of operations and maintenance to determine how the airport (which is an ARC DV) can accommodate an A-380. Apparently, Singapore Airlines is considering bringing their A-380 into your airport three times weekly. How do you approach this task? What are some options available to the airport? How would you seek FAA approval?

2. You are the airport director of a commercial service airport that tends to be overly congested. In discussions with the ATC tower chief, she feels that aircraft are remaining on the runway too long. What can be done about this? Can the airport actually enhance capacity without building a new runway? If so, how?

3. Looking for a challenge and an opportunity to utilize your 30 years of airport management experience in a unique way, you have been hired by a newly established airport authority that is in the design phase of building a new commercial service airport for a beachfront community. Preliminary air service studies have shown the region can produce demand for 2–3 million enplaned passengers annually, with the vast majority being domestic. The design firm is seeking your thoughts on the terminal configuration. Considering the possible types of terminals, what would you recommend and why?

4. As the airport manager at a GA airport, you desire to retain a management consultant to (a) develop a strategic plan, (b) perform an air service analysis, and (c) assist with other tasks that may require the need of this consultant. How would you select such a consultant?

5. You have been hired as an engineering/design consultant for a new commercial-service airport to replace an older commercial-service airport that is now landlocked. The airport will be located in northern Florida and serve no less than 4 airlines and 5 million enplaned passengers annually. Discuss how you would decide on the pavement type, the runway design, the terminal design, whether common-use would be appropriate, etc.

References and Resources for Further Study

American Association of Airport Executives. 2005. "Body of Knowledge Module 2. Planning, construction, and environmental." Washington, DC: AAAE.

Belliotti, R. 2008. "ACRP Synthesis 8: Common Use Facilities and Equipment at Airports." Washington, DC: Transportation Research Board.

de Neufville, R. and A. Odoni. 2003. *Airport Systems: Planning Design and Management.* New York: McGraw Hill.

Federal Aviation Administration (FAA). 2005a. *Engineering Materials Arresting Systems for Aircraft Overruns.* AC 150/5220-22A. Washington, DC: FAA.

———. 2005b. *Runway Length Requirements for Airport Design.* AC 150/5325-4B. Washington, DC: FAA.

———. 2007a. *Quality Control of Construction for Airport Grant Projects.* AC 150/5370-12A. Washington, DC: FAA.

———. 2007b. "United States Standard for Terminal Instrument Procedures." FAA Order 8260.3B.

———. 2009. *Predesign Prebid, and Preconstruction Conferences for Airport Grant Projects.* AC 150/5300-9B. Washington, DC: FAA.

———. 2011a. *Operational Safety on Airports During Construction.* AC 150/5370-2F. Washington, DC: FAA.

———. 2011b. *Standards for Specifying Construction of Airports.* AC 150/5370-10F. Washington, DC: FAA.

———. 2014. *Airport Design.* AC 150/5300-13A. Washington, DC: FAA.

Los Angeles World Airports. 2012. "Comprehensive Annual Financial Report." Retrieved from http://www.lawa.org/uploadedFiles/LAWA/pdf/LAWA_Comprehensive_Annual_Financial_Report_2012.pdf

Richards, J. 2008. "Common Use Technology Trumps Physical Expansion at Fresno." Retrieved from http://www.airportimprovement.com/article/common-use-technology-trumps-physical-expansion-fresno

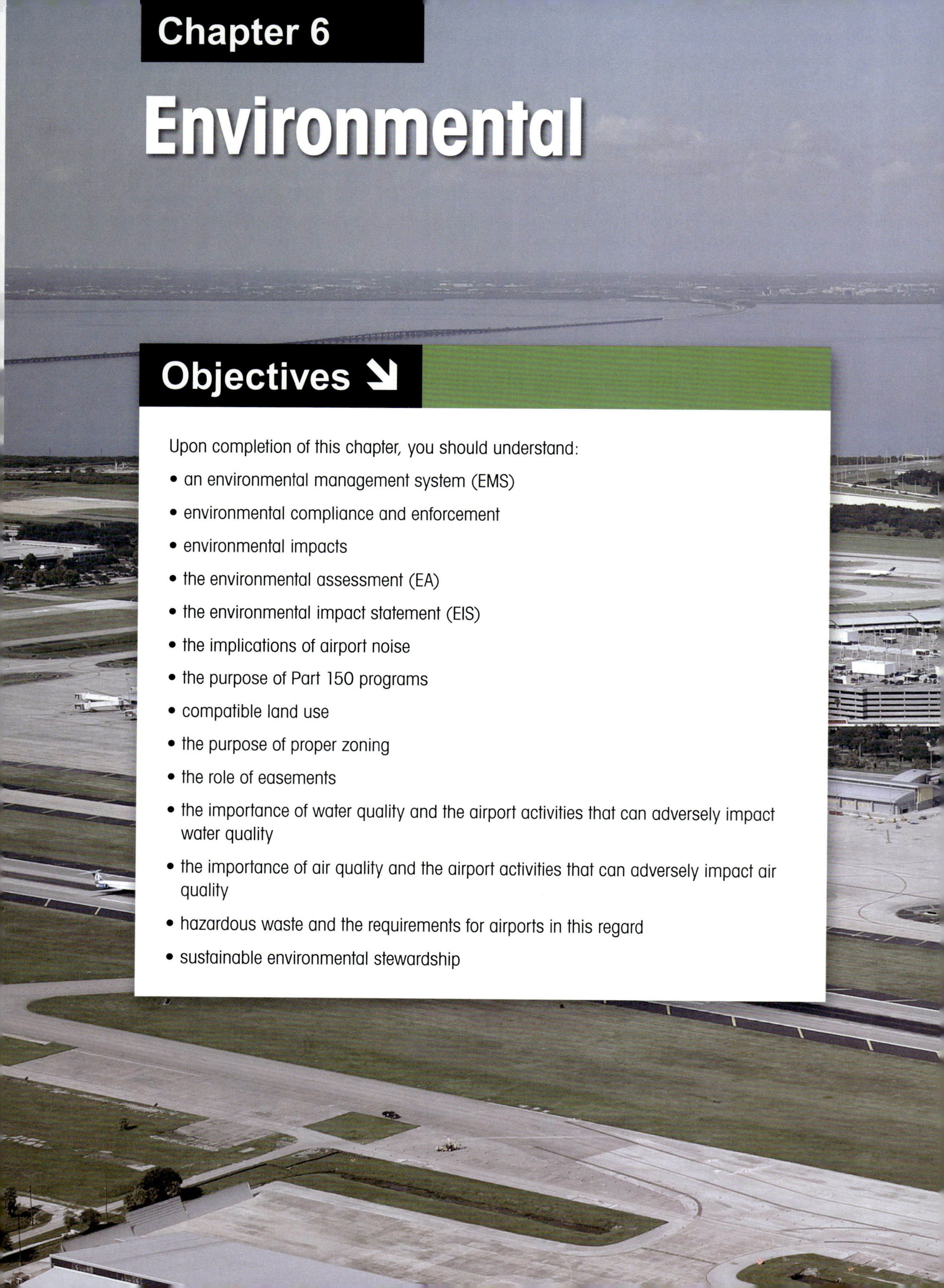

Chapter 6

Environmental

Objectives

Upon completion of this chapter, you should understand:

- an environmental management system (EMS)
- environmental compliance and enforcement
- environmental impacts
- the environmental assessment (EA)
- the environmental impact statement (EIS)
- the implications of airport noise
- the purpose of Part 150 programs
- compatible land use
- the purpose of proper zoning
- the role of easements
- the importance of water quality and the airport activities that can adversely impact water quality
- the importance of air quality and the airport activities that can adversely impact air quality
- hazardous waste and the requirements for airports in this regard
- sustainable environmental stewardship

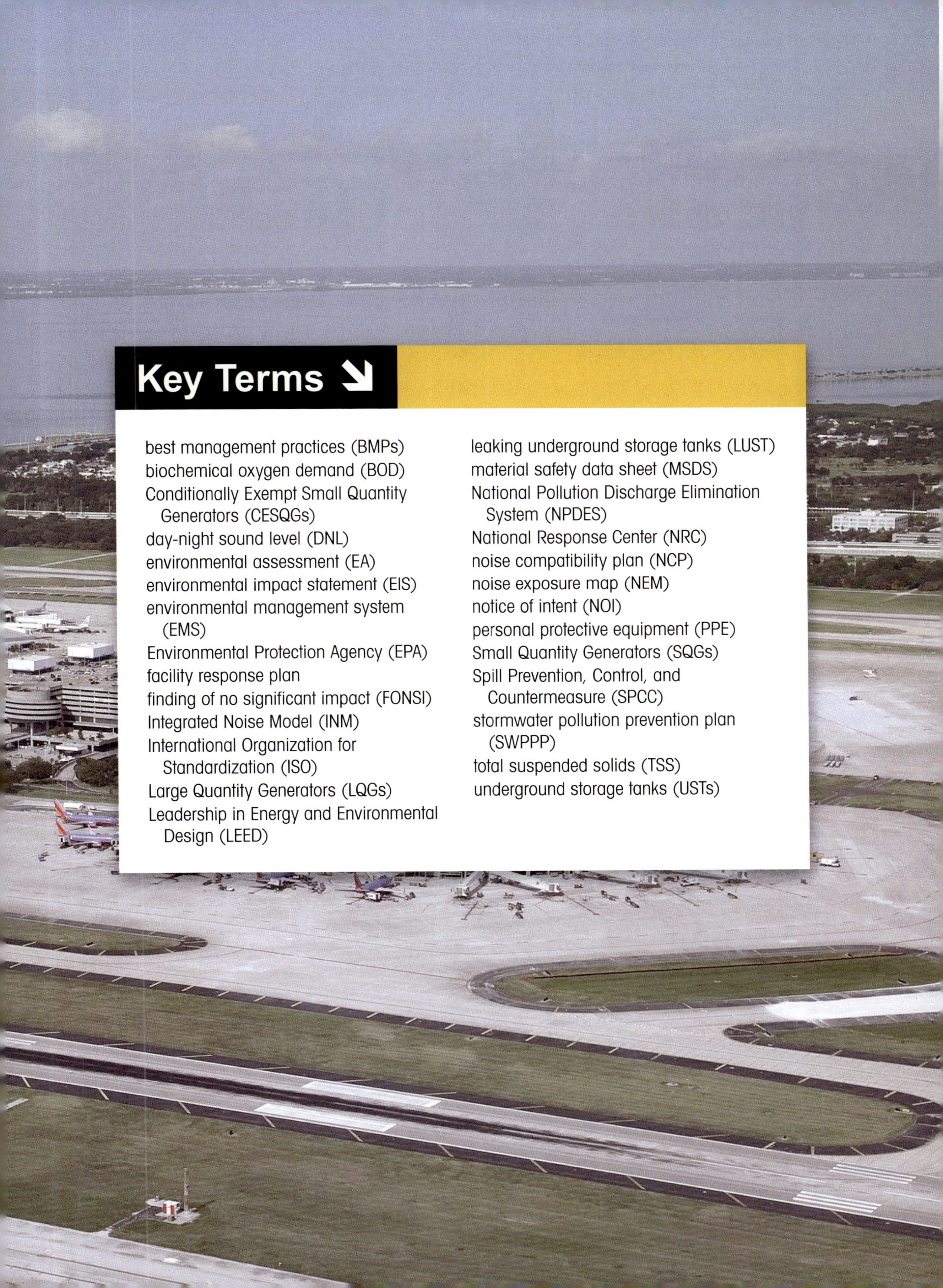

Key Terms

- best management practices (BMPs)
- biochemical oxygen demand (BOD)
- Conditionally Exempt Small Quantity Generators (CESQGs)
- day-night sound level (DNL)
- environmental assessment (EA)
- environmental impact statement (EIS)
- environmental management system (EMS)
- Environmental Protection Agency (EPA)
- facility response plan
- finding of no significant impact (FONSI)
- Integrated Noise Model (INM)
- International Organization for Standardization (ISO)
- Large Quantity Generators (LQGs)
- Leadership in Energy and Environmental Design (LEED)
- leaking underground storage tanks (LUST)
- material safety data sheet (MSDS)
- National Pollution Discharge Elimination System (NPDES)
- National Response Center (NRC)
- noise compatibility plan (NCP)
- noise exposure map (NEM)
- notice of intent (NOI)
- personal protective equipment (PPE)
- Small Quantity Generators (SQGs)
- Spill Prevention, Control, and Countermeasure (SPCC)
- stormwater pollution prevention plan (SWPPP)
- total suspended solids (TSS)
- underground storage tanks (USTs)

In Chapter 6

Environmental Regulations **239**

Environmental Management System **239**

Compliance and Enforcement **240**

Impacts **241**
- Environmental Assessment 242
- Environmental Impact Statement 243

Noise **243**

Compatible Land Use **251**

Zoning **252**

Easements **253**

Water Quality **254**
- Stormwater Discharge 256
- Aircraft and Pavement Deicing 257

Air Quality **259**

Hazardous Waste **261**

Sustainable Environmental Stewardship ... **265**

Concluding Thoughts **268**

Chapter Summary **268**

Review Questions **271**

Scenarios **272**

References and Resources for Further Study **273**

FEATURES

Boston Logan International Airport's Soundproofing Program **249**

By adopting a proactive approach to soundproofing residential homes and schools, Boston Logan is minimizing the impact of aircraft noise on the surrounding communities.

Denver International Airport Glycol Recovery System **257**

A glycol recovery system has allowed the airport to meet new EPA rules while accommodating airline needs for aircraft deicing.

San Francisco International Airport Terminal 2 .... **267**

By becoming the first airport terminal to achieve LEED Gold status, SFO has shown a commitment to sustainability.

Environmental Regulations

Environmental impacts can result from a number of activities and facilities on airports, such as stormwater discharge, weed and pest control, runway and taxiway deicing, aircraft rescue firefighting training, various underground and aboveground fuel storage tanks, electrical equipment and vaults, aircraft maintenance, vehicle maintenance, asbestos in buildings, restaurant or building maintenance, and grease, solvents, and other chemicals. Airports must be aware of—and strive to maintain compliance with—the numerous local, state, and federal environmental regulations and policies. It is important to remember that even though an airport typically has numerous tenants, such as airlines, fixed base operators, and maintenance providers, the airport acts as the landlord and is responsible for ensuring that tenants comply with the various regulations and policies on airport property. Additionally, airports can be forced to remediate environmental issues on property returned to the airport via lease expirations, terminations, or bankruptcy. In the end, the airport operator is responsible for what occurs on airport property.

Environmental Management System

FAA Advisory Circular (AC) 150/5050-8, *Environmental Management Systems for Airport Sponsors*, provides guidance to airports in developing a comprehensive **environmental management system (EMS)**. An EMS, which serves as the foundation for a strategic and proactive approach to ensuring environmental compliance, is generally based on the **International Organization for Standardization (ISO)** 14001 EMS standard. Based on the principles of process control, reduced consumption of resources, and environmental compliance, an EMS is designed to allow airports to balance environmental performance with business objectives through a process of continual improvement. Specifically, it incorporates the "Plan-Do-Check-Act" (P-D-C-A) cycle. During the "Plan" phase, the airport's overall environmental program is defined. During the "Do" phase, the strategies of the EMS (including training) are fully implemented. The "Check" phase involves monitoring environmental program performance to verify results and the achievement of objectives. Finally, during the "Act" phase, elements needing improvement are identified and a plan is developed and committed to for improving upon these areas (FAA, 2007; McGormley et al., 2011). Benefits of an EMS include:

1. Increased overall efficiency and accountability
2. Reduced costs and reduction of potential liability
3. Increased employee awareness of environmental responsibilities
4. Improved community relations

(AAAE, 2010, p. 135)

To develop an effective EMS, airports take the following steps:

1. Establish an environmental compliance philosophy.
2. Communicate compliance goals to employees, tenants, and the community.
3. Identify and assess the current level of compliance through an audit.
4. Establish programs to attain compliance.
5. Create processes and procedures to correct and maintain compliance.
6. Establish and implement strategies for building environmental capacity (AAAE, 2010, p. 135)

Similar to a safety management system (SMS), the EMS is becoming a standard practice at airports desiring to formalize their approach to proactive environmental management. Although the EMS is voluntary, airports are aware of the potential for environmental liability and the EMS is a best management practice in the airport industry to minimize this liability.

Compliance and Enforcement

Compliance with environmental regulations is imperative for airports. It is important for airports to effectively manage this compliance to avoid any liability associated with non-compliance. A good-faith effort is important in environmental compliance. If an airport has made such an effort, liability is minimized, even decreasing the likelihood of an airport manager being prosecuted for noncompliance by either the government or a private citizen. It is also crucial that the airport manager know the regulatory requirements and implement policies and procedures to ensure compliance. These two items are integral to a comprehensive environmental management program (AAAE, 2010).

The foundation of a good-faith effort requires airports to ensure tenant and contractor compliance through initial bid specifications and/or requests for proposals, periodic inspections and audits, and lease and contract agreements. Although requiring compliance initially through bid specifications and lease and contract agreements is a step in the right direction, airports must regularly ensure compliance through inspections and audits. An audit involves examining the current level of environmental compliance both within the organization and among various airport tenants. The audit should reveal any areas of non-compliance so that these areas can be addressed in light of the environmental requirements. Without an audit, no baseline (current level of compliance) can be established and continued oversight of environmental compliance is not possible. Additionally, providing an employee/tenant training program and maintaining good records is important (AAAE, 2010).

Additionally, airports typically maintain environmental impairment liability insurance. Even with good-faith efforts and a comprehensive environmental management program in place, airports may experience environmental liability due to actions by tenants. Therefore, an insurance policy designed to protect the airport from liability and potential cleanup costs related to environmental issues is important (AAAE, 2010).

The federal environmental regulations allow for civil and criminal liability exposure for environmental noncompliance. Citizens are able to pursue civil enforcement (which may result in fines or other financial penalties), while government agencies can pursue civil or criminal enforcement (which may result in fines and/or imprisonment). Civil enforcement pursued by a federal agency may take the form of either administrative or court action. Penalties for civil violations are based on each infraction and per day that it exists. Thus, violations that have been occurring for multiple days could result in significant financial fines. Environmental regulations are "without regard to fault," meaning that an airport manager or other personnel can be found guilty of noncompliance even if there was not intent to commit a crime. Also, in addition to the airport manager, employees of an airport (or other organization) can be found guilty, with these individual employees being held personally liable. To determine if an employee is personally liable, the following three factors must be considered:

1. Ability to make timely discovery of the problem
2. Power to direct the activities of persons who control the mechanisms causing the problem
3. Ability to prevent and abate the damage

(AAAE, 2010, p. 132)

Impacts

The impacts to the environment resulting from an airport's many activities and operations can be significant and must be addressed. But just as likely, environmental impacts from airport development projects can be significant and must be addressed prior to initiating the development project. The National Environmental Policy Act of 1969 (NEPA) requires airports (among other industries) to completely consider the environmental impacts of a proposed project prior to initiating it. NEPA also requires coordination with federal agencies and public participation during the planning and environmental review process. FAA Order 5050.4B, "National Environmental Policy Act (NEPA) Implementing Instructions for Airport Projects," provides guidance to airports in complying with NEPA (AAAE, 2010).

When utilizing NEPA to evaluate the proposed environmental impacts of a planned project, several different environmental actions are possible. First, a project may be categorically excluded if, according to FAA Order 5050.4B, projects of that type have been found under normal circumstances to have no potential for significant environmental impact. Two categories of environmental exclusions are possible—those projects that are unlikely to involve extraordinary circumstances and those that are likely to involve extraordinary circumstances. Typical projects that are categorically excluded and unlikely to involve extraordinary circumstances include grants to prepare an environmental assessment or environmental impact statement; approval of noise exposure maps or noise compatibility plans; approval of PFCs; and the acquisition of security equipment, safety equipment or snow removal equipment. If extraordinary circumstances are present, a normally categorically excluded action may result in significant environmental impacts (Figure 6-1). Typical projects that are categorically excluded but likely to involve extraordinary circumstances include parking areas, taxiways or taxilanes, roads, runway grooving, equipment storage buildings or T-hangars, airfield lighting installation or upgrades, construction of cargo buildings, and construction of deicing or anti-icing facilities (AAAE, 2010).

Figure 6-1. Airport construction project in an environmentally sensitive area (burrowing owl nesting area).

(Lee Brown, Fort Lauderdale-Hollywood International Airport.)

ENVIRONMENTAL ASSESSMENT

If a project is either not categorically excluded or is categorically excluded but likely to involve extraordinary circumstances, then an **environmental assessment (EA)** may be required. An EA involves a comprehensive analysis of the environmental effects of the proposed project. This requires a study of the site to be impacted and any wildlife, vegetation, etc., that may be impacted, as well as any geographical features (such as wetlands) that may be impacted. Typical projects that would justify an EA include helicopter facilities or operations, land acquisition, new airports, new runways, major runway strengthening, major runway extension, conversion of land protected under the Farmland Protection Act, and projects involving waters or wetlands.

ENVIRONMENTAL IMPACT STATEMENT

The EA results in one of two findings—either no significant impacts or significant impacts. If the EA determines there will be no significant impacts, a **finding of no significant impact (FONSI)** is prepared. This is, of course, the best case scenario. An airport may be able to take certain mitigation measures to allow a FONSI to be issued, in which case the FONSI will be dependent on these measures (AAAE, 2010).

On the other hand, if the impacts of the proposed project are determined to be significant, an **environmental impact statement (EIS)** may be required. In this case, the airport will file a **notice of intent (NOI)** with the FAA indicating that an EIS is forthcoming. The EIS identifies the projected impacts, and presents the environmental impacts that the project and the reasonable alternatives to the proposed project would cause. Additionally, the EIS presents methods to minimize the environmental impacts, as well as innovative uses of technology to mitigate the impacts (AAAE, 2010).

In general, few airport projects or actions require the preparation of an EIS. Often, it may be possible to alter a planned project to avoid significant environmental impacts. If alternatives are available, it is always preferable to choose the alternative with the fewest environmental impacts. If an EIS is necessary, however, the FAA will assume responsibility for preparing the EIS for AIP-funded projects, with input provided by the airport.

Noise

Noise can be a major community annoyance, and many airports can point to noise as their single greatest environmental impact on the community. Although noise can emanate from many sources at an airport, aircraft are the greatest contributor to the noise problem. Many individuals associate aircraft noise with lack of safety, often calling the airport to report, "the planes are so loud, they're about to crash into my house!" Thus, noise is an emotionally charged issue that must be proactively addressed by airports, often requiring delicate complaint-resolution skills.

Aircraft noise is measured on the decibel (dB) scale (see Figure 6-2). One decibel is equal to 20 micropascals (a unit of pressure), which is equivalent to the faintest audible sound heard by a person with very good hearing in an extremely quiet room. The scale ranges from zero to 130 decibels (which is the threshold of pain for the human ear). The decibel scale is logarithmic, meaning that sound pressure increases by powers of ten. For example, 10 decibels is 10 times greater than 1 decibel, while 30 decibels is 1,000 times louder than 1 decibel. To the human ear, loudness would appear to double for every increase of 10 decibels (AAAE, 2010).

The decibel scale, however, does not account for the frequency of sound, the duration of sound, or the human response to the sound. Additionally,

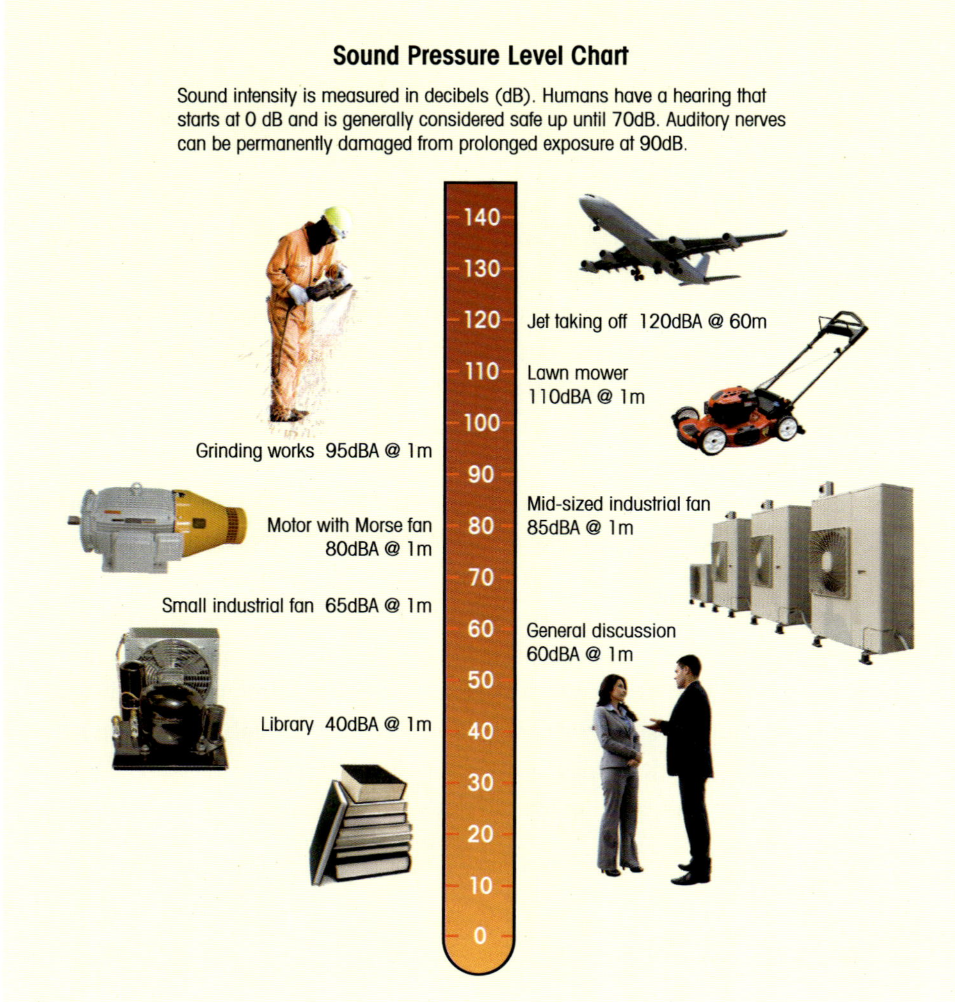

Figure 6-2. Aircraft noise related to the decibel scale.

traditional methods to measure noise simply measure each noise event. While people certainly respond to the noise of single events, it is important to measure the long-term effects of prolonged noise exposure. In consideration of this, the FAA has adopted a cumulative noise metric—the average **day-night sound level (DNL)** in A-weighted decibels. DNL is the 24-hour average sound level in A-weighted decibels for the period midnight to midnight, obtained after the addition of ten decibels to sound levels occurring between midnight and 7 a.m., and between 10 p.m. and midnight. The purpose of the ten-decibel penalty from 10 p.m. to 7 a.m. is to account for the increased annoyance during late night and early morning hours. A-weighting takes into consideration the frequency of sound.

The human ear is sensitive to frequencies ranging from 20 to 20,000 hertz (cycles per second). Research has shown that people tend to be more sensitive to higher frequencies (treble) than lower frequencies (bass). This discrimination by the human ear against lower frequencies can be taken into consideration by weighting decibels. By weighting decibels to reduce the influence of low and high frequency sound, the measurement more closely approximates the response of the human ear to sound, and is known as dBA or LA (FAA, 1983).

Historically, noise has not always been such a challenge for airports. However, with the introduction of jet aircraft in the 1960s, noise immediately became a significant issue for many airports. As a result, in 1969, the FAA introduced 14 CFR Part 36 to create certification standards for the design of turbojet and transport category aircraft. The main purpose of the regulation was to reduce aircraft noise at its source—the engines. First, all aircraft having Stage 1 noise characteristics (meaning older, noisier-technology engines) were required to be removed from operation by 1975. The 1990 Airport Noise and Capacity Act placed limits on aircraft having Stage 2 characteristics (engines using newer technology than Stage 1, but still noisy) and weighing more than 75,000 pounds maximum takeoff weight (MTOW), resulting in the majority of Stage 2 aircraft being phased out of service by December 31, 1999 (although a limited number of exemptions were allowed to operate after that date). Stage 3 standards began applying to all certificated aircraft in November 1975. Currently, the FAA has aircraft standards up to Stage 4 for jet aircraft. The international community is looking to approve a more stringent standard, which will be Stage 5. Stage 5 will apply to new type certificates after December 31, 2017, and December 31, 2020, depending on the weight of the aircraft (AAAE, 2010; FAA, n.d.).

Even with these various noise standards, as turbojet aircraft activity has increased over the years and as residential development has moved closer to airports, the noise problem has been consistently increasing for airports. According to the FAA (1983, p. 2), "Noise is one of the greatest threats to aviation today." Therefore, airports have been pressured by the community and the federal government to address the effects of aircraft noise and adopt methods to become more compatible with the community.

The 1992 Airport and Airway Safety, Capacity, Noise Improvement, and Intermodal Transportation Act required the FAA to study the social, economic, and health effects of noise at the 65 dB, 60 dB, and 55 dB DNL noise areas to determine the specific noise level at which adverse impacts on populations were experienced. Based on research, the FAA adopted the 65 dB DNL standard, attempting to balance the protection of the public with competing economic and technological considerations (AAAE, 2010).

Although voluntary, the 14 CFR Part 150 program is one effective response to the noise problem at airports. Part 150 contains the procedures, standards, and methodology addressing the development, submission, and review of **noise exposure maps (NEM)** and **noise compatibility plans (NCP)**. It also presents a single system for the measurement of airport noise and a single system for determining the exposure of individuals to airport noise. Similarly, FAA Advisory Circular 150/5020-1, *Noise Control and Compatibility Planning for Airports*, presents guidance to airports in addressing the noise problem (McGormley et al., 2011; FAA, 1983).

Prior to developing a NEM, noise measurement must be carried out. Rather than attempting to accomplish this with a simple handheld sound level meter, accurate noise measurement requires the use of a multi-component system. These systems consist of microphones (for measuring noise events), calibrators (for checking the A-weighting filtering), tripods, precision sound level meters, a graphic level recorder, a camera, etc. The microphones of an accurate noise measurement system are placed in strategic locations throughout the community. A daily DNL reading is first recorded, measuring noise each second during a 24-hour period, with the ten decibel penalty added to noise at night. The cumulative total of all the readings over the 24-hour period are then averaged on an hourly and daily basis. Airports develop yearly DNL numbers as a basis for Part 150 studies (AAAE, 2010; FAA, 1983).

With the noise measurements recorded and the A-weighted DNL determined, the noise metrics can be graphically mapped into a NEM (see Figure 6-3). This map will show not only the airport, but also the surrounding community, and will represent both present and future noise patterns and land uses. Often, several different NEMs are prepared, such as for the baseline current year, five years with no noise mitigation, and subsequent maps showing the impacts of various noise mitigation measures. Also important is a consideration and explanation of ambient noise and background community noise. With the 65 dB DNL, 70 dB DNL, and 75 dB DNL noise contours overlaid on the map, it is easy to visually determine those land uses exposed to higher-than-acceptable noise levels. According to Part 150, all types of land use are considered to be compatible with noise levels less than 65 dB DNL. However, residential land uses and places of public assembly (such as hospitals, schools, and churches) are considered incompatible with noise levels higher than 65 dB DNL. Commercial, recreational, and industrial land uses are not as noise-sensitive and are generally compatible with higher noise exposure levels. The FAA recommends that airports own all property within the 75 dB DNL or greater contours (AAAE, 2010; FAA, 1983).

Once prepared, the NEM must be submitted to the FAA for approval. The benefit of receiving FAA approval is that the airport's liability for noise is

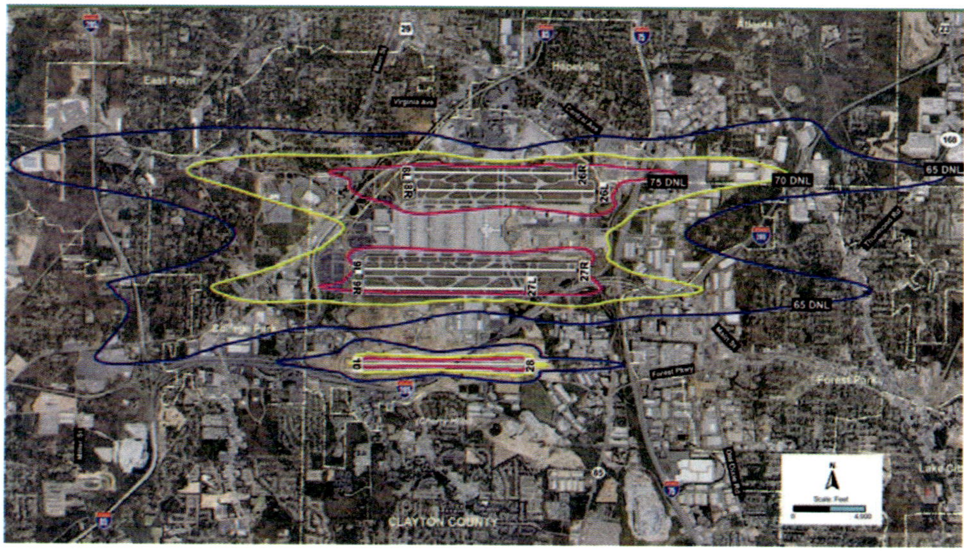

Figure 6-3. Noise exposure map.

(Hartsfield-Jackson International Airport.)

limited or eliminated. For instance, an individual who acquires an interest in property within the 65 dB DNL contour after FAA approval of a noise exposure map cannot recover damages for noise unless it can be shown that a significant change (defined as an increase in DNL of 1.5 dB if the new DNL is above 65 dB) in the aviation noise levels has occurred (AAAE, 2010; FAA, 1983).

In addition to the NEM, a full Part 150 study will also prepare a noise compatibility plan. This is particularly important if the NEM identifies noise-sensitive areas within the 65 dB DNL or greater contours (also known as incompatible land use). An NCP, which is typically updated every 3 to 5 years, will present a number of noise mitigation and land use management measures to mitigate the effects of airport noise and seek optimal accommodation of both airport operations and community activities within acceptable safety, economic and environmental parameters. This typically requires efforts to reduce existing incompatible land uses in the vicinity of the airport and prevent the introduction of new incompatible land uses in the future.

The reduction of airport noise is generally accomplished via:

1. Reduction of noise at the source (such as quieter aircraft and prohibition of auxiliary power units [APUs] in operation at the gate)
2. Relocation of the source of the noise in either space or time (such as night-time curfews or displaced threshold)
3. Acoustical changes to the area receiving the noise (such as soundproofing of homes in the community)

(AAAE, 2010, p. 185)

Some of the most common noise mitigation measures adopted by airports include:

1. *Denial of use to aircraft not meeting federal noise standards*—Involves limiting access to an airport to aircraft that conform with certain 14 CFR Part 36 standards. Although most turbojets and propeller-driven light airplanes already meet federal standards, implementing an airport restriction that forces some airport users to retrofit or replace aircraft contrary to federal requirements should be avoided.
2. *Capacity limits based on noise*—Could involve restrictions based on cumulative noise impact (adjusting operations so as not to exceed a cumulative noise contour), certificated noise levels (threshold noise levels that might vary by day and night, based on certificated noise levels by aircraft), or estimated single event noise levels (based on guidance in FAA AC 36-3, *Estimated Airplane Noise Levels in A-weighted Decibels*).
3. *Noise abatement takeoff or approach procedures*—Could involve runway selection, takeoff and landing profiles and power settings, and approach or departure paths (see Figure 6-4). FAA approval is required.
4. *Landing fees based on noise*—Involves basing all or a portion of the landing fee on the noise level of the individual aircraft, thus apportioning the fees to the relative noise "cost" of the operation to the airport. This strategy

encourages the use of quieter aircraft while producing additional revenue to offset noise-induced expenses. To avoid discrimination, the noise fee for each aircraft should be based upon standard single event noise ratings for the aircraft, such as those published in AC 36-3. Alternatively, an airport operator can provide a reward, in the form of a discount or reduction in landing fees, to air carriers who go to extra lengths to reduce noise generated by their aircraft.

5. *Noise barriers (shielding)*—Engine run-ups, specifically associated with aircraft maintenance, generate significant noise, often during the more sensitive nighttime hours. Shielding involves sound barriers, berms, or engine run-up enclosures.
6. *Acquisition of land or interests therein*—Involves purchasing full or partial interest in land that is critical to achieving or maintaining an airport's noise compatibility.
7. *Complete or partial curfews*—Involves restrictions on some or all flights during certain periods of the day (such as 2200 hours to 0700 hours) through restrictions based on noise threshold and certificated aircraft noise levels. This strategy should only be used as a last resort, due to the negative effects it has on aviation and the community's benefit from aviation.
8. *Soundproofing of homes and/or businesses*—Generally used for homes in noise-impacted areas, this involves sealing gaps/leaks, installing higher-efficiency windows, insulated doors, and possibly providing more wall insulation, especially in one room of preference in the home (typically a bedroom). Soundproofing decisions should be made on a case-specific basis with individuals having acoustical and architectural expertise. It should be noted that even once a residence is soundproofed, outdoor activities remain subject to existing noise levels.
9. *Off-airport land use plans and controls*—Involves proper zoning to prevent incompatible land use.

(FAA, 1983)

Figure 6-4. Airport noise abatement sign.

Boston Logan International Airport's Soundproofing Program

Boston Logan International Airport and the airport's operator, Massport, have implemented one of the most significant airport soundproofing programs in the country. Designed to minimize the impact of airport noise on the surrounding communities, Massport's Residential Sound Insulation Program has soundproofed 11,000 dwelling units, including 5,500 homes and 36 schools, since the program began in 1983, which equates to an investment of $170 million. Massport provides architects, contractors, and acoustical specialists, as well as all materials and labor needed to complete the project. Soundproofing options include weatherization and window and door upgrades. Additionally, homeowners can opt to have Massport create a room of preference in the home, with extra sound insulation, including acoustically treated exterior walls and ceilings. Massport uses the 65 DNL contour to determine residential soundproofing eligibility. Massport is quick to point out that residents may experience noise from the airport, but not qualify for soundproofing if the home is outside the FAA-defined 65 DNL contour.

(Massport, n.d.)

Regardless of which measures are selected, any noise compatibility measure must meet certain objectives. The measure must:

1. Achieve the goal of reducing non-compatible land uses around the airport
2. Not derogate safety or adversely affect the safe and efficient use of airspace
3. Not unjustly discriminate against an airport user
4. Not create an undue burden on interstate or foreign commerce
5. Not adversely affect other powers and responsibilities of the FAA Administrator as prescribed by law

(AAAE, 2010, p. 187)

Similar to the NEM, the NCP is reviewed by the FAA, who will then accept or reject each alternative. Once approved by the FAA, the airport becomes eligible for noise set-aside funding from the Airport Improvement Program (AIP). Items eligible for AIP funding include soundproofing, property or easement acquisition, runway and taxiway extensions, new runways, and new taxiways. Higher priority is placed on projects in 75 dB DNL or greater contours (FAA, 1983).

To effectively gauge the success of a noise compatibility program, the airport typically installs a continuous airport noise monitoring system. In contrast to a temporary noise measurement system (which is designed to initially measure noise to develop noise contours), a permanently installed noise monitoring system is used to track the impacts of noise compatibility measures that have been implemented and refine airport noise contours as appropriate. This system should be able to provide continuous measurement of dBA at the site, provide hourly and daily noise data, and provide single event maximum A-weighted sound level data. Many airports have incorporated advanced geographic information system (GIS) displays combined with flight track monitoring software to pinpoint the exact aircraft responsible for a particular noise event and even graphically see the flight track (including the altitude of the aircraft) over homes and businesses. This is especially helpful for following up on noise complaints (FAA, 1983).

It is important to remember that any Part 150 program is locally developed and is not considered a federal program. Additionally, airports undertaking a Part 150 study should understand some of the pitfalls. First, a Part 150 study can create controversy in the community as citizens are provided the opportunity to voice objections to airport noise. The airport must also endeavor to avoid creating unrealistic expectations among citizens in the community. In other words, noise will not "disappear" simply due to the Part 150 study. Third, the Part 150 process requires cooperative participants. Rather than everyone getting their way, some concessions are necessary to provide the most benefit for the most people (AAAE, 2010).

Although voluntary, Part 150 programs are strongly recommended by the FAA, especially if any of the following four conditions are met:

1. Significant amounts of noise-affected incompatible land use
2. The receipt of serious noise complaints
3. A threat from urban development pressure to increase incompatible land use near the airport
4. The introduction of major changes in airport facilities or operations that are likely to shift or increase noise patterns

(AAAE, 2010, p. 184)

A complete Part 150 plan will consist of the following elements:

1. A copy of the noise exposure map and its supporting documentation
2. A categorization of the parties responsible for implementation
3. The development of a noise compatibility program which meets Part 150 standards
4. The actual or anticipated effect of the program on reducing noise exposure
5. A description of how the recommendations may change previously adopted action
6. A schedule for implementation of the program
7. Costs of program implementation and anticipated sources of funding
8. Provision for revising the program if necessary
9. A description of public participation and the consultation process used during the program's development

(AAAE, 2010, p. 185)

An important component of noise mitigation at airports is the ability to predict noise impacts associated with the addition of new aircraft and new runways, for instance, as well as the reduced noise impacts that will result when certain noise compatibility measures are adopted. To accomplish these predictions with any degree of accuracy, computer-based mathematical modeling is required. The standard prediction analysis tool for use by airports is the FAA's **Integrated Noise Model (INM)**. The INM calculates the total impact of aircraft noise at or around airports. Specifically, the INM produces noise exposure contours that are used to produce NEMs and aid the airport in land use compatibility planning. INM easily interfaces with GIS to provide a graphical overlay of the surrounding area in consideration of the noise contours. The noise contours developed by the INM do not represent actual noise measurements; therefore, noise measurements should be verified by ground-based noise measuring equipment. As with all computer programs, the accuracy of the outputs is dependent upon the accuracy of the inputs. This requires the user to input accurate data on flight tracks, flight procedures, aircraft types, and schedule of operations. Additionally, the effects of local topography, weather, and buildings can cause variations in noise levels among points on the same contour. For these reasons, the accuracy of INM is ±3 dB in the 75 DNL dB contour and ±5 dB in the 65 dB contour (AAAE, 2010; FAA, 1983).

Compatible Land Use

One of the stated objectives of the Part 150 process is to develop and ensure compatible land uses around airports. Land use refers to the present or planned utilization of a given parcel of land. For any airport, land adjacent to the airport may be characterized as compatible-use or incompatible-use. It is extremely important for airports to maximize compatible-use and minimize incompatible-use. This is important, as incompatible land use around an airport will certainly create headaches for the airport manager. Consider a large residential development immediately adjacent to a very active airport runway. This incompatible land use will not only result in a large number of noise complaints, it would interfere with future development of the airport. Typically, schools, residences, churches, public health facilities, and concert halls are considered incompatible land use. Factories, warehouses, storage yards, and open farmland are generally compatible land use. Offices, shopping centers, recreation areas, or hotels may be considered compatible or incompatible depending on noise levels at the site, proximity to the airport, etc. (see Table 6-1).

Table 6-1. Compatible and incompatible land use around airports.

Land Use Noise Sensitivity Matrix				
		55–65 DNL	65–75 DNL	75+ DNL
Residential	1–2 Family	Compatible	Incompatible	Incompatible
	Multi-Family	Compatible	Incompatible	Incompatible
	Mobile Homes	Compatible	Incompatible	Incompatible
	Dorms, etc.	Compatible	Incompatible	Incompatible
Institutional	Churches	Compatible	Incompatible	Incompatible
	Schools	Compatible	Incompatible	Incompatible
	Hospitals	Compatible	Incompatible	Incompatible
	Nursing Homes	Compatible	Incompatible	Incompatible
	Libraries	Compatible	Incompatible	Incompatible
Recreational	Sports/Play	Compatible	Compatible	Incompatible
	Arts/Instructional	Compatible	Incompatible	Incompatible
	Camping	Compatible	Compatible	Incompatible
Commercial	All Uses	Compatible	Compatible	Compatible
Industrial	All Uses	Compatible	Compatible	Compatible
Agricultural	All Uses	Compatible	Compatible	Compatible

(FAA) Per 14 CFR Part 150: Compatible / Incompatible

It is important, therefore, that airports incorporate the concept of land use compatibility into the development of the airport. Aware of this, airports typically incorporate land use compatibility into the master planning process. Additionally, the airport layout plan would graphically represent uses of land that is considered compatible. Even so, there are many airports nationwide with significant land-use compatibility issues. Oftentimes, these issues could have been prevented with proper zoning by the municipality.

Zoning

To ensure compatible land use around airports, zoning regulations must be adopted and implemented. Zoning is, in fact, the most common land use control. Zoning is an exercise of the police powers of the state, as delegated to local governments, designating the uses permitted on each parcel of land within the zoning jurisdiction. It normally consists of a zoning ordinance which specifies land development and use constraints. Zoning is, by definition, a local responsibility. With proper zoning, proper land use compatibility can be promoted, while the land remains in private ownership, on the tax rolls, and economically productive (FAA, 1983).

Rather than zoning land for specific uses in a disorganized fashion, proper zoning should be based on a plan. This plan will consider the total needs of the community along with the specific needs of the airport. In essence, it is not in the best interest of homeowners or the airport to locate a residential area in a noise-affected area. Thus, proper zoning can prevent this from occurring. Rather than being viewed negatively, zoning can and should be viewed positively. It can be used constructively to increase the value and productivity of affected land. For zoning to be viable, however, there should be a reasonable present or future need for each designated use (FAA, 1983).

Although proper zoning is highly recommended in order to prevent incompatible land use around airports, zoning is not without pitfalls. First, zoning is not a permanent solution to the land use compatibility issue around airports. Requests for zoning changes can be applied for, with zoning changed by local officials. Also, zoning can actually allow incompatible land use around an airport, such as in the case of communities adopting cumulative zoning in which all "higher" uses of land (residential) is permitted in "lower" use districts (such as commercial or industrial). Zoning is also typically not retroactive, meaning that changing zoning primarily to prohibit a use that is already in existence is normally not possible. Lastly, airport noise impacts may span more than one jurisdiction, requiring a coordinated approach to zoning between these various communities (FAA, 1983).

It is imperative for the airport manager to work collaboratively with the municipal zoning commission or planning department to ensure that zoning regulations are adopted to prevent incompatible land use in the proximity of the airport. For instance, to prevent a cellular phone tower from being erected two miles away from the airport in the approach corridor (which could interfere with 14 CFR Part 77 surfaces), the airport must educate the local zoning commission or planning department as to land uses that would be incompatible with the operation of the airport. If successfully carried out, the municipality would deny the request to erect a cell phone tower at that location. If not successfully carried out, the tower may be erected and the FAA may determine it to be a hazard to air navigation, requiring the airport to displace a threshold, for instance. Clearly, this is not in the airport's best interest. Therefore, a proactive approach to zoning is absolutely necessary for airports (FAA, 1983).

Easements

Somewhat related to zoning, an easement is a right held by one person to make use of the land of another for a limited purpose. An avigation easement allows for flights of aircraft over the property, whereas a noise easement allows for aircraft to generate noise over the property. Easements can be quite effective in assuring compatible land use around airports. Airports may acquire easements via purchase, condemnation, and dedication. Although the concept of purchase is obvious, the concepts of condemnation and dedication are more novel. Condemnation for an easement is similar to full condemnation via eminent domain. The condemnation process involves court action (resulting in higher costs) and generates significant negative publicity and ill will on the part of the home or land owner. Dedication refers to the concept of subdivision regulations including a provision for dedicating private land or easements on private land for public purposes.

A significant advantage of easements is their permanent nature, in contrast to the temporary nature of land use zoning. Additionally, easements can typically be obtained for a fraction of the total value of the land, making them much less expensive than acquisition of the land. However, an easement does not reduce the noise impacts on people or convert incompatible land uses to compatible uses (FAA, 1983).

Water Quality

Maintaining the quality of water, especially in the nation's rivers and lakes, is the main purpose of the Clean Water Act of 1977. The Clean Water Act, through presidential executive order, prohibits the discharge of pollutants into a waterway from a point source unless a permit (issued by the **Environmental Protection Agency [EPA]** or other authorized agency) allows such a discharge. The **National Pollution Discharge Elimination System (NPDES)** permit program is the means of regulating point source discharge of pollutants into the nation's navigable waterways. In contrast to non-point source pollution (which results from runoff, precipitation and drainage), point-source discharges of industrial process water, noncontact cooling water, and collected or channeled stormwater runoff require a NPDES permit (see Figure 6-5). In essence, discharges or runoff that are made directly to surface waters require a NPDES permit.

Figure 6-5. Runoff with environmental pollutants being discharged to waterways can affect water quality.

(Wikimedia Commons; see credit on page 624)

Airports may inadvertently create a discharge of oil into the environment through fueling activities, maintenance activities, handling of drums, and filling of aboveground and underground storage tanks. Largely due to the Exxon-Valdez oil spill incident on March 24, 1989, the Oil Pollution Act of 1990 requires the development of a **facility response plan** that addresses a worst-case discharge of oil into the environment. The facility response plan will clearly demonstrate the ability of the airport to clean up spills of any sizes from its facilities, including access to the necessary personnel and equipment to do so. This is especially important if the airport is located near navigable waterways. Additionally, the 1990 Act requires airports to develop **Spill Prevention, Control and Countermeasure (SPCC)** plans if they have an aboveground oil storage capacity greater than 1,320 gallons or a buried oil storage capacity greater than 42,000 gallons, and a reasonable potential for a discharge into or upon navigable waters of the United States. The SPCC Plan, which must be certified by a professional engineer (except by small airports which may "self-certify"), is intended to prevent any discharge of oil into or upon navigable waters of the United States or adjoining shorelines. The typical contents of an SPCC Plan are as follows:

1. Contents, volumes, and locations of bulk oil storage containers
2. Container construction
3. Secondary containment measures
4. Drainage controls
5. Overfill and spill prevention measures
6. Container inspection and testing methods
7. Security measures to prevent vandalism
8. Spill control and containment countermeasures
9. Potential spill volumes and pathways
10. Training requirements

(McGormley et al., 2011, p. 35)

Generally, the requirements of the Oil Pollution Act are addressed at airports via:

1. a spill prevention task force;
2. a system or structure for containing spills;
3. a quality control program for the transfer and storage of fuel;
4. development of a training program for those involved in product transfer; and
5. the resource capability to handle any size of spill.

(AAAE, 2010, p. 136)

STORMWATER DISCHARGE

Stormwater discharge can represent the most significant source of water pollution at an airport. After a heavy rain, chemicals such as hydraulic fluid, deicing chemical, diesel fuel, jet fuel, and aviation gasoline are washed from the pavement and swept into the stormwater drainage system. It is therefore very important for airports to properly design and install stormwater drainage systems to mitigate the environmental effects of stormwater discharge. If not, surface water and groundwater can become contaminated. In addition to precipitation-induced pollution, airports can inadvertently contaminate groundwater through the storage, handling, and disposal of wastes; through leaking petroleum storage tanks; and by salt or sand stockpiles, landfills, septic tanks, and agricultural practices. The protection of groundwater is best achieved by preventing contaminants from reaching the groundwater aquifer (AAAE, 2010).

Due to the acres of paved surfaces at an airport, as well as the significant concentration of various chemicals on airport pavement, airports are required by the NPDES permit program to obtain an NPDES permit for stormwater discharge. Prior to obtaining a permit, an airport must develop a **stormwater pollution prevention plan (SWPPP)**, which provides a comprehensive approach to managing airport stormwater discharge, including stormwater discharge from all tenant areas. The SWPPP requires the airport to monitor discharges, maintain appropriate records, and report unusual discharges.

Four types of stormwater permit applications are available:

1. General
2. Individual
3. Multi-sector general
4. Construction

If an airport has over 50,000 operations annually, it must develop a stormwater prevention plan and adhere to **best management practices (BMPs)**. In essence, BMPs are those devices, systems, and practices considered proven and effective at minimizing water pollution and managing stormwater. Individual states may have additional requirements that apply to airports with less than 50,000 operations. Of these four types of stormwater permits, the construction type is required when an airport engages in rehabilitation or expansion activities that involve five or more acres.

AIRCRAFT AND PAVEMENT DEICING

Airports located in geographic areas of the country susceptible to snow and ice must not only maintain pavement (runways and taxiways) in a "no worse than wet" condition, but they must also engage in, or allow for, aircraft deicing. In maintaining pavement, various types of chemicals or liquids may be used for preventing or removing accumulations of snow and ice. The FAA has approved both fluid and solid deicers/anti-icers for use on the airside. Approved fluids include glycol-based, potassium acetate-based, and potassium formate-based fluids. Approved solid compounds include airside urea, sodium formate, and sodium acetate. In comparison to airside urea, sodium formate and sodium acetate products are more effective with colder pavement temperatures. The urea deicing function is practical only at temperatures above approximately 15°F due to the decreasing melting rates below this temperature. Additionally, agricultural-grade urea is also acceptable. In the powdered form, airside urea is typically mixed with sand. Chloride salts, similar to those used on highways or in parking lots, are not permitted on airports (AAAE, 2011).

Deicing/anti-icing chemicals are not without environmental impacts. In fact, deicing/anti-icing chemicals commonly used on airfields degrade rapidly due to chemical and biological processes. These processes often cause a large drop in the dissolved oxygen levels of receiving waters off the airport. As a result, the Environmental Protection Agency (EPA) has issued new technology-based effluent limitations guidelines and new source performance standards to control discharges of pollutants from airport deicing operations. Specifically, existing and new primary airports with 1,000 or more annual jet departures that generate wastewater associated with airfield pavement deicing are to use non-urea-containing deicers, or alternatively, meet a numeric effluent limitation for ammonia (AAAE, 2011; EPA, 2014).

Denver International Airport Glycol Recovery System

Denver International Airport has large deicing pads installed near the departure runway thresholds to allow for efficient deicing of aircraft just prior to takeoff. With the environmental considerations associated with aircraft deicing fluids, the airport also installed capture drains at the deicing pads to allow capture of a concentrated mixture of the glycol-based deicing fluid, which then flows via gravity-flow to an onsite recycling plant. During the 2009–2010 deicing season, 71 percent of sprayed aircraft deicing fluid was collected, and 72 percent of the collected aircraft deicing fluid was recycled—11 percent higher than the Environmental Protection Agency's proposed new rules. Diluted fluid (less than 1 percent glycol) is sent to an offsite wastewater treatment facility. In 2009, the airport realized a cost savings of $1.4 million over the fees for disposal at the municipal sewage treatment plant.

(Roberts and Evans, 2011)

Airports that regularly engage in aircraft deicing commonly have one or more dedicated aircraft deicing facilities. Chemicals used in aircraft deicing include propylene glycol and ethylene glycol. Aircraft deicing is accomplished by spraying one of several types of heated aqueous solutions (water and ethylene/polypropylene glycol) onto critical aircraft surfaces (see Figure 6-6). The heat of the solution and the force of the spray melt and remove the ice, snow, and frost, and the antifreeze properties of the solution prevent refreezing (AAAE, 2011).

Figure 6-6.
Aircraft deicing.

(Wikimedia Commons; see credit on page 624)

However, aircraft deicing chemicals create negative environmental impacts, especially if they reach a body of water. Each glycol compound is known for its **biochemical oxygen demand (BOD)** and for its aquatic toxicity. For example, although the propylene glycol in aircraft deicing fluid is biodegradable, it generates a high biochemical oxygen demand during decomposition, lowering oxygen levels so extensively that healthy biotic communities occupying those water bodies are at risk. Of the glycols, Type IV has a higher toxicity and higher BOD than Type I. Type IV, known as ethylene glycol, is listed as a hazardous substance by the EPA. Ethylene glycol will degrade more quickly than propylene glycol. In addition, other contaminants may be mixed in with the glycol, such as additives, oil, grease and fuel; these can affect BOD, total organic carbon (TOC), **total suspended solids (TSS)**, pH, and flow rate limits. As a result, airports have found it necessary to address environmental requirements for the retention, collection, and/or treatment of the fluid (AAAE, 2011).

Air Quality

Airports are known for generating a substantial amount of air pollutant emissions from both mobile and stationary sources. Mobile sources include aircraft, ground support equipment (GSE), auxiliary power units (APUs), motor vehicles, and construction equipment (see Figure 6-7). Stationary emissions may be from either fuel combustion or fuel evaporation. Stationary sources include fuel tanks, refueling facilities, emergency generators, boilers, space heaters, paint booths, and deicing facilities (McGormley et al., 2011).

At the federal level, both the EPA and the FAA regulate the air quality at airports. Specifically, the EPA:

- Approves state air quality plans
- Develops regulations and polices pertaining to air pollution
- Designates areas with respect to attainment of outdoor air quality standards
- Enforces violations of federal air quality regulations
- Sets air emissions standards for engines, fuels, and other emissions sources
- Sets outdoor air quality standards for air pollutants

The FAA:

- Certifies aircraft engines, fuels, pilots, and airports
- Conducts research on aviation-related environmental issues
- Enforces violations of aircraft environmental practices and standards
- Serves as lead federal agency on many environmental assessments of airport-related developments, improvements, and other actions
- Sets emissions standards for aircraft engines and fuels (jointly with EPA) (McGormley et al., 2011, p. 15)

Figure 6-7. Aircraft exhaust.

(Wikimedia Commons; see credit on page 624)

The federal requirements applicable to air quality include the Airport and Airway Improvement Act of 1982 and the Clean Air Act of 1970. First, the Airport and Airway Improvement Act of 1982 addresses airport development projects with projected air quality impacts. These projects can only receive funding and approval if (a) there are no reasonable alternatives to the project that would avoid the projected environmental impact and (b) reasonable mitigation measures will be implemented to account for the adverse impacts. Additional federal requirements are found in the Clean Air Act of 1970, as amended. Title I of the act authorizes the EPA to safeguard human health and environmental welfare with respect to air pollution. The EPA must make an endangerment finding on air pollutants that cause or contribute to air pollution or endanger the public health.

The EPA also promulgates National Ambient Air Quality Standards (NAAQS) for carbon monoxide, nitrogen dioxide, sulfur dioxide, ozone, particulate matter with mean diameters of 10 micrometers or less, particulate matter with mean diameters of 2.5 micrometers or less, and lead. States are required to monitor outdoor air quality to determine the level of compliance with NAAQS. If non-attainment areas are identified, a state must prepare and submit a State Implementation Plan (SIP) that presents emission reduction strategies. If an airport is located in a non-attainment area, it must comply with the local SIP and show that airport operations and development do not adversely affect the area's ability to meet air quality standards (McGormley et al., 2011).

Although no federal regulations currently govern greenhouse gas emissions, in 2009 the EPA declared that greenhouse gases are an endangerment to human health or environmental welfare, which allows the EPA to begin regulating greenhouse gases under the Clean Air Act. Although it remains to be seen how the EPA will regulate greenhouse gas emissions, possible options include a market-based emissions cap-and-trade system, or emissions or fuel standards for sources of greenhouse gases. Likewise, although there are currently no federal regulations on the emissions of ultrafine particulate matter (defined as those exhaust emission particles measuring 0.1 micrometers or less in diameter), research has proven that airports, and in particular jet turbine aircraft, are significant contributors of ultrafine particulate matter. Airports must, therefore, monitor developments regarding greenhouse gas emissions and ultrafine particulate matter and be prepared to assume a proactive role in minimizing the harmful environmental effects of these emissions (McGormley et al., 2011).

Hazardous Waste

The Comprehensive Environmental Response, Compensation, and Liability Act of 1980 (CERCLA), also known as "Superfund," and subsequent modifications (Superfund Amendments and Reauthorization Act of 1986 [SARA]) established criteria for closed and abandoned hazardous waste sites; allowed for the liability of individuals and/or companies found responsible for the release of hazardous waste (generally including toxic, flammable, corrosive, or environmentally harmful substances); and perhaps most significantly, created a funding source that provides for the cleanup of hazardous waste sites when the responsible individuals and/or companies either cannot be located or are no longer in existence. The Superfund is important because inactive sites may still release hazardous substances into the environment, requiring that they be cleaned up. If the company or organization responsible for the toxic waste site is no longer in business or financially able to fund the cleanup, the Superfund is available to fund the cleanup effort. According to Superfund, potentially responsible parties include:

1. The owner or operator of a facility.
2. Any person, who at the time of disposal of any hazardous substance, owned or operated any facility where the hazardous wastes were disposed.
3. Any person who arranged for hazardous substance treatment or disposal.
4. Any person who arranged for the transport of hazardous substances for treatment or disposal.
5. Any person who accepts or accepted hazardous substance for transport to disposal or treatment facilities, incineration vessels, or other selected sites (AAAE, 2010, pp. 141–142).

The Superfund law is rather broad and applies to hazardous waste for as long as it exists and remains hazardous. Acting as the landlord, airport management remains responsible for all hazardous waste that is generated (or exists) on the airport. This is true regardless of when the waste was created and even if the airport manager was not responsible for generating or placing the hazardous waste on airport. This is important, because if the airport acquires property with hazardous waste that was not cleaned up prior to the acquisition, the airport may be liable for cleanup costs. Although the Superfund law requires current owners of contaminated property to adequately clean up the site, this does not always occur. In addition to the requirements of CERCLA, SARA requires emergency response plans that contain procedures for fuel spills and hazardous waste exposure, as well as allowing for public participation in the decision-making process regarding remediation methods for contamination cleanup. Under SARA, federal facilities became subject to Superfund as well (AAAE, 2010).

The Emergency Planning and Community Right-to-Know Act (EPCRA) is another piece of legislation that affects airports in the environmental area. Under EPCRA, states are required to establish local chemical emergency preparedness programs, making these programs available to the public. Additionally, anyone manufacturing, processing, storing, or using hazardous substances is required to report this information to appropriate state and local officials.

Under the Occupational Safety and Health Act of 1970, airports are required to have a **material safety data sheet (MSDS)** for each hazardous chemical present on the airport. MSDS are intended to provide workers and emergency personnel with procedures for handling that substance in a safe manner, and include information on the chemical's melting point, boiling point, and/or flash point, toxicity, health effects, first aid, reactivity, storage, disposal, protective equipment, and spill-handling procedures (Figure 6-8). The EPCRA requires airports with chemicals covered by MSDS to comply with regular hazardous chemical inventory reporting requirements.

The Resource Conservation and Recovery Act of 1976 (RCRA)—actually an amendment to the Solid Waste Disposal Act of 1965—is another environmental law affecting airports. Designed to provide a framework for managing and recycling wastes, the RCRA applies to airports that generate or transport hazardous wastes, as well as those that operate a facility for the storage, treatment, or disposal of hazardous wastes. The EPA is given authority, in part, by the RCRA. In regulating hazardous substances, the EPA requires extensive record keeping, warning labels on waste containers, and transport manifests when hazardous wastes are being transported for disposal (AAAE, 2010).

Hazardous waste generators under RCRA are categorized based on the volume of hazardous waste generated.

Figure 6-8. Right to know station, including availability of material safety data sheets for hazardous chemicals and substances in use at this workplace.

(Lee Brown, Fort Lauderdale-Hollywood International Airport.)

- **Conditionally Exempt Small Quantity Generators (CESQGs)**—Generate less than 100 kg per month. Authorized to accumulate no more than 1,000 kg at any time.
- **Small Quantity Generators (SQGs)**—Generate more than 100 kg per month, but less than 1,000 kg per month. Authorized to accumulate no more than 6,000 kg in any 180-day period.
- **Large Quantity Generators (LQGs)**—Generate more than 1,000 kg of waste per month. Authorized to accumulate no more than 6,000 kg in any 90-day period.

Special permits may allow for greater accumulation limits. Additionally, stored waste is required to be taken off-site or treated within 180 days (270 days if the treatment plant is 200 miles or further away), unless a permit allows for storage, treatment, and disposal on-site. An airport is prohibited from disposing of waste on the airport unless a permit allowing for such disposal has been obtained. Of course, if hazardous waste is generated and/or stored on the airport, it is imperative for the airport to prevent accidental release of the hazardous substances into the environment. Prevention of a hazardous substance release is most effectively ensured with a preparedness and prevention plan. This plan will detail emergency communication methods, firefighting equipment and response, and the types of hazardous waste to be generated and the storage locations on airport (McGormley et al., 2011).

In addition, the 1984 Hazardous and Solid Waste Amendments to RCRA address **underground storage tanks (USTs)**, specifically establishing requirements for tank design, release/leak detection, and **leaking underground storage tanks (LUSTs)**. USTs at airports typically contain jet fuel, used oil, fuel oil, diesel, or gasoline. Although most states have developed state-specific UST requirements, the EPA regulates the states without such a program. Owners of USTs are required to register their tanks with either their state or the EPA (in the absence of a state program). In addition to registering the tank ownership, location, facility type, and contact information, owners of USTs must provide evidence of financial ability to address leaks and other environmental concerns associated with the UST, as well as compensate third parties for accidental releases of petroleum and CERCLA hazardous substances from the UST. For the installation of new USTs, owners must certify compliance with tank and piping installation requirements, cathodic protection, financial responsibility, and release/leak detection (Figure 6-9) (McGormley et al., 2011).

If there is an accidental release of a hazardous substance (covered under CERCLA) or an extremely hazardous substance (covered under EPCRA) in excess of its reportable quantities and anticipated to affect areas that are beyond the facility boundaries, airports are required to notify their local emergency planning committee and the state emergency response commission. Releases of hazardous substances (under CERCLA) also require notification to the **National Response Center (NRC)**. Notification will contain the name of

Figure 6-9. Installation of underground storage tank.

(©iStock.com/bissell)

the substance, an estimate of the quantity released, time and duration of the release, known or anticipated acute or chronic health risks associated with the substance, etc. If a release is solely within the airport boundaries or federally permitted, this reporting is not required (McGormley et al., 2011).

Federal regulations have also been adopted to manage the registration, manufacturing, transportation, sale, labeling, storage, application, and disposal of pesticides in the United States. The Federal Insecticide, Fungicide, and Rodenticide Act of 1947 (as amended) (FIFRA) addresses these aspects of pesticide management. Airports typically apply pesticides to control vegetation and pests. Although an airport may contract out these services, if an airport handles pesticides in-house, airport management must ensure that FIFRA is complied with. For airports, the most applicable aspects of FIFRA include storage and labeling, as well as application and disposal. The regulation requires

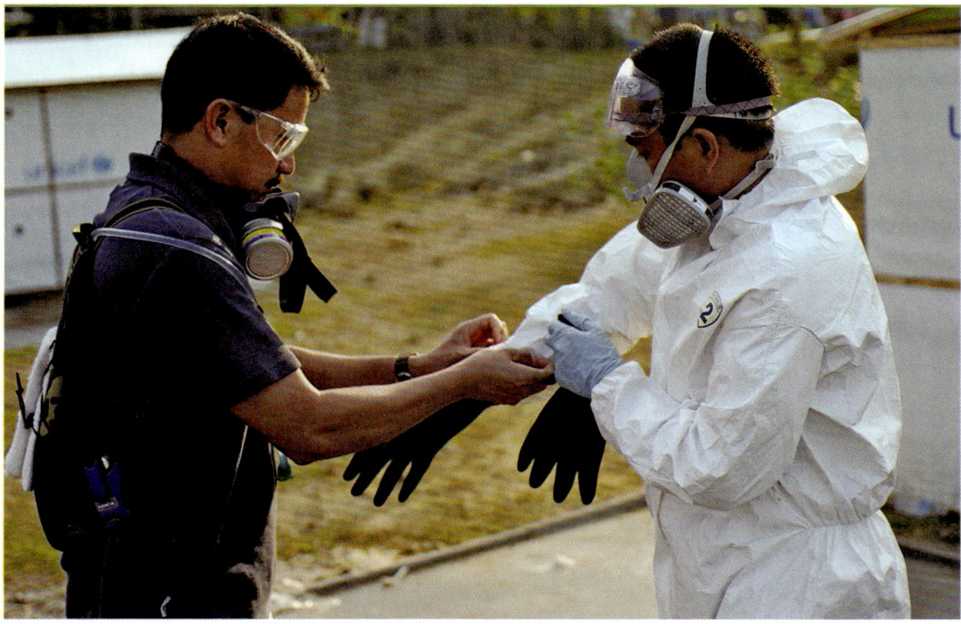

Figure 6-10. Personal protective equipment.

(Wikimedia Commons; see credit on page 624)

pesticides to be stored in an approved container/package and be properly labeled with the pesticide registration number, health hazards, and warnings. Individuals applying pesticides classified as "restricted-use" must either be certified as a commercial or private applicator or be supervised by a certified commercial or private applicator. Additionally, any individual applying pesticides should wear proper **personal protective equipment (PPE)** as specified on the product labeling (see Figure 6-10). Disposal of containers used to apply pesticides must be triple rinsed or pressure rinsed prior to disposal. Unused pesticides may be recycled by adhering to universal waste management procedures (McGormley et al., 2011).

Sustainable Environmental Stewardship

Proactive environmental stewardship offers numerous environmental, social, and financial benefits, including:

- Reduced life cycle costs of capital assets
- Reduced operating costs
- Reduced environmental footprint
- Optimization for new and better technologies
- Reduced costs of asset development
- Enhanced bond ratings
- Reduced environmental, health, and safety risks
- Improved work environment for employees, leading to higher productivity
- Better customer service and satisfaction
- Enhanced relationships with the surrounding community

Airport sustainability has been defined as "a holistic approach to managing an airport so as to ensure the integrity of economic viability, operational efficiency, natural resource conservation, and social responsibility of the airport." (McGormley et al., 2011, p. 101). Sustainability planning at airports incorporates a proactive approach to environmental stewardship and affects every effort the airport takes. Sustainability planning involves:

- *Developing a sustainability vision or policy*—In concert with the airport mission, this will set forth the direction of the airport regarding environmental stewardship.
- *Conducting a baseline assessment/gap analysis*—Determining the airport's current environmental impacts is essential in identifying opportunities for improvement. By examining current conditions and then determining where gaps exist, it is easier to determine areas for improvement.
- *Establishing goals and objectives*—Goals and objectives flow from the sustainability vision and are developed on consultation with stakeholders.

- *Setting performance targets*—Setting performance targets and metrics is important to meet established goals and objectives. Typical environmental performance metrics include potable water use per square foot of building area or passenger, electricity consumption per square foot of building area or passenger, and rate of recycling waste as a percentage of total waste generated.
- *Identifying sustainability practices*—This involves identifying reasonable and practical sustainability practices considering the airport's available resources. In evaluating which initiatives would be most beneficial, useful criteria include the priorities of the airport, benefits and costs of each practice, resources required to implement and maintain each practice, and the potential cost savings or return on investment.
- *Implementing practices*—This involves implementing the selected initiatives by identifying priority projects, funding them, and developing schedules and individual responsibilities.
- *Regularly measuring, reporting, and reevaluating*—Using metrics previously developed, the airport is able to measure progress and ascertain the performance of its sustainability program.

(McGormley et al., 2011, pp. 102–103)

A number of airports have adopted specific environmental stewardship practices that have proven successful in generating both positive environmental benefits and positive goodwill and community relations. One such practice is the pursuit of **Leadership in Energy and Environmental Design (LEED)** accreditation. Developed by the U.S. Green Building Council (USGBC), LEED provides building owners and operators with a framework for identifying and implementing practical and measurable green building design, construction, operations and maintenance solutions. Specifically, LEED certification provides independent, third-party verification that a building, home or community was designed and built using strategies aimed at achieving high performance in key areas of human and environmental health: sustainable site development, water savings, energy efficiency, materials selection, and indoor environmental quality. Among airports, Terminal 2 at San Francisco International Airport was the first airport terminal in the United States to achieve LEED Gold certification. Highlights include dining options that feature locally grown and organic foods, hydration stations, eco-friendly child play areas, natural light, cleaner air, connection to mass transit, zero waste, water conservation, paperless ticketing, and use of sustainable building materials. Since Terminal 2 at San Francisco International Airport, other airports have developed new LEED facilities. For example, in January 2014, the newly constructed aircraft rescue and firefighting station at Southwest Florida International earned the LEED Gold Certification due to energy-efficient lighting and mechanical systems, low-flow water fixtures, a rainwater reclamation system that collects and stores water to be used for landscaping irrigation, recycling and separating of construction debris and

San Francisco International Airport Terminal 2

In 2011, San Francisco International Airport's Terminal 2 (T2) was the first airport terminal in the United States to achieve LEED Gold status. LEED references the Leadership in Energy and Environmental Design by the U.S. Green Building Council (USGBC). The 640,000 square foot T2 has many unique features, including a wide array of natural and organic culinary offerings; more than 400 computer plug-in outlets and intuitive, comfortable work-station seating; eco-friendly art installations from local artists that highlight the natural world and double as children's play areas; and convenient "hydration stations" that allow travelers to refill reusable water bottles post-security. Additionally, T2 produces cleaner air due to a special displacement ventilation system; natural sunlight enhances the interior lighting; and a paperless ticketing system reduces waste and adds convenience. T2 provides a car-free connection with direct connection to Bay Area Rapid Transit (BART); is zero-waste, replacing traditional garbage cans with waste stations incorporating compartments for composting, recyclables and trash; and conserves water via a dual plumbing system that allows for reclaimed water from the airport's water treatment facility to be used for toilets and other uses throughout the airport, as well as plumbing fixtures that use 40 percent less water than typical fixtures.

(San Francisco International Airport, 2011)

waste, and the use of reflective building materials and allowance of natural light into the building (McCarron, 2011).

Another practice involves encouraging alternative transportation means for employees and passengers. For example, airports may encourage more frequent use of public transportation by providing public transit incentives for employees and ensure convenient connections to public transportation by passengers. Additionally, bicycle lanes, special parking areas for electric/hybrid vehicles, and storage racks for bicycles could be installed. Airports have also encouraged use of compressed natural gas-powered buses, electric vehicles, and three-wheeled bikes for maintenance employees.

Yet another practice involves encouraging biodiversity. Airports can do this by planting native, non-wildlife attracting landscaping that needs less irrigation than non-native species. Airports may also partner with local environmental organizations.

Airports may also adopt measures to counteract climate change and reduce the airport's carbon footprint by becoming more energy efficient. By conducting an energy audit, the airport can determine where energy is used at the airport. Examples of energy efficient measures include escalator sleep-mode settings, motion-activated lighting in infrequently used areas, Energy Star computers and equipment, and fluorescent and LED lighting.

A relatively new trend among airports involves capitalizing on renewable energy sources such as solar, wind, and geothermal. Often the most visible of these are installations of photovoltaic (PV) module installations. Quite a few airports have installed PV arrays, including Denver International Airport (DIA), Fresno Yosemite International Airport (FAT), and Tallahassee Regional Airport (TLH). PV installations can be quite expensive, however, in essence requiring that 20+ years of electricity is paid for up front. In the case of TLH, in 2010 the purchase and installation of a 25 kilowatt (kW) system was $125,000, while a 75 kW system was $350,000 to $400,000. Return on investment (ROI) was estimated at 40 years for a 25 kW system and 34 years for a 75 kW system, although these timeframes will be significantly lessened (to 8.6 years and 23.8 years, respectively) with an energy efficiency and conservation block grant. At Fresno Yosemite International Airport, the solar installation is expected to supply 40 percent of the airport's energy needs, saving the airport $13 million over 20 years. Regardless of which environmental stewardship practices are adopted, airports can directly lessen their impact on the environment in a publicly acceptable way by pursuing sustainable environmental stewardship (McGormley et al., 2011).

Concluding Thoughts

Airports are responsible for complying with numerous environmental regulations. Whether it be noise, land use compatibility, zoning, water quality, air quality, or hazardous waste, it is imperative for airport managers to understand the importance of environmental compliance and develop policies and procedures to ensure that all businesses on the airport meet environmental requirements.

Chapter Summary

- An environmental management system (EMS) is the foundation for a strategic and proactive approach to ensuring environmental compliance and is becoming a standard practice at airports desiring to formalize their approach to proactive environmental management.
- The foundation of a good-faith effort requires airports to ensure tenant and contractor compliance through initial bid specifications and/or requests for proposals, periodic inspections and audits, and lease and contract agreements.
- Environmental regulations are "without regard to fault," meaning that an airport manager or other personnel can be found guilty of noncompliance even if there was not intent to commit a crime.

- The National Environmental Policy Act of 1969 required airports (among other industries) to completely consider the environmental impacts of a proposed project prior to initiating it.
- A project may be categorically excluded from the environmental impact study requirements if, according to FAA Order 5050.4B, projects of that type have been found under normal circumstances to have no potential for significant environmental impact.
- If a project is either not categorically excluded or is categorically excluded but likely to involve extraordinary circumstances, then an environmental assessment may be required.
- The EA results in one of two findings—either no significant impacts or significant impacts. If the former, a finding of no significant impact (FONSI) is prepared. If, on the other hand, the impacts of the proposed project are determined to be significant, an environmental impact statement (EIS) may be required.
- The FAA has adopted a cumulative noise metric—the average day-night sound level (DNL) in A-weighted decibels. DNL is the 24-hour average sound level in A-weighted decibels for the period midnight to midnight.
- 14 CFR Part 150 contains the procedures, standards, and methodology addressing the development, submission, and review of noise exposure maps and noise compatibility plans.
- According to Part 150, all types of land use are considered to be compatible with noise levels less than 65 dB DNL.
- The reduction of airport noise is generally accomplished via (a) reduction of noise at the source, (b) relocation of the source of the noise in either space or time, and (c) acoustical changes to the area receiving the noise.
- Although voluntary, Part 150 programs are strongly recommended by the FAA if the airport has (a) significant amounts of noise-affected incompatible land use, (b) the receipt of serious noise complaints, (c) a threat from urban development pressure to increase incompatible land use near the airport, or (d) the introduction of major changes in airport facilities or operations that are likely to shift or increase noise patterns.
- The standard prediction analysis tool for use by airports, the FAA's Integrated Noise Model, calculates the total impact of aircraft noise at or around airports. The INM produces noise exposure contours that are used to produce NEMs and aid the airport in land use compatibility planning.
- Maintaining the quality of water, especially in the nation's rivers and lakes, is the main purpose of the Clean Water Act of 1977.
- The National Pollution Discharge Elimination System permit program is the means of regulating point source discharge of pollutants into the nation's navigable waterways.

- The Oil Pollution Act of 1990 requires the development of (a) a facility response plan that addresses a worst-case discharge of oil into the environment and (b) a Spill Prevention, Control and Countermeasure (SPCC) plan if the airport has an aboveground oil storage capacity greater than 1,320 gallons or a buried oil storage capacity greater than 42,000 gallons, and a reasonable potential for a discharge into or upon navigable waters of the United States.
- Airports are required by the National Pollution Discharge Elimination System permit program to obtain an NPDES permit for stormwater discharge. Prior to obtaining a permit, an airport must develop a stormwater pollution prevention plan.
- The FAA has approved both fluid and solid deicers/anti-icers for use on pavements. Approved fluids include glycol-based, potassium acetate-based, and potassium formate-based fluids. Approved solid compounds include airside urea, sodium formate, and sodium acetate.
- Chemicals used in aircraft deicing include propylene glycol and ethylene glycol.
- The EPA approves state air quality plans; develops regulations and polices pertaining to air pollution; designates areas with respect to attainment of outdoor air quality standards; enforces violations of federal air quality regulations; sets air emissions standards for engines, fuels, and other emissions sources; and sets outdoor air quality standards for air pollutants.
- The Comprehensive Environmental Response, Compensation, and Liability Act of 1980, also known as "Superfund," and subsequent modifications (Superfund Amendments and Reauthorization Act of 1986) established criteria for closed and abandoned hazardous waste sites, allowed for the liability of individuals and/or companies found responsible for the release of hazardous waste, and created a funding source that provides for the cleanup of hazardous waste sites when the responsible individuals and/or companies either cannot be located or are no longer in existence.
- Under the Occupational Safety and Health Act of 1970, airports are required to have material safety data sheets for each hazardous chemical present on the airport. MSDS are intended to provide workers and emergency personnel with procedures for handling that substance in a safe manner, and include information on the chemical's physical properties, toxicity, health effects, first aid, etc.
- The 1984 Hazardous and Solid Waste Amendments to RCRA address underground storage tanks, specifically establishing requirements for tank design, release/leak detection, and leaking underground storage tanks.
- Sustainability planning involves developing a sustainability vision or policy, conducting a baseline assessment/gap analysis, establishing goals and objectives, setting performance targets, identifying sustainability practices, implementing practices, and regularly measuring, reporting, and reevaluating.

Review Questions

1. What are some of the airport activities that can result in environmental impacts?
2. Explain an environmental management system, including the benefits and steps in development.
3. What is required of airports by the National Environmental Policy Act of 1969?
4. Explain the environmental impact statement.
5. Explain the decibel scale.
6. What standard noise metric is used to measure aircraft noise?
7. Explain the purpose of 14 CFR Part 150.
8. What is the purpose of a noise compatibility plan?
9. What are the most common noise mitigation measures?
10. Explain how a continuous airport noise monitoring system works.
11. Under what conditions is a Part 150 program strongly recommended?
12. Explain the Integrated Noise Model (INM).
13. Explain compatible land use.
14. Explain the purpose of easements.
15. What are the typical components of a Spill Prevention, Control and Countermeasure plan?
16. Explain the chemicals used in maintaining airport pavements during snow and icing conditions.
17. Explain the chemicals used in deicing aircraft.
18. What is the purpose of material safety data sheets?
19. Under what situations would the National Response Center (NRC) be notified?
20. Explain what sustainability planning involves.

Scenarios ↘

1. As the new environmental manager at Blue Junction Airport, you have been asked to develop an environmental management system. First, what are the benefits of doing so? Second, how would you develop such a system?
2. A former FBO operator at your airport has left behind several underground storage tanks on their former leasehold. One was used for Avgas and one for Jet-A fuel. Now that the airport is planning to redevelop the area once occupied by this FBO, what must be done with these underground tanks? If problems are discovered (i.e., leaking tanks with contaminated soil), how should this be resolved? What if the former FBO operator can't be located or is bankrupt and no longer in business?
3. With a Part 150 study recently completed, it is obvious that several residential areas surrounding the airport are affected by noise (included in the 70 dB DNL contour). What options are available to the airport to minimize the impacted areas?
4. With the EPA's new technology-based effluent limitations guidelines and new source performance standards to control discharges of pollutants from airport deicing operations, you are tasked with minimizing the environmental impact of airfield pavement deicing at your airport. What are your options for ensuring compliance?
5. What options are available to you to reduce emissions at your airport? Consider emissions from aircraft APUs at the gate, ground support equipment, airport vehicles, public transit, etc.

References and Resources for Further Study

American Association of Airport Executives (AAAE). 2010. "Body of Knowledge Module 2. Planning, construction, and environmental." Washington, DC: AAAE.

———. 2011. "ACE Operations Module 4: Hazardous Materials, FOD, Wildlife, ARFF, Winter Operations, and Security." Alexandria, VA: AAAE.

Environmental Protection Agency (EPA). 2014. "Airport Deicing Effluent Guidelines." Retrieved from http://water.epa.gov/scitech/wastetech/guide/airport/index.cfm

Federal Aviation Administration (FAA). n.d. "Details on FAA Noise Levels, Stages, and Phaseouts." Retrieved from http://www.faa.gov/about/office_org/headquarters_offices/apl/noise_emissions/airport_aircraft_noise_issues/levels/

———. 1983. *Noise Control and Compatibility Planning for Airports*. AC 150/5020-1. Washington, DC: FAA.

———. 2002. *Estimated Airplane Noise Levels in A-weighted Decibels*. AC 36-3. Washington, DC: FAA.

———. 2007. *Environmental Management Systems for Airport Sponsors*. AC 150/5050-8. Washington, DC: FAA.

Massport. n.d. "Mitigating Airport Noise in the Community." Retrieved at http://www.massport.com/environment/environmental-reporting/noise-abatement/sound-insulation-program/

McCarron, M. 2011. Media Advisory, "SFO's Terminal 2 Certified LEED Gold." Retrieved from http://www.flysfo.com/web/page/about/news/pressrel/2011/sf1186.html

McGormley, R. W., J. A. Lengel, D. E. Seal, J. N. Foster, M. Kenney, P. K. Sanford, B. J. Siwinski, C. Lurie, E. Humblet. 2011. "ACRP Report 43: Guidebook of Practices for Improving Environmental Performance at Small Airports." Washington, DC: Transportation Research Board. Retrieved from http://onlinepubs.trb.org/onlinepubs/acrp/acrp_rpt_043.pdf

Roberts, D. and G. Evans. 2011. "Recycling: DEN's Sustainable Approach." Retrieved from http://www.aviationpros.com/article/10290507/recycling-dens-sustainable-approach?page=2

San Francisco International Airport. 2011. "SFO's Terminal 2 Certified LEED® Gold." News release. Retrieved from http://www.flysfo.com/media/press-releases/sfos-terminal-2-certified-leed%C2%AE-gold

Chapter 7

Operations

Objectives

Upon completion of this chapter, you should understand:

- the airports to which 14 CFR Part 139 applies
- the classes of Part 139 airports
- the airport certification manual (ACM) and its typical contents
- each of the sections of 14 CFR Part 139 and the conditions to which certificated airports must adhere
- the purpose of a snow and ice control plan (SICP)
- the aircraft rescue and firefighting (ARFF) index, equipment and agents, and operational requirements
- the airport emergency plan (AEP)
- wildlife hazard management
- the NOTAM system
- airport communications
- the impacts of new generation aircraft

Key Terms

active control
airport certification manual (ACM)
airport emergency plan (AEP)
Airport/Facility Directory (A/FD)
airport operating certificate (AOC)
ARFF Index
Class I
Class II
Class III
Class IV
habitat management
new large aircraft (NLA)
Notice to Airmen (NOTAM)
scheduled operation
snow and ice control plan (SICP)
turret
unscheduled operation
wildlife attractant
wildlife strike

In Chapter 7

Introduction **277**

Title 14 CFR Part 139 .... **277**

- Records 281
- Personnel 282
- Paved Areas 283
- Unpaved Areas... 284
- Safety Areas 285
- Marking, Signs, and Lighting 286
- Snow and Ice Control.................................... 287
- ARFF: Index Determination............................. 289
- ARFF: Equipment and Agents 290
- ARFF: Operational Requirements 291
- Handling and Storing of Hazardous Substances and Materials 295
- Traffic and Wind Direction Indicators 296
- Airport Emergency Plan................................. 296
- Self-Inspection Program 298
- Pedestrians and Ground Vehicles.................... 299
- Obstructions 301
- Protection of NAVAIDs 301
- Public Protection 302
- Wildlife Hazard Management.......................... 302
- Airport Condition Reporting............................ 304
- Identifying, Marking, and Lighting Construction and Other Unserviceable Areas.................... 305
- Noncomplying Conditions 306

Airport Communications........................ **306**

Wildlife Hazard Management **308**

New Generation Aircraft.........................**312**

Concluding Thoughts.............................**314**

Chapter Summary **314**

Review Questions..................................**317**

Scenarios...**318**

References and Resources for Further Study **319**

FEATURES

Ronald Reagan Washington National Airport Emergency Exercise.............................. 297

A full-scale emergency exercise in compliance with 14 CFR §139.325

Orlando International Airport's Wildlife Hazard Management Program 310

Efforts to minimize wildlife hazards at Orlando International Airport have enhanced safety for airport users.

Introduction

Airports, by their nature, are operations-driven. It is the operation of aircraft that justifies the existence of an airport. Although airports across the United States vary in size and operational activity, airport operators must focus on providing safe airports that are properly maintained. This chapter discusses the operation of public-use airports in the United States (Figure 7-1).

Figure 7-1. San Francisco International Airport, a public-use, publicly-owned Part 139 certificated airport.

(©iStock.com/StephanHoerold)

Title 14 CFR Part 139

The federal regulation that applies to the commercial service airports in the United States is 14 CFR Part 139, Certification of Airports. This regulation applies to all airports serving scheduled air carrier aircraft with more than 9 seats and unscheduled air carrier aircraft with more than 30 seats. Part 139 does not apply to:

- GA airports (meaning those airports not being served by air carriers)
- Airports serving scheduled air carrier operations only by reason of being designated as an alternate airport
- Airports operated by the United States
- Airports located in the State of Alaska that only serve scheduled operations of small air carrier aircraft and do not serve scheduled or unscheduled operations of large air carrier aircraft (small aircraft have a certificated maximum takeoff weight of 12,500 pounds or less)
- Airports located in the state of Alaska during periods of time when not serving operations of large air carrier aircraft
- Heliports

(FAA, 2004, p. 1)

Among those airports to which Part 139 does apply, four classes of airports exist. These classes are:

- **Class I**—Serve scheduled operations of large air carrier aircraft and unscheduled passenger operations of large air carrier aircraft and/or scheduled operations of small air carrier aircraft.
- **Class II**—Serve scheduled operations of small air carrier aircraft and unscheduled passenger operations of large air carrier aircraft.
- **Class III**—Serve scheduled operations of small air carrier aircraft.
- **Class IV**—Serve unscheduled passenger operations of large air carrier aircraft.

(FAA, 2004)

As of 2015, there were 393 Class I airports, 33 Class II airports, 31 Class III airports, and 82 Class IV airports, resulting in 544 certificated airports nationwide. As evident by these numbers, most of the certificated airports in the United States are capable of serving any type of operation and size of aircraft as may be necessary.

A **scheduled operation** is any common carriage passenger-carrying operation for compensation or hire conducted by an air carrier for which the air carrier or its representatives offer in advance the departure location, departure time, and arrival location. An **unscheduled operation** is any common carriage passenger-carrying operation for compensation or hire, using aircraft designed for at least 31 passenger seats, conducted by an air carrier for which the departure time, departure location, and arrival location are specifically negotiated with the customer or the customer's representative. Unscheduled operations include any passenger-carrying supplemental operation conducted under 14 CFR Part 121 and any passenger-carrying public charter operation conducted under 14 CFR Part 380. In simple terms, an unscheduled operation is typically a charter of some sort, whereas a scheduled operation occurs at the same time each week, allowing anyone to plan to take a scheduled flight (FAA, 2004).

For an airport to operate under Part 139, it must apply for and obtain an **airport operating certificate (AOC)** from the FAA. Obtaining an AOC requires developing an **airport certification manual (ACM)** that addresses each of the requirements in Part 139. The ACM provides specific local guidance unique to that airport and explains how the airport will comply with each of the requirements of Part 139. Since Part 139 is a regulation that applies to airports, large and small, the airport develops an ACM to notify the FAA how their specific airport will comply with the regulation. Thus, although there are similarities among various airports' ACMs, each ACM is unique to the airport for which it is developed.

It is a best practice to address each section of Part 139 Subpart D, in order, in the ACM. Many airports develop their ACM using the exact same numbering as the sections in Subpart D. The FAA likes an ACM that has the same structure as Subpart D, and this can easily be done by incorporating the same numbering system as the regulation. Typically, the ACM is prepared in a three-ring binder, allowing for subsequent revisions of specific pages without the need to revise the entire manual. Each page of the ACM is approved and signed by the FAA. A page control table at the front of the manual allows the airport and the FAA to make certain the manual is current, based on future page revisions. Once prepared, the ACM is submitted to the FAA for approval. Once approved, the ACM is updated regularly with any revised pages submitted to the FAA for approval.

A key point to remember when preparing an ACM is that it should be comprehensive, yet conservative. The ACM, once approved by the FAA, becomes an extension of the regulation and the airport will be held responsible for complying with this extension of the regulation. For instance, if Part 139 requires a self-inspection once each day, but the airport states in the ACM that three will be conducted each day, the airport will in fact be held to the three-per-day standard, even though it is contrary to the regulation. Part 139 contains minimum requirements, and the airport should meet these minimums. Exceeding these minimums is admirable, but formalizing in the ACM the specific manner by which the minimums will be exceeded is not recommended.

To be eligible for an AOC, airports must (a) provide written documentation that air carrier service will begin on a certain date, (b) submit an ACM, and (c) be found properly and adequately equipped and able to provide a safe airport operating environment in accordance with Part 139 and the ACM. It should be noted that not all airports are eligible to obtain an AOC, even if they prepare and submit an ACM. The FAA is only interested in providing an AOC to airports that will serve air carriers, whether scheduled or unscheduled. Once obtained, an AOC is effective until the airport surrenders it or the FAA suspends or revokes it. Although an AOC has no expiration date, certificated airports are required to ensure their ACM is current at all times. Each page of the ACM will have an approval date (typically in the form of a date block with the initials of the FAA certification inspector approving the page).

Each ACM is required to have certain elements that address each of the required areas of Part 139. Interestingly, Class I, Class II, and Class III airports are each required to include the same elements in their ACM. However, Class IV airports are not required to include seven of the elements that other Classes of Part 139 airports are required to include. See Table 7-1 for the required certification manual elements.

Subpart D of Part 139, entitled Operations, presents the specific requirements for certificated airports relating to daily airport operations. In essence, Subpart D presents the "real meat" of the regulation as it pertains to airports.

Table 7-1. Required elements in an airport certification manual.

Manual elements	Airport certificate class			
	Class I	Class II	Class III	Class IV
1. Lines of succession of airport operational responsibility	X	X	X	X
2. Each current exemption issued to the airport from the requirements of this part	X	X	X	X
3. Any limitations imposed by the Administrator	X	X	X	X
4. A grid map or other means of identifying locations and terrain features on and around the airport that are significant to emergency operations	X	X	X	X
5. The location of each obstruction required to be lighted or marked within the airport's area of authority	X	X	X	X
6. A description of each movement area available for air carriers and its safety areas, and each road described in §139.319(k) that serves it	X	X	X	X
7. Procedures for avoidance of interruption or failure during construction work of utilities serving facilities or NAVAIDS that support air carrier operations	X	X	X	
8. A description of the system for maintaining records, as required under §139.301	X	X	X	X
9. A description of personnel training, as required under §139.303	X	X	X	X
10. Procedures for maintaining the paved areas, as required under §139.305	X	X	X	X
11. Procedures for maintaining the unpaved areas, as required under §139.307	X	X	X	X
12. Procedures for maintaining the safety areas, as required under §139.309	X	X	X	X
13. A plan showing the runway and taxiway identification system, including the location and inscription of signs, runway markings, and holding position markings, as required under §139.311	X	X	X	X
14. A description of, and procedures for maintaining, the marking, signs, and lighting systems, as required under §139.311	X	X	X	X
15. A snow and ice control plan, as required under §139.313	X	X	X	
16. A description of the facilities, equipment, personnel, and procedures for meeting the aircraft rescue and firefighting requirements, in accordance with §§139.315, 139.317 and 139.319	X	X	X	X
17. A description of any approved exemption to aircraft rescue and firefighting requirements, as authorized under §139.111	X	X	X	X
18. Procedures for protecting persons and property during the storing, dispensing, and handling of fuel and other hazardous substances and materials, as required under §139.321	X	X	X	X

Table 7-1. *(continued)*

Manual elements	Airport certificate class			
	Class I	Class II	Class III	Class IV
19. A description of, and procedures for maintaining, the traffic and wind direction indicators, as required under §139.323	X	X	X	X
20. An emergency plan as required under §139.325	X	X	X	X
21. Procedures for conducting the self-inspection program, as required under §139.327	X	X	X	X
22. Procedures for controlling pedestrians and ground vehicles in movement areas and safety areas, as required under §139.329	X	X	X	X
23. Procedures for obstruction removal, marking, or lighting, as required under §139.331	X	X	X	X
24. Procedures for protection of NAVAIDS, as required under §139.333	X	X	X	
25. A description of public protection, as required under §139.335	X	X	X	
26. Procedures for wildlife hazard management, as required under §139.337	X	X	X	
27. Procedures for airport condition reporting, as required under §139.339	X	X	X	X
28. Procedures for identifying, marking, and lighting construction and other unserviceable areas, as required under §139.341	X	X	X	
29. Any other item that the Administrator finds is necessary to ensure safety in air transportation	X	X	X	X

RECORDS

First, §139.301, Records, requires airports to maintain personnel training records, as required by §§139.303 and 139.327, for 24 consecutive calendar months. Emergency personnel training records for aircraft rescue and firefighting and emergency medical service personnel, as required by §139.319, must be retained for 24 consecutive calendar months. Records of airport fueling agent inspections, as required by §139.321, must be maintained for 12 consecutive calendar months. Records of fueling personnel training, as required by §139.321, must be maintained for 12 consecutive calendar months.

Figure 7-2. 14 CFR Part 139 specifies requirements for records that must be maintained and furnished to the FAA upon request.

(Wikimedia Commons; see credit on page 624)

Records of self-inspections, as required by §139.327, must be maintained for 12 consecutive calendar months. Records of training given to pedestrians and ground vehicle operators with access to movement areas and safety areas, as required by §139.329, must be maintained for 24 consecutive calendar months. Records of each accident or incident in movement areas and safety areas involving an air carrier aircraft and/or ground vehicle, as required by §139.329, must be maintained for 12 consecutive calendar months. Records of airport condition information dissemination, as required by §139.339, must be maintained for 12 consecutive calendar months. Each of the records required to be maintained under §139.301 must be furnished to the FAA upon request, which usually occurs once annually during the annual certification inspection (Figure 7-2) (FAA, 2004).

PERSONNEL

14 CFR §139.303, Personnel, requires airports to provide sufficient and qualified personnel to comply with the requirements of the airport's ACM. Personnel who access movement areas and safety areas and perform duties in compliance with the ACM and Part 139 must be trained prior to the initial performance of duties and at least once every 12 consecutive calendar months thereafter in at least the following areas:

- Airport familiarization, including airport marking, lighting, and signs systems
- Procedures for access to, and operation in, movement areas and safety areas
- Airport communications, including radio communication between the air traffic control tower and personnel, use of the common traffic advisory frequency if there is no air traffic control tower or the tower is not in operation, and procedures for reporting unsafe airport conditions
- Duties required under the airport certification manual and the requirements of Part 139.
- Any additional subject areas required under §§139.319, 139.321, 139.327, 139.329, 139.337, and 139.339, as appropriate.

Airports must also equip these personnel with sufficient resources necessary to perform the functions required of them according to the ACM (Figure 7-3). Generally, new operations personnel spend three to six months receiving on-the-job training, including learning the layout of the airfield, the airport's inspection program, Security Identification Display Area (SIDA) and movement area training, and familiarization with the ACM, emergency response manual (ERM), etc.

Figure 7-3. Airport operations vehicle.

PAVED AREAS

Section 139.305, Paved Areas, requires airports to maintain and promptly repair the pavement of each runway, taxiway, loading ramp, and parking area on the airport that is available for air carrier use. Specifically, airports are required to maintain pavement as follows:

- The pavement edges must not exceed 3 inches difference in elevation between abutting pavement sections and between pavement and abutting areas.
- The pavement must have no hole exceeding 3 inches in depth nor any hole the slope of which from any point in the hole to the nearest point at the lip of the hole is 45 degrees or greater, as measured from the pavement surface plane, unless, in either case, the entire area of the hole can be covered by a 5-inch diameter circle (Figure 7-4).
- The pavement must be free of cracks and surface variations that could impair directional control of air carrier aircraft, including any pavement crack or surface deterioration that produces loose aggregate or other contaminants. (FAA, 2004)

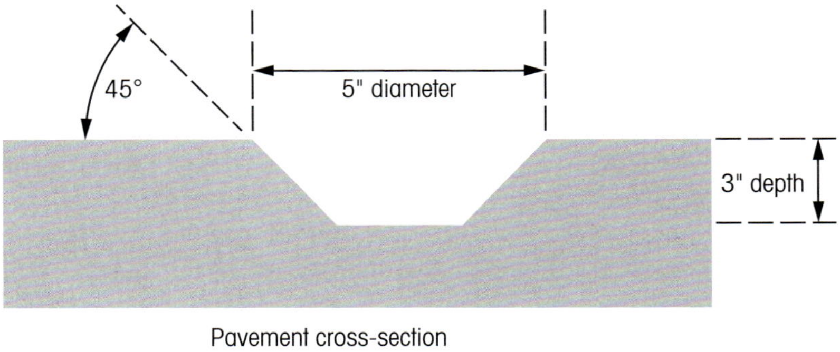

Figure 7-4. Tolerances not to be exceeded for paved areas.

Additionally, mud, dirt, sand, loose aggregate, debris, foreign objects, rubber deposits, chemicals, and other contaminants must be removed promptly and as completely as practical. Pavement must also be sufficiently drained and free of depressions to prevent ponding that obscures markings or impairs safe aircraft operations. Section 139.305 does not apply to the control of snow and ice accumulations. Paved areas are inspected daily and often generate the most work orders for repair. Whether flexible or rigid, pavement reaches the end of its useful life and starts deteriorating, requiring rehabilitation or repair (see Figure 7-5). It is often airport operations personnel who keep tabs on the pavement as part of the inspection program and initiate this repair as needed (FAA, 2004).

Figure 7-5. Pavement in need of repair.

UNPAVED AREAS

14 CFR §139.307, Unpaved Areas, requires airports to maintain and promptly repair the surface of each gravel, turf, or other unpaved runway, taxiway, or loading ramp and parking area on the airport that is available for air carrier use (see Figure 7-6). Specifically, airports are required to maintain unpaved areas as follows:

- No slope from the edge of the full-strength surfaces downward to the existing terrain must be steeper than 2:1.
- The full-strength surfaces must have adequate crown or grade to assure sufficient drainage to prevent ponding.
- The full-strength surfaces must be adequately compacted and sufficiently stable to prevent rutting by aircraft or the loosening or build-up of surface material, which could impair directional control of aircraft or drainage.
- The full-strength surfaces must have no holes or depressions that exceed 3 inches in depth and are of a breadth capable of impairing directional control or causing damage to an aircraft.
- Debris and foreign objects must be promptly removed from the surface. (FAA, 2004)

Often, unpaved areas are not inspected as frequently as paved areas yet they are important nonetheless. A best practice involves walking these unpaved areas on a regular basis to detect any depressions or holes that could impair the directional control of aircraft.

Figure 7-6. Unpaved area.

SAFETY AREAS

14 CFR §139.309, Safety Areas, requires airports to provide and maintain, for each runway and taxiway that is available for air carrier use, adequate safety areas. These areas must be maintained as follows:

- Each safety area must be cleared and graded and have no potentially hazardous ruts, humps, depressions, or other surface variations.
- Each safety area must be drained by grading or storm sewers to prevent water accumulation.
- Each safety area must be capable under dry conditions of supporting snow removal and aircraft rescue and firefighting equipment and of supporting the occasional passage of aircraft without causing major damage to the aircraft.
- No objects may be located in any safety area, except for objects that need to be located in a safety area because of their function. These objects must be constructed, to the extent practical, on frangibly mounted structures of the lowest practical height, with the frangible point no higher than 3 inches above grade.

Safety areas are notorious for being overlooked during the daily self-inspection. After all, these areas surround runways and taxiways and time does not always allow for a daily drive of these areas. Often, the inspector simply inspects these areas from a distance each day while driving down the runway or taxiway. However, just with unpaved areas, it is a best practice to regularly walk the safety areas to ensure there are no depressions or holes that would impair the directional control of aircraft if there were an excursion from the runway or taxiway. If safety areas are ignored and not properly maintained, the airport may be noted for a discrepancy during the annual Part 139 inspection.

MARKING, SIGNS, AND LIGHTING

14 CFR §139.311—Marking, Signs, and Lighting—requires airports to provide and maintain marking systems, sign systems, and lighting systems for air carrier operations. Specifically, airport marking systems must at a minimum consist of:

- Runway markings meeting the specifications for takeoff and landing minimums for each runway
- A taxiway centerline
- Taxiway edge markings, as appropriate
- Holding position markings
- Instrument landing system (ILS) critical area markings

Airport sign systems must consist of at least the following:

- Signs identifying taxiing routes on the movement area
- Holding position signs
- Instrument landing system (ILS) critical area signs
- Each of these required signs must be internally illuminated at all Class I, II, and IV airports, with holding position signs and ILS critical area signs requiring illumination at all Class III airports.

Airport lighting systems are required for air carrier operations when the airport is open at night, during conditions below visual flight rules (VFR) minimums, or in Alaska, during periods in which a prominent unlighted object cannot be seen from a distance of 3 statute miles or the sun is more than six degrees below the horizon. Airport lighting systems must consist of at least the following:

- Runway lighting that meets the specifications for takeoff and landing minimums for each runway.
- One or more of the following taxiway lighting systems:
  - › Centerline lights
  - › Centerline reflectors
  - › Edge lights
  - › Edge reflectors
  - › An airport beacon
  - › Approach lighting that meets the specifications for takeoff and landing minimums for each runway, unless provided and/or maintained by an entity other than the certificate holder (such as the FAA)
  - › Obstruction marking and lighting, as appropriate, on each object within its authority that has been determined by the FAA to be an obstruction

Airports are also required under §139.311 to maintain each marking, sign, or lighting system installed and operated on the airport, which includes cleaning, replacing, or repairing any faded, missing, or nonfunctional item; keeping each item unobscured and clearly visible; and ensuring that each item provides an accurate reference to the user. Additionally, airports must ensure that all lighting on the airport—including lighting used on aprons, vehicle parking areas, roadways, fuel storage areas, and buildings—is adequately adjusted or shielded to prevent the lighting from interfering with the visibility of air traffic control and aircraft operators (FAA, 2004).

Other than pavement, the most significant areas of focus during the daily self-inspection (day and night) are markings, signage, and lighting. These three components provide directional information to pilots and drivers of ground vehicles and must meet FAA standards and be maintained in proper condition. As with any of the components of Subpart D of Part 139, if operations personnel discover an issue, a work order is issued for resolution by maintenance, or if it is an emergency situation, maintenance is called for immediate response. A NOTAM may be issued as appropriate.

SNOW AND ICE CONTROL

At airports located in geographic areas of the United States where snow and ice are experienced, §139.313, Snow and Ice Control, requires airports to prepare, maintain, and carry out a **snow and ice control plan (SICP)** (see Figure 7-7). The SICP is the guidebook the airport utilizes during winter operations and must, according to §139.313, include instructions and procedures for:

- Prompt removal or control, as completely as practical, of snow, ice, and slush on each movement area;
- Positioning snow off the movement area surfaces so all air carrier aircraft propellers, engine pods, rotors, and wing tips will clear any snowdrift and snowbank as the aircraft's landing gear traverses any portion of the movement area;
- Selection and application of authorized materials for snow and ice control to ensure that they adhere to snow and ice sufficiently to minimize engine ingestion;
- Timely commencement of snow and ice control operations; and
- Prompt notification, in accordance with §139.339, of all air carriers using the airport when any portion of the movement area normally available to them is less than satisfactorily cleared for safe operation by their aircraft (FAA, 2004).

Snow and ice removal is a full-time job during the winter at airports located in regions of the country that are susceptible to winter conditions. Airports routinely experiencing icing conditions or annual snow accumulations of 6 inches or more should have a SICP. Elements of the SICP include: preseason preparation, snow committee composition, snow desk or snow control center location, equipment, personnel training, weather reports, field condition reports, clearance criteria, clearance priorities, supervision, and communications. An SICP

Figure 7-7.
Airport snow removal.

(Glory2045/Bigstock.com)

must be flexible enough to allow snow and ice removal operations to change according to changing weather and operational needs. Additionally, airports will have a Snow Control Center (SCC) (sometimes referred to as the "Snow Desk") as part of their SICP. The SCC is a centralized facility for coordinating all snow and ice control activities. The SCC facilitates communication between the ATCT, snow and ice control equipment, supervisors' vehicles, and other support elements vital to a safe winter operation.

Snow and ice can be removed in one of two ways, either mechanically or chemically (see Figure 7-8). Mechanical methods for removing snow and ice include:

1. Rotary blowers or throwers
2. Plows
3. Broom sweepers
4. Loaders

Figure 7-8.
Rotary plow.

Chemical methods involve material spreaders that disperse deice/anti-ice granules or liquid. Airports in snow-prone areas such as Salt Lake City, Denver, Milwaukee, and New York have millions of dollars invested in snow removal equipment.

ARFF: INDEX DETERMINATION

Part 139 also specifies aircraft rescue and firefighting (ARFF) requirements. Specifically, §139.315, Aircraft Rescue and Firefighting: Index Determination, states that certificated airports must have an **ARFF Index** and includes the manner by which this index is determined. The index is determined by the length of air carrier aircraft and the average daily departures of air carrier aircraft. The ARFF Index specifies the required number of ARFF vehicles and required amount of extinguishing agents (see Table 7-2).

Table 7-2. ARFF Index determination.

The index is determined by a combination of: 1. The length of air carrier aircraft and 2. Average daily departures of air carrier aircraft.
For the purpose of Index determination, air carrier aircraft lengths are grouped as follows: 1. Index A includes aircraft less than 90 feet in length. 2. Index B includes aircraft at least 90 feet but less than 126 feet in length. 3. Index C includes aircraft at least 126 feet but less than 159 feet in length. 4. Index D includes aircraft at least 159 feet but less than 200 feet in length. 5. Index E includes aircraft at least 200 feet in length.

According to §139.315, if there are five or more average daily departures of air carrier aircraft in a single index group serving that airport, the longest aircraft with an average of five or more daily departures determines the index required for the airport. When there are fewer than five average daily departures of the longest air carrier aircraft serving the airport, the index required for the airport will be the next lower index group than the index group prescribed for the longest aircraft. For example, if there are three average daily departures of B-767 aircraft (Index D) and two average daily departures of B-717 aircraft (Index B), the ARFF Index for the airport would be Index C, even though the airport in this case is not served by any Index C aircraft. The minimum ARFF Index for certificated airports will be Index A. Additionally, Class III airports may comply with the ARFF Index requirements by providing a level of safety comparable to Index A that is approved by the FAA.

ARFF: EQUIPMENT AND AGENTS

Section 139.317, Aircraft Rescue and Firefighting: Equipment and Agents, specifies the response equipment and type and amount of extinguishing agents required for each index. There are several standard extinguishing agents in use at airports. First, a sufficient quantity of water is carried, which is the main reason ARFF trucks are so large. Water is generally not used by itself, but is mixed at the time of application with aqueous film forming foam (AFFF) (in 3% or 6% concentrate) to form a blanket of foam which starves a fire of

---

Unless otherwise authorized by the Administrator, the following rescue and firefighting equipment and agents are the minimum required for the Indexes referred to in §139.315:

(a) Index A. One vehicle carrying at least—

(1) 500 pounds of sodium-based dry chemical, halon 1211, or clean agent; or

(2) 450 pounds of potassium-based dry chemical and water with a commensurate quantity of AFFF to total 100 gallons for simultaneous dry chemical and AFFF application.

(b) Index B. Either of the following:

(1) One vehicle carrying at least 500 pounds of sodium-based dry chemical, halon 1211, or clean agent and 1,500 gallons of water and the commensurate quantity of AFFF for foam production.

(2) Two vehicles—

(i) One vehicle carrying the extinguishing agents as specified in paragraphs (a)(1) or (a)(2) of this section; and

(ii) One vehicle carrying an amount of water and the commensurate quantity of AFFF so the total quantity of water for foam production carried by both vehicles is at least 1,500 gallons.

(c) Index C. Either of the following:

(1) Three vehicles—

(i) One vehicle carrying the extinguishing agents as specified in paragraph (a)(1) or (a)(2) of this section; and

(ii) Two vehicles carrying an amount of water and the commensurate quantity of AFFF so the total quantity of water for foam production carried by all three vehicles is at least 3,000 gallons.

(2) Two vehicles—

(i) One vehicle carrying the extinguishing agents as specified in paragraph (b)(1) of this section; and

(ii) One vehicle carrying water and the commensurate quantity of AFFF so the total quantity of water for foam production carried by both vehicles is at least 3,000 gallons.

(d) Index D. Three vehicles—

(1) One vehicle carrying the extinguishing agents as specified in paragraphs (a)(1) or (a)(2) of this section; and

(2) Two vehicles carrying an amount of water and the commensurate quantity of AFFF so the total quantity of water for foam production carried by all three vehicles is at least 4,000 gallons.

(e) Index E. Three vehicles—

(1) One vehicle carrying the extinguishing agents as specified in paragraphs (a)(1) or (a)(2) of this section; and

(2) Two vehicles carrying an amount of water and the commensurate quantity of AFFF so the total quantity of water for foam production carried by all three vehicles is at least 6,000 gallons.

Figure 7-9. ARFF equipment requirements.

(14 CFR §139.317)

oxygen, suppresses fuel vapors, and cools the fire. In essence, AFFF attacks all three sides of the fire triangle. Dry chemical, either sodium-based or potassium-based, is also used. Purple K is a common potassium-based dry chemical in use by ARFF. The requirements are presented in Figure 7-9.

In addition to specifying the equipment, §139.317 specifies the foam discharge capacity. First, each ARFF vehicle used to comply with Index B, C, D, or E requirements with a capacity of at least 500 gallons of water for foam production must be equipped with a **turret.**[1] Each vehicle with a water tank capacity of between 500 to 2,000 gallons must have a turret discharge rate between 500 and 1,000 gallons per minute. For vehicles with water tank capacities of at least 2,000 gallons, the turret discharge rate must be between 600 and 1,200 gallons per minute. For each ARFF vehicle required to carry dry chemical, halon 1211, or clean agent, the minimum discharge rates are 5 pounds per second for a hand line and 16 pounds per second for a turret. Lastly, for ARFF vehicles required to carry AFFF, a sufficient amount of AFFF must be carried to enable mixing with twice the water required to be carried by the vehicle (Figure 7-10) (FAA, 2004).

Figure 7-10. 3,000-gallon ARFF truck.

(Nan Phanitsuda Sophonpanasak, Denver International Airport)

ARFF: OPERATIONAL REQUIREMENTS

Operational requirements for ARFF are specified in §139.319, Aircraft Rescue and Firefighting: Operational Requirements. First, if there is an increase in the average daily departures or the length of air carrier aircraft to the extent that the airport's index changes, the airport must comply with the increased requirements. Also, this section allows an airport to reduce the ARFF level corresponding to the index group of the longest air carrier aircraft being operated, during those times when only air carrier aircraft shorter than the normal index are being operated. However, this is subject to specific procedures (including full recall of the ARFF capability) being included in the airport certification manual. Additionally, the reductions may not be implemented unless notification to air carriers is provided in the ***Airport/Facility Directory*** **(A/FD)** or via

[1] A device which allows for extinguishing agent to be dispersed from either a roof mount or bumper mount.

Notices to Airmen (NOTAMs), and by direct notification of local air carriers. The *Airport/Facility Directory*, which is updated every 56 days, is a government publication that is published per FAA region providing detailed information about public airports, seaplane bases, heliports, military facilities, and selected private-use airports in that region. NOTAMs are the official manner in which to convey airport condition information to pilots. NOTAMs may be issued by airport personnel or the FAA via Flight Service.

This section also requires each required ARFF vehicle to be equipped with two-way voice radio communications that allows for communication with all other required emergency vehicles, the ATCT, the CTAF when an ATCT is not in operation or there is no ATCT, and fire stations, as specified in the airport emergency plan. ARFF vehicles are required to be equipped with a flashing or rotating beacon and painted or marked in high-contrast colors. Additionally, vehicles must be maintained so as to be available and operationally capable during all air carrier operations. At airports located in geographical areas subject to prolonged temperatures below 33 degrees Fahrenheit, the vehicles must be provided with cover or other means to ensure equipment operation and discharge under freezing conditions. If any required vehicle becomes inoperative to the extent that it cannot perform as required, it must be replaced immediately with equipment having at least equal capabilities. If replacement equipment is not immediately available, the regional airports division manager and each air carrier using the airport must be notified. Also, if the required index level of capability is not restored within 48 hours, the airport operator (unless otherwise approved by the FAA) must limit air carrier operations to those compatible with the index corresponding to the remaining operative ARFF equipment (Figure 7-11).

14 CFR §139.319 also requires that ARFF equipment respond to an aircraft accident in a timely manner. Specifically, at least one required ARFF vehicle must reach the midpoint of the farthest runway serving air carrier aircraft from its assigned post within three minutes from the time of alarm. The ARFF vehicle must also begin application of extinguishing agent during this time.

Figure 7-11. ARFF facility.

All other required vehicles must arrive and begin application of extinguishing agent within four minutes from the time of alarm. ARFF response time is tested annually by the FAA during the airport's Part 139 certification inspection.

Section 139.319 also requires ARFF personnel to be properly equipped and trained to perform the duties required of their position (see Figure 7-12). Training must take place prior to initial performance of duties and every 12 consecutive calendar months thereafter. The curriculum for this initial and recurrent training must include:

- Airport familiarization, including airport signs, marking, and lighting
- Aircraft familiarization
- Rescue and firefighting personnel safety
- Emergency communications systems on the airport, including fire alarms
- Use of the fire hoses, nozzles, turrets, and other appliances required for compliance with this part
- Application of the types of extinguishing agents required for compliance with this part
- Emergency aircraft evacuation assistance
- Firefighting operations
- Adapting and using structural rescue and firefighting equipment for aircraft rescue and firefighting
- Aircraft cargo hazards, including hazardous materials/dangerous goods incidents
- Familiarization with firefighters' duties under the airport emergency plan

Figure 7-12. Engine fire in an ARFF aircraft trainer being extinguished.

Additionally, §139.319 requires all ARFF personnel to participate in a live fire drill prior to initial performance of duties and every 12 consecutive calendar months thereafter (see Figure 7-13). There must also be at least one person available during air carrier operations who is trained and current in basic emergency medical care, including 40 hours of training covering:

- Bleeding
- Cardiopulmonary resuscitation
- Shock
- Primary patient survey
- Injuries to the skull, spine, chest, and extremities
- Internal injuries
- Moving patients
- Burns
- Triage

Figure 7-13. Live ARFF burn training.

(Nan Phanitsuda Sophonpanasak, Denver International Airport)

Records of this training must be maintained for 24 consecutive calendar months after completion of training. In addition to having sufficient personnel on duty to comply with the requirements of Part 139, airports must have an alerting system in place to notify ARFF personnel of any existing or impending emergency requiring their assistance. Each ARFF vehicle is also required to carry (or have access to) the "North American Emergency Response Guidebook" published by the U.S. Department of Transportation (or similar). Lastly, §139.319 requires airports to provide and maintain emergency access roads that are capable of supporting ARFF vehicles.

Depending on the airport, ARFF personnel may be specific only to the ARFF function, may also serve a public safety function role as police officers, or may also serve as operations personnel. Typically, job specialization is more pronounced at larger airports, meaning that ARFF personnel would generally be responsible only for ARFF. Unlike snow removal equipment, all certificated airports must invest in ARFF equipment, with today's modern ARFF trucks costing over $1 million.

HANDLING AND STORING OF HAZARDOUS SUBSTANCES AND MATERIALS

Section 139.321, Handling and Storing of Hazardous Substances and Materials, is designed to address both hazardous cargo and fuel. If a certificated airport acts as a cargo handling agent, procedures for the protection of persons and property during the storing or handling of any hazardous material must be developed. Although it is uncommon for an airport to act as a cargo handling agent, if it does, it must provide for at least:

- Designated personnel to receive and handle hazardous substances and materials
- Assurance from the shipper that the cargo can be handled safely, including any special handling procedures required for safety
- Special areas for storage of hazardous materials while on the airport

It's much more likely for an airport to handle fuel. If so, standards must be developed to protect against fire and explosion in the storing, dispensing, and handling of fuel. Fueling agents on the airport must be held to these same standards, requiring regular surveillance of fueling activity to verify compliance. These standards must address:

- Bonding
- Public protection
- Control of access to storage areas
- Fire safety in fuel farm and storage areas
- Fire safety in mobile fuelers, fueling pits, and fueling cabinets
- Training of fueling personnel in fire safety
- The fire code of the public body having jurisdiction over the airport.

In addition, §139.321 requires airports to inspect the physical facilities of each airport tenant fueling agent at least once every 3 consecutive months, with records being maintained for at least 12 consecutive calendar months. Fire safety training must be given to at least one supervisor with each fueling agent prior to initial performance of duties and at least every 24 consecutive calendar months thereafter. Those employees who fuel aircraft, accept fuel shipments, or otherwise handle fuel are able to receive initial on-the-job training from their supervisor, as well as recurrent instruction every 24 consecutive calendar months. To verify that required training has taken place, each certificated airport must obtain a written confirmation of this training once every 12 consecutive calendar months. Airports are required to maintain this record for 12 consecutive calendar months.

TRAFFIC AND WIND DIRECTION INDICATORS

Section 139.323, Traffic and Wind Direction Indicators, requires certificated airports to maintain the following:

- A wind cone that visually provides surface wind direction information to pilots. For each runway available for air carrier use, a supplemental wind cone is required to be installed at the end of the runway or at least at one point visible to the pilot while on final approach and prior to take-off. For airports open for air carrier operations at night, the wind direction indicators and supplemental indicators must be lighted (see Figure 7-14).
- A segmented circle, landing strip indicator, and a traffic pattern indicator must be installed around a wind cone for each runway with a right-hand traffic pattern at certificated airports if air carrier operations are conducted without a control tower in operation.

Figure 7-14. Lighted wind cone.

AIRPORT EMERGENCY PLAN

Section 139.325, Airport Emergency Plan, requires certificated airports to develop and maintain an **airport emergency plan (AEP)**. The AEP must include procedures (including a communications network) for prompt response to all emergencies, sufficient detail to provide adequate guidance to each person who must implement the AEP, and an emergency response for the largest air carrier aircraft in the airport's index group. Specifically, and in accordance with AC 150/5200-31, *Airport Emergency Plan*, the AEP must include instructions for responses to:

- Aircraft incidents and accidents;
- Terrorism incidents;
- Structural fires, and fires at fuel farms and fuel storage areas;
- Natural disasters, including hurricane, earthquake, tornado, volcano, flood;
- Hazardous materials incidents;
- Sabotage, hijack, and other unlawful interference with operations;
- Failure of power for movement area lighting;
- Water rescue situations; and
- Crowd control

The AEP must also include provisions for medical services; contact information and emergency capability of hospitals and medical facilities in the local community; contact information for rescue squads, ambulance services, military installations, and government agencies that have agreed to provide medical assistance and/or transportation; an inventory of surface vehicles and aircraft available to transport injured and deceased persons; a list of hangars or buildings that can be used to accommodate uninjured, injured, and deceased persons; and procedures for removing disabled aircraft.[2] Additionally, the AEP must provide for the marshalling, transportation, and care of ambulatory injured and uninjured accident survivors; the removal of disabled aircraft; emergency alarm or notification systems; coordination of airport and control tower functions relating to emergency actions; and the rescue of aircraft accident victims from significant bodies of water or marshlands adjacent to the airport that are crossed by the approach and departure paths of air carriers.

Once the AEP is developed, all certificated airports must:

- Coordinate the plan with law enforcement agencies, rescue and firefighting agencies, medical personnel and organizations, the principal tenants at the airport, and other persons who have responsibilities under the plan;
- Ensure that all airport personnel having duties and responsibilities under the plan are familiar with their assignments and are properly trained;
- At least once every 12 consecutive calendar months, review the plan with all of the parties with whom the plan is coordinated, to ensure that all parties know their responsibilities and that all of the information in the plan is current (often referred to as a tabletop exercise); and
- If a Class I certificated airport, hold a full-scale airport emergency plan exercise once every 36 consecutive calendar months.

Ronald Reagan Washington National Airport Emergency Exercise

A recent full-scale emergency exercise at Ronald Reagan Washington National Airport was held to meet the 14 CFR Part 139 requirement for Class I airports to exercise the airport emergency plan. A training aircraft was used at the southern end of the airport to simulate a crashed aircraft (Alert III). The exercise, which required months of planning and coordination across multiple jurisdictions and disciplines, consisted of more than 50 responding emergency vehicles, including mutual aid from 13 surrounding fire departments to transport victims to hospitals, nearly 150 volunteers who were moulaged to simulate injuries sustained in the accident, boats used as part of a river rescue, and helicopters for support and rapid transport to area hospitals.

(Metropolitan Washington Airports Authority, 2013)

[2] Refer to ACRP Synthesis 38, Expediting Aircraft Recovery at Airports.

Planning for a full-scale emergency exercise at a certificated airport requires months of preparation. Some airports begin planning for this exercise one year in advance. Not only must an accident scenario be developed, but an aircraft has to be arranged, volunteers need to be coordinated, a date must be set, and all interested parties must be invited to participate. On the day of the event, everyone responds to the accident site in response to a "simulated Alert III" just as if there were a real accident (see Figure 7-15). The exercise tests everyone's response. Afterward, a thorough debriefing is held to discuss what worked well and what didn't work well. Changes can then be made so that personnel are better prepared in the future.

Figure 7-15. Full-scale emergency exercise.

(Jordan Biegler, Tampa International Airport)

SELF-INSPECTION PROGRAM

Section 139.327, Self-Inspection Program, presents the requirements for airports to self-inspect on a daily basis to ensure Part 139 compliance. Specifically, certificated airports are required to inspect:

- daily, except as otherwise required by the airport certification manual;
- when required by any unusual condition, such as construction activities or meteorological conditions, that may affect safe air carrier operations; and
- immediately after an accident or incident.

To meet these requirements, certificated airports must provide sufficient, qualified personnel; equipment to be used by these personnel in conducting inspections; procedures, facilities, and equipment to disseminate information to air carriers; and a reporting system to ensure prompt correction of unsafe airport conditions (including wildlife strikes) noted during an inspection. Personnel responsible for meeting the requirements of §139.327 must receive initial and recurrent training (every 12 consecutive calendar months) in at least the following topic areas:

- Airport familiarization, including airport signs, marking and lighting
- Airport emergency plan
- Notice to Airmen (NOTAM) notification procedures
- Procedures for pedestrians and ground vehicles in movement areas and safety areas
- Discrepancy reporting procedures

Additionally, §139.327 requires certificated airports to maintain a record of each inspection (showing the conditions found and all corrective actions taken) for a period of 12 consecutive calendar months. Airports must also maintain training records for 24 consecutive calendar months showing a description of the training and the date on which the training took place.

Of all the responsibilities of operations personnel, conducting self-inspections is the most significant. This is the manner by which airports ensure their compliance with Part 139 and maintain a safe airport. At larger Part 139 airports, a complete self-inspection may take two to three hours or more. Some airports, such as Los Angeles International Airport, actually have operations personnel assigned to the airfield for their entire shift. At the majority of certificated airports, however, once the self-inspection is complete, operations personnel respond to the airfield as needed throughout the shift.

PEDESTRIANS AND GROUND VEHICLES

Section 139.329, Pedestrians and Ground Vehicles, presents requirements necessary for certificated airports to provide protection for pedestrians and ground vehicles in the movement areas and safety areas. Specifically, certificated airports must:

- Limit access to movement areas and safety areas to those pedestrians and ground vehicles necessary for airport operations.
- Establish and implement procedures for the safe and orderly access to, and operation in, movement areas and safety areas by pedestrians and ground vehicles, including provisions identifying the consequences of noncompliance with the procedures by an employee, tenant, or contractor.
- When an air traffic control tower is in operation, ensure that each pedestrian and ground vehicle in movement areas or safety areas is controlled by one of the following:
  - › Two-way radio communications between each pedestrian or vehicle and the tower;
  - › An escort with two-way radio communications with the tower accompanying any pedestrian or vehicle without a radio; or

- › Measures authorized by the FAA Administrator for controlling pedestrians and vehicles, such as signs, signals, or guards, when it is not operationally practical to have two-way radio communications between the tower and the pedestrian, vehicle, or escort.
- When an air traffic control tower is not in operation, or there is no air traffic control tower, provide adequate procedures to control pedestrians and ground vehicles in movement areas or safety areas through two-way radio communications or prearranged signs or signals.
- Ensure that each employee, tenant, or contractor is trained on proper procedures (including consequences of noncompliance) prior to moving on foot, or operating a ground vehicle, in movement areas or safety areas (Figure 7-16).

Figure 7-16. Contractor on the movement area.

(Lee Brown, Fort Lauderdale-Hollywood International Airport)

In compliance with §139.327, certificated airports are required to maintain a record of training on each individual (including a description and date of training) for 24 consecutive calendar months after the termination of an individual's access to movement areas and safety areas. Additionally, certificated airports are required to maintain a description and date of any accidents or incidents in the movement areas and safety areas involving air carrier aircraft, ground vehicles, or a pedestrian for 12 consecutive calendar months from the date of the accident/incident.

OBSTRUCTIONS

Section 139.331, Obstructions, requires certificated airports to ensure that each object within its authority that has been found to be an obstruction to air navigation (as a result of a Part 77 analysis) be removed, marked, or lighted, unless determined to be unnecessary by the FAA. Lighted obstructions are checked by operations personnel during a self-inspection.

PROTECTION OF NAVAIDS

Section 139.333, Protection of NAVAIDs, requires certificated airports to protect navigational aids from interference and other detrimental impacts (see Figure 7-17). Specifically, certificated airports must:

- Prevent the construction of facilities on the airport that would adversely impact the operation of an electronic or visual NAVAID and air traffic control facilities on the airport;
- Protect all NAVAIDs located on the airport from vandalism and theft;
- Prevent, to the extent possible, interruption of visual and electronic signals of NAVAIDs.

Figure 7-17. NAVAID protected by fencing to prevent vandalism and theft.

PUBLIC PROTECTION

Section 139.335, Public Protection, requires certificated airports to protect the public from entering areas that are unsafe and from the effects of jet blast and propwash. Specifically, certificated airports must install safeguards to prevent inadvertent entry to the movement area by unauthorized persons or vehicles and protect persons and property from aircraft blast (see Figure 7-18). Fencing that meets TSA and FAA regulations is considered a sufficient safeguard.

Figure 7-18. Airport blast fence.

WILDLIFE HAZARD MANAGEMENT

Section 139.337, Wildlife Hazard Management, presents the requirements for certificated airports to manage wildlife to prevent any dangerous aircraft strikes with wildlife. In addition to the requirement to take immediate action whenever wildlife hazards are discovered, certificated airports are required to carry out a wildlife hazard assessment when any of the following events occur on or near the airport:

- An air carrier aircraft experiences multiple wildlife strikes;
- An air carrier aircraft experiences substantial damage that adversely affects the structural strength, performance, or flight characteristics of the aircraft as a result of striking wildlife;
- An air carrier aircraft experiences an engine ingestion of wildlife; or
- Wildlife of a size, or in numbers, capable of causing any of these events is observed to have access to any airport flight pattern or aircraft movement area (see Figure 7-19).

If required, the wildlife hazard assessment must be carried out by a wildlife damage management biologist who has professional training and/or experience in wildlife hazard management at airports. The wildlife hazard assessment will contain at least the following:

- An analysis of the events or circumstances that prompted the assessment.
- Identification of the wildlife species observed and their numbers, locations, local movements, and daily and seasonal occurrences.
- Identification and location of features on and near the airport that attract wildlife.
- A description of wildlife hazards to air carrier operations.
- Recommended actions for reducing identified wildlife hazards to air carrier operations.

Figure 7-19. Airport wildlife.

(Lee Brown, Fort Lauderdale-Hollywood International Airport)

Once completed, the wildlife hazard assessment is submitted to the FAA for approval, as well as a determination of whether the airport needs a wildlife hazard management plan. In determining whether a wildlife hazard management plan is needed, the FAA will consider the wildlife hazard assessment, actions recommended in the assessment to reduce wildlife hazards, the aeronautical activity at the airport, views of the airport and users, and any other known factors. If the FAA determines that an airport needs a wildlife hazard management plan, a plan should be developed that provides measures to alleviate or eliminate wildlife hazards to air carriers, is approved by the FAA, and becomes part of the ACM.

Specifically, a wildlife hazard management plan must include:

- A list of the individuals having authority and responsibility for implementing each aspect of the plan.
- A list prioritizing the following actions identified in the wildlife hazard assessment and target dates for their initiation and completion:
    - Wildlife population management;
    - Habitat modification; and
    - Land use changes.
- Requirements for and, where applicable, copies of local, state, and federal wildlife control permits.
- Identification of resources that the certificate holder will provide to implement the plan.

- Procedures to be followed during air carrier operations that at a minimum include:
  - designation of personnel responsible for implementing the procedures;
  - provisions to conduct physical inspections of the aircraft movement areas and other areas critical to successfully manage known wildlife hazards before air carrier operations begin;
  - wildlife hazard control measures; and
  - ways to communicate effectively between personnel conducting wildlife control or observing wildlife hazards and the air traffic control tower.
- Procedures to review and evaluate the wildlife hazard management plan every 12 consecutive months or following an event previously described, including:
  - the plan's effectiveness in dealing with known wildlife hazards on and in the airport's vicinity, and
  - aspects of the wildlife hazards described in the wildlife hazard assessment that should be reevaluated.
- A training program conducted by a qualified wildlife damage management biologist to provide airport personnel with the knowledge and skills needed to successfully carry out the wildlife hazard management plan.

AIRPORT CONDITION REPORTING

Section 139.339, Airport Condition Reporting, requires certificated airports to report airport conditions to air carriers. This requires airports to have in place a system of collecting and disseminating airport condition information, typically the NOTAM system. Specifically, airports are required to provide information on the following airport conditions:

- Construction or maintenance activity on movement areas, safety areas, or loading ramps and parking areas.
- Surface irregularities on movement areas, safety areas, or loading ramps and parking areas.
- Snow, ice, slush, or water on the movement area or loading ramps and parking areas.
- Snow piled or drifted on or near movement areas contrary to §139.313.
- Objects on the movement area or safety areas contrary to §139.309.
- Malfunction of any lighting system, holding position signs, or ILS critical area signs required by §139.311.
- Unresolved wildlife hazards as identified in accordance with §139.337.
- Non-availability of any rescue and firefighting capability required in §§139.317 or 139.319.
- Any other condition as specified in the airport certification manual or that may otherwise adversely affect the safe operations of air carriers.

Certificated airports are required to maintain records of each dissemination of airport condition information to air carriers for a period of 12 consecutive calendar months. Generally, operations personnel are responsible for issuing NOTAMs as needed. It is always better to err on the side of safety and issue a NOTAM to report unsafe conditions to pilots, rather than not issue a NOTAM.

IDENTIFYING, MARKING, AND LIGHTING CONSTRUCTION AND OTHER UNSERVICEABLE AREAS

Section 139.341—Identifying, Marking, and Lighting Construction and Other Unserviceable Areas—requires certificated airports to properly mark and light (if appropriate):

- each construction area and unserviceable area that is on or adjacent to any movement area or any other area of the airport on which air carrier aircraft may be operated (see Figure 7-20);
- each item of construction equipment and each construction roadway, which may affect the safe movement of aircraft on the airport; and
- any area adjacent to a NAVAID that, if traversed, could cause derogation of the signal or the failure of the NAVAID.

Additionally, certificated airports are required to develop procedures to prevent interruption of utilities (including cables, wires, conduits, pipelines, or other underground facilities) during any construction work on the airport. Procedures typically require a review of all appropriate utility plans prior to construction.

Figure 7-20. Low-profile barricades in use for an airport construction project.

NONCOMPLYING CONDITIONS

Section 139.343, Noncomplying Conditions, states that whenever Part 139 requirements cannot be met by a certificated airport to the extent that unsafe conditions exist on the airport, the airport must limit air carrier operations to those areas of the airport not rendered unsafe by those conditions. Note that this requirement (and all Part 139 requirements) refers to air carrier operations. Thus, it would be possible to allow GA operations in an area that does not meet Part 139 standards. In this case, however, the airport operator would still be certain not to allow any aircraft activity in areas that are considered unsafe. Indeed, the airport operator is responsible for maintaining a safe and secure airport; thus, if an area is under construction or has an unsafe condition, it is the responsibility of the airport operator to NOTAM that area closed to prevent inadvertent entry by aircraft (whether air carrier or GA) into an area that would cause damage to the aircraft or result in loss of directional control of the aircraft.

Airport Communications

Airports have often been characterized as "small cities." Indeed, many of the larger airports generate some of their own power; have their own police force, system of governance, and form of transportation; generate their own sources of revenue; are self-contained with food, beverage and retail establishments; etc. For a "small city" or airport to operate effectively, sufficient communication must be in place. In fact, one key to an efficiently run airport is a well-developed communication system.

On the surface, this would appear easy to accomplish. It is important to keep in mind, however, that an airport serves two types of customers. First, internal customers include all of the individuals employed by the entity that owns and operates the airport. If the airport is owned and operated by an airport authority, for instance, internal customers would be the employees of the airport authority. Although these employees are often thought of simply as employees, when airport leadership and employees in all departments view each other as internal customers, morale typically improves, efficiency is enhanced, and the airport is able to better meet the needs of the other customer group—the external customers.

To be sure, external customers are the ones typically thought of as customers, because they represent passengers and meeters and greeters, as well as employees of the various tenants on the airport (including airlines, FBOs, maintenance organizations, concessionaires, and others). It is important for an airport to effectively communicate with these external customers so that the airport is perceived not only as a well-managed and welcoming facility, but also as a great place to work and conduct business. Effectively communicating with external customers requires the airport to hold regular tenant meetings;

issue NOTAMs as appropriate; adopt a policy of transparency with regards to fees, rates, and charges; and regularly communicate priority issues via memos, meetings, and other forms of communication.

In addition to those external customers that airport personnel interact with daily, external customers also include citizens and businesses in the surrounding community, whether or not these groups ever visit the airport. It is important for the airport to consider local businesses in meeting the air transportation needs of the region. Local business leaders often play an important role in securing new or additional commercial air service. Also, as will be discussed in more detail in Chapter 11, communicating with the community is imperative if the airport wants to experience positive relations with the community. Often, negative community relations are not perceived as being detrimental until the public hearing phase of an airport project. Yet these relations may be so negative as to derail the entire project. Communicating with the community involves issuing press releases, inviting community groups to tour the airport and attend regular noise meetings, and being responsive to community needs and concerns.

When considering airport communications and their role in the operation of the airport, many airports (especially larger ones) have a dedicated airport communications center (see Figure 7-21). Although the airport communications center is referred to differently among airports (including the "Center," "Comm Center" or "Airport Command Center"), the role of the "Center" is much the same among airports. Typically, the Center serves as the central receiving point for all phone calls from the public (whether emergency or routine in nature). These phone calls include calls made by airport patrons within the terminal.

Additionally, the Center has a phone line used by ATCT to report emergencies (often referred to as the "netline" or "crash phone"). This netline is a direct line that allows ATCT to pick up the phone and report the details of an aircraft emergency (often referred to as "Alert I," "Alert II," and "Alert III") to the Center, as well as ARFF stations and possibly others including police, any mutual aid agencies, and operations. Often, however, the Center records the pertinent information (such as airline/operator, flight number, aircraft type,

Figure 7-21. Airport communications center.

(Lee Brown, Fort Lauderdale-Hollywood International Airport)

fuel on board, souls on board, intended runway, and estimated time of arrival) and then relays this information to appropriate personnel (such as operations, police, maintenance, and senior airport leadership). At a minimum, however, each airport ARFF station must have landline access to enable ARFF personnel to receive the information as early as possible so that they can ensure a rapid response as first responders to the scene.

In addition to answering phone calls, the Center plays an important role in monitoring airport systems and facilities. Depending on the size of the airport, the Center may be staffed 24/7 with two to six operators (also known as "dispatchers"). These individuals typically sit at a computer with one or more monitors, located in a large room with a number of larger monitors (typically in the form of large, flat-panel screens). These allow the operators to monitor people movers (shuttles, monorails, trams, moving sidewalks, escalators, and elevators), fire alarm systems, access control systems, lightning warning systems, fuel systems, and more. Additionally, the operators have the ability to control hundreds of security cameras (many with full pan-tilt-zoom functionality) that enable them to observe terminal areas, gate areas, airfield areas, parking areas, etc. Airports typically have hundreds of cameras to record passenger activity, accidents, medical events, security breaches, and criminal activity such as thefts, assaults, etc. When a significant event occurs (such as a security breach), the operators are able to find the correct camera to bring up the event on the monitor. Often, for those personnel desiring more information, but not necessarily wanting to respond to the scene, they can visit the Center to observe the event in progress. During these events, a picture (or video image) truly is worth a thousand words.

With all of this capability, the Center plays an important role in logging all events that occur on the airport. Typically in the form of an incident log, the operator first receiving a phone call about an aircraft emergency or other incident begins an entry in the computer to record all details and actions related to the incident. Often, airport operations personnel relay information to the Center operator to make this entry more complete. Once the incident is resolved, this chronological log is useful for any debriefing sessions that might be held.

Wildlife Hazard Management

As spelled out earlier in this chapter, 14 CFR §139.337 details the requirements of certificated airports to properly manage wildlife and alleviate wildlife hazards to aircraft. According to the FAA, wildlife is defined as, "Any wild animal, including without limitation any wild mammal, bird, reptile, fish, amphibian, mollusk, crustacean, arthropod, coelenterate, or other invertebrate, including any part, product, egg, or offspring thereof, as well as feral animals and domestic animals out of the control of their owners" (FAA, 2007, p. 22). Hazardous wildlife is defined as, "Species of wildlife (birds, mammals, reptiles), including feral animals and domesticated animals not under control, that are associated with aircraft strike problems, are capable of causing structural damage to airport facilities, or act as attractants to other wildlife that pose a strike hazard." (See Figure 7-22) (FAA, 2007, p. 22)

In practical terms, wildlife hazards at airports are typically managed by airport operations personnel. Although many certificated airports have developed wildlife hazard management plans, even those airports without such a plan are required by Part 139 to alleviate wildlife hazards whenever they are detected. FAA Advisory Circular (AC) 150/5200-33, *Hazardous Wildlife Attractants On or Near Airports*, contains guidance on the attractants at airports that can contribute to wildlife hazards. According to this advisory circular, a **wildlife attractant** is "Any human-made structure, land-use practice, or human-made or natural geographic feature that can attract or sustain hazardous wildlife within the landing or departure airspace or the airport's AOA. These attractants can include architectural features, landscaping, waste disposal sites, wastewater treatment facilities, agricultural or aquaculture activities, surface mining, or wetlands" (FAA, 2007, p. 22).

In general, airport wildlife management programs (whether formalized in a wildlife hazard management plan or not) are built upon two components: habitat management and active control. **Habitat management** is a planned activity that includes identifying the habitat, considering modifying or eliminating the habitat, and incorporating any changes into a long-term land-use management practice. This may include altering grass height; removing trees, ponds, building ledges, and other unnecessary perches or roosting areas; installing fencing at least 7 feet high (10–12 feet at airports with deer problems) with three-strand barbed wire; placing glycol storage basins and storm water ponds underground or providing netting or wires over them to keep birds out; draining all areas of standing water; designing ponds with a 4:1 slope; and using sweepers to remove worms from the airport's hard surfaces (see Figure 7-23).

Figure 7-22. Airport wildlife.

Figure 7-23. Habitat management technique showing the use of mylar tape across a wetland to prevent Canada geese nesting.

(Alaska DOT)

Orlando International Airport's Wildlife Hazard Management Program

Orlando International Airport (MCO), which is surrounded primarily by residential areas, industrial parks, major roadways, and commercial businesses, is known to have significant wildlife concerns. In addition to operations personnel who constantly monitor the airfield for wildlife activity, MCO has employed a wildlife biologist to manage the wildlife program at the airport since 1996. The airport has been reporting wildlife strikes to the FAA since 1990. Today, the wildlife biologist and a staff of two wildlife control specialists daily address wildlife hazards at the airport.

Passive wildlife management techniques include regular mowing, perimeter fence inspections and maintenance, daily foreign object debris (FOD) inspections, installing perching deterrents, proper disposal of dead animal remains, and maintaining ditch/pond vegetation. Active wildlife management techniques include harassing or dispersing of wildlife using vehicles, using pyrotechnics, and taking lethal control when necessary. Lethal control techniques also take place outside the airport perimeter fence when large mammals, such as deer and coyote, are observed near the fence line. Annually, the deer populations outside the perimeter fence on adjacent airport property are reduced. As expected at a Florida airport, birds are a significant wildlife hazard at MCO. The four most hazardous bird species within the AOA are cattle egrets, turkey vultures, ring-billed gulls, and sandhill cranes. The most frequently struck bird species, from 2003 to 2014, were tree swallows (73 strikes), cattle egrets (61 strikes), killdeer (59 strikes), barn swallows (55 strikes), mourning doves (41 strikes), and turkey vultures (36 strikes). The reason for the difference in these two metrics is because even though tree swallows are the most often struck species, they are not considered the most hazardous because of their small size. When struck, these small birds cause little to no damage to an aircraft. Regardless, wildlife control personnel at MCO must maintain constant vigilance and actively work to minimize wildlife hazards to aircraft on the AOA.

(Greater Orlando Aviation Authority, 2015)

Active control includes harassing, scaring, dispersing, frightening, or trapping wildlife, or the use of lethal control. Specific techniques can include bird distress-call tapes, pyrotechnic devices, propane cannons, whistles, decoys, shotgun blasts with screamer shells, and high-pressure water from fire hoses. Chemicals can also be used to cause dispersal and movement of flocks. Lethal control or the killing of wildlife through the use of chemicals, firearms, or other mechanical means normally requires a depredation permit from a state or federal fish and wildlife service. Because birds and animals adapt to these various strategies, it is important for airports to implement both habitat modification and active control, while also varying the techniques used with each (see Figure 7-24).

Figure 7-24. Equipment used for active control of wildlife.

Even with the implementation of these various wildlife control techniques, a wildlife strike may still occur at an airport. According to FAA Advisory Circular 150/5200-32, *Reporting Wildlife Aircraft Strikes*, a **wildlife strike** has occurred when:

1. A pilot reports striking one or more birds or other wildlife.
2. Aircraft maintenance personnel identify aircraft damage as having been caused by a wildlife strike.
3. Personnel on the ground report seeing an aircraft strike one or more birds or other wildlife.
4. Bird or other wildlife remains, whether in whole or in part, are found within 200 feet of a runway centerline, unless another reason for the animal's death is identified.
5. An animal's presence on the airport had a significant negative effect on a flight (i.e., aborted takeoff, aborted landing, high-speed emergency stop, aircraft left pavement area to avoid collision with animal) (see Figure 7-25).

Pilots, airport operations personnel, aircraft maintenance personnel, or anyone else who has knowledge of a strike is encouraged to report it to the FAA. Wildlife strikes may be reported to the FAA using the paper FAA Form 5200-7, "Bird/Other Wildlife Strike Report," or electronically at the Airport Wildlife Hazard Mitigation web site: http://wildlife-mitigation.tc.faa.gov. All reported strikes are then edited and entered into the National Wildlife Aircraft Strike Database, which allows for trend analysis by species, airport, etc. Worldwide, wildlife strikes have cost the civil aviation industry an estimated $1.2 billion annually. Each year in the United States, wildlife strikes to U.S. civil aircraft cause about $500 million in aircraft damage and about 500,000 hours of civil aircraft downtime (FAA, 2004).

Figure 7-25. Bird strikes can result in costly aircraft damage, as shown in the blades of this turbine engine, and downtime.

(Wikimedia Commons; see credit on page 624)

New Generation Aircraft

Airports are also being confronted with new generation aircraft, including **new large aircraft (NLA).** Currently, the Airbus A380 and Boeing 747-8 are two aircraft that are considered NLA. Specifically, the A380-800 (which is built by Airbus Industries) is 239 feet long with a 261-foot wingspan, a maximum takeoff weight of 1,235,000 pounds, and capacity for 555 to 822 passengers (depending on seating configuration) (see Figure 7-26). The Boeing 747-8 (which is built by Boeing Corporation and is considered the largest commercial aircraft built in the United States) is 250 feet long with a 224-foot wingspan, a maximum takeoff weight of 975,000 pounds, and capacity for 467 to 581 passengers (depending on seating configuration). These two NLA contrast to the much smaller, narrow-body B737-600, for example, which is 102 feet long with a 117-foot wingspan, a maximum takeoff weight of 145,500 pounds, and capacity for 108 to 130 passengers (depending on seating configuration). Considering the A380 and 747-8, it is obvious that NLA require significant consideration before commencing operations at an airport. Airports must consider the dimensions of runways and taxiways, and capacity of the terminal building, including customs and border protection, TSA passenger screening, baggage claim, ticketing, concessions, and conveniences such as restrooms.

Although Chapter 5 discusses airport design criteria, airports expecting to serve NLA that do not currently meet the design standards required for these aircraft must either alter the airfield to the extent that will allow the NLA to operate unrestricted or must file a request for Modification of Standards (MoS) with the FAA. Typically, MoS's address taxiway-to-taxiway centerline separation, runway-to-taxiway centerline separation, object free areas, taxiway widths, and runway widths. The FAA must approve a MoS to enable the airport to serve an NLA without modifying the airfield to meet the design criteria for the NLA.

Specifically regarding airport operations, once an NLA begins serving an airport, special procedures usually must be adopted to ensure the safety of the NLA and other aircraft while the NLA is in operation. An airport that serves an A380 may, for instance, need to close a taxiway while the aircraft is taxiing (necessary for separation and jet blast). The airport may also consider the runway used by the aircraft closed until an inspection can be completed. Consider, for instance, the A380 (with the 261-foot wingspan) operating on a 150-foot wide runway. Even with paved runway shoulders, once the aircraft rotates on takeoff, debris may be lifted and deposited onto the runway, requiring an inspection and the removal of this debris prior to allowing any subsequent aircraft operations. Clearly, NLA require not only special considerations in the design aspects of the airport, but also in daily operations at the airport.

Figure 7-26. Airbus A380.

(Nan Phanitsuda Sophonpanasak, Denver International Airport)

Concluding Thoughts

The effective management of an airport requires keen attention to operations. Specifically, adhering to 14 CFR Part 139, which is mandatory for certificated airports, requires a focus on airport operations. Even small, non-certificated airports, however, must focus on operations to ensure a safe airport environment. This chapter has provided insight into the requirements of Part 139 as it relates to airport operations.

Chapter Summary

- The federal regulation that applies to the commercial service airports in the United States is 14 CFR Part 139, Certification of Airports. This regulation applies to all airports serving scheduled air carrier aircraft with more than 9 seats and unscheduled air carrier aircraft with more than 30 seats.
- Part 139 has four classes of airports:
  - (a) Class I—Serve scheduled operations of large air carrier aircraft and unscheduled passenger operations of large air carrier aircraft and/or scheduled operations of small air carrier aircraft;
  - (b) Class II—Serve scheduled operations of small air carrier aircraft and unscheduled passenger operations of large air carrier aircraft;
  - (c) Class III—Serve scheduled operations of small air carrier aircraft; and
  - (d) Class IV—Serve unscheduled passenger operations of large air carrier aircraft.
- All Part 139 certificated airports must obtain an airport operating certificate from the FAA. First, however, an airport must develop an airport certification manual which addresses each of the requirements in Part 139. The ACM, once approved, becomes an extension of the regulation.
- Section 139.305, Paved Areas, requires airports to maintain and promptly repair the pavement of each runway, taxiway, loading ramp, and parking area on the airport that is available for air carrier use.
- Section 139.307, Unpaved Areas, requires airports to maintain and promptly repair the surface of each gravel, turf, or other unpaved runway, taxiway, or loading ramp and parking area on the airport that is available for air carrier use.
- Section 139.309, Safety Areas, requires airports to provide and maintain, for each runway and taxiway that is available for air carrier use, adequate safety areas.
- Section 139.311, Marking, Signs, and Lighting, requires airports to provide and maintain marking systems, sign systems, and lighting systems for air carrier operations.

- At airports located in geographic areas of the United States where snow and ice are experienced, §139.313, Snow and Ice Control, requires airports to prepare, maintain, and carry out a snow and ice control plan.
- Section 139.317, Aircraft Rescue and Firefighting: Equipment and Agents, specifies the response equipment and type and amount of extinguishing agents required for each index.
- Section 139.319 requires that ARFF equipment respond to an aircraft accident in a timely manner, with the first truck arriving and initiating fire extinguishing within three minutes and all others within four minutes.
- Section 139.321, Handling and Storing of Hazardous Substances and Materials, addresses both hazardous cargo and fuel. If a certificated airport acts as a cargo handling agent, procedures for the protection of persons or property during the storing or handling of any hazardous material must be developed. Generally however, airports are not cargo handling agents; thus, standards must be developed to protect against fire and explosion in the storing, dispensing, and handling of fuel.
- Section 139.323, Traffic and Wind Direction Indicators, requires certificated airports to maintain a wind cone that visually provides surface wind direction information to pilots (with additional wind cones required for air carrier runways and lighted for air carrier operations at night) and a segmented circle, landing strip indicator, and a traffic pattern indicator for each runway with a right-hand traffic pattern at certificated airports if air carrier operations are conducted without a control tower in operation.
- Section 139.325, Airport Emergency Plan, requires certificated airports to develop and maintain an airport emergency plan that includes instructions for (a) aircraft incidents and accidents; (b) terrorism incidents; (c) structural fires, including fires at fuel farms and fuel storage areas; (d) natural disasters; (e) hazardous materials incidents; (f) sabotage, hijack, and other unlawful interference with operations; (g) failure of power for movement area lighting; (h) water rescue situations; and (i) crowd control.
- Section 139.327, Self-Inspection Program, presents the requirements for airports to self-inspect on a daily basis to ensure Part 139 compliance.
- Section 139.329, Pedestrians and Ground Vehicles, presents requirements necessary for certificated airports to provide protection for pedestrians and ground vehicles in the movement areas and safety areas.
- Section 139.331, Obstructions, requires certificated airports to ensure that each object within its authority that has been found to be an obstruction to air navigation (as a result of a Part 77 analysis) be removed, marked, or lighted, unless determined to be unnecessary by the FAA.
- Section 139.335, Public Protection, requires certificated airports to protect the public from entering areas that are unsafe and from the effects of jet blast and propwash.

- Section 139.337, Wildlife Hazard Management, presents the requirements for certificated airports to manage wildlife to prevent any dangerous aircraft strikes with wildlife. In addition to the requirement to take immediate action whenever wildlife hazards are discovered, certificated airports are required to carry out a wildlife hazard assessment in the case of certain specific events (such air carrier aircraft experiencing multiple wildlife strikes or incurring substantial damage from a wildlife strike) occurring on or near the airport.
- Section 139.339, Airport Condition Reporting, requires certificated airports to report airport conditions to air carriers.
- Section 139.341, Identifying, Marking, and Lighting Construction and Other Unserviceable Areas, specifies the construction and unserviceable areas; construction equipment and roadways; and areas adjacent to a NAVAID that certificated airports are required to properly mark and light (if appropriate).
- Section 139.343, Noncomplying Conditions, states that whenever Part 139 requirements cannot be met by a certificated airport to the extent that unsafe conditions exist on the airport, the airport must limit air carrier operations to those areas of the airport not rendered unsafe by those conditions.
- Airports serve two types of customers: Internal customers are the individuals employed by the entity that owns and operates the airport. External customers are the ones typically thought of as customers, because they represent passengers and meeters and greeters, as well as employees of the various tenants on the airport.
- The communications center is the hub of communications for the airport and is the central receiving point for all phone calls from the public, aircraft accident/emergency communications, and monitoring of airport systems and facilities.
- In general, airport wildlife management programs are built upon two components: habitat management and active control.
- In AC 150/5200-32, *Reporting Wildlife Aircraft Strikes*, guidance is provided to airport operators regarding the reporting of wildlife strikes.
- To accommodate new large aircraft, airports must consider the dimensions of runways and taxiways, and capacity of the terminal building, including customs and border protection, TSA passenger screening, baggage claim, ticketing, concessions, and conveniences such as restrooms.

Review Questions ↘

1. To which airports does 14 CFR Part 139 not apply?
2. Explain the various classes of Part 139 airports.
3. Explain the airport certification manual, including its purpose and its role.
4. Which subpart of Part 139 presents most of the guidance regarding airport operations?
5. Explain the various recordkeeping requirements of Part 139.
6. In which areas must personnel who access movement areas and safety areas and perform duties in compliance with the airport certification manual be trained?
7. Explain the standards to which paved areas must be maintained at certificated airports.
8. What are the minimum markings that make up an airport marking system at certificated airports?
9. Explain how to determine the ARFF Index for a certificated airport.
10. List the required Part 139 training areas for ARFF personnel.
11. What fire fuel safety standards must be developed at certificated airports?
12. What is required of certificated airports in 14 CFR §139.327, Self-Inspection Program?
13. Under what circumstances are certificated airports required to conduct a wildlife hazard assessment?
14. List the components of a wildlife hazard management plan.
15. For what conditions are certificated airports required to report to air carriers, according to §139.339?
16. Explain the types of customers that an airport serves and the manner by which these customers should be served.
17. Explain the function of the airport communications center.
18. What is a wildlife attractant, according to the FAA?
19. Under what situations is a wildlife strike considered to have occurred, according to AC 150/5200-32?

Scenarios

1. As the manager of a small general aviation airport, you are being pressured by the city manager to pursue commercial airline service. Although your airport is located only 48 miles (by road) from a major commercial service airport, the city manager feels that your community of 100,000 can support commercial airline service to cities such as Atlanta and St. Louis. Remember, your airport is not currently able to accommodate commercial airline service because it is not Part 139 certificated. What must be done to obtain Part 139 certification? How do you relay these requirements (and associated costs) to the city manager?

2. As you prepare for your annual Part 139 certification inspection, you know you need to make sure every aspect of your airport is in compliance with the regulation and your ACM. Develop a "to-do" list for your staff to make certain that your airport is ready for this important annual inspection.

3. As the result of a recent Part 139 certification inspection by an FAA inspector, your aircraft received three discrepancies: (1) Hazardous ruts in the 36L safety area; (2) Inadequate response by ARFF in the timed response drill (first truck arriving in 3 minutes, 20 seconds, and all others within 4 minutes); and (3) Faded mandatory surface painted signs at the Taxiway B, C, D entrances to runway 36R. The FAA inspector is requesting an action plan from your airport to immediately correct these discrepancies. Develop this plan, as well as a longer-term plan to prevent similar discrepancies in the future.

4. Your airport received FAA approval of the newly developed Wildlife Hazard Management Plan 13 months ago. However, since the plan has been implemented, bird strikes at your airport are on the rise. What is your next step?

5. You are the director of operations at a small-hub, ARFF Index B airport. Your airport employs 8 operations personnel responsible for Part 139 compliance, a city-contracted ARFF crew, 23 airport police officers, and requisite maintenance and other personnel. Develop a training program to comply with 14 CFR §139.301 and §139.303. If any assumptions are made, please state those assumptions.

References and Resources for Further Study

American Association of Airport Executives. 2005. "Body of Knowledge Module 3: Airport Operations, Security, and Maintenance." Washington, DC: AAAE.

de Neufville, R. and A. Odoni. 2003. *Airport Systems: Planning Design and Management.* New York: McGraw Hill.

Federal Aviation Administration (FAA). 1997. *Measurement, Construction, and Maintenance of Skid-Resistant Airport Pavement Surfaces.* AC 150/5320-12C. Washington DC: FAA.

———. 2004. Title 14 Code of Federal Regulations, Part 139, Airport Certification. Washington, DC: FAA.

———. 2007. *Hazardous Wildlife Attractants On or Near Airports.* AC 150/5200-33B. Washington, DC: FAA.

———. 2009. National Plan of Integrated Airport Systems (NPIAS).

———. 2013. *Reporting Wildlife Aircraft Strikes.* AC 150/5200-32B. Washington, DC: FAA.

Greater Orlando Aviation Authority. 2015. "Wildlife Hazard Site Visit Report." Retrieved from http://www.orlandoairports.net/east_airfield/2015/Appendix_H.pdf.

Metropolitan Washington Airports Authority. 2013. "Full-Scale Emergency Preparedness Exercise at Reagan National Airport on Saturday, Sept. 21." News Release. Retrieved from http://www.metwashairports.com/6552.htm

Transportation Research Board. 2012. "ACRP Synthesis 38: Expediting Aircraft Recovery at Airports." Washington, DC: TRB. Retrieved from http://onlinepubs.trb.org/onlinepubs/acrp/acrp_syn_038.pdf

Chapter 8

Maintenance

Objectives ↘

Upon completion of this chapter, you should understand:

- inspections and preventive maintenance at airports
- the types of airside maintenance performed at airports
- the types of landside maintenance performed at airports
- the purpose of an airport pavement management program (PMP) and the general types of pavement distress
- the benefits of contracted maintenance services

Key Terms

airport pavement management program (PMP)
continuous friction measuring equipment (CFME)
decelerometer (DEC)
heating, ventilation, and air conditioning (HVAC)
hot mix asphalt (HMA)
Portland cement concrete (PCC)
preventive maintenance (PM)

In Chapter 8

Introduction **323**

Inspections.. **323**

Preventive Maintenance........................ **323**

Maintenance Equipment........................ **324**

Recordkeeping **324**

Airside Maintenance **325**
- Runway Rubber Removal 326
- Pavement Management 329

Landside Maintenance **337**
- Fleet Maintenance 337
- Landscaping.. 338
- Building Maintenance 338
- Electrical Maintenance 339
- HVAC 339
- Systems Maintenance.................................. 340
- Contract Services 340

Concluding Thoughts........................... **340**

Chapter Summary **341**

Review Questions................................ **343**

Scenarios... **344**

References and Resources for Further Study **345**

FEATURES

Texas DOT Routine Airport Maintenance Program 330

By funding matching grants at airports throughout Texas, pavement and airside maintenance are better ensured.

Introduction

In addition to accommodating daily operations, airports are required to adequately maintain the airport to ensure a safe and secure operating environment. Typically, larger airports have separate maintenance departments that handle both landside and airside maintenance. However, even the smallest GA airport has maintenance needs. Maintenance performed at airports includes preventive maintenance and maintenance issues of a routine or urgent nature.

Inspections

One of the first components of airport maintenance involves inspections. As part of maintaining an airport, regular inspections of the facilities, including the many pieces of equipment, must be conducted. Although airport operations personnel will typically conduct inspections focused on the airfield (especially self-inspections as required by 14 CFR Part 139), maintenance personnel typically conduct inspections of landside facilities (including loading bridges; automated gates and doors; people mover systems; **heating, ventilation, and air conditioning [HVAC]** systems; emergency generators; electrical vaults; and water supply systems). These inspections are conducted regularly and according to the schedule developed for the airport's facilities and equipment. Often, a maintenance employee on the overnight shift (also known as midnight shift or graveyard shift) spends the majority of the shift conducting inspections and performing routine, preventive maintenance on various equipment and systems. It should be noted that without regular inspections, issues might not be addressed until equipment or system failure occurs, which can, of course, result in interruption of necessary services. Thus, inspections are an important component of an effective airport maintenance program.

Preventive Maintenance

Similar to performing preventive maintenance on a vehicle (such as regular oil changes), airports engage in **preventive maintenance (PM)** to keep facilities, equipment, and systems operating normally. In fact, PM has been shown to reduce maintenance costs and minimize service interruptions. Possibly the most visible PM program involves airfield pavement (discussed later in this chapter). To maximize the life of airfield pavement, it must be maintained. This includes crack sealing, pavement overlays, etc. Airports also carry out PM on lighting—both on the airfield and in terminal buildings, offices, curbside, and parking structures. Lighting programs may include replacing fixtures, replacing bulbs (known as re-lamping), replacing wiring controls, and repainting fixtures. Additionally, by measuring lighting circuit voltage, any loss of electrical current can be discovered and corrected to prevent system failure (Grothaus et al., 2009).

In reality, PM is carried out on numerous airport facilities, equipment, systems, and airport vehicles. Without PM, airport personnel would just wait until systems and equipment break down and then respond with repairs. In essence, PM is a proactive approach to maintenance. Interestingly, vehicles used on airports endure difficult driving conditions with continuous stop-and-go driving and can accumulate thousands of miles each year. Especially for police, ARFF, operations, and maintenance personnel, these vehicles must be reliable and able to perform sufficiently in time-sensitive situations. Regular PM is key to ensuring that reliability (Grothaus et al., 2009).

Maintenance Equipment

Airports typically have large numbers of maintenance equipment, including mowers, sweepers, tractors, friction measuring equipment, snow removal equipment, wildlife management equipment, painting equipment, dump trucks and various types of excavating equipment, lighted Xs, etc. This maintenance equipment must be accounted for, typically via an annual inventory process. Each piece of equipment will either have an asset tag (with a unique number) and/or a vehicle identification number (VIN). Airports know that each piece of equipment must be (a) properly maintained and (b) replaced at the end of its useful life. Therefore, airports develop equipment maintenance schedules that dictate the number of hours, uses, or cycles between maintenance on the equipment. Airports must also plan for the replacement of equipment as it nears the end of its useful life. With a revolving equipment schedule (which includes an inventory of equipment listed by year and the replacement schedule based on age and use), an airport can plan ahead for equipment needs, and appropriately budget for these needs and replace equipment as needed.

Recordkeeping

Similar to the airport operations department, the airport maintenance department must maintain accurate records. According to Grothaus et al. (2009), "The value of establishing written forms, logs, or checklists, documenting efforts, and maintaining organized files cannot be stressed enough." Maintenance recordkeeping allows an airport maintenance department to track maintenance expenses, analyze maintenance trends, and generally stay organized. Records of inspections, training, and maintenance efforts should be maintained for one year.

From an operational perspective, perhaps the most important records are records of maintenance work requests (known as "work orders") that have been submitted and records of the resolution of these work requests. Specifically, for maintenance work orders submitted to resolve discrepancies discovered during the daily self-inspection (or any other inspection), the FAA requires that records of the work request, as well as records of work performed to resolve the issue, be maintained for 12 consecutive calendar months. Many airport maintenance departments have electronic work order systems that are integrated with the operations department, allowing operations personnel to submit a work request and immediately receive a work order number. This work order number then allows the individual submitting the work order to follow up on the issue and verify when it is resolved (and thus, for example, cancel NOTAMs as appropriate).

Airside Maintenance

Maintenance at airports is performed on both the airside and the landside. On the airside, maintenance must be carried out in a number of areas, including:

- Runway and taxiway pavement (spall repair, joint sealing, and FOD removal)
- Pavement markings (repainting)
- Signs (relamping and sign panel replacement)
- Lighting (relamping)
- Wind socks (replacing wind sock and lighting)
- Obstruction lights (relamping)
- NAVAIDs (including relamping)
- Grass (mowing and spraying)
- Safety areas (mowing, leveling/grading, and erosion control)
- Aprons (sweeping for FOD, maintaining markings and signage, and maintaining loading bridges)

On the landside, significant maintenance is also required, including:

- Parking structures and areas (pavement maintenance and lighting replacement)
- Access roads (including pavement maintenance)
- Signage (including relamping and revising)
- Terminal buildings (maintaining restrooms, public areas, airline offices, ticket counter areas, and baggage claim areas)
- Curbsides (including curb maintenance).

Some airports have one maintenance department with the same personnel responsible for both airside and landside maintenance. Other airports have divisions within their maintenance department that allow for some personnel to specialize in airside maintenance, while other personnel specialize in landside maintenance. The degree of specialization is typically related to the size of the airport. Larger airports tend to have more specialized personnel, while smaller airports have more generalized personnel. In fact, an airport could be so small as to have only one employee—the airport manager. In this case, that person may be responsible for all airport issues, including maintenance.

Yet another possibility is an airport that contracts out some or all airport maintenance. Indeed, depending on the resources, organizational structure, and desired task or project of the airport, it may be beneficial to contract out maintenance. Some airports may not have the financial resources to hire sufficient in-house personnel on a full-time basis to perform required maintenance activities. Other airports may have sufficient resources, but may simply prefer to contract out certain maintenance (especially maintenance performed infrequently, such as rubber removal). Some airports are structured very lean, with many activities being performed by private contractors (such as janitorial, vehicle parking operation, ARFF, and landscaping services). Yet other airports have sufficient in-house personnel, but contract out certain projects due to the infrequency with which they need to be performed or the need for specially skilled personnel and/or special equipment. One example of this arrangement is rubber removal. If an airport performs runway rubber removal only every three months, for instance, and considering the very unique high-pressured water equipment required for this task, contracting this task to a private contractor may make great sense for an airport. Regardless of the reasons, many airports realize great benefit from contracting out various maintenance tasks.

RUNWAY RUBBER REMOVAL

Certificated airports are required by 14 CFR §139.305 to promptly remove any contaminants on paved surfaces as completely as practicable. Contaminants, often referred to as foreign object debris (FOD), can be detrimental to aircraft in a number of ways (see Figure 8-1). Loss of friction on a paved surface can result in loss of directional control. FOD can damage engines and airframes, possibly even resulting in an aircraft accident.[1]

Skid resistance refers to the ability of a pavement to provide a surface with desired friction characteristics under all weather conditions. Skid resistance is affected by the polishing action of aircraft traffic and ground vehicles, contaminants on the pavement, fuel or other fluid spillage, rubber deposits, pavement texture, paint markings, and pavement abnormalities. Wet pavement, snow- or ice-covered pavement, and pavement with rubber deposits or other contaminants can result in aircraft hydroplaning or can create an unacceptable loss of traction. Such a loss of traction can result in poor braking performance and possible loss of directional control. Hydroplaning occurs when tires lose contact

[1] See ACRP Synthesis 26: Current Airport Inspection Practices Regarding FOD.

Figure 8-1. FOD on runway.

(John Padgett, Nashville International Airport)

with the pavement due to pavement contamination of some form—such as water, snow, ice, oil, deice fluid, or rubber deposits.

For many airports, rubber deposits from the tires of landing aircraft are the contaminant most often to blame. To minimize this, periodic rubber removal is required, especially in the touchdown areas. Generally, when 40 percent of the grooves in the runway are equal to or less than 1/8 inch in depth and/or width for a distance of 1,500 feet, rubber removal is required.

Rubber can be removed from runways via one of the following methods:

1. High-pressure water spray
2. Use of chemical solvents
3. High-velocity abrasive impact techniques
4. Mechanical grinding

According to FAA Advisory Circular (AC) 150/5320-12, rubber removal should be conducted according to the frequencies shown in Table 8-1.

Table 8-1. Recommended rubber removal frequencies.

Number of Daily Turbojet Aircraft Landings per Runway End	Suggested Rubber Deposit Removal Frequency
Less than 15	2 years
16 to 30	1 year
31 to 90	6 months
91 to 150	4 months
151 to 210	3 months
Greater than 210	2 months

A more accurate method to determine friction loss due to pavement contamination (and the subsequent timing of rubber removal) is to conduct friction evaluations. This should be done for all runways that accommodate jet aircraft. The timing of friction evaluation will vary among airports and possibly even among runways at a specific airport. According to AC 150/5320-12, friction surveys should take place according to the schedule in Table 8-2.

Table 8-2. Recommended friction survey frequencies.

Number of Daily Minimum Turbojet Aircraft Landings per Runway End	Minimum Friction Survey Frequency
Less than 15	1 year
16 to 30	6 months
31 to 90	3 months
91 to 150	1 month
151 to 210	2 weeks
Greater than 210	1 week

Friction evaluations may be conducted using the following types of airport friction-measuring equipment:

1. **Decelerometers (DEC)**—Provide a spot check of the pavement surface, rather than a continuous graphic record of friction. On pavements with patches of frozen contaminants, decelerometers may be used only on the contaminated areas. A minimum of three braking tests are required in each zone to determine the average friction value for that zone. This will result in a minimum of nine tests for a complete runway friction survey. The vehicle speed for conducting the friction survey should be 20 mph (FAA, 1997).
    a. *Electronic*—Eliminates potential human error by automatically computing and recording friction averages for each one-third of the runway. Also provides a printed record of the friction survey data. Much preferred over mechanical.
    b. *Mechanical*—Typically considered only as a backup to an electronic decelerometer, as they require longer runway downtime and do not provide automatic friction averages or a printed copy of data.
2. **Continuous friction measuring equipment (CFME)**—Recommended for pavement surfaces covered with contaminants, as it provides a continuous graphic record of the pavement surface friction characteristics with friction averages for each one-third zone of the runway length. May be either self-contained or towed. Generally, a runway friction survey is conducted for the full length of the runway to determine the average friction value for each zone. The survey may be conducted at any speed up to 40 mph, although some CFME should be operated at slower speeds based on manufacturer recommendations (Figure 8-2). (FAA, 1997)

Figure 8-2. Self-contained continuous friction measuring equipment.

(Lee Brown, Fort Lauderdale-Hollywood International Airport)

PAVEMENT MANAGEMENT

As discussed earlier, airport pavement, specifically runways, require regular maintenance. To properly maintain airport pavement, airports typically develop an **airport pavement management program (PMP)**. A PMP enables airports to make cost-effective decisions about pavement maintenance and rehabilitation. Although airports receiving federal AIP grants are required to develop and maintain an effective PMP, the FAA encourages all airports to develop maintenance programs as a means of preserving their facilities. Rather than simply determining the present condition of airport pavement, the PMP also predicts the future condition of pavement through the use of a pavement condition indicator. This provides a consistent, objective, and systematic procedure for establishing facility policies, setting priorities and schedules, allocating resources, and budgeting for pavement maintenance and rehabilitation. Rather than reacting to pavement maintenance needs as they arise, this system enables airports to be more proactive in this regard.

Indeed, pavement deteriorates over time, and by projecting the rate of deterioration, a life-cycle cost analysis can be made for various alternatives. The airport can then determine the best alternative and the optimal time to implement the chosen alternative. As time progresses, the condition of pavement deteriorates and the cost to rehabilitate it greatly increases. In this case, performing proactive, preventive maintenance is less expensive than deferring maintenance.

According to FAA Advisory Circular 150/5380-7B, *Airport Pavement Management Program (PMP)*, an effective PMP includes the following components:

- *Pavement structure.* Knowing when the pavement was originally built, the structural composition (material and thickness), and subsequent overlays, rehabilitation, etc., is key to analyzing problems and designing solutions. "As built" records should provide this information. If they are not available or if records are suspect, it will be necessary to core the existing pavement to establish the thickness and composition of the structural layers.
- *Maintenance history.* A history of performed maintenance and its associated costs will provide valuable information on the effectiveness of various maintenance procedures on flexible and rigid pavements. The cost of each maintenance procedure is necessary when performing a life-cycle cost analysis.
- *Traffic data.* Data about the number of operations and types of aircraft using the pavement is necessary when analyzing probable causes of deterioration and when considering alternate maintenance and repair procedures.
- *Pavement condition data.* A fundamental component of any pavement management program is the ability to track pavement condition. This requires an evaluation process that is objective, systematic, and repeatable. A pavement condition rating system provides a rating of the surface condition of a pavement with implications of structural performance.

Texas DOT Routine Airport Maintenance Program

The Texas Department of Transportation (TDOT) has developed a Routine Airport Maintenance Program (RAMP) that makes available a $50,000 annual matching grant for airports in the state to be used for lower cost airside and landside improvements. Airside improvements receive first priority for funding. Examples of airside maintenance projects include pavement crack sealing; pavement slurry seal/fog seal/ rejuvenator; pavement markings; limited pavement failure repairs; drainage maintenance; sweeping; herbicide/pesticide, including fire ant control and mesquite tree eradication; replacement bulbs/lamps for airside lighting fixtures and approach aids; repair and maintenance of beacon, lighting, approach aids; and parts replacement for AWOS not covered under warranty.

A new grant is required each fiscal year prior to work being performed. If an airport manager would like a grant, initial contact with the State Aviation Division must be made. This contact will include a description of the project for which the grant is being requested and the estimated cost of the project, if known.

(Texas Department of Transportation, n.d.)

The PMP should also be capable of:

- *Predicting future pavement condition.* Condition predictions are necessary in developing optimum, multi-year maintenance and rehabilitation (M&R) plans.
- *Determining optimum M&R plans for a given budget.* A PMP should be capable of producing an optimum M&R plan that identifies where and when M&R is required and approximately how much it will cost. This data will assist in setting priorities that fit predetermined M&R budgets.
- *Determining budget requirements to meet management objectives.* Typical management objectives include maintaining pavements above a specified condition and eliminating major M&R requirements over a specified number of years.
- *Facilitating the formulation and prioritization of M&R projects.* In addition to developing optimum M&R plans at the section level, a PMP should facilitate the formulation and prioritization of M&R projects. Engineering judgment, however, remains a key component in transforming the optimum M&R plans into practical executable projects.

Much of the guidance for the actual maintenance of airport pavements can be found in FAA Advisory Circular 150/5380-7B, but much guidance is also contained in AC 150/5320-17, *Airfield Pavement Surface Evaluation and Rating Manuals*. This AC provides guidance on understanding and rating the surface condition of flexible and rigid airfield pavements and provides a simple system to visually rate the condition of airfield pavement.

Airport pavements are designed to accommodate certain traffic loads and if those loads exceed the design loads, the life of the pavement can be considerably reduced. Normal distresses in the pavement structure result from surface weathering, fatigue effects, and differential movement in the underlying subbase over a period of years. In addition, faulty construction techniques, substandard materials, or poor workmanship can accelerate the pavement deterioration process. As a result, airport pavements require routine maintenance, rehabilitation, and upgrading.

Pavement distress can be grouped into the following five categories:

1. Cracking
2. Joint seal damage
3. Disintegration
4. Distortion
5. Loss of skid resistance

Within these five main categories, specific types of pavement distress may occur, and these types vary based on the type of pavement (flexible or rigid).

Most common on runways at commercial-service airports, rigid pavement may experience the following types of pavement distress within the five main categories:

1. Cracking—evidenced by singular cracks or patterns of cracks in the pavement (see Figure 8-3).
   - Longitudinal, transverse and diagonal cracks—caused by repeated loads and shrinkage stresses.
   - Corner breaks—caused by load repetition, combined with loss of support and curling stresses.
   - Durability "D" cracking—caused by variable expansion aggregates in the pavement that are unable to withstand environmental factors, such as freeze-thaw cycles.
   - Shrinkage cracking—formed during the setting and curing of concrete.
2. Joint seal damage—evidenced by damage to the joint seal between slabs (see Figure 8-4). In effect, it is any condition that allows infiltration of water or soil/rocks to accumulate in the joint. It is caused by improper joint width, use of incorrect sealant, incorrect application, and/or improper joint cleaning prior to sealing.
   - Stripping of joint sealant
   - Extrusion of joint sealant
   - Hardening of the filler
   - Loss of bond to the slab edges
   - Absence of joint seal

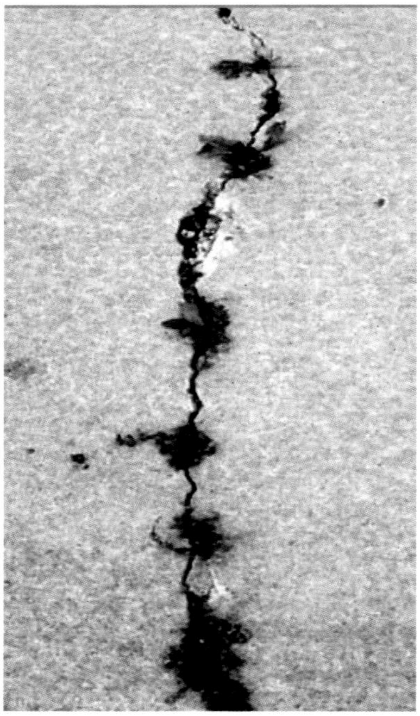

Figure 8-3. Pavement cracking.
(From FAA AC 150/5320-17)

Figure 8-4. Joint seal damage.
(From FAA AC 150/5320-17)

3. Disintegration—evidenced by the breakup of pavement into small, loose particles (see Figure 8-5). It is caused by improper curing and finishing, unsuitable aggregates, and improper mixing of concrete.
   - Scaling, map cracking, and crazing—caused by improper curing or finishing or freeze-thaw cycles.
   - Joint spalling—caused by excessive stresses at the joint or crack resulting from infiltration of incompressible materials or weak concrete at the joint, combined with traffic loads.
   - Corner spalling—caused by the same mechanisms that leads to joint spalling.
   - Shattered slab/intersecting cracks—caused by overloading due to traffic and/or inadequate foundation support.
   - Blowups—caused by insufficient width of a joint, occurring most often in thin pavement, drainage structures, asphalt overlay, and hot weather.
   - Popouts—caused by freeze-thaw action in combination with expansive aggregates.
   - Patching—an intentional repair whereby the original pavement has been removed and replaced by a filler material. A patch is considered a defect in the pavement, regardless of how well it is performing.

4. Distortion—evidenced by a change in the pavement surface's original position, such as what may result from foundation settlement, expansive soils, and frost-susceptible soils (see Figure 8-6).
   - Pumping—caused by a deflection of the slab when loaded, as well as poor joint-load transfer, poor joint seal, and/or presence of groundwater.
   - Settlement or faulting—caused by upheaval or nonuniform consolidation of the underlying pavement layer material, resulting from frost heave, loss of load transfer device (such as a key or dowel), or swelling soils.
5. Loss of skid resistance—evidenced by lower friction coefficients.
   - Polished aggregates—caused by using pavement aggregates that become polished quickly under traffic or are naturally polished at time of construction. Solved by crushing the aggregate prior to use.
   - Contaminants—caused by rubber deposits, oil spills, and other contaminants.

Figure 8-5. Severe spalling along joint and crack of concrete pavement, which generates FOD.

(From FAA AC 150/5320-17)

Figure 8-6. Pavement distortion.

(From FAA AC 150/5320-17)

Flexible pavement experiences the following types of pavement distress within the five main categories:

1. Cracking (see Figure 8-7)
   - Longitudinal and transverse cracks—caused by shrinkage or contraction of HMA surface, which is hastened by oxidation, age hardening, thermal fluctuations, and poorly constructed paving lane joints.
   - Block cracking—caused by contraction of asphalt and daily temperature cycling. Not associated with traffic loads.

- Reflection cracking—caused by expansion and contraction of pavement, which is the result of temperature and moisture changes or traffic loads.
- Alligator or fatigue cracking—caused by fatigue failure of the HMA surface under repeated traffic loading.
- Slippage cracks—caused by a low-strength surface mix or poor bond between the surface and next layer of pavement, appearing when braking or turning wheels cause the pavement surface to slide and deform.

Figure 8-7. Alligator crack pattern on asphalt pavement, caused by failure of the entire pavement due to traffic loading (fatigue).

(From FAA AC 150/5320-17)

2. Joint seal damage
   - None; asphalt has no need for joints.
3. Disintegration (see Figure 8-8)
   - Raveling and weathering—the wearing away of the pavement surface caused by the dislodging of aggregate particles and the loss of asphalt binder.
   - Potholes—caused by fatigue of the pavement surface, often more severe in northern climates. Potholes are uncommon with airfield pavement.
   - Asphalt stripping—caused by moisture infiltration into the HMA pavement structure leading to "stripping" of the bituminous binder from the aggregate particles.
   - Jet blast erosion—caused by jet blast that has burned or carbonized the bituminous binder.
   - Patching and utility cut patch—an intentional repair in which the original pavement has been removed and replaced by a filler material. A utility cut results when the original pavement was cut for the installation of underground utilities. A patch is considered a defect in the pavement, regardless of how well it is performing.

Figure 8-8. Flexible pavement disintegration.

(From FAA AC 150/5320-17)

4. Distortion (see Figure 8-9)
    - Rutting—caused by a permanent deformation in any one of the pavement layers or subgrade, resulting from the consolidation or displacement of the materials due to traffic loads.
    - Corrugation—caused by a lack of stability in the mix and a poor bond between material layers.
    - Shoving—caused by a lack of stability in the mix or lateral stresses produced by adjacent PCC pavement during expansion.
    - Depression—caused by traffic heavier than that for which the pavement was designed, localized settlement of the underlying pavement layers, or poor construction methods.
    - Swelling—caused by frost action surrounding dissimilar material types in the subgrade or by swelling soil.

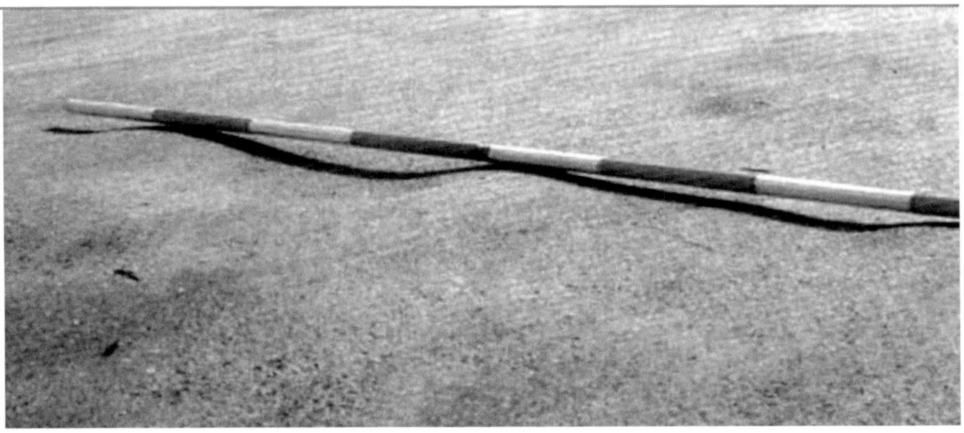

Figure 8-9. Distortion caused by heavy traffic.

(From FAA AC 150/5320-17)

5. Loss of skid resistance (see Figure 8-10)
   - Polished aggregate—caused by using pavement aggregates that quickly become polished under traffic or are naturally polished at time of construction. Solved by crushing the aggregate prior to use.
   - Contaminants—caused by rubber deposits, oil spills, and other contaminants.
   - Bleeding—caused by excessive amounts of asphalt binder in the mix and/or low air-void content, occurring when asphalt binder fills the voids in the mix during hot weather and then expands out onto the surface of the pavement.
   - Fuel/oil spillage—continuous fuel/oil spillage on a HMA surface will soften the surface. Minor fuel/oil spillage will only result in minor damage.

As seen from the list, flexible pavement and rigid pavement experience different specific types of pavement distress. Distress may be caused by traffic loads, environmental conditions, poor installation or maintenance practices, and contaminants. For instance, flexible pavement such as **hot mix asphalt (HMA)** can be softened by continuous exposure to fuel or oil spillage. However, rigid pavement such as **Portland cement concrete (PCC)**, will only experience a reduction in surface friction, but will not be damaged by the contaminant. Therefore, in addition to airport needs (based on aircraft utilization such as traffic loads), available financial resources, and required pavement maintenance, when considering the installation of pavement, the airport should factor into its decision-making process the types of pavement distress that may be experienced with a particular type of pavement.

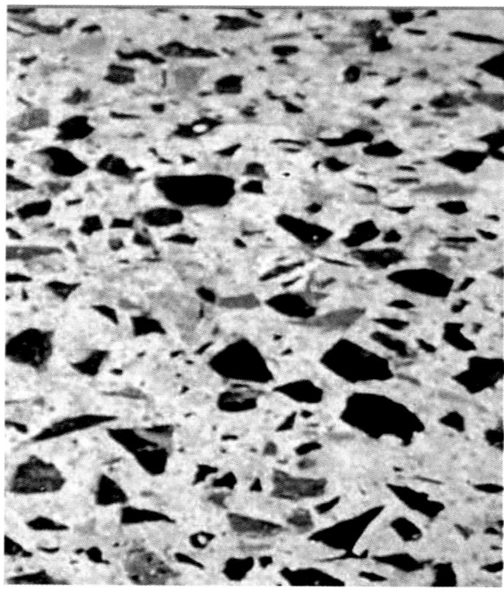

Figure 8-10. Polished pavement surface.

(From FAA AC 150/5320-17)

Landside Maintenance

In addition to maintaining the airside, airports have significant landside maintenance responsibilities as well. It is often the landside components that are most visible to the public. Therefore, it is crucial for airport maintenance to include both airside and landside components.

FLEET MAINTENANCE

Although many airport vehicles are used on the airside, fleet maintenance is generally considered a component of landside maintenance. Airports often have large fleets of vehicles. Personnel in operations, police, ARFF, and maintenance have airport vehicles they use on a daily basis. Amazingly, vehicles can accumulate thousands of miles per month while being driven around on the airport, which may consist of only a few hundred acres. To ensure reliability and long life, these vehicles must be maintained. Oil must be changed, tires must be replaced, fluids must be serviced, etc. At larger airports with fleets of dozens or a hundred or more vehicles, it generally is more economical and timely to have airport personnel service these vehicles on the airport. Thus, a fleet maintenance department is often created and housed in a garage with several service bays to ensure airport vehicles are serviced in a timely fashion (see Figure 8-11). This facility may be located near the ARFF facility, the airfield maintenance facility, or some other convenient location on the airport. Although the facility may be accessed from the airside, it often has access to a local street so that personnel working in the facility can drive from off-airport to the facility to report for work.

Figure 8-11. Fleet maintenance facility.

(Paha_L/Bigstock.com)

LANDSCAPING

Airports often have grand entrances with green lawns, trees, water features, and extensive landscaping (see Figure 8-12). Such landscaping offers significant aesthetic benefits, but also comes at a cost and must be maintained. The airport can either perform this maintenance with in-house airport personnel or contract landscape maintenance to a third party. The choice is typically driven by the expense associated with maintaining the landscaping. At airports with extensive landscaping, maintaining it is a full-time job and may require several to a dozen or more individuals. Contracts for this landscape maintenance may total several hundred thousand dollars or more annually.

Figure 8-12. Airport landscaping.

BUILDING MAINTENANCE

All airport buildings will at some time have maintenance needs, requiring personnel dedicated to building maintenance. Airports often have multiple buildings housing hundreds of thousands of square feet. Terminal buildings accommodate thousands of passengers on a daily basis, many using restrooms, concessions, and common areas including seating and other lounge areas. It is imperative to maintain these areas in good condition so the airport is aesthetically pleasing. Although this may also be contracted out—especially at smaller airports—it is often performed by in-house personnel. Maintenance needed in terminal buildings includes ensuring that toilets are unclogged, signs and overhead lights are illuminated, torn carpet is repaired, and escalators are maintained. By having personnel dedicated to maintaining the buildings (often numerous buildings), the airport can avoid service disruptions and ensure positive customer perception.

ELECTRICAL MAINTENANCE

Electricians are always needed to address the unique electrical maintenance needs at an airport. Electrical maintenance personnel may be divided into landside electrical maintenance and airside electrical maintenance, or all electrical maintenance personnel may have responsibility for both of these areas. On the airside, the extensive airfield lighting systems (consisting of runway, taxiway, and ramp lighting; illuminated signs; rotating beacon, visual approach aids; etc.) often require nightly attention (Figure 8-13). At many airports, the midnight shift provides the perfect opportunity for electrical personnel to spend time on the airfield replacing lamps, inspecting lighting, etc. On the landside, there are often thousands of lighting fixtures, both within terminals and parking garages, that require regular attention. Occasionally, a major relamping project may be undertaken to replace all bulbs, as they may fade over time.

Figure 8-13. Electrical maintenance being performed by electrician with airport operations observing.

(Brett Fay, Lakeland Linder Regional Airport)

HVAC

Due to the large heating, ventilation, and air conditioning (HVAC) systems at airports, especially in the larger terminal buildings, maintenance personnel specifically skilled in operating and maintaining HVAC systems generally are part of the maintenance department. Often, these individuals spend a large portion of their time performing preventive maintenance on these systems, including changing filters, taking air pressure readings, etc. Consider the TSA requirement for 100 percent screening of checked baggage post-9/11. Airports initially put large explosive-detection machines at the ticketing level, which placed large demands on the air conditioning system due to the heat they generated. HVAC personnel became aware of this and stepped up inspections of AC systems as a result.

SYSTEMS MAINTENANCE

At commercial-service airports, personnel are also usually assigned to maintain various airport systems. These systems include elevators and escalators, boarding bridges, ground power units (including pre-conditioned air and 400 Hz electrical at the aircraft gate), and baggage handling systems. Systems such as escalators run continuously and must be regularly maintained to minimize outages. Since some airport systems are rather complex, airports have found it beneficial to have specially trained personnel dedicated to maintaining these systems. For instance, an airport may have personnel dedicated only to maintaining escalators and elevators. Due to the complexity of these systems, it could be beneficial to contract this responsibility out to a skilled third party, such as Schindler, a manufacturer of escalators and elevators.

CONTRACT SERVICES

Any of the maintenance services presented in this chapter can be contracted out. At smaller airports with few staff, many or all of these maintenance services might be contracted out. As an example, all airports have the need for janitorial services. However, is the need great enough to justify hiring part- or full-time personnel solely dedicated to this task? It may be. However, smaller airports and even larger airports may decide to contract out janitorial services. As stated earlier, the decision to fulfill certain maintenance needs by contracting out is most commonly driven by the financial expense of hiring in-house personnel and paying benefits versus contracting out to a third party. Therefore, the degree of contracted maintenance will vary among airports. Some airports have found it very beneficial to maintain large maintenance departments with personnel skilled in the many areas needed by the airport to properly maintain its various systems and equipment. Others have found it beneficial to contract out a large portion of maintenance, greatly relying on third parties and maintaining a minimal in-house maintenance staff. Generally, contracting out costs more than maintaining in-house personnel, but contracting can provide great benefits to the airport.

Concluding Thoughts

For airports to operate without disruption, proper maintenance must be performed on a daily basis. This is true for large, commercial-service airports as well as small, GA airports. Whether maintenance is contracted out or performed by in-house personnel, airport maintenance is not an afterthought—rather, it is part of the daily operation of the airport.

Chapter Summary

- Although airport operations personnel typically will conduct inspections focused on the airfield (especially self-inspections as required by 14 CFR Part 139), maintenance personnel typically conduct inspections of landside facilities.
- Airports conduct preventive maintenance on numerous airfield facilities and systems.
- Maintenance recordkeeping allows an airport maintenance department to track maintenance expenses, analyze maintenance trends, and generally stay organized.
- Maintenance at airports is performed on both the airside and the landside.
- Hydroplaning occurs when tires lose contact with the pavement due to pavement contamination of some form, such as water, snow, ice, oil, deice fluid, or rubber deposits.
- Rubber can be removed from runways via high-pressure water spray, use of chemical solvents, high-velocity abrasive impact techniques, or mechanical grinding.
- Friction evaluations may be conducted using either decelerometers or continuous friction measuring equipment.
- To properly maintain airport pavement, airports typically develop an airport pavement management program, which provides a consistent, objective, and systematic procedure for establishing facility policies, setting priorities and schedules, allocating resources, and budgeting for pavement maintenance and rehabilitation.
- Pavement distress can be caused by traffic loads, environmental conditions, poor installation or maintenance practices, and contaminants.
- Categories of pavement distress include cracking, joint seal damage, disintegration, distortion, and loss of skid resistance.
- Fleet maintenance is the act of maintaining airport vehicles.
- Airports with extensive landscaping must maintain this landscaping on a regular basis.
- Airport buildings must be maintained to accommodate passengers and employees.
- HVAC systems require regular preventive maintenance.
- Airports may choose to contract out maintenance services.

Review Questions

1. Explain the role of preventive maintenance at airports, including some specific examples of PM.
2. What is the value of recordkeeping in the airport maintenance department?
3. What are some examples of maintenance performed on the airside and landside?
4. Discuss some of the reasons for contracting out certain types of maintenance at an airport.
5. Explain the purpose of rubber removal, including the four methods that can be used and recommended frequencies.
6. Explain the various types of airport friction measuring equipment.
7. Explain the role of an airport pavement management program.
8. Explain the components of an airport pavement management program.
9. What should an airport pavement management program be capable of?
10. List the five categories of pavement distress.
11. List the specific types of flexible pavement distress and explain how each type is evidenced.
12. List the specific types of rigid pavement distress and explain how each type is evidenced.
13. What is the purpose of fleet maintenance at airports?
14. Why should airports expend resources on maintaining landscaping?
15. Explain the importance of building maintenance at airports.
16. Explain the purpose of electrical maintenance.
17. What impact did the post-9/11 requirements have on airport HVAC systems?
18. What types of systems must be maintained at commercial service airports?
19. Explain contract services.
20. When would an airport choose to contract out maintenance instead of performing maintenance in-house?

Scenarios

1. As the newly hired director of maintenance at a small hub airport, it becomes clear to you that your predecessor was not very organized, leading to areas of the airport not being properly maintained. You see the need to develop a comprehensive maintenance program, including both airside and landside components. What would this program look like?
2. As director of maintenance at a large hub airport with extensive landscaping along the entrance to the airport, recent discussions have centered on whether to continue performing this landscape maintenance in house or contract it out. Without knowing the financial specifics involved, explain the pros and cons of in-house maintenance and contract maintenance.
3. As manager of airside maintenance at a medium hub airport, you have been tasked with developing an airport pavement management program. Explain what this PMP would look like.
4. As director of operations at a medium hub commercial service airport with 210 jet operations per day, what schedule for rubber removal will you develop? How regularly will you conduct friction evaluations to determine if the runway friction coefficient is degraded due to rubber contamination? What type of friction measurement equipment will you use?
5. As director of maintenance at a small hub airport, you have been asked by the airport's executive director to develop a landside maintenance program. What areas will you consider? How will you develop this program? Discuss whether you will decide to conduct maintenance in-house or via contract personnel.

References and Resources for Further Study

American Association of Airport Executives. 2005. "Body of Knowledge Module 3: Airport Operations, Security, and Maintenance." Washington, DC: AAAE.

deNeufville, R. and A. Odoni. 2003. *Airport Systems: Planning Design and Management.* New York: McGraw Hill.

Federal Aviation Administration (FAA). 1997. *Measurement, Construction, and Maintenance of Skid-Resistant Airport Pavement Surfaces.* AC 150/5320-12C. Washington, DC: FAA.

———. 2004. *Airfield Pavement Surface Evaluation and Rating Manuals.* AC 150/5320-17. Washington, DC: FAA.

———. 2007. *Guidelines and Procedures for Maintenance of Airport Pavement.* AC 150/5380-6B. Washington, DC: FAA.

———. 2009. National Plan of Integrated Airport Systems (NPIAS).

———. 2014. *Airport Pavement Management Program.* AC 150/5380-7B. Washington, DC: FAA.

Grothaus, J., T. Helms, S. Germolus, D. Beaver, K. Carlson, T. Callister, R. Kunkel, and A. Johnson, 2009. "ACRP Report 16: Guidebook for Managing Small Airports." Washington, DC: Transportation Research Board.

Texas Department of Transportation. n.d. "2015 Routine Airport Maintenance Program (RAMP) Grants." Retrieved from http://ftp.dot.state.tx.us/pub/txdot-info/avn/ramp_grants.pdf

Transportation Research Board. 2011. "Current Airport Inspection Practices Regarding FOD." Washington, DC: TRB. Retrieved from http://onlinepubs.trb.org/onlinepubs/acrp/acrp_syn_026.pdf

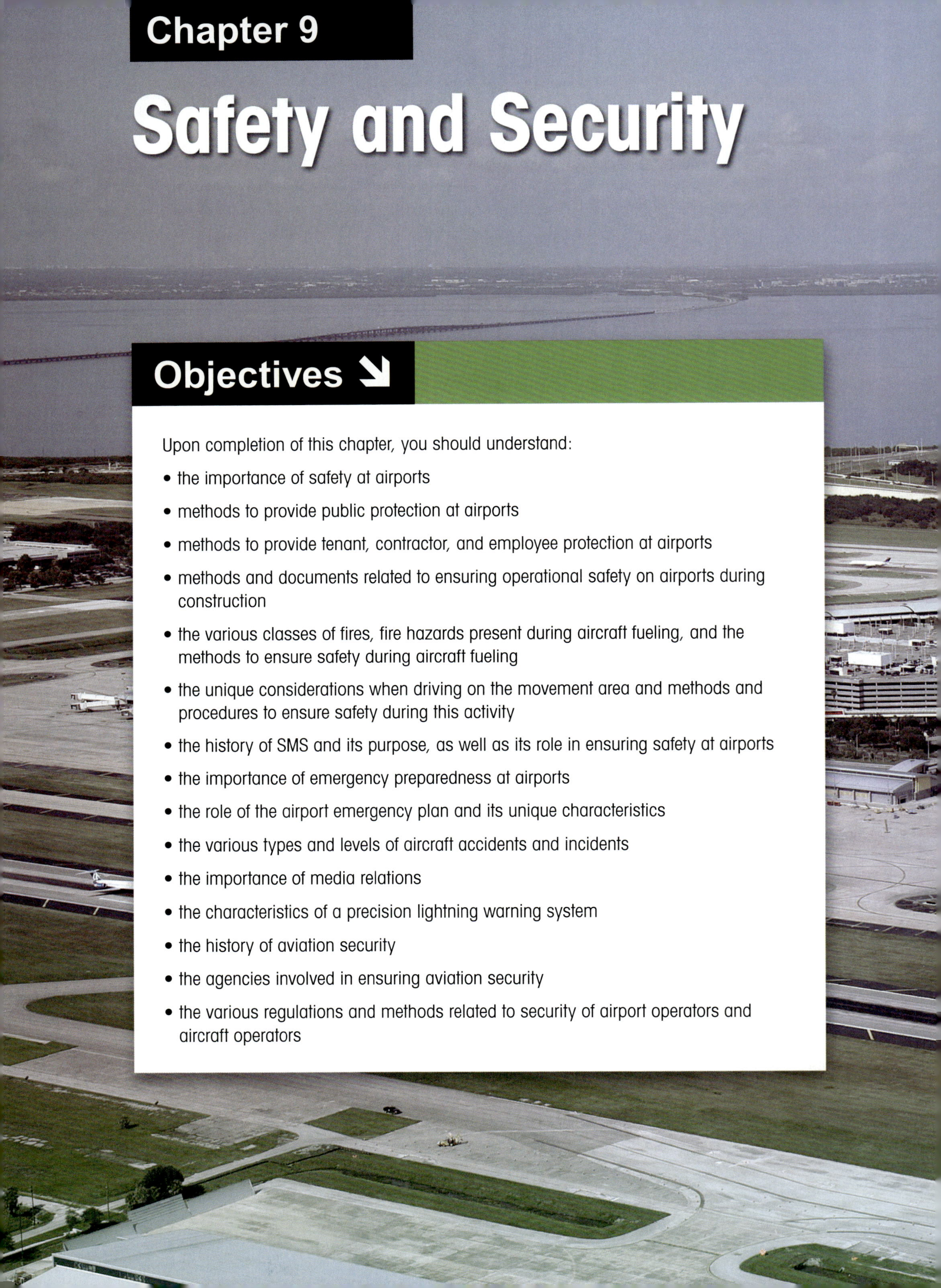

Chapter 9

Safety and Security

Objectives

Upon completion of this chapter, you should understand:

- the importance of safety at airports
- methods to provide public protection at airports
- methods to provide tenant, contractor, and employee protection at airports
- methods and documents related to ensuring operational safety on airports during construction
- the various classes of fires, fire hazards present during aircraft fueling, and the methods to ensure safety during aircraft fueling
- the unique considerations when driving on the movement area and methods and procedures to ensure safety during this activity
- the history of SMS and its purpose, as well as its role in ensuring safety at airports
- the importance of emergency preparedness at airports
- the role of the airport emergency plan and its unique characteristics
- the various types and levels of aircraft accidents and incidents
- the importance of media relations
- the characteristics of a precision lightning warning system
- the history of aviation security
- the agencies involved in ensuring aviation security
- the various regulations and methods related to security of airport operators and aircraft operators

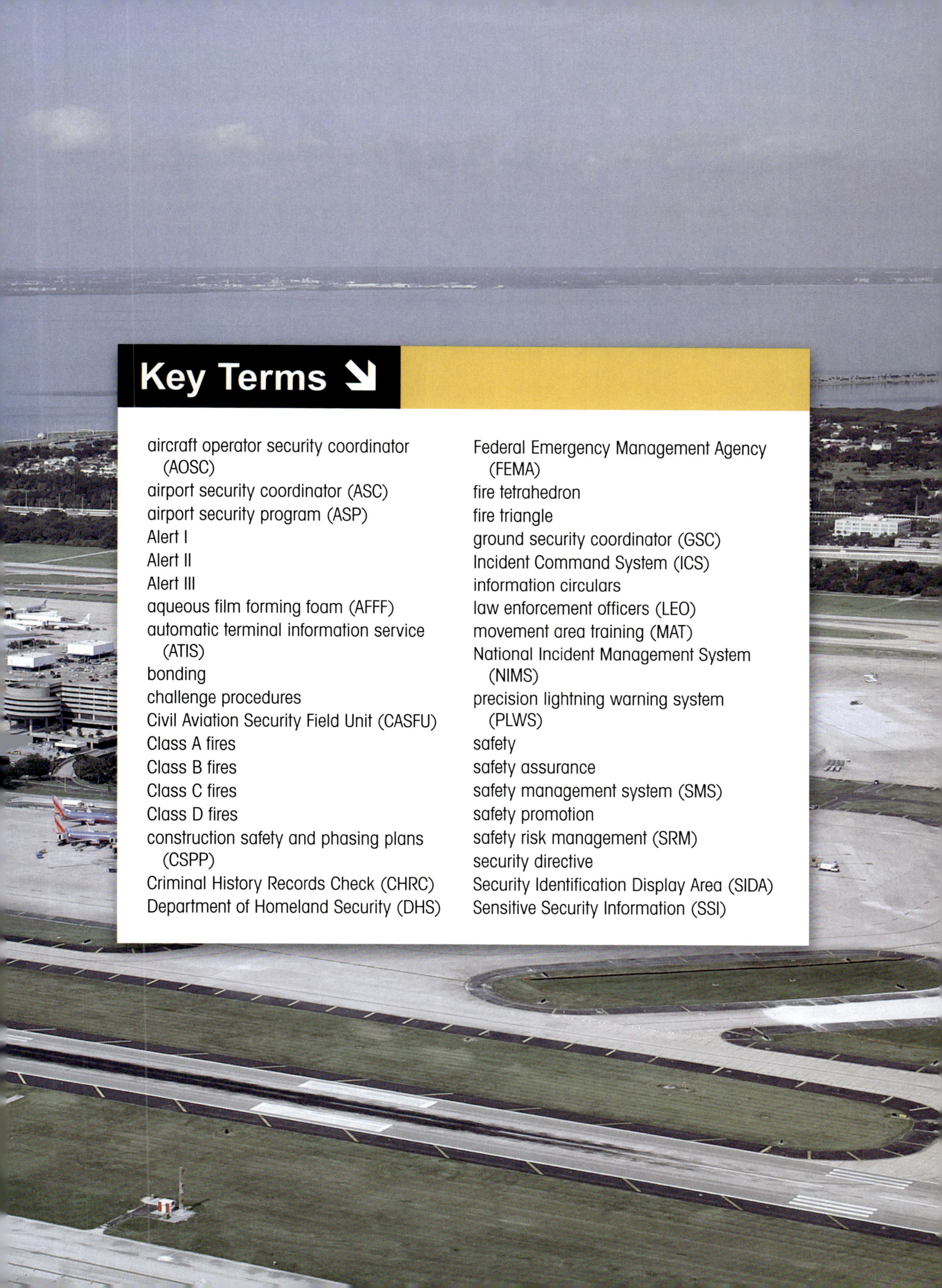

Key Terms

aircraft operator security coordinator (AOSC)
airport security coordinator (ASC)
airport security program (ASP)
Alert I
Alert II
Alert III
aqueous film forming foam (AFFF)
automatic terminal information service (ATIS)
bonding
challenge procedures
Civil Aviation Security Field Unit (CASFU)
Class A fires
Class B fires
Class C fires
Class D fires
construction safety and phasing plans (CSPP)
Criminal History Records Check (CHRC)
Department of Homeland Security (DHS)
Federal Emergency Management Agency (FEMA)
fire tetrahedron
fire triangle
ground security coordinator (GSC)
Incident Command System (ICS)
information circulars
law enforcement officers (LEO)
movement area training (MAT)
National Incident Management System (NIMS)
precision lightning warning system (PLWS)
safety
safety assurance
safety management system (SMS)
safety promotion
safety risk management (SRM)
security directive
Security Identification Display Area (SIDA)
Sensitive Security Information (SSI)

In Chapter 9

Safety **349**
- Public Protection 349
- Tenant, Contractor, and Employee Protection 350
- Aircraft Fueling 352
- Driving on the Movement Area 356
- SMS 357
- Emergency Preparedness 362
- Lightning Warning System 366

Security **367**
- Historical Overview 367
- Agencies 370
- Security Regulations 372
- General Aviation Airport Security 380

Concluding Thoughts **383**

Chapter Summary **384**

Review Questions **387**

Scenarios **388**

References and Resources for Further Study **389**

FEATURES

Tampa International Airport's Precision Lightning Warning System 367

By installing a lightning warning system, employees at this airport are safer while working on the ramp.

Safety

Safety, which is an environment of risk mitigation, an awareness of accident causes, and an environment free of accidents, is imperative for airports. Although aviation will never be completely free of accidents and incidents (which are often due to human error), airports can and should make certain that the airport operating environment is as safe as possible at all times. 14 CFR Part 139 is the FAA's attempt to regulate this safe airport operating environment, although not all airports are Part 139 certificated. In fact, only about 550 airports nationwide fall under Part 139. But whether or not an airport must comply with Part 139, there are certain procedures and practices that can be adopted by all airports to ensure a safe airport operating environment.

PUBLIC PROTECTION

First, airports must protect the public from the hazards present in the airport operating environment (see Figure 9-1). 14 CFR §139.335 actually requires certificated airports to provide:

- Safeguards to prevent inadvertent entry to the movement area by unauthorized persons or vehicles; and
- Reasonable protection of persons and property from aircraft blast.

This can be ensured with appropriate blast fences, runway protection zones, perimeter fencing, access-controlled gates and doors, natural barriers, etc. Since there is no requirement for GA airports to comply with Part 139, some GA airports do an inadequate job of protecting the public from the hazards of the airport operating environment. Although a three-foot high chain link fence with a gate that is always open may allow the public to better observe aircraft activity and enjoy the airport, it is incumbent upon the airport operator to protect the public from the hazards present in the airport operating environment, and this is woefully inadequate. Indeed, the general public is not aware of the hazards present in aircraft noise, moving tugs, moving aircraft, spinning propellers, etc. Airports have actually been found by courts to be an "attractive nuisance." Although they may attract children and adults alike, airports

Figure 9-1. Public protection signage.

that do not implement safeguards to protect the public from airport-specific hazards are exposed to liability in this area.

TENANT, CONTRACTOR, AND EMPLOYEE PROTECTION

Additionally, airports must ensure the protection of tenants and contractors. Although this is usually easier to accomplish on the landside (such as within the terminal), ensuring such protection on the airside (such as on the airfield) is more difficult. One manner in which to do this is to restrict tenants operating on the airside to the ramps. This includes catering companies driving large catering trucks to and around aircraft gates; fuelers driving tanker trucks or smaller refuelers; and airline employees driving tugs, maintenance vehicles, and other ground support equipment (GSE). Almost universally, employees of these tenants are authorized to drive on the ramp (non-movement areas), but are not authorized to operate on movement areas (taxiways and runways). Although this greatly minimizes the risk of runway incursions by not allowing these individuals access to the movement areas, they also do not benefit from movement area training (MAT). In essence, they receive the same training that skycaps and airline customer service agents receive—**Security Identification Display Area (SIDA)** training. This SIDA training includes the proper procedures for wearing a SIDA badge and challenge procedures (among other items), but generally does not cover runway and taxiway lighting, runway markings, and other airfield-specific items. As a result, it is important for airports to ensure that tenants and contractors that operate on the airside are aware of airport rules and regulations (specifically as they pertain to driving on the airside, including speed limits, service roads, vehicle driving lanes, and movement/non-movement boundary markings).

There have been instances at airports in which an airline employee drove a tug into the movement area, possibly to chase an escaped cat or dog, or to retrieve a cap blown in the wind. However, without having MAT and authorization to enter the movement area, this action is prohibited without an approved escort. It is imperative for all individuals with driving privileges on the airside to be properly trained and educated in this regard. 14 CFR §139.329 actually requires certificated airports to limit access to movement areas and safety areas only to those pedestrians and ground vehicles necessary for airport operations. As part of this, airports must develop procedures for noncompliance, and these procedures should be part of the training for individuals with driving privileges on the airside.

Similarly, it is important for airports to develop procedures to protect contractors (especially those working on the airside). The best source of guidance in this area is FAA Advisory Circular 150/5370-2, *Operational Safety on Airports During Construction*. Specifically, AC 150/5370-2 states that airports must (a) restrict movement of construction vehicles and personnel to permitted construction areas by flagging, barricading, erecting temporary fencing, or providing escorts, as appropriate and as specified in the **construction safety and**

phasing plans (CSPP) and the safety plan compliance documents (SPCD); and (b) ensure that no contractor employees, employees of subcontractors or suppliers, or other persons enter any part of the AOA from the construction site unless authorized.

The CSPP should include specific vehicle and pedestrian requirements, such as:

1. Construction site parking, including designated vehicle parking areas for contractor employees to prevent any unauthorized entry of persons or vehicles onto the AOA.
2. Construction equipment parking: an area for all equipment to be located outside the OFZ and active runway and taxiway safety areas. Additionally, equipment should not interfere with imaginary surfaces contained in 14 CFR Part 77.
3. Access and haul roads that are clearly marked to prevent inadvertent entry by construction vehicles to areas open to airport operations.
4. Marking and lighting of vehicles in accordance with FAA Advisory Circular 150/5210-5, *Painting, Marking, and Lighting of Vehicles Used on an Airport.*
5. Description of proper vehicle operations on various areas under normal, lost communications, and emergency conditions.
6. Required escorts.
7. Training requirements for vehicle drivers to ensure compliance with the airport operator's vehicle rules and regulations. Guidance is contained in FAA Advisory Circular 150/5210-20, *Ground Vehicle Operations on Airports.*
8. Situational awareness, which involves being aware of aircraft at all times, as well as the location of all escorted vehicles if an escort is being provided.
9. Two-way radio communication procedures, including the use of appropriate radio frequencies at airports with and without ATCT. When operating vehicles on or near open runways or taxiways, construction personnel must understand the critical importance of maintaining radio contact, as directed by the airport operator, with airport operations, ATCT, common traffic advisory frequency (CTAF), and **automatic terminal information service (ATIS)**. ATIS is a dedicated frequency that broadcasts noncontrol information in an automated fashion to reduce frequency congestion and controller workload with the need for repetitive broadcasts of this same information to multiple users. Vehicular traffic crossing active movement areas must be controlled either by two-way radio with the ATCT, escort, flagman, signal light, or other means appropriate for the particular airport. Additionally, proper radio usage, proper phraseology, and light gun signals must be included.
10. Maintenance of the secured area of the airport, including fencing and gates, badging requirements, and 49 CFR Part 1542 standards for access control, movement of ground vehicles, and identification of construction contractor and tenant personnel (if appropriate).

    (FAA, 2011)

As stated in AC 150/5370-2, an airport operator has overall responsibility for all activities on the airport, including construction activity; therefore, it is imperative for airports to adequately develop and implement procedures to protect contractors working on the airside. One specific manner in which airports do this is by requiring contractors to install two barricade lines around their construction sites on the airside. The barricade line closest to the construction site is designed as a visual barrier to keep personnel inside the authorized construction area. The second barricade line is placed closest to active movement areas and is designed to keep aircraft out of the construction area (see Figure 9-2).

Figure 9-2. Construction personnel conducting runway painting, with barricade lines visible.

AIRCRAFT FUELING

Safety during fueling is critical, as unsafe procedures during fueling can create extremely hazardous situations. 14 CFR §139.321 requires certificated airports to establish and maintain standards authorized by the FAA for protecting against fire and explosions in storing, dispensing, and otherwise handling fuel. These standards must address training of fueling personnel in fire safety; bonding; public protection; control of access to storage areas; fire safety in fuel farm and storage areas; fire safety in mobile fuelers, fueling pits, and fueling cabinets; and the fire code of the jurisdiction having authority over the airport.

Basic to ensuring safety during fueling operations on airports is awareness of the **fire triangle** (see Figure 9-3). The triangle contains the following three elements: heat, fuel, and oxygen. If any of these three elements are removed, the fire will be extinguished. In general terms, heat may be removed by cooling the fire, as is possible with the use of water on **Class A fires**. The fuel source may be removed by eliminating the wood or paper fueling the Class A fire (such as making a fire break ahead of a forest fire). Oxygen can be removed by use of certain chemical fire extinguishers, such as carbon dioxide (which displaces oxygen). Although the fire triangle is appropriate for learning the components necessary to start a fire, the **fire tetrahedron** is necessary to learn how a fire continues to burn (see Figure 9-4). The fourth side is a chemical chain reaction. If uninterrupted, this chain reaction will maintain a fire. The chemical chain reaction can only be interrupted by application of certain extinguishing agents.

Aircraft fuel fires are not Class A fires, however. Class A fires are composed of ordinary combustibles (such as wood or paper). **Class B fires** are composed of flammable and combustible liquids (such as greases and gas). **Class C fires** are composed of energized electrical equipment. **Class D fires** are composed of combustible metals (magnesium and sodium). Water, which has a cooling effect, is most effective in extinguishing Class A fires. Carbon dioxide, which smothers the fire as it displaces oxygen, is effective on Class B or Class C fires. Dry chemical, which is a mixture of specially treated sodium bicarbonate, also deprives the fire of oxygen and is effective on Class B and C fires. For Class B fires (such as fuel fires), foam is most effective (see Table 9-1).

Figure 9-3. Fire triangle.

Figure 9-4. Fire tetrahedron.

Also known as **aqueous film forming foam (AFFF)**, this extinguishing agent is a blend of bicarbonate of soda and aluminum sulfate. When applied, AFFF creates an aqueous film on the fuel surface that prevents evaporation and hence, reignition of the fuel once it has been extinguished by the foam (see Figure 9-5). Additionally, the film can self-heal and reseal areas that are disturbed by falling debris. AFFF effectively blankets a fire with a layer of foam, thus cooling the fire and starving it of oxygen. It is primarily used on Class B fires, such as on-airport fuel fires, but may also be effective on Class A fires. However, foam is not effective on vertical surfaces or pressure fires (such as broken fuel lines). AFFF is now in use on all U.S. Navy aircraft carriers and by major airports, refineries, and other areas where potentially catastrophic fuel fires can occur.

Halon is a liquefied gas which breaks the chemical reaction by interrupting the supply of oxygen. Due to the ability of Halon to degrade the ozone layer, a replacement, Halitron, has been invented that is more environmentally friendly

Table 9-1. Classes of combustibles.

Class of Fire	Type of Combustible	Example	Common Extinguishing Agents
A	Common combustibles	Wood, paper, cloth, etc.	Water; chemical foam; dry chemical*
B	Flammable liquids and gases	Gasoline, propane and solvents	Carbon dioxide (CO_2); halon**; dry chemical; aqueous film forming foam (AFFF)
C	Live electrical equipment	Computers, appliances	CO_2; halon; dry chemical
D	Combustible metals	Magnesium, lithium, titanium	Dry powder (suitable for the specific combustible metal involved)
K	Cooking media	Cooking oils and fats	Wet chemical (Potassium acetate based)

* Dry chemicals, CO_2 and halon can be used on Class A fires, but may not be effective on their own. They need to be supplemented with water.

** Halon extinguishers are no longer made but some may still be in use. Dangerous gases are formed when halon is used to extinguish fires. Wear proper respiratory equipment, particularly in enclosed spaces. After use, do not allow anyone to enter the area until it has been well ventilated.

Figure 9-5. Aqueous film forming foam (AFFF).

(Jeff Price)

and very effective for aircraft engine fires and aircraft brake fires. For class D fires, only specialized agents such as METL-X and G-1 powder are effective.

Airports must ensure that training for all fuelers focuses on regularly minimizing the risk of fire (Figure 9-6). Liquid fuels, such as AvGas and Jet-A, emit vapors that can ignite when the flashpoint is reached. The flashpoint of AvGas is -50 degrees Fahrenheit, while Jet-A has a 100 degree Fahrenheit flashpoint. As a result, the vapors released from these two fuels will be at or above the flashpoint in almost every circumstance in which they'll be handled. All mobile fuelers should be equipped with air filter/flame arrestor equipment and a leak-free exhaust system which terminates into a standard baffle muffler at the front of the vehicle. Line service personnel should only wear clothing composed of 100 percent cotton. Fabrics such as silk, polyester, nylon, and wool generate static, which can produce a spark that may ignite fuel or fuel vapors. Additionally, refueling personnel should not carry any type of igniting device on their person or within 100 feet of any fuel tank or refueler. Only high-quality non-galvanized metal funnels should be used. **Bonding**, which grounds the fueler to the aircraft via a metal cable or wire, is imperative during fueling operations. Static can build up on an aircraft during flight and while fuel is flowing through a hose and nozzle. Thus, bonding is necessary to equalize these charges and prevent an errant spark. Personnel must also remain aware of additional ignition sources, including hot brakes, hot engine surfaces, jet engine exhaust, thunderstorms and lightning, portable electrical devices, fixed electrical equipment, and exposed light bulbs.

Even with adequate training and proper procedures, airports may experience a fuel spill (see Figure 9-7). Typically, fuel spills can occur if a fueler has been filled beyond its capacity at the fuel farm, an aircraft has vented a significant amount of fuel, or a fueler has been moved while connected to an aircraft or fuel farm. If a spill does occur, it is important to stop the flow of fuel. If possible, a fire extinguisher must be placed upwind of the spill. Next, a supervisor or the

Figure 9-6. Aircraft fueling.

airport fire department must be notified. In addition, it's necessary to ensure that fueling vehicles are not moved and equipment is not started or turned off (due to a possible backfire). If trained and properly equipped, personnel may begin cleaning up the spill. Typically, a spill cart will need to be brought on scene to enable proper cleanup of the spill. It is important to have ARFF or fire extinguishers standing by, as the vapors may ignite (Prather, 2009).

Figure 9-7. Fuel spill at the aircraft gate, with ARFF on scene, although not visible in the photograph.

DRIVING ON THE MOVEMENT AREA

Driving on the movement areas of the airfield presents a unique set of complex factors that require personnel authorized to drive on the AOA to be well-trained. In addition to SIDA training, 14 CFR §139.303 requires all personnel who access movement areas and safety areas and perform duties in compliance with the airport's ACM to be trained in at least the following areas:

- Airport familiarization, including airport marking, lighting, and signs system.
- Procedures for access to, and operation in, movement areas and safety areas.
- Airport communications, including radio communication between the air traffic control tower and personnel, use of the common traffic advisory frequency if there is no air traffic control tower or the tower is not in operation, and procedures for reporting unsafe airport conditions.
- Duties required under the airport certification manual and Part 139.
- Any additional areas as appropriate.

Often, those employees with access to the movement areas will include employees in the areas of operations, maintenance, ARFF, and police. Almost universally, the employees with access to the movement areas are employed by the airport operator. These employees must complete **movement area training (MAT)**. This training will produce employees who are knowledgeable of airfield markings, signage, lighting, and procedures to enable safe driving on the AOA. This will include the right-of-way that aircraft always maintain, communication procedures with ATCT, escort procedures, and the need to maintain constant situational awareness on the AOA. With vehicles operating on the movement areas, there is an increased risk of runway incursions. Thus, training will focus on making sure that all employees with access to the movement areas are very familiar with procedures necessary to avoid such an incursion. Indeed, ensuring safety on the airfield requires proper training of all personnel authorized to operate on the AOA, while restricting the number of personnel authorized to operate on the AOA (see Figure 9-8).

Figure 9-8. Airport operations vehicle on the AOA.

SMS

On October 7, 2010, the FAA issued a notice of proposed rulemaking (NPRM) requiring a **safety management system (SMS)** for certificated airports. The rule would require certificated airports to establish an SMS for their entire airfield environment (including movement and non-movement areas) to improve safety at airports hosting air carrier operations. This proposal would require a certificate holder to submit an implementation plan and implement an SMS within certain timeframes. This NPRM stemmed from the November 2005 amendment to ICAO Annex 14, Volume I (Airport Design and Operations) that required member states (countries) to have certificated international airports establish an SMS. The United States is one such member state and the FAA is the U.S. regulatory agency responsible for enforcing this requirement. The NPRM allowed for public comment until January 5, 2011, which was then extended to July 5, 2011. More than 150 comments were submitted.

The FAA also funded two pilot studies to explore SMS at airports. In the first pilot study, 22 larger airports participated. Nine airports participated in the second pilot study, which focused on SMS at smaller airports. In these first two pilot studies, the consultants were generally retained by the airport to develop an SMS manual, but the airports were not required to implement the SMS. More recently, the FAA funded an Implementation Pilot Study which consisted of 14 airports that participated in either the first or the second pilot study and involved actually implementing the SMS that was already developed.

Even though the NPRM was issued in 2010, by May 2015, the FAA had not revised Part 139 to require SMS at certificated airports, nor had the agency issued a final rule in response to the NPRM and the comments received. So airports remain in a holding pattern, so to speak. Airports have been issued some guidance on this topic, however. Specifically, in 2007 the FAA published Advisory Circular 150/5200-37, *Introduction to SMS for Airport Operators*. This AC was designed to introduce the concept of a SMS for airport operators. This was necessary, especially since the SMS concept requires a more proactive, top-down approach to safety, which is a relatively new concept to U.S. airports. Additionally, in June 2012, the FAA issued a draft advisory circular (150/5200-37A) entitled "Safety Management Systems for Airports." Comments were due to the FAA by August 31, 2012. As of May 2015, the FAA had not released this AC in its final form, nor issued any regulatory guidance for airports requiring the development and implementation of SMS. Readers are encouraged to visit the SMS section of the FAA website (www.faa.gov/about/initiatives/sms/) for the most current information regarding SMS efforts for airports.

What is SMS? According to AC 150/5200-37, an SMS is a formalized approach to managing safety by developing an organization-wide safety policy, developing formal methods of identifying hazards, analyzing and mitigating risk, developing methods for ensuring continuous safety improvement, and creating organization-wide safety promotion strategies. Specifically, an SMS consists of the following four elements (see Figure 9-9):

- Safety policy and objectives
- Safety risk management
- Safety assurance
- Safety promotion

Safety Policy and Objectives

The safety policy, which is a formal commitment to safety expressed by senior management, is the foundation of an effective SMS. If senior management has not formally expressed a commitment to safety, it will be difficult to obtain "buy-in" from employees on the front line. To establish specific safety objectives, an airport will typically appoint a safety manager to oversee the SMS and ensure accountability within the organization. With a solid foundation of the safety policy and objectives, an airport will better be able to develop a positive "safety culture." In positive safety cultures, there are clear reporting lines, clearly defined duties and well understood procedures. Personnel will fully understand their responsibilities and know what to report, to whom, and when (FAA, 2007).

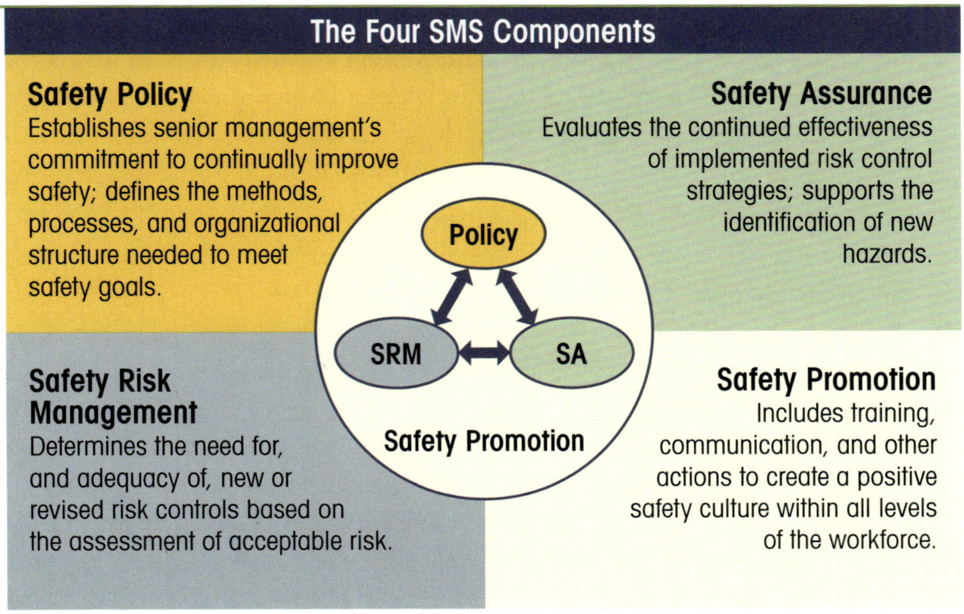

Figure 9-9. Elements of a safety management system (SMS). (FAA)

Safety Risk Management

Safety risk management (SRM) is the main cornerstone of SMS. SRM requires a proactive approach to safety, rather than reacting after an accident or incident has occurred. The five phases in the SRM process are:

1. Describe the system.
2. Identify the hazards.
3. Determine the risk.
4. Assess and analyze the risk.
5. Treat the risk.

Phase 1, describing the system, requires consideration of the airport's current safety program as required by Part 139 and outlined in the ACM. Knowing the baseline safety status of the airport is important in knowing how much progress needs to be made to develop an SMS and a supportive safety culture (FAA, 2007).

Phase 2, identifying the hazards, requires an assessment of hazards of the system. Properly identifying hazards requires operational expertise, training in SMS, a simple hazard analysis tool, and adequate documentation of the process. In essence, the hazard identification stage considers all the possible sources of system failure (FAA, 2007).

Phase 3, determining the risk, requires each hazard to be identified to determine what risks exist that may be related to the hazards. In this phase, all potential risks associated with each hazard are identified and documented. There is no determination of the severity or potential of the risk occurring (FAA, 2007).

Phase 4, assessing and analyzing the risk, requires the airport operator to estimate the level of risk by using a predictive risk matrix. Risk is defined as the composite of the predicted severity and likelihood of the outcome or effect (harm) of the hazard in the worst credible system state. In order to assess the risk of an accident or incident occurring, severity and likelihood must be determined. Hazards are ranked according to the severity and the likelihood of their risk. The likelihood of an event is broken down into frequent, probable, remote, extremely remote, and extremely improbable. The severity of an event is broken down into no safety effect, minor, major, hazardous, and catastrophic. Depending on where an event/activity falls on the predictive risk matrix, various levels of risk may be possible (FAA, 2007).

Risk severity can be broken down into three levels. These levels of risk include high, medium, and low. A high risk activity is considered unacceptable. In this instance, the activity cannot be undertaken unless hazards are further mitigated so that risk is reduced to a medium or low level. A medium risk activity presents an acceptable level of risk. In this instance, the activity can continue, but tracking and management are required. Finally, a low risk activity presents the target level of risk. Low risk activities are acceptable without restriction or limitation, and the identified hazards are not required to be actively managed, but are documented (see Figure 9-10) (FAA, 2007).

Phase 5, treating the risk, requires the airport operator to develop options to mitigate the risk and alternative strategies for managing a hazard's risk(s). Generally, these strategies are designed to address medium-risk and high-risk hazards. Strategies may include avoidance, assumption, control, or transfer. Of course, risk mitigation may require a management decision to approve, fund, schedule, and implement one or more risk mitigation strategies. This phase is specifically designed for the airport operator to mitigate hazards (FAA, 2007).

An example of the SRM process at an airport could involve the construction of a new parallel taxiway at a two-runway airport. In identifying hazards,

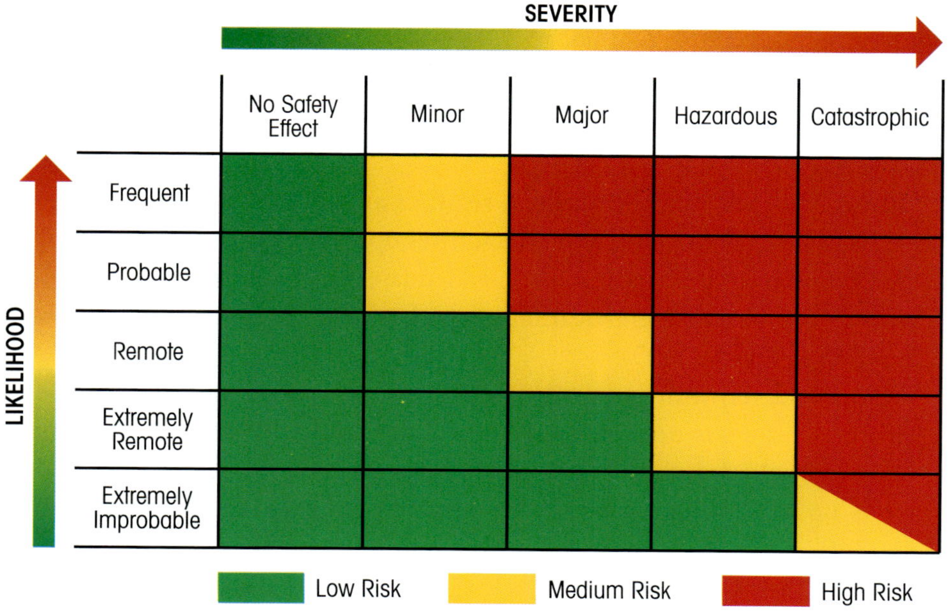

Figure 9-10. Hazard risk matrix.

(From FAA AC 150/5200-37.)

personnel may think about runway incursions caused by contractors; construction equipment or stockpiled materials interfering with safety areas or 14 CFR Part 77 surfaces or NAVAIDs; security vulnerabilities from open gates; utilities being interrupted due to excavation; etc. Once hazards are identified, the risk represented by each hazard must be determined. For example, the risk associated with a runway incursion may stem from a contractor driving across the runway without authorization from ATCT. The predictive risk matrix is used to then determine the severity and likelihood of the risk. It is actually highly likely that a runway incursion can occur as contractors are driving in the movement area. And, this could result in deaths in the worst possible case. For those falling into medium or high risk categories, a plan must be developed to treat the risk. For example, maybe a training plan could be developed for contractors. Or a snow fence could be erected to provide a visible marker for contractor personnel. Another option would be to completely close the runway to prevent this possibility. Of course, the costs of closing the runway to airport operations must be weighed against the benefits of leaving it open.

Safety Assurance

Safety assurance is the process of oversight once the SMS has been established. Specifically, safety assurance includes self-auditing, external auditing, and safety oversight. Considering the many tenants and different activities on airports, safety oversight is often best achieved through auditing and surveillance practices. Additionally, the SMS should include a non-punitive safety reporting system to allow individuals to report hazards and other issues with no fear of reprisal. The reports submitted should be used by the safety manager to identify and address safety deficiencies. The safety reporting system may also identify and correct non-conformance to safety policy (FAA, 2007).

Safety Promotion

Even with a well-developed SMS, without promotion of the SMS and the processes associated with it, airport safety is not likely to be enhanced. Therefore, **safety promotion** becomes integral to the effective implementation of an SMS. Safety promotion includes (a) training and education, (b) safety communication, and (c) safety competency and continuous improvement.

Safety training and education should include (a) a documented process to identify training requirements, (b) a validation process that measures the effectiveness of training, (c) initial (general safety) job-specific training, (d) recurrent safety training, (e) indoctrination/initial training incorporating SMS, and (f) training that includes human factors and organizational factors. Safety communication can include products such as safety seminars, safety letters, safety notices/bulletins, lessons learned, safety reporting drop boxes, and electronic reporting through web sites or email (FAA, 2007).

EMERGENCY PREPAREDNESS

Emergencies, defined as "any occasion or instance, natural or man-made that warrants action to save lives and protects property and public health," can happen at any time (FAA, 2009, p. 1). Airports in particular are prone to emergencies, due to the critical phases of flight that occur on and in the immediate vicinity of airports. In fact, according to the FAA (2009, p. 1):

> An airport incident can occur anywhere, at any time—day or night, under any weather condition, and in varying degrees of magnitude; it can occur instantaneously or develop slowly; it can last only a few minutes or go on for days. It can be natural, such as a hurricane or earthquake, or it can be "man-made", such as a hazardous materials spill, civil unrest, terrorism, major fire, or power outage.

Being fully prepared for an emergency at an airport is necessary to ensure a safe airport environment. Emergencies can occur at an airport at any time and emergency preparedness is crucial to ensuring an effective response to and recovery from an airport emergency. This is best accomplished with an airport emergency plan.

Airport Emergency Plan

14 CFR §139.325 requires certificated airports to develop an airport emergency plan. The AEP is necessary to ensure that procedures are in place to effectively respond to and resolve an emergency on the airport. FAA Advisory Circular 150/5200-31, *Airport Emergency Plan*, provides guidance to airport operators for the development and implementation of an AEP. This lengthy AC, at almost 300 pages, provides detailed guidance in the ten functional sections of an AEP: command and control, communications, alert notification and warning, emergency public information, protective actions, law enforcement/security, firefighting and rescue, health and medical, resource management, and airport operations and maintenance. Additionally, the AC provides detailed information on how to develop plans and procedures for the nine hazards that are detailed in chapter 7.

Developing an AEP is similar to developing an ACM in that the AEP is usually written in exact conformance to the AEP AC. The AEP must also be approved by the FAA and is usually prepared in a 3-ring binder with a page control chart for ease in revision. The AEP is designed to provide guidance to all interested personnel in how to appropriately respond to any number of airport emergencies (see Figure 9-11).

A 2010 change to the AEP AC requires airports to comply with the **National Incident Management System (NIMS)** in developing their AEP and in responding to emergencies. The NIMS provides a set of standardized organizational procedures, including the **Incident Command System (ICS)**, multiagency coordination systems, and public information systems—as well

Figure 9-11. Airport emergency response.

(Nan Phanitsuda Sophonpanasak, Denver International Airport)

as requirements for processes, procedures, and systems designed to improve interoperability among jurisdictions and disciplines in various areas. According to FEMA, the ICS is a "management system designed to enable effective and efficient domestic incident management by integrating a combination of facilities, equipment, personnel, procedures, and communications operating within a common organizational structure" (FEMA, 2015). The NIMS focuses on preparedness, communications, management of resources, and incident management. Specifically, NIMS guides departments and agencies at all levels of government, nongovernmental organizations, and the private sector in managing incidents involving all threats and hazards to minimize loss of life, loss of property and harm to the environment. At an airport, NIMS is especially useful when multiple jurisdictions—such as on-airport ARFF, off-airport fire rescue from multiple stations, police, highway patrol, etc.—respond to an accident. The **Federal Emergency Management Agency (FEMA)** offers NIMS training via their online Emergency Management Institute.

Emergency Training and Airport Familiarization

It is important that an airport that serves air carriers (more than nine seats if scheduled or at least 31 seats if unscheduled) have an effective training program in place for those involved in emergency response. This is required by Part 139, and typically applies to ARFF personnel. Operations personnel and other responders may also benefit from this training, however. Specifically, 14 CFR §139.319 requires certificated airports to train ARFF personnel in the areas specified in chapter 7.

Aircraft Accidents and Incidents

Often, those emergencies on the airport that have the greatest impact are those involving aircraft. An aircraft accident is defined as "Any occurrence associated with the operation of an aircraft that takes place between the time a person boards the aircraft with the intention of flight and the time such person has disembarked, in which a person suffers death or serious injury as a result of the occurrence or in which the aircraft, including cargo aircraft, receives substantial damage" (FAA, 2009, p. 109). An aircraft incident is defined as "an occurrence other than an accident that affects or could affect the safety of operations" (FAA, 2009, p. 109). Part 139 not only requires the development and implementation of an AEP, but it also requires certificated airports to have sufficient and trained personnel, equipment, and extinguishing agents to respond to aircraft accidents and incidents (see Figure 9-12).

Figure 9-12.
Aircraft emergency.

There are typically three levels of alert used at airports to convey emergency information to ARFF, operations, Comm Center, and other airport personnel in the emergency communication chain. These alert levels indicate to responders the seriousness of the potential or actual emergency.

1. **Alert I** (Local Standby Alert)—An aircraft with a known or suspected operational defect may or may not be landing at your airport. This is notification only. No response is required. All units involved will be manned and will standby in quarters.
2. **Alert II** (Full Emergency Alert)—An aircraft is known or suspected to have an operational defect that affects normal flight operations to the extent that there is danger of an accident. All units respond to pre-designated positions (see Figure 9-13).
3. **Alert III** (Aircraft Accident Alert)—An aircraft incident/accident has occurred on or in the vicinity of the airport. All designated emergency response units proceed to the scene in accordance with established plans and procedures.

   (FAA, 2009)

Once the alert is declared, responders report to their standby positions (if necessary) or respond to the actual scene of the accident. Generally, Alert II is the most common level of alert at airports. For an Alert II, ARFF responds to various locations along the runway (short of the mandatory hold short line) to enable rapid response to the runway and site of an aircraft accident (if necessary). Airport operations personnel respond to standby at the approach end of the runway (short of the mandatory short line). As the aircraft flies over the threshold, the operations vehicle immediately drives onto the runway to conduct an inspection of the runway surface behind the aircraft. Either at this time or pre-arranged with ATC, the operations agent closes the runway to prevent the ATCT from sending any other aircraft to that runway (either for arrival or departure). Considered a special inspection, the operations agent inspects the runway for any debris left by the aircraft involved in the emergency (including hydraulic fluids, rubber debris, etc.). However, as the aircraft slowly decelerates on the runway, the operations agent gives way to ARFF equipment, which are considered first responders and should be in first position to extinguish an aircraft fire. If the aircraft lands safely and is able to taxi on its own power to the gate, the airport operations agent will be the last vehicle to clear the runway and will verify the runway is reopened and available for use, while at the same time securing the Alert. According to AC 150/5200-31, the airport operator must ensure that the airport, or portions thereof, is not reopened after an accident or incident until the airport operator has ensured that (a) aircraft operating areas are secure; (b) aircraft movement areas that are to be reopened have been properly inspected; and (c) adequate aircraft rescue and firefighting protection is available for aircraft operations (FAA, 2009).

Figure 9-13. Standby areas for alert.

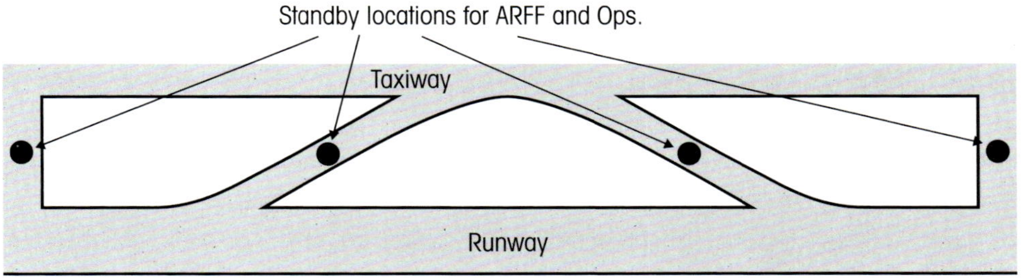

Media Relations

With any airport emergency, the media will usually have a vested interest in obtaining information and visiting the airport to get information out to the public (Figure 9-14). Therefore, airports must be prepared to respond to the media in a proactive manner. Some airports actually develop media or public relations plans. These plans guide airport personnel in how to best respond to the media after an accident or incident, as well as proactively develop positive community relations utilizing the media. Such media plans will include areas for media staging, and procedures for issuing press releases, interacting with media personnel, and providing escorts to media personnel. AC 150/5200-31 proposes that an airport's AEP include an emergency public information section. Many airports also employ a public information officer who has the responsibility for interacting with the media and keeping them informed of any emergency events on airport.

Figure 9-14. Live broadcast from a media satellite truck located at an airport parking deck.

LIGHTNING WARNING SYSTEM

Airports located in areas prone to lightning (such as Florida) may install a **precision lightning warning system (PLWS)**. These systems utilize several sources of data, such as satellite lightning strike data and field mill sensors, which measure voltage potential. More advanced systems have the ability to predict when lightning may occur, rather than producing an alarm after the fact. Airports with a PLWS typically have remote enunciators installed on terminal buildings that are visible and audible to personnel on the ramp. Airlines may also have displays in their respective operations offices that generate an audible and lighted warning on the display unit. With a PLWS, the risks associated with lightning strikes to personnel are reduced. However, lightning can still strike the pavement, resulting in damage to the pavement that must be repaired.

Tampa International Airport's Precision Lightning Warning System

The state of Florida has the most lightning-related fatalities of any state in the United States. At commercial-service airports, where airline employees are outdoors 18–20 hours or more per day, those working at Florida airports receive much greater exposure to the potential for a lightning strike. To address this, in 1996, the owner and operator of Tampa International Airport, the Hillsborough County Aviation Authority, in cooperation with the Tampa Airport Managers Association (TAMA), contracted with Global Atmospherics (now Vaisala) for the installation and maintenance of a precision lightning warning system (PLWS) at a cost of $176,537. The system receives data from three sources: national satellite lightning strike data and two electronic field mill sensors, which measure voltage potential. Rather than only alert personnel after a lightning strike, this system has the ability to predict when a lightning strike may occur. Although the initial installation included remote alarm display systems (RADS) placed in airline operations offices, in 2002, at a cost of $82,940, the airport additionally installed remote enunciators (RE) consisting of audible horns and beacons installed on the ramp-side exteriors of the airside terminals to also inform personnel on the ramp of lightning danger. This system has greatly enhanced ramp safety before, during, and after stormy weather, as personnel no longer need to guess whether or not it is safe to be outside, but now can confidently decide whether or not to consider the ramp closed based on alerts provided by the PLWS.

(Vaisala Precision Lightning Warning System, n.d.)

Security

Although maintaining safety at airports is imperative, ensuring a secure airport is no less important. Indeed, due to the ever-evolving threats to airport security, the federal government has developed a number of regulations to ensure security at airports, especially those Part 139 airports serving air carriers.

HISTORICAL OVERVIEW

Airport security has evolved since the beginning of the industry. Although very few events related to aviation security occurred in the early days, once passenger travel became a reality, security threats were introduced. These threats were typically in the form of hijackings. The first recorded hijacking of an aircraft took place in 1931 in Arequipa, Peru, but hijackings reached their all-time high in 1970. The early hijackings were generally motivated by the potential for monetary gain via the taking of hostages, or the desire to seek asylum. In the later years, hijackings were carried out for political purposes (Price and Forrest, 2010).

In addition to the hijacking threat, bombings have also been a threat to aviation security. The first bombing of a U.S. airliner occurred on November 1, 1955, on a DC-6 that had departed Stapleton International Airport. Motivated by the desire to collect life insurance proceeds, Jack Graham placed a bomb in baggage belonging to his mother, which caused an explosion that resulted in 44 deaths. Airline bombings continued throughout the following decades, although they were not as frequent as hijackings (Price and Forrest, 2010).

Subsequent events include the 1985 hijacking of TWA Flight 847 and the bombing of Air India Flight 182. In 1987, an irate former airline employee killed his former supervisor (who was a passenger on the flight) and the flight crew of PSA 1771 over San Diego, California, resulting in the crash of the aircraft and 43 deaths. On December 21, 1988, a bomb was detonated on Pan Am Flight 103, killing a total of 270, including all of the passengers and 11 citizens of Lockerbie, Scotland. On September 11, 2001, in the largest and most dramatic aviation terrorist attacks in the history of aviation, four U.S. commercial aircraft were hijacked. The hijackers crashed two of the aircraft into the two towers of the World Trade Center, resulting in complete destruction of both buildings. The third plane crashed into the Pentagon and the fourth crashed in a field in Pennsylvania. The death toll included all passengers and crew on the four aircraft, as well as people on the ground, especially in the World Trade Center. Close to 3,000 individuals lost their lives and more than 6,000 were injured. Osama bin Laden and the terrorist organization Al Qaeda was held responsible for the attacks (Price and Forrest, 2010).

As a result of these events over the years, the U.S. Congress, some U.S. presidents, and the federal government have responded in various ways in an attempt to prevent future attacks and minimize threats to aviation security. However, the most significant piece of legislation that continues to affect aviation security in the United States is the Aviation and Transportation Security Act (ATSA) of 2001. This act was signed into law on November 19, 2001, which was a little more than two months after the 9/11 terrorist attacks. Most significantly, the act created the Transportation Security Administration (TSA) and transferred all civil aviation security responsibilities to the TSA. Prior to the ATSA, civil aviation security was the responsibility of the FAA, in the form of a Civil Aviation Security Field Unit (CASFU) at the airport level, and the passenger screening function was the responsibility of the airlines. Although the airlines generally contracted the screening function out to private security companies, the failure of an inadequate screening system allowed the terrorists to smuggle weapons on board the aircraft and carry out the attacks on 9/11. Thus, Congress decided that a new federal security agency should assume that responsibility. ATSA also created the position of federal security director at each commercial service airport, with oversight responsibility for passenger, baggage and cargo screening; airport security risk assessments; crisis management; etc. In addition, the act allowed for federal air marshals and required the screening of 100 percent of checked baggage for explosives by December 31, 2002 (Figure 9-15) (Price and Forrest, 2010).

Figure 9-15. Baggage screening.

Even with the implementation of the ATSA of 2001, threats to aviation security remain and have resulted in additional attacks and attempted attacks on the U.S. aviation system. On December 22, 2001, Richard Reid attempted unsuccessfully to ignite explosives concealed in his shoes while on an American Airlines flight from Paris to Miami. As a result of this incident, the TSA began requiring passengers to remove their shoes to be separately screened. On December 25, 2009, on a Northwest Airlines flight from Amsterdam to Detroit, Michigan, Umar Farouk Abdulmutallab attempted to detonate plastic explosives hidden in his underwear. As a result of this incident, the TSA began quickly deploying advanced imaging screening technology that could "see" through articles of clothing worn by passengers. Although this technology had first been deployed by the TSA in 2007, this 2009 attempted bombing created a sense of urgency for more widespread deployment of this technology. There are two types of advanced imaging technology—millimeter wave and backscatter. As of 2012, there were more than 640 imaging technology units in use at approximately 165 airports nationwide (Figure 9-16) (Price and Forrest, 2010; TSA, n.d.[a]).

Figure 9-16. TSA screening checkpoint.

In order for the TSA to stay ahead of emerging security threats and prevent terrorist attacks that are either aimed at or utilize the aviation system, a multi-layered approach has been necessary. These layers have included Visible Intermodal Prevention and Response (VIPR), Travel Document Checker, behavior detection officers (BDO), Secure Flight, federal air marshals (FAMs), Federal Flight Deck Officer (FFDO) program, employee screening, and checkpoint screening technology. According to the TSA, the use of technology is an important component in this multi-layered approach. As of 2012, the TSA was using technology in the following forms:

1. Paperless boarding pass
2. Biometrics
3. Bottle liquids scanners
4. CastScope (for screening of casts and prosthetics)
5. Explosive detection system
6. Explosives trace detection
7. Threat image projection
8. Imaging technology

   (TSA, n.d.[c])

AGENCIES

There are several agencies involved with securing aviation. Prior to the TSA, the FAA was responsible for securing aviation and the airlines were responsible for screening passengers and carry-on baggage, often contracting this function out to private security firms. In the early days, the Federal Aviation Agency, which was created by the 1958 Federal Aviation Act, assumed the responsibilities of the Civil Aeronautics Authority. Although safety was the foundation of their responsibilities, aviation security soon became a responsibility, as well. Prior to the Federal Aviation Agency assuming responsibility for aviation security, however, the U.S. Immigration and Naturalization Service assumed this responsibility. Specifically, with the first U.S. aircraft hijackings in 1961, the federal government began using armed guards on civilian aircraft. These armed guards were actually border patrolmen recruited from the U.S. Immigration and Naturalization Service. That same year, President Kennedy signed an amendment to the Federal Aviation Act of 1958 making it a crime to hijack an aircraft, interfere with an active flight crew, or carry a dangerous weapon aboard an air carrier aircraft. To help enforce these revisions to the Act, and allow the Federal Aviation Agency to assume responsibility for aviation security, a special corps of FAA safety inspectors began training for duty aboard airline flights. In March 1962, the Federal Aviation Agency's first "peace officers" were sworn in as special U.S. deputy marshals. These men worked as safety inspectors for the FAA flight standards organization and carried out their role as armed marshals on flights only when specifically requested to do so (FAA, 2010a).

In 1967, the Department of Transportation began operations and the Federal Aviation Agency became the Federal Aviation Administration (FAA). As security threats continued to increase and evolve, the FAA continued to assume responsibility for aviation security. After eight airliners were hijacked to Cuba in January 1969, the FAA created the Task Force on Deterrence of Air Piracy. One product of this task force was the development of a hijacker "profile" that could be used, along with metal detectors (magnetometers), during the screening of passengers. However, after a hijacking by Arab terrorists in September 1970 during which four airliners were blown up, a comprehensive anti-hijacking program, which included a federal marshal program, was introduced by President Nixon that same September (Rumerman, n.d.). After thwarted attempted bombings and subsequent hijackings in 1972, the FAA issued an emergency rule making inspection of carry-on baggage and scanning of all passengers by airlines mandatory by the start of 1973. This emergency rule was subsequently incorporated into law with the signing of an anti-hijacking bill in August 1974 (Rumerman, n.d.).

Much of the work of the FAA in the area of aviation security was conducted by the FAA Civil Aviation Security Office. At airports, this work was carried out by **Civil Aviation Security Field Units (CASFUs)**. These field units were in charge of ensuring the security of local airports, as well as responding to security threats and events as they occurred.

However, as a result of the 9/11 terrorist attacks, the Homeland Security Act was signed into law in 2002. This Act created the **Department of Homeland Security (DHS)**, which is a new cabinet-level department in the executive branch. The mission of the DHS is threefold: to (a) help prevent terrorist attacks in the United States, (b) reduce the country's vulnerability to terrorism, and (c) assist in recovery after an attack. Although the TSA is part of the DHS, the department houses 22 separate government agencies, including the United States Coast Guard, the Secret Service, the Federal Emergency Management Agency, Immigration and Customs Enforcement (ICE), and Customs and Border Protection (CBP).

In terms of aviation security, the most important of these agencies is the TSA. Although the TSA works to ensure the security of aviation, rail, transit, highway, and pipeline sectors, their role in ensuring aviation security is a role familiar to any airline passenger. The TSA employs nearly 50,000 transportation security officers who screen more than 1.7 million passengers each day at more than 450 airports nationwide. The TSA also screens 100 percent of checked baggage for explosives, having screened approximately 4 billion checked bags since inception. The TSA also deploys approximately 2,800 behavior detection officers at airports across the country, leading to more than 2,200 arrests since inception. Additionally, the TSA utilizes more than 400 explosives specialists in aviation and multimodal environments and thousands of federal air marshals who are deployed every day on both domestic and international flights. The TSA also trains and deploys explosives detection canine teams to assist airports and mass transit systems with ensuring security (TSA, n.d.[d]).

SECURITY REGULATIONS

Prior to 9/11 and the subsequent creation of the TSA, aviation security regulations were contained with Title 14 of the Code of Federal Regulations (CFR). However, the Aviation and Transportation Security Act of 2001 transferred the federal regulations concerning aviation security from the FAA to the TSA, and also moved them from Title 14 to Title 49 of the CFR. Often referred to as the Transportation Security Regulations, the aviation security regulations are contained in the Title 49 CFR Part 1500 series.

Title 49 CFR Part 1503—Investigative and Enforcement Procedures

The regulation that governs investigative and enforcement procedures for investigations conducted by the TSA for violations of security regulations is 49 CFR Part 1503. If an individual or business entity violates any of the transportation security regulations, enforcement may be carried out under Part 1503. Enforcement actions can include civil or criminal penalties (Price and Forrest, 2010).

Title 49 CFR Part 1520—Protection of Sensitive Security Information

Due to the nature of aviation security, there are plans and procedures that should not be made available to the general public or anyone other than those with a need-to-know. As a result, 49 CFR Part 1520 is designed to protect this **Sensitive Security Information (SSI)** and restrict its release only to individuals or entities that have a legitimate need-to-know. If the person needs the information to carry out security duties (or is in training to carry out security duties), to supervise or manage individuals carrying out security duties, or to advise others who are authorized to receive SSI, the individual has a need-to-know. Airport operators and aircraft operators are explicitly prohibited from releasing SSI without the approval of the TSA. SSI includes records (whether in written form, drawings, maps, audio or videotape, film or photographs) and vulnerability assessments (which includes any examination of a transportation system, vehicle, or facility to determine its vulnerability to security threats) (Price and Forrest, 2010).

Title 49 CFR Part 1540—General Rules

Title 49 CFR Part 1540 contains definitions and also delegates the authority over aviation security to the TSA. Issues such as fraud, tampering or compromising a security system, interfering with security personnel, carrying weapons or explosives on board an airplane, and passenger screening, are addressed (Price and Forrest, 2010).

Title 49 CFR Part 1542—Airport Security

Due to the need for secure airports, especially at Part 139 airports serving air carriers, 49 CFR Part 1542 was developed. This regulation, in a different form than the old 14 CFR Part 107, is the main regulation that guides airport operators in securing their airports. Part 1542 includes the role and responsibilities of the **airport security coordinator (ASC)**; access control systems; personnel identification systems including the Criminal History Records Check process; law enforcement personnel and response requirements; contingency planning; and incident response. Additionally, Part 1542 addresses the identification and use of security areas (including the AOA, the secured area, and the Security Identification Display Area) and barriers designed to prevent unauthorized access to the security areas. It also grants inspection authority to the TSA and allows the agency to test airport security systems (Price and Forrest, 2010).

The ASC assumes the primary role for ensuring airport compliance with transportation security regulations, especially Part 1542. The individual serving as the ASC is the primary airport contact for the federal government, specifically the TSA. The ASC is tasked with developing the airport's **airport security program (ASP)**. The ASP is designed to address the unique characteristics of each airport. Each page of the ASP must be approved and signed by the airport's federal security director. The ASP will address the duties and responsibilities of individuals responsible for carrying out the plan. Each Category X and I airport is required to conduct a tabletop exercise of the ASP every two years, while Category II, III, and IV airports must exercise the ASP once every three years (Price and Forrest, 2010).

The airport security program can be one of three forms—complete, supporting, or partial. The program required is generally based on the size and activity of the airport, as determined by passenger enplanements and factors such as proximity to major population centers, the type of operations at the airport, and the desires of the TSA. A complete security program is required at most Category X through Category II airports (as defined by enplanements), whereas supporting and partial programs are required at Category III and IV airports. A complete security program requires adherence to the 21 sections as spelled out in Part 1542. A supporting program requires adherence to the sections relating to ASC, law enforcement requirements, recordkeeping, contingency plans, SSI, and incident management. A partial program requires the same sections as a supporting program, with the exception of contingency plans (Price and Forrest, 2010).

Additionally, the ASC administers the airport's access control system, the personnel identification system (to be applied in the SIDA), and tenant security programs. Specifically, the ASC is responsible for:

1. Being available on a 24-hour basis as the airport's primary and immediate contact for communications with the TSA.
2. Ensuring that security functions, procedures, and processes are in compliance with Part 1542.

3. Correcting conditions not in compliance with Part 1542 and adhering to changes mandated by TSA security directives (SDs).
4. Reviewing and controlling the results of Criminal History Records Checks and security threat assessments.
5. Processing applications from individuals applying for unescorted access to the SIDA areas.
6. Sharing security information with air carrier station managers and foreign air carrier operators.

Having an effective access control system is also an important requirement of Part 1542. This regulation requires airports to control access to security areas to prevent unauthorized individuals from having access to these areas. Although this can be accomplished through the use of locks on doors and gates with keys issued to authorized personnel, many airports employ a very complex access control system consisting of badge/card readers, personal identification number (PIN) pads, and even biometric components (such as fingerprint, iris, or hand geometry). The goal of an airport access control system is to selectively grant access and prevent unauthorized access. With only a lock/key access control mechanism, if an employee resigns or is fired and does not return their key, all locks have to be rekeyed. However, with computer-based access control systems, the employee's badge can simply be eliminated from the system, thereby preventing any further access. With PIN-based systems, if a badge is lost or stolen, the individual attempting access with the lost or stolen badge will be unsuccessful if the PIN is not known. However, a PIN could be intentionally shared and a badge could be loaned to provide an unauthorized person with access. With a biometric-based system, even if a PIN is shared and a badge is lost, stolen, or loaned, an individual would be prevented access if they do not have the identical biometric signature (in the form of an iris, fingerprint, or hand geometry) (Price and Forrest, 2010).

Part 1542 also specifies the requirements for personal identification media (often referred to as SIDA badges). First, this media must include a full-face photo of the individual, the individual's full name, the individual's employer, and an identification number unique to that individual. Second, the media must clearly signify the scope of the individual's access and movement privileges (see Figure 9-17). Airports often adopt various colors to signify the various access levels. For instance, red may be used for personnel that will stay in the terminal or within the "shadow" of the terminal on the ramp. Green may be used to signify those individuals authorized to be on the ramp around aircraft. Blue may be used to signify those authorized to access the movement areas. Third, the media must be of sufficient size and appearance to be visible to others, enabling challenge procedures to be carried out. **Challenge procedures** refer to the requirement for personnel to verify the authority of any person not displaying approved identification media. An individual without approved

Figure 9-17. Airport employee's SIDA badge.

Figure 9-18. Airport operations conducting a SIDA challenge to verify this individual's authorization to be in the SIDA area.

identification media must be under escort by an authorized individual. Personnel must wear their SIDA badge at all times above waist level while in the secured area or SIDA (see Figure 9-18) (Price and Forrest, 2010).

A requirement of the Aviation and Transportation Security Act of 2001 was for personnel of all airport operators, aircraft operators, and foreign air carriers with access to the SIDA to undergo a fingerprint-based **Criminal History Records Check (CHRC)**. In fact, any individual who will have unescorted access to a SIDA or a sterile area, or who will have the authority to authorize others to have unescorted access, is required to undergo a fingerprint-based CHRC with a result that does not reveal any prior convictions or findings of not-guilty-by-reason-of-insanity of a disqualifying criminal offense. The 28 disqualifying offenses are:

1. Forgery of certificates, false marking of aircraft, and other aircraft registration violations
2. Interference with air navigation
3. Improper transportation of a hazardous material
4. Aircraft piracy
5. Interference with flight crewmembers or flight attendants
6. Commission of certain crimes aboard aircraft in flight
7. Carrying a weapon or explosive aboard an aircraft
8. Conveying false information and threats
9. Aircraft piracy outside the special aircraft jurisdiction of the United States
10. Lighting violations involving transporting controlled substances
11. Unlawful entry into an aircraft or airport area that serves air carriers or foreign air carriers contrary to established security requirements
12. Destruction of an aircraft or aircraft facility
13. Murder
14. Assault with intent to murder
15. Espionage
16. Sedition
17. Kidnapping or hostage taking
18. Treason
19. Rape or aggravated sexual abuse
20. Unlawful possession, use, sale, distribution, or manufacture of an explosive or weapon
21. Extortion
22. Armed or felony unarmed robbery
23. Distribution of, or intent to distribute, a controlled substance
24. Felony arson
25. Felony involving a threat
26. Felony involving willful destruction of property; importation or manufacture of a controlled substance; burglary; theft; dishonesty, fraud or misrepresentation; possession or distribution of stolen property; aggravated assault; bribery; or illegal possession of a controlled substance punishable by a maximum term of imprisonment of more than one year
27. Violence at international airports
28. Conspiracy or attempt to commit any of the criminal acts listed above

If the airport finds that the result of an applicant's CHRC indicates an arrest for a disqualifying criminal offense without disposition (guilty or not guilty), it is important to investigate further to determine whether the arrest resulted in a disqualifying offense. This must be determined before granting unescorted access authority. If there is no disposition or the disposition did not result in a finding of guilty or not guilty by reason of insanity, the applicant would not be disqualified from unescorted airport access (Price and Forrest, 2010).

Part 1542 also requires airports to provide **law enforcement officers (LEO)** to assist in carrying out the ASP and support the TSA at the passenger screening checkpoints. LEOs in use at airports must have arrest authority, be identifiable in uniform, be armed with and authorized to use a firearm, have completed a law enforcement officer training program, and be trained in the responsibilities of LEOs in carrying out the ASP (see Figure 9-19) (Price and Forrest, 2010).

The TSA typically communicates security information to the airport operator either in the form of a **security directive** or information circular. Security directives mandate measures with which airports must comply. Airport operators are required to acknowledge receipt of the security directive within the time prescribed and also to notify the TSA of the manner in which the airport will comply with the security directive. If unable to implement the measures required in the SD, the ASC must propose alternative measures to the TSA for approval within the time prescribed in the security directive. **Information circulars** contain advisory information and do not require implementation of any measures by the airport, other than possibly a heightened sense of security or awareness of specific threats highlighted in the information circular (Price and Forrest, 2010).

Figure 9-19. Airport law enforcement officer.

Title 49 CFR Part 1544—Aircraft Operator Security

Similar to airport operators, aircraft operators are required to designate an **aircraft operator security coordinator (AOSC)** and this individual will be the main point of contact for the airline to the TSA. The AOSC is also responsible for developing the Aircraft Operator Standard Security Program (AOSSP) for the airline. The airline will also have a **ground security coordinator (GSC)** to oversee security for each passenger and cargo flight. The AOSSP will be designed to fit the needs of the airline, considering size of aircraft and number of passenger seats. An aircraft operator security program can be one of five types: full, partial, all-cargo, private charter, or twelve-five.

Full programs apply to aircraft operators with (a) seating configurations of 61 or more seats, or (b) seating configurations of 60 or fewer seats when operating to/from a sterile area. Indeed, full programs apply to most scheduled operators in the United States and require the aircraft operator to:

1. Screen individuals and carry-on bags.
2. Screen checked baggage.
3. Screen cargo.
4. Ensure that TSA has conducted screening of persons, carry-on and checked baggage, and cargo.
5. May use metal detectors to screen persons if part of the security program.
6. May use X-ray system for checked baggage if authorized by TSA.
7. Must use explosive detection system for checked baggage on international flights if authorized by the TSA.
8. Designate an aircraft operator security coordinator and a ground security coordinator for each flight.
9. Provide for law enforcement officer support.
10. Carry armed LEOs.
11. Carry prisoners.
12. Transport FAMs.
13. Prevent unauthorized access to exclusive area and the aircraft.
14. Conduct security inspection of the aircraft before placing in passenger operations.
15. Carry out provisions of the exclusive area agreement.
16. Conduct a security threat assessment for personnel with access to air cargo.
17. Conduct a search of the aircraft before departure.
18. Conduct CHRCs for those with unescorted access, screeners, and those with access to checked baggage or cargo.
19. Conduct CHRCs of flight crew members.
20. Use an airport-approved identification system.
21. Provide training for ground and in-flight security coordinator and crewmembers.

22. Provide training for individuals with security duties such as the ground security coordinator.
23. Restrict access to flight deck.
24. Have contingency plans.
25. Have bomb and air piracy threat procedures.
26. Comply with and protect security of SDs and ICs.
27. Use approved screeners and screening programs if not using TSA personnel. (Price and Forrest, 2010, pp. 120–122)

Partial programs apply to scheduled and public charter passenger operations with (a) seating configurations of 31 to 60 seats that do not enplane or deplane into a sterile area or (b) seating configurations of less than 60 seats to/from/outside the United States that do not enplane or deplane into a sterile area. Partial programs do not require the screening of persons and property. An airport operator may, however, require that passengers and property are screened prior to allowing passenger access to the airport's sterile area (Price and Forrest, 2010).

All-cargo operators are held to the all-cargo security program. A significant portion of this program involves the screening of cargo. Through the Implementing Recommendations of the 9/11 Commission Act of 2007, which was signed into law on August 3, 2007, TSA required cargo screening and as of October 2008, 100 percent of cargo being transported on narrow-body aircraft was being screened. Due to the significant amount of cargo being transported by air in the United States and the difficulty in screening this cargo, as of May 2012, 50 percent of air cargo on passenger carrying aircraft is screened, and 100 percent of the cargo on 96 percent of the flights originating in the United States is screened (TSA, n.d.[b]).

The Private Charter Standard Security Program (PCSSP) is an abbreviated program for private charter operators that requires screening of all passengers and accessible baggage prior to boarding the aircraft. Part 121 and 135 operators operating private charters with aircraft of a maximum certificated takeoff weight greater than 45,500 kg (100,309.3 pounds), or with at least 61 passenger seats, must ensure that all passengers and accessible baggage are screened prior to boarding the aircraft. However, to assist the private charter operator, this screening may be carried out by "non-TSA" screeners who have completed TSA-approved private charter screener training. These private charter operators must also develop a security program that includes use of metal detection devices, X-ray systems, security coordinators, law enforcement personnel, accessible weapons, CHRC, training for security coordinators and crewmembers, training for individuals with security-related duties, and training and procedures for bomb or air piracy threats (Price and Forrest, 2010).

For charter operators utilizing aircraft with a maximum certificated takeoff weight of more than 12,500 pounds, the "Twelve-Five rule" applies. The Aviation and Transportation Security Act of 2001 required the Under Secretary of Transportation for Security to implement a security program for charter air carriers with a maximum certificated takeoff weight of 12,500 pounds or more. A final rule was published in 2002 requiring certain aircraft operators using aircraft with a maximum certificated takeoff weight of 12,500 pounds or more to carry out security measures, including conducting CHRC on their flight crew members and restricting access to the flight deck. According to the final rule, "certain aircraft operators" were defined as those conducting operations in scheduled or charter service, carrying passengers or cargo or both. Aircraft operators falling under this rule are required to implement a Twelve-Five Standard Security Program (TFSSP).

Title 49 CFR Part 1546—Foreign Air Carrier Security

Part 1546 applies to security at foreign air carriers. Unless authorized by the TSA, foreign air carriers are not allowed access to SSI materials. Foreign air carriers also do not follow and are not allowed access to the domestic air carrier Aircraft Operator Standard Security Program (AOSSP). On the other hand, foreign air carriers are required to comply with a Model Security Program (MSP) (Price and Forrest, 2010).

Title 49 CFR Part 1548—Indirect Air Carrier Security

Indirect air carriers are those shippers that routinely ship cargo on air carriers either as part of their business or as their business. Indirect air carriers can be one of two types. First, direct shippers place the cargo on a truck and send it directly to the airport, where it is placed on an aircraft to be flown to its ultimate destination. Second, freight forwarders place the cargo on a truck, which delivers the cargo to a consolidation facility, and subsequently forwards that freight to an airport sorting center. These carriers must appoint security coordinators and have an approved Indirect Air Carrier Standard Security Program (IACSSP) (Price and Forrest, 2010).

GENERAL AVIATION AIRPORT SECURITY

The TSA does not regulate security at GA airports. However, in May 2004 the TSA issued Information Publication (IP) A-001, *Security Guidelines for General Aviation Airports*. Although GA airports are not obligated to utilize this IP, they are encouraged to do so by the TSA. The IP can actually be very helpful for the GA airport manager in not only determining the airport's current security posture, but also adopting tools and procedures to enhance this security posture (see Figure 9-20).

Specifically, the IP discusses the vulnerability of GA airports and the specific airport characteristics that affect an airport's risk to security threats. These characteristics include:

1. Airport location—A facility's proximity to mass population areas or sensitive sites (such as military installations, nuclear and chemical plants, centers of government, monuments, and international ports) can affect its security posture.
2. Based aircraft—A smaller number of based aircraft increases the likelihood that illegal activities would be identified more quickly than at airports with a large number of based aircraft.
3. Runways—Airports with longer paved runways are able to serve larger aircraft and consequently should be more security conscious.
4. Operations—The number and types of operations that are conducted at an airport call for different approaches to security.

(TSA, 2004)

Figure 9-20. General aviation airport perimeter fence.

The IP includes an Airport Characteristics Measurement Tool with points assigned to various levels of risk in each of these four categories. If an airport uses this tool, a specific point level will be determined. With the point level, Appendix B of the IP can be used to determine TSA-suggested airport security enhancements. These enhancements can be in any of the following areas:

1. Personnel
   a. Passengers/visitors
   b. Flight schools and student pilots
   c. Aircraft renters
   d. Transient pilots
2. Aircraft

3. Airports and facilities
    a. Hangars
    b. Locks
    c. Perimeter control
    d. Lighting
    e. Signs
    f. Identification system
    g. Airport planning
4. Surveillance
    a. Airport community watch program
    b. Reporting procedures
    c. Airport security committee
    d. Law enforcement officer (LEO) support
    e. Closed circuit television (CCTV)
    f. Intrusion detection systems (IDS)
5. Security procedures and communications
    a. Security procedures
    b. Threat level increases
    c. Threat communication system
6. Specialty operations
    a. Agricultural aircraft operations
    b. Airport tenant facilities
    c. Aircraft and vehicle fueling facilities
    d. Military facilities

    (TSA, 2004)

To assist GA airports with developing a set of security procedures, Appendix G of the IP includes a sample set of GA airport security procedures. The IP can prove beneficial for GA airports, especially those that have not truly considered the security threats present at their airport and implemented efforts to improve their airport's security posture.

In response to IP A-001, some states have begun regulating security at the GA airports in their state. For example, in 2006 the state of Ohio passed the Ohio Terrorism Law requiring each public-use GA airport in the state to develop a written security plan based on the template provided by the state. A copy of this plan is required to be submitted by any airport in the state seeking improvement grants from the Ohio DOT.

Additionally, in May 2011, the TSA issued a revised version of their "Recommended Security Guidelines for Airport Planning, Design and Construction." Used along with the IP A-001, these guidelines are effective for airports in considering the design implications of security measures, and provide design guidance for layout and boundaries; airside; landside; terminal; passenger, baggage, and cargo screening; access, alarms, and biometrics; and video surveillance and detection (TSA, 2011).

Although the TSA does not regulate security at GA airports, the agency does reach into GA with oversight of flight training providers and their students through the TSA's alien flight training/citizenship validation rule. This requires flight training providers to verify students' proof of U.S. citizenship, or ensure that TSA approval to train is received prior to beginning training. The intent of this requirement is to ensure that foreign students seeking training at flight schools regulated by the FAA do not pose a threat to aviation or national security. Additionally, anyone who interacts with flight training students must receive both initial and recurrent security awareness training approved by the TSA. The flight training provider can utilize the TSA's security awareness program or develop their own program if it complies with TSA requirements. These additional requirements for flight training providers can be challenging and add a layer of complexity to the flight training process (for students and providers alike) that did not exist prior to 9/11.

Figure 9-21. AOPA airport watch sign.

(Aircraft Owners and Pilots Association)

Another effort to enhance the security posture of GA airports is the AOPA Airport Watch program, which has been industry initiated and developed in partnership with the TSA (Figure 9-21). This program consists of warning signs, informational literature, and a training video to teach pilots and airport employees how to enhance security at their airports. It is based on the concept that those working at a GA airport and the pilots with based aircraft best know who belongs and can keep an eye out for suspicious persons and activities. The program provides a toll-free telephone number to report suspicious persons or activities: 866-GA-SECURE.

Concluding Thoughts

All airports, whether commercial service or general aviation, are typically focused on two areas: safety and security. Although these terms are often used together, maintaining the safety of the airport requires attention to different areas than what is required to maintain the security, and vice versa. Regardless, each of these two areas is important, requiring airport leadership to simultaneously focus on both.

Chapter Summary

- 14 CFR Part 139 requires certificated airports to provide (a) safeguards to prevent inadvertent entry to the movement area by unauthorized persons or vehicles, and (b) reasonable protection of persons and property from aircraft blast.
- Airports must also ensure operational safety on airports during construction. This is best accomplished by restricting movement of construction vehicles and personnel to permitted construction areas through various means, as appropriate and as specified in the CSPP and SPCD, and ensuring that no contractor employees, employees of subcontractors or suppliers, or other persons enter any part of the air operations area from the construction site unless authorized.
- Class A fires are composed of ordinary combustibles (such as wood or paper).
- Class B fires are composed of flammable and combustible liquids.
- Class C fires are composed of energized electrical equipment.
- Class D fires are composed of combustible metals.
- For Class B fires (such as fuel fires), aqueous film forming foam (AFFF) is most effective.
- Liquid fuels, such as AvGas and Jet-A, emit vapors that can ignite when the flashpoint is reached. The flashpoint of AvGas is -50 degrees Fahrenheit; Jet-A's flashpoint is 100 degrees Fahrenheit.
- Bonding is necessary during aircraft fueling to dissipate static buildup and prevent an errant spark.
- A safety management system (SMS) is a formalized approach to managing safety by developing an organization-wide safety policy. An SMS consists of a safety policy and objectives, safety risk management, safety assurance, and safety promotion.
- Safety risk management requires a proactive approach to safety, rather than reacting after an accident or incident has occurred.
- Safety assurance is the process of oversight once the SMS has been established.
- Safety promotion involves promotion of the SMS and the processes associated with it.
- 14 CFR §139.325, Airport Emergency Plan, requires certificated airports to develop an airport emergency plan, which is necessary to ensure that procedures are in place to effectively respond to and resolve an emergency on airport. FAA AC 150/5200-31 provides airport operators with detailed information on how to develop plans and procedures to respond to aircraft accidents and incidents, bomb incidents, structural fires, and six other specific categories of hazards detailed in §139.325.

- 14 CFR §139.319 requires that ARFF personnel are trained in airport familiarization, aircraft familiarization, rescue and firefighting personnel safety, airport emergency communications systems, use of the fire hoses, nozzles, turrets, and other appliances, application of extinguishing agents required for compliance, emergency aircraft evacuation assistance, firefighting operations, use of structural rescue and firefighting equipment for aircraft rescue and firefighting, aircraft cargo hazards, and familiarization with firefighters' duties under the AEP.
- Alert I is used to indicate that an aircraft that is known or suspected to have an operational defect may or may not be landing at your airport. This is notification only. No response is required.
- Alert II is used to indicate an aircraft that is known or is suspected to have an operational defect that affects normal flight operations to the extent that there is danger of an accident (i.e., aircraft with a declared emergency is inbound to your airport).
- Alert III is used to indicate an aircraft incident/accident has occurred on or in the vicinity of the airport, requiring full response.
- Airports must be prepared to respond to media inquiries in a positive and proactive manner.
- A precision lightning warning system uses satellite lightning strike data and field mill sensors to measure voltage potential and provide some degree of likelihood for lightning strikes in the local area.
- The Aviation and Transportation Security Act (ATSA) was signed into law on November 19, 2001, creating the Transportation Security Administration and transferring all civil aviation security responsibilities to the TSA.
- As of 2012, the TSA was using technology for paperless boarding passes, biometrics, bottle liquids scanners, screening of casts and prosthetics, explosive detection system, explosives trace detection, threat image projection, and imaging technology.
- The Homeland Security Act, signed into law in 2002, created the Department of Homeland Security, which is the current home of the TSA.
- 49 CFR Part 1503 is titled Investigative and Enforcement Procedures.
- 49 CFR Part 1520 is titled Protection of Sensitive Security Information.
- 49 CFR Part 1540 is titled General Rules.
- 49 CFR Part 1542 is titled Airport Security. It requires an airport security coordinator, an airport security program, an access control system, personal identification media, challenge procedures, Criminal History Records Checks (CHRC) for personnel desiring unescorted access to the SIDA, and law enforcement officers.
- 49 CFR Part 1544, titled Aircraft Operator Security, requires aircraft operators to designate an aircraft operator security coordinator and a ground security coordinator, as well as an Aircraft Operator Standard Security Program.

- 49 CFR Part 1546 is titled Foreign Air Carrier Security.
- 49 CFR Part 1548 is titled Indirect Air Carrier Security.
- All-cargo operators are held to the all-cargo security program.
- Security at general aviation airports is not regulated by the TSA; however, TSA's Information Publication A-001, *Security Guidelines for General Aviation Airports*, addresses the vulnerability of GA airports and the specific airport characteristics that affect an airport's risk to security threats.

Review Questions ↘

1. Explain methods airports may use to protect the public from the hazards associated with the airport operating environment.
2. What are the vehicle and pedestrian requirements that should be included in construction safety and phasing plans at airports?
3. Explain the fire triangle.
4. What are Class A fires?
5. What are Class B fires?
6. What are Class C fires?
7. What are Class D fires?
8. Explain the purpose of bonding.
9. Explain the four elements of an SMS.
10. Explain the five phases of the safety risk management process.
11. Explain the National Incident Management System.
12. Explain the three levels of alert typically used at airports to convey information about aircraft emergencies.
13. Explain the purpose and function of a precision lightning warning system (PLWS).
14. What act created the Transportation Security Administration (TSA)?
15. What cabinet-level department in the executive branch was created by the Homeland Security Act of 2002?
16. What is an airport security coordinator responsible for?
17. Explain challenge procedures.
18. What capabilities must law enforcement officers at airports have?
19. Explain the Private Charter Standard Security Program (PCSSP).
20. What characteristics are addressed in TSA IP A-001, *Security Guidelines for General Aviation Airports*?

Scenarios ↘

1. As a newly-hired airport operations supervisor, you are asked to develop consequences for individuals that are found not in compliance with the airport's rules and regulations regarding access to and operation in movement areas and safety areas. Explain the program you would develop, to include various levels of noncompliance and the consequences associated with each level.

2. As a director of operations with a proactive safety mindset employed at a medium hub airport, you have decided to develop a safety management system. After speaking with other airports, you feel that this program can be developed in-house. How would you initiate such a project? Who would be mainly responsible for developing the SMS? Who would be involved in the process? What steps would you take?

3. As the airport security coordinator at a large hub airport, you are the sole individual responsible for ensuring compliance with TSA security directives. Consider the following SDs and specify how your airport would comply:
   a. All vehicles parking within 600 feet of the main terminal must be physically searched. (Your short-term parking garage has three levels equivalent to 1,500 spaces within 600 feet of the main terminal.)
   b. No baggage or items may be left unattended within the terminals.
   c. All employees, in addition to passengers with boarding passes, must be searched prior to entering the sterile area of the terminal.
   d. No metal knives may be present in the sterile area of the terminal.

4. Develop a fuel spill response plan for your airport, to include airport operations, police, ARFF, airline personnel, and the airport fueling company. Consider each of these stakeholders and the role they would be required to play if a fuel spill were to occur.

5. Utilizing the hazard risk matrix presented in this chapter, conduct an assessment for each of the following. In addition to the assessment, develop strategies to mitigate risk:
   a. Haul route across an active taxiway during an airfield construction project.
   b. Active taxiway crossing point due to the service road intersecting taxiways A and B.
   c. Airline mechanics taxiing aircraft from the ramp across an active runway to the maintenance hangar.
   d. Electrical maintenance performing lighting inspections three nights per week.
   e. Temporary tower erected during the annual airshow and fly-in.
   f. Closing a taxiway for three days for the upcoming AOPA Aviation Summit.
   g. Creating two new temporary helipads on taxiway T for the Super Bowl traffic.
   h. Aircraft taxiing to the new ground run-up enclosure adjacent to taxiway C.

References and Resources for Further Study

American Association of Airport Executives. 2005. "Body of Knowledge Module 3. Airport Operations, Security and Maintenance." Washington, DC: AAAE.

deNeufville, R. and A. Odoni. 2003. *Airport Systems: Planning Design and Management.* New York: McGraw Hill.

Federal Aviation Administration (FAA). 2002. *Ground Vehicle Operations on Airport.* AC 150/5210-5D.

———. 2007. *Introduction to Safety Management Systems (SMS) for Airport Operators.* AC 150/5200-37. Washington, DC: FAA.

———. 2009. *Airport Emergency Plan.* AC 150/5200-31C. Washington, DC: FAA.

———. 2010(a). "History." Retrieved April 18, 2012 from http://www.faa.gov/about/history/brief_history/

———. 2010(b). *Painting, Marking and Lighting Vehicles Used on Airport.* AC 150/5210-5D. Washington, DC: FAA.

———. 2011. *Operational Safety on Airports During Construction.* AC 150/5370-2. Washington, DC: FAA.

Federal Emergency Management Agency. 2015. "National Incident Management System." Retrieved from http://www.fema.gov/national-incident-management-system

Prather, C.D. 2009. *General Aviation Marketing and Management: Operating, Marketing, and Managing an FBO.* Malabar, FL: Krieger.

Price, J. and J. Forrest. 2010. "Airport operations, security, and maintenance." Washington, DC: AAAE.

Rumerman, J. n.d. "Aviation Security." U.S. Centennial of Flight Commission. Retrieved April 18, 2012 from http://www.centennialofflight.net/essay/Government_Role/security/POL18.htm

Transportation Security Administration (TSA). 2004. *Security Guidelines for General Aviation Airports.* Information Publication A-001. Retrieved April 22, 2012 from http://www.tsa.gov/assets/pdf/security_guidelines_for_general_aviation_airports.pdf

———. 2011. *Recommended Security Guidelines for Airport Planning, Design and Construction.*

———. n.d.(a) "Advanced imaging technology." Retrieved April 17, 2012 from http://www.tsa.gov/approach/tech/ait/index.shtm

———. n.d.(b) "Air Cargo." Retrieved April 21, 2012 from http://www.tsa.gov/stakeholders/air-cargo

———. n.d.(c) "Innovation and technology." Retrieved April 17, 2012 from http://www.tsa.gov/about-tsa/technology

———. n.d.(d). "What is TSA?" Retrieved April 18, 2012 from http://www.tsa.gov/about-tsa

"Vaisala Precision Lightning Warning System (PLWS)." n.d. Retrieved from Reference: http://app.tampaairport.com/about/media/PLWS-Summary.pdf

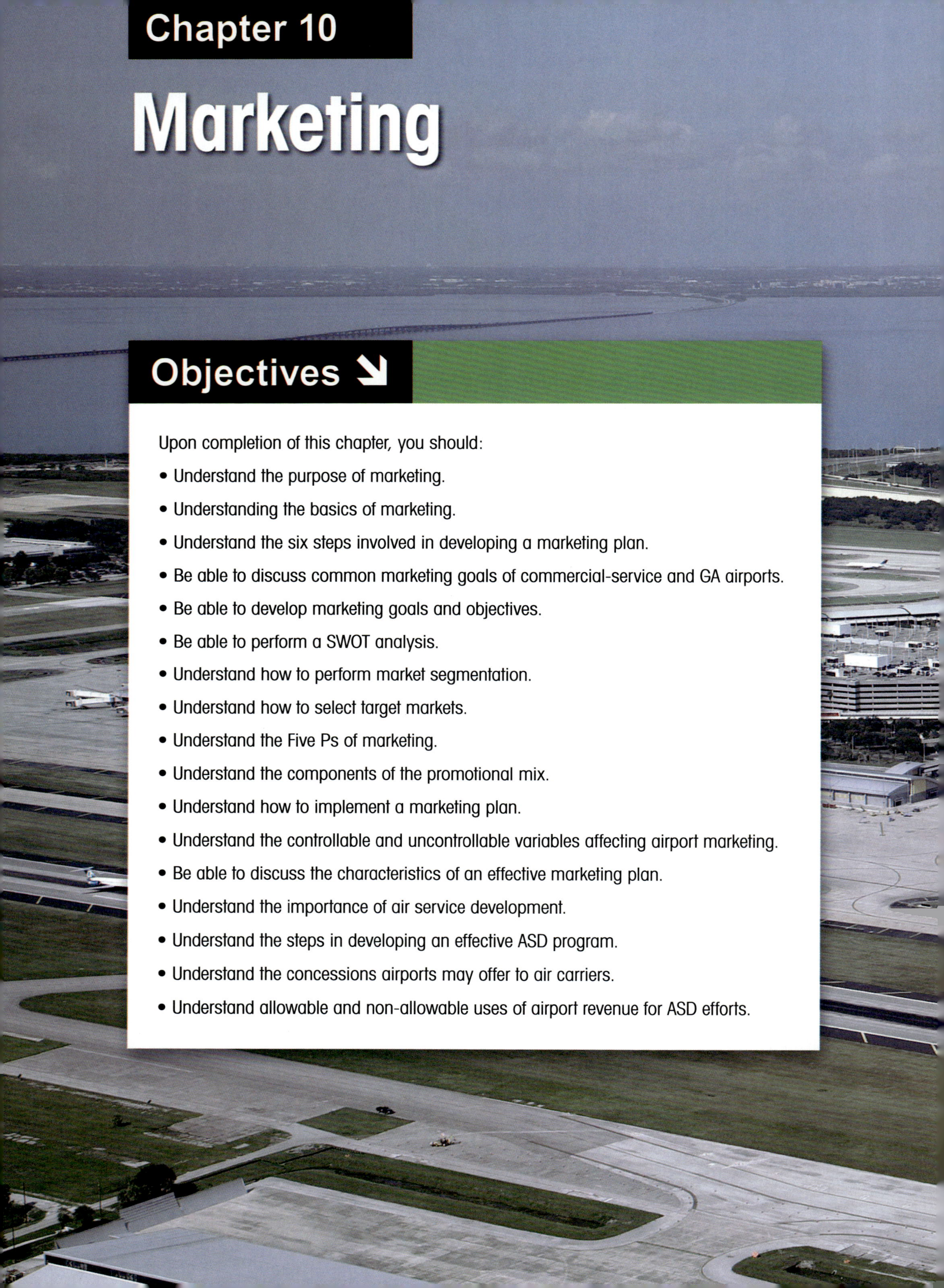

Chapter 10

Marketing

Objectives

Upon completion of this chapter, you should:

- Understand the purpose of marketing.
- Understanding the basics of marketing.
- Understand the six steps involved in developing a marketing plan.
- Be able to discuss common marketing goals of commercial-service and GA airports.
- Be able to develop marketing goals and objectives.
- Be able to perform a SWOT analysis.
- Understand how to perform market segmentation.
- Understand how to select target markets.
- Understand the Five Ps of marketing.
- Understand the components of the promotional mix.
- Understand how to implement a marketing plan.
- Understand the controllable and uncontrollable variables affecting airport marketing.
- Be able to discuss the characteristics of an effective marketing plan.
- Understand the importance of air service development.
- Understand the steps in developing an effective ASD program.
- Understand the concessions airports may offer to air carriers.
- Understand allowable and non-allowable uses of airport revenue for ASD efforts.

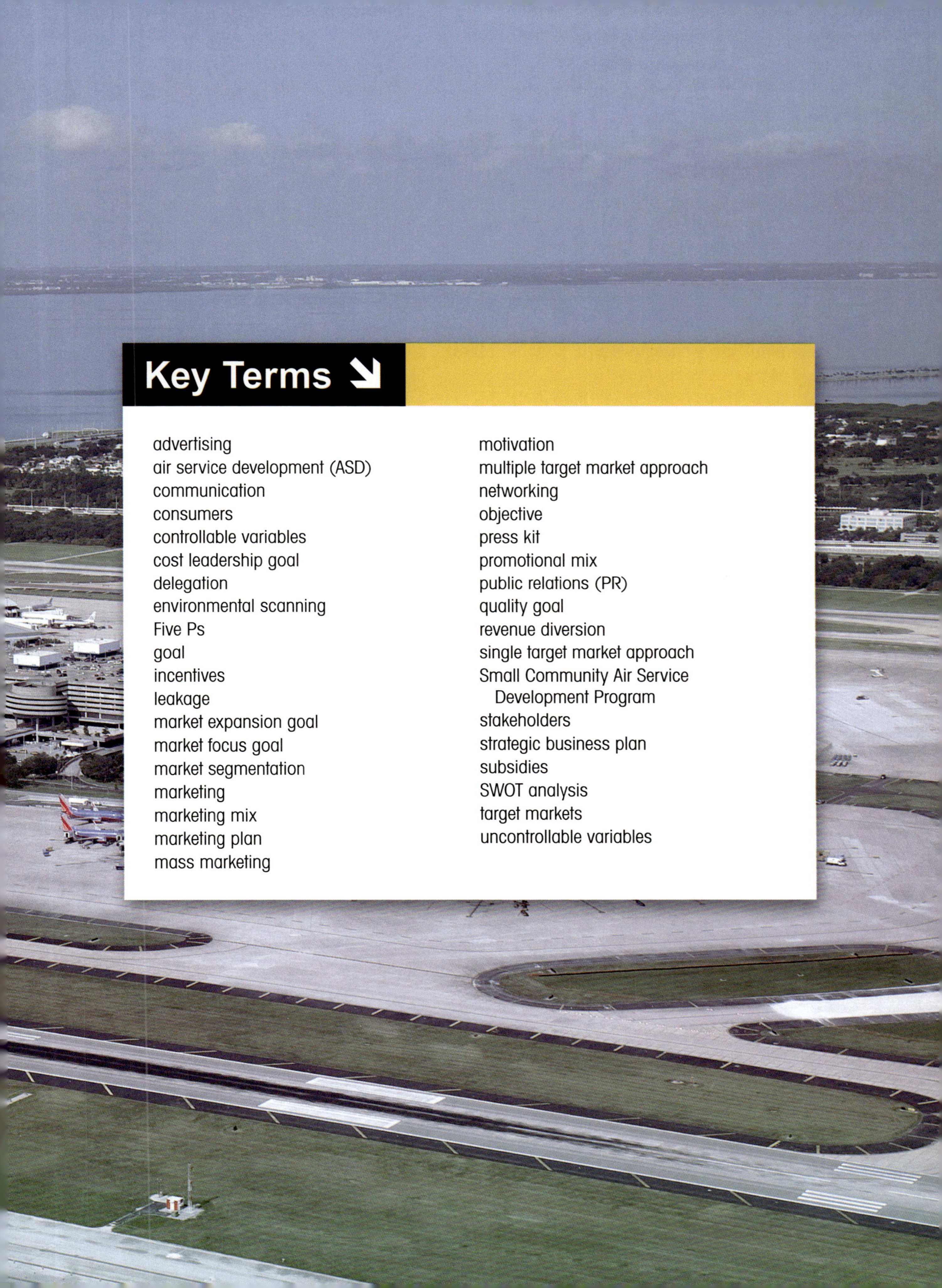

Key Terms ↘

- advertising
- air service development (ASD)
- communication
- consumers
- controllable variables
- cost leadership goal
- delegation
- environmental scanning
- Five Ps
- goal
- incentives
- leakage
- market expansion goal
- market focus goal
- market segmentation
- marketing
- marketing mix
- marketing plan
- mass marketing
- motivation
- multiple target market approach
- networking
- objective
- press kit
- promotional mix
- public relations (PR)
- quality goal
- revenue diversion
- single target market approach
- Small Community Air Service Development Program
- stakeholders
- strategic business plan
- subsidies
- SWOT analysis
- target markets
- uncontrollable variables

In Chapter 10

Purpose of Marketing **393**

Marketing Basics **394**

Developing a Marketing Plan **395**

Determine Goals and Objectives 396

Assess Resources and Perform a SWOT Analysis 398

Revise Goals and Objectives 399

Segment the Market 399

Select Target Markets 399

Establish a Unique Marketing Mix 400

Variables **408**

Implementing the Plan **410**

Characteristics of an Effective Marketing Plan **411**

Air Service Development **412**

Concluding Thoughts **417**

Chapter Summary **417**

Review Questions **419**

Scenarios **420**

References and Resources for Further Study **421**

FEATURES

Jackson County Airport's Marketing Plan 395

This marketing plan was developed in an effort to increase airport business and revenues.

Revenue Diversion at Los Angeles World Airports.... 414

In an effort to increase tourism and business activity, LAWA was found to have diverted revenue from the airport to the city's convention and visitors bureau.

Purpose of Marketing

Marketing is defined as those sets of plans developed by a firm and the activities carried out based on these plans that are specifically designed to influence the behavior of consumers. The term "**consumers**" typically refers to those individuals making purchases, but may also refer to the firm's target audience. Indeed, some firms, including airports, may engage in marketing to generate goodwill or stimulate support. Marketing can prove beneficial even if the firm has nothing to sell. As Sean Mauger states, "Marketing is the art of identifying and understanding customer needs and creating solutions that deliver satisfaction to the customers, profits to the producers and benefits for the stakeholders." (Kramer et al., 2010, p. 2)

Essentially, customer satisfaction is the ultimate objective of the marketing process. And it will be challenging for a company to provide customer satisfaction if customer needs are not adequately understood. Firms rely on marketing to build stronger relationships with current customers and discover new target markets on which to capitalize. Most importantly, customers, not marketers, primarily determine what they need, want, and are willing to buy. Although savvy marketing can motivate impulse purchasing, generally the customer has certain needs and wants and the role of marketing is to both identify and satisfy those needs and wants (see Figure 10-1).

Unlike a retailer that focuses solely on attracting and retaining customers, airports must focus on the many stakeholders they serve. As a result, marketing approaches among airports can be quite different based on the stakeholders being targeted. Whether utilizing a comprehensive marketing strategy or simply placing an advertisement in the newspaper, all marketing approaches have commonalities among them. This chapter provides marketing concepts and practices that are common to airports of any size and any targeted audience.

Figure 10-1. A satisfied customer—the ultimate objective of the marketing process.

(©iStock.com/Trish233)

Marketing Basics

In meeting customer needs and endeavoring to provide customer satisfaction, airports are in a unique situation to focus on tenants, airline passengers, and/or the community. In fact, airports can utilize marketing to reach a number of **stakeholders**, including the community, passengers, meeters and greeters, current and potential tenants (including airlines, fixed base operators, maintenance providers, corporate operators), and various business prospects. An airport's justification for marketing to these various groups is as follows:

- Community
  - Generate goodwill and support for the airport.
  - Generate awareness of the airport and its economic impacts on the economy.
- Passengers
  - Convey the availability of airport services.
  - Convey information about airport news and events.
  - Attract more passengers.
- Meeters and greeters
  - Convey information about parking services.
  - Convey information about airport construction projects that may affect access and circulation of vehicles.
  - Convey information about concessions that meeters and greeters may be able to utilize.
- Current tenants
  - Generate support for airport capital development plans.
  - Convey the financial basis for fees, rates, and charges.
  - Motivate new services by tenants, including new routes, aircraft, and services by airlines.
  - Retain current tenants.
- Potential tenants
  - Motivate new services by tenants, including new airline service.
  - Attract new tenants to the airport by conveying information about airport facilities, fees, services, and potential market for tenant products/services.
- Business prospects
  - Generate investment in the airport.
  - Motivate use of airport facilities and services.

(Kramer et al., 2010)

Jackson County Airport's Marketing Plan

The Jackson County Airport—Reynolds Field, located in south central Michigan, developed an airport marketing plan in 2011. As a GA airport currently situated on over 700 acres providing air traffic control services, car rentals, a restaurant, aviation fuel and aircraft repair, flight training, and a variety of other airport-based businesses, the airport desired to overcome impacts of a sluggish economy, rising aviation fuel prices, and a poor business climate. The marketing plan was developed through the work of an advisory council, which included representatives from airport-based businesses. In addition to performing an issue analysis and SWOT analysis, the council collected 77 surveys from airport customers by placing surveys in the airport restaurant. Marketing strategies developed as part of this marketing plan included: (a) encourage and enhance partnerships and collaboration efforts; (b) encourage young people to get involved with airport events and aviation in general; (c) market the airport as a venue for special events and as a location for community meetings and gatherings; (d) initiate a "branding" study to create an airport brand; (e) research the feasibility of a modern electronic sign for the main airport entrance; and (f) encourage the availability of a based business that offers aircraft rentals and perhaps light sport aircraft sales and instruction. Although this plan is representative of a small, GA airport, even small airports need to be strategic about marketing their services and promoting the benefits of the airport to the community.

(Jackson County—Reynolds Field Airport. 2011)

Developing a Marketing Plan

Preparing an airport marketing plan takes significant focus and effort. If well designed, a properly developed airport marketing plan will answer the following questions:

- What are the marketing goals?
- Who are the target audiences?
- What is the message the airport intends to communicate?
- What methods of communication will the airport use to reach its audience?
- What staffing and financial resources will support the effort?
- How will the airport measure success?

(Kramer et al., 2010, p. 6)

It's often said that if you fail to plan, you plan to fail. This pearl of wisdom could be applied to marketing. Without a plan, an airport will be "shooting in the dark" and likely waste valuable resources with ineffective marketing. In essence, a **marketing plan** is imperative if an airport wants to realize success in their marketing efforts. Although the process is not complex, preparing a marketing plan does involve six specific steps:

Step 1: Determine goals and objectives.

Step 2: Assess resources and perform a Strengths-Weaknesses-Opportunities-Threats (SWOT) analysis.

Step 3: Revise goals and objectives as necessary.

Step 4: Segment the market.

Step 5: Select target markets.

Step 6: Establish a unique marketing mix aimed at a particular audience.

a. Product or service
b. Price
c. Channel of distribution (place)
d. Promotion (advertising, sales promotion, personal selling, and publicity)
e. Passion

(Prather, 2009; Kramer et al., 2010)

DETERMINE GOALS AND OBJECTIVES

Step 1 requires the airport to determine goals and objectives. A **goal** will generally encompass the "big picture" of the marketing effort, such as attracting an air carrier, increasing the number of based aircraft, increasing fuel sales, or minimizing vacancies in the airport business park. **Objectives**, on the other hand, are more specific and may include attracting an air carrier operating with non-stop capability to a specific hub airport, a specific aircraft type, or seating capacity. Although an airport may develop a long list of marketing goals, it is important to separate the various goals into distinct categories and develop a marketing plan with aspects focused on each of these categories. Without this, marketing efforts may prove confusing. For instance, marketing efforts to increase fuel sales will be quite different from marketing efforts to attract an air carrier, and the marketing plan should reflect this (Prather, 2009).

The most common marketing goals across all industries include: (a) market expansion, (b) market focus or segmentation, (c) cost leadership, and (d) quality. For commercial-service airports or those desiring to attract air carriers, a **market expansion goal** can refer to increasing enplanements, typically from other markets, and/or increasing air carriers or air service. For GA airports, a goal of market expansion may refer to increasing based aircraft or new tenants. A **market focus goal** refers to either focusing on a particular type of customer or specializing in a particular service. For airports, the focus may be on international passengers or attracting light sport aircraft. A **cost leadership goal** refers to the desire to have the lowest costs in an area. For airports, this may mean the lowest fuel prices, the lowest landing fees, or the lowest hangar rental fees. A **quality goal** can revolve around quality products or services, and for airports often refers to the goal of offering exceptional customer service. In fact, airports often pride themselves in the exceptional level of customer service they offer. A 2008 study of airports found the following marketing goals at commercial-service airports, in order of popularity:

1. Attract passengers.
2. Promote positive view of the airport in the community.
3. Improve air service.
4. Retain existing carriers.
5. Attract new businesses to the airport.

(Kramer et al., 2010).

A 2008 study of GA airports found the following marketing goals, in order of popularity:

1. Attract new business to the airport.
2. Promote positive view of airport in the community.
3. Retain current airport tenants.
4. Attract more GA or business activity.
5. Promote airport to funding sources.

(Kramer et al., 2010).

Although these lists show similarities in the marketing goals of commercial-service and GA airports, there clearly are differences as well. In airport marketing, the key factor for airports to consider is what they are hoping to achieve with their marketing efforts. It is also important for the goals and objectives to integrate with the airport's **strategic business plan**. Such a plan outlines the overall mission and vision of the airport, as well as its overall goals and objectives. Developing marketing goals and objectives that are at odds with the airport's mission would be a mistake. Although goals may not be, marketing objectives should be quantified and stated in understandable terms. For example, rather than simply desiring to attract an air carrier, it is helpful to express this in terms of desiring an air carrier that can provide a particular level of service with a certain number of seats by a certain date. A benefit of developing specific objectives is that the airport can measure the level of success of marketing efforts by determining to what degree the various objectives have been achieved. Vague objectives will leave airport personnel wondering whether or not (or to what degree) they were successful in their marketing efforts (Prather, 2009; Kramer et al., 2010).

It's important for airports to consider the stakeholders as they develop goals and objectives. As an airport begins thinking like a stakeholder, it is much easier to develop effective marketing goals and objectives. Statements that may stimulate the development of goals and objectives include:

- Our tenants think…
- Our customers think…
- The community thinks…
- Our airport is known for…
- We are proud of…
- We strive to…
- We want our customers to…
- This airport should…

ASSESS RESOURCES AND PERFORM A SWOT ANALYSIS

Step 2, although often seen as a time-consuming step that airports would rather avoid, requires airports to (a) assess the resources available for the marketing efforts and (b) perform a **SWOT analysis** (see Figure 10-2). An airport may perform step 2(a) simply by asking, "What's our budget?" but it is also helpful to examine the personnel and financial resources available to commit to the marketing plan. Step 2(b) requires a candid examination of the strengths and weaknesses of the airport, as well the opportunities and threats confronting the airport. This exercise can help an airport consider what they have to offer various stakeholders. Strengths and weaknesses are typically internal to the organization, while opportunities and threats refer to issues in the external environment. For instance, if a GA airport has an objective of attracting an air carrier, it will be beneficial to use the SWOT approach to evaluate the airport from the perspective of a potential air carrier. This exercise forces the airport to think like the air carrier to which they will be marketing, likely resulting in a more effective marketing plan. Strengths may include the airport's location, ILS availability, modern terminal building, support of air carrier service by the community, etc. Weaknesses may include lack of an ATC tower, lack of automobile parking, or lack of aircraft deicing services. Opportunities and threats

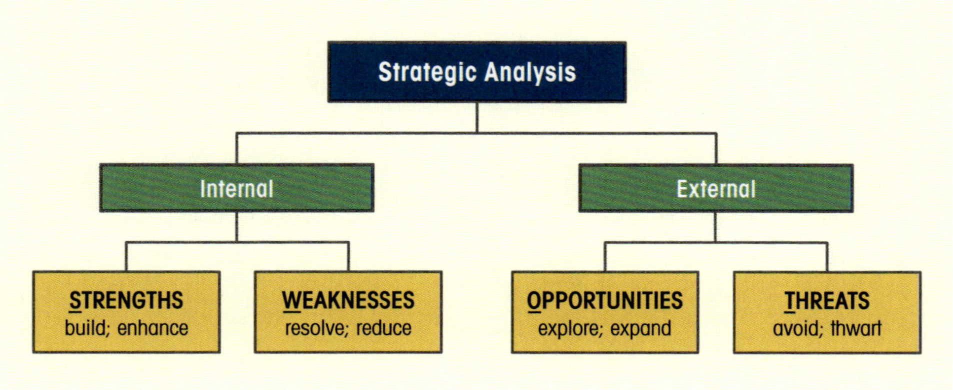

Figure 10-2. SWOT analysis.

may apply more to the airport than the air carrier. Opportunities may include potential air carrier service and an FAA contract tower. Threats may include the close proximity of an airport with existing air carrier service (Prather, 2009; Kramer et al., 2010).

Although a SWOT analysis is usually completed as part of the airport's strategic business plan, it is beneficial to conduct such an analysis as part of the marketing plan. Additionally, although a SWOT analysis is often performed by airport personnel, it may be helpful to obtain customer feedback on the strengths and weaknesses of the airport. Without doing this, airport personnel will simply be guessing what stakeholders consider to be the strengths and weaknesses. This feedback can be obtained from customers via surveys, comments on social media, comment cards in the terminal, or random personal interviews in the terminal. Feedback can be obtained from tenants via surveys or tenant events (Kramer et al., 2010).

REVISE GOALS AND OBJECTIVES

In step 3, the airport has the opportunity to revise goals and objectives based on the results of the SWOT analysis. Oftentimes, the airport will uncover weaknesses or threats that will require a revision to the original marketing goals. If no revisions are necessary, the original goals and objectives may stand. However, this is the time to make revisions, not once thousands of dollars are spent on marketing efforts.

SEGMENT THE MARKET

In step 4, the airport further defines the market by segmenting it. **Market segmentation** is the process of breaking down the total market into smaller, more homogeneous groups with similar needs that the airport can satisfy. For instance, an airport desiring air carrier service can segment the market into major carriers and regional carriers. Regional carriers could be further segmented by the route structure, which will eventually allow the airport to focus on those carriers that would most likely be willing to add that airport to their existing route structure (Prather, 2009).

SELECT TARGET MARKETS

In step 5, **target markets** are selected. Although segmenting the market aids the airport in further defining the focus of its marketing efforts, selecting a target market allows the airport to pinpoint the object of the airport's marketing mix. This could take the form of a single target market approach or a multiple target market approach. A **single target market approach** requires the airport to select one primary market segment as the airport's target market. Although this approach allows the airport to narrow its focus, it also involves more financial risk than if the airport diversifies into multiple target markets. A **multiple target market approach** requires the airport to select two or more market segments, with each being treated as a separate target market. Although this approach allows for more diversification, each target market will also require a unique marketing mix. It is important to note that selecting a target market allows the airport to engage in targeted marketing rather than mass marketing. **Mass marketing** does not attempt to differentiate between the market segments, and instead aims toward all segments—a "shotgun" approach, which is effective in certain circumstances (Prather, 2009).

Examples of possible target markets for an airport include:

- Local passengers
- Destination passengers
- Airlines
- Local businesses
- Transient pilots
- Aircraft owners with registered aircraft in the region
- Flight schools in the area
- Affiliate service centers of the local FBO
- Aviation specialists (e.g., maintenance & repair, helicopters, offshore oil rig support, aircraft painting)
- Existing tenants
- Tenant leads
- Schools and colleges
- Government groups
- Congressional delegation

(Kramer et al., 2010)

ESTABLISH A UNIQUE MARKETING MIX

In step 6, the final step, airports develop a unique marketing mix. The **marketing mix** refers to the set of controllable marketing variables that the airport uses to achieve marketing goals and objectives. This involves everything the airport does to influence the demand for its product or influence the behavior of the target market. Specifically, the marketing mix consists of the following "**Five Ps**":

1. Product or service
2. Price
3. Place (channel of distribution)
4. Promotion (public relations, advertising, and networking)
5. Passion

Product or Service

The first P represents "*product or service*"—the combination of benefits, physical features, and services designed to satisfy the needs or wants of the identified target market. In other words, what specifically is the airport marketing? In marketing to prospective air carriers, the airport will want to emphasize the demand that exists in the form of potential passengers.

Price

The second P, *price*, refers to the value of a good or service. Since customers perceive price as the sacrifice or cost they must pay, marketers must maintain the price level equal to or less than the amount customers are willing to pay to experience the perceived satisfaction provided by the product or service. This cost-benefit relationship plays a major role in pricing strategies. If an airport is marketing to prospective air carriers, these carriers must be convinced that airport fees, rates, and charges, as well as aircraft operating costs (also measured as costs per enplaned passenger), will be sufficiently less than the revenues they may realize on the routes to be established, based on load factors and ticket prices.

Place

The third P, *place*, refers to delivering the product and services to customers in a timely manner. In addition to a convenient airport location, the appropriate products and services must be available for each target market in the correct amount when customers need them. Obviously, a prospective air carrier will be interested in whether the geographic location of the airport integrates with the air carrier's existing routes structure.

Promotion

The fourth P, *promotion*, involves systematic decision making related to all aspects of the development and management of an airport's promotional effort. Promotion is any form of communication used to inform, persuade, or remind people about products, services, image, ideas, or community involvement. Promotion is the heart of marketing. Although an airport marketing plan may contain any or all of the components of the promotional mix (depending on the specific goals and objectives of the airport's marketing plan), the **promotional mix** available to airports consists of:

1. Public relations
2. Advertising
3. Networking

Public relations (PR) refers to the act of relating to the public. AOPA defines PR as "everything the airport is and does that addresses or affects the public interest." (Kramer et al., 2010, p. 69). In reality, PR involves the public opinion. Whether or not an airport engages in PR, the public likely already holds an opinion of the airport. Engaging in PR allows the airport the opportunity to proactively and positively influence that opinion. Tools available to influence the public opinion include:

- Earned media (includes press kits, press releases, interviews, public service announcements, featured articles and stories, and awards and special recognition)
- Public speaking (includes speaking at local community events and presentations at conferences or tradeshows)
- Other print communications (includes airshows, open houses, and educational programs)
- Events (includes contests and drawings, free services and amenities, giveaway items, reduction of rates and charges)
- Sponsorships and volunteering (includes sponsoring interns and students, board participation, supporting non-profit community events, and volunteering in the community)
- Other print materials (includes customer satisfaction surveys, print and electronic newsletters, economic impact studies, testimonials, and white papers)

A form of earned media that can be quite effective is a "**press kit**." A press kit is a tool for proactively utilizing the media for marketing and generating positive community support. In today's internet-driven culture, press kits are often in electronic form, a technological enhancement to the old stack of published materials. The internet allows anyone to access an airport's press kit on its website at any time, which also reduces or completely eliminates the expense associated with mailing press kits—a common practice in the days before the widespread use of the internet.

An airport press kit may include any or all of the following:

- A website or physical cover with the airport's brand (logo, key message, graphics, and colors)
- Information for media inquiries
  - Office hours
  - Phone numbers
  - How to request an interview
  - Parking and "live broadcast trucks"
  - Airport access
- Fact sheet about the airport
- Image library (photos of the airport)
- Airport newsletter
- News releases
- Staff biographies

- Members of the airport governing group (airport commission or authority)
- Airport tenants and businesses
- Airport statistics
- Airport financial records
- Business cards and stationery that carry the airport's brand are used in the press kit

  (Kramer et al., 2010)

Although developing a press kit takes time and possibly some contracted marketing expertise, it is an opportunity to distribute airport information and positive news in a proactive manner to those in the media that can provide free promotion of the airport. Press kits can equally benefit commercial-service and GA airports.

Yet another effective form of earned media is the press release. Press releases are free and can be quite effective at getting the word out about the airport. Effective press releases address who, what, when, where, and why. It requires skill to develop an effective press release. Important elements of a press release include a strong lead-in sentence, the use of quotes to give it a personal touch, and highlights that have human interest (see Figure 10-3).

The media, through their typically wide distribution (i.e., readership, viewership, or listenership) can generate positive and negative press for the airport. Therefore, it is important to fully utilize the media to ensure that all press about the airport is positive. Media contacts may include:

- News stations
- Television programs/features
- Public service announcements
- Radio programs
- Newswires
- Newspapers

Advertising tools are different than PR tools in that they are intentionally designed, paid for, and placed by the advertising sponsor. Advertising tools consist of:

- Internet and websites (includes airport websites, email distributions, and internet advertising)
- Print media (includes print ads in newspapers, magazines, and trade journals; direct mail; brochures; business cards and stationary; testimonials)
- Signage (includes billboards, posters, banners, and display signage)
- Multi-media tools (includes radio, television, and video)

Figure 10-3. Sample press release guidelines.

Airport Logo
NEWS RELEASE
Date: (The date the release is being distributed.)
FOR IMMEDIATE RELEASE
For more information, contact:
(Name, Department, Title)
(Phone Number)
(Email Address)—optional

SUBJECT: (A brief topic or event description, typically 5 words or less.)

The body of the press release is very basic; who, what, where, when and why. The first paragraph of the press release should contain in brief detail what the press release is about.

The second paragraph explains, in detail: who cares; why you should care; where one can find the event being promoted; and when the event will happen. The second paragraph also usually includes a quote that gives the release a personal touch. "Touchy-feelies" go a long way with journalists. Press releases and news stories are boring to journalists without a "human interest."

The third and generally final paragraph identifies department contact information and where the reader can get information, i.e., website, telephone numbers, etc.

The content of the press release should be typed in a clear, basic font (Times New Roman is preferred). The release should be about a page and generally no more than 400 to 500 words. If a press release exceeds one page, the second page should indicate "Page Two" in the upper right-hand corner, and "more" should appear at the bottom of the first page. Journalistic standards have set basic parameters to define the end of a press release: Three "#" symbols ("###") centered directly underneath the last line indicate the end of the release. Finally, verify your facts and check your spelling. Once a mistake is printed or reported in the media it is difficult to get it corrected.

###

(Kramer et al., 2010, p. 73)

Although multi-media tools can reach a wide audience, they can be quite expensive. An effective alternative is the internet and development of a website. Today, many potential customers conduct research and fact-finding on the internet, which makes this advertising tool very effective.

Networking comprises the third and final category of marketing tools. Networking refers to the process of building contacts and relationships through various means. This includes:

- Business, civic, and non-profit groups
- Professional organizations
- Tradeshows and conferences
- Strategic partnerships
- Lobbying

(Kramer et al., 2010)

Often, it is important for an airport manager to engage in networking with each of these groups. However, networking with local business, civic, and non-profit groups allows the airport to generate significant community goodwill. As stated by Kramer et al. (2010, p. 120), airports that engage in networking are able to:

- Continuously remind the community of the airport's value and role in the economic activity of the community.
- Create goodwill that makes it easier to resolve difficult airport–community issues.
- Build lasting relationships with organizations that have a vested interest in the airport's long-term vitality.
- Recruit champions, volunteers, marketers, and partners of the airport.
- Educate and excite the "next generation" of airport leaders and champions.

The specific promotional mix selected by an airport may be free or may cost a substantial amount of money. Although smaller, GA airports often operate on a tighter marketing budget than larger commercial-service airports, all airports must establish a marketing budget and strive to remain within that budget. Airports oftentimes fund their marketing budget with their retained earnings. However, there are alternative sources of funding for airport marketing, including grants, cash donations, in-kind contributions, and cost sharing. The most common grant source is the **Small Community Air Service Development Program** through the DOT. This program provides funding to airports in conducting air service development studies and funding marketing to attract new carriers or enhance existing air carrier service (Kramer et al., 2010).

Regardless of how funds are pooled to support an airport marketing plan, airports must develop and adhere to a marketing budget. Fortunately, many of the components of a promotional mix that can be quite successful to an airport's marketing efforts are inexpensive. The available components and their level of cost are as follows:

- Free/minimal cost
  - Press releases
  - Editorials
  - Travel-related articles
  - E-mail newsletter
  - Chamber speeches
  - Networking
  - Testimonials
- Some cost
  - Website
  - Promotions
  - Receptions
  - Open house
  - Social media
- More cost
  - Radio
  - Newspaper ads
  - Billboards
- Most cost
  - TV Ads

  (Kramer et al., 2010)

Of all of the components available to an airport today, the internet allows for broad and often inexpensive exposure. A website may be designed to serve as a brochure, presenting various information about the airport (such as airlines, parking options, food and beverage choices, maps of the facilities, etc.). A website may also be more strategically designed as a marketing tool, with changing content (such as flight times, new airline services/routes, etc.) and links to the airport's presence on social networking sites such as Facebook and Twitter. Generally, a dynamic website that visitors can interact with will be more productive for the airport and successfully contribute to the airport's marketing efforts. Although an airport can utilize a website with little financial expense (other than domain registration, hosting, web design services, and staffing to maintain currency of the site), a myriad of advertising options are also available on the internet, although some of these can be quite expensive. Online advertising is typically based on the amount a firm will pay for each impression and/or click. Often, a fixed fee is charged for a certain number of impressions and another fee is charged if a visitor clicks on the ad.

In addition to a website, a relatively recent trend in promoting an airport involves the use of social media. Although websites are integral for getting information to customers and prospective customers, the various forms of social media (including Facebook, Twitter, and other platforms) allow airports the ability to interact with customers in real-time—holding contests, answering questions, posting photos and videos, and more. Social media has changed the manner in which companies are marketed and customers research products and services. The key in effectively using social media is to interact regularly (preferably daily) and make it fun for individuals to interact with the airport. To build a large fan base, the airport can pay for advertisements on Facebook, for example, and set a daily ad budget paying on a per-click basis.

In addition, airports may develop an application (app), allowing customers and prospective customers to install an airport-specific app on their smartphone. These apps may have flight information, parking information, maps of terminals, and more (see Figure 10-4).

Small airports most often rely on developing an airport website, generating newspaper articles, and issuing press releases to comprise their promotional mix. Commercial-service airports, on the other hand, most often develop an airport website, generate articles in newspapers and magazines, issue press releases, and produce radio ads. The use of billboards is also a popular marketing tool for commercial-service airports, especially when introducing new airline service (although the airline may assist with or completely handle billboard efforts). Networking is also used by airports, although this often is among industry peers, rather than with customers the airports are trying to reach. In this case, airport personnel may attend events sponsored by agencies such as AAAE, Airports Council International (ACI) – North America (NA), and state airport associations. However, if trying to target potential passengers, an airport manager may network by speaking at a Rotary Club meeting or speaking with chamber of commerce members. If trying to reach potential air carriers, an airport manager may attend events such as Network USA and other events at which airline representatives would be present (Kramer et al., 2010).

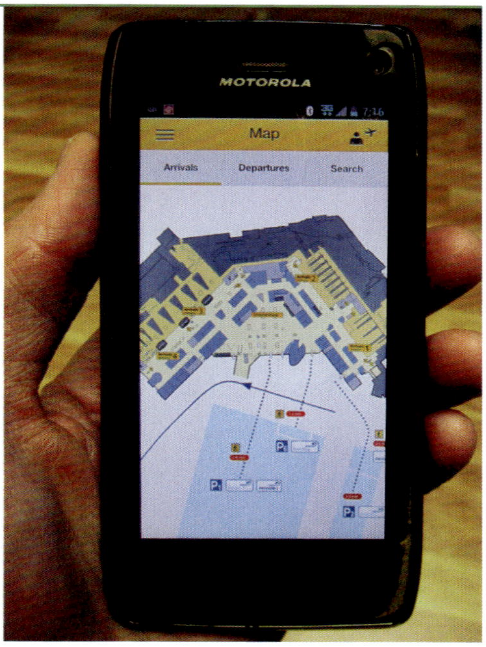

Figure 10-4. Airport app displaying an airport map.

Passion

The fifth of the "Five Ps" is *passion*, which is often intangible, but important nonetheless. When marketing the airport, it is important that passion about the airport and future potential is evident. If passion is lacking, it will be difficult to motivate stakeholders. How can an air carrier be motivated to begin service at an airport if the airport (or marketing) director lacks any passion about the airport or the air carrier? As an example, infomercials have historically been very effective at selling large numbers of products due in part to the passion exhibited by the presenter/host. Fortunately, those in aviation are generally quite passionate about the industry in which they work, which should benefit marketing efforts.

It is important for an airport to consider each of the Five Ps when developing a marketing plan. Potential customers will be considering each of the Five Ps (although maybe not explicitly), so it is imperative for the airport to do the same.

Variables

In any environment, there are variables that affect our level of success. Some of these variables can be controlled (such as our level of training, quality of running shoes, and clothing as we run in a marathon). Other variables are uncontrollable (such as the weather, the number of competing runners, etc.). This is also true of marketing. Although airports can control the money they dedicate toward marketing, the goals and objectives they adopt, and the marketing messages they choose (i.e., **controllable variables**), they must also contend with many **uncontrollable variables**.

The uncontrollable variables are those factors affecting the airport's performance that cannot be directed by marketing efforts. Any marketing plan, regardless of the expense involved, can fail if adversely influenced by uncontrollable variables. Therefore, it is important for an airport to regularly monitor the external environment and adjust the marketing plan as necessary. This process of continually acquiring information about trends occurring externally to the airport is referred to as **environmental scanning**. Typical uncontrollable variables include:

- Consumer demographics
- Competition
- Government regulations
- The economy
- Technology
- Media
- Public interest groups

First, although a firm has control over the selection of a target market, it cannot control the characteristics of the population. As demographics (such as age, income levels, marital status, occupation, race, education, and place and type of residence) change, airports can only react to these changes. It is important to anticipate changes in demographics and react as necessary.

Second, competitors can affect the success of any marketing effort. Especially among airports, potential passengers from a market area may drive to another airport (leakage) for lower-priced flights or better service. Competition can be experienced in one of three forms:

1. Direct competition between companies offering similar products and services.
2. Competition between companies that offer products or services that can be substituted for one another.
3. Competition for limited financial resources.

Third, governmental regulation can impact marketing success. In addition to the federal laws involving antitrust, discriminatory pricing, unfair trade practices, and occupational health and safety, the aviation industry must comply with numerous regulations promulgated by the Federal Aviation Administration. Occasionally, these laws change. In addition to federal laws, state and local governments have their own political climates that may adversely affect airport marketing efforts.

Fourth, the current state of the economy can greatly affect marketing efforts. For instance, if an airport is endeavoring to increase enplanements, but the country is enduring a recession, many individuals may choose not to fly because they cannot afford to. Indeed, an economic recession, high unemployment, and the rising cost of credit all affect purchasing power. On the other hand, if the country is enjoying a high rate of economic growth, marketing will likely be more successful.

Fifth, technological innovation can affect marketing success. The aviation industry has always been on the leading edge of technological change. Many technological advances are beyond the control of individual firms, especially smaller ones. However, unless they keep pace with improved technology, they will no longer remain competitive.

Sixth, the media can influence marketing success. In particular, the media can influence the behavior of consumers. The media can also provide positive or negative coverage of a company or an industry. Airports can, on the other hand, capitalize on the media's power by sharing positive news (as previously discussed).

Lastly, public interest groups can affect marketing success. The number of public interest groups has increased significantly during the past two decades. Hundreds of other consumer interest groups—private and governmental—operate at the national, state, and local levels. Some airports have been confronted with environmental groups opposing an airport expansion, so the existence, power, and influence of public interest groups is a real threat.

Implementing the Plan

Regardless of how much time and effort was required to develop the marketing plan, success will be not be realized if customers don't purchase goods and services, new airlines don't begin service, or fuel sales do not increase (depending on the specific marketing objectives). Therefore, once a plan is developed, it must be implemented—or put into action. Implementation of marketing plans requires three phases:

1. Delegation
2. Communication
3. Motivation

Delegation is necessary because it will be difficult for one person to do it all. Delegation is carried out both formally through organizational structure and informally through the daily assignment and sharing of tasks. In addition to determining appropriate duties, delegation requires matching the capabilities and preferences of employees to those duties. In other words, delegation is only successful when the duties to be performed have been clearly specified, and appropriate personnel have been assigned to perform those duties. For instance, one employee in the marketing department may be skilled at developing websites and utilizing social media, while another may be a skilled and passionate presenter and negotiator (Prather, 2011).

The implementation of a marketing plan also requires proper **communication**. Some in the organization may not be aware of the new marketing goals or the plans implemented to achieve those goals. Through proper communication, the firm can create shared understanding among individuals. Rather than solely the upper-level management sharing ideas, it is beneficial if information flows across the organizational hierarchy (among departments, for instance). As an example, the airport operations department should be informed if an air carrier is considering starting service with a larger aircraft, as it may impact the airport's ARFF Index or require a modification to standards based on the airport's airport reference code. Marketing plans are best implemented in a work environment that fosters a complete and open flow of information. Methods to improve communications include:

- *Information Dissemination*: Up-to-date organizational charts, telephone directories, a company newsletter, an in-house library of industry material, and a policy for releasing information as quickly as possible to avoid rumor.
- *Instruction*: Training programs, formal performance appraisals, sessions with supervisors, and financial assistance for educational pursuits.
- *Interaction*: Informal company gatherings and interdepartmental committees.

Even so, delegating and communicating will not necessarily lead to marketing success. **Motivation** is also key. It is important that efforts are undertaken to motivate employees to perform the tasks expected of them and buy in to the marketing goals and objectives. Employees can actually contribute to marketing success—or alternatively, if they do not believe in the marketing goals and objectives, they may hinder marketing efforts. Obtaining buy-in is important, not only to the success of the airport, but also to the success of the marketing efforts. Allowing employees to provide input into the marketing plan will likely enhance buy-in. The key is to design motivation efforts that assist employees in carrying out the marketing objectives of the airport.

Additionally, once implemented, it is important to determine the success of marketing efforts. Measuring success requires regular monitoring and evaluation of the plan. This requires an airport to stay abreast of the promotional mix in place, as well as the progress being made toward the marketing goals and objectives. For example, if a goal was to increase fuel sales, the airport will want to maintain a daily, weekly, and monthly total in gallons of fuel sold and the amount of gross sales. More specifically, the airport may want to track gallons of fuel sold to each customer, whether based or transient. By regularly monitoring the plan and the progress toward goals and objectives, mid-course corrections can be made to enhance marketing success.

Characteristics of an Effective Marketing Plan

Although marketing plans are as diverse as the airports that develop them, there are common characteristics of effective plans. These characteristics include:

- *Customer and service centered.* The main focus of the plan must be on meeting the demand(s) of its target audience(s).
- *Differentiates itself from competitors.* If possible, the airport should differentiate itself from its competitors and spell out unique reasons why users should select this airport over rivals.
- *Easily communicated.* The plan needs to be simple and clear to target audiences and also to airport staff so they can easily understand and talk about it.
- *Motivating.* A successful plan will be adopted enthusiastically by airport stakeholders.
- *Flexible.* The plan should be sufficiently broad to embrace a variety of marketing activities and to allow for mid-course corrections and unforeseen changes in the marketplace.

(Kramer et al., 2010, p. 53)

The main determinant of the success of any marketing plan is the degree to which the plan achieves the goals and objectives developed. Hence the need for specific and measurable objectives, as previously discussed.

Air Service Development

Although marketing plans can be designed to achieve a number of objectives, one of the most common objectives for airports with commercial air service—as well as those desiring to attract commercial air service—involves **air service development (ASD)**. This term comprises all activities that are designed to enhance commercial passenger service at an airport. Airports with existing airline service focus on maintaining the service presently in place, as well as increasing flights and carriers. Airports without existing airline service focus on attracting air carrier service. Airports desiring air service or additional air service know the benefits that air service can bring to the community, including the economic impacts (such as investment and employment).

The key to developing an effective ASD program is understanding how carriers make decisions as to which airports they will serve. Air carriers are profit-driven. Thus, airport costs (fees, rates, and charges) and potential revenues (passenger numbers the market will bear) are critical to an airline's decision. For example, regardless of how much a community is driven to attract airline service, if the numbers don't add up for the airline, ASD efforts may be unsuccessful. Many carriers today actually expect concessions (in the form of discounted or waived landing fees, low terminal rental rates, etc.) when initiating new service to an airport not currently served by the carrier. The air carriers see these concessions as a form of "risk sharing" between the airport and the airline. Thus, airports desiring initial air carrier service must use caution in having revenues as the sole impetus. It likely will take some time before these revenues are realized, based on the airline concessions granted and the success of the airline service.

When attempting to attract air carrier service, airports study the amount of "leakage" present. **Leakage** refers to the number of passengers that leave the local area to patronize another commercial-service airport to board a flight. Even well-developed airports with significant levels of airline service typically encounter some amount of leakage. Most leakage is due to other airports offering more choices, including nonstop flights, convenient departure and arrival times, and more frequent flights. However, some leakage may occur due to seemingly insignificant items such as long-term parking fees. Small airports in particular face several major challenges, including:

- Proximity to airports with service by major air carriers
- Proximity to airports with low-cost air carrier service
- Small isolated populations with little demand
- Fragmentation of the local passenger traffic base among competing nearby airports
- Predominantly inbound markets that rely on tourism

(Martin, 2009)

Another reality for airports to consider is that smaller communities generally have insufficient demand for air carrier service. That being said, the Essential Air Service (EAS) program provides federal subsidies to air carriers to serve smaller underserved communities. Developed in response to the Airline Deregulation Act of 1978, the EAS program was designed to aid smaller communities that were likely to lose air service as a result of airline deregulation. In selecting an EAS carrier, the DOT considers (a) service reliability, (b) contractual and marketing arrangements with larger carriers at a nearby hub airport, (c) interline arrangements with larger carriers at the hub, and (d) community views (DOT, n.d.).

As of 2013, the DOT subsidized commuter airline service to approximately 160 rural communities across the country that otherwise would not receive any scheduled air service. This amounted to approximately $123 million. Even so, communities continue to lose airline service (especially during difficult economic times). After filing a 90-day notice of intent to suspend service, a carrier may leave a community. If a replacement carrier is not found, that community will lose service altogether. In 2008 alone, 38 airports in the United States lost all air carrier service (DOT, n.d.).

Recent reforms to the EAS program prohibit the DOT from providing EAS to communities whose annual passenger subsidies are greater than $1,000 per passenger, regardless of their distance from the nearest hub airport. Additionally, the requirement that communities receive EAS on 15-seat or larger aircraft has been waived. Now, no new communities can enter the program should they lose their unsubsidized service. Additionally, in order to remain in the EAS program, effective in fiscal year 2013, subsidized communities must maintain an average of ten passenger enplanements per service day. There is an exception for communities in Alaska and Hawaii, and for those that are more than 175 driving miles from the nearest large or medium hub airport.

Due to the precarious nature of air service, especially in smaller communities, it is imperative for airports to proactively engage air carriers to maintain existing service or attract new service. This is accomplished via ASD programs.

An effective ASD program is based on the following steps:

1. Identify deficiencies (including air carrier pricing, capacity, aircraft type, and reliability).
2. Identify major stakeholders.
3. Identify available resources (including financial resources and human resources).
4. Establish and validate goals (should be reasonable and based on community needs).
5. Select ASD strategy and techniques.
6. Present a compelling case to the airlines.
7. Evaluate.

(Martin, 2009)

Two main ASD strategies exist. The first involves increasing airport revenue by promoting passenger demand. The second involves increasing air carrier service, in which case airports are typically prepared to offer concessions to the airline. Concessions may include:

- *Minimum airline revenue guarantees*—Agreements that establish a target amount of revenue that a carrier will receive for operating a particular service to a particular destination over a given length of time.
- *Guaranteed ticket purchases*—Travel bank in which businesses or individuals deposit funds in a bank account that are used for purchasing tickets on the target airline during a given period of time.
- *Cost subsidies*—Include waivers of fees or discounted landing fees during a promotional period.
- *Marketing and advertising*—Purchased on behalf of the airline's new service and designed to build awareness and develop demand.
- *Non-financial (in-kind) contributions*—Products, goods, or services that would normally have to be paid for, but instead are donated by third-party providers (such as local advertising or newspaper/TV coverage).
- *Hire ASD consultant*—A consultant that can provide aviation industry information, analyze changes in the local market, and conduct air service analysis studies.

(Martin, 2009)

Revenue Diversion at Los Angeles World Airports

Grant Assurance 25 states, "All revenues generated by the airport and any local taxes on aviation fuel established after December 30, 1987, will be expended by it for the capital or operating costs of the airport; the local airport system; or other local facilities which are owned or operated by the owner or operator of the airport and which are directly and substantially related to the actual air transportation of passengers or property; or for noise mitigation purposes on or off the airport." Yet, airports sometimes engage in revenue diversion, which is prohibited by Grant Assurance 25. For example, in 2009, the Los Angeles World Airports (LAWA), owner and operator of Los Angeles International Airport, was accused by the FAA of improperly diverting funds to L.A. Inc., the city's convention and visitors bureau. After a routine audit of airport funds by the FAA in July 2008, the FAA questioned whether Los Angeles World Airports had illegally provided more than $38.8 million to L.A. Inc. for marketing services since 2002. Although the airport was able to provide justification for some of the funds, the Los Angeles City Council agreed to return more than $21.2 million from L.A. Inc. to LAWA to settle the claims. Additionally, the FAA required LAWA to develop a more clearly defined marketing plan that specifically relates to airport amenities, airlines and advantages for travelers as mandated by federal regulations. In addition, the agency was required to document those expenditures.

(FAA, 2014; Weikel, 2009)

Specifically to provide guidance to federally-obligated airports in establishing an incentive program for air carriers, the FAA has published the *Air Carrier Incentive Program Guidebook* (FAA, 2010). Although this guidebook recognizes the value in providing incentives to air carriers, the FAA stresses that airports may not use airport revenue to promote any kind of general economic development. This would be considered "**revenue diversion**," which is prohibited by the FAA at federally-obligated airports. According to the guidebook, allowable uses of revenues include:

- The full costs of activities directed at promoting competition at an airport
- Public and industry awareness of airport facilities and services
- New air service and competition at the airport (other than direct subsidy of air carrier operations)
- A share of promotional expenses such as marketing, advertising, and related activities designed to increase travel using the airport, which includes specific information about the airport.

Non-allowable uses of airport revenues include:

- Destination or tourism marketing
- Any activities, materials, or expenses for general economic development not related to the airport
- Marketing or promotional activities unrelated to airports or airport systems (FAA, 2010)

It should be noted that the FAA allows air carrier **incentives** (which include any fee reduction, fee waiver, or use of airport revenue for acceptable promotional costs), but prohibits **subsidies** (which include direct payment of airport revenue to a carrier or to any provider of goods or services to that carrier, in exchange for additional service by the carrier). Additionally, if an airport decides to offer incentives only to new entrants, but not existing (incumbent) air carriers, incentives must not last longer than one year. This includes new entrants that begin serving a route already served by an incumbent. In this case, the airport could offer incentives to the new entrant, but would not be required to do the same for the incumbent as long as the one year time frame is not exceeded. Furthermore, airports may not target specific types of carriers (such as low-cost) or specific carriers (such as Southwest Airlines) by offering incentives. Incentives, if offered, must be made available for new service, regardless of the type or carrier. Additionally, incentives must be based on the airport destinations the airport wishes to support, not specific type of aircraft. For example, an airport may not make an incentive contingent upon use of a turbojet aircraft (FAA, 2010).

According to the FAA, acceptable incentives include:

- Reduced or zero landing fees
- Reduced or zero terminal rents
- Reduced or no fuel flowage fees

Incentives that are not acceptable include:

- Paying for leased property not owned by the airport on behalf of the air carrier
- Making a direct payment to an air carrier to help defray start-up costs
- Providing interest-free loans to an air carrier
- Tying incentives to ticket prices
- Providing a cash incentive to passengers who depart on the first leg of their journey from the airport
- Promising to purchase a set number of tickets from the air carrier (although this may be allowed under the Small Community Air Service Development Program)
- Guaranteeing the number of seats that will be filled
- Guaranteeing gross passenger revenue
- Offering incremental discounts based on increased weight for a previously scheduled flight

In sum, according to the FAA, an air carrier incentive program may not

- Guarantee gross passenger revenue
- Guarantee ticket sales
- Influence ticket prices
- Include direct payments to carriers from airport revenue
- Offer incremental discounts based on weight for existing service
- Offer incentives based on incremental weight or increased number of seats on existing flights
- Result in higher charges to other carriers to support the incentive program
- Use PFCs or federal grants (other than those from the Small Community Air Service Development Program) to cover costs associated with incentives (FAA, 2010)

Once goals are established and a strategy and techniques are decided upon, it is time for the airport to make a compelling case to the airlines. This should take the form of a "business case" and should be based on realistic information that includes information not normally available to the airline. Generally, this would include community- and airport-specific information that the airline would find useful, but not have available. The case should also include a route forecast, which includes the airport's best estimate of the projected level of success, a comparison to similar routes flown by competitors, and economic and demographic data. This case is most often presented to the airline at their corporate headquarters via a Microsoft PowerPoint presentation and a hard-copy, bound proposal. The presentation should be tailored to those in attendance and given by a knowledgeable and passionate airport professional (typically the director of marketing or director of air service development). Airports are encouraged not to bring local elected officials, as they often do not add any objective substance to the presentation and may actually introduce political bias that could hinder efforts (Martin, 2009).

Concluding Thoughts

Airports must engage in effective marketing programs to proactively attract airlines, maintain satisfied customers, and enhance public perception. This requires a multi-pronged effort, often requiring a dedicated marketing professional and/or marketing department. Even with the implementation of a marketing plan, it is important for airports to measure progress toward the achievement of marketing objectives. Changes to the plan can then be made to more effectively reach target markets and maintain highly satisfied customers.

Chapter Summary

- Marketing is the art of identifying and understanding customer needs and creating solutions that deliver satisfaction to the customers, profits to the producers, and benefits for the stakeholders.
- Customer satisfaction is the ultimate objective of the marketing process.
- Developing a marketing plan requires determining goals and objectives; assessing resources and performing a SWOT analysis; revising goals and objectives; segmenting the market; selecting target markets; and establishing a unique marketing mix.
- The most common marketing goals include market expansion; market focus or segmentation; cost leadership; and quality.
- A SWOT analysis requires assessing the airport's strengths, weaknesses, opportunities, and threats.
- Market segmentation is the process of breaking down the total market into smaller, more homogenous groups with similar needs that the airport can satisfy.
- Although segmenting the market aids the airport in further defining the focus of its marketing efforts, selecting a target market allows the airport to pinpoint the object of the airport's marketing mix.
- The five Ps consist of (1) product or service, (2) price, (3) place, (4) promotion, and (5) passion.

- The promotional mix consists of public relations, advertising, and networking.
- Tools available to influence the public opinion include earned media, public speaking, other print communications, events, sponsorships and volunteering, and other print materials.
- Advertising tools include internet and websites; print media; signage; and multi-media tools.
- Networking is the process of building contacts and relationships through various means, which can include business, civic, and non-profit groups; professional organizations; tradeshows and conferences; strategic partnerships; and lobbying.
- Typical uncontrollable variables include consumer demographics, competition, government regulations, the economy, technology, media, and public interest groups.
- Implementation of a marketing plan requires delegation, communication, and motivation.
- Effective marketing plans are customer and service centered; differentiating from competitors; easily communicated; motivating; and flexible.
- One of the most common objectives for airports with commercial air service, as well as those desiring to attract commercial air service, involves air service development (ASD).
- The key to developing an effective ASD program is understanding that air carriers are profit-driven and make decisions based on potential revenues.
- The Essential Air Service (EAS) program provides federal subsidies to air carriers to serve smaller underserved communities.
- An effective ASD program is based on identifying deficiencies; identifying major stakeholders; identifying available resources; establishing and validating goals; selecting ASD strategy and techniques; presenting a compelling case to the airlines; and evaluating efforts.
- Airline concessions may include minimum airline revenue guarantees; guaranteed ticket purchases; cost subsidies; marketing and advertising; non-financial contributions; and hiring an ASD consultant.
- Revenue diversion is prohibited by the FAA at federally-obligated airports.
- The FAA allows air carrier incentives, but prohibits subsidies.

Review Questions ↘

1. What is marketing?
2. What is the ultimate objective of marketing?
3. What questions would a well-developed marketing plan answer?
4. Explain the six steps required to develop a marketing plan.
5. What is the difference between a goal and an objective?
6. Explain the SWOT analysis.
7. What are the five Ps?
8. What is the purpose of an airport press kit?
9. What advertising tools are available to airports?
10. What networking tools are available to airports?
11. What is the purpose of the Small Community Air Service Development Program?
12. Which components of the promotional mix are the least expensive?
13. Explain the three phases required to implement a marketing plan.
14. What are some characteristics of effective marketing plans?
15. Explain some challenges faced by small airports.
16. What steps are necessary in developing an effective air service development program?
17. What are allowable uses of revenues in developing an incentive program for air carriers?
18. What is the difference between incentives and subsidies?
19. What air carrier incentives are not acceptable to the FAA?
20. What are some considerations when preparing a presentation to an air carrier to secure air service?

Scenarios ↘

1. As the director of marketing at a small hub airport, you have been asked by the airport director to develop a marketing plan to secure scheduled airline service by an additional air carrier. Currently, one carrier has 100 percent of the market share at your airport. Develop this marketing plan, using the guidance in this chapter.
2. Currently, you serve as the airport manager of a small GA airport. The city manager recently asked you to do your best to make the airport financially self-sufficient. As it stands now, the airport operates at a $100,000 per year deficit, requiring financial support by the city. The airport does own and operate the FBO (with fueling, parking, and other line services as well as flight training services) and has twenty T-hangars that are 70 percent occupied. Develop a marketing plan with the aim of making the airport financially self-sufficient.
3. Visit a local airport, study their services, and perform a SWOT analysis from the perspective of a potential air carrier.
4. As director of community relations, you have been asked by the airport director to issue a press release announcing new non-stop service by an incumbent carrier, Twice Air, to Honolulu. Write this press release.
5. As director of marketing, you have been busy attempting to recruit an air carrier at your Part 139-certificated airport since the only air carrier serving the airport eliminated service three years ago. Develop an air service development plan, including concessions that you would be willing to make available to an air carrier that begins service.

References and Resources for Further Study

Department of Transportation. n.d. "Essential Air Service." Retrieved from http://www.dot.gov/policy/aviation-policy/small-community-rural-air-service/essential-air-service

Federal Aviation Administration (FAA). 2010. *Air Carrier Incentive Program Guidebook: A Reference for Airport Sponsors.* Retrieved from http://www.faa.gov/airports/airport_compliance/media/air-carrier-incentive-2010.pdf Washington, DC: FAA.

———. 2014. Grant Assurances Airport Sponsors. Retrieved from http://www.faa.gov/airports/aip/grant_assurances/media/airport-sponsor-assurances-aip.pdf

Jackson County—Reynolds Field Airport. 2011. "Marketing Plan 2011." Retrieved from http://www.co.jackson.mi.us/Agencies/airport/docs/Marketing_Plan_Jackson_County_Airport.pdf

Kramer, L., P. Fowler, R. Hazel, M. Ureksoy, and G. Harig. 2010. "Marketing Guidebook for Small Airports." ACRP Report 28. Washington, DC: Transportation Research Board.

Martin, S. 2009. "Passenger Air Service Development Techniques." ACRP Report 18. Washington, DC: Transportation Research Board.

Prather, C. D. 2009. *General Aviation Marketing & Management: Operating, Marketing, and Managing an FBO.* Malabar, FL: Krieger.

Weikel, Dan. 2009. "L.A. to return $21.2 million to LAX's operator." Los Angeles Times, December 17. Retrieved from http://articles.latimes.com/2009/dec/17/local/la-me-airport-money17-2009dec17

Chapter 11

Governmental, Legal, and Public Relations

Objectives

Upon completion of this chapter, you should understand:

- the role of governmental relations in airport management
- the national level of government with which airport managers interact
- the state level of government with which airport managers interact
- the local level of government with which airport managers interact
- the State Block Grant Program
- the manner in which airport managers interact with airport boards and municipal officials
- Robert's Rules of Order
- the purpose of the notice of proposed rulemaking process
- the role of FAA orders
- the role of FAA advisory circulars, including those ACs important for airport operations personnel
- available airport law resources
- the regulatory agencies in the aviation industry
- the aviation industry trade associations
- the role of public relations in airport management

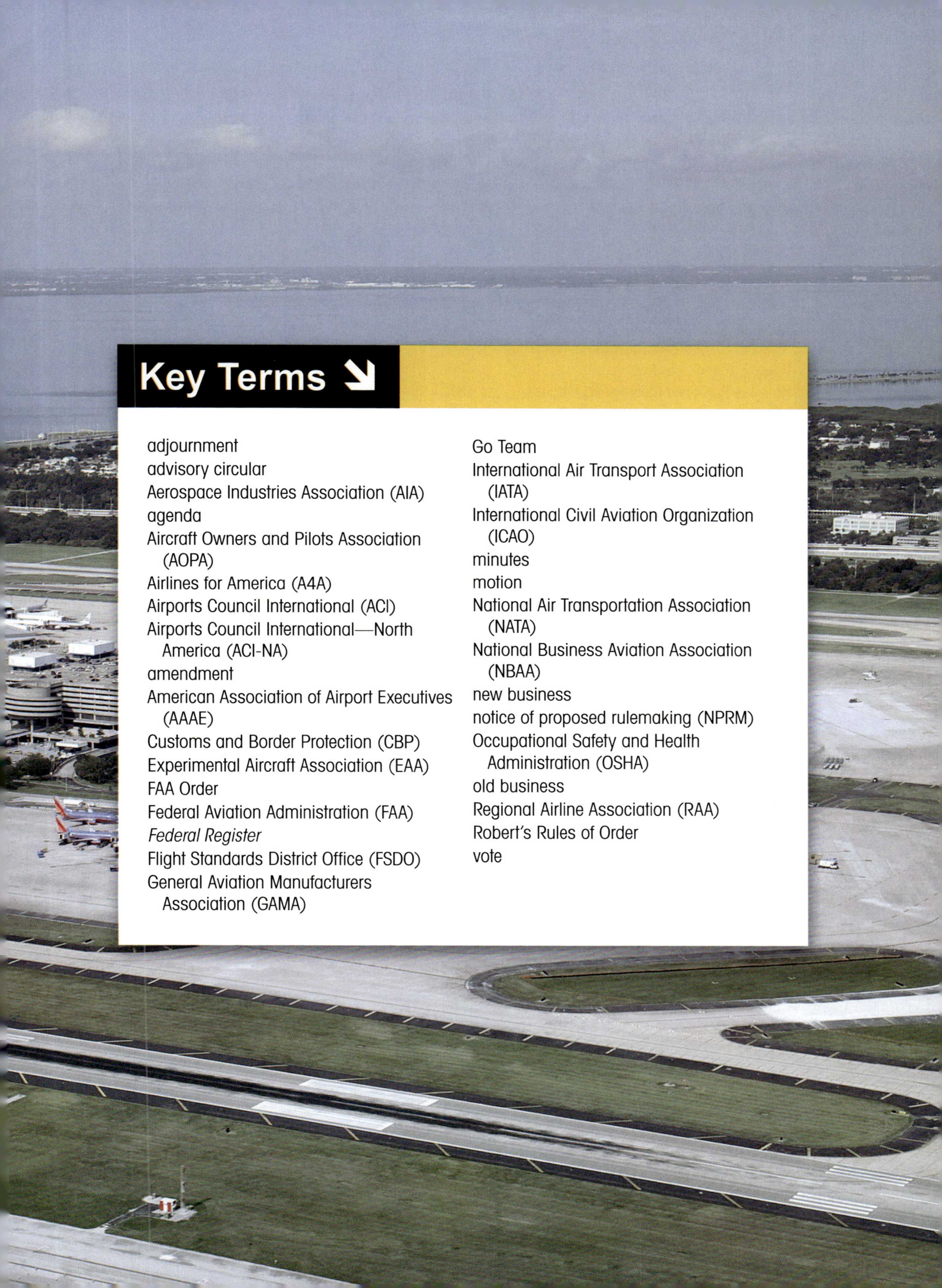

Key Terms ↘

adjournment
advisory circular
Aerospace Industries Association (AIA)
agenda
Aircraft Owners and Pilots Association (AOPA)
Airlines for America (A4A)
Airports Council International (ACI)
Airports Council International—North America (ACI-NA)
amendment
American Association of Airport Executives (AAAE)
Customs and Border Protection (CBP)
Experimental Aircraft Association (EAA)
FAA Order
Federal Aviation Administration (FAA)
Federal Register
Flight Standards District Office (FSDO)
General Aviation Manufacturers Association (GAMA)
Go Team
International Air Transport Association (IATA)
International Civil Aviation Organization (ICAO)
minutes
motion
National Air Transportation Association (NATA)
National Business Aviation Association (NBAA)
new business
notice of proposed rulemaking (NPRM)
Occupational Safety and Health Administration (OSHA)
old business
Regional Airline Association (RAA)
Robert's Rules of Order
vote

In Chapter 11

Governmental Relations **425**
- National, State, and Local Relations 425
- Communication with Airport Boards and Municipal Officials 429
- Robert's Rules of Order 429
- Notice of Proposed Rulemaking Process 431
- FAA Orders 432
- FAA Advisory Circulars 432
- Airport Law Resources 436
- Regulatory Agencies 438

Industry Relations **444**
- Industry Trade Associations 444
- Grassroots Efforts.. 448

Public Relations **448**
- Community Relations 448
- Media Relations 450
- Customer Service 451
- Events.. 452
- Social Media... 452

Concluding Thoughts........................... **452**

Chapter Summary **453**

Review Questions................................ **457**

Scenarios... **458**

References and Resources for Further Study **459**

FEATURES

New Hampshire Airport Block Grants 428

New Hampshire, through the state's Department of Transportation Bureau of Aeronautics, provides airport improvement grants to qualifying airports throughout the state.

Governmental Relations

Public-use airports in the United States are typically owned and operated by governmental entities (generally municipalities). Therefore, by the very nature of the airports they manage, airport directors and senior airport personnel are usually very politically aware. Whether their airport is large or small, commercial-service or GA, these personnel are aware of the need for positive and proactive governmental relations.

NATIONAL, STATE, AND LOCAL RELATIONS

Although public-use airports are generally owned and operated by local municipalities, some are owned and operated by the state in which they are located. In the past, the federal government also owned and operated some public-use, commercial-service airports. For example, the FAA owned and operated Ronald Reagan Washington National Airport and Washington Dulles International Airport prior to 1987, at which time the airports were transferred to the Metropolitan Washington Airports Authority under a 50-year lease authorized by the Metropolitan Washington Airports Act of 1986. Regardless of the entity owning and operating an airport, it is crucial for the airport director to communicate with and recognize the role of other governmental units.

National

At the national level, the FAA handles all aspects of the nation's aviation system. In fact, the mission of the FAA is to provide the safest, most efficient aerospace system in the world. The FAA carries out this mission through the following departments at its headquarters in Washington, DC:

- Airports
- Air Traffic Organization
- Aviation Safety
- Chief Counsel
- Civil Rights
- Commercial Space Transportation
- Communications
- Financial Services
- Government and Industry Affairs
- Human Resources Management
- Information Services
- NextGen
- Policy, International Affairs and Environment

- Regions & Center Operations
- Security and Hazardous Materials
  (FAA, 2012)

Additionally, the FAA is comprised of the following field and regional offices:

- Aircraft Certification Offices (ACO)
- Airports Regional Offices
- Flight Standards District Offices (FSDO)
- Manufacturing & Inspection District Offices (MIDO)
- Aircraft Evaluation Groups (AEG)
- International Field Offices and Units (IFO) (IFU)
- Certificate Management Offices (CMO)
- Regional Offices
- Security and Hazardous Materials Offices
- Mike Monroney Aeronautical Center
- FAA Academy
- Center for Management and Executive Leadership
- Logistics Center
- William J. Hughes Technical Center
  (FAA, 2012)

Although the FAA is headquartered in the nation's capital, it is directly involved with airports at the local level through various departments and offices. For instance, the Airports office has responsibility for all programs related to airport safety and inspections, and standards for airport design, construction, and operation (including international harmonization of airport standards). Additionally, the Airports office is responsible for national airport planning and environmental and social requirements, and establishes policies related to airport rates and charges, compliance with grant assurances, and airport privatization.

State

Each state typically has a state aviation department or aeronautics agency (see Figure 11-1). The role of this department/agency is to promulgate statewide rules and regulations governing aviation and airports in the state, administer federal- and state-aid funds for public-use airports, play a role in the design of airport construction and maintenance projects, and ensure the continued and integrated growth of airports in the state. States also typically facilitate safety inspection efforts at all non-certificated public airports and some private airports. Many state aviation agencies have the following departments (although some may be combined):

- *Planning*—Initiates, compiles and monitors activities of the agency; initiates, develops, monitors and maintains statewide airport capital improvement projects; and ensures each airport maintains approved long range planning and environmental documents for sustainable airport facilities throughout the state.
- *Finance and Grant Management*—Maintains, releases and approves grants and loans. If the state is one of ten states nationwide that is a block grant state, the state aviation agency will also handle all AIP grants and funding to airports in the state (see below).
- *Engineering*—Works with airports and their consultants on maintenance and construction projects, and assists with securing equipment.
- *Air Service*—Carries out projects dedicated to the improvement and promotion of air service in the state.
- *Flight Operations*—Responsible for state-owned aircraft, providing flight services for the governor and other state personnel on state business.

Figure 11-1. State aviation headquarters, Tennessee.

It should be noted that if a state participates in the State Block Grant Program, the state aviation agency is responsible for administering Airport Improvement Program grants at nonprimary commercial service, reliever, and general aviation airports throughout the state. Rather than the FAA distributing federal AIP funds to individual airports, a lump sum (block grant) is provided to the state, with funds then provided to the state's individual airports based on project needs and priority. As of 2015, the following ten states were members of the State Block Grant Program:

- Georgia
- Illinois
- Michigan
- Missouri
- New Hampshire
- North Carolina
- Pennsylvania
- Tennessee
- Texas
- Wisconsin

Local

Public-use airports are typically owned and operated at the local level. Whether a city, county, city/county, parish, authority, or some other form of municipal entity, the local level is the level at which ownership and daily operation of public-use airports typically occurs. This is as it should be, as the local municipalities have the most vested interest in maintaining a local airport. Indeed, the local community receives the most significant benefits (economic and otherwise) from the airport.

That being said, the local airport manager plays an important role, which revolves around governmental and public relations. Governmental relations is integral for the airport manager. As discussed, officials in the federal government,

New Hampshire Airport Block Grants

As one of ten states in the FAA State Block Grant Program, New Hampshire, through the New Hampshire Department of Transportation Bureau of Aeronautics, serves as the FAA-equivalent airport grant funding agency for airports in the state. A member of the FAA's State Block Grant Program since FY2008, the Bureau "has a better understanding of local issues and needs that are used to help determine project and funding priorities. By giving the state the funding assistance, the FAA gives the Bureau the flexibility to redistribute these funds for non-primary airport improvements based, in part, on local needs" (NHDOT, 2009). Just as in non-block grant states, all airports receiving funding through the block grant must be included in the NPIAS for eligibility. During FY2014, New Hampshire provided \$3.1 million in block grants to eight airports throughout the state. Funded projects included installation of perimeter fencing, land acquisition, equipment acquisition, master plan update, PAPI installation, obstruction analysis, and obstruction removal/lighting. The state also utilized \$140,000 to update the state Airport Information Management System.

state government, and local government are all involved with airport management and operation. To obtain federal airport funding and ensure a successful Part 139 inspection, the airport manager should coordinate effectively with FAA officials. To obtain state funding and ensure the airport's capital development needs are reflected in a state airport system plan, the airport manager must communicate effectively with state aviation officials, as well as other officials at the state level (including the governor and secretary of transportation). At the local level, the airport manager should educate local officials as to the benefits of the airport to the community, as well as stress the financial needs of the airport to secure municipal funding.

COMMUNICATION WITH AIRPORT BOARDS AND MUNICIPAL OFFICIALS

An airport may be governed by an airport board or commission, or may fall under the city council and/or the board of county commissioners. Whether the airport is governed by a specific body, or falls under a more general decision-making body, airport managers must continually communicate with these officials to make certain that airport needs (as well as community benefits) are well understood. It is only by effective communication with these officials that the airport will enjoy more political success. And this often equates to funding decisions.

It should be noted that some airports have an airport advisory board, which is different than the boards or commissions previously discussed. An airport advisory board is only advisory in nature, and although it is beneficial for the airport director to recognize their expertise and contributions (usually as volunteers), the airport director is the professional hired to manage the airport and should only consider input from the advisory board as advice, rather than orders that must be carried out.

ROBERT'S RULES OF ORDER

Airport personnel (especially at the senior level) spend a considerable amount of time in meetings. Some of these meetings consist of only a few individuals and are rather informal. However, other meetings may be formal (such as airport board meetings or airport commission meetings) (Figure 11-2). In such instances, the chairman of the meeting and all participants should adhere to a standard and formalized process for conducting the meeting. The most common guide for conducting meetings in this way is known as **Robert's Rules of Order**.

The parliamentary authority outlined in Robert's Rules of Order, first published in 1876, is widely recognized and adhered to as the most effective and formal means of holding meetings of civic, charitable and governmental organizations. The Rules include guidelines for debate and discussion, amendments,

Figure 1.
Typical air... meeting room.

(©iStock.com/OJO_Images)

handling motions, voting, nominations, elections, and more. For an airport manager or chair, the most important Rules to remember are:

- Call the meeting to order—This officially starts the meeting. This phrase informs all attendees that informal discussion should end, as the meeting has begun. "This meeting of the Airport Authority is now called to order."
- **Agenda**—It is important for all meetings to be governed by an agenda. If possible, the agenda should be sent to attendees prior to the meeting to allow for preparation.
- **Old Business**—Each meeting may have old, unfinished business from a past meeting that needs to be resolved. This is typically the first item on the agenda. Often, the previous meeting's minutes (record of discussion, motions, etc.) are presented and voted on for approval. This allows minutes to be corrected for inaccuracies before becoming official.
- **New Business**—Each meeting will typically have new items or business to discuss. These are grouped together on the agenda and discussed in a certain order of priority, typically as determined by the chair of the meeting. If an item on the agenda is expected to generate lengthy discussion, it may appear first or last (again, depending on the chair's desire).
- Discussion—With both old and new business, the chair should allow for discussion on the item. "Any discussion?"
- **Motion**—A motion is made, and then seconded, when a participant would like to bring an item up for a vote. "So moved." Or "I would like to make a motion that …."
- **Amendment**—Occasionally, a motion may be amended after discussion. In that case, it is the responsibility of the individual recommending the amendment of the motion to state the amendment, which will then be voted upon.
- **Vote**—Immediately after a motion is made and seconded on an item, if there is no further discussion, a vote is held. Generally, this is via, "All in favor, signify by saying aye." (Wait for vote.) "All opposed, with like sign." (Wait for vote.)

- **Adjournment**—After an opportunity is provided for any other discussion or new items of business, the meeting can be adjourned by the chair.
- **Minutes**—Throughout the meeting, the secretary (or other assigned individual) should keep minutes, which is a record of votes, amendments, discussions, etc. In that way, a record of the meeting and business conducted during the meeting can be maintained. These minutes will then be voted on for approval at the next meeting. Often, the minutes for a meeting are sent to attendees soon after the meeting to allow for correction of any inaccuracies prior to being voted on at the next meeting.

It should be noted that some meetings may be conducted very informally, without the formality of Robert's Rules of Order. This is up to the chair (or the individual calling the meeting). However, it is important for all airport managers to be knowledgeable in Robert's Rules of Order, as they will invariably be called upon to chair a formal meeting at which these Rules should be adhered to. If the airport manager does not follow the Rules at such a meeting, a great deal of credibility—and control of the meeting—may be lost.

NOTICE OF PROPOSED RULEMAKING PROCESS

The process whereby new regulations or revised regulations are first introduced is the **notice of proposed rulemaking (NPRM)** process. All NPRMs are published in the ***Federal Register***, which is the official journal of the U.S. government and contains most routine publications and public notices of government agencies. It is published daily throughout the year, except for federal holidays. The *Federal Register* is compiled by the Office of the Federal Register (within the National Archives and Records Administration) and is printed by the Government Printing Office (although it is also made available online). The NPRM process allows for public comment by a certain deadline before a final rule is issued. Airport managers must be aware of the *Federal Register* and stay current with any aviation NPRMs that are published. Although organizations such as AAAE will often ask for comments and submit a unified response on behalf of their membership, it is important for airport managers to not only read NPRMs that affect airports and the aviation industry, but also take time to submit comments to make their voices heard.

In writing a comment to an NPRM, it is important to address the effect the NPRM would have on the airport, including financial, managerial, operational, etc. Emotionally laden comments will not be taken as seriously as comments written in a professional tone that address both the pros and cons of a proposed rule. Comments must address the docket number and may be submitted online at www.regulations.gov, via mail, hand delivery, or fax. Once the comment deadline has passed, the responsible agency will review all of the comments and decide whether to make changes to the proposed rule, leave it unchanged as initially proposed, or issue a supplemental NPRM allowing comments on the revised proposed rule. All final rules promulgated by a federal agency and published in the *Federal Register* are ultimately reorganized by topic or subject matter and codified in the Code of Federal Regulations (CFR). A sampling of recent airport-related notices published in the *Federal Register* include:

- Approval of Noise Compatibility Program for Philadelphia International Airport
- Notice of Record of Decision on the Final Environmental Impact Statement that Evaluated the Proposed Airfield Improvement Project at Palm Beach International Airport, Palm Beach County, FL
- Notice of Release From Federal Grant Assurance Obligations at Fresno Yosemite International Airport, Fresno, CA
- Request for Public Comment, Raleigh County Memorial Airport, Beckley, WV
- Noise Exposure Maps; Cleveland Hopkins International Airport, Cleveland, OH
- NPRM—Safety Management Systems for Certificated Airports

FAA ORDERS

The FAA provides guidance internally typically through orders. An **FAA order** may address the siting of temporary control towers, the administration of the AIP program, the establishment of instrument approaches, or numerous other topics. Although an airport manager is able to view FAA orders on the FAA website, these orders are generally not important to the airport manager, as they simply provide insight into internal FAA guidance. However, if an airport manager is seeking to understand FAA rationale or procedures, reading FAA orders on the topic may prove insightful.

FAA ADVISORY CIRCULARS

Much more beneficial for the airport manager are FAA **advisory circulars** (ACs). Although the term "advisory" may seem to indicate that these are publications providing optional advice to airports, advisory circulars present the acceptable means (in accordance with the FAA Administrator) for complying with a regulation or other requirement. Specifically, ACs provide a means of fulfilling the applicable mandatory requirements set out in AIP grant assurances, passenger facility charge (PFC) assurances, and regulations. Airport personnel are most familiar with the ACs in the Part 150–Airports series, which covers a myriad of topics. Table 11-1 shows the ACs in this series as of 2014.

Table 11-1. FAA advisory circulars in the Part 150–Airports series.

Although all ACs in the Part 150 series are important, the ACs most pertinent to those involved in airport operations are indicated in bold type and highlighted yellow.

AC Number	AC Title
150/5220-21	Aircraft Boarding Equipment
150/5390-2	Heliport Design
150/5200-36	Qualifications for Wildlife Biologist Conducting Wildlife Hazard Assessments and Training Curriculums for Airport Personnel Involved in Controlling Wildlife Hazards on Airports
150/5220-26	Airport Ground Vehicle Automatic Dependent Surveillance-Broadcast (ADS-B) Out Squitter Equipment
150/5300-17	Standards for Using Remote Sensing Technologies in Airport Surveys
150/5370-10	Standards for Specifying Construction of Airports
150/5370-11	Use of Nondestructive Testing in the Evaluation of Airport Pavements
150/5370-15	Airside Applications for Artificial Turf
150/5340-30	Design and Installation Details for Airport Visual Aids
150/5345-28	Precision Approach Path Indicator (PAPI) Systems
150/5345-56	Specification for L-890 Airport Lighting Control and Monitoring System (ALCMS)
150/5370-2	**Operational Safety on Airports During Construction**
150/5345-39	Specification for L-853, Runway and Taxiway Retroreflective Markers
150/5100-13	Development of State Standards for Nonprimary Airports
150/5335-5	Standardized Method of Reporting Airport Pavement Strength–PCN
150/5345-47	Specification for Series to Series Isolation Transformers for Airport Lighting Systems
150/5100-19	Guide for Airport Financial Reports Filed by Airport Sponsors
150/5220-10	Guide Specification for Aircraft Rescue and Fire Fighting (ARFF) Vehicles
150/5220-16	Automated Weather Observing Systems (AWOS) for Non-Federal Applications
150/5370-17	Airside Use of Heated Pavement Systems
150/5220-25	Airport Avian Radar Systems
150/5210-23	ARFF Vehicle and High Reach Extendable Turret (HRET) Operation, Training and Qualifications
150/5210-24	**Airport Foreign Object Debris (FOD) Management**
150/5220-17	Aircraft Rescue and Fire Fighting (ARFF) Training Facilities
150/5000-16	Announcement of Availability of the Guide for Private Flyers U.S. International Airports
150/5210-13	Airport Water Rescue Plans and Equipment
150/5345-3	Specification for L-821, Panels for the Control of Airport Lighting
150/5345-10	Specification for Constant Current Regulators and Regulator Monitors
150/5345-44	Specification for Runway and Taxiway Signs
150/5345-12	Specification for Airport and Heliport Beacons
150/5200-35	Submitting the Airport Master Record in Order to Activate a New Airport

Table 11-1. *(continued)*

AC Number	AC Title
150/5345-51	Specification for Discharge-Type Flashing Light Equipment
150/5340-1	**Standards for Airport Markings**
150/5340-18	**Standards for Airport Sign Systems**
150/5000-15	Announcement of Availability of Airport-Related Research and Development Products
150/5210-5	Painting, Marking, and Lighting of Vehicles Used on an Airport
150/5220-24	**Foreign Object Debris Detection Equipment**
150/5300-9	Predesign, Prebid, and Preconstruction Conferences for Airport Grant Projects
150/5320-6	Airport Pavement Design and Evaluation
150/5340-26	Maintenance of Airport Visual Aid Facilities
150/5345-54	Specification for L-884, Power and Control Unit for Land and Hold Short Lighting Systems
150/5380-9	Guidelines and Procedures for Measuring Airfield Pavement Roughness
150/5200-12	**First Responders Responsibility for Protecting Evidence at the Scene of an Aircraft Accident/Incident**
150/5210-17	Programs for Training of Aircraft Rescue and Firefighting Personnel
150/5200-31	**Airport Emergency Plan (Consolidated AC includes Change 2)**
150/5210-19	Driver's Enhanced Vision System (DEVS)
150/5300-18	General Guidance and Specifications for Submission of Aeronautical Surveys to NGS: Field Data Collection and Geographic Information System (GIS) Standards
150/5345-46	Specification for Runway and Taxiway Light Fixtures
150/5220-23	Frangible Connections
150/5200-30	**Airport Winter Safety And Operations**
150/5210-14	Aircraft Rescue Fire Fighting Equipment, Tools and Clothing
150/5300-15	Use Of Value Engineering For Engineering And Design Of Airport Grant Projects
150/5345-26	FAA Specification For L-823 Plug And Receptacle, Cable Connectors
150/5210-18	Systems for Interactive Training Of Airport Personnel
150/5370-6	Construction Progress and Inspection Report—Airport Improvement Program (AIP)
150/5360-12	Airport Signing and Graphics
150/5210-15	Aircraft Rescue and Firefighting Station Building Design
150/5320-15	Management Of Airport Industrial Waste
150/5000-13	Announcement Of Availability: RTCA Inc., Document RTCA-221
150/5210-7	Aircraft Rescue and Fire Fighting Communications
150/5300-14	Design of Aircraft Deicing Facilities
150/5200-28	**Notices to Airmen (NOTAMS) for Airport Operators**
150/5370-12	Quality Control of Construction for Airport Grant Projects

Table 11-1. *(continued)*

AC Number	AC Title
150/5370-16	Rapid Construction of Rigid (Portland Cement Concrete) Airfield Pavements
150/5380-6	**Guidelines and Procedures for Maintenance of Airport Pavements**
150/5050-8	Environmental Management Systems for Airport Sponsors
150/5345-13	Specification for L-841 Auxiliary Relay Cabinet Assembly for Pilot Control of Airport Lighting Circuits
150/5345-50	Specification for Portable Runway and Taxiway Lights
150/5300-16	General Guidance and Specifications for Aeronautical Surveys: Establishment of Geodetic Control and Submission to the National Geodetic Survey
150/5220-18	Buildings for Storage and Maintenance of Airport Snow and Ice Control Equipment and Materials
150/5340-5	Segmented Circle Airport Marker System
150/5345-52	Generic Visual Glideslope Indicators (GVGI)
150/5200-33	**Hazardous Wildlife Attractants On or Near Airports**
150/5345-49	Specification L-854, Radio Control Equipment
150/5345-55	Specification for L-893, Lighted Visual Aid to Indicate Temporary Runway Closure
150/5200-29	Announcement Of Availability Of Airport Self-Inspection DVD
150/5070-6	**Airport Master Plans**
150/5345-45	Low-Impact Resistant (LIR) Structures
150/5200-37	**Introduction to Safety Management Systems (SMS) for Airport Operators**
150/5190-6	Exclusive Rights at Federally Obligated Airports
150/5220-9	Aircraft Arresting Systems
150/535-42	Specification for Airport Light Bases, Transformer Housings, Junction Boxes, and Accessories
150/5320-5	Surface Drainage Design
150/5370-13	Off-Peak Construction of Airport Pavements Using Hot-Mix Asphalt
150/5345-5	Circuit Selector Switch
150/5345-43	Specification for Obstruction Lighting Equipment
150/5380-7	**Airport Pavement Management Program**
150/5190-7	**Minimum Standards for Commercial Aeronautical Activities**
150/5200-34	Construction or Establishment of Landfills near Public Airports
150/5100-17	Land Acquisition and Relocation Assistance for Airport Improvement Program Assisted Projects
150/5100-14	Architectural, Engineering, and Planning Consultant Services for Airport Grant Projects
150/5220-22	Engineered Materials Arresting Systems (EMAS) for Aircraft Overruns
150/5345-53	Airport Lighting Equipment Certification Program
150/5325-4	Runway Length Requirements for Airport Design
150/5200-32	**Reporting Wildlife Aircraft Strikes**

Table 11-1. *(continued)*

AC Number	AC Title
150/5070-7	The Airport System Planning Process
150/5020-2	Guidance on the Balanced Approach to Noise Management
150/5320-17	**Airfield Pavement Surface Evaluation and Rating Manuals**
150/5210-6	Aircraft Fire and Rescue Facilities and Extinguishing Agents
150/5230-4	**Aircraft Fuel Storage, Handling, and Dispensing on Airports**
150/5345-27	Specification for Wind Cone Assemblies
150/5210-22	**Airport Certification Manual (ACM)**
150/5200-18	**Airport Safety Self-Inspection**
150/5210-21	Announcement of Availability: Airport Surface Safety Training Programs for Mechanics and Ramp Personnel
150/5210-20	**Ground Vehicle Operations on Airports**
150/5345-7	Specification for L-824 Underground Electrical Cable for Airport Lighting Circuits
150/5370-14	Hot Mix Asphalt Paving Handbook
150/5360-14	Access to Airports By Individuals With Disabilities
150/5320-12	Measurement, Construction, and Maintenance of Skid Resistant Airport Pavement Surfaces
150/5395-1	Seaplane Bases
150/5000-9	Announcement of Availability Report No. DOT/FAA/PP/92-5, Guidelines for the Sound Insulation of Residences Exposed to Aircraft Operations
150/5220-20	**Airport Snow and Ice Control Equipment**
150/5300-13	**Airport Design**
150/5360-13	Planning and Design Guidelines for Airport Terminal Facilities
150/5190-4	A Model Zoning Ordinance to Limit Height of Objects Around Airports
150/5150-2	Federal Surplus Personal Property for Public Airport Purposes
150/5060-5	**Airport Capacity And Delay**
150/5020-1	**Noise Control and Compatibility Planning for Airports**
150/5360-9	Planning and Design of Airport Terminal Facilities at Non-Hub Locations
150/5050-4	Citizen Participation in Airport Planning
150/5300-7	FAA Policy on Facility Relocations Occasioned by Airport Improvements or Changes

AIRPORT LAW RESOURCES

Due to the significant pieces of legislation, regulations, and other guidance at the federal, state, and even local level, it is imperative for the airport manager to maintain an awareness of issues affecting the airport on the legislative front. Larger airports may employ an individual in a Legal Counsel role to handle legal affairs, and/or an individual in a legislative affairs role to ensure the airport is aware of any pending or existing legislation that would affect the airport.

Various industry associations, such as the American Association of Airport Executives and Airports Council International—North America, also have a legislative affairs or airport law department to keep member airports informed of important issues.

One excellent source for guidance on airport law is the Legal Research Program of the Airport Cooperative Research Program. This FAA-funded program contracts with consultants who produce reports and digests on a number of airport topics related to airport law. As of 2015, these included the following Legal Research Digests (LRD):

- LRD No. 1, Compilation of Airport Law Resources (February 2008)
- LRD No. 2, Theory and Law of Airport Revenue Diversion (June 2008)
- LRD No. 3, Survey of Laws and Regulations of Airport Commercial Ground Transportation (July 2008)
- LRD No. 4, Compilation of Digest—Parts 13 and 16 Determinations and Related Documents (November 2008)
- LRD No. 5, Responsibility for Implementation and Enforcement of Airport Land-Use Zoning Restrictions (April 2009)
- LRD No. 6, The Impact of Airline Bankruptcies on Airports (June 2009)
- LRD No. 7, Airport Governance and Ownership (August 2009)
- LRD No. 8, The Right to Self-Fuel (December 2009)
- LRD No. 9, Case Studies on Community Challenges to Airport Development (July 2010)
- LRD No. 10, Analysis of Federal Laws, Regulations and Case Law Regarding Airport Proprietary Rights (August 2010)
- LRD No. 11, Survey of Minimum Standards: Commercial Aeronautical Activities at Airports (February 2011)
- LRD No. 12, Fair Disclosure of Airport Impacts in Real Estate Transfers (November 2011)
- LRD No. 13, An Index and Digest of Decisions: Compilation of Airport Law Resources (March 2012)
- LRD No. 14, Achieving Airport-Compatible Land Uses and Minimizing Hazardous Obstructions in Navigable Airspace (April 2012)
- LRD No. 15, Compilation of State Airport Authorizing Legislation (August 2012)
- LRD No. 16, Procurement of Airport Development and Planning Contracts (September 2012)
- LRD No. 17, State and Federal Regulations that May Affect Initiatives to Reduce Airports' GHG Emissions (December 2012)
- LRD No. 18, Buy America Requirements for Federally Funded Airports (March 2013)
- LRD No. 19, Legal Issues Related to Developing Safety Management Systems and Safety Risk Management at U.S. Airports (January 2013)

- LRD No. 20, Airport Responsibility for Wildlife Management (August 2013)
- LRD No. 21, Compilation of U.S. Department of Transportation (DOT) and U.S. Federal Aviation Administration (FAA) Airport Legal Determinations and Opinion Letters (September 2013)
- LRD No. 22, The Role of the Airport Sponsor in Airport Planning and Environmental Reviews of Proposed Development Projects Under the National Environmental Policy Act (NEPA) and State Mini-NEPA Laws (May 2014)
- LRD No. 23, A Guide for Compliance with Grant Agreement Obligations to Provide Reasonable Access to an AIP-Funded Public Use General Aviation Airport (February 2015)
- LRD No. 24, Sovereign Immunity for Public Airport Operations (April 2015)

REGULATORY AGENCIES

The aviation industry initially was self-regulated. In essence, there were no formal regulations governing issues such as safety of flight, airspace, and airports. A little more than 100 years later, however, the industry has become heavily regulated. The history of the aviation industry was presented in chapter 1. This section presents the agencies that have an effect on the aviation industry.

CAA and CAB

In the early years, with no federal agency in charge of aviation, the system was quite disorganized and often characterized by an "anything goes" attitude. That changed in 1926 with the passage of the Air Commerce Act. In 1938, the Civil Aeronautics Act transferred the federal civil aviation responsibilities from the Department of Commerce (which had been assuming the responsibility of fostering air commerce, issuing and enforcing air traffic rules, licensing pilots, certificating aircraft, establishing airways, and operating and maintaining aids to air navigation since 1926) to a new independent agency, the Civil Aeronautics Authority (CAA). In addition to these responsibilities, the CAA had new authority to regulate airline fares and to determine the routes that air carriers would serve. This economic regulation was designed to promote the growth of the commercial airline industry and protect consumers (Preston, n.d.).

In 1940, the CAA was split into two agencies: the Civil Aeronautics Administration (CAA) and the Civil Aeronautics Board (CAB). The CAA was responsible for ATC, airman and aircraft certification, safety enforcement, and airway development, while the CAB was responsible for safety rulemaking, accident investigation, and economic regulation of the airlines. In 1941, the CAA began assuming responsibility for takeoff and landing operations at airports. Finally, in 1946, the CAA was assigned the added task of administering the first federal-aid airport program (Preston, n.d.).

FAA, DOT, and NTSB

The Federal Aviation Agency was created by the Federal Aviation Act of 1958. As discussed in Chapter 1, several very visible midair collisions served as the impetus for this Act. In June 1956, there was a midair collision over the Grand Canyon between a United Airlines DC-7 and a TWA Lockheed L-1049. In April 1958, a United Airlines DC-7 experienced a midair collision with a U.S. Air Force fighter jet. Then in May 1958, a Vickers Viscount was involved in a midair collision with a Lockheed T-33 being operated by the Air National Guard over Brunswick, Maryland. These three midair collisions resulted in a total 189 fatalities. The newly created FAA was granted broad authority to combat aviation hazards. Additionally, the FAA assumed safety rulemaking from the CAB and had sole responsibility for developing and maintaining a common system of air navigation and air traffic control (civil and military).

Even with the newly created FAA, concern remained about the lack of a coordinated transportation system. Therefore, in 1966, Congress authorized the creation of the Department of Transportation (DOT), which combined all major federal transportation responsibilities. The DOT began operations on April 1, 1967. Also on that day, the Federal Aviation Agency became one of several model organizations within DOT and was renamed the **Federal Aviation Administration (FAA)**. Today, the DOT consists of the following departments/agencies:

- Office of the Secretary of Transportation
- Federal Aviation Administration
- Federal Highway Administration
- Federal Motor Carrier Safety Administration
- Federal Railroad Administration
- Federal Transit Administration
- Maritime Administration
- National Highway Traffic Safety Administration
- Office of Inspector General
- Pipeline and Hazardous Materials Safety Administration
- Research and Innovative Technology Administration
- Saint Lawrence Seaway Development Corporation
- Surface Transportation Board

Clearly, the FAA is the most involved with aviation, and as a result, this is the DOT agency that airport personnel most often interact with.

The DOT Act of 1966 also transferred the accident investigation role of the Civil Aeronautics Board to the new National Transportation Safety Board (NTSB), which was an independent agency within the DOT. In 1974, the NTSB was established as a completely separate entity outside of the DOT via

The Independent Safety Board Act of 1974. The NTSB promotes transportation safety via:

- Congressionally mandated independence and objectivity;
- Accident investigations and safety studies;
- Airman and mariner certification appeals;
- Advocating and promoting safety recommendations; and
- Assisting victims of transportation accidents and their families.

The NTSB has five board members, each nominated by the President and confirmed by the Senate to serve five-year terms. A member is designated by the President as chairman and another as vice chairman for two-year terms. The chairmanship requires separate Senate confirmation.

The NTSB is concerned with all transportation safety, which obviously includes aviation safety. As a result, airport personnel may be called upon to work with the NTSB if an accident occurs at the airport. The NTSB investigates and reports on all U.S. air carrier accidents, commuter and air taxi accidents, midair collisions, serious mishaps involving government aircraft, and all fatal general aviation accidents. The NTSB also investigates accidents involving both civilian and military aircraft, and accidents involving military aircraft where the functions of the FAA are at issue. Internationally, the NTSB investigates major accidents involving U.S. air carriers and U.S.-manufactured air carrier aircraft under the auspices of the **International Civil Aviation Organization (ICAO)**. The NTSB typically delegates to the FAA (commonly a **Flight Standards District Office [FSDO]**) the investigation of non-fatal, general aviation accidents involving fixed-wing aircraft of less than 12,500 pounds, home-built aircraft, crop dusters, and rotorcraft.

If an accident occurs and the NTSB conducts the investigation, it will be either a field office investigation or a headquarters investigation. Fatal general aviation crashes, as well as some air carrier and commuter accidents with relatively minor injuries, are often investigated by a single field investigator from one of the NTSB's regional offices. On the other hand, major accidents are handled by a "**Go Team**" from NTSB headquarters in Washington, DC. The "Go Team" consists of an Investigator-In-Charge (IIC) and technical specialists. Committees known as "groups" have responsibility for specialized components of the investigation, and may include an operations group, structures group, maintenance group, air traffic control group, weather group, and witness group. The investigation of a major air carrier accident also typically includes a member of the Board and a public affairs officer, who will assume responsibility of media relations.

During a major investigation, daily meetings are held to review progress in the investigation. Notes are taken, draft reports are discussed, and various theories as to the cause of the crash are explored. It should be noted that the Board does not conduct investigations for the purpose of determining all causes with certainty. NTSB investigations are terminated after finding the "probable" cause. Field investigations result in a factual report, from which the investigator recommends a probable cause determination to the Board. The Board then reviews field investigation reports and votes to adopt, reject or modify the probable cause determination recommended by a field investigator. With major accident investigations led by NTSB Go Teams, each group chairman prepares a report and submits it to the Investigator-In-Charge. The Investigator-In-Charge then prepares a draft NTSB report and submits it to the Board for review. The Board may conduct public hearings to gain more insight into the cause of the accident. The Board then meets and determines probable cause, resulting in a published final report.

DHS and TSA

In addition to aviation safety, the federal government is involved with securing the aviation system. The events of September 11, 2001, forever changed the landscape of aviation security in the United States. As a result of those events, Congress passed the Aviation and Transportation Security Act on November 19, 2001. This Act established the Transportation Security Administration (TSA) and gave it three major mandates:

- Secure all modes of transportation;
- Recruit, assess, hire, train, and deploy Security Officers for 450 commercial airports from Guam to Alaska in 12 months; and,
- Provide 100 percent screening of all checked luggage for explosives by December 31, 2002.

Prior to this, the airlines were responsible for passenger and baggage screening. However, as a result of the events of September 11, Congress felt that the airlines were doing an inadequate job. In reality, the screening functions had been contracted out to numerous security companies of varying capabilities that often paid minimum wages and offered minimal training to screeners. Further concentrating national security efforts, the Department of Homeland Security was created on November 25, 2002, by the Homeland Security Act of 2002. As part of this Act, the TSA was moved from the DOT to the new Department of Homeland Security (DHS) in March 2003.

As of 2015, the TSA employed 50,000 transportation security officers that screen 2 million passengers each day at more than 450 airports nationwide (see Figure 11-3). The TSA also deployed approximately 2,800 behavior detection officers at airports across the country, utilized more than 400 TSA explosives specialists, deployed thousands of federal air marshals on domestic and international flights each day, and both trained and deployed approximately 800 explosives detection canine teams to airports and mass transit systems across the nation (TSA, n.d.[b]; TSA, n.d.[c]).

Prior to the creation of the TSA, airport managers dealt with the FAA and typically the FAA Civil Aviation Security Field Unit (CASFU) locally regarding airport security matters. Today, however, airport personnel interact regularly

Figure 11-3. Transportation Security Administration (TSA) screening checkpoint.

(Wikimedia Commons; see credit on page 624)

with the TSA regarding airport and airline security. Locally, the Federal Security Director (FSD) is the ranking TSA authority responsible for leadership and coordination of TSA security activities. The Assistant Federal Security Director—Regulatory Inspection serves as the principal advisor to the Federal Security Director on all matters concerning enforcement and compliance with security directives pertaining to airport and aviation security for Category X and Large Category I and II Airports. This Assistant FSD—Regulatory Inspection manages an inspection program for compliance by airlines, vendors, and other airport tenants and business interests with airport and aviation security policies and requirements. The Assistant Federal Security Director—Screening has responsibility for passenger security screening, managing a staff of security screeners, checkpoint supervisors, and screening managers who conduct screening, manage screening operations, and administer laws, regulations, and policies pertaining to TSA's aviation security program (TSA, n.d.[a]).

ICAO

The International Civil Aviation Organization (ICAO) is a specialized agency of the United Nations, and was established on December 7, 1944, via the Chicago Convention (also known as the Convention on International Civil Aviation). The purpose of ICAO is to promote the safe and orderly development of international civil aviation throughout the world through the creation of standards and regulations necessary for aviation safety, security, efficiency and regularity, as well as for aviation environmental protection. The ICAO is comprised of 191 member states, including the United States.

Although the ICAO operates on an international scale, and an airport manager will interact almost universally with the FAA and TSA, it is helpful to be aware of the role of ICAO and standards and recommended practices that are generated by ICAO. Often, the activities of the FAA can be traced back to

ICAO recommendations or requirements. Consider safety management systems (SMS) as an example. The ICAO first required SMS for the management of safety risk in air operations, maintenance, air traffic services and aerodromes in Annexes 1, 6, 8, 11, and 14 beginning in 2001. The FAA SMS rulemaking process then stemmed from this ICAO requirement.

CBP

In addition to the TSA, **Customs and Border Protection (CBP)** plays an important role in securing the borders and protecting the United States from threats. The CBP represents the largest law enforcement agency within the Department of Homeland Security with more than 58,000 employees serving both nationwide and overseas. The primary mission of the CBP is to prevent terrorists and terrorist weapons from entering the United States, while allowing legitimate travel and trade. This involves apprehending individuals attempting to enter the United States illegally; minimizing the flow of illegal drugs and other contraband; protecting agricultural and economic interests from harmful pests and diseases; protecting American businesses from theft of intellectual property; and regulating and facilitating international trade, collecting import duties, and enforcing U.S. trade laws (U.S. Customs and Border Protection, 2010).

Airport managers and personnel will likely interact with the CBP during the processing of passengers and crew on inbound international flights. The CBP has very strict access requirements for airport personnel needing access to the Federal Inspection Station (FIS) area, generally requiring airport personnel to undergo additional background checks and receive a special FIS access clearance. Airports are required to maintain areas where inbound international passengers can be screened separately by CBP and remain segregated from domestic passengers until after being allowed access to the United States. This is typically in the form of separate international arrivals terminals or in the basement (or ramp level) of an existing terminal building.

OSHA

Lastly, the **Occupational Safety and Health Administration (OSHA)** was established by the Occupational Safety and Health Act of 1970. The role of OSHA is to assure safe and healthful working conditions for workers by setting and enforcing standards and by providing training, outreach, education, and assistance. As part of the Department of Labor, OSHA is most concerned with protecting workers and ensuring a safe working environment. As a result, airports are required to provide personal protective equipment (PPE) to workers, material safety data sheets (MSDS) for personnel handling various chemicals, etc.

Industry Relations

In addition to interacting with governmental entities (both at the federal, state, and local levels), airport managers and personnel may also join various industry associations. Industry associations generally support their members by providing representation in Washington, DC, information on issues affecting members, and networking opportunities with other members. In essence, industry trade associations serve their members by ensuring effective industry relations.

INDUSTRY TRADE ASSOCIATIONS

AAAE

The **American Association of Airport Executives (AAAE)** was established in 1928 and currently represents nearly 5,000 individual members, including 3,000 airport professionals representing nearly 850 different airports. AAAE has evolved into a multi-functioning organization that not only represents airports' interests to those on Capitol Hill, but also provides a number of services to airports and individual members.

First, AAAE has an active legislative affairs team referred to as the Airport Legislative Alliance. The role of the Legislative Alliance is to represent airports nationwide by petitioning Congress for increased AIP funds and increased PFCs, as well as keeping the membership informed of changes in the political landscape, including newly elected officials and proposed and approved legislation. The role of the Legislative Alliance is a very typical role for industry associations that are based in the Washington, DC, area. Similar to the Legislative Alliance, AAAE also has a Regulatory Affairs Department, which is focused on representing airports before key executive agencies, including the Department of Transportation, the Federal Aviation Administration, and the Environmental Protection Agency.

AAAE's Transportation Security Policy team represents airports before key federal leaders in aviation security and homeland security. The team also keeps airports informed on the most recent issues affecting aviation security. This team created the Transportation Security Clearinghouse (TSC), which is a non-profit arm of AAAE that operates in partnership with the TSA to ensure security threat assessments (STA) and Criminal History Record Checks (CHRC) are accomplished for aviation workers who require access to the secure areas of airports. According to AAAE, the TSC is the nation's largest civilian clearinghouse, processing over 1.3 million TSA-mandated security threat assessments and more than half a million biometrically based Criminal History Records Checks annually (AAAE, n.d.).

One of AAAE's strengths lies in the hundreds of meetings, conferences and training events the association holds each year. Whether in the form of their annual conference, regional conferences, Basic or Advanced Airport Safety and Operations Specialist (ASOS) Schools, or Certified Member or Airport

Certified Employee (ACE) training, AAAE provides plenty of opportunities each year for members to enhance their knowledge of the industry or specific topics and network with other airport professionals.

AAAE also has additional tools that are helpful in training airport professionals, such as Interactive Employee Training (IET) and Airport News and Training Network (ANTN) Digicast. These industry training tools are widely utilized by airports. IET is an airport-specific, on-site training program that an airport contracts with AAAE to develop. However, ANTN is a web-based training platform that any airport can gain access to by paying a subscription fee. In addition, AAAE's publications such as *Airport Report Today*, *Airport Magazine*, and *Aviation News Today* are all extremely beneficial for airport professionals.

ACI and ACI-NA

In addition to AAAE, the **Airports Council International (ACI)** exists to represent airports on a global scale. According to ACI, they are the only global trade representative of the world's airports. ACI was established in 1991 and represents the world's airports to governments and international organizations such as ICAO. Prior to the formation of ACI in 1991, the world's airports were represented by the Airport Associations Coordinating Council (AACC). ACI also develops standards, policies and recommended practices for airports, and provides information and training opportunities for airport personnel. To better represent North American airports, ACI created **ACI-North America (ACI-NA)**. It was formed in 1948 as the Airport Operators Council (AOC). The purpose of ACI-NA is to represent airports throughout North America to federal decision makers in Washington, DC, keep airports up-to-date on issues affecting them, conduct research for the benefit of airports, and provide networking, training, and educational opportunities.

AOPA

The main industry association representing GA pilots and GA aircraft owners is the **Aircraft Owners and Pilots Association (AOPA)**. The AOPA has a membership of more than 400,000 pilots and aviation enthusiasts in the United States. According to AOPA, the organization is the largest, most influential aviation association in the world. AOPA supports GA by advocating on behalf of members; educating pilots, nonpilots, and policy makers; supporting activities that ensure the long-term health of general aviation; fighting to keep general aviation accessible to all; and securing sufficient resources to ensure success. AOPA also provides member services such as legal services, advice, and other assistance; insurance; aircraft buying assistance; aircraft financing; and networking and educational opportunities. This is often the first organization that student pilots join.

EAA

The **Experimental Aircraft Association (EAA)** also represents pilots and owners of aircraft. The EAA was initially founded in 1953 by a group of individuals who were interested in building their own airplanes. Today, however, the EAA membership includes pilots and owners of antiques, classics, warbirds, aerobatic aircraft, ultralights, helicopters, and contemporary manufactured aircraft. Less of a lobbying organization, the EAA is designed to develop camaraderie among those who fly, build, and restore recreational aircraft. Various local chapters often host monthly fly-ins, pancake breakfasts, and Young Eagle flights. Most popular with those who are 8 to 17 years old, the Young Eagle program provides free flights in a GA aircraft by EAA volunteers which are designed to introduce children to aviation.

NBAA

The **National Business Aviation Association (NBAA)** represents businesses that own and operate aircraft used for business purposes. Founded in 1947 and based in Washington, DC, the NBAA is the leading organization for companies that rely on general aviation aircraft to help make their businesses more efficient, productive and successful. NBAA represents more than 10,000 companies and provides more than 100 products and services to the business aviation community, including the NBAA Business Aviation Convention and Exhibition, the world's largest civil aviation trade show.

A4A

Airlines for America (A4A), formerly known as the Air Transport Association (ATA), is an industry association representing U.S. airlines. Founded by a group of 14 airlines in 1936, A4A endeavors to promote a business and regulatory environment that ensures safe and secure air transportation in the United States. The organization is designed to enable U.S. airlines to flourish, stimulating economic growth locally, nationally and internationally. In the past, this organization has been at odds with AAAE on important economic issues, such as raising the cap on PFCs. Generally, AAAE supports lifting or raising the cap, while A4A is against this.

IATA

The **International Air Transport Association (IATA)** is an international trade body created over 60 years ago by a group of airlines. Today, IATA represents some 240 airlines comprising 84 percent of total air traffic. To some degree, it could be argued that the IATA is the international arm of A4A, although they are not related.

NATA

The **National Air Transportation Association (NATA)** represents aviation service businesses such as fixed base operators, charter providers, aircraft management companies (including those supporting fractional shareholders), maintenance and repair organizations, flight training providers, and airline service companies. NATA was established in 1940 and promotes safety and the success of aviation service businesses through its advocacy efforts before government, the media and the public. It also provides various programs for the benefit of members, such as the NATA Safety First program—a line service safety training program.

RAA

The **Regional Airline Association (RAA)** is an industry association that represents smaller, regional airlines. The RAA also represents manufacturers of products and services supporting the regional airline industry to Congress, the DOT, the FAA and other federal agencies. It could be said that in effect the RAA is the regional arm of A4A, although they are not related. With more than 13,000 regional airline flights every day, regional airlines operate more than 50 percent of the nation's commercial service.

AIA

The **Aerospace Industries Association (AIA)** represents manufacturers and suppliers of civil, military, and business aircraft, helicopters, unmanned aircraft systems, space systems, aircraft engines, missiles, material and related components, equipment, services, and information technology. Although the AIA may not be an association that an airport manager would be acquainted with, it is one of the oldest associations in the aviation industry, having been established in 1919.

GAMA

Established in 1970, the **General Aviation Manufacturers Association (GAMA)** represents over 70 of the world's leading manufacturers of fixed-wing general aviation airplanes, engines, avionics, and components. The purpose of GAMA is to foster and advance the general welfare, safety, interests and activities of general aviation. This includes promoting a better understanding of general aviation and the important role it plays in economic growth and in serving the transportation needs of communities, companies and individuals worldwide.

GRASSROOTS EFFORTS

Most important to the future of general aviation are efforts at the grassroots level by many of the various industry trade associations to make aviation more attractive. Consider "GA Serves America" by AOPA. This site is designed to educate visitors about the benefits of GA and the many ways in which GA is used to serve America. AOPA also developed the "Be a Pilot" program, designed to increase the number of student pilots. EAA developed "Reach for the Sky," a brochure designed to generate interest in flying. Various associations have also developed teacher's modules for grades K–12 designed to provide teachers with curriculum to introduce students to aviation. These efforts have experienced varying levels of success. What is important to note is that the industry has taken responsibility for promoting general aviation, rather than relying on the FAA to handle this.

Public Relations

In addition to relating to the government and industry, airport managers must also relate to the public. In fact, public relations is integral to the success of an airport in the eyes of the community. Regardless of the number of non-stop airline flights or available automobile parking spots, if the community does not have a positive image of the airport, it can be quite detrimental to the airport. Indeed, a public relations disaster is not the goal of any airport manager.

COMMUNITY RELATIONS

First, the airport must be relatable to the community. Especially for GA airports, the at-large community often has no interest in the airport and sees the airport as only supporting the hobby of the rich. Worse, if the airport is not financially self-sufficient, the community may have a very negative view of it as a drain of community resources. Therefore, it is important, for the airport manager and other senior airport personnel to be present in the community, proactively delivering a positive message of the value of the airport and its benefits to the community. This may include presentations at the Chamber of Commerce, Rotary Club, schools, and other community groups. It should involve an overview of the services provided by the airport, including air ambulance, aircraft firefighting, and flight training. If the airport has conducted an economic impact study, it is important to present these positive findings as well. In short, community relations involves educating the community. To do this effectively, the airport manager must remain proactive.

Role and Value of Interest Groups

An interest group is defined as any voluntary association that seeks to publicly promote and create advantages for its cause. Interest groups may include corporations, charitable organizations, civil rights groups, neighborhood associations, and professional and trade associations. Fortunately, an interest group may be very supportive of an airport, such as the Cattaraugus County-Olean Airport Support Group in Ischua, New York:

> "The purpose of the Cattaraugus County-Olean Airport Support Group, formed in 2005, is to act as a driving, unified and proactive advisory force to ensure promotion of the airport as a key area resource, the upgrade of general facilities maintenance and execution of an ongoing capital improvement program. Specific areas of focus include:
>
> - Acting as a facilitator between the county, the city, airport users and airport supporters, providing continuous open channels of communication.
> - Aggressively educating the county, city and public at large, providing accurate and factual information regarding the importance of the airport to the entire area.
> - Providing technical support to the city and airport staff in selection and prioritization of general facilities maintenance, equipment upgrades and capital improvements.
> - Providing technical assistance to the city in acquisition of federal, state, county and private funding.
> - Advising and assisting the city, jointly with the Greater Olean Area Chamber of Commerce (GOACC), with promotional advertising and organizing airport promotional events—air shows, fly-ins, open houses, tourism literature, Web site design, etc."
>
> (Cattaraugus County Olean Airport, n.d.)

Another example of a supportive airport interest group is the Grove Airport Support Group in Grove, Oklahoma:

> "The mission of the Grove Airport Support Organization is to promote our airport to the community at large by executing annual events such as the Fly-In Breakfast and Fly-by-the-Pound, Promote Aviation Safety through seminars and identifying areas of potential facility improvements for the Grove, OK aviation and business community."
>
> (Grove Airport Support Group, n.d.).

Much to the dismay of airport managers, however, interest groups can also show negative support for the airport. Perhaps the most unified national voice against aircraft and airport noise is Stop the Noise. A non-profit origination based in Harvard, Massachusetts, the organization works to "restore quiet to the skies above our communities by causing FAA to enforce existing regulations regarding aerobatic flight and by working to bring about changes in the FAA regulations and in the FAA culture" (Stop the Noise, 2008). There are also numerous anti-airport organizations at the local level. Citizens Against Airport

Pollution, in San Jose, California, is "dedicated to protecting and restoring the environmental quality of the Santa Clara Valley. We focus on noise, air and water quality, as well as other critical environmental issues to keep our neighborhoods clean and quiet" (Citizens Against Airport Pollution, 2012). They have filed lawsuits against the City of San Jose to prevent airport expansion, claiming a lack environmental review, significant noise, and detrimental impacts on wildlife. A sampling of other interest groups that oppose airport expansion and noise include Residents Against Airport Expansion in Delco (Delaware County, Pennsylvania); Concerned Residents Against Airport Pollution in Santa Monica, California; and the New Jersey Coalition Against Aircraft Noise.

Clearly, interest groups that support an airport are much easier for an airport manager to work with. Interest groups that oppose an airport can generate substantial negative press and create considerable difficulties for the airport manager. As a result, the airport manager must make efforts to reach out to these groups and endeavor to find common ground. Ignoring their efforts will likely create a major public relations issue for the airport.

MEDIA RELATIONS

Airport managers must recognize the power of the media. Even in small communities with one GA airport, the local media has a significant impact on the community and can greatly affect the community's perception of the airport, either in a positive or negative sense. It is important to utilize the media for the benefit of the airport in a proactive way, rather than attempting to respond to negative media publicity after the fact. Some ways to do this include press releases, inviting the media to the airport for a tour, contacting the media with "stories" that are newsworthy, and developing a relationship with transportation reporters. All of these are proactive efforts on the part of the airport manager. In other words, it is best not to sit and hope that news coverage will be positive. Rather, the airport manager can actually generate positive press by feeding positive stories and news to the right person in the media (see Figure 11-4).

Figure 11-4. Media relations.

(auremar/Shutterstock.com)

CUSTOMER SERVICE

Customer service is one area which has suffered neglect in recent years. Consider the phone call to a national cable network, insurance company, or satellite provider. Inevitably, the caller will be greeted by an automated voice and presented with a dizzying array of menu choices from which to select. Eventually, and with enough patience, the caller may be granted an opportunity to speak with an actual person. Almost universally, callers feel this is poor customer service. However, companies have transitioned to automated phone systems to increase efficiency and more effectively direct calls to the correct person. It is important, therefore, for companies (including airports) to balance efficiency with the need for positive customer service.

Excellent airport customer service has been defined as "the synergy created when an airport's ability to exceed its customers' needs and expectations consistently matches its customers' perception that their needs and expectations are well met" (Paternoster, 2007, p. 218). It is important for airports to adopt a practice of exceeding customer expectations. For a period of time, Tampa International Airport's motto was "Going above and beyond." By adopting this slogan, the airport made it clear to passengers, tenants, and the community that customer service was a top priority and all efforts would be taken to exceed customer expectations.

Although there is a great deal of guidance available on customer service, the ten rules below perhaps best summarize what airports should be endeavoring to do on the customer service front:

- Understand the customer.
- Be a good listener.
- Identify and anticipate needs.
- Make customers feel important and appreciated.
- Help customers understand your methods and procedures.
- Learn how to say "Yes."
- Know how to apologize.
- Give more than expected.
- Get regular feedback.
- Treat internal customers (employees) well.

Although these rules may seem obvious, points such as regarding employees as internal customers may not be as obvious. Airports often focus on passengers and tenants, but may forget that internal employees are also customers. It is important to treat fellow coworkers with the same level of respect, understanding, and appreciation as you would treat your customers. After all, if employees aren't happy and morale is low, they in turn will not treat customers well, which will lead to lost revenues, lost customers, and lost opportunities for providing exceptional customer service.

EVENTS

Events are yet another way to generate publicity for an airport. Typically, these events are in the form of an airshow, open house, fly-in, or grand opening of a terminal or other facility. They can also be in the form of banquets, holiday parties, or conferences. By holding an event and inviting the general public, the airport is able to enhance the public perception of the airport and give something back to the community. Events can be expensive, so a careful analysis of costs and benefits will be necessary, but airports are often willing to incur the expenses associated with such events due to the positive publicity they produce.

SOCIAL MEDIA

The most recent form of public relations involves online media in the form of social interaction. In fact, a large percentage of the U.S. population utilizes various forms of social media (with Facebook being the most popular). Other services such as Twitter, LinkedIn, and Pinterest are also popular and being used by some airports. In essence, if current and potential customers are online, why shouldn't airports meet these customers online? Social media has allowed airports to effectively interact with current and potential customers in real-time.

Airports can effectively utilize social media by creating a Facebook page and keeping it current with new information. Contests and other giveaways will generate interest and allow the page to increase in popularity. Some airports effectively utilizing social media such as Facebook have a staff person dedicated to maintaining the page and can even post status updates on parking garage availability, security screening wait times, and food and beverage specials. Other airports have developed applications (apps) that allow customers to check on flight times/status, parking availability, maps of terminals, etc.

Concluding Thoughts

It is important for airport leadership to be politically aware both internally and externally. In other words, airport professionals should not only be able to interact and develop mutually beneficial relationships at the federal, state, and local levels, as well as with industry trade associations, but also be aware of the media and current and prospective customers/passengers. This requires airport professionals to be politically aware and in tune with the external environment.

Chapter Summary

- The State Block Grant Program, administered by the FAA, provides a lump sum to the state, which then provides funds to the individual airports within the state based on project needs and priority.
- Whether a city, county, city/county, parish, authority, or some other form of municipal entity, the local level is the level at which ownership and operation of public-use airports typically occurs.
- Whether there is a specific body that governs the airport or the airport falls under a more general decision-making body, airport managers must continually communicate with these officials to make certain that airport needs (as well as community benefits) are well understood.
- The parliamentary authority outlined in Robert's Rules of Order is widely recognized and adhered to as the most effective and formal means of holding meetings of civic, charitable and governmental organizations.
- The process whereby new regulations or revised regulations are first introduced is the notice of proposed rulemaking (NPRM) process.
- The manner by which the FAA provides guidance internally is typically through FAA orders.
- FAA advisory circulars (ACs) provide advice to airports on the acceptable means (in accordance with the FAA Administrator) for complying with a regulation or other requirement.
- The NTSB typically delegates to the FAA (commonly a FSDO) the investigation of non-fatal, general aviation accidents involving fixed-wing aircraft of less than 12,500 pounds, home-built aircraft, crop dusters and rotorcraft.
- Major accidents are handled by a "Go Team" (from NTSB Headquarters) that consists of an Investigator-In-Charge and technical specialists.
- The Department of Homeland Security (DHS) was created on November 25, 2002, by the Homeland Security Act of 2002. As part of the Act, the Transportation Security Administration (established by the Aviation and Transportation Security Act on November 19, 2001) was moved from the DOT to the new DHS.
- The International Civil Aviation Organization (ICAO), a specialized agency of the United Nations, was established on December 7, 1944, via the Chicago Convention to promote the safe and orderly development of international civil aviation throughout the world through the creation of standards and regulations necessary for aviation safety, security, efficiency and regularity, as well as for aviation environmental protection.

- Customs and Border Protection (CBP) plays an important role in securing the borders and protecting the U.S. from threats, representing the largest law enforcement agency within the DHS, with more than 58,000 employees serving both nationwide and overseas.
- The Occupational Safety and Health Administration (OSHA) was established by the Occupational Safety and Health Act of 1970 and aims to assure safe and healthful working conditions for workers by setting and enforcing standards and by providing training, outreach, education, and assistance.
- The American Association of Airport Executives (AAAE) was established in 1928 and currently represents nearly 5,000 individual members, including 3,000 airport professionals representing nearly 850 different airports.
- The Airports Council International (ACI) exists to represents airports on a global scale, while ACI—North America represents North American airports.
- The main industry association representing GA pilots and GA aircraft owners is the Aircraft Owners and Pilots Association (AOPA).
- The Experimental Aircraft Association (EAA) also represents pilots and owners of aircraft, especially smaller recreational, homebuilt, and experimental aircraft.
- The National Business Aviation Association (NBAA) represents businesses that own and operate aircraft used for business purposes.
- Airlines for America (A4A), formerly known as the Air Transport Association (ATA), is an industry association representing U.S. airlines.
- The International Air Transport Association (IATA) is an international trade body created over 60 years ago by a group of airlines.
- The National Air Transportation Association (NATA) represents aviation service businesses such as fixed base operators, charter providers, aircraft management companies, maintenance and repair organizations, flight training providers, and airline service companies.
- The Regional Airline Association (RAA) is an industry association that represents smaller, regional airlines.
- The Aerospace Industries Association (AIA) represents manufacturers and suppliers of civil, military, and business aircraft, helicopters, unmanned aircraft systems, space systems, aircraft engines, missiles, material and related components, equipment, services, and information technology.
- The General Aviation Manufacturers Association (GAMA) represents over 70 of the world's leading manufacturers of fixed-wing general aviation airplanes, engines, avionics, and components.

- Public relations is integral to the success of an airport in the eyes of the community.
- An interest group is defined as any voluntary association that seeks to publicly promote and create advantages for its cause, and may include corporations, charitable organizations, civil rights groups, neighborhood associations, and professional and trade associations.
- The local media has a significant impact on the community and can greatly affect the community's perception of the airport, either in a positive or negative sense.
- Excellent airport customer service has been defined as the "the synergy created when an airport's ability to exceed its customers' needs and expectations consistently matches its customers' perception that their needs and expectations are well met."
- Events, such as an airshow, fly-in, or terminal grand opening, are yet another way to generate publicity for an airport.
- The most recent form of public relations involves online media in the form of social interaction, and airports that are on the leading edge of customer service have tapped into the various forms of social media to interact with their customers.

Review Questions ↘

1. Explain the typical role of state aviation agencies.
2. Explain the State Block Grant Program (including listing participating states).
3. Explain the role of an airport advisory board.
4. Explain Robert's Rules of Order (including the most important Rules to remember).
5. Explain the purpose of a "notice of proposed rulemaking."
6. Explain the purpose of advisory circulars (ACs).
7. In what ways does the National Transportation Safety Board promote transportation safety?
8. Under what circumstances would the NTSB delegate accident investigation authority to a Flight Standards District Office?
9. What were the three original mandates for the Transportation Security Administration (TSA)?
10. Which individuals would an airport manager most likely interact with regarding passenger screening at an airport?
11. Explain the role of the International Civil Aviation Organization (ICAO).
12. Explain the role of the Occupational Safety and Health Administration (OSHA).
13. Explain the purpose of the American Association of Airport Executives (AAAE).
14. Explain the purpose of the National Business Aviation Association (NBAA).
15. Explain the purpose of Airlines for America (A4A).
16. Explain the role and value of interest groups.
17. Explain how an airport manager can ensure effective media relations.
18. Explain how an airport manager can ensure positive customer service.
19. Explain the role of events in generating publicity for an airport.
20. Explain how an airport can effectively use social media in offering positive customer service.

Scenarios

1. As the airport manager of a small, GA airport, you are preparing for the monthly airport board meeting. The meeting topics will include old business (approval of minutes from past meeting), and new business (issuing an RFP for a new FBO operator; pay raise of 3 percent for staff, which total 5 employees not including yourself; a review of the number of noise complaints received during the past quarter; and an update on the new terminal construction project). Prepare an agenda for this meeting, and talk through the actions to be held during the meeting using Robert's Rules of Order.
2. As the airport manager of a city-owned and operated airport, you must present your budget request to the city manager and city council each year just as other city department heads must do. To ensure your airport gets a fair share of funds, what are some "selling points" you can bring forth during your presentation to the city manager and city council?
3. As an airport manager of a small, GA airport, which industry trade associations would you be a member of as an individual, and which would your airport be a member of as an organization, and why?
4. As an airport manager of a large, commercial-service airport, which industry trade associations would you be an individual member of, and which would your airport be an organization member of, and why?
5. You are the newly appointed airport manager of a small, GA airport that has been neglected by the community. In fact, the community has been pressuring the mayor to close the airport and turn it into a city park. What approach would you take to change this public perception? Prepare a detailed public relations strategy.

References and Resources for Further Study

American Association of Airport Executives. n.d. "Transportation Security Clearinghouse." Retrieved from http://www.aaae.org/federal_affairs/transportation_security_policy/tsc.cfm

Cattaraugus County Olean Airport. n.d. "Support Group." Retrieved from http://oleanairport.org/support/

Citizens Against Airport Pollution. 2012. "Mission Statement." Retrieved from http://www.caap.org/

Federal Aviation Administration (FAA). 2012. "Offices." Retrieved from http://www.faa.gov/about/office_org/

Grove Airport Support Group. n.d. "Grove, OK Municipal Airport." Retrieved from https://sites.google.com/site/groveokmunicipalairport/

New Hampshire Department of Transportation (NHDOT). 2009. "Block Grant Program." Retrieved from http://www.nh.gov/dot/org/aerorailtransit/aeronautics/programs/blockgrants.htm

Paternoster, J. 2007. "Excellent airport customer service meets successful branding strategy." *Airport Management* 2 (3): 218–226.

Preston, E. n.d. The Federal Aviation Administration and Its Predecessor Agencies. Retrieved from http://www.centennialofflight.net/essay/Government_Role/FAA_History/POL8.htm

Stop the Noise. 2008. "Who we are." Retrieved from http://stopthenoise.org/

Transportation Security Administration (TSA). n.d.(a) "Airport Security Careers." Retrieved from http://www.tsa.gov/careers/airport-security-careers

———. n.d.(b) "TSA by the numbers." Retrieved from http://www.tsa.gov/sites/default/files/publications/pdf/tsabythenumbers_final.pdf

———. n.d.(c) "What is TSA?" Retrieved from http://www.tsa.gov/about-tsa

U.S. Customs and Border Protection. 2010. "We are CBP!" Retrieved from http://www.cbp.gov/xp/cgov/careers/customs_careers/we_are_cbp.xml

Chapter 12

Properties, Contracts, and Commercial Development

Objectives

Upon completion of this chapter, you should understand:

- the role of agreements in airport management
- the purpose and meaning of aeronautical lease agreements
- airline operating agreements
- the difference between signatory and non-signatory airlines
- the purpose of majority-in-interest provisions
- airline lease agreements
- residual-cost and compensatory rate-making methodologies
- the role of concessionaires and the manner by which airports earn revenues from concessionaires
- FBO agreements
- the purpose and role of minimum standards
- land leases
- MOUs and LOAs
- the terms and conditions of agreements
- rules and regulations
- self-fueling
- through-the-fence operations
- exclusive rights
- how to effectively interact with tenants
- the aeronautical and non-aeronautical commercial development of airports
- Disadvantaged Business Enterprise

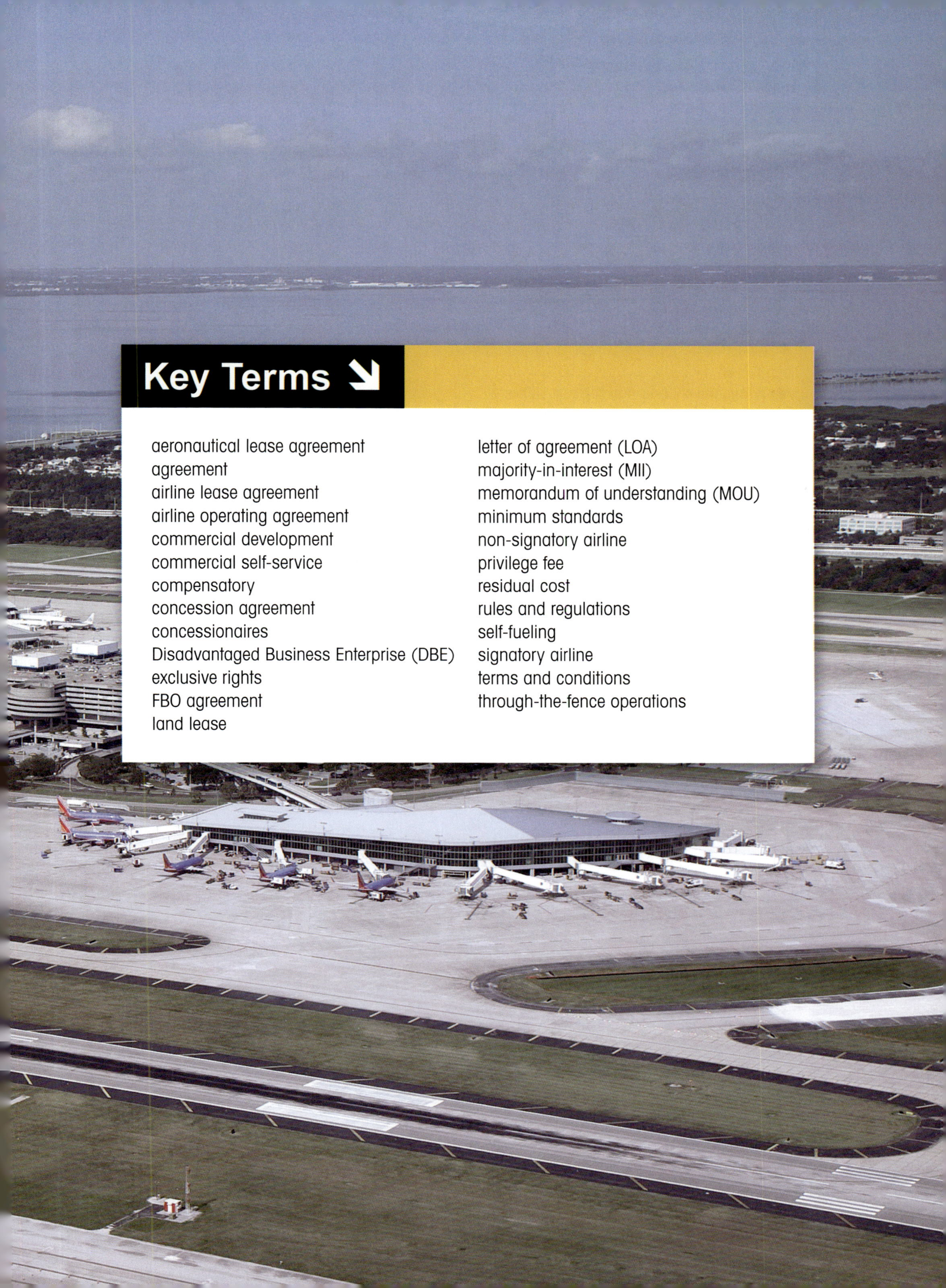

Key Terms ↘

- aeronautical lease agreement
- agreement
- airline lease agreement
- airline operating agreement
- commercial development
- commercial self-service
- compensatory
- concession agreement
- concessionaires
- Disadvantaged Business Enterprise (DBE)
- exclusive rights
- FBO agreement
- land lease
- letter of agreement (LOA)
- majority-in-interest (MII)
- memorandum of understanding (MOU)
- minimum standards
- non-signatory airline
- privilege fee
- residual cost
- rules and regulations
- self-fueling
- signatory airline
- terms and conditions
- through-the-fence operations

In Chapter 12

Agreements **463**
- Airline Agreements 463
- Concession Agreements 466
- FBO Agreements 467
- Land Lease 471
- Memorandums of Understanding and Letters of Agreement 472
- Considerations 472

Interacting with Tenants **478**

Commercial Development **479**
- Aeronautical 481
- Non-Aeronautical 481

Disadvantaged Business Enterprise **483**

Information Systems **483**

Concluding Thoughts **484**

Chapter Summary **485**

Review Questions **487**

Scenarios **488**

References and Resources for Further Study **489**

FEATURES

The Columbus Regional Airport Authority Signs New Airline Lease Agreements 465

New airline lease agreements provide guarantees to the airport as well as the airlines.

Smyrna Airport Business Park 480

By developing an airport business park, this airport has generated additional revenues from airport land.

Agreements

Airports often own hundreds of acres of land and accommodate dozens of tenants that provide a number of different services. Since these vendors operate on land owned by the airport and airports recover revenue as a result of this, airports enter into **agreements** to clearly spell out the expectations, liabilities, lease rates, and other terms and conditions related to tenants being on airport property. In the world of business, including airport business, verbal agreements and understandings are not sufficient. Written agreements are the formal practice used to specify agreements and understandings between two or more parties. Although agreements with airport-based vendors, tenants, and others are quite common, airports may also enter into agreements with entities off-airport, such as nearby military bases or community organizations. In essence, lease agreements and operating agreements exist to protect the airport from uses that are detrimental to its operation and development, and arrange for revenues to be recovered from those operating on airport property.

Each agreement is specific to the tenant/vendor and the unique purpose of the agreement. **Aeronautical lease agreements** are generally designed for two types of airport users: commercial operators/tenants and non-commercial operators/tenants. In essence, commercial operators/tenants are individuals or entities that provide goods or services for a profit. Non-commercial tenants, on the other hand, are individuals or entities not using the airport in a for-profit manner. In practice, agreements can be very simple, perhaps totaling no more than one page. More commonly, however, agreements are rather complex, numbering 10–20 pages or more in length. Regardless of their length and purpose, agreements generally contain some common elements:

- Specific information about the property the tenant is allowed to use
- Responsibilities for utilities and other costs
- Language allowing property inspections for lease compliance
- Conditions under which the lease may be terminated
- Financial terms of the agreement
- Expiration dates for the agreement
- Escalation clause allowing rates to be revisited and adjusted over time or in the event of a significant change

AIRLINE AGREEMENTS

One of the most common agreements at commercial-service airports is the airline agreement. Airlines generally will be party to two agreements at an airport: an operating agreement and lease agreement.

First, the airline will enter into an **airline operating agreement** to obtain the authorization to land at the airport. This agreement will specify any landing fees, passenger facility charges to be collected, the process and deadlines by which revenues must be submitted, use of the airport, etc. In an effort to differentiate between airlines that may operate only one or two flights per week or seasonally and those that operate on a daily basis, airports have developed the terms signatory and non-signatory.

Signatory airlines enter into a fixed term agreement with the airport, and as a result, gain benefits such as lower landing fees (Figure 12-1). At Orlando International Airport, for example, to be categorized as a signatory airline, the airline must lease at least one preferential gate and other space in the terminal that is deemed sufficient by the executive director and totals at least 5,000 square feet. **Non-signatory airlines** operate limited or seasonal service and generally do not enter into a signatory agreement, so they are required to pay slightly higher landing fees and per-use fees for their use of the airport facilities. Non-signatory airlines at Orlando International Airport include airlines providing scheduled service to the airport, airlines operating from the airport's common facilities, airlines operating from the facilities of a fixed base operator (FBO), and cargo carriers using facilities other than the terminal facilities generally on a per-use basis.

Figure 12-1. Signatory air carrier.

Majority-in-interest (MII) provisions refer to the degree of control given by the airport to the signatory airlines allowing these airlines to approve or disapprove capital expenditures and possibly even provide input into the budget, including fees, rates, and charges. MII provisions are more common at residual-cost airports than those with compensatory approaches (discussed later in this chapter). Signatory airlines generally have majority-in-interest.

Typical components of an airline operating agreement include:

- Definitions
- Term
- Rights of airline

- Maintenance, operation, use and condition of airport
- Airline rates and charges
- Other fees and charges
- Rules and regulations
- Indemnity and insurance
- Assignment and sub-use
- Taxes
- Default and cancellation
- Prohibited uses
- Federal grants and non-discrimination
- Miscellaneous

Second, airlines generally enter into an **airline lease agreement** (for land and/or facilities) occupied by the airline. A land lease is used for a maintenance hangar, reservations call center, or other facility that occupies airport land. An airport will generally never sell any land to a tenant, so if a tenant needs to have a facility on-airport, a land lease is entered into for the purpose of specifying the exact terms and conditions associated with the airline occupying airport-owned land. Land leases are usually on a per-acre or per-thousand-square-feet basis (depending on the amount of land being occupied). A facility lease is used for baggage claim space, a baggage claim office, ticket counter space, gate space, operations offices, and airline offices that occupy space in an airport-owned building, typically a terminal. Facility leases are generally on a per-square-foot

The Columbus Regional Airport Authority Signs New Airline Lease Agreements

In 2009, the Columbus Regional Airport Authority, owner and operator of Port Columbus International Airport, signed a new five-year airline lease agreement with the ten signatory airlines serving Port Columbus, which include Air Canada Jazz, AirTran, American, Chautauqua, Continental, Delta, Midwest, Southwest, United, and US Airways. The new lease agreement expanded revenue sharing with the airlines while holding down rent, landing fees and other airline charges. Specifically, the new agreement required the airport authority to share 75 percent of its annual net operating income after debt service and capital fund requirements with the airlines. The revenue sharing was to be paid to the airlines in the form of rent credits. In this way, the cost of doing business at the airport for airlines would be offset, while providing an incentive for airlines to maintain and expand service. In essence, higher airline activity would result in greater revenue sharing and, therefore, reduced airport charges. The former airline lease agreement included a fixed, pre-negotiated credit regardless of net revenues to the airport, which did not incentivize greater airline activity. The new agreement allows for a larger sum to be provided to the airlines tied to activity levels.

(Columbus Regional Airport Authority, 2009)

basis, with the monthly lease rate being based upon the price per square foot and the amount of square feet the airline occupies.

Additionally, airports must choose one of two general rate-making methodologies. Airline agreements and the rates and charges that airlines are assessed can be developed on a residual-cost basis or compensatory basis. These two methodologies differ in the manner in which airlines accept responsibility, possess authority over capital projects and budgets, and are assessed rates and charges (such as landing fees). Although the specific methodology in use at an airport is closely tied to revenues (addressed in chapter 13), the methodology also has an effect on airline agreements. Specifically, the **residual cost** approach requires airlines to collectively assume significant financial risk by agreeing to pay any costs of running the airport that are not allocated to other users or covered by nonairline sources of revenue. In essence, the airport measures revenues from all sources other than the airlines, and the amount necessary to then "break-even" is charged to the airlines in the form of landing (or other) fees. The residual cost approach is popular among smaller, less busy airports that often don't have significant sources of nonairline revenues, such as food and beverage concessions, auto parking, etc. With this approach, the airport is always assured of breaking even, but at the same time, the airport gives up some control over capital development to the airlines. In essence, the airlines have veto power over any expenditures that will result in higher landing fees to them.

The **compensatory** approach, on the other hand, requires the airport to assume the major financial risk of running the airport, with the airlines charged fees and rental rates based on the actual costs of the facilities and services that they use. With this approach, the airport is not guaranteed to break even, but on the other hand, it can generate substantial revenues. Thus, this approach is more popular at larger airports with significant sources of nonairline revenues.

CONCESSION AGREEMENTS

Airports also have tenants that offer food, beverages, or products (such as books, retail goods, etc.). These tenants are considered **concessionaires** (see Figure 12-2). Due to these concessionaires both occupying space within an airport-owned facility (such as a terminal building) and earning revenues on airport-owned property, a **concession agreement** is entered into. This agreement will specify the area that may be occupied by the concessionaire, and the percentage of revenues and any minimum privilege fee that will be payable to the airport, including the process and deadlines by which these payments must be submitted. A **privilege fee** is often paid to the airport by the concessionaire for the privilege of conducting business at the airport. Even if the concessionaire doesn't earn any revenues, the airport will still be paid a privilege fee and lease rate for the space occupied by the concessionaire.

Figure 12-2. Airport concessions.

Although concession agreements vary in length and scope, the typical components of an agreement include:

- Premises
- Term
- Rent, fees, reporting, records, and audits
- Permissible uses
- Standard of operation
- Disadvantaged Business Enterprise
- Construction and capital investment
- Maintenance, utilities, and repairs
- Cash deposit and surety bond
- Insurance and indemnification
- Termination without cause
- Default and remedies
- Assignment and sublease
- General provisions

FBO AGREEMENTS

If an airport has a fixed base operator on site, the airport will enter into an agreement with this tenant. The FBO will not only occupy either an airport-owned or (more often) an FBO-owned building on airport property, but will also earn revenues and engage in services such as flight instruction, aircraft sales, aircraft charter, aircraft maintenance, line service, etc. (Figure 12-3). The

Figure 12-3.
Fixed base operator (FBO).

FBO agreement must address the facility use and land use of the FBO, as well as the commercial aeronautical services offered by the FBO. Whereas each airline will generally have two agreements in effect with an airport (operating agreement and land or facility lease), airports often combine the facility/land lease and the operating agreement into one agreement with an FBO. This agreement will specify the facility or land occupied by the FBO and the lease rate for that space; the services to be offered by the FBO; and any other revenues the airport will collect from the FBO (usually a fuel flowage fee per gallon of aviation fuel sold by the FBO—to be discussed in chapter 13).

Components of an FBO agreement may include:

- Property description
- Building construction
- Term
- Rent and user fees
- Insurance
- Lessee Rights
- Maintenance of buildings
- Right to inspect
- Lease transfer
- Laws and regulations
- Hold harmless
- Quiet enjoyment
- Signs
- Obstruction lights
- Fair and nondiscriminatory services
- Nonexclusive rights

- Affirmative action
- Aircraft service by owner or operator
- Hours of operation
- Airport closings
- Snow removal
- Taxes
- Airport development
- Lessor's rights
- Obstructions
- Subordination of provision
- Performance bonds
- Financial disclosure
- Default
- Rights after termination
- Arbitration

One unique aspect of FBOs operating on an airport is the development of **minimum standards** to which an FBO must adhere. Not only will minimum standards set minimum service and quality levels, but these standards will also aid in preventing economic discrimination and the granting of an exclusive right to conduct aeronautical activities at the airport, both of which are violations of federal and state grant obligations. Airports are encouraged by the FAA to ensure providers of aeronautical services (such as FBOs) meet certain standards. It is in the airport's best interest to hold all aeronautical operators/providers on the airport to a high level of quality, which will reflect positively on the airport and ensure top-quality services for users. Beyond simply hoping that this occurs, however, airports develop minimum standards, incorporate these standards into the agreement they enter into with the provider, and regularly audit or inspect the provider to make certain these standards are being met.

Although the development of minimum standards is optional, the FAA strongly recommends that airports hold FBOs to certain standards, and thus has developed Advisory Circular 150/5190-7, *Minimum Standards for Commercial Aeronautical Activities* (FAA, 2006). According to the FAA, minimum standards are meant to ensure a safe, efficient and adequate level of operation and services to the public. However, these standards must be reasonable and not unjustly discriminatory.

Specifically, 150/5190-7 states that minimum standards should be developed to "promote safety in all airport activities, protect airport users from unlicensed and unauthorized products and services, maintain and enhance the availability of adequate services for all airport users, promote the orderly development of airport land, and ensure efficiency of operations" (FAA, 2006, p. 3). When developing minimum standards, it is important to consider each aeronautical activity and the operating environment at the airport. In essence, minimum standards should be tailored to each specific aeronautical activity at the airport. For the FAA to support an airport's minimum standards, the airport must:

1. Apply standards to all providers of aeronautical services, from full service FBOs to single service providers;
2. Impose conditions that ensure safe and efficient operation of the airport in accordance with FAA rules, regulations, and guidance;
3. Ensure standards are reasonable, not unjustly discriminatory, attainable, uniformly applied and reasonably protect the investment of providers of aeronautical services to meet minimum standards from competition not making a similar investment;
4. Ensure standards are relevant to the activity to which they apply; and
5. Ensure standards provide the opportunity for newcomers who meet the minimum standards to offer their aeronautical services within the market demand for such services.

(FAA, 2006, p. 4)

The advisory circular contains specific questions to be answered in developing minimum standards. These questions address fuel sales; personnel requirements; airport and passenger services; flight training activities; aircraft engine/accessory repair and maintenance; skydiving; ultralight vehicles and light sport aviation; and fractional aircraft ownership. Clearly, not all of these activities may be present on an airport; thus, airports will need to develop minimum standards unique to their own activities (Figure 12-4) (FAA, 2006).

Items to consider in developing minimum standards are shown in Table 12-1.

Figure 12-4.
On-airport business.

Table 12-1. Considerations for developing minimum standards.

Category	Considerations
Fuel sales	Fuel tank locations and access Use of fuel trucks Fuel capacity and types of fuel for various aircraft Fuel supply Liability insurance for fueling operator
Personnel requirements	Number of trained and qualified personnel Training and qualifications of personnel
Flight training activities	Type of flight training offered Office space the school is required to maintain Full- or part-time training Type of aircraft Aircraft storage and maintenance provisions Coordination and contact with Flight Standards District Office
Aircraft engine accessory repair and maintenance	Types of services offered to the public Repair station ratings Qualifications of repair station employees Space requirements Standard parts storage space Lighting and ventilation requirements Safe spray painting, cleaning, or machining space
Skydiving, ultralight or sport aviation	These aeronautical activities must be accommodated at federally-obligated airports; however, airports may prohibit or limit these activities based on the operational safety of the airport, subject to FAA approval.

(Center for Transportation Studies, 2007, p. 2)

LAND LEASE

General **land leases** are utilized for any organization/entity that uses land on an airport. If this use is on a long-term, daily basis, the land lease may be incorporated into another agreement, such as an FBO agreement. However, if an organization, such as the Experimental Aircraft Association (EAA), only needs to utilize a specific portion of airport land for a one-week period (such as for an airshow), a land lease is created and entered into to specify liabilities, expectations, and other terms and conditions.

Generally, a land lease for short-term use will include:

- Leasehold
- Terms and conditions
- Lease payments
- Insurance
- Use of premises
- Utilities

- Repairs, maintenance, and appearance
- Alterations and improvements
- Waiver
- Time is of the essence
- Default
- Termination of use
- Mortgaging of leasehold
- Indemnity

MEMORANDUMS OF UNDERSTANDING AND LETTERS OF AGREEMENT

Although not as extensive as leases and other formal agreements, a **memorandum of understanding (MOU)** or **letter of agreement (LOA)** may be developed to specify terms of understanding or agreement between two parties. An MOU is generally less formal and can even be used for internal terms of understanding. For instance, an MOU may be developed to specify areas of agreement between an airport and union employees (such as police officers), or an airport and its community advisory group. An LOA may be more formal and is usually between the airport and an external organization—such as, for example, the FAA for an informal runway use program, or the EAA for an airshow/fly-in.

All MOUs and LOAs have common elements, such as the initial foundation, phrased in terms of "Whereas" statements. The action items are phrased as "Therefore" statements. In essence, an MOU or LOA simply states areas of agreement, cooperation, or understanding between both parties signing the document. It may have a defined term (such as one year) or an indefinite term.

CONSIDERATIONS

In developing use, lease, and operating agreements, airport staff must consider a number of items. These considerations are integral to ensuring a fair agreement that cannot be challenged and would be upheld by the FAA. In fact, airlines have challenged airports in the past by filing complaints with the FAA. Tenants other than airlines have also filed complaints. Informal complaints are filed under 14 CFR Part 13 (investigated by FAA regional staff), while formal complaints are filed under 14 CFR Part 16 (investigated by FAA headquarters). Parties filing under Part 16 must be substantially affected by the alleged noncompliance. Occasionally, these complaints have resulted in an FAA determination that the airport was not in compliance with grant assurances or federal regulations. Therefore, in developing an agreement, it is crucial to address specific considerations.

Terms and Conditions

Terms and conditions refer to the general items spelled out in the agreement. These terms and conditions can cover a number of topics, such as:

Subordination to federal and state obligations—All agreements should clearly state that the agreement is subordinate to the airport's federal and state obligations. It must also specify that tenants must comply with current and future federal grant assurances and conditions of state aid. Subordination to local ordinances and codes may be specified as well.

Use of premises—Agreements must specify the area that is being leased on the airport, as well as specifying the use of those leased premises. This includes what services are to be provided by the party to the agreement, as well as those activities that are prohibited. It is also important to include the non-exclusive right to conduct certain aeronautical activities. For instance, if the airport currently has one FBO, it should be made clear that a second FBO may be added in the future and/or that tenants can conduct self-fueling, etc.

Term—The term of agreements should be long enough for a tenant to fully amortize their initial investment, but not so long that it relinquishes the airport owner's control over the property. A term of 20–25 years is common, with anything over 30 years being uncommon. Depending on the agreement's purpose, an FBO agreement may be for only 3–5 years with several 1–3 year extensions. It is important for agreements to include an escape clause which allows the airport owner to terminate the lease if the land is needed for airport improvement or other purposes. There will always be a stipulation that the agreement can be cancelled due to noncompliance with the agreement. If appropriate, agreements should also contain a reversion clause stipulating that upon termination of the lease, all improvements (financed by the tenant or otherwise) revert back to the airport, regardless of how the lease is terminated.

Rates—Rates specified in agreements should be fair, reasonable, and competitive. Clearly, rates will vary depending on size, function, location, and level of improvements to the land and facilities being leased. Rates should result in maximum revenue, while also including an escalation clause which allows the rate to be increased over the term of the lease. This rate of escalation is usually tied to the Consumer Price Index (CPI) or another mechanism that the airport chooses, provided that the escalation is uniformly applied to all tenants.

Airport operation, maintenance, and development—Airport agreements should not interfere with the airport owner's ability to operate, maintain, and develop the airport. The airport must retain the right to temporarily close the airport or any of the facilities and to construct any new facilities. The airport should also be willing to terminate or amend a lease or agreement as necessary to allow for future development of the airport. Additionally, although the airport owner should protect its right to operate, maintain, and develop the airport, it should be clear that the airport owner is not responsible for maintaining privately leased areas. The lessee should be responsible for general maintenance, repairs, and grounds upkeep, as well as improvements on leased land.

Security requirements—It is important for tenants and parties of agreements to be aware of the security requirements of the airport. Security is everyone's responsibility, including tenants on the airport. Leases and other documents should require compliance with any current or future aviation-specific, state or federally-mandated security requirements.

Tenant liabilities—It is important for the airport to be protected from liabilities incurred by the tenant. To ensure adequate protection, agreements should include a hold harmless clause and adequate insurance requirements, with a minimum level of comprehensive liability insurance for the activities to be carried out by the party to the agreement. Likewise, agreements should contain an environmental/hazardous substance contamination clause that will hold tenants responsible for any damaging environmental impact they may cause.

Economic nondiscrimination—Agreements should also require tenants to engage in reasonable and nondiscriminatory practices. FAA grant assurance number 22, Economic Nondiscrimination, presents specific language for such a requirement.

Inspections—Agreements should require tenants to allow the airport owner or representative access to the leased premises for both announced and unannounced inspections. This is necessary to confirm compliance with the lease, airport rules and regulations, minimum standards, and any applicable local, state, and federal codes, statutes, ordinances, rules, regulations and/or grant assurances. If the tenant prevents the airport owner or representative from gaining access for such an inspection, this should be grounds for termination of the agreement.

Rules and Regulations

In addition to minimum standards for commercial aeronautical activities, airports develop **rules and regulations** that set the standards for airport users. Although these may be in the form of local ordinances, it is beneficial for rules and regulations to be developed as a stand-alone document specific to the airport. Rules and regulations may address vehicle and pedestrian rules; air traffic patterns; security; sanitation; restriction of access to certain areas; fire protection; fueling of aircraft; storage of hazardous materials; hangar use; personal conduct; commercial and non-commercial activity; First Amendment activities; fire and safety; aeronautical activities; motor vehicles; commercial ground transportation; and penalties.

One topic which is most commonly included in rules and regulations is First Amendment activities. In the past, airports have had to confront those using an airport terminal for First Amendment activities such as picketing, petitioning, etc. As an example, the Hillsborough County Aviation Authority (Tampa, Florida) has incorporated the following statement on First Amendment activities within their rules and regulations:

> The Authority has neither intended to operate the passenger terminal complex as a public forum for First Amendment activities nor allowed any such expressive activities to be conducted freely on its premises. The passenger terminal complex is not a traditional public forum for the conduct of First Amendment activities, and the Authority has not consented, agreed, operated or designated its facilities in such a manner so as to consent or agree that such facilities are or were a public forum.
> (HCAA, 2011, p. 11)

Self-Fueling

Aircraft owners and operators have the right to service their own aircraft. In fact, an aircraft owner or operator may "tie down, adjust, repair, refuel, clean, and otherwise service his/her own aircraft, provided the service is performed by the aircraft owner/operator or his/her employees with resources supplied by the aircraft owner or operator" (FAA, 2007, p. 4). This right includes the right to self-fuel. **Self-fueling** involves the fueling of aircraft on a corporate hangar ramp or other location on airport by the owner or operator (or own employees) of the aircraft. Self-fueling and other self-services cannot be contracted out to another party. Additionally, fuel used for self-fueling purposes can be obtained by the aircraft owner from a source of his/her preference. It is important for the FBO to understand this right, as the FBO will very possibly be losing fuel sales as a result (Prather, 2009).

Although an airport must allow for self-fueling, reasonable rules and regulations or standards can be implemented and must be adhered to by the aircraft owner or operator when servicing his/her own aircraft. If unreasonable restrictions are imposed on the aircraft's owner or operator regarding the servicing of their own aircraft, an exclusive rights violation may have occurred.

Due to the complexities involved and the liabilities assumed, self-fueling activities often require separate standards, most appropriately specified in an individual operating directive or policy. It is important to understand that commercial self-service is different than self-fueling. Self-fueling refers to "the fueling or servicing of an aircraft...by the owner (or operator) of the aircraft with his or her own employees and using his or her own equipment" (FAA, 2007, pp. 9–10). It is this right that is protected at all federally obligated airports.

Commercial self-service, on the other hand, allows owners and operators of aircraft to taxi to a fuel pump on the airport and fuel up in a self-service format. As stated by the FAA, commercial self-service is "a fueling concept that enables a pilot to fuel an aircraft from a commercial fuel pump installed for that purpose by a fixed base operator (FBO) or the airport sponsor" (FAA,

2007, p. 4). Some airports without an FBO may only have fueling in a commercial self-service format. Other airports may have an FBO and a commercial self-service fuel pump. Owners and operators of aircraft then have a choice of whether to fuel up in a full-service fashion at the FBO or a self-service fashion at the self-serve pump. Often, fuel at self-serve pumps is priced lower than at the full-service FBO, to reflect the "do-it-yourself" savings. It should be noted that airports may or may not provide for commercial self-service fueling.

Through-the-Fence Operations

Through-the-fence operations refer to those activities that permit an individual or organization access to the airfield without actually being located on the airfield. Thus, although the individual or organization has access to the airfield, the airport exercises no control over this individual or organization. According to the FAA, through-the-fence "permits access to the public landing area by independent operators offering an aeronautical activity or to owners of aircraft based on land adjacent to, but not a part of, the airport property" (FAA, 2006, p. 7).

Consider a local electronics supplier located off airport that has contracted with a Cessna 210 pilot to pick up a small shipment each morning and fly the shipment to a supplier at another airport. This arrangement could be conducted "through the fence," in which the local electronics supplier literally uses a box installed in a cut-out of the perimeter fence next to the FBO that enables something to be placed in the box from off airport, and then enables the pilot on the AOA side of the ramp to pick this shipment up and load it onto the aircraft. Another example of through-the-fence operations can be found at residential airparks. In this arrangement, individuals have access to the airport and can taxi their aircraft from their homes to the taxiways and runways, and yet the airport exercises no authority over these individuals. Generally, all airport tenants, whether an airline or a private individual with an aircraft in a private hangar or tie-down, must comply with the airport's rules and regulations. However, the airport has no authority to require a private individual or company located off-airport to comply with the airport's rules and regulations.

In 2011, the FAA issued an interim policy on residential through-the-fence (RTTF) access agreements at federally-funded airports. The policy outlined the requirements that airport sponsors were required to follow to continue RTTF agreements at federally funded airports. Specifically, this policy addressed situations in which people who own residential property with aircraft storage facilities near an airport have access to the airport from off-airport property.

The interim policy required airport sponsors with existing agreements to develop an airport access plan that outlined how the airport will meet its obligations to operate as a public-use airport, including how the airport sponsor would meet standards for control of the airport, safety of operations, self-sustainability, and nondiscriminatory airport rates. For those airports without RTTF access agreements, new RTTF agreements were prohibited. According to the FAA,

"RTTF agreements that are not consistent with the FAA's new policy may introduce safety risks by creating direct access to runways or taxiways, impede a sponsor's ability to collect appropriate fees, or limit the airport's ability to address future growth" (FAA, 2011). This policy only applied to federally-funded airports, and did not include non-federally obligated, privately-owned airports.

In February 2012, these requirements were formally codified in the FAA Modernization and Reform Act of 2012. Section 136 of this law permits general aviation airports, as defined by the statute, to enter into residential through-the-fence agreements with property owners or an association representing property owners. These agreements must comply with specific terms and conditions contained in the law. Further, in July 2013, the FAA issued another policy on RTTF, which replaced the 2011 interim policy. This 2013 policy addressed through-the-fence access to a federally-obligated airport from an adjacent or nearby property, when that property is used as a residence. Specifically, for the co-location of homes and aeronautical businesses, airports are required to execute two separate agreements with the homeowner. One agreement must address the duration, rights, and limitations of the homeowner's residential through-the-fence access, and the second agreement must be consistent with the FAA's current policies on commercial through-the-fence activities and ensure the off-airport business does not result in unjust economic discrimination for on-airport aeronautical service providers (FAA, 2013). Readers are encouraged to verify the current status of through-the-fence by visiting the FAA website pertaining to this topic at http://www.faa.gov/airports/airport_compliance/residential_through_the_fence/

Exclusive Rights

Airports are required by federal grant assurances to avoid granting exclusive rights. **Exclusive rights** are defined as "a power, privilege, or other right excluding or debarring another from enjoying or exercising a like power, privilege, or right. An exclusive right can be conferred either by express agreement, by the imposition of unreasonable standards or requirements, or by any other means" (FAA, 2007, p. 8). The prohibition on granting exclusive rights is spelled out in FAA Grant Assurance 23, Exclusive Rights. It states, "[the airport operator] will permit no exclusive right for the use of the airport by any person providing, or intending to provide, aeronautical services to the public" (FAA, 2012, p. 11). In essence, the FAA's position is that if an airport has been developed or improved with federal funding, the airport needs to be operated for the use and benefit of the public, which means it should be available for all types, kinds, and classes of aeronautical activity and without granting an exclusive right. The intent of the prohibition on exclusive rights is to promote fair competition at federally obligated, public-use airports for the benefit of aeronautical users.

Note that even with this prohibition, an airport can have just one FBO, for example. This is specifically addressed in Grant Assurance 23. The providing of services by one FBO is not considering granting an exclusive right if (a) it would be unreasonably costly, burdensome, or impractical for more than one fixed based operator to provide such services and (b) if allowing more than one fixed based operator to provide such services would require the reduction of space leased pursuant to an existing agreement between such single fixed based operator and such airport. Also, an airport sponsor can deny a prospective aeronautical service provider the right to engage in an on-airport aeronautical activity for reasons of safety and efficiency (for instance, no parachute activity allowed at a busy, commercial-service airport).

Interacting with Tenants

An airport without tenants is an airport that likely is struggling financially. Granted, many airports have no "real" tenants, such as an airline, FBO, or aircraft maintenance provider. Even so, these airports may have tenants in the form of based aircraft, even if all of these aircraft are owned by private individuals. If an airport has no tenants, and charges no landing fees or fuel flowage fees, the airport has little feasible way of earning revenues. Therefore, tenants on airports are more common than not, and the presence of tenants requires airport staff to interact with them.

How should airport staff interact with tenants? The answer is professionally and fairly, yet firmly and in a straightforward manner. This requires airport staff to remain professional at all times and appreciate the role tenants play on the airport and in the local community. Each tenant must also be treated fairly. This is not the time to show favoritism, because word will get out that—for example—one tenant was allowed to conduct commercial activities out of their private hangar, while other tenants were prohibited from doing the same. The key in being fair is to utilize the airport's rules and regulations, and apply this equally across the board. In fact, experience has shown that tenants will respect airport staff for equally applying rules and regulations to all tenants. Being firm and straightforward is required as well, as some tenants may try to convince or persuade airport staff that their activities are not that bad after all. In fact, some tenants can be very persuasive in convincing airport staff of how their activities or practices actually benefit the airport.

Managing an airport does require the ability to be flexible and make decisions on a per-case basis; being 100 percent black-and-white in the interpretation of rules and regulations may not be in the best interest of the airport. For instance, airport rules and regulations, similar to federal regulations, cannot be specific to every situation that may arise at an airport. For example, if the rules and regulations prohibit commercial activities from being conducted in a private hangar, and this is discovered by airport staff, the individual must be instructed to cease the activity, but a certain amount of time may be allowed for this individual to cease the activity. Additionally, even though the activity is in violation of the lease agreement, and grounds exist to terminate the lease, the airport does benefit (in the form of revenues) from the tenant's occupation of the premises, so the lease would not necessarily be terminated because of the activity. Thus, the goal is to maintain tenants on the airport and ensure compliance with the rules and regulations, but the manner in which tenants are treated and provided opportunities to cease and desist activities that are not in compliance with the rules and regulations is important.

Commercial Development

Airports often have hundreds, or perhaps thousands, of acres of land. An airport may choose to put this land to work rather than leave it vacant. **Commercial development** defines this concept. To properly develop airport land, the FAA recommends the following:

- Develop a service plan for providing the access and utility improvements for land that could be utilized.
- Establish a strategy for funding the infrastructure improvements required for commercial development.
- Airport marketing can be instrumental in developing land and leasing airport property.
- Develop a good relationship with your community economic development entity and/or chamber of commerce.

(Briggs, 2012)

Many smaller airports (with or without commercial airline service) have ensured financial self-sufficiency by developing land and/or making it available for commercial services. Although some airports are more successful than others in this regard, promoting the use of airport land for commercial activities provides a number of benefits for various stakeholders. First, this will generate additional revenues for the airport. Second, by making more aeronautical services available, users of the airport will benefit. Third, bringing in additional businesses on the airport will result in jobs and tax revenues for the community (and state).

The airport must have in mind intended uses of land before promoting the commercial development of the airport. This will often be spelled out in the airport master plan. For instance, land adjacent to a taxiway is often best used by an FBO, corporate hangars, aircraft maintenance hangars, or private aircraft hangars. Land on airport that is not in close proximity to taxiways and ramps may be best used as a business/office park, golf course, or industrial building. The airport may possibly have several hundred acres that could be set aside for a home improvement store or retail shopping center. A go-cart track or miniature golf course are other possibilities. To effectively develop the airport with

Smyrna Airport Business Park

The Smyrna-Rutherford County Airport Authority, owner and operator of the GA/Reliever Smyrna Airport, in an effort to better utilize airport land and generate additional revenues, developed the 400 acre Smyrna Airport Business Park. This master-planned development offers aviation sites with direct access to the AOA, and is appropriate for corporate headquarters and commercial or industrial needs. According to the business park website, the park provides attractive lease rates/terms, access to three major interstates, all utilities, high-speed internet, and more than 60 acres of ramp space. For firms interested in developing a site within the business park, the steps to success are to schedule an initial visit, obtain a copy of property guidelines, submit a letter of interest, develop and sign a land lease agreement with the airport, develop engineering and architectural design plans, obtain approval of the plans, begin construction, and eventually move in.

(Smyrna-Rutherford County Airport, n.d.)

commercial activities, it is important for airport staff to think outside the box. Recognize that airports will rarely sell their land; rather, the airport will enter into a long-term land use which allows the commercial developer to build a facility on airport property, or the airport agreeing to build the facility, with regular land lease payments being paid to the airport.

One important consideration to remember is that commercial development on the airport may compete with commercial development in the local community. For instance, if an airport develops a business/office park on airport property, this park will compete with any other available commercial space for lease or sale in the local community. Real estate development is not without risk, especially if millions of dollars are invested to build a facility before the first tenant is signed up. There are more than several examples of airports that have invested significant sums of money to develop airport land and the facilities sit vacant today. To avoid this risk, airports should make land available for development, but prospective tenants should pay to build the facility of their choice and then enter into a land lease for the land occupied by the facility. Often, after a certain number of years (30–50, for instance) the facility may revert back to the airport. After all, the tenant will not be able to haul the building with them if they move to another location off airport.

It should be noted that airports generally do not pay real estate taxes. However, real estate taxes generally are assessed and must be paid for hangars and other improvements built by airside users on long-term land leases.

AERONAUTICAL

Aeronautical development of the airport includes facilities and services that benefit airport users (owners and operators of aircraft). The most common form of aeronautical development includes an FBO. An airport may only have one FBO, which is not considered an exclusive right if there is only enough activity (demand) on the airport for one FBO to be successful. However, many airports have more than one FBO. In any event, having an FBO on airport is an aeronautical form of commercial development that will benefit both the airport in the form of revenues and users in the form of desired aeronautical services.

In addition to FBOs, other aeronautical forms of commercial development may be considered. This may include aircraft maintenance facilities, aircraft paint shops, avionics shops, aircraft hangars, flight schools, etc. In reality, an airport should consider any businesses or use of airport property compatible with airport operations that will benefit airport users.

NON-AERONAUTICAL

An airport may also consider development with non-aeronautical forms of commercial activity—that is, businesses and activity that are not directly aeronautical, but still produce benefits. However, a balance is required between aeronautical and non-aeronautical use of the airport. Specifically, non-aeronautical use must not interfere with the aviation use of the airport. Airports must ensure that the use of the property does not jeopardize future airport development, and does not create or contribute to a flight hazard.

Although it may seem that an airport is no place for non-aeronautical activity, many airports have non-aeronautical forms of activity and realize substantial revenues from this activity. Consider that many airports have prime real estate that may be in demand by various businesses and developers, even without need for use of the airport. For instance, food, beverage, and retail concessionaires are very common at airports and represent forms of non-aeronautical activity. Consider a restaurant that just happens to be located in the airport terminal. This restaurant is no more involved in aeronautical activity than that same restaurant located in the downtown area of the community. It just happens that one is located on an airport. Consider shoeshine vendors, massage parlors, toy stores, and postal facilities located on airport property. These are all forms of non-aeronautical activity, and yet they have a very real place on an airport.

These examples of non-aeronautical activity are located within an airport terminal; generally, uses of airport property outside of the terminal buildings will be aeronautical in nature. However, there are airports with a golf course, a regional postal sort facility, a go-cart track, or a home improvement store on their property. One of the most common non-aeronautical uses of airport property is agricultural activity. Although this activity can generate revenues for the airport, there are some factors to consider:

- *Location and height of crops*—Agreements should specify that crops be of low height so as not to interfere with Part 77 surfaces, or visual NAVAIDs.
- *Wildlife attractant*—Generally, grain crops (including corn) can attract wildlife that can be hazardous to aircraft. It is helpful to require agricultural operators to submit crop plans to the airport for approval to prevent hazardous wildlife attractants from being planted and grown on airport property.
- *Equipment*—Equipment used in agricultural activities should also be addressed in the agreement. Specifically, the agreement should address routes to and from the leased area, as well as security requirements (clearances, closing and securing airport gates, etc.), parking, and storage of equipment.
- *Damages*—Lease agreements should require an agricultural operator to prevent damages to airport property, to include ruts, depressions, and the creation of foreign object debris. On the other hand, the airport should not provide for damages to the agricultural operator if crops are damaged or destroyed for reasons such as airport maintenance, operational, or development purposes.
- *Lease rates and terms*—In determining the lease rate for the ground on which agricultural activity will take place, it is important to charge fair market value. In other words, the airport should charge rates similar to those charged for other farmland in the area. Short-term leases for agricultural activities are beneficial, possibly numbering less than five years, with two- to three-year terms preferred. Again, it is important to include an escape clause that will allow the airport to terminate the lease in case the land is needed for other (such as aeronautical) purposes.

(Wisconsin Department of Transportation, 2011)

Often, the following non-aeronautical forms of commercial development can result in substantial revenues for the airport. The more innovative the use, often the higher are the profits for the airport.

- Blueberry farm—Georgia's largest blueberry farm is located on an airport.
- Solar panels—San Francisco, Long Beach, Denver and other airports are allowing for solar "farms" to be built on airport property. These may provide electricity for the airport or the land can be made available to the local utility company with revenues returning to the airport.
- Wind turbines—Boston Logan International Airport has 20 six-foot tall wind turbines on airport property.
- Golf course—Dallas Fort Worth International Airport has two 18-hole championship golf courses on airport property. Other airports with golf courses on airport property include Oakland International Airport (California), Huntsville International Airport (Alabama), and Los Angeles International Airport (California).

Disadvantaged Business Enterprise

Disadvantaged Business Enterprise (DBE) programs are not unique to airports. In fact, the Federal Aviation Administration, Federal Highway Administration, and Federal Transit Administration are three operating administrations within the U.S. Department of Transportation that have a DBE program. The DOT Office of Small and Disadvantaged Business Utilization (OSDBU) oversees these DBE programs. 49 CFR Part 23, Participation of Disadvantaged Business Enterprise in Airport Concessions, and Part 26, Disadvantaged Business Enterprise: Program Improvements, specify the requirements for an airport DBE program.

Specifically for airports, all construction, professional services, and procurement contracts which are funded in whole or in part by federal dollars from the U.S. DOT require the airport to maintain a viable DBE program to promote and maintain a level playing field for all DBEs to compete for and perform on these federally funded contracts. Airports must adhere to nondiscriminatory practices, remove any barriers which may impede DBE participation, assist in the development of DBE firms to compete successfully, ensure that the DBE program is narrowly tailored in accordance with applicable laws, and implement DBE eligibility standards which are consistent with 49 CFR Parts 23 and 26.

Information Systems

Airports are driven by information. Airline information includes gate assignments, baggage claim assignments, arrival and departure information, ticket counter information, and weather information. Airport information includes system information (escalators, elevators, shuttles, monorails, fire alarm systems, access control systems, lightning warning systems, deicing systems), operational information (NOTAMs, training records, etc.), and more. All of this information must be accurate, relayed in a timely manner, and oftentimes integrated (such as in the case of information from several airlines that is integrated into a single source of flight information to benefit patrons of a cell phone waiting lot).

Larger airports often have well-developed information technology (IT) departments. Employees in an IT department develop internal information systems that include personal computers for employees in all airport departments, servers that allow for an internal network (intranet), and a website for the airport. These employees also ensure that the significant amount of information being processed each day at an airport is made available to those who need to know. Integrating data from numerous airlines so that all airport patrons can benefit is also a major responsibility.

Concluding Thoughts

Airports often consist of hundreds of acres of land, with many businesses and activities present. It is imperative to develop agreements to properly govern these businesses, generating revenue for the airport and protecting the airport from any liabilities that may arise. Additionally, airport leadership must be proactive in developing the commercial potential of the airport. These requirements create the need for airport leaders to be well-versed in properties, contracts, and commercial development of airport property.

Chapter Summary

- Lease agreements and operating agreements exist to protect the airport from uses that are detrimental to its operation and development, and arrange for revenues to be recovered from those operating on airport property.
- Aeronautical lease agreements are generally designed for two types of airport users: commercial operators/tenants and non-commercial operators/tenants.
- Airlines generally must sign an operating agreement (for the right to land and operate at the airport) and a lease agreement (for facilities occupied at the airport).
- Airlines will be categorized either as signatory (if exclusively leasing gates on a regular basis, for example) or non-signatory (if offering limited or seasonal service and only needing space on a per-use basis).
- Majority-in-interest provisions refer to the degree of control given by the airport to the signatory airlines to approve or disapprove capital expenditures and possibly even provide input into the budget.
- Airline agreements and the rates and charges that airlines are assessed can be developed on a residual-cost basis (requiring airlines to collectively assume significant financial risk by agreeing to pay any costs of running the airport that are not allocated to other users or covered by nonairline sources of revenue) or compensatory basis (requiring the airport to assume the major financial risk of running the airport, with the airlines charged fees and rental rates based on the actual costs of the facilities and services that they use).
- A concession agreement specifies the area that may be occupied by the concessionaire, the percentage of revenues and any minimum privilege fee that will be payable to the airport, and the process and deadlines by which these payments are submitted.
- The FBO agreement addresses the facility use and land use of the FBO, as well as the commercial aeronautical services offered by the FBO.
- Minimum standards set minimum service and quality levels, but these standards will also aid in preventing economic discrimination and the granting of an exclusive right to conduct aeronautical activities at the airport, both of which are violations of federal and state grant obligations.
- General land leases are utilized for any organization/entity that uses land on airport.

- A memorandum of understanding or letter of agreement may be developed to specify terms of understanding or agreement between two parties. An MOU is generally less formal and an LOA more formal.
- "Terms and conditions" refer to the general items spelled out in the agreement.
- In addition to minimum standards for commercial aeronautical activities, airports develop rules and regulations that set the standards for airport users.
- An airport must allow for self-fueling—the fueling of an aircraft on a corporate hangar ramp or other location on airport by the owner or operator (or own employees) of the aircraft.
- Commercial self-service, which is not required, allows owners and operators of aircraft to taxi to a fuel pump on the airport and fuel up in a self-serve manner.
- Through-the-fence operations refer to those activities that permit an individual or organization access to the airfield without actually being located on the airfield.
- Airports are required by federal grant assurances to avoid granting exclusive rights, which are defined as "a power, privilege, or other right excluding or debarring another from enjoying or exercising a like power, privilege, or right."
- Aeronautical development of an airport includes facilities and services that benefit airport users (owners and operators of aircraft).
- Non-aeronautical development of the airport includes businesses and activities that are not intended to specifically benefit airport users.
- Agricultural activity on airport requires consideration of location and height of crops, wildlife attractants, equipment, damages, lease rates and terms.
- All construction, professional services, and procurement contracts funded in whole or in part by federal dollars from the U.S. DOT require the airport to maintain a viable Disadvantaged Business Enterprise program to promote and maintain a level playing field for all DBEs to compete for and perform on these federally funded contracts.

Review Questions ↘

1. What are the two main purposes of lease agreements and operating agreements?
2. What is the most common agreement at commercial-service airports?
3. Differentiate between signatory airlines and non-signatory airlines.
4. Explain majority-in-interest provisions.
5. Differentiate between airline operating agreements and airline lease agreements.
6. Explain the residual cost methodology.
7. Explain the compensatory methodology.
8. What are concessionaires?
9. What is a privilege fee?
10. Explain minimum standards (including items to consider).
11. Explain the land lease (including typical components).
12. What are MOUs and LOAs?
13. Explain rules and regulations.
14. What is self-fueling?
15. Explain exclusive rights.
16. How should airport personnel interact with tenants?
17. What are the FAA recommendations regarding commercial development of airport land?
18. Differentiate between aeronautical and non-aeronautical uses of airport land.
19. What factors should be considered with on-airport agricultural activity?

Scenarios

1. As airport director, you have been approached by a regional airline desiring to serve the airport with three flights per week to a coastal city. This service will only be in effect from May through August each year. Consider whether this airline will likely be a signatory or non-signatory, will have majority-in-interest, and will benefit from common-use. Also consider the types of agreement(s) that will need to be in place prior to this airline commencing service. Are there any other considerations?

2. As the newly hired director of general aviation, you have been asked by the airport executive director to develop minimum standards to put in place prior to the new FBO commencing operations. What would these minimum standards cover? How would you ensure FBO quality without being unjustly discriminatory?

3. As the director of business development at your airport, you have been tasked with commercially developing airport property. Rather than focusing solely on aeronautical, you have decided to also focus on non-aeronautical uses of airport property. What specific uses would you consider and how would you develop property for both aeronautical and non-aeronautical purposes?

4. A corporate flight department located at the airport for which you serve as airport director just submitted a request to begin self-fueling on their private ramp. Your airport currently has one FBO with full-service fueling (Jet-A and Avgas) and a self-serve fuel pump (Avgas only). How do you respond to their request?

5. You are the director of operations at a medium hub, commercial-service airport. This airport is served by Delta Airlines, Southwest Airlines, Frontier, and Allegiant. Currently, the airport has dedicated gates, holdrooms, ticket counters, baggage belts, baggage service offices, etc. for the exclusive use of these airlines. However, the airport often receives charter operators that need these facilities, but do not serve the airport frequently enough to justify exclusive-use space. The airport has only retained one small ticket counter, one gate (with loading bridge) to accommodate narrow-body aircraft, and one baggage claim belt for use by these charter operators. At times, you have not had the facilities needed to accommodate multiple charter operators at once. Your director has asked for your analysis on how to handle charter operators and use of airport space from this point forward. What do you recommend?

References and Resources for Further Study

Briggs, J. 2012. "How Airports Make Money and What's New in Compliance." Retrieved from http://www.faa.gov/airports/northwest_mountain/airports_news_events/annual_conference/2012/media/how_airports_make_money_and_whats_new_in_compliance.pdf

Center for Transportation Studies. 2007, Summer. "Navigating airport leases and agreements." *AirTap Briefings*. Minneapolis, MN: University of Minnesota.

Columbus Regional Airport Authority. 2009. "Expanded Revenue Sharing a Unique Feature of 5-Year Port Columbus-Airline Lease Agreement." News release, December 7. Retrieved from http://columbusairports.com/files/press-releases/20091207_expanded_revenue_sharing_a_unique_feature_of_5_year_port_columbus_airline_lease_agreement.pdf

Federal Aviation Administration (FAA). 2006. *Minimum Standards for Commercial Aeronautical Activities*. AC 150/5190-7. Washington, DC: FAA.

———. 2007. *Exclusive Rights at Federally-Obligated Airports*. AC 150/5190-6. Washington, DC: FAA. Retrieved from http://www.faa.gov/documentLibrary/media/advisory_circular/150-5190-6/150_5190_6.pdf

———. 2011. "FAA issues residential through-the-fence policy." Retrieved from http://www.faa.gov/news/updates/?newsId=62676&omniRss=news_updatesAoc

———. 2012. "Grant Assurances Airport Sponsors." Retrieved from http://www.faa.gov/airports/aip/grant_assurances/media/airport-sponsor-assurances-aip.pdf

———. 2013. Compliance Guidance Letter 2013-01, FAA Review of Existing and Proposed Residential Through-the-Fence Access Agreements. Retrieved from http://www.faa.gov/airports/airport_compliance/residential_through_the_fence/media/cgl2013_1RTTF.pdf

Hillsborough County Aviation Authority. 2011. "Rules and Regulations for Tampa International Airport." Retrieved from http://m.www.tampaairport.com/about/general_aviation/policies/r330.pdf

Prather, C. D. 2009. "The Right to Self-Fuel." *Legal Research Digest* 8: Retrieved from http://ntl.bts.gov/lib/43000/43800/43861/acrp_lrd_008.pdf

Smyrna-Rutherford County Airport, n.d. "Business Site Opportunities." Retrieved from http://www.smyrnaairport.com/business_sites

Wisconsin Department of Transportation. 2011. "Airport leases: An airport owner and management reference document."

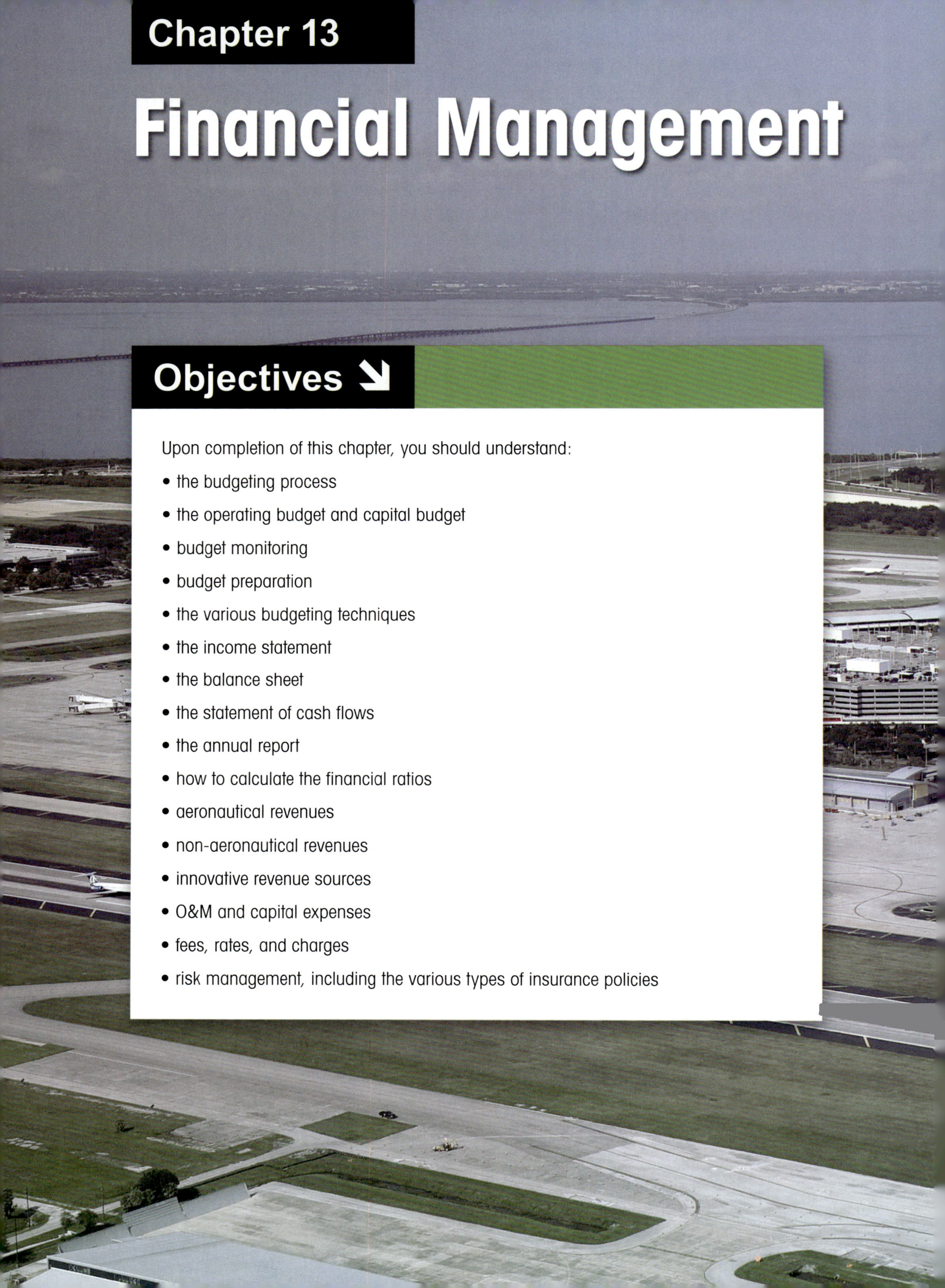

Chapter 13

Financial Management

Objectives

Upon completion of this chapter, you should understand:

- the budgeting process
- the operating budget and capital budget
- budget monitoring
- budget preparation
- the various budgeting techniques
- the income statement
- the balance sheet
- the statement of cash flows
- the annual report
- how to calculate the financial ratios
- aeronautical revenues
- non-aeronautical revenues
- innovative revenue sources
- O&M and capital expenses
- fees, rates, and charges
- risk management, including the various types of insurance policies

Key Terms ↘

activity-based budgeting
aeronautical revenues
annual report
assets
balance sheet
budget
budget monitoring
capital budgeting
capital expenditures
capital improvement plan (CIP)
consolidated rental car facilities (CONRAC)
cost of sales
current assets
current liabilities
current ratio
debt service safety margin
debt-to-asset ratio
depreciation
dividends
expenses
fees, rates, and charges
financial plan
financial ratios
financial statements
financing activities
fiscal year
fixed assets
fixed expenses
food and beverage (F&B) concession
fuel flowage fees
gross profit
hydrant fuel system fee
income statement
income tax
indemnification
insurance
interest expense
interest income
investing activities
landing fees
liabilities
line-item budgeting
long-term liabilities
lump sum budgeting
net profit
net take-down ratio
non-aeronautical revenues
noncurrent assets
non-operating revenues
operating activities
operating budget
operating expenses
operating ratio
operations and maintenance (O&M)
owner's (or shareholder's) equity
performance-based budgeting
program plan budgeting
retail concessions
return on assets ratio
revenue/cost-centered budgeting
revenues
risk management
statement of cash flows
statement of changes in equity
target-based budgeting
traditional budgeting
variable expenses
variance report
zero-based budgeting

In Chapter 13

Budgeting Overview ... 493

Budget Development ... 493
- Operating Budget ... 494
- Capital Budget ... 495
- Budget Process and Monitoring ... 495
- Budget Preparation ... 496
- Budget Techniques ... 497

Revenues ... 498
- Aeronautical Revenues ... 498
- Non-Aeronautical Revenues ... 501
- Non-Operating Revenues ... 507
- Innovative Revenue Sources ... 507

Expenses ... 508
- O&M ... 508
- Capital ... 509

Financial Statements ... 509
- Balance Sheet ... 509
- Income Statement ... 513
- Statement of Cash Flows ... 516
- Statement of Changes in Equity ... 518
- Relationship Among Financial Statements ... 518
- Annual Report ... 519
- Financial Ratios ... 520

Establishing Fees, Rates and Charges ... 524

Risk Management ... 526
- Liability ... 526
- Insurance ... 527

Concluding Thoughts ... 528

Chapter Summary ... 529

Review Questions ... 531

Scenarios ... 532

References and Resources for Further Study ... 533

FEATURES

Self-Sustained Enterprise Fund at Boise Airport ... 494

By being an enterprise fund, this airport is responsible for setting fees and charges to cover all expenses.

Dallas Fort Worth International Airport Gas Exploration ... 508

In an effort to tap natural resources and generate alternative revenues, DFW is allowing natural gas wells on airport land.

Budgeting Overview

Airports are financial enterprises. In reality, they serve as financial engines for the communities in which they operate. Just as an aircraft engine needs specific amounts of fuel, requiring the pilot to pre-plan for this required fuel, the airport financial engine requires financing as well as planning for this financing. This planning occurs in the form of a **budget**. Just as individuals develop budgets to manage personal finances, airports develop budgets to manage their finances. This is even more imperative with revenues and expenditures amounting to tens of millions of dollars, as is the case for many airports nationwide. An airport budget is intended to guide the airport in projecting revenues and expenditures for the year, while also keeping track of monthly progress in light of the budget to prevent the airport from spending more than projected revenues will allow.

Simply, a budget utilizes accounting data to plan for future operational and capital expenditures (as well as revenues). This **financial plan** becomes a fundamental tool used by management in making decisions that will have an impact on the airport's finances. Without a budget, the airport is likely to spend too much and run out of money prior to the end of the year. It goes without saying that a well-developed budget is a very effective tool for airport managers.

Budget Development

Prior to developing a budget, the airport establishes a **fiscal year**. The fiscal year is the 12-month year used for accounting purposes, which may or may not coincide with the calendar year. Once established, the dates coinciding with the fiscal year will not change. Although the fiscal year may be identical to the calendar year (January 1 to December 31), it typically is not (July 1 to June 30, or October 1 to September 30 are popular fiscal year dates). The purpose in having an alternate fiscal year is to enable the airport to close out the year and accounting statements at a time other than the end of the calendar year (which coincides with holidays). The FAA has a fiscal year of October 1 to September 30.

The development of a budget begins months prior to the start of a new fiscal year. Often, each department director is involved and tasked with developing funding requests, both of an operational and a capital nature. Department requests are generally higher than what may actually be included in the approved budget, but as the various airport departments submit their "wish lists," their needs and wants are made known to management. Clearly, all requested expenditures must be in line with projected revenues for the next year.

OPERATING BUDGET

The **operating budget** focuses on expenses and revenues associated with ongoing operations of the airport. The operating budget may include both revenues and expenditures or only expenditures. The functional areas generally included in the operating budget consist of airfield, terminal, landside, and general/administrative. To determine expenditures in each of these areas, employees may be asked to keep track of hours spent on various tasks, as well as supplies used. Salaries/wages may be included in a departmental operating budget, or this may be included in the airport's overall operating budget.

The operating budget is key to making sure each airport department spends within their means, especially for day-to-day operations. In fact, when departmental budgets are discussed, the operating budget is most often referred to. By definition, some airport departments such as maintenance and operations may have very large operating budgets. Other departments, such as finance or human resources, may have smaller operating budgets. Although the airport will have an overall operating budget, the unique operating budget developed for each department is more detailed and specific to the particular department. In fact, departmental budgets are essential; otherwise, each department's expenditures are likely to get lost in the airport's overall operating budget.

According to AAAE (2010, p. 112), in developing an operating budget, airport management must:

- Plan for the operational needs of the organization.
- Obtain resources from the airport's operating environment.
- Distribute those resources throughout the organization.
- Track the resource expenditures to ensure they are used effectively and efficiently.

Self-Sustained Enterprise Fund at Boise Airport

The City of Boise owns and operates Boise Airport, located in Boise, Idaho. The airport's website explains that the airport is a self-sustained enterprise fund department of the City of Boise. As such, no local tax funding contributes to the airport. Airport revenues are generated by fees and charges, as well as federal grant funding. Additionally, as a non-profit entity, all revenues above expenses are reinvested into the city's aviation operations.

In addition to revenue generated by airport fees and charges, Boise Airport is also the beneficiary of FAA grants. Since 1952, those grants have totaled more than $136 million and have funded projects such as runway and terminal improvements, land acquisition, noise abatement, security enhancements, baggage system upgrades, fire equipment, and basic infrastructure investment.

(Boise Airport, n.d.)

In practice, this requires airport management not only to prioritize operating expenditures in developing the operating budget, possibly deferring expenditures into future years, but also to track month-to-month expenditures once the operating budget is approved. Remember, airlines serving the airport are most concerned about their costs (often characterized as costs per enplaned passenger—CPE), and as a result, airport management must be conservative in developing operating budgets.

CAPITAL BUDGET

Unlike operating budgeting, **capital budgeting** focuses only on capital projects. These are long-term expenditures such as terminals, parking garages, new runways/taxiways, ARFF trucks, etc. Capital budgeting involves an examination of long-term capital needs and a prioritization of those needs based on realistic costs, resulting in a yearly capital budget (often for 3 to 5 years into the future). The multi-year plan becomes the airport's **capital improvement plan (CIP)**, which then integrates with state and national plans, such as the National Plan of Integrated Airport Systems (NPIAS).

Although the operating budget is used daily by a department director to track expenditures and make certain the department stays within budget, the capital budget is used less frequently and only to track big ticket items that are purchased much less frequently—maybe once per year. Even so, if only $1 million was budgeted for an ARFF truck, for example, it is important that no more than $1 million is spent on this piece of equipment. The capital budget will reveal this.

BUDGET PROCESS AND MONITORING

Once a budget is prepared, is must be continually monitored. Just as individuals prepare personal budgets and don't wait until the end of the year to check on their progress toward the budget, airports don't wait until the end of the year to check on progress toward their budgets. **Budget monitoring** at airports takes place monthly, and even daily. An airport's finance department continually pays invoices and records revenues, and as part of that, tracks progress against the budget. A **variance report** shows actual expenditures as a percentage of the budgeted amount. This is useful, for example, so that if the year is half over and more than 50 percent of the budgeted amount for a particular area has been spent, changes in spending will likely need to be made to avoid either spending more than the budgeted amount or running out of money before the end of the year. Likewise, if an ARFF truck is budgeted for and is purchased in April, the variance report will show 100 percent of that budget amount spent before mid-year. The difference between the actual revenues and expenses and the budgeted revenues and expenses is the variance. Each area director needs to remain aware of the budget for their area and the progress made toward that budgeted amount—i.e., the variance.

BUDGET PREPARATION

Preparing an airport budget is a multi-step process that typically occurs over several months. If an airport's new fiscal year begins on October 1, for example, preparation of the coming year's budget may begin in the spring. The first step is for the airport to review its current financial picture, including revenues and expenses for the current year. Next, revenues are estimated for the coming year. Airports, specifically those served by air carriers, have very passenger-dependent revenues. A commercial-service airport can, for instance, consider current revenues based on a certain number of enplaned passengers. If the number of enplaned passengers increases by 3 percent in the coming year, revenues can also be projected to increase by a specific percentage.

Next, fixed and variable expenses must be projected for the coming year. **Fixed expenses** are those expenses that don't change (such as debt service), while **variable expenses** change from month to month (for example, utilities). As part of this, capital equipment requests are presented. Each department prepares requests (operating and capital) and then submits these requests to the finance department and/or airport director, who then reviews each department's requests. Requests are prioritized and they may not all be approved. Eventually, approved requests are incorporated into the airport's budget. This process may require some give-and-take, requiring patience, negotiating skills, and justification for any requested expenditures (especially for capital items). In the end, department directors must accept the budget as approved by the airport's governing body, even if they don't completely agree with it (see Figure 13-1).

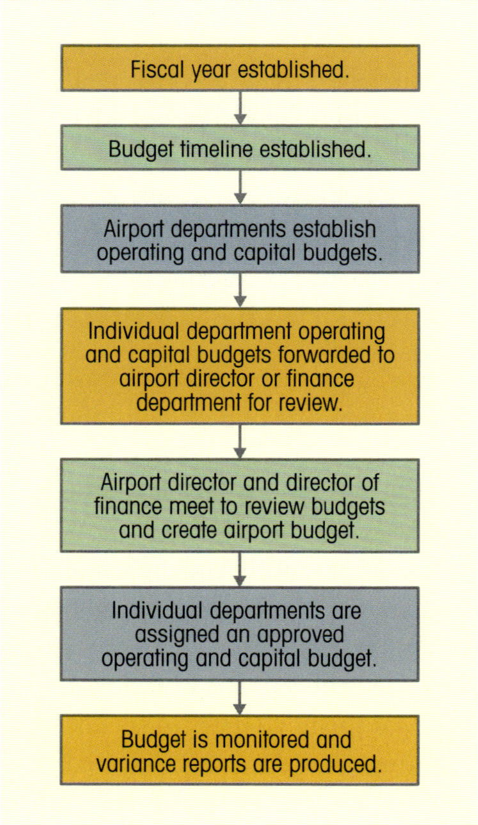

Figure 13-1. Airport budgeting process.

BUDGET TECHNIQUES

Budgets can be prepared in a number of ways. The various techniques used are often dependent on management preference. This means that it's possible for a department director to be familiar with utilizing a certain technique to develop a department budget at one airport, only to accept a department director position at another airport and be required to use a different budget preparation technique. The various budgeting techniques include:

- **Traditional budgeting—**Based on a percentage increase or decrease of revenues and expenditures, which builds from the current year budget. This is also known as incremental budgeting, in reference to incremental increases or decreases from the current year budget. A 3–5 percent increase from year to year is common.
- **Lump sum budgeting**—More common at GA airports, this budgeting technique involves a lump sum of money that the airport then uses its judgment in expending throughout the year.
- **Activity-based budgeting**—Presents costs as a ratio of the number of full-time employees to the required action or work in a specific budget category. Allocates funds to specific activity areas.
- **Performance-based budgeting**—Based on the allocation of funds according to outcomes associated with specific goals. If performance goals are met or exceeded, funding at the highest levels will be made available.
- **Program plan budgeting**—Focuses on cost-benefit analyses. Takes a long-term view of projects and their associated costs, breaking them down into yearly operating budgets. It is centered on a functional or organizational area, identifying facilities, personnel, or equipment needed.
- **Zero-based budgeting**—Each budget is developed from zero, as if no current budget exists, which requires a careful analysis of all revenues and expenditures. Each department must prioritize, rank, and justify needs.
- **Target-based budgeting**—Similar to zero-based budgeting, but allows more flexibility. Revenues are estimated with an associated cap placed on expenditures based on the revenue estimate.
- **Revenue/cost-centered budgeting**—Focuses on break-even needs associated with revenue and cost centers. This requires care in developing cost and revenue centers, as well as allocating revenues and costs to these areas.
- **Line-item budgeting**—A very detailed form of budgeting in which all expenditures are broken down into cost centers, with a chart of accounts. A detailed numbering and coding system is developed for each line item.

  (AAAE, 2010)

Revenues

In simple terms, **revenues** are the money earned or collected at or by the airport. Similar to the salary/wages that individuals earn, airports earn revenues for the services and facilities they provide. Airports are generally not in the business of selling products, but they are in the business of providing services (fueling, valet parking, police, ARFF, etc.) and facilities (parking structures, terminal buildings, runways, taxiways, ramps, etc.). These services and facilities are in demand and cost money to provide, and thus charges can be assessed on those using these services and facilities. Revenues can be in the form of aeronautical or non-aeronautical.

AERONAUTICAL REVENUES

To provide runways, taxiways, ramp areas, and safety areas, and maintain these areas, airports incur significant costs. It costs a considerable amount of money to design and construct large expanses of paved areas. It costs more money to install signage, markings, and lighting. The pavement, as well as signage, marking, and lighting, must then be maintained. Grass must be cut, pavement must be repaired, markings need to be repainted, lights burn out and require replacement, etc. Additionally, personnel must be hired and paid to carry out these maintenance tasks, as well as inspect the airfield. All told, an airport spends tens of thousands to millions of dollars annually to provide an airfield that allows safe and efficient use of the airport by various users. As expenses are incurred in this area, revenues must be earned to cover these costs. Since these are aeronautical expenses, **aeronautical revenues** are charged to cover these expenses. In essence, aeronautical revenues are those revenues earned from aeronautical users and aeronautical activity.

Landing Fees

At airports that serve air carriers, the most common aeronautical source of revenue is **landing fees**. In fact, landing fees typically account for almost one quarter of airport operating revenues. This is the most effective way to recover those expenses necessary to provide and maintain the airfield (see Figure 13-2).

Landing fees are assessed per 1,000 pounds of certificated maximum gross landing weight (CMGLW) of aircraft. This is important for two reasons. First, air carriers are charged based on their activity at the airport, as well as the size of the aircraft they fly. Admittedly, larger, heavier aircraft place higher levels of stress on airfield pavements. Therefore, they must pay more. Second, the landing fee is based on certificated landing weight, not actual landing weight. Thus, an aircraft could be full of passengers (100 percent load factor) or empty (0 percent load factor) and in both of these cases, the same landing fee would be assessed for the same aircraft. This is important because it means airports

Figure 13-2. The landing of an air carrier aircraft, generating landing fee revenues for the airport.

need not be concerned about airline load factors and actual passengers on board (at least concerning landing fees) when assessing landing fees.

Airports collect millions of dollars in landing fees annually. Landing fees may range from pennies to several dollars or more per thousand pounds CMGLW. As discussed in Chapter 12, landing fees for signatory airlines are generally somewhat less than landing fees for non-signatory airlines. At Orlando International Airport, for example, 2015 landing fees were assessed to airlines at the rate of $1.5901 per 1,000 pounds CMGLW (Greater Orlando Aviation Authority, 2014).

Fuel Fees

Airlines are required to pay the market rate for fuel at an airport. Airport fuel systems, although typically installed by the airport, are often managed and maintained by an airline or private operator, such as Aircraft Service International Group (ASIG). Some airports/airlines/operators also assess a **hydrant fuel system fee** (for those underground systems served by fuel hydrants at each gate). This fee is on a per-gallon basis, with a large portion of the fee designed to cover the rent, operations, and maintenance of the hydrant fuel system. At Orlando International Airport, for example, the hydrant fuel system fee was $0.0348 per gallon in 2015 (Figure 13-3).

Although landing fees are easily assessed on scheduled air carriers that have entered into an operating agreement with the airport, collecting landing fees from GA aircraft, especially transient users, is difficult if not impossible. Consider a GA aircraft that performs only one touch-and-go. How would a landing fee be collected from this pilot? To counteract this difficulty and yet also charge GA aircraft for their use of the airfield, **fuel flowage fees** may be charged. These fees are assessed on a per-gallon basis for each gallon of Avgas and Jet fuel

Figure 13-3. Fueling of an air carrier aircraft.

(aberenyi/Bigstock.com)

that is pumped into GA aircraft at the airport. Since the airport has an agreement in place with the FBO (or owner of the self-service pump), fuel flowage fees can be collected and then submitted to the airport on a regular (typically monthly) basis. In this way, GA aircraft share in the cost burden of providing and maintaining the airfield. Although exact fuel flowage fees vary, $0.05 to $0.20 per gallon is common. Often lowest at commercial service airports that generate substantial landing fees from air carriers, the fuel flowage fee at Orlando International Airport in 2015, for example, was assessed at the rate of $0.025 per gallon. Just as with state and local fuel taxes, the fuel flowage fee is part of the per gallon advertised price. Therefore, users generally have little idea as to how much fuel flowage fee they're paying as they fuel their aircraft. As long as the total price per gallon is acceptable, the user will purchase fuel (and pay fuel flowage fees in the process).

Land Lease and Terminal Rent

Discussed in Chapter 12, land and terminal rent could be characterized as either aeronautical or non-aeronautical. In the aeronautical sense, airlines pay a significant amount each month to airports for the use of space in terminals. This space includes ticket counter space, baggage claim space, ticket counter office space, operations office space, baggage claim office space, etc. Additionally, an airline or corporate operator will likely lease the land on which their hangar sits. These revenues factor into the airport revenue equation and typically account for one quarter of airport operating revenues.

NON-AERONAUTICAL REVENUES

Non-aeronautical revenues are earned from non-aeronautical activities and non-aeronautical uses of the airport. Although airports exist to service aeronautical activities, due to the presence of passengers as well as meeters and greeters, non-aeronautical activities (such as retail stores, food and beverage providers, shoe shine shops, and parking structures) are often part of the airport environment. Consider those activities that may result in revenues even if no planes were flying. In fact, airports continued to earn revenues (albeit substantially reduced) during the three days in which the nation's aviation system was shut down following the September 11, 2001, terrorist attacks. Cars remained in parking garages, interest was earned on airport savings accounts, meeters and greeters and employees may have purchased food and beverages, etc.

Parking

The most significant source of non-aeronautical revenues is associated with automobile parking. In fact, automobile parking revenues generally account for one quarter of all airport operating revenues. As hundreds of thousands or even millions of individuals park at an airport annually, they utilize parking facilities, often in the form of parking garages, that were expensive to construct and must be maintained (Figure 13-4). Although off-airport parking facilities not associated with the airport may be available to those needing long-term parking, in many cases there are few options for someone needing to park a car on either a short-term or long-term basis. At least in the United States, Americans love their cars. And although mass transit is effective in some metropolitan areas, in the vast majority of cities and airports across the country, people prefer to drive their personal vehicle when going to the airport. It is often more convenient and even though it may cost to park at the airport, Americans often choose to do so.

Figure 13-4. Airport parking garage.

As a result of this demand and the need to provide parking facilities, airports charge parking fees and earn significant revenues in this way. Often, patrons have the opportunity to choose from short-term parking, long-term parking, and possibly remote or satellite long-term parking. Many larger airports now offer (on a complimentary basis) cell phone waiting lots that allow meeters and greeters to wait for family, friends, and business associates to arrive on a flight without having to pay for short-term parking or congesting the arrivals curbside.

The daily parking rates at Orlando International Airport are presented in Table 13-1.

Table 13-1. Orlando International Airport parking rates.

Parking Area	Hourly Rate	Daily Rate
North Park Place (Blue Lot)	Grace period for first 10 minutes; then $4 for 11 minutes to 3 hours	$10 (maximum stay 120 days)
South Park Place (Red Lot)	Grace period for first 10 minutes; then $4 for 11 minutes to 3 hours	$10 (maximum stay 120 days)
Terminal Garage	Grace period for first 20 minutes; $2 for 21 to 40 minutes; then $1 for each additional 20 minutes (or any part thereof from the time of entry)	$17 (maximum stay 60 days)
Terminal Top	Grace period for first 20 minutes; $2 for 21 to 40 minutes; then $1 for each additional 20 minutes (or any part thereof from the time of entry)	$17 (maximum stay 60 days)
Curbside Valet	$7 per hour (or any part thereof) up to a maximum of $25	$25 (maximum stay 60 days)
Hyatt Valet	$4 for the first 20 minutes (or any part thereof); then $1 per additional 20-minute period (or any part thereof) up to 3 hours; then $25 per 24-hour period (or any part thereof)	$25
Express Pick-up/Drop-Off	$1 per 30 minutes up to 2 hours; then $5 per hour (or any part thereof)	
Hotel Self-Parking	N/A	$12
Hotel Valet Parking	N/A	$16

Based on these rates, Orlando International Airport earned $50 million in parking revenues in 2014. Combined with rental car revenues of $87 million and other ground transportation revenues of $11 million, total ground transportation revenues represented 37% of 2014 operating revenues. This category represents the largest share of 2014 operating revenues, with revenues from signatory airlines representing the second largest share of operating revenues at 28% (Orlando International Airport, n.d.; Greater Orlando Aviation Authority, 2015).

Rental Car

Especially at airports, which serve as transportation centers, rental cars are often in great demand. This is particularly true at origin and destination (O&D) airports, as most arriving passengers are staying in the area and unless they are being picked up by an acquaintance, or take a hotel shuttle, taxi, or public transportation, a rental car will be needed. As with all facilities, services, and products provided at an airport, rental car companies are charged for their access to the airport and/or the airport land they occupy. This is often in the form of a concession fee or airport access fee, and rental car companies do pass this charge on to customers. This is why it is more expensive to rent a car on-airport compared to an off-airport location. As stated earlier, in 2014, rental car revenues at Orlando International Airport amounted to $87 million. These revenues represent the airport's collection of a 10% privilege fee of rental car gross receipts. Clearly, the Orlando area is one of the nation's largest rental car markets.

A relatively new trend in rental car concessions is the use of **consolidated rental car facilities**, often abbreviated CONRAC (i.e., **con**solidated **r**ent **a** **c**ar). A CONRAC is designed to consolidate all rental car companies into one facility for the convenience of both the rental companies and passengers. Phoenix Sky Harbor International Airport, for example, has a significant CONRAC that is located away from the passenger terminals, requiring passengers to board a shuttle bus for a ride to the CONRAC to retrieve their rental car. Nashville International Airport, on the other hand, has a smaller CONRAC that is located across the street from the main terminal building, allowing passengers to walk to retrieve their rental car (see Figure 13-5).

Figure 13-5. Nashville International Airport consolidated rental car facility (CONRAC).

Retail Concessions

Anyone who has waited for an hour or more at an airport has likely taken advantage of the airport's **retail concessions**. Some airports have invested significant sums of money into renovating one or more terminal buildings and incorporating retail concessions for the benefit of passengers, meeters and greeters, and employees alike. In fact, airports such as Minneapolis-St. Paul International Airport have refined the shopping mall concept by incorporating brand name stores and dedicating a significant amount of square footage to retail concessions. The MSP Airport Mall meets the needs of many individuals as they wait to catch a flight, purchase souvenirs, buy gifts for children, etc. (see Figure 13-6).

Airports generally earn revenues from retail concessions by assessing a privilege fee (for the privilege of doing business at the airport) and a percentage of gross sales. With these two types of fees, the airport earns revenue from the concessionaire even if it has zero sales for a given month. However, if the concessionaire does well financially, the airport will also benefit by collecting a percentage of the concessionaire's gross sales. In 2014, Orlando International Airport earned $19.9 million in general merchandise concession revenues.

Figure 13-6. Airport retail concessions.

Food and Beverage Concessions

The majority of airline passengers have, at one time or another, visited a **food and beverage (F&B) concession** at an airport. These concessions meet the demand of airport patrons for a place to get refreshed with food and/or beverages. Indeed, as passengers are frequently a captive audience and have no other options for obtaining food and beverages, providing quality food and beverage concessions is integral for airports, especially those with commercial service.

The trend at airports has been to incorporate not only national brands (such as Subway, Burger King, McDonald's, Starbucks, and Chili's), but also local and regional brands (such as Whitt's Barbeque, Rhythms Café, and Grandaddy's Bar). The most important concept is to provide choices for patrons, and ensure that the concessions are well-located so that regardless of the gate or terminal, passengers have convenient access to food and beverage concessions. This is even more important post-9/11, as only ticketed passengers and employees can access the terminal past the security screening checkpoint. Another important component is to offer pricing as close to "street-pricing" as possible. In other words, prices should not be excessive, and should be similar to prices at the same establishments off airport property. In 2014, Orlando International Airport earned $18.1 million in food and beverage concession revenues (Figure 13-7).

Figure 13-7. Airport food and beverage concessions.

Services

In addition to the typical food and beverage and retail concessions at airports, there has been a transition in recent years toward offering more personal services at airports. These services may include shoe shine, hair salon, nail salon, massage spa, business center, airline clubs/lounge, credit union/bank, currency exchange, yoga studio/gym, traveler's insurance, etc. (Figure 13-8). These services are greatly appreciated by passengers who often do not have ready access to off-airport services. Adding services concessions within an airport terminal can create a more welcoming environment and enhance traveler productivity, while reducing stress. In 2014, Orlando International Airport earned $11.6 million in services concession revenues.

Figure 13-8. Airport shoe shine, a common airport services concession.

Advertising

Airports often have advertising present within the passenger terminal buildings (see Figure 13-9). This advertising serves three purposes. First, it provides an interesting graphical aesthetic within the terminal building providing passengers and meeters and greeters (as well as employees) something visually appealing to look at. Second, due to the significant number of passengers and others that serve as a captive audience within a terminal building, the advertiser often receives significant "bang for the buck" with their advertising dollar. Third, advertisers pay for the space they utilize and as a result, the airport earns advertising revenues.

Figure 13-9. In-airport advertising.

In recent years, airports have capitalized on advertising revenues by making more airport space available for advertisers. Options include wall wraps, jet bridges, banners, dynamic LED signage, etc. With a captive audience of thousands daily, companies wishing to project their image or message to this audience find airport advertising an attractive option. Meanwhile, airports are enjoying the revenues that come with that advertising. Typically, an airport contracts with a firm to manage all airport advertising, outsourcing the task to experts and yet still enjoying the revenues associated with it. In 2014, Orlando International Airport earned $13.5 million in "other terminal area" concessions, which includes advertising revenues.

NON-OPERATING REVENUES

Non-operating revenues refer to those earned revenues that have little to do with the operation of the airport. For example, think about interest on a savings account. Even if the airport is closed (due to a hurricane or some other event), revenue will continue to be earned on a savings account in which the airport has money invested. Generally, non-operating revenues are a minor part of the overall revenues earned by airports.

INNOVATIVE REVENUE SOURCES

Although traditional sources of revenue will continue to form the "bread and butter" of airport revenues, many airports have started exploring more innovative revenue sources. Oftentimes, these are the traditional revenue sources with a "twist." It may appear that some of these options require expenditures, which might be true; however, they are all designed to increase revenues—whether immediately or eventually. The options are limited only by the imagination of airport management and FAA grant assurances. Some sources that have been tapped by airports include:

- *Airport parking*—valet parking, customer loyalty programs, monthly parking rates, web-based parking systems, automated payment options.
- *Rental car*—privilege fees, terminal rental, land leases, customer facility charges, consolidated rental car facilities.
- *Terminal concessions*—branded merchandise and food and beverage, upscale dining, kiosks, self-serve newsstands.
- *Advertising programs*—touch screen directories, jet bridge and airfield advertising, Wi-Fi applications.
- *Natural resources/agricultural activity*—oil drilling, mining, farming activity.

Dallas Fort Worth International Airport Gas Exploration

In 2007, Dallas Fort Worth International Airport (DFW) became the site of the largest natural gas exploration project at a major U.S. airport. DFW is located on the Barnett Shale formation, one of America's largest natural gas fields. Almost all of DFW's 18,000 acres are available for exploration, with more than 9,000 of those acres available for surface drilling. Working with Chesapeake Energy, as many as 300 wells may eventually be established on airport land, each one a safe distance from the AOA. The first well was to be drilled to an average vertical depth of about 8,000 feet. At that point, the well bore would turn horizontal, with an anticipated lateral length of approximately 4,000 feet parallel to the ground above, resulting in a total well bore length of more than 12,000 feet to the lower Barnett Shale formation. Airport leadership pursued this partnership with Chesapeake Energy to create jobs and business opportunities for local firms, as well as generate innovative sources of revenue, which will keep costs down for the airlines that operate at DFW. Chesapeake paid DFW a $186 million initial bonus and will continue to pay a 25% revenue-sharing royalty on all natural gas produced from the airport's leasehold.

(Dallas Fort Worth International Airport, 2007)

Expenses

The other side of the financial equation consists of expenses. Indeed, airports incur substantial expenses each day. If the revenues earned are not higher than the expenses, the airport will be unable to pay bills without borrowing money. Just as in personal finances, if financial difficulties are encountered, two options are available: increase revenues or decrease expenses. It is often more straightforward to decrease expenses than to increase revenues. The airport exerts more control over the money it spends than the money others spend (its revenues).

O&M

Operations and maintenance (O&M) expenditures refer to the expenses incurred on a daily basis that are necessary to ensure the operation and maintenance of the airport. What is unique about O&M is that capital expenditures are not included. Therefore, O&M includes almost all expenses that are not capital in nature. It does not include expenses for new ARFF trucks, new taxiways, new terminals, or new parking facilities. Rather, it includes expenses such as salaries, utilities, landscaping, vehicle maintenance, paint for airfield markings, etc. These are daily expenses associated with the operation and maintenance of the airport. It should be noted that funds available through AIP, PFCs, and the debt markets cannot be used for O&M expenses. Therefore, it is important for airports to become and to stay financially self-sufficient to ensure all O&M expenses are covered.

CAPITAL

Unlike O&M, **capital expenditures** include those "big-ticket" items such as new ARFF trucks, new taxiways, new terminals, new parking facilities, etc. An airport will generally have a capital improvement plan that includes all capital expenditures over a period of 3 years, 5 years, or more. Once the projected capital expenditures are known, the airport can pursue funding for these capital expenditures. Capital projects and equipment often require millions of dollars, so fortunately for airports, various funding sources can be pursued for all or a portion of these expenditures (see Chapter 14).

Financial Statements

Financial statements are used to convey financial information about an airport (or any organization, for that matter) to stakeholders, shareholders, citizens, business leaders and others who may desire such information. Without financial statements, it would be almost impossible to gauge the financial strength of an airport. Interested parties would have a lot of numbers, but not be able to make sense out of them. Additionally, marketing can paint the airport in a positive light, but numbers don't lie (as long as the financial statements were independently audited and prepared according to generally accepted accounting principles).

BALANCE SHEET

As seen in Figure 13-10, the **balance sheet** (or statement of net assets) reflects what a company owns and what it owes at a fixed point in time. This financial statement is considered a "snapshot" of the company's assets, liabilities, and owner's equity on the day the statement was prepared. Although it doesn't necessarily indicate the degree to which profits were earned (as the income statement does), it does indicate the net worth of the firm (which should be positive).

The balance sheet is divided into two sections:

1. Assets
2. Liabilities and net assets (or shareholder's equity if the company has issued shares of stock)

Assets include all the goods and property owned by the company, as well as uncollected amounts due (receivables). More specifically, assets include physical property (such as plants, trucks, equipment and inventory), cash, and investments, as well as intangible items (such as trademarks and patents). Assets can be held (cash), sold (either temporarily as with parking spaces, or permanently as with food and beverages), or used to make more products or services that can be sold (e.g., office supplies to print newsletters). In addition, assets can be

STATEMENTS OF NET ASSETS
SEPTEMBER 30, 2011 AND 2010

	2011	2010
ASSETS		
CURRENT ASSETS		
Unrestricted:		
Cash and Cash Equivalents	$ 37,335,514	$ 35,575,345
Restricted:		
Cash and Cash Equivalents	75,395,482	79,434,134
Investments	88,957,117	88,556,620
Accounts Receivable, Net	2,507,445	4,155,888
Passenger Facility Charges Receivable	5,132,140	5,310,138
Government Grants Receivable	888,018	1,227,162
Accrued Interest Receivable	1,240,127	1,218,320
Prepaid Insurance and Other Assets	3,097,682	3,186,885
Total Restricted Assets	177,218,011	183,089,147
Total Current Assets	214,553,525	218,664,492
NONCURRENT ASSETS		
Capital Assets:		
Land	188,357,353	183,696,379
Construction in Progress	34,024,271	95,570,824
Building, Equipment and Improvements	1,896,774,284	1,816,858,809
Total	2,119,155,908	2,096,126,012
Less: Accumulated Depreciation	(865,201,264)	(797,214,197)
Total Capital Assets, Net	1,253,954,644	1,298,911,815
Debt Issue Costs (Net of Accumulated Amortization of $7,627,897 and $6,656,015, Respectively)	6,300,398	7,161,872
Other Receivables	129,536	137,923
Total Noncurrent Assets	1,260,384,578	1,306,211,610
Total Assets	$ 1,474,938,103	$ 1,524,876,102
LIABILITIES AND NET ASSETS		
CURRENT LIABILITIES		
Payable from Unrestricted Assets:		
Accounts Payable – Construction	$ 894,798	$ 3,659,298
Accrued Airline Revenue Sharing	6,163,906	4,919,104
Total Current Liabilities Payable from Unrestricted Assets	7,058,704	8,578,402
Payable from Restricted Assets:		
Accounts Payable – Construction	2,877,791	9,118,931
Accounts Payable – Trade	3,778,158	2,597,060
Accrued Expenses	8,342,055	9,122,362
Accrued Interest Payable	86,460	96,488
Current Maturities of Revenue Bonds Payable	50,720,000	47,290,000
Current Maturities of Suntrust Notes and Commercial Paper Notes	-	7,000,000
Deferred Revenue and Other Liabilities	3,523,081	1,617,002
Total Current Liabilities Payable from Restricted Assets	69,327,545	76,841,843
Total Current Liabilities	76,386,249	85,420,245
NONCURRENT LIABILITIES		
Long-Term Portion of Revenue Bonds Payable, Net	602,318,747	655,206,849
Suntrust Notes and Commercial Paper Notes	88,053,335	78,180,000
Other Liabilities	4,022,952	5,171,503
Total Noncurrent Liabilities	694,395,034	738,558,352
Total Liabilities	770,781,283	823,978,597
NET ASSETS		
Invested in Capital Assets, Net of Related Debt	616,438,897	626,604,861
Restricted	57,441,113	47,295,701
Unrestricted	30,276,810	26,996,943
Total Net Assets	$ 704,156,820	$ 700,897,505

Figure 13-10. Statement of Net Assets.

(Hillsborough County Aviation Authority)

current or noncurrent. **Current assets** (such as cash) are generally consumed or sold within one year. These can be unrestricted or restricted. Unrestricted assets can be used for any purpose, whereas restricted assets are set aside for a specific purpose or not easily converted to cash (such as PFCs). **Noncurrent assets** are not expected to be converted to cash within one year, or are expected to be sold beyond one year. Included in noncurrent assets, **fixed assets** (or capital assets) are those assets that will remain on the books for years into the future. Fixed assets include land, ARFF trucks, and terminal buildings. Often, accumulated **depreciation** is subtracted from noncurrent assets to reveal the true worth of fixed assets. Depreciation is the practice of dispensing against income the cost of a fixed asset over its estimated useful life. As an example, if straight-line depreciation is used for an ARFF truck that cost $1 million and has a useful life of ten years, the statement of net assets would show a depreciation amount of $100,000 annually.

Using the sample statement of net assets presented in Figure 13-10, when unrestricted assets are added to restricted assets, we arrive at total current assets for 2011:

	Total Unrestricted Assets:	$37,335,514
+	Total Restricted Assets:	$177,218,011
=	Total Current Assets:	$214,553,525

Likewise, when capital assets are added to debt issue costs and other receivables, and after accumulated depreciation is subtracted, we arrive at total noncurrent assets for 2011:

	Total Capital Assets:	$2,119,155,908
–	Accumulated Depreciation:	$865,201,264
=	Total Capital Assets, Net:	$1,253,954,644
+	Debt Issue Costs:	$6,300,398
+	Other Receivables:	$129,536
=	Total Noncurrent Assets:	$1,260,384,578

By adding total current assets to total noncurrent assets, we arrive at total assets:

	Total Current Assets:	$214,553,525
+	Total Noncurrent Assets:	$1,260,384,578
=	Total Assets:	$1,474,938,103

On the other side of the coin, **liabilities** are the amounts of money that are owed by the company. This includes bank loans, rent for use of a building, money owed to suppliers for materials, payroll a company owes to its employees, environmental cleanup costs, or taxes owed to the government. Liabilities also include obligations to provide goods or services to customers in the future (for example, tickets sold by airlines for a flight to occur at some point in the future). Similar to assets, liabilities can be current or long-term. **Current liabilities** are obligations a company expects to pay off within the year. Current liabilities can be paid from unrestricted assets or restricted assets. **Long-term liabilities** are obligations due more than one year in the future, and they are usually paid from bonds or other loans (commercial paper).

Owner's (or shareholder's) equity is sometimes called capital, net worth, or net assets. It is the amount remaining if a company sold all of its assets and paid off all of its liabilities. This leftover money belongs to the shareholders, or the owners, of the company. If a company distributes part or all of the equity, these are known as **dividends**. Airports that are publicly owned and operated do not have shareholders and therefore do not distribute dividends.

Using the sample statement of net assets presented in Figure 13-10, when total current liabilities payable from unrestricted assets are added to total current liabilities payable from restricted assets, we arrive at total current liabilities for 2011:

	Total Current Liabilities Payable from Unrestricted Assets:	$7,058,704
+	Total Current Liabilities Payable from Restricted Assets:	$69,327,545
=	Total Current Liabilities:	$76,386,249

When total current liabilities are added to total noncurrent liabilities, we arrive at total liabilities for 2011:

	Total Current Liabilities:	$76,386,249
+	Total Noncurrent Liabilities:	$694,395,034
=	Total Liabilities:	$770,781,283

Taking into account total net assets, we see evidence that Assets = Liabilities + Owner's Equity or Net Assets in 2011. This is an accounting rule and should always be true.

	Total Liabilities:	$770,781,283
+	Total Net Assets:	$704,156,820
=	Total Assets:	$1,474,938,103

INCOME STATEMENT

One of the most useful financial statements is the **income statement** (or statements of revenues, expenses, and changes in net assets). The purpose of this statement is to show how much money a company earned and spent during a given period of time. An income statement is generally a one-year statement, reflecting income and expenses during the year. The bottom line of an income statement shows the difference between revenues and expenses, resulting in the "**net profit**" of the business. Revenues, before expenses are taken out, are considered "**gross profits**" or "gross revenues." Net profits are clearly much more telling as to the financial performance of the business and will reveal if the business has made money or lost money, after paying all expenses. It is common for a business to earn substantial revenues, but once expenses are taken into account, the business actually loses money for the year. If a company has stock outstanding, earnings will also be quantified on a per-share basis, known as "earnings per share." Publicly held airports do not issue stock; thus, there would be no earnings per share shown on the airport income statement.

The first component of the income statement is **revenues**. This reflects the total amount of money brought in from sales of products or services. For airports, revenues are usually categorized based on the area in which they're earned (such as airfield, terminals, general aviation, etc.). Remember, it is "gross" at this point because expenses have not yet been deducted. After revenues, an amount will be shown for any earned revenues the company doesn't expect to collect. This could be due, for example, to sales discounts or merchandise returns. Once returns and allowances (more common in retail) are deducted from the gross revenues, net revenues is the result.

Expenses are presented next. If there is a cost of sales, it would be presented. **Cost of sales** represents the amount of money the company spent to produce the goods or services it sold during the accounting period. Next, costs of sales are subtracted from net revenues to arrive at a subtotal called gross profit or sometimes "gross margin." It's considered "gross" because there are certain expenses that haven't yet been deducted. **Operating expenses** related to the operation of the company are presented next. These expenses include salaries, research costs, and marketing expenses. Operating expenses are uniquely different from "costs of sales," because operating expenses are not directly associated with the production of products or services being sold. For airports, operating expenses are often categorized (similar to revenues) into the category in which they're incurred. Depreciation and amortization will also be reflected in the income statement.

After all operating expenses have been deducted from gross profit, "income from operations" or operating profit or loss will result. Interest income and interest expense must then be accounted for. **Interest income** is earned on interest-bearing savings accounts and money market funds, just as private individuals earn money on savings accounts. **Interest expense**, however, is interest paid on money borrowed. Depending on how the income statement is structured, interest income and interest expense may be shown separately or combined. The interest income and expense are then added or subtracted from the operating profits to arrive at operating profit before income tax. Lastly, **income tax** must be accounted for. Although municipalities, and airports, are likely exempt from income taxes, these taxes are paid by privately airport operators. Once income tax is deducted, the airport's net profit (net income or net earnings) or net losses will be reflected. In essence, did the company make or lose money during the year?

Using the sample "Statements of Revenues, Expenses, and Changes in Net Assets" presented in Figure 13-11, we see that operating revenues come from many sources, including the airfield, terminal buildings, airside buildings, commercial landside, cargo, auxiliary airports, general aviation, and federal reimbursements. Likewise, when considering operating expenses, the categories are identical, with the exception of the passenger transfer system, and roads and grounds. To calculate whether the airport experienced an operating profit or operating loss, we subtract total operating expenses from total operating revenues for 2011:

Total Operating Revenues:	$169,515,761
– Total Operating Expenses:	$92,496,355
= Operating Profit:	$77,019,406

When signatory airline net revenue sharing is taken into consideration, as well as depreciation and amortization, we arrive at either an operating loss or operating profit. Parentheses are used to denote negative numbers.

Operating Profit:	$77,019,406
– Signatory Airline Net Revenue Sharing:	$6,163,906
– Depreciation and Amortization:	$81,962,284
= Operating Loss:	($11,106,784)

It is this bottom line, the net operating profit or loss, that the income statement (or statements of revenues, expenses, and changes in net assets) is used to calculate.

The sample statement also has a "Change in Net Assets" section, which is not true of income statements. This section is designed to calculate the effect of non-operating revenues and expenditures on the airport's assets. Commonly, the income statement consists of operating revenues and expenditures, as well as non-operating revenues and expenditures. In our sample, however, they appear in a separate section showing their effect on net assets from the beginning to the end of the year.

Figure 13-11. Statements of Revenues, Expenses, and Changes in Net Assets.

(Hillsborough County Aviation Authority)

STATEMENTS OF REVENUES, EXPENSES AND CHANGES IN NET ASSETS
YEARS ENDED SEPTEMBER 30, 2011 AND 2010

	2011	2010
OPERATING REVENUES		
Airfield	$ 13,655,170	$ 12,513,751
Terminal Building	39,671,549	37,141,682
Airside Buildings	16,687,814	16,564,311
Commercial Landside	83,767,454	79,771,340
Cargo	1,982,430	2,174,119
Auxiliary Airports	923,252	928,361
General Aviation	1,631,769	1,484,868
Federal Reimbursements	1,230,326	1,230,326
Other	9,965,997	8,640,559
Total Operating Revenues	169,515,761	160,449,317
OPERATING EXPENSES		
Airfield	9,223,485	8,195,258
Terminal Building	25,276,659	25,371,635
Airside Buildings	19,492,202	19,642,185
Commercial Landside	21,768,151	20,102,180
Cargo	608,623	612,322
Auxiliary Airports	1,368,615	1,417,325
General Aviation	835,588	844,160
Passenger Transfer System	3,715,518	3,626,579
Roads and Grounds	7,363,652	7,875,890
Other	2,843,862	2,111,242
Total Operating Expenses	92,496,355	89,798,776
Signatory Airline Net Revenue Sharing	6,163,906	4,919,104
Operating Income before Depreciation and Amortization	70,855,500	65,731,437
Depreciation and Amortization	81,962,284	81,714,186
OPERATING LOSS	(11,106,784)	(15,982,749)
NONOPERATING REVENUES AND EXPENSES		
Investment Income	3,611,822	7,345,605
Bonds and Commercial Paper Interest Expense	(30,305,423)	(29,122,601)
Total Nonoperating Expenses - Net	(26,693,601)	(21,776,996)
CHANGE IN NET ASSETS BEFORE CONTRIBUTIONS	(37,800,385)	(37,759,745)
CAPITAL CONTRIBUTIONS		
Passenger Facility Charges	33,191,463	33,032,091
Federal and State Grants	7,868,237	17,310,665
Other Contributions	-	1,066,903
Total Capital Contributions	41,059,700	51,409,659
CHANGE IN NET ASSETS	3,259,315	13,649,914
Total Net Assets - Beginning of Year	700,897,505	687,247,591
TOTAL NET ASSETS - END OF YEAR	$ 704,156,820	$ 700,897,505

STATEMENT OF CASH FLOWS

The third financial statement that is prepared by companies is the **statement of cash flows**, which shows the exchange of money between the company and other organizations, entities, and individuals. In essence, the statement of cash flows reflects the flow of cash both into and out of the company. Cash flows are important in reflecting the degree to which a company spends more or less money than it makes. A company needs to have enough cash on hand to pay its expenses and purchase assets. Although the income statement will indicate whether or not a company made a profit (considering all revenues and expenses), the statement of cash flows indicates management of cash, including the degree to which the company generated cash.

Although the statement of cash flows stands on its own, it does reflect information from the company's balance sheet and income statement. A statement of cash flows reflects cash flows from (a) operating activities, (b) investing activities, and (c) financing activities.

Operating activities refer to the operation of the business. This first section of the statement of cash flows analyzes a company's cash flow from net income or losses, reconciling net income to the actual cash the company received from or used in its operating activities. This requires adjusting net income for any non-cash items (depreciation expenses) and adjusting for any cash that was used or provided by other operating assets and liabilities.

Cash flows from **investing activities** are the second section of the statement of cash flows. This includes purchases or sales of long-term assets (such as property, plant and equipment), as well as investment securities. An investment in a piece of machinery would appear as a cash outflow from investing activities if cash was used. If investments were sold for cash, the proceeds from the sales would show up as a cash inflow from investing activities.

Cash flows from **financing activities** are the third section of the statement of cash flows. Financing activities include selling stocks and bonds (cash inflow) and borrowing from banks (cash outflow). This section may be minimal or rather lengthy, depending on the degree of financing activities engaged in by the airport.

Using the sample "Statements of Cash Flows" presented in Figure 13-12, we see the three main sections for 2011. Note that due to the nature of cash flows, there may be flows into the airport (represented by positive numbers) or out of the airport (represented by negative numbers). Based on this, the subtotals may be positive or negative:

Net Cash Provided by Operating Activities:	$74,996,267
+ Net Cash Used by Capital and Related Financing Activities:	($80,512,461)
+ Net Cash Provided by Investing Activities:	$3,237,711
= Net Change in Cash and Cash Equivalents:	($2,278,483)

Once these are determined, the cash and cash equivalents at the end of the year can be determined. As seen in the sample, the negative $2,278,483 lowers the cash and cash equivalents from the beginning of the year from $115,009,479

Figure 13-12. Statements of Cash Flows.

(Hillsborough County Aviation Authority)

STATEMENTS OF CASH FLOWS
YEARS ENDED SEPTEMBER 30, 2011 AND 2010

	2011	2010
CASH FLOWS FROM OPERATING ACTIVITIES		
Operating Cash Receipts from Customers	$ 170,691,406	$ 155,738,871
Cash Payments to Suppliers for Goods and Services	(64,906,326)	(64,919,225)
Cash Payments to Employees for Services	(32,019,139)	(32,806,551)
Cash Receipts from Federal Reimbursements	1,230,326	1,230,326
Net Cash Provided by Operating Activities	74,996,267	59,243,421
CASH FLOWS FROM CAPITAL AND RELATED FINANCING ACTIVITIES		
Proceeds from Issuance of 2011 Suntrust Notes	88,053,335	-
Proceeds from Issuance of Commercial Paper Notes	-	6,180,000
Redemption of Commercial Paper Notes	(85,180,000)	-
Payments of Suntrust Notes and Commercial Paper Issuance Costs	(133,086)	(7,424)
Principal and Interest Paid on Revenue Bond Refunding	-	(5,655,776)
Principal Paid on Revenue Bond Maturities and Commercial Paper Notes	(47,290,000)	(40,225,000)
Interest Paid on Revenue Bonds and Commercial Paper Notes	(36,702,872)	(38,669,533)
Acquisition and Construction of Capital Assets	(40,845,067)	(96,235,516)
Net Proceeds from Direct Financing Lease and Other Assets	8,387	17,328
Federal and State Grants	8,207,381	18,466,297
Passenger Facility Charges	33,369,461	32,479,400
Net Cash Used by Capital and Related Financing Activities	(80,512,461)	(123,650,224)
CASH FLOWS FROM INVESTING ACTIVITIES		
Purchases of Investment Securities	(85,020,369)	(98,667,663)
Proceeds from Maturities of Investment Securities	85,418,857	101,397,696
Income Received on Investments	2,839,223	2,861,522
Net Cash Provided by Investing Activities	3,237,711	5,591,555
NET CHANGE IN CASH AND CASH EQUIVALENTS	(2,278,483)	(58,815,248)
Cash and Cash Equivalents - Beginning of Year	115,009,479	173,824,727
CASH AND CASH EQUIVALENTS - END OF YEAR	$ 112,730,996	$ 115,009,479
RECONCILIATION OF OPERATING LOSS TO NET CASH PROVIDED BY OPERATING ACTIVITIES		
Operating Loss	$ (11,106,784)	$ (15,982,749)
Adjustments to Reconcile Operating Loss to Net Cash Provided by Operating Activities:		
Depreciation and Amortization	81,962,284	81,714,186
(Increase) Decrease in Accounts Receivable	1,648,443	(1,939,855)
(Increase) Decrease in Prepaid Insurance and Other Assets	89,203	(223,910)
Increase (Decrease) in Accounts Payable - Trade	1,181,098	(1,315,094)
Increase (Decrease) in Accrued Expenses, Deferred Revenue, and Other Liabilities	1,222,023	(3,009,157)
Net Cash Provided by Operating Activities	$ 74,996,267	$ 59,243,421
NONCASH ACTIVITIES		
Unrealized Gain on Investments	$ 798,985	$ 4,426,138
Amortization of Bond Premium - Net	$ (3,348,672)	$ (3,687,400)
Amortization of Deferred Loss on Bond Refundings	$ 1,207,094	$ 1,385,606
Other Capital Contributions	$ -	$ 1,066,903

to $112,730,996. This statement also takes the operating loss of $11,106,784 from the Statement of Revenues, Expenses, and Changes in Net Assets and provides a reconciliation of operating loss to net cash provided by operating activities.

STATEMENT OF CHANGES IN EQUITY

The fourth financial statement is known as the **statement of changes in equity**, or the statement of retained earnings. This statement details the change in owners' equity or retained earnings over an accounting period by detailing the changes or movement in reserves which make up the shareholders' or owners' equity. Since most public-use airports in the United States do not have shareholders, the statement of changes in equity is not often seen in an airport's annual report. The statement of retained earnings, while not as common as the previous financial statements discussed, may be seen as it relates simply to changes in the airport's retained earnings.

RELATIONSHIP AMONG FINANCIAL STATEMENTS

Although it is tempting to consider each financial statement in isolation, in reality, they are closely related to each other. The balance sheet begins the period and once profits and losses are calculated, these are fed into the income statement and cash flow statement. Next, as capital is raised and dividends paid (for those firms with shares of issued stock), this affects the statement of changes in equity and the cash flow statement. Finally, gains and losses recognized directly in equity affect the statement of changes in equity, while cash flow used in investing activities and cash flow from financing debt affect the cash flow statement. Lastly, the balance sheet at the end of the period is impacted from these activities (see Figure 13-13).

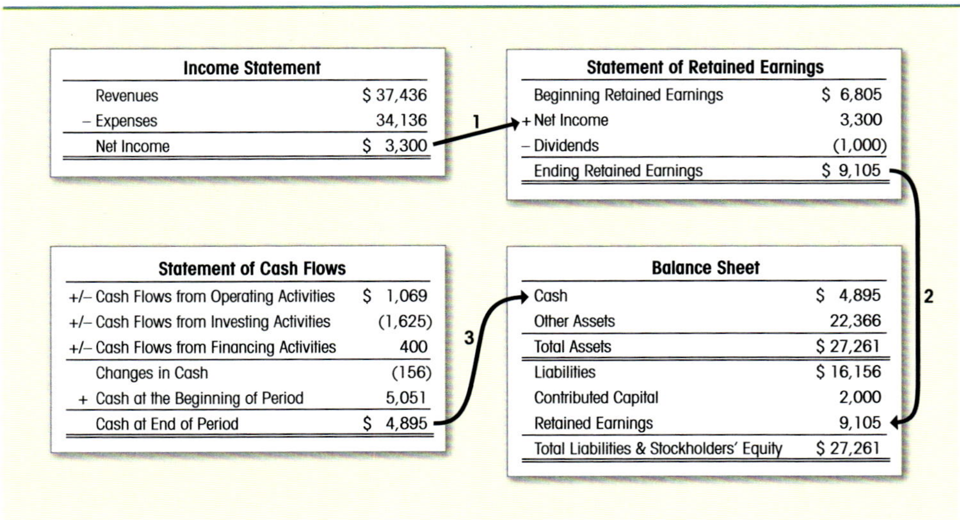

Figure 13-13. Relationships among financial statements.

ANNUAL REPORT

The U.S. Securities and Exchange Commission (SEC) requires companies with more than $10 million in assets and a class of equity securities that is held by more than 500 owners to file Form 10-K (**Annual Report**) each year. This report provides a comprehensive summary of the company's performance. When discussions center around an annual report, however, they are usually referring to the very glossy and image-rich document that presents the year's highlights and financial statements to shareholders, stakeholders, the media, and others interested in the company. Publicly owned and operated airports prepare an annual report for the benefit of citizens, business leaders, and others interested in the financial health of the airport, as well as the airport's accomplishments during the past year. The annual report will also provide a glimpse into the future of the airport.

Although airport annual reports vary in length and information provided, and may be so unique that they are unlike any other, the following elements are rather common:

- *Letter from the chairman or executive director:* This letter is a general letter from top management that highlights successes from the past year, possibly presents some challenges faced, and closes on a positive note and maybe even includes a thank you to the airport's team of employees for their hard work during the year.
- *Sales and marketing:* This section contains detailed information about the airport's facilities and services, accomplishments, airlines, destinations, and a description of major divisions and groups and their areas of responsibility.
- *Ten-year summary of financial results:* Rather than present only one year of financial data, an airport may include a presentation of financial results over a ten-year period. Trends can be uncovered by reviewing financial results over this longer horizon.
- *Management discussion and analysis:* Management often discusses significant financial trends during the past few years and may offer explanations for any poor performance.
- *Letter of CPA opinion:* Financial statements must be audited by an independent qualified Certified Public Accountant (CPA). There will generally be a letter from the CPA certifying the review/audit and expressing any qualifications with the financial statements or the manner by which they were prepared. These letters are almost always positive. Any concerns or issues should be worked through with the CPA before the annual report is produced.
- *Financial statements:* The "meat" of the annual report is the financial statements. At minimum, the income statement, balance sheet, and cash flow statement should be included. Almost as important as the statements are the footnotes, which often contain extremely important information that cannot be included in the statements.

- *Footnotes:* Provides more detailed information about the financial statements.
- *List of directors and officers:* Although this list may appear at the front of the report, listing directors and officers of the airport provides insight into the management structure. Officers may include the president, chief executive officer, vice presidents, senior directors, etc.

FINANCIAL RATIOS

To make sense among all the financial numbers and to allow for comparisons between airports, various **financial ratios** have been developed. By using financial ratios, the financial strength of small airports can be compared to large airports, or to the entire industry. Breaking down all the dollars and cents to a ratio can be very helpful in conducting such comparisons. Without these, it could be argued that larger airports have more assets and make more money than smaller airports. Yet comparing airports using the various financial ratios allows equal comparisons to easily be made. Although a number of ratios can be developed and utilized, the following are the most common ratios used in the airport industry.

Return on Assets Ratio

$$\text{Return on Assets} = \frac{\text{Net Profits}}{\text{Total Assets}}$$

The **return on assets ratio** provides insight into the productivity of the airport's assets. The greater the net profits, the greater the ratio. Thus, higher ratios are preferred, with ratios closer to 1.0 desired. A ratio above 1.0 means the airport is earning more in net profits than they own in assets, which is indicative of a high level of productivity.

Using the sample financial statements (Figures 13-10, 13-11), the return on assets ratio is -0.007. This extremely low ratio is the result of an operating loss of over $11 million. In essence, this airport not only has no return on assets, but has a negative return. The ratio below zero should raise a red flag.

$$-0.007 = \frac{(\$11{,}106{,}784)}{\$1{,}474{,}938{,}103}$$

Current Ratio

$$\text{Current Ratio} = \frac{\text{Current Assets}}{\text{Current Liabilities}}$$

The **current ratio** is used to measure the difference between the amount of current assets and current liabilities. This ratio provides an indication as to the ability of the airport to pay current liabilities with current assets. Higher current ratios are preferred. With twice as many current assets as current liabilities, for example, a ratio of 2.0 would result. A ratio of 0.5 would result if an airport owes twice as much as it owns (in the form of current assets).

Using the sample financial statements (Figure 13-10), the current ratio is 2.81. In essence, this airport has almost three times as many current assets as it has current liabilities. So although it had an operating loss for the year (and a very low return on assets ratio), it has more than sufficient assets (mostly consisting of cash and investments) to cover current liabilities.

$$2.81 = \frac{\$214,553,525}{\$76,386,249}$$

Operating Ratio

$$\text{Operating Ratio} = \frac{\text{Operating Expenses + Maintenance Expenses}}{\text{Operating Revenue}}$$

The **operating ratio** measures the share of revenues absorbed by operating and maintenance costs. A low ratio is preferred. A higher ratio (close to 1.0) indicates that little additional revenue is available for capital expenditures. Depending on the financial statements, maintenance expenses may be incorporated into total operating expenses.

Using the sample financial statements (Figure 13-11), the operating ratio is 0.55. In essence, a little more than half of operating revenues are absorbed by operating expenses. Although this ratio could be lower (and thus, stronger), it shows that there are operating revenues remaining after covering operating expenses.

$$0.55 = \frac{\$92,496,355 + 0}{\$169,515,761}$$

Net Take-Down Ratio

$$\text{Net Take-Down Ratio} = \frac{\left[\text{Total Revenue} - \left(\begin{matrix}\text{Operating}\\\text{Expenses}\end{matrix} + \begin{matrix}\text{Maintenance}\\\text{Expenses}\end{matrix}\right)\right]}{\text{Total Revenue}}$$

Although similar to the operating ratio, the **net take-down ratio** also takes into account non-operating revenues (interest income, for example). It is, as a result, a broader measure of airport revenues remaining after payment of operating expenses.

Using the sample financial statements (Figure 13-11), the net take-down ratio is 0.47. This ratio is similar to the operating ratio for this airport because non-operating revenues were only \$3,611,822, which is only 2 percent of the total revenues.

$$0.47 = \frac{[(\$169,515,761 + \$3,611,822) - (\$92,496,355 + 0)]}{(\$169,515,761 + \$3,611,822)}$$

$$0.47 = \frac{\$173,127,583 - \$92,496,355}{\$173,127,583}$$

Debt-to-Asset Ratio

$$\text{Debt-to-Asset Ratio} = \frac{\text{Gross Debt} - \text{Bond Principal Reserves}}{\text{Net Fixed Assets} + \text{Working Capital}}$$

The **debt-to-asset ratio** measures the total assets provided by creditors. In this formula, gross debt = total debt = total liability. Bond principal reserves will often be presented within the notes to financial statements. Net fixed assets is calculated by deducting accumulated depreciation from fixed assets (or noncurrent assets), shown on the sample statement as "total capital assets, net." Working capital is current assets minus current liabilities. A low ratio indicates each dollar of debt is secured with more dollars of assets. A high ratio would indicate a highly leveraged airport, which is not preferred. This is important in case assets have to be sold to pay off bondholders.

To obtain bond principal reserves, see Notes to Financial Statements Excerpt in Figure 13-14. Using this and the sample financial statements (Figure 13-10), the debt-to-asset ratio is 0.49. Rather than being too low or high, this ratio indicates this airport has about twice as much in assets as in debt.

$$\frac{\$770{,}781{,}283 - (\$46{,}203 + \$89{,}107{,}264)}{\$1{,}253{,}954{,}644 + (\$214{,}553{,}525 - \$76{,}386{,}249)}$$

$$= \frac{\$681{,}627{,}816}{\$1{,}253{,}954{,}644 + \$138{,}167{,}276}$$

$$= \frac{\$681{,}627{,}816}{\$1{,}392{,}121{,}920}$$

$$= 0.49$$

Debt Service Safety Margin

$$\text{Debt Service Safety Margin} = \frac{\text{Gross Revenues} - \left(\text{Operating Expenses} + \text{Maintenance Expenses} + \text{Annual Debt Service}\right)}{\text{Gross Revenues}}$$

The **debt service safety margin** measures the percentage of revenues available to service new debt, as well as the financial reserves available in the event of the airport experiencing unexpectedly low revenues. Debt must be "serviced" by paying interest and eventually paying off the bonds. The margin refers to a "safety net" to service the debt, which includes paying interest on the outstanding bonds. A high ratio indicates a larger safety net. Annual debt service is found in the notes to financial statements.

To obtain annual debt service, see Notes to Financial Statements Excerpt in Figure 13-14. Using this and the sample financial statements (Figure 13-11), the debt service safety margin is -0.02. With a negative debt service safety margin, this airport is paying more in operating expenses and annual debt service than it makes in gross revenues. In fact, for this airport, the annual debt service of

Figure 13-14. Notes of Financial Statements Excerpt.

(Hillsborough County Aviation Authority)

RESTRICTED ASSETS

The Trust Agreement, among other things, requires all airport revenues, excluding PFCs, grants, bond proceeds and their earnings, and revenues from certain nontrust funded projects, be deposited in the Revenue Fund, the establishment of certain trust accounts, and defines the priority and flow of cash receipts. Certain of these trust accounts require specified balances and are restricted as to use. Bond proceeds issued for construction are held by a trustee appointed by the Authority per the bond agreement. Debt Service and Debt Reserve accounts are held by a trustee designated by the Trust Agreement and are pledged as collateral for debt service. A summary of the balances in these accounts as of September 30, 2011 and 2010 is as follows:

	2011	2010
Restricted for Debt Service:		
Bond Principal, Interest, and Redemption Sinking Fund	$ 46,203	$ 57,641
Bond Reserve Fund	89,107,264	88,489,083

DEBT AND OTHER NON-CURRENT LIABILITIES

Revenue Bonds

The total principal maturities and debt service requirements for all revenue bonds through the year 2038, as of September 30, 2011 are as follows:

Year Ending September 30	Principal	Interest	Total Debt Service
2012	$ 50,720,000	$ 33,674,481	$ 84,394,481
2013	53,205,000	31,109,119	84,314,119
2014	56,055,000	28,402,094	84,457,094
2015	58,985,000	25,464,006	84,449,006
2016	54,560,000	22,418,631	76,978,631
2017–2021	186,465,000	71,765,950	258,230,950
2022–2026	56,685,000	43,406,763	100,091,763
2027–2031	43,950,000	30,181,650	74,131,650
2032–2036	57,070,000	17,071,050	74,141,050
2037–2038	27,395,000	2,257,375	29,652,375
Total	$ 645,090,000	$ 305,751,119	$ 950,841,119

\$84,394,481 almost equals operating expenses of \$92,496,355. This ratio is particularly insightful for potential investors as they examine the likelihood the airport will be able to pay interest on bonds. In this case, this airport is not a particularly strong investment.

$$\frac{\$169{,}515{,}761 + \$3{,}611{,}822 - (\$92{,}496{,}355 + 0 + \$84{,}394{,}481)}{\$169{,}515{,}761 + \$3{,}611{,}822}$$

$$= \frac{\$173{,}127{,}583 - (\$176{,}890{,}836)}{\$173{,}127{,}583}$$

$$= \frac{(\$3{,}763{,}253)}{\$173{,}127{,}583}$$

$$= -0.02$$

Establishing Fees, Rates and Charges

In order to cover the costs associated with operating and maintaining an airport, airports implement various fees, rates, and charges. The term "**fees, rates, and charges**" refers to numerous items, depending upon the activity and the agreement. Some airports have established hundreds of unique fees, rates and charges. At Dallas/Fort Worth International Airport, for example, the FY2015 schedule of charges includes:

- Aircraft Operations
  - Landing fee rates
  - Common-use gate turn times
  - Terminal aircraft parking fees
  - Penalty for failure to move aircraft from a common-use gate
  - Exemption to airfield charges
  - Corporate aviation charges
- Terminal Rental Rates
  - Airline terminal rates
  - Terminals B/E & D, Common gate use charges
  - Terminal hardstand operations
  - Common-use charges for preferential leaseholders
  - Federal Inspection Service (FIS) Fees
- Ground Rental and Foreign Trade Zone
  - Ground rental
  - Foreign Tradezone
- Parking Charges
  - Public parking charges
  - Off-airport charges
  - Exemptions from parking charges
  - Vehicular access charges
  - Other parking charges
- Ground Transportation
  - Operating authority fees
  - Access fees
  - Meet and greet service fees
  - Central queue service fees
  - Mystery shop reimbursement
- Public Safety Medical and Service
  - Aircraft rescue and firefighting (ARFF) and structural fire training
  - Emergency medical service (EMS)

- Fingerprinting for identification
- Towing and impoundment charges
- Indoor firearms range
- Copies of accident (crash) report
- Airport identification/access badges and fingerprinting services
- AOA Vehicle Access Permits
- AOA access control devices (GENIES)

- Utilities and Maintenance Services
  - Heating and cooling services
  - Electrical and natural gas
  - Water
  - Trash
  - International waste disposal
  - Maintenance charge
- Environmental Cost Recovery
  - Actions occurring on designated source isolation deicing pads
  - Actions occurring outside designated source isolation deicing pads
  - Gate/Ramp Demerit rating system—Individual permit
- Development Charges
  - Construction permit fees
  - Landscape fees
- Concessionaire Charges
  - Operating and maintenance charges (O&M)
  - Employee transportation charge (ETC)
  - Other costs
  - Food court common area maintenance (FCCAM)
  - Trash removal charge
  - Marketing assessment
  - Grease interceptor amortization
  - Security surcharge
  - Grease interceptor maintenance
  - Warehouse
  - Tenant rules and regulations
- Other Charges
  - Signage
  - Commercial filming, photography, videotaping, and airfield escort services
  - Conference room rental rates
  - Off-airport rental car companies common bus services

- Trunked radio system charge
- Employee transportation charge
- Employee hangars
- Rent-a-car facility and transportation charges
- Rent-a-car facility tenants and off airport rental car tenants

With each of these fees, rates, and charges, the airport is simply attempting to recover the costs associated with providing the facilities and services listed. Transparency in this area, especially with the airlines, is important.

Risk Management

With the many risks presented by aviation activity, as well as on-airport tenants (airlines, food and beverage concessions, FBOs, etc.), it is important for airports to proactively engage in managing risk. Indeed, **risk management** is necessary to protect the airport from liability—arising both from the airport's activities and from that of tenants. This begins by purchasing general liability insurance and requiring all tenants to name the airport as an additional insured in that tenant's commercial operator's insurance.

LIABILITY

Airports can be found liable for a number of reasons. This may include an aircraft accident on airport property, a vehicle crash on airport property, or a person's fall on an escalator. In addition to purchasing the appropriate insurance coverage, airports typically include indemnity language in all contracts with tenants and operators. This is definitely where attorneys get involved. Sample **indemnification** language might read as follows:

> Tenant shall indemnify, defend, save and hold harmless ABC Airport, its departments, agencies, directors, trustees, boards, commissions, officers, officials, agents, and employees (hereinafter referred to as "Indemnitee") from and against any and all claims, actions, liabilities, damages, losses, or expenses (including court costs, attorneys' fees, and costs of claim processing, investigation and litigation) (hereinafter referred to as "Claims") for bodily injury or personal injury (including death), or loss or damage to tangible or intangible property caused, or alleged to be caused, in whole or in part, by the negligent or willful acts or omissions of Tenant or any of its owners, officers, directors, agents, employees or subcontractors. This indemnity includes any claim or amount arising out of or recovered under the Workers' Compensation Law or arising out of the failure of such contractor to conform to any federal, state or local law, statute, ordinance, rule, regulations or court decree. It is the specific intention of the parties that the Indemnitee shall, in all instances, except for

Claims arising solely from the negligent or willful acts or omissions of the Indemnitee, be indemnified by Tenant from and against any and all claims. It is agreed that Tenant will be responsible for primary loss investigation, defense and judgment costs where this indemnification is applicable. In consideration of the award of this contract, the Tenant agrees to waive all rights of subrogation against ABC Airport, its officers, officials, agents and employees for losses arising from the work performed by the Tenant for ABC Airport.

INSURANCE

Insurance can be purchased with varying coverage limits, deductibles, and the resulting premiums. Coverage limits may be as little as $1 million, although coverage limits of up to $10 million or more are common. It is said that insurance is something you purchase hoping you'll never have to use it. With airports, due to the inherent risks involved with aviation activity, insurance premiums can be very expensive. Although an airport can be self-insured (meaning they set aside enough cash to cover an accident), it is often more cost-effective to purchase an insurance policy to meet the airport's needs. At a minimum, an airport will need insurance policies in place to cover property damage and bodily injury or death, not only for airport employees, but all stakeholders interacting at the airport.

The various types of policies available for airports (and tenants) include:

- *Commercial General Liability*—Coverage for general liabilities associated with the operation of the airport.
- *Business Automobile Liability*—Coverage for liability associated with operating automobiles for business purposes.
- *Worker's Compensation and Employer's Liability*—Coverage associated with worker's compensation claims, including injuries sustained while at work.
- *Professional Liability (Errors and Omissions)*—Coverage for management staff to provide some degree of protection against poor decisions or omissions of pertinent information.
- *Airport/Aircraft Liability*—Coverage for liability associated with operation of aircraft on the airport.
- *Airport Premises Liability*—Coverage for tenants operating on airport premises.
- *Property Insurance*—Coverage to provide protection if airport property is damaged.
- *Product Liability*—Coverage for products sold by the airport, including fuel and other fluids, for example.

In addition to the main policies in force, the airport can purchase "riders" to cover unique needs, such as coverage for public events, construction projects, fly-ins or air shows, or filming activities. For example, air meet rain insurance can provide an airport a certain benefit if rain, for example, interrupts or cancels the airshow and greatly lowers attendance. For this type of policy to pay benefits, a certain amount of rain must fall during a specified time period. Typically, the airport will require the tenant or entity engaging in the unique activity to provide evidence of coverage as well.

Concluding Thoughts

Airport professionals should have a working knowledge of finance and be able to apply that knowledge to making decisions about airport operating and capital budgets. It is also important to have a focus on increasing revenues and developing alternative revenue streams, while also controlling expenditures. Airports must become and remain financially healthy, and it is the airport director's responsibility to ensure this occurs.

Chapter Summary

- The operating budget focuses on expenses and revenues associated with ongoing operations of the airport.
- The capital budget focuses only on capital projects, such as terminals, parking garages, new runways/taxiways, ARFF trucks, etc.
- Preparing an airport budget is a multi-step process that occurs over several months.
- Fixed expenses are those expenses that don't change (such as debt service), while variable expenses change from month to month (for example, utilities).
- Traditional budgeting is commonly based on a percentage increase or decrease of revenues and expenditures, which builds from the current year budget.
- Lump sum budgeting involves a lump sum of money that the airport then uses its judgment in expending throughout the year.
- Activity-based budgeting presents costs as a ratio of the number of full-time employees to the required action or work in a specific budget category and allocates funds to specific activity areas.
- Performance-based budgeting allocates funds according to outcomes associated with specific goals.
- Program plan budgeting focuses on cost-benefit analyses and takes a long-term view of projects and their associated costs, breaking them down into yearly operating budgets.
- Zero-based budgeting is developed from zero, as if no current budget exists, which requires a careful analysis of all revenues and expenditures.
- Target-based budgeting is similar to zero-based budgeting, but allows for more flexibility.
- Revenue/cost-centered budgeting focuses on break-even needs associated with revenue and cost centers.
- Line-item budgeting is a very detailed form of budgeting in which all expenditures are broken down into cost centers, with a chart of accounts.
- Financial statements are used by airports to convey financial information about the airport to stakeholders, shareholders, citizens, business leaders and others who may desire such information.
- The income statement reveals how much money was earned and spent during a given time period (typically one year).
- The balance sheet reveals the assets, liabilities, and owner's equity of the airport.
- The statement of cash flows reveals the money that was exchanged between the airport and other organizations, entities, and individuals.

- The annual report provides a comprehensive summary of the company's performance.
- Financial ratios are used to gauge the financial performance of an airport and allow for easy comparison among airports, regardless of size.
- Revenues are either aeronautical (e.g., landing fees, fuel fees, and land lease and terminal rent) or non-aeronautical (e.g., parking, rental cars, retail concessions, food and beverage concessions, and advertising).
- Airports adopt innovative revenue-generating techniques to enhance revenues and capitalize on the land and facilities that are available.
- There are two types of airport expenditures: (1) operations and maintenance (O&M) and (2) capital.
- Airports establish fees, rates, and charges to earn revenues from tenants and airport users.
- Risk management requires airports to mitigate liability and obtain appropriate insurance.

Review Questions ↘

1. What is the purpose of a budget?
2. Define fiscal year.
3. Explain the operating budget.
4. Explain the capital budget.
5. What is the capital improvement plan (CIP)?
6. What is the purpose of budget monitoring?
7. Explain the budget preparation process.
8. What is the purpose of financial statements?
9. Explain the income statement.
10. Explain the balance sheet.
11. Explain the statement of cash flows.
12. What is the purpose of the annual report?
13. What is the purpose of financial ratios?
14. Define aeronautical revenues, including the various types.
15. Define non-aeronautical revenues, including the various types.
16. Define non-operating revenues.
17. Explain operations and maintenance (O&M) expenditures.
18. Explain capital expenditures.
19. Explain risk management.
20. What insurance policies are available for airports and tenants?

Scenarios ↘

1. As the director of finance at a large-hub airport, you are tasked with developing the airport's budget each year. The fiscal year is from July 1 to June 30. As you get back to work after the first of the year, you know a new budget needs to be developed for next fiscal year. What steps will you take? What timeline will you develop for this process? How will you ensure the timeline is adhered to and a cost-effective budget is developed for the new fiscal year? Which budgeting technique would you prefer?
2. As the airport manager of a small hub airport, you are faced with declining revenues and reduced air service. It is imperative that you do whatever is necessary to reduce expenditures and increase revenues. What are some considerations for you in this regard?
3. As airport manager of a small airport with significant flight training activity (two on-airport flight schools) and aeronautical events (monthly fly-ins), you are concerned whether or not you are doing enough to manage risk. What insurance policies would be necessary? What are some other thoughts to manage risk?
4. Calculate the Return on Assets Ratio, Current Ratio, Operating Ratio, Net Take-Down Ratio, Debt-to-Asset Ratio, and Debt Service Safety Margin using the following data. Once calculated, interpret these ratios to gauge the financial strength of this hypothetical airport.

Current Assets	\$300,526,887
Fixed Assets	\$1,537,558,689
Accumulated Depreciation	\$399,987
Current Liabilities	\$289,668,983
Noncurrent Liabilities	\$1,210,558,325
Operating Expenses	\$1,800,669
Maintenance Expenses	\$431,698
Operating Revenue	\$32,558,559
Nonoperating Revenue	\$5,000,689
Bond Principal Reserves	\$2,589,332
Annual Debt Service	\$358,611

5. As director of finance at a medium hub airport served by three air carriers, your director has asked you to develop a fair, but financially sustainable schedule of fees, rates, and charges. Your medium hub airport is typical of many medium hub airports with regard to services and facilities provided. Considering the financial information provided in scenario 4, the list of fees, rates, and charges categories at DFW within this chapter, and internet resources, what will your schedule look like? What will your approach be to setting fees, rates, and charges? What other data might you need to fully meet your director's request?

References and Resources for Further Study

American Association of Airport Executives. 2010. "Body of Knowledge Module 1. Finance and Administration." Washington, DC: AAAE.

Boise Airport. n.d. "Budget." Retrieved from http://www.iflyboise.com/airport-guide/about-the-airport/budget/

Dallas Fort Worth International Airport. 2007. "Chesapeake Energy Corporation Taps First Natural Gas Well at DFW International Airport." News release, May 22. Retrieved from https://www.dfwairport.com/pressroom/Chesapeake_Energy_Corporation_Taps_First_Natural_Gas_Well_Airport.pdf

Greater Orlando Aviation Authority. 2014. Air Carrier Guide. Retrieved from http://orlandoairports.net/aviation/docs/aircarrierguide.pdf#page=9

Greater Orlando Aviation Authority. 2015. *Comprehensive Annual Financial Report for the years ended September 30, 2014 and 2013.* Retrieved from http://orlandoairports.net/finance/cafr/CAFR_2014.pdf

Kemp, S. and Dunbar, E. 2003. *Budgeting for Managers.* McGraw Hill.

Merrill Lynch. 2000. *How to Read a Financial Report.* Retrieved from http://www.scribd.com/doc/11755202/Merrill-Lynch-How-to-Read-a-Financial-Report#scribd

Moore, C. and Ashford, N. 2013. *Airport Finance.* New York: Springer.

Morris, K. M. and Morris, V. B. 2004. *The Wall Street Journal Guide to Understanding Money and Investing.* 3rd ed. New York: Fireside.

Morris, K. M. and Morris, V. B. 2004. *The Wall Street Journal Guide to Understanding Personal Finance: Mortgages, Banking, Taxes, Investing, Financial Planning, Credit, Paying for Tuition.* 4th ed. New York: Fireside.

Orlando International Airport. n.d. "Parking." Retrieved from http://www.orlandoairports.net/ops/parking.htm

Chapter 14

Funding and Financial Impacts

Objectives

Upon completion of this chapter, you should understand:

- the sources of capital development funding
- the need for matching funds
- the role of bonds in airport funding
- bond ratings
- the types of bonds
- the alternative minimum tax (AMT)
- PFCs
- the AIP
- the grant application process
- the role of grant assurances
- the role of internally-generated funds
- the role of state and local sources
- the method used to determine the economic impact of airports
- the impacts of airline bankruptcies on airports
- the role of performance management and benchmarking

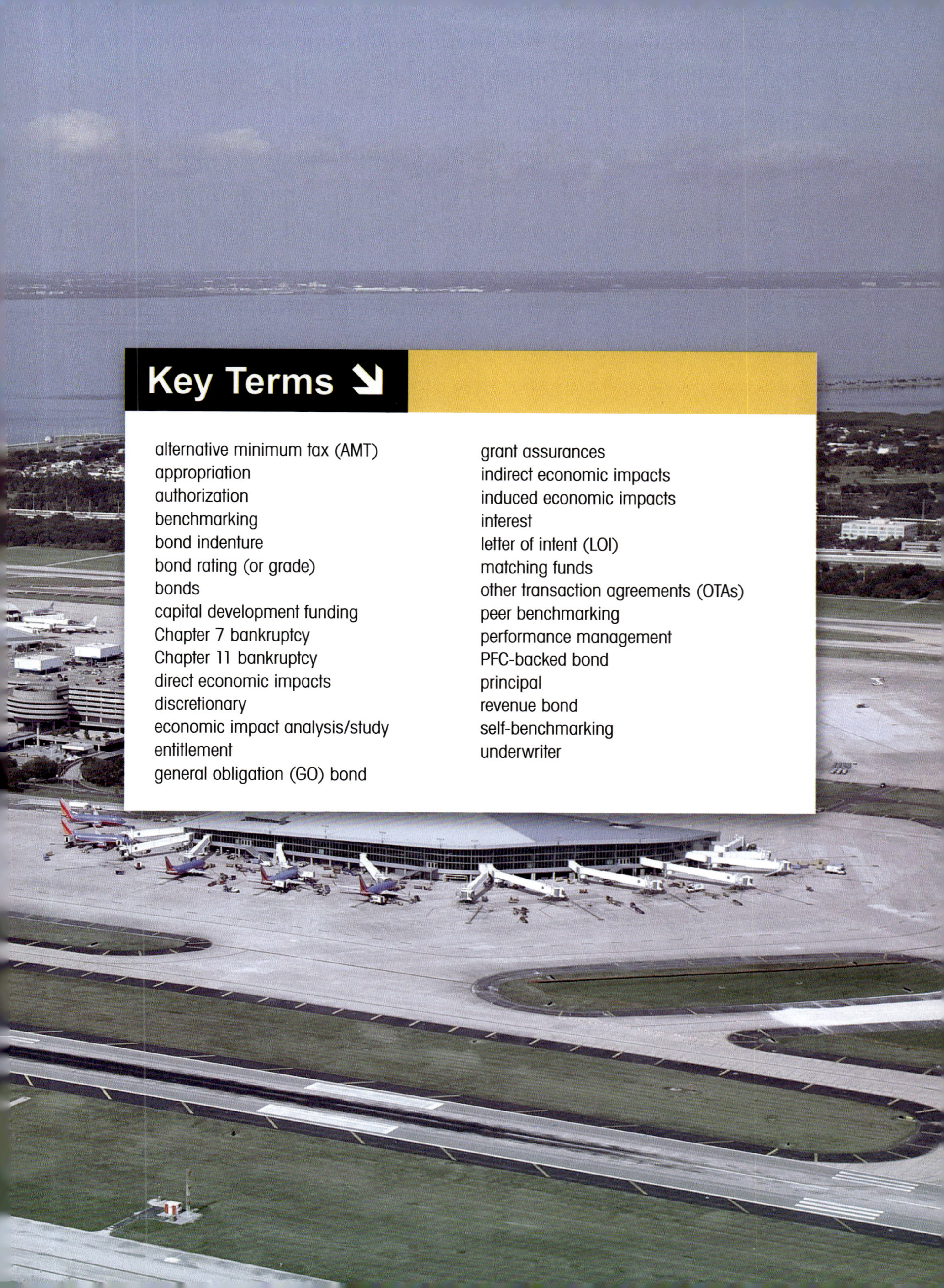

Key Terms

alternative minimum tax (AMT)
appropriation
authorization
benchmarking
bond indenture
bond rating (or grade)
bonds
capital development funding
Chapter 7 bankruptcy
Chapter 11 bankruptcy
direct economic impacts
discretionary
economic impact analysis/study
entitlement
general obligation (GO) bond
grant assurances
indirect economic impacts
induced economic impacts
interest
letter of intent (LOI)
matching funds
other transaction agreements (OTAs)
peer benchmarking
performance management
PFC-backed bond
principal
revenue bond
self-benchmarking
underwriter

In Chapter 14

Introduction **537**

Sources of Capital Development Funding **537**

- Proceeds of Bonds and Other Forms of Debt 538
- PFC Revenues 542
- AIP Grants 544
- Internally-Generated 548
- State and Local Sources 548

Economic Impact of Airports **549**

Impacts of Airline Bankruptcies on Airports **549**

Performance Management and Benchmarking **551**

Concluding Thoughts **553**

Chapter Summary **553**

Review Questions **555**

Scenarios **556**

References and Resources for Further Study **557**

FEATURES

Impact of Delta/Northwest Merger on Memphis International Airport 550

Once a thriving Northwest Airlines hub airport, Memphis International has experienced significant negative impacts from the Delta/Northwest merger.

Introduction

For airports to carry-out capital improvement in the form of new runways, new taxiways, new terminals, ground run-up enclosures, etc., funding must be secured. Depending on the extent of the project, costs can total tens of millions of dollars to one billion dollars or more. Adequate capital development funding is integral to enabling an airport to expand, improve facilities, and better develop infrastructure. This chapter focuses on sources of funding, as well as issues such as grant assurances, revenue diversion, and the economic impacts of airports.

Sources of Capital Development Funding

Funds for airport development are derived from a variety of sources, and include federal, state, and local grants; bond proceeds; passenger facility charges; airport-generated funds (from landing and terminal fees, parking, and concessions revenue); and tenant and third-party financing. During the early 2000s, **capital development funding** at airports was financed 50% via bonds, 29% via AIP, 17% via PFCs, 4% via state and local contributions, and 4% via airport revenue (see Figure 14-1).

With these many sources of capital development funding, airports often mix and match funds. Indeed, it is rare for an airport to receive 100% of the funding needed for a capital development project from a single source. **Matching funds** is the term used to refer to the act of securing multiple sources of funds for a capital development project. Vision 100 (the FAA Reauthorization Act signed on December 12, 2003) raised the federal share for capital projects from 90% to 95% for airports smaller than large-hub and medium-hub, and for airports in states participating in the State Block Grant Program (Georgia, Illinois, Michigan, Missouri, New Hampshire, North Carolina, Pennsylvania, Tennessee, Texas, and Wisconsin). The federal share for most projects at large and medium hub airports is 75% (80% for noise compatibility projects). Airports are responsible for securing additional funds to finance a project to total 100% (Kirk, 2010).

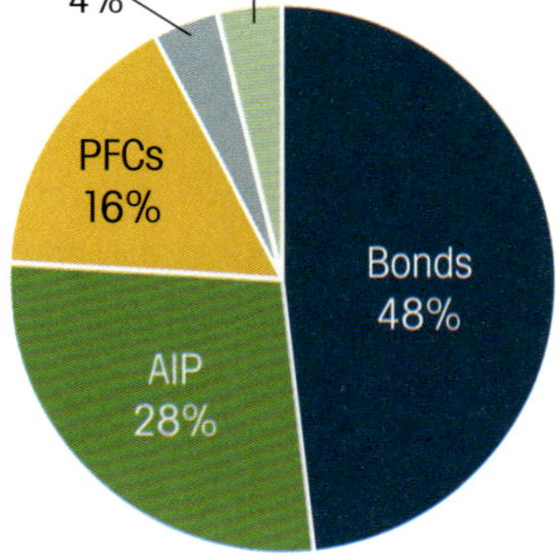

Figure 14-1. Sources of capital development funding (early 2000s).

PROCEEDS OF BONDS AND OTHER FORMS OF DEBT

Bonds, in the simplest form, represent IOUs. An investor loans money to an airport and in return gets an IOU in the form of a bond. A bond is nothing more than a piece of paper that specifies the principal amount, the interest rate, duration, and repayment terms. The **principal** is the amount the investor loaned. If the bonds are issued at $5,000 face value, an investor loaning $10,000 to the airport would receive two $5,000 bonds in return. The investor is investing money to earn a return, which is tied to the **interest** rate or coupon rate. For example, a $5,000 bond paying 5% would result in a payment of $250 annually to the investor for each $5,000 bond owed. Although this example uses an annual payment as an example, the airport may pay interest monthly, quarterly, semi-annually, or annually. The duration of the bond specifies the number of years until the bond matures. Upon maturity, the investor is repaid the full amount of the face value of the bond. This means, of course, that the investor gets 100% of their money back. At this point, the airport satisfies the IOU.

Bonds are a very common form of capital funding, and airport bond issues are often in the amount of hundreds of millions of dollars. Airports have authorization to issue bonds through the **bond indenture** (also known as the bond resolution or bond ordinance). The bond indenture defines the definition and computation of airport revenues and expenses, as well as the funds and accounts set aside for the payment of interest and principal on the bonds (debt service), and the covenants between the issuing entity and the bondholders, including a rate covenant that requires the airport operator to set rates and charges at sufficient levels to produce enough revenues to service the debt (Nichol, 2007).

Generally, institutional investors purchase airport bonds. They may be mutual funds, investment banks, or wealthy investors, but the average individual investor would likely not own any airport bonds. Bond issues are handled by an **underwriter** or several underwriters, generally in the form of large investment banks. The airport has no preference for the investors that purchase the bonds, as all will be treated the same, according to the terms of the bond issue.

Although the terms of the bond issue will be developed by the airport in consultation with the underwriter(s) based on current market conditions, it should be noted that bonds behave in certain ways. To investors, two items are important. First, the interest rate being paid is foundational. All investors desire their money to work for them and create more money, and as interest is paid by the airport, the investor makes money for their "loan" to the airport. During the recession of 2009–2011, banks were paying 1% or less on savings accounts, and certificates of deposit were not earning much more. However, in these circumstances, a bond paying 3% may be more attractive to an investor compared to lower-yielding investments.

The next item that is important, however, is the grade of bond. In other words, to what degree can the investor be assured that the airport issuing the bonds will not go bankrupt and will indeed satisfy the IOU according to the terms of the bond issue? Several agencies grade or rank bonds, and this is useful to investors in judging the financial strength of the airport issuing the bonds and the likelihood that the bonds will be satisfied according to the terms of the bond issue. Not all airports are financially strong, and ratings assigned to a bond issue should reveal this.

The three major credit rating agencies (Moody's Investors Service, Fitch Ratings, and Standard & Poor's) evaluate bonds and assign a **rating (or grade)** based on several fundamental factors relevant to the issuer's long-term and short-term risk profile (see Table 14-1).

Table 14-1. Investment grade bond ratings.

Moody's		S&P		Fitch		rating description
Long-term	Short-term	Long-term	Short-term	Long-term	Short-term	
Aaa	P-1	AAA	A-1+	AAA	F1+	Prime
Aa1		AA+		AA+		High grade
Aa2		AA		AA		
Aa3		AA-		AA-		
A1		A+	A-1	A+	F1	Upper medium grade
A2		A		A		
A3	P-2	A-	A-2	A-	F2	
Baa1		BBB+		BBB+		Lower medium grade
Baa2	P-3	BBB	A-3	BBB	F3	
Baa3		BBB-		BBB-		
Ba1	Not prime	BB+	B	BB+	B	Non-investment grade speculative
Ba2		BB		BB		
Ba3		BB-		BB-		
B1		B+		B+		Highly speculative
B2		B		B		
B3		B-		B-		
Caa1		CCC+	C	CCC	C	Substantial risks
Caa2		CCC				Extremely speculative
Caa3		CCC-				Default imminent with little prospect for recovery
Ca		CC				
		C				
C		D	/	DDD	/	In default
/				DD		
/				D		

Ratings are developed by asking the following two questions:

1. What is the risk to the debt/bondholder of not receiving timely payment of principal and interest?
2. How does the level of risk compare with that of all other debt securities?

Answering these two questions requires certain steps. First, the rating agency has a meeting with airport management to ascertain the history of the airport, airport mission and vision, management structure, management quality and experience, debt structure, and financial strength. This meeting often lasts from several hours to a full day. A tour of the airport and surrounding area may also occur. Next, the rating committee meets to consider the findings from the meeting with management and introduce the relevant risk factors and other issues that should be considered. According to Moody's, "the role of the lead analyst at the rating committee meeting is to present the rating recommendation and rationale, and to ensure that all relevant issues related to the credit are presented and discussed." (Moody's, n.d.). After 60–90 days of analysis, discussions, and evaluation, the rating will be publicly released, and subsequently an interest rate and other terms of the bond issue will be established.

General Obligation Bonds

A common form of bond for municipalities nationwide, including many airports, is the **general obligation (GO) bond**. The GO bond is supported by the overall tax base of the issuing entity. For airports owned and operated by cities, counties, or states, the state or municipality pledges general revenues (from the tax base) to back the bonds and service the debt (pay interest and ultimately repay the face value of the bonds). Taxpayer approval is required. Many airports, however, are owned and operated by an authority or other entity without the ability to levy taxes. In that case, GO bonds could still be issued, although airports that do not have tax revenue would back the bonds with airport sources of revenue (Nichol, 2007).

GO bonds are an important form of financing, especially for smaller airports. Some reasons for this include:

- Stronger credit with lower interest rates—Generally, a bond backed by the full faith and credit of a municipality is stronger than a bond backed solely by revenues, which may be uncertain. As a result, the GO bond issue will generally have a stronger rating, which then requires the airport to pay lower interest rates to attract investors. A bond rated AAA can be issued for 3%, for example, while a C-rated bond may need to pay 12% to attract investors to such a risky investment.
- Lower issuance costs
- No coverage requirement

Revenue Bonds

Although not as popular among airports several decades ago, **revenue bonds** are much more common today, especially at commercial-service airports earning substantial revenues each year. The key requirement for the issuance of revenue bonds is the ability of the issuing entity to earn revenues. This type of bond is based on the concept that facilities should be paid for by those who use them, with the facilities backed by the revenues generated. An example is a newly built toll road. Likely, revenue bonds were issued to build the road and a toll is charged to generate the revenues necessary to service the debt and ultimately pay off the bonds. Revenue bonds do not require voter approval as do GO bonds.

Bonds Backed by PFCs

Although it is more common for revenue bonds to be backed by general airport revenues, the FAA does allow airports to issue revenue bonds that are guaranteed by specific revenues, such as passenger facility charges. Known as **PFC-backed bonds**, these bonds require the airport to have authorization to collect PFCs. Airports must apply for approval to collect PFCs ($4.50 maximum per enplaned passenger) and the application must specify a specific use for the PFCs collected under the application. Often, PFCs are collected to provide capital funding for a specific project, and yet PFCs may not be adequate to completely fund the project. In this instance, the airport can issue revenue bonds backed by the PFCs, so that some of the PFCs can be used to pay interest on the bonds until the facility constructed with the PFCs is completed and revenues begin to be realized, at which time those revenues can be used to service the debt (pay bond interest and face value at maturity).

Since PFC revenue is tied directly to passenger traffic, and considering the volatility of passenger traffic since the terrorist attacks of September 11, 2001, PFC-backed bonds are not as common today. A more common approach is for an airport to issue double-barrel PFC bonds. This can include combining PFC revenues with general airport revenues to repay the bonds, or pledging general airport revenues as a backup if PFC funds fall. In either case, airports must consider the impacts of declining passengers on their ability to service the debt.

Bonds to be Paid with Future Grants

Another financing option allows an airport to issue bonds based on future grant funds that will be received. In order to do this, the airport needs to have received a **letter of intent (LOI)** from the FAA. In essence, an LOI is a commitment by the FAA to provide funding for a multi-year project. For major capital projects, most of the expenses occur during the first few years. However, the duration of an LOI may be five or ten years, with equal funding amounts provided yearly. To make up for the shortfall in funding during the initial years of a project, an airport may issue bonds to be serviced with future grant funds. This solves the immediate need for funding during the first few years of a project when expenditures are more than the LOI authorizes. Of course, multi-year funding tied to an LOI is contingent upon AIP appropriations and authorizations, which introduces some degree of uncertainty (Nichol, 2007).

TSA Grants for Baggage Screening Infrastructure

Screening of checked baggage for explosives is now a requirement in the United States, and although some airports still have large explosive detection machines on the ticketing level, the trend is for airports to install in-line detection systems. However, these expensive systems often require substantial funding. The TSA has made grants available on a limited basis since 2003, funded in part by federal user fees. These grants have been issued either as multi-year LOIs or one-year grants known as **other transaction agreements (OTAs)** to fund baggage screening infrastructure. Some airports have creatively issued bonds to be repaid with annual TSA LOI grant funds, using the bond proceeds to build the in-line systems (Nichol, 2007).

AMT Issues

The **alternative minimum tax (AMT)** was designed to ensure that all taxpayers pay at least a minimum amount of federal taxes on their income, preventing individual taxpayers from taking unfair advantage of the various federal tax preferences and incentives. Tax-exempt governmental bonds are not subject to the AMT, whereas private activity bonds are subject to the AMT. Private activity airport bonds are designed to allow a private entity to enter the tax-exempt bond market to raise funding for a capital project at a public-use airport. By issuing bonds not subject to the AMT, bonds can be issued at lower interest rates, which benefits the airport as it lowers debt service.

PFC REVENUES

Passenger facility charges are extremely popular among commercial-service airports in the United States to pay for capital projects. Although AIP funds are more typically used for airfield projects, PFCs are being increasingly used for landside projects (including interest payments), with less than 20% being used for airfield projects. In FY2008, for example, 45.4% were used for landside (mostly terminal) projects, 22.1% for interest on bonds, 20.8% for airside projects, 5.9% for access (mostly roads), and 5.7% for noise projects. PFCs allow airports that support millions of passengers annually to tap into a significant revenue source authorized by the FAA by assessing a facility charge on each passenger.

The Aviation Safety and Capacity Expansion Act of 1990 authorized the collection of PFCs in the amount of $1, $2, or $3 on each paying passenger boarding an aircraft at their airports. PFCs were capped at $3.00 per enplaned passenger, with a $12 limit on the total PFCs that a passenger could be charged per round-trip. Large and medium hub airports had their AIP apportionments reduced by 50% of their projected PFC revenues until they had forgone 50% of their apportionments. This requirement makes more AIP funding available for smaller airports that don't have the same capability to collect PFCs as do larger airports with tens of millions of enplanements annually (Kirk, 2010).

The Aviation Investment and Reform Act for the 21st Century (AIR 21) increased the PFC ceiling to $4.50. To impose a PFC above $3, an airport must show that the funded projects will make significant improvements in air safety, increase competition, or reduce congestion or noise impacts on communities and that these projects could not be funded by using the airport's AIP formula funds or through AIP discretionary grants. Large and medium hub airports imposing PFCs above the $3 level give back 75% of their AIP entitlements. Beginning in FY2001, PFCs at large and medium hub airports could not be approved unless they had submitted a written competition plan to the FAA. As of 2009, there were 56 large hub and medium hub airports and 252 smaller airports authorized to collect the $4.50 PFC.

It should be noted that the airline industry, especially as represented by Airlines 4 America (A4A), oppose PFCs and oppose raising the cap on PFCs. Airlines have argued that PFCs are actually costs incurred by the airlines, rather than the passengers. In today's price-competitive environment, a several-dollar difference in the price of a round-trip airline ticket can make the difference in whether a prospective passenger chooses one airline or another. Although a PFC is, in reality, incorporated into the price of the ticket, paid for by the passenger, airlines argue that they bear the cost of the PFC. Interestingly, airlines today charge fees for checked baggage, food, premium seats, and more. In the second quarter of 2014, U.S. passenger airlines collected a total of $900 million in baggage fees (representing 2.0 percent of total operating revenue) and $753 million from reservation change fees (representing 1.7 percent of total operating revenue). For 2013, passenger airlines collected a total of $3.3 billion in baggage fees (representing 1.7 percent of total operating revenue) and $2.8 billion from reservation change fees (representing 1.4 percent of total operating revenue). Why then should an airport not collect several dollars per enplaned passenger using their airport facilities in an effort to maintain those facilities? Thankfully, the FAA has recognized this need; thus, the approval of PFCs for the airport industry (BTS, n.d.).

AIP GRANTS

The Airport Improvement Program (AIP) provides a significant source of funding for capital development at airports. The Airport and Airway Trust Fund, established by the Airport and Airway Revenue Act of 1970, provides the revenues used to both fund AIP projects and administer the AIP. Revenues flow into the trust fund from the following sources:

- 7.5% ticket tax (domestic passenger or rural domestic passenger)
- $4.00 domestic flight segment tax
- 6.25% tax on cargo waybills
- 4.3 cents per gallon on commercial aviation fuel
- 19.3 cents per gallon on general aviation gasoline
- 21.8 cents per gallon on general aviation jet fuel
- $17.50 international arrival tax
- $8.70 plus applicable domestic tax rate for flights between continental U.S. and Alaska or Hawaii
- 7.5% of value of miles on frequent flyer mileage awards

(FAA, 2014)

The actual amount of AIP funding available each year is determined by Congress as they authorize obligation authority to distribute the trust fund resources to airports. It is important to note the difference between authorization and appropriation. Specifically, an **authorization** provides the legal authority for the federal government to undertake a program. Authorizations can be for three or five years, or only one year. An example of multi-year funding is the Vision 100–Century of Aviation Reauthorization Act of 2003, which created multi-year funding by authorizing AIP for fiscal years 2004 through 2008. An **appropriation**, on the other hand, is separately enacted by Congress each fiscal year to provide actual funding for a program. Although it is not common, Congress can authorize AIP at a specific level and then appropriate it at a lower level. When the system works well, authorizations and appropriations would be equal.

As indicated in Chapter 4, an airport must be included in the NPIAS to be eligible for AIP funding. The 2011–2015 Plan contains no less than $52.2 billion in AIP-eligible infrastructure development needs among NPIAS airports. These significant needs are driven by (a) increased traffic, resulting in the need to expand facilities; (b) rehabilitation or reconstruction of infrastructure due to use and age of facilities; and (c) improved aircraft technology, requiring airports to update or replace equipment and infrastructure. Cost estimates in the NPIAS are generated by airport master plans and state system plans that are typically prepared by planning and engineering firms for airport sponsors. Although the NPIAS is utilized by the FAA in administering the AIP program, never have all of the financial needs presented in the report been fully met with AIP funding (FAA, 2012b).

Since 1992, almost two-thirds of AIP grant funds have been used for airfield projects on airports, including runways, taxiways, aprons, and safety-related projects. AIP-eligible projects include improvements related to enhancing airport safety, capacity, security, and environmental concerns—which generally encompasses most airfield capital improvements or repairs and in some specific situations, also includes terminals, hangars, and non-aviation development. Professional services that are necessary for eligible projects (including planning, surveying, and design) are also AIP-eligible (Kirk, 2010).

Entitlements

Primary airports receive funding based on the number of enplaned passengers. This is an automatic amount of funding based purely on the number of passengers enplaned at the airport. In essence, these are funds to which airports are "entitled." **Entitlements** vary based on the following:

- $7.80 for each passenger boarding up to 50,000 passengers;
- $5.20 for each additional passenger boarding up to 100,000 passengers;
- $2.60 for each additional passenger boarding up to 500,000 passengers;
- $0.65 for each additional passenger boarding up to 1,000,000 passengers; and
- $0.50 for each additional passenger boarding from 1,000,001 passengers and up.

Primary airports will receive $1 million at a minimum. The maximum funding amount is $26 million. New airports receive the minimum for their first fiscal year of operation. Indeed, entitlements are the main type of federal AIP funding that commercial-service airports can plan for each year.

Discretionary

In essence, **discretionary** funds are funds left over after entitlements have been distributed. One-third of AIP funds are actually allocated to discretionary. Although the term would imply these funds are used at the "discretion" of Congress, in fact, there are three set-asides that airports can regularly count on. These include the airport noise set-aside (35% of discretionary funds), the military airport program (4%), and grants for reliever airports (2/3 of 1%). In practice, about 75% of the grants made from the discretionary fund are used to preserve and enhance capacity, safety, and security at primary and reliever airports and to carry out airport noise compatibility planning and programs at these airports. From the remaining 25%, $5 million is set aside for the testing and evaluation of innovative aviation security systems. In recent years, discretionary funds have ranged from roughly 24%–30% of total AIP funding (Kirk, 2010).

Grant Application Process

All grants have an application process. Even for college students searching for federal aid to support college expenses, a Free Application for Federal Student Aid (FAFSA) is required. Airports seeking federal grants are no different. Several years before applying for an AIP grant, an airport begins the process by identifying potential projects, consulting with the Airport District Office (ADO), determining the level of environmental review, determining whether the ALP needs updating, and coordinating with airport users. Simplified, the steps to undertake prior to applying for a grant include:

- Submit five-year Capital Improvement Plan (CIP) to ADO.
- Develop a project schedule.
- Develop a project scope.

By communicating with the ADO, the airport will submit these items and apply for the grant. Next steps include:

- Complete environmental review.
- Hire consultants and design project.
- Advertise and award contract.
- Construct project.
- Submit grant closeout documentation.

Note that even with AIP entitlements, airports are required to have a project on their ALP. In other words, airports are not given AIP funding simply to have. The funding must be used for AIP-eligible projects.

Grant Assurances

"Free" money (in the form of grants) often comes with "strings" attached. These "strings" for airports receiving federal grants from the FAA are known as **grant assurances**. When funds are accepted from the FAA, certain obligations (or assurances) must be complied with, which then become part of the final grant offer.

The grant assurances include the following topics:

- General
- Duration and Applicability
- Sponsor Certification
    - › General federal requirements
    - › Responsibility and authority of the sponsor
    - › Sponsor fund availability
    - › Good title
    - › Preserving rights and powers
    - › Consistency with local plans

- Consideration of local interest
- Consultation with users
- Public hearings
- Air and water quality standards
- Pavement preventive maintenance
- Terminal development prerequisites
- Accounting system, audit, and record keeping requirements
- Minimum wage rates
- Veteran's preference
- Conformity to plans and specifications
- Construction inspection and approval
- Planning projects
- Operation and maintenance
- Hazard removal and mitigation
- Compatible land use
- Economic nondiscrimination
- Exclusive rights
- Fee and rental structure
- Airport revenues
- Reports and inspections
- Use by government aircraft
- Land for federal facilities
- Airport layout plan
- Civil rights
- Disposal of land
- Engineering and design services
- Foreign market restrictions
- Policies, standards, and specifications
- Relocation and real property acquisition
- Access by intercity buses
- Disadvantaged business enterprise
- Hangar construction
- Competitive access (see Appendix B: Grant Assurances)

(FAA, 2014b)

The duration of these obligations depends on the type of recipient, the useful life of the facility being developed, and other conditions stipulated in the assurances. Specifically, grant assurances remain in effect throughout the useful life of the facilities developed or equipment acquired for an airport development or noise compatibility program project, not to exceed 20 years. The grant assurances for airport sponsors, as of 2014, were 20 pages long and are reprinted for your reference in Appendix B.

INTERNALLY-GENERATED

In addition to external sources of funding, airports generate internal funds (i.e., net income) that may be set aside for various purposes, including capital development projects. Airports with significant concession revenues (including food and beverage, retail, parking, etc.) will generate more internal funds than airports without these revenue-generating services. Thus, it is good practice for airports to capitalize on the captive audience of passengers in the terminal (as well as meeters and greeters) and offer concessions to meet the needs of these patrons.

Often, internally-generated funds provide the airport-required match for a federal grant/loan. Of course, an airport must generate net profits in order to have funds that can be used for this purpose. Often, an airport will create a fund (similar to a savings account) where funds are deposited for future use. These funds are then accessed as needed to match grant funds (or for other uses).

STATE AND LOCAL SOURCES

Although federal funding is the largest source of public funding nationwide for airports, it is only one level of funding available. Indeed, funding for airports may also be available at the state and local levels. All states have a state aviation agency, often in the form of a state department of transportation with an aviation or aeronautics branch. Funding for airports may be available from this agency. Commonly, airport funding at the state level is provided by revenues received from a state tax on aviation fuel. With this, providers of aviation fuel incorporate the state fuel tax into the price per gallon and then submit these funds to the state on a regular basis. The state then uses these funds to redistribute back to airports for capital improvement projects. This is especially important for GA airports that do not have access to PFCs, for example.

Local municipalities may also make funds available for airports. Although many airports are entities of the city, county, parish, or municipality—and funds for operating expenses (such as salaries, utilities, etc.) are distributed to the airport if needed to ensure the airport breaks even financially—the municipality may or may not provide funds for capital development of the airport. Airports often compete with many important municipal services, such as schools, police, fire, parks, etc. As an airport competes with these other municipal services for funding, it is important to educate municipal officials as to the positive benefits the airport brings to the community and the justification of the capital project.

Economic Impact of Airports

Airports are often tremendous economic engines for the communities in which they operate. This is obvious with extremely busy airports, such as Los Angeles International Airport, Hartsfield-Jackson Atlanta International Airport, Chicago O'Hare International Airport, and Dallas/Fort Worth International Airport. However, even smaller airports (with or without commercial-service) generate positive economic impacts. It's important for airports to conduct **economic impact analysis** so that these economic impacts are quantitatively determined and can be shared with municipal officials and the local community. This is especially important for smaller airports that often face opposition in the community. Sharing the good news of the positive economic impacts of the airport is a worthwhile endeavor.

Economic impact studies determine direct economic impact, as well as indirect and induced economic impact. Easiest to determine, **direct economic impacts** consist of the amount of spending that will remain within the local economy. Although some mistake direct economic impacts as the total dollars initially spent on a purchase, if a portion of these revenues is being sent to company headquarters in another state, that portion should not be included in an estimate of direct economic impacts. Thus, direct economic impacts may be less than actual revenues.

Indirect economic impacts are those impacts that result when a business makes purchases from other businesses. For example, as patrons purchase goods from airport vendors, those vendors will then make more purchases from suppliers to replenish inventory. The financial benefit to the suppliers comprises the indirect impacts.

Finally, **induced economic impacts** result from the expenditures of employee wages. For example, the employees working at an airport food and beverage concession are paid a wage and these employees in turn use these wages to purchase products and services in the local community. With an understanding of these three types of economic impacts, one can see the importance of "buying locally."

Impacts of Airline Bankruptcies on Airports

The instability of the airline industry has had substantial impacts on airports. For instance, in the months following September 11, 2001, and during the economic recession which began in 2007, many airlines completely eliminated service in smaller communities and cut back capacity at larger airports, through the use of smaller aircraft or a loss of routes or frequency of service.

Additionally, airlines with serious financial difficulty may declare bankruptcy. According to U.S. bankruptcy laws, a company may declare either Chapter 7 or Chapter 11 bankruptcy (in reference to the specific chapter of bankruptcy law). **Chapter 7 bankruptcy** is also known as liquidation or straight bankruptcy. With Chapter 7, the airline is planning to go out of business. Assets are sold, creditors are paid, and the airline then ceases to exist. This is usually a last-ditch effort after other attempts have been made at financially "repairing" the business.

The bankruptcy process which aims to allow the airline to continue operating is known as **Chapter 11 bankruptcy**. In this case, a bankruptcy judge is appointed and the airline is given time to reorganize its finances into a more stable position. Often, employee labor agreements are renegotiated, airport leases are renegotiated (with facilities possibly given up), retirement plans are altered, etc. If all goes well, the airline emerges from Chapter 11 bankruptcy in a stronger position to compete effectively. Occasionally, another airline or investor purchases the airline during the bankruptcy process. The bankrupt airline may think it is better to stay afloat, even if it means being absorbed by another airline, than to cease operations indefinitely.

Although Chapter 7 bankruptcy has a detrimental impact to airports that completely lose service by the bankrupt airline, an airline declaring bankruptcy under either Chapter 7 or 11 can create serious concern for airport management, especially if that airline serves their airport and leases facilities and space. To better cope with future airline bankruptcies, many airports have adopted

Impact of Delta/Northwest Merger on Memphis International Airport

Memphis International Airport (MEM) was once the home of a Northwest Airlines hub. However, Delta Airlines and Northwest Airlines merged in 2008. With Atlanta, the site of Delta's major hub, only 370 miles to the east of Memphis, Delta announced that effective September 2013, MEM would no longer be a hub for the combined airline. This move resulted in the loss of about three-dozen flights and about 230 jobs. The reduction marked the first time in nearly 30 years that MEM would find itself without a major passenger airline hub. As a result of the merger and Delta's decision to drop MEM as a hub, passenger enplanements declined 29.4 percent between 2008 and 2012. International enplanements declined 75.7 percent. Adjusted for inflation, the total direct economic impact of MEM in FY2012 was approximately 15.5 percent less than it was in FY2007. In reality, it made little sense for Delta to maintain two hubs in such close proximity to each other. Even so, the loss of the Northwest hub has been a significant setback for the Memphis International Airport, which now has lower passenger enplanements than it did in 2008. Fortunately, cargo is growing and the airport ranks number one in the country for total cargo handled. Mainly thanks to FedEx, cargo was up 3.8 percent from just over 4.3 billion pounds in 2008 to nearly 4.5 billion pounds in 2012. With revenue per pound averaging $2.66, this equates to more than $11.9 billion in revenue associated with cargo enplaned in Memphis.

("An Economic Assessment," n.d.; Mutzabaugh, 2013)

shorter lease terms and shorter-term use agreements. In this way, the airport is afforded more flexibility in addressing airline bankruptcies.

With possible effects similar to airline bankruptcy, a merger of two airlines may result in reduced airline service at an airport. For instance, the two merged airlines will likely consolidate operations and routes, which may negatively impact an airport. Consider an airport served by only two airlines. If these two airlines merge, the airport is now served by only one airline. With no competition, airfares may increase, and the space needed by the one airline will likely be less than the space previously needed by the two airlines combined. Thus, lease revenues would be reduced.

Performance Management and Benchmarking

To assist with determining the strength of performance (financial or otherwise) of the airport, airports often integrate **performance management** and **benchmarking**. Indeed, it can be quite helpful to airport management to know how the competition is performing and what they are doing to acquire new air service, increase parking revenues, etc. According to the Infrastructure Management Group (2010, p.10):

> Measuring and managing performance is crucial to airport success. Performance measurement is not just about identifying and tracking some numbers; it is ultimately about managing to achieve results. Performance measurement is a cyclical process that starts with identifying the ultimate outcomes an airport wants to achieve, such as safety, customer service, and financial success.

Airports use airport performance indicators (API) to judge their performance among peer airports. Although airports may be interested in different metrics or measurements, the following are common APIs (by category) in use among airports today:

- Airfield operations
  - Aircraft operations
- Air service
  - Cargo tons—Change over prior period
  - Enplanements—Change over prior period
  - Nonstop destinations—Change in number of domestic and international
  - Passenger flights—Change in number of domestic and international
- Concessions
  - Concession revenue to the airport as percent of total operating revenue
  - Concession revenue to the airport per enplaned passenger
  - Rental car revenue to the airport per destination passenger

- Financial
  - Airline cost per enplaned passenger
  - Airport cost per enplaned passenger
  - Bond rating
  - Days unrestricted cash on hand
  - Debt per enplanement
  - Debt service coverage ratio
  - Non-aeronautical operating revenue as percent of total operating revenue
  - Non-aeronautical operating revenue per enplanement
  - Operating cost per enplanement
- General aviation
  - Based aircraft
  - Fuel use/sales—Change over prior period
  - Hangar rental and ground lease income
- Human resources
  - Minority/Women/DBE participation rate; actual versus cost
  - Salary + Wages + Benefits cost as a percent of total operating cost
  - Salary + wages + Benefits cost per airport employee
  - Employee turnover
- Parking
  - Parking revenue to the airport per originating passenger
- Planning/construction
  - Construction projects—Actual versus budgeted costs of significant projects
- Properties/contracts
  - Landing fee rate
- Safety risk management
  - Employee accidents and injuries—Lost work days
- Service quality
  - Customer satisfaction with airport

(Hazel, Blais, Browne, & Benzon, 2011).

As airports attempt to measure their performance among their peers, benchmarking is crucial. In practice, this can include both self-benchmarking and peer benchmarking. **Self-benchmarking** allows an airport to determine how well it is doing internally, compared perhaps to prior years or quarters. **Peer benchmarking**, on the other hand, requires the airport to compare its performance with peer airports. The APIs listed above are used in both techniques, with most APIs suited to self-benchmarking, some suited to peer benchmarking, and some suited to both (Hazel, et al., 2011).

Concluding Thoughts

Airports typically have capital development needs that amount of millions of dollars. Fortunately, an airport may obtain funding for these projects from a variety of sources. However, the airport director must be proactive and diligent in pursuing funding from these sources. Additionally, although AIP funding is "free" funding, it does come with strings attached in the form of grant assurances. It is imperative for the airport to comply with these numerous assurances to avoid jeopardizing future AIP funds.

Chapter Summary

- Funds for airport development are derived from a variety of sources and include federal, state, and local grants; bond proceeds; passenger facility charges; airport-generated funds (from landing and terminal fees, parking, and concessions revenue); and tenant and third-party financing.
- Bonds represent an IOU, and require the bond issuer to pay regular interest and eventually pay off the bond principal.
- A bond issue is assigned a rating or grade by one or more of the bond rating agencies to enable potential investors to determine the strength of the firm issuing the bonds.
- The general obligation (GO) bond is a common form of bond for municipalities nationwide, including many airports, and is supported by the overall tax base of the issuing entity.
- The revenue bond is becoming more common among airports and is supported by revenues of the issuing entity.
- The PFC-backed bond is a form of revenue bond that is supported by PFCs assessed by the airport.
- Bonds issued on future grant funds require a letter of intent from the FAA.
- The alternative minimum tax was designed to ensure that all taxpayers pay at least a minimum amount of federal taxes on their income, preventing individual taxpayers from taking unfair advantage of the various federal tax preferences and incentives. Tax-exempt governmental bonds are not subject to the AMT.
- PFCs allow airports that support millions of passengers annually to tap into a significant revenue source authorized by the FAA by assessing a facility charge on each passenger.
- The Airport Improvement Program (AIP), funded by the Airport and Airway Trust Fund, generates funding for AIP-eligible capital development at airports.

- AIP entitlements are based on passenger enplanements, whereas AIP discretionary funds are at the discretion of Congress and include funds for noise programs, the military airport program, reliever airports, and projects that enhance capacity, safety, and security.
- The grant application process includes submitting a five-year CIP, developing a project schedule, developing a project scope, completing an environmental review, hiring a consultant and designing the project, advertising and awarding the contract, constructing the project, and submitting grant closeout documentation.
- Grant assurances are the "strings" attached to an AIP grant, requiring the airport to comply with numerous requirements.
- Internally generated funds can be set aside to provide some or all of the matching funds for a grant.
- State and local funding may also be available to airports for capital development.
- Economic impact studies determine direct economic impact, as well as indirect and induced economic impact.
- Chapter 7 bankruptcy is also known as liquidation or straight bankruptcy. With Chapter 7, the airline is planning to go out of business.
- Chapter 11 bankruptcy allows the airline to continue operating, and requires the airline to reorganize operations.
- Airports often integrate performance management and benchmarking to assist in determining the strength of their performance (financial or otherwise). Benchmarking is crucial in measuring performance against peer airports.
- Airports use airport performance indicators to judge their performance among peer airports.

Review Questions ↘

1. List the sources available to airports in securing funding for capital development.
2. Explain the typical breakdown of capital development funding sources.
3. Explain matching funds.
4. Define bond indenture.
5. Explain the role of the underwriter.
6. What two questions are first asked by the rating agencies when rating a bond issue?
7. Define general obligation (GO) bonds.
8. Why are GO bonds an important form of financing, especially for smaller airports?
9. Define revenue bonds.
10. Define PFC-backed bonds.
11. Define bonds to be backed by future grants.
12. Define alternative minimum tax.
13. Explain passenger facility charges.
14. Define AIP entitlements funds.
15. Define AIP discretionary funds.
16. Describe the grant application process.
17. Explain grant assurances.
18. What impact do airline bankruptcies have on airports?
19. Explain Chapter 7 and Chapter 11 bankruptcies.
20. Explain performance management and benchmarking.

Scenarios

1. As airport manager of a nonhub airport with 23,000 enplanements annually, you are faced with a CIP that has over $6 million in capital improvements planned for the next five years. What options are available to secure funding? Based on the size of the airport, which options are most practical?
2. As the CFO of a large hub airport with 30 million enplanements, you are considering applying for authorization to collect a $4.50 PFC. Your airport is currently authorized to collect a $3.00 PFC. Would it be more advantageous to collect a $4.50 PFC, considering the AIP funding that would have to be foregone?
3. As the newly hired director of performance management at a large hub airport, you are considering how to best measure the performance of the airport. This will require benchmarking and comparison to peer airports. Which airport performance indicators (API) will you use and why?
4. The airport for which you serve as director of finance is preparing a $110 million bond issue. You are tasked with preparing for a visit by a bond rating agency. How do you prepare? Develop a schedule for their two-day visit.
5. The community has recently been vocal in their opposition of the airport for which you serve as airport director. They seem to think your airport does nothing for the local community. Although your airport is only a GA airport, it clearly plays an important role in the community. Conduct online research on airport economic impacts. Review some airport economic impact studies and begin preparing your response to the community. Your goal is to determine your airport's economic impacts and show how beneficial your airport is to the local economy.

References and Resources for Further Study

Bureau of Transportation Statistics (BTS). n.d. Airline Financial Data Press Releases. Retrieved from http://www.rita.dot.gov/bts/sites/rita.dot.gov.bts/files/press_releases/airline_financial_data.html

"An Economic Assessment of the Impact of the Memphis International Airport." n.d. Accessed May 2015 at http://memphis.edu/sbber/pdfs/impactstudies/mem_economic_impact_2012_executive_summary.pdf

Federal Aviation Administration (FAA). 2012a. "Overview: What is AIP?" Retrieved from http://www.faa.gov/airports/aip/overview/

———. 2012b. 2013–2017 National Plan of Integrated Airport Systems (NPIAS). Retrieved from http://www.faa.gov/airports/planning_capacity/npias/reports/

———. 2014a. "Current Aviation Excise Tax Structure." Retrieved from http://www.faa.gov/about/office_org/headquarters_offices/apl/aatf/media/14.1.17ExciseTaxStructureCalendar2014.pdf

———. 2014b. Grant Assurances Airport Sponsors. Retrieved from http://www.faa.gov/airports/aip/grant_assurances/media/airport-sponsor-assurances-aip.pdf

Hazel, R. A., J. D. Blais, T. J. Browne, and D. M. Benzon. 2011. "Resource Guide to Airport Performance Indicators." ACRP Report 19A. Washington, DC: Transportation Research Board.

Infrastructure Management Group. 2010. "Developing an Airport Performance-Measurement System." ACRP Report 19. Washington, DC: Transportation Research Board.

Kirk, R. 2010. "Airport Improvement Program: Reauthorization Issues for Congress." Congressional Research Service.

Moody's. n.d. "How to Get Rated." Retrieved from https://www.moodys.com/ratings-process/How-to-Get-Rated/002001

Mutzabaugh, B. 2013. "Delta to pull plug on Memphis hub after Labor Day." *USA Today*, June 4. Retrieved from http://www.usatoday.com/story/todayinthesky/2013/06/04/delta-air-lines-to-pull-plug-on-memphis-hub/2390515/

Nichol, C. 2007. "Innovative Finance and Alternative Sources of Revenue for Airports." ACRP Synthesis 1. Washington, DC: Transportation Research Board.

Chapter 15

Future Challenges and Opportunities

Objectives ↘

Upon completion of this chapter, you should be able to explain the challenges and opportunities presented by:

- airline bankruptcies and mergers.
- new large aircraft.
- capital development funding.
- unfunded federal mandates.
- passenger leakage.
- customer service.
- sustainability.
- airside congestion.
- unmanned systems.

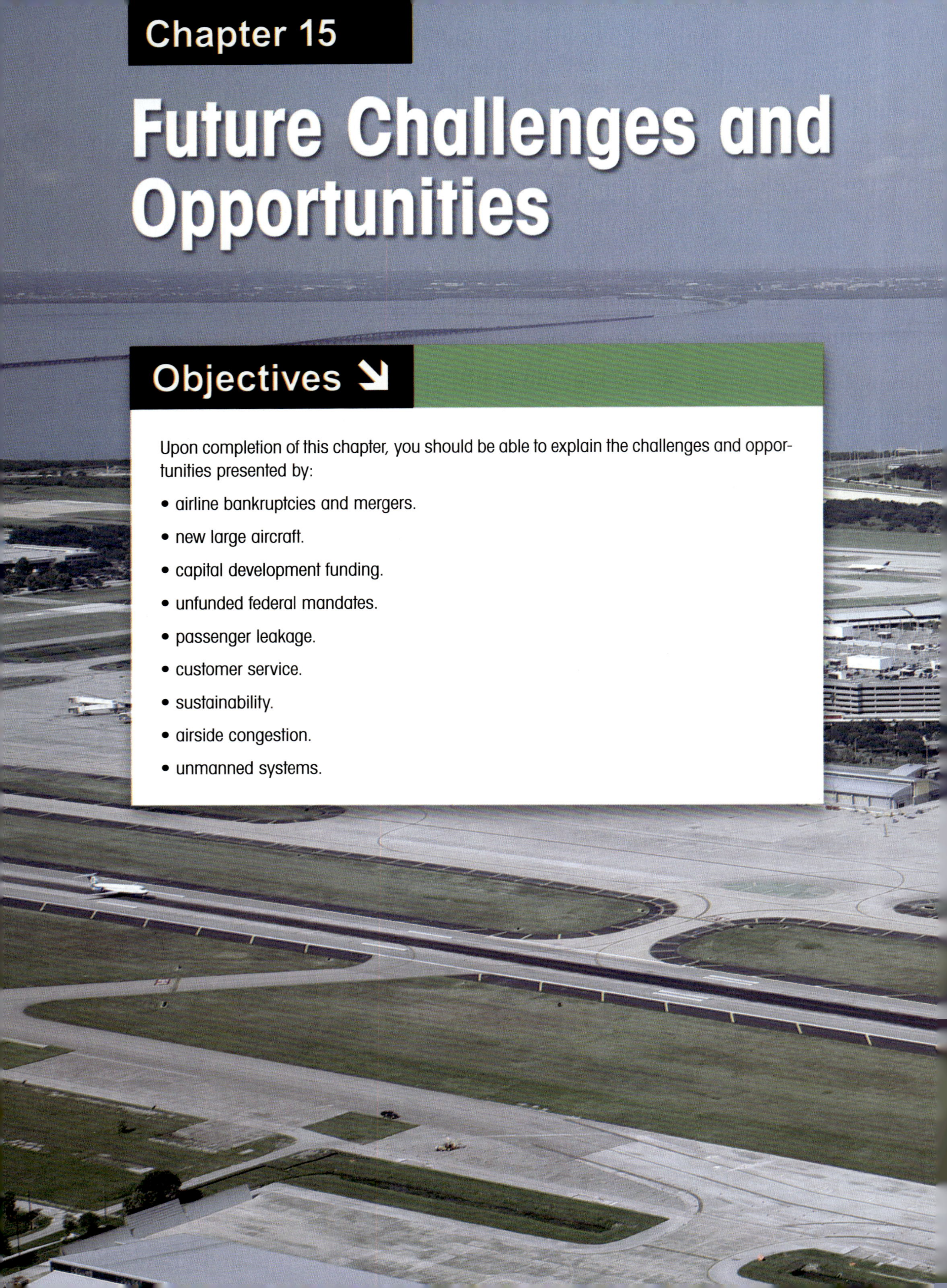

Key Terms

costs per enplaned passenger (CPE)

unmanned aircraft system (UAS)

In Chapter 15

Introduction 561

Airline Bankruptcies and Mergers............ 561

New Large Aircraft 562

Capital Development Funding 563

Unfunded Federal Mandates 564

Passenger Leakage 565

Customer Service 566

Sustainability Initiatives 567

Airside Congestion................................ 568

Unmanned Aircraft Systems................... 569

Concluding Thoughts.............................570

Chapter Summary 571

Review Questions................................. 572

Scenarios... 573

References and Resources for Further Study 573

FEATURES

Passenger Retention Analysis at Gillette–Campbell County Airport 565

One airport's effort to determine, and thereby minimize, passenger leakage.

Introduction

One thing all airport leaders have in common is the need to meet future challenges they and their airports will face. The aviation industry is dynamic, requiring airport leaders to forecast, adjust plans as necessary, and proactively meet future challenges. To be successful, this requires an "outside-the-box" mindset. Airport leaders who adopt the attitude of "we've always done it that way" and who have an "old school" mentality will likely multiply the challenges they face. On the other hand, airport leaders who innovate, lead with an outstretched hand, and stay in touch with industry trends will be much better able to meet future challenges head on.

Airline Bankruptcies and Mergers

The airline industry is in an ever-evolving state. Especially since deregulation of the industry in 1978, we have witnessed numerous bankruptcies, mergers, and acquisitions. The airline industry of today is a far cry from that of 1978. As a result, airports have been forced to adjust to this dynamic industry. Although GA airports exist to serve the GA industry, commercial-service airports mainly serve air carriers. And even with a substantially larger revenue base than most GA airports, these commercial-service airports are at the mercy of the air carriers and the seemingly monthly announcements of bankruptcies, mergers, etc.

All of this activity in the industry does not lead to expansion. Rather, it leads to consolidation of the industry. And this consolidation greatly impacts airports. For instance, consider the commercial-service airport served by only one air carrier. What if that sole air carrier declares bankruptcy? That airport will suddenly be faced with no commercial service, which can be severely detrimental to a community. Or consider an airport that is served by two air carriers, each having about 50 percent of the market. What if these two carriers merge? Suddenly, this airport will be served by only one air carrier, and due to routes previously shared by the two carriers, the airport may see a reduction in service beyond the anticipated 50 percent previously had by the independent air carrier.

In essence, commercial-service airports have a vested interested in maintaining a healthy airline industry with numerous carriers. Competition is good for business, resulting in lower airfares for consumers and more of a cushion for an airport. Airports served by a dozen or so air carriers are in a much better position than airports served by a sole air carrier. Airports would like to avoid "putting all their eggs in one basket." This requires airports to cater to their air carriers, just as they cater to passengers and meeters and greeters.

Just how should an airport do this? First, airports should focus on minimizing costs for airlines, often measured in terms of **cost per enplaned passenger (CPE)**. This includes landing fees, terminal rent, baggage claim rent, and other fees charged to the airlines. Although airports are expected to charge airlines reasonable fees for the facilities they use, if an airport focuses on increasing non-aeronautical revenues, more reasonable fees can be charged to the airlines. Additionally, airports should practice excellent customer service to the airlines. On a practical level, this means possibly creating an airline station manager's committee or association. Additionally, any work requests or immediate repairs phoned in by an airline to the airport should be addressed in a timely manner. The airlines should feel they are well taken care of and appreciated by the airport. It is also helpful for senior airport personnel to visit with the airlines at their corporate headquarters at least annually. Proactively stressing the positive attributes of the airport and community to the airline's route planners and senior leadership can develop and continue a positive relationship that may serve the airport well into the future. For instance, if an airline begins to experience financial difficulty and consider service cutbacks, a supportive airport may receive a more favorable review than an airport that is not as supportive.

In sum, senior airport personnel should view airlines serving their airport as partners in the health of the airport. Having sufficient airline service for the community will actually make the airport director appear quite successful. Many airport boards and communities place sufficient airline service as a top priority, meaning they equate this airline service with success on the part of the airport director. The irony is that oftentimes the airport director has little to do with the airline service at an airport, although the success of this individual is judged in light of this service. True, the airport director can meet with airline route planners and senior leadership, but airlines are for-profit enterprises and if there is not enough demand in a community to ensure the airline will at least break even, the airline won't begin service regardless of the airport director's good intentions. Incentives (such as reduced or no landing fees for a short period time, such as six months) may entice a carrier to take a chance on a community, but if revenues don't materialize, the airline won't hesitate to pull out.

New Large Aircraft

In past years, airports were not too concerned with aircraft that might exceed the airport's limits. At least at most commercial-service airports, little thought generally was given to the load limits of runways, taxiways, and ramps; wingtip clearances for aircraft maneuvering the airfield; or passenger loads on terminal buildings. However, in today's world of larger aircraft able to accommodate up to almost 900 passengers, airport leaders must consider the impact of these new large aircraft on their airport—both airside and landside.

FAA Advisory Circular 150/5300-13A, *Airport Design* (introduced in Chapter 5), clearly spells out the aircraft approach category, airplane design group, and visibility minimums that make up the runway design code. The Airbus A380 is the first civilian aircraft that falls into Airplane Design Group VI (Figure 15-1). Prior to the A380 entering service, Group V was the largest category of civilian aircraft that would be expected to serve an airport. What

Figure 15-1. Airbus A380.

(Nan Phanitsuda Sophonpanasak, Denver International Airport)

challenges do this new Group VI aircraft bring to an airport? Design criteria will be impacted, as adequate wingtip clearance, for example, is provided for this and other large aircraft.

Although an airport may request a modification to standards (as discussed in Chapter 7), an airport desiring to meet the design requirements of a Group VI aircraft will be required to alter various components of the airfield. For instance, an existing E-V airport will need to expand the runway from 150 feet in width to 200 feet in width to become an E-VI airport. Additionally, taxiways will need to be widened from 70 feet to 100 feet in width. Bringing an entire airfield up to these standards requires a substantial investment. And if the Group VI aircraft will only service the airport several times per week, an airport may decide to petition the FAA for a modification to standards.

Also consider the impacts on the landside of the new large aircraft. Traditionally, when a Boeing 737 parks at a gate, only about 130 passengers unload. However, if an A380 parks at the gate, more than 500 (and up to 853) may unload. This large number of passengers will impact the restrooms, food and beverage, retail, people movers, baggage claim, rental cars, taxis, hotel shuttles, etc. In essence, a fully loaded A380 will have the same impact on the landside as more than six arriving 737s. On the airfield, however, the A380 represents one operation, just as a 737 does.

Capital Development Funding

Airports are always planning 10–20 years into the future to meet projected demand, which is why an airport master plan commonly has a 20-year planning horizon. If an airport were to wait until projected demand is realized before breaking ground on a new terminal or parking garage, for instance, it would be too late. From planning to completion, large capital development projects take years to complete, so planning ahead is imperative. Due to this, it seems that many airports (especially commercial-service) always have a construction project underway. This capital development can be expensive and capital development funding must be in place for such projects.

As explained in Chapter 14, capital development funding can come from many different sources, including bonds, PFCs, AIP, internally generated, and state and local sources. Possibly the most challenging of these for airports is AIP funding. This is true even today. For the 2013–2017 timeframe, for example, $42.5 billion in AIP-eligible capital development projects were identified in the NPIAS, which amounts to $8.5 billion annually. However, AIP grants rarely total much more than $3 billion annually. This amounts to more than $5.5 billion in annual airport capital development needs that are not met by AIP grants. Clearly, this is a huge shortfall. Although it would not be feasible for the FAA to grant more AIP funds to airports than the Airport and Airway Trust Fund can generate, it is important for airport leadership to convey the importance of capital development funding to elected representatives who may have an impact on securing more funding for airports in the future.

Airports have been forced to either obtain funding from other sources (such as bonds, PFCs, and retained earnings) or forgo planned improvements. In particular, PFCs have been helpful, with collections typically exceeding $2 billion annually. However, this challenge is not likely to go away; as construction costs increase and airport capital development needs grow, funding for capital development will become increasingly needed.

Unfunded Federal Mandates

Unfunded federal mandates refers to regulatory requirements that are mandatory, cost money to meet, and yet don't have any funding tied to them. In essence, airports are asked by the FAA or TSA to adopt a certain measure, which may cost hundreds of thousands of dollars or more to implement, and then are required to find the money to implement the measure. Although certain airports may have sufficient revenues to meet these mandates, others may have difficulty in securing the financing needed to comply.

The challenge for airports is that they are tasked with a new regulation or requirement, and yet are forced to find their own source of funds to pay for the projects, personnel, or other expenses associated with meeting the new regulation or requirement. A simple example was the requirement for airports in the FAA southeast region to mark runway closures with a raised, lighted "X." Prior to this requirement, there were inexpensive ways to mark closed runways, such as with yellow-painted plywood secured with sandbags. With the new requirement, airports were forced to purchase lighted Xs at a cost of about $50,000 each. Where did this money come from? True, an airport could obtain funding through various sources, but the FAA didn't send a $100,000 check to each of the certificated airports in the southern region to purchase the required lighted Xs.

Unfunded federal mandates will require airport leadership to be more innovative in securing funds to comply with these mandates. Proactive airport leaders have found that it is wise to develop a contingency fund for unplanned expenses, including unfunded mandates.

Passenger Leakage

Commercial-service airports must always remain aware of their passenger enplanements. This number changes regularly and can impact the categorization of the airport (such as large hub) as well as funding. In essence, passenger leakage refers to individuals living in the local area or metropolitan statistical area (MSA) that, rather than take a flight out of their local airport, choose instead to drive an hour or several hours away to take a flight out of another airport. By driving out of the local area and taking a flight out of a competing airport, the local airport experiences leakage because the airport "lost" a potential passenger.

Airport leaders agree that passenger leakage such as this cannot be completely eliminated. Individuals have freedom of choice. They can choose to fly out of Airport A or Airport B. They can also choose to drive, take the bus, or choose not to go. Another factor involves the motivation for choosing to fly out of another airport. Airfares greatly affect this decision. Non-stop flights also have an impact on this decision.

Passenger Retention Analysis at Gillette–Campbell County Airport

Located in Gillette, Wyoming, Gillette–Campbell County Airport, through their consultant, performed a passenger retention analysis in March 2013. This airport, a nonhub airport, enjoyed 32,714 enplaned passengers in 2014 and was served by two air carriers—Delta and United. With a catchment area of 40,433, Gillette had nonstop service to two major hubs, Denver and Salt Lake City. According to the study, Gillette–Campbell County Airport retained 59 percent of all passengers over the survey period. However, the study found that passengers leaked to Rapid City, South Dakota, a two-hour drive, as well as Denver, Colorado, a nearly six-hour drive. Passengers leaking to Rapid City most often chose United, Delta, or American. Passengers leaking to Denver most often chose air carriers that do not serve Gillette, often low-cost carriers like Frontier and Southwest. The study found that leakage of passengers from Gillette is decreasing overall, likely due to the finding that average airfares in Gillette are falling, with the price gap between Gillette and nearby airports shrinking. Generally, passengers drive to another airport outside their local area for either lower airfares or more direct and better service. Airports that address these issues, in coordination with air carriers, can minimize leakage.

(Gillette Campbell County Airport, 2013)

Consider these factors that may affect an individual's decision on which flight to take:

- Airline (frequent flyer miles, safety record, baggage fees, etc.)
- Number of intermediate stops (non-stops are usually much preferred)
- Time of departure (convenient departure times are much preferred)
- Airfare (lower cost a priority)
- Airport parking and services (pricing, convenience, etc.)
- Distance from competing airport (number of miles the individual must drive, with cost of fuel part of the decision)

Even with these variables, airport leaders agree that airports can make a concerted effort to minimize leakage. Advertising campaigns can be initiated to encourage individuals in the local area to choose their local airport. Any new airline service (including seasonal, new airlines, or increased frequency) should be advertised heavily in the local community. An airline may pay for this, but the airport can also play a part in "selling" the airport to the local community. In other words, it is important to make it a difficult decision for an individual considering driving to an airport outside the local area. The easy decision should be to utilize the local airport (see Figure 15-2).

Figure 15-2. Advertising air service: Emphasizing low fares may help reduce passenger leakage.

(Wikimedia Commons; see credit on page 624)

Customer Service

On all levels, airport employees' priority must be to provide exceptional customer service. Especially today, with the extensive use of technology (including automated phone systems) and numerous charges for what was free in the past (such as airline baggage fees), customer service in some areas of the aviation industry is almost nonexistent. With this realization, airports can step up and provide a positive customer experience, even for passengers who have had a poor experience with an airline in the past.

Providing exceptional customer service requires a daily focus on the customer (both internal and external) and this begins with the commitment of senior airport leadership. It requires employees to anticipate customer needs and work to satisfy those needs before the customer even asks. There are FBOs in this country that are well-known for providing exceptional customer service and it often means that their personnel anticipate customer needs, strive to meet those needs, and exceed customer expectations—treating everyone as if they are the CEO of a company arriving onto the ramp (flight crew included). To encourage exceptional customer service, the airport director could, for example, begin a new customer service initiative with customer service training for employees, and an award program for employees going above and beyond.

Customer service will remain a future challenge for airports because as new employees are hired and others resign or retire, the culture of the organization may change, requiring a constant reprioritizing of airport values, including customer service. Additionally, customer service can begin to suffer as employees become comfortable and somewhat uninvolved over the years. If the airport director initiates a new customer service initiative with training provided to employees, but then does nothing else, it will be only a matter of years (if not months) before customer service will suffer once again. And especially if the airport has a negative culture, it will take time to change the culture and obtain buy-in from employees regarding the benefits of providing exceptional customer service. It does, after all, require additional effort on the part of employees. But this is effort well expended.

Sustainability Initiatives

Airports also must remain aware of public perception. This often revolves around the impact airports have on the environment. Proactive airport leaders are aware of this and remain committed to reducing their airport's carbon footprint. Fortunately, airports have various options for accomplishing this.

A common sustainability initiative involves the use of renewable sources of energy. This may include the use of solar, wind, water, geothermal, and biomass. Of these renewable sources, airports have most commonly capitalized on solar energy, for several reasons. Airports often occupy hundreds if not thousands of acres with ready access to the sun (Figure 15-3). Also, photovoltaic panels can

Figure 15-3. Use of solar power as a source of renewable energy at an airport.

(bspguy/Bigstock.com)

be installed close to the ground, minimizing any concerns with height restrictions (unlike with wind turbines). Of course, a solar power installation can be expensive, requiring the airport leader to be innovative in securing funds for such a worthwhile project.

In addition to capitalizing on renewable sources of energy, airports proactive in this area have developed environmentally friendly buildings, such as LEED-certified terminal buildings. These may include air filtration systems, low flow or waterless toilets, natural light via skylights, low energy consumption lighting, sustainable building materials, etc. To achieve this, airport leaders must specify the need for an environmentally friendly building in the initial planning stages as architects and engineers are developing the plans for the building.

Aircraft noise is always a challenge for airports and airport leaders must remain aware of the impacts of negative publicity associated with aircraft noise. Initiatives can be undertaken to minimize aircraft noise, including noise abatement programs, hiring a noise officer, installing a noise monitoring system, and building a ground run-up enclosure to allow aircraft to be powered above idle while on the ground, with much of the resulting noise absorbed and deflected upward.

In sum, environmental challenges will never cease, requiring airport leaders to be proactive in this area. Likely, this will become even more important in the future, especially as discussions of global warming continue.

Airside Congestion

Some airports, especially commercial-service airports located in major metropolitan areas, experience times when demand exceeds capacity, resulting in delays and even congestion on the airfield (Figure 15-4). With AIP funding levels below what would be required at many airports to increase capacity with airfield improvements, airports may not be increasing capacity at the rate needed by the airlines. Generally, airports only have so much land and room to expand. For example, San Diego International Airport has only one runway and doesn't have land for another. Thus, the airport's available land constrains its

Figure 15-4. Airfield congestion.

capacity today and in the future. Other airports, like Hartsfield-Jackson Atlanta International Airport, have created more capacity by building new runways and airfield features such as end-around taxiways and high-speed exits, but the sheer number of operations and enplanements (along with airlines' tightly bunched schedules) ensure that airfield demand exceeds capacity at certain times.

As such, congestion on the airfield will continue to challenge airport leaders in the future. It will be important for airport leaders to not only adopt efforts to increase capacity and better utilize existing capacity, but also petition the airlines to de-peak their flight schedules so that arrivals and departures are not so bunched. Clearly, if airlines schedule ten arrivals at 8:30, delays will result. However, if those ten arrivals are spread out over even a ten-minute period, the airfield could possibly accommodate the demand with minimal or no delay.

Unmanned Aircraft Systems

An **unmanned aircraft system (UAS)** includes the unmanned aircraft (UA) and all of the associated support equipment, such as control station, data links, telemetry, communications and navigation equipment, required to operate the unmanned aircraft. The UA is the flying portion of the system, flown by a pilot via a ground control system, or autonomously through use of an on-board computer, communication links, and any additional equipment that is necessary for the UA to operate safely. Although the military has been using UAS dating back to WWI, commercial use of UAS is a much more recent phenomenon (FAA, 2015).

According to the FAA, "Unmanned aircraft systems (UAS) are inherently different from manned aircraft. Introducing UAS into the nation's airspace is challenging for both the FAA and aviation community, because the U.S. has the busiest, most complex airspace in the world" (FAA, 2015). However, after approving six UAS test sites in 2014/2015, the FAA issued an NPRM, Operation and Certification of Small Unmanned Aircraft Systems, on February 23, 2015. This NPRM presents proposed guidelines for commercial use of UAS that weigh less than 55 pounds. According to this proposed rule, among other requirements, the operation of small UAS must remain within visual line of sight by the operator or visual observer, operation will be restricted to daylight only, UAS may operate at a maximum altitude of 500 feet AGL, and operators will be required to obtain an unmanned aircraft operator certificate with a small UAS rating.

Clearly, the UAS landscape is continuing to evolve, with many significant changes expected in the near future. There is great demand by firms of all types to operate UAS in the national airspace system for profit-driven purposes. Airports leaders must remain current on this continually changing landscape and determine what impact, if any, UAS will have on their airport and aircraft operations. Although UAS are being integrated into the national airspace system, albeit cautiously by the FAA, airport leaders will need to stand up to protect their airports and ensure the safety of aircraft operating into and out of their facility. That being said, an airport leader should not simply avoid this reality. For the innovative airport leader, the increasing popularity of UAS may present significant opportunities for new and enhanced uses of the airport and airport property.

Concluding Thoughts

Airport leaders of the future will need to be innovative, proactive, and well-aware of current aviation trends affecting the airport industry. Although some of this can be learned, this textbook does not attempt to be the sole resource for the airport professional. For those students desiring to enter the airport industry, it is important to learn the history, the terms and concepts, and the practical application of this knowledge. The scenarios in this textbook were designed to allow the reader to apply knowledge gained toward solving real-world issues. Likewise, the case studies were designed to provide practical insight into real-world airport issues that were encountered and successfully resolved. In addition to this resource, it is important to learn from professionals active in the industry, whether through an internship or a less-formal shadowing arrangement. It is only through practical knowledge and actual airport experience that airport professionals will be prepared to meet the future challenges of the airport industry.

Chapter Summary

- The airline industry is dynamic and quite volatile, with mergers and acquisitions commonplace, especially in a post-deregulated environment.
- Airports serving air carriers should strive to minimize cost per enplaned passenger.
- The impacts of new large aircraft, such as the A380, must be considered in terminal design, airfield design, landside access, etc.
- The methods by which to fund capital development, and the amount of funding available for capital development, will remain a challenge for airports.
- Unfunded federal mandates are becoming the norm, and airports will be required to develop alternative financing strategies to fund compliance with these mandates.
- Air carrier airports are always concerned about passenger leakage, especially if an airport is located within driving distance to an alternative air carrier airport. Thus, creative strategies of minimizing passenger leakage must be considered to minimize this to the extent possible.
- In the service-oriented airline industry, airports must place an emphasis on meeting customer needs. Offering top-notch customer service requires consistently exceeding customer expectations.
- Environmental concerns are now a mainstream topic and airports that focus on implementing green initiatives will be welcomed by the community.
- As the industry grows, and few (if any) new air carrier airports are built, congestion will continue to increase. Airports must creatively adopt strategies to minimize congestion whenever possible, as this will provide benefits to airlines, passengers, air traffic control, other users, and the airport itself.
- Unmanned aircraft systems and their integration in the national airspace system continues to evolve, requiring airports to remain current on this topic.

Review Questions

1. Considering the current industry climate, which airlines are likely to merge and why?
2. Explain the manner in which airline mergers are beneficial for consumers.
3. Explain the manner in which airline mergers are detrimental to consumers.
4. Should airlines that are on the verge of bankruptcy be allowed to go out of business?
5. In what ways do new large aircraft create better efficiencies for airports?
6. Explain the challenges for airports of new large aircraft.
7. Discuss the importance of adopting an innovative mindset in securing capital development funding.
8. Why is more than one source of capital development funding often necessary to fully fund a project?
9. If unfunded mandates are such a concern, what can airport professionals do to meet this challenge?
10. Why is customer service such a challenge for airports?
11. Describe a poor customer service experience you've had.
12. Explain passenger leakage.
13. How can an airport prevent leakage?
14. Explain why customer service is important.
15. Why are many airports adopting green initiatives?
16. What are the most common green initiatives adopted by airports?
17. How common is airside congestion at commercial-service airports?
18. What are some methods to ease airside congestion at airports?
19. What are some methods to ease landside congestion at airports?
20. What do you consider to be the most significant challenge confronting airports over the next ten years, and why?

Scenarios ↘

1. As executive director of a large hub airport, you are in the middle of a master plan update. As part of this process, you have asked the consultant responsible for the master plan update to consider future challenges that your airport may face. Why is this important? Are there any challenges not addressed in this chapter that you feel could affect your airport in the future? Why?
2. As the director of planning at a large hub, Group V airport, you are told by the executive director that Singapore Airlines may begin service with A380 aircraft in 6–9 months. What options are available to you in accommodating this aircraft?
3. As the director of marketing at a small hub airport, your job performance is judged in part by the number of passengers enplaned at the airport. Concern has been expressed by the amount of leakage, as many potential passengers in the local area drive two hours south to take flights that are oftentimes less expensive. Passenger enplanements at your airport have declined 9 percent from the previous year since low-fare service was introduced by Allegiant at this other airport. How do you counteract this leakage? Develop a plan to confront this challenge head on.

References and Resources for Further Study

Federal Aviation Administration. 2015. "Unmanned Aircraft Systems." Retrieved from https://www.faa.gov/uas/

Gillette Campbell County Airport. 2013. Passenger Retention Analysis. Retrieved at http://www.ccgov.net/ArchiveCenter/ViewFile/Item/129

Appendix A

Case Studies

Airport Solar Farm 575

Airport Emergency Exercise 579

Airport Operations Department Administrative Challenges 581

Airfield Lighting 589

Aircraft Laser Strike 594

Airport Noise 598

Airport Solar Farm

Developed by Gene Conrad, C.M. & Brett Fay, C.M.
Lakeland Linder Regional Airport

BACKGROUND

High operational costs continue to be a major issue for airports across the country and can create significant obstacles to achieving financial self-sufficiency. With energy rates continuing to rise, reducing the cost of electricity at airports has never been more important. In a continuing effort to lower energy costs and reduce environmental impacts, the Lakeland Linder Regional Airport began discussing the possibility of a large solar panel installation to be located on the airport in late 2007. The concept involved creating a 40-acre solar farm on the western edge of the airport property, outside of the Airport Operations Area. To ensure the realization of this new alternative energy source, the airport would need to secure funding and address a wide range of issues and challenges.

FUNDING

The first major step in building this solar farm was to secure funding for the project. The funding would be established through a unique public–private partnership between the City of Lakeland and Sun Edison. In the agreement, Sun Edison would pay for the construction of the solar farm and the City of Lakeland would purchase the electricity for a long term fixed rate over the next twenty five years. The airport would provide the land for the solar farm in exchange for energy credits at a rate of two cents per kilowatt-hour (kWh). This agreement would generate nearly $250,000 annually for the airport with no cost associated with planning or construction. With clear benefits to the airport and surrounding communities, a suitable location would need to be agreed upon.

LOCATION

It was decided that determining a suitable location for the airport solar farm would be critical to the overall success of the project. After conducting a site survey and review of the airport master plan, the airport determined that locating the solar field just outside of the existing runway protection zone (RPZ) for runway 9/27 would be the optimal location. This determination was based on several critical factors. First, the solar panels would require an east/west orientation to track the sun throughout the day and maximize efficiency. Next, all equipment would need to be located in an area that would not create any interference with navigational aids or air traffic operations. Finally, selecting a location that would not hinder the future development plans for the airport was critical. The final location resulted in a site that would meet all requirements for both the airport and the project. After determining a final location, several potential safety concerns were identified and would need to be thoroughly evaluated before the project could move forward.

Figure A-1.
Solar farm with airport in the background.

(Brett Fay, C.M.)

GLARE

Safety in and around the airport environment is paramount and remains at the forefront of any decision regarding site selection and location. The airport had been proactive in addressing any potential safety concerns early in the project development phase. However, due to the location of the solar panels, the Federal Aviation Administration was concerned that light reflecting from the solar panels had the potential to cause glare for pilots landing or departing Runway 9/27. Subsequently, the airport conducted a "glare analysis" to determine any potential negative effects on pilot visibility. The results of the analysis concluded that photovoltaic panels absorb nearly two-thirds of all light reaching the panels. In addition, new solar panels have an anti-reflective coating which further reduces the amount of sunlight reflected. The result is highly efficient solar panels that produce a glare potential similar to that of grassy vegetation (see Figure A-2).

ENVIRONMENTAL

In addition to safety issues, the airport made a concerted effort to identify any potential environmental hazards that might be associated with the project. Even when a project is inherently environmentally friendly, there can be unintended environmental impacts associated with the construction. The City of Lakeland conducted an environmental study that identified several issues requiring

Figure A-2. Reflectivity of common surface materials compared to solar panels.

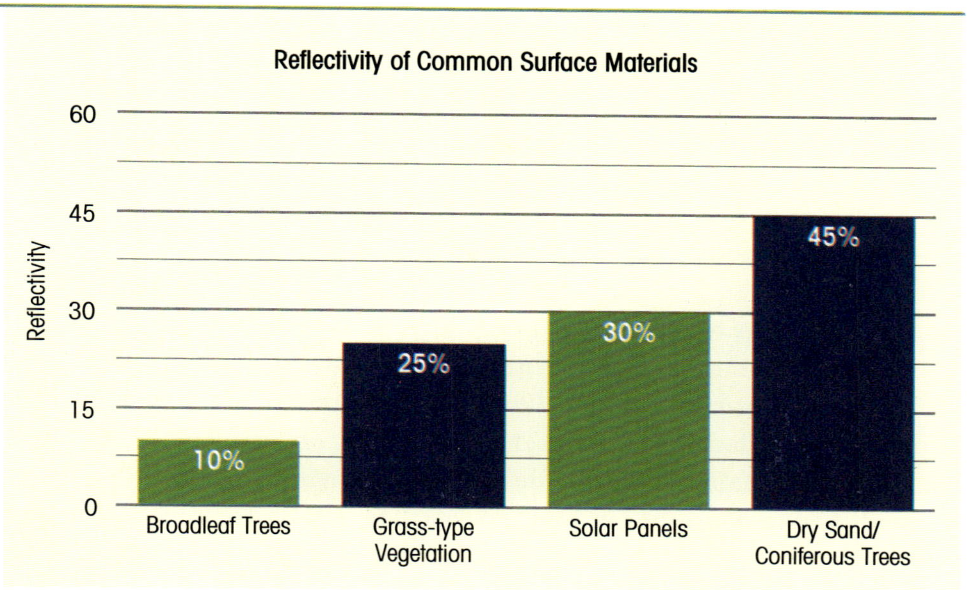

mitigation. First, several "gopher tortoise" burrows found on the development site would require relocation. The gopher tortoise is a protected species of burrowing tortoise native to the state of Florida and all relocations must be conducted by trained and certified personnel. Additionally, minor clearing and earth work would be required to prepare the site for the installation phase. As a result, a local ordinance to prevent deforestation required more than 350 trees to be planted at a location to be determined by the airport.

WILDLIFE HAZARDS

Special care was also taken to investigate the potential for wildlife hazards or attractants resulting from the project. The primary concern was that the solar panels themselves could potentially become a roosting or nesting environment for birds or other wildlife. Through careful research and utilization of a certified wildlife hazard biologist, the airport determined that no significant wildlife hazards or attractants resulted from the solar farm installation.

CONSTRUCTION

The construction phase of the project was divided into two distinct phases and handled by a contractor. Ground was broken on phase one on September 14, 2011, and was completed in less than four months, with phase two beginning just a few months later. The entire construction was conducted completely outside the air operations area, which alleviated security access issues and minimized construction coordination challenges common with any construction project inside the AOA.

RESULTS

On October 15, 2012, the Lakeland Linder Regional Airport, in partnership with Lakeland Electric and Sun Edison, flipped the switch to activate over 18,000 solar panels. This solar farm is the first of its kind at an airport in the FAA southern region and has become a model for airports throughout the country that are seeking innovative energy solutions that promote self-sustainability. This new green power source added more than 9 million kWh of solar electricity per year to the local power grid while creating more than 90 local construction jobs during the installation. The farm will generate over $250,000 in energy credits annually, nearly eliminating the airport's electricity costs. The farm will also reduce carbon dioxide emissions by an estimated 324 million pounds over 25 years. This is the equivalent of removing over 31,000 cars from the road. Additionally, the farm will generate enough electricity to power over 22,000 homes for an entire year. The addition of this 40-acre solar farm at the Lakeland Linder Regional Airport highlights the magnitude and significance of "green" airport initiatives as well as the positive impacts these types of initiatives can have on the environment and local communities.

Airport Emergency Exercise

Developed by Jordan A. Biegler, A.A.E.
Hillsborough County Aviation Authority

The successful resolution of aircraft accidents near or on an airport involves not just the airport, but all mutual aid agencies in the community. For an effective response to take place, actions must occur prior to the emergency that can prevent, alleviate, or diminish the potential effects of a disastrous situation and enhance emergency response. 14 CFR Part 139 requires Class I airports to conduct a full-scale emergency exercise once every 36 consecutive calendar months to test these actions and the resources of mutual aid partners.

To meet this requirement, Pensacola International Airport conducted a full-scale emergency exercise in March 2012. This exercise was designed to assess the operational capability of the airport's emergency plan by requiring actual utilization of all resources, equipment, and personnel that would normally be available.

Despite potential policy, operational, or jurisdictional differences among agencies located off-airport, it was critical to actively involve the community in the exercise planning process from the beginning. To achieve this, personnel at Pensacola International Airport began by inviting all agencies willing to assist in planning, conducting, and evaluating the exercise to participate in a Concepts and Objectives Meeting. The purpose of the meeting was to reach out to agencies in the community for involvement and address their initial concerns. During this meeting, an exercise planning committee was formed. This committee consisted of numerous agencies crucial to a coordinated emergency response, including law enforcement, rescue and firefighting, emergency medical services, county emergency management, area hospitals, air carriers, and volunteer organizations. The goal was to bring these players together to help establish an exercise scenario and plan the exercise.

The committee followed guidance set forth in the U.S. Department of Homeland Security (DHS) Homeland Security Exercise and Evaluation Program (HSEEP). This led to effective management of all aspects of exercise development including needs assessments, scope and purpose of the exercise, setting measurable goals and objectives, creating exercise evaluation guides, solving logistical concerns, hazard mitigation, and public and media notifications.

The planning committee carried out and evaluated an ambitious exercise with participants from more than twenty organizations taking part in at least one of the three simultaneously occurring exercise scenes (see Figure A-3). Just one example of the complexity and scale of the exercise was the exercise crash scene, which involved a Mobile Aircraft Firefighting Training Device (MAFTD) simulating an aircraft crash, along with 150 volunteers complete with stage blood and mock injuries playing the role of victims. In the end, the Pensacola International Airport and members of the exercise planning committee not only fulfilled FAA and TSA regulatory requirements, but meaningfully contributed to emergency preparedness in the community. The successful collaboration from numerous organizations involved is evidence of the growing public safety partnership among multiple jurisdictions, area hospitals, Pensacola International Airport, and its airline partners. The exercise served as a conduit for participating agencies to test their own goals, while the airport was able to test and later refine the effectiveness of its AEP.

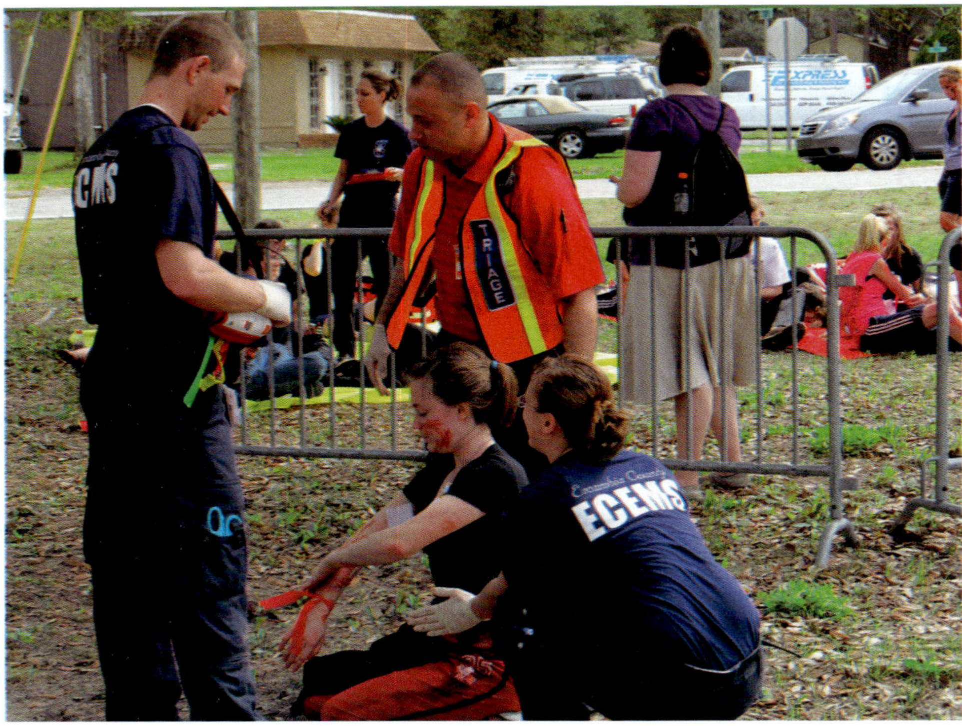

Figure A-3. Volunteers serving as victims during an emergency exercise.

(Jordan Biegler, A.A.E.)

Airport Operations Department Administrative Challenges

Developed by Richard Steele, C.M.
Los Angeles World Airports

AIRPORT OPERATIONS DEPARTMENT OVERVIEW

This airport is a medium hub, FAA Class I, TSA Category I airport. The FAA air traffic control tower (ATCT) is open 24 hours per day. The airfield includes two intersecting runways, and five parallel taxiways with appropriate intersecting taxiways. There are four fuel handling companies and one fuel farm on the property. The operations department includes an Airside Operations Section, Communications Center Section, and the Airport ID Badging Section. Airside Operations and the Communications Center must be staffed 24 hours per day. Airside Operations responsibilities include airfield operations and terminal operations. There is a separate Landside Operations Department during the regular work week, but the Airside Operations personnel cover the landside functions after-hours and on weekends and holidays. There is a $5,000 line item for training in the department operating and maintenance (O&M) budget. There are a total of 15 operations personnel with responsibilities divided as follows:

- ***Airside Operations Section:*** Five operations supervisors documented as being trained in compliance with 14 CFR Part 139 to conduct duties under the airport certification manual (ACM), which includes requirements of Subpart D—Operations of Part 139, as well as respond to all 49 CFR Part 1542—Airport Security related incidents.
- ***Communications (Comm.) Center Section:*** One communications center supervisor and seven operations coordinators/dispatchers who are responsible for monitoring the access control system, digital video surveillance system (DVSS), facility fire alarm system, crash phone ring down system, and other covert alarm systems. The Comm. Center dispatches airport operations, airport fire (ARFF), airport police, and airport maintenance to emergency and non-emergency events related to the airport emergency plan (AEP) and 49 CFR 1542—Airport Security. Eighty percent of the Comm. Center personnel's daily functions include operating the Justice Department Interface Controller (JDIC) to run driver's licenses, license plates, weapon serial numbers, VIN numbers, etc. for airport police.
- ***Airport ID Badging Section:*** Two badging administrative assistants who process all documentation related to 2,500 badge airport employees consisting of tenants, contractors, agencies, and airport authority employees.

IMMEDIATE TASKS

The Airside Operations Department had to successfully complete the following tasks within 12 months.

1. Executive management explained they were not pleased with how the Operations Department was previously being managed. There were continuous problems with the department identifying significant airfield discrepancies late in the year, just prior to the annual 14 CFR Part 139 inspection related to markings, signage, lighting, pavement, and safety areas. The Finance Department seemed to be continuously jumping through hoops to fund these last-minute repairs. Executive management did not feel that the Operations Department personnel knew what they were looking for during the daily inspections. Executive management also expected the department to focus on three cornerstones as it redirected down a new path:
   - Safety
   - Security
   - Financial Efficiency
2. Within the next two weeks, the NCAA BCS Championship Football game would be hosted in an adjoining city. The last time the BCS Championship game was hosted in this area, it brought in an additional 150 GA aircraft requiring ramp services and parking. Due to the teams in this year's game, the FBOs were expecting 250 aircraft, likely requiring the closure of multiple taxiways for aircraft parking.
3. The next phase of the airport's camera system upgrade project was due to be presented to the airport authority commission within two months. This long-term project started three years prior, and involved converting the system from analog to digital, adding additional cameras, and adding servers for video storage. The presentation required a written explanation of the next project phase, a PowerPoint presentation, and submission of the final bid with an itemized breakdown.
4. The annual 14 CFR Part 139 required tabletop exercise must be completed within three months in order to meet the 12 consecutive month requirement.
5. The next fiscal year budget proposal was due within the next three months.
6. During the recent 14 CFR Part 139 inspection, the airport received a total of four Part 139 discrepancies after several years of receiving zero discrepancies. All discrepancies must be corrected within the next six months.
7. The FAA has released a revised airport emergency plan advisory circular (AC). AC 150/5200-32C requires all Part 139 airports to update their AEP by the summer of the following year. Significant progress needs to be made by the end of this year to include the establishment of working groups.
8. The FAA Runway Safety Action Team (RSAT) has identified some action items that the airport needs to correct by the end of the current year.

ACTION PLAN AND INITIAL MEETINGS

Due to the limited resources available, these eight tasks were a significant challenge. First, it was important to prioritize projects for this year. It was also necessary to ensure that:

1. Everyone in the department understood the upcoming tasks for the department
2. Everyone understood executive management's expectations
3. Tasks were delegated while understanding each employee's needs and areas of strength
4. A preliminary plan was developed to navigate through this year with input from department personnel and guidance from fellow managers.

Within two weeks, an all-personnel department meeting, referred to as an "all-hands" meeting, was held and included all airside operations sections, the Landside Operations Department (three employees), and the Security Department (one employee). The only personnel not in attendance at the meeting were the three to four personnel that were either on graveyard shift or on their day off. These individuals were met with on an individual basis in the days following this meeting. The tasks and executive management's expectations were discussed in the meeting, as well as a preliminary plan and expectations to successfully complete the eight tasks.

During the meeting, everyone was asked, "What initially motivated you to work in airport operations." Ninety percent of them said it was either due to the "challenge" or because "no two days at the airport were alike." Personnel possessed a wide range of backgrounds, including former airline employees, TSA employees, police officers, paramedic dispatchers, prison security guards, parking cashiers, and airport operations. With such a well-rounded team, the manager decided to schedule individual meetings to learn about each person's interests; what motivated them to come to work every day; their experiences; educational background; and training received at the airport. The manager also expressed his support to the entire team.

After individual meetings with all of the airside operations personnel, the manager felt he had a good understanding of everyone's strengths, experiences, educational background, and interests. He matched up specific department responsibilities with the employee that had the most experience, education, and/or interest in each area—including airfield markings, signage, and lighting; AEP; ACM; camera systems; access control systems; airfield pavement; etc. Each person was established as a "champion" or "lead" for a certain area, and if something came up related to their responsibility, the manager and individual would discuss the task and together establish a plan and milestones. It should be noted that these assignments were in addition to the daily airfield/terminal inspections, emergency responses, dispatching, and documentation required of personnel as part of their regular responsibilities.

The manager held weekly, minimum 30-minute meetings with each person who directly reported to him to discuss how they were doing personally, discuss new and ongoing items, and update the tasks they were working on. In this way, the manager maintained a good idea of the department's week-to-week progress along the critical path to the task milestones and final goals. Of course, some meetings had to be rescheduled or canceled due to operational needs, but the team stayed on track.

During this process, the manager identified areas to focus on:

1. ***Training***—The Department was not investing in department personnel. Some of the airside supervisors had gone to the American Association of Airport Executives (AAAE) Basic and Advanced Airport Safety and Operations Specialist (ASOS) courses, but that was the extent of the initial and recurring technical training related to 14 CFR Part 139. Most personnel in the Airside and Comm. Center sections had received their initial on-the-job training, but nothing since. There were no ongoing meetings, safety meetings, team meetings, etc. Training in the following areas was lacking:
   - Technical training—related to 14 CFR Part 139, 49 CFR Part 1542, systems functionality, Microsoft products, and department procedures.
   - Personal training and development—related to leadership, supervisory skills, workplace conduct, and industry qualifications/certifications.
2. ***Documentation***—related to training, meeting notes, agendas, reports, and daily logs.
3. ***Processes and Procedures***—some written policies and procedures were in place, but most were out of date.

TASK COMPLETION SUMMARY

1. **Executive Management's Concerns (due date = long-term):**
   Two key items were identified to address these concerns:
   a. Training:
      i. The department desperately needed resources for training other than on-the-job training (OJT). Prior to that year, the 12 consecutive month training requirements by 14 CFR §139.303 were being completed one to two weeks prior to the annual Part 139 inspection. It only took approximately 2 hours to cover all of the topics, and they would not be revisited in a formal setting until just prior to the subsequent year's inspection. Technical knowledge was being lost. The manager immediately established a monthly all-hands meeting to address this.
      ii. Each meeting discussed at least one 14 CFR Part 139 topic and one 49 CFR Part 1542 topic. The manager conducted the training for the first few months and then began assigning each supervisor a topic to present in the following months. This helped supervisors build their

knowledge and hone their skills in public speaking. Later that year, airport maintenance personnel were included in the training sessions so that they would become familiar with advisory circulars and FAA requirements.

iii. In addition to the internal training, strides were made with executive management to increase the department's annual training budget from $5,000 to $21,000. The airport subscribed to the AAAE Aviation News and Training Network (ANTN), and scheduled each supervisor to attend at least one off-site conference or working group related to 14 CFR Part 139 each year. ANTN had current videos which covered all 14 CFR §139.303 training topics such as the self-inspection program, airfield condition reporting, and standards for markings, signage, lighting, pavement, and safety areas.

iv. Law enforcement dispatchers in the Comm. Center were scheduled to attend a three-week Peace Officers Standards and Training (POST) course to receive their certification.

v. Within two years, the airport approved for operations supervisors to complete their Airport Certified Employee (ACE)—Operations certificate, and operations coordinators to complete their ACE—Communications certificate.

b. Airfield Audits:

i. To address the issue of late identification of airfield discrepancies, the manager began assigning the leads for airfield items (markings, signage, lighting, pavement, safety areas, obstructions, and NAVAIDs), to conduct audits between January and February of each year. This required personnel to get out of the vehicles and measure, identify, and report all discrepancies.

ii. In this way, the airport could then identify and project discrepancies such as paint build-up, faded signage, faded light lenses, etc., which could be accounted for before the next fiscal year budget planning cycle ended.

2. **NCAA BCS Bowl (due date = 2 weeks):**

a. Pre-planning meetings had occurred, but there was still uncertainty about the exact number of aircraft to plan for. The manager assigned an operations supervisor with the assistance of an operations coordinator to take the lead on coordinating a Unified Incident Command (IC) for the event. The IC consisted of FBO management, the FAA tower manager, airport police, and ARFF personnel. The closure of movement areas for aircraft parking based on priority was established.

b. The FBOs reported a combined total of approximately 250 GA aircraft that operated between two FBOs within a span of 3 days.

c. There were no aircraft incidents, accidents, or incursions during this event.

3. **Camera System Project Presentation (due date = 2 months):**
   a. One of the operations supervisors was very familiar with the old and first phases of the camera system project. He provided historical information regarding the old camera system and recent modifications in a report.
   b. The manager met with airport police, TSA, and the Comm. Center supervisor to identify where the next cameras needed to be placed by order of priority.
   c. The manager prepared the report and presentation material, and presented the information to the airport authority commissioners.
   d. The project was approved to move forward and was successfully completed on time and under budget.
4. **Annual 14 CFR Part 139 Tabletop Exercise (due date = 3 months):**
   a. The manager assigned two operations supervisors to develop the scenario; coordinate logistics with assistance from the purchasing department; send invitations; and coordinate with the involved airline.
   b. The FAA Airport Certification Inspector indicated that the exercise met all requirements under 14 CFR Part 139.
5. **Budget Planning (due date = 3 months):**
   a. The department did not have a structured format for budget preparation. One of the operations supervisors developed a Microsoft Excel spreadsheet to track invoices and purchase orders, which allowed the manager to accurately assess how much the department was spending and show any increases, decreases, and forecasting.
   b. The manager reached out to all current vendors for budgetary quotes on consumables and repairable items.
   c. The manager confirmed with service providers if service costs would remain the same or increase.
   d. The manager received budgetary quotes from prospective vendors on new purchases that might be made in the next fiscal year.
   e. The manager attempted to request the addition of more full-time employees (FTE), but was unsuccessful the first year. Three more FTEs were added the following year.
   f. The manager provided brief justifications for all O&M and capital project items.
   g. Executive management was impressed with the research, which made the approval process less painful.
6. **Four 14 CFR Part 139 Discrepancies (due date = 6 months):**
   a. There were several discrepancies related to markings, signage, lighting, and items that were "not fixed by function" inside the runway safety areas (RSA).
   b. All of the items required coordination with the engineering department, maintenance department, and/or ARFF.

c. One discrepancy ultimately resulted in the need for a Modification to Standard (MOS) which was later approved due to the non-standard application of hold position markings on intersecting runways not approved for land and hold short operations (LAHSO).

d. All discrepancies were repaired by the due date. The next three year inspection results included 8 discrepancies in year 1, 1 discrepancy in year 2, and 0 discrepancies in year 3.

7. **AEP Revision (due date = 1.5 years):**

   a. The entire AEP had to be reformatted and rewritten.

   b. The manager assigned an operations supervisor to lead the AEP revision working group, with the manager assisting as well.

   c. Due to the airport's geographical location, four cities and the county had a stake in the airport. This meant that all law enforcement and fire agencies had to be consulted and agree on how a response to accidents/incidents explained in the hazard-specific section of the AEP would be handled.

   d. Some of the other agencies and organizations that were included in specialized meetings included the NTSB, FBI, FAA ATCT, FAA So Cal Center (SCC), TSA, American Red Cross, coroner's office, air carriers, air cargo carriers, and concessions.

   e. AEP working group meetings were initially scheduled monthly, but the frequency was increased to every two weeks closer to the due date.

   f. The airport's AEP was submitted to the FAA Airports Division on time. It was returned to the airport by the FAA within two weeks indicating no corrections were needed. Training of personnel then began on the new AEP.

8. **RSAT Action Items (due date = 3 months to 3 years):**

   a. The RSAT can be compared to a proactive approach to aircraft accidents/incidents and incursions. These teams work with local FAA ATCT, airport personnel, and tenants to identify hazardous areas and mitigate the possibility of a future accident.

   b. The items identified by the RSAT ranged from the relocation of signage and equipment from RSAs, to relocating neighboring company floodlights so as not to shine toward the runway approach, to erecting blast fences.

   c. The manager assigned one operations supervisor to take the lead and coordinate the efforts to complete the action items assigned to the airport operator.

   d. This required continued coordination with neighboring businesses, the local FAA ATCT, tenants, and the engineering, maintenance, finance, and accounting departments.

   e. All action items due that year were completed.

The department was successful at completing the assigned tasks due to six primary reasons:

1. The manager had a great team of motivated employees who all brought something valuable to the department.
2. The landside department manager and security manager had previously worked as airside operations supervisors
3. Prior to the manager's promotion to the airside manager position, he had already established good working relationships with personnel in the engineering department, maintenance department, police department, and airport fire department (ARFF).
4. The manager also had a good working relationship with a majority of the airport tenants.
5. The manager had established an airport information exchange email group the prior year, allowing for the exchange of information with approximately 30 other airports nationwide. This provided a forum for surveying other airport professionals if questions arose.
6. The manager had completed reading the book *Strengths Based Leadership* written by Tom Rath and Barry Conchie. This book explains that three key findings were apparent during the authors' research. The most effective leaders:
    a. Are always investing in strengths;
    b. Surround themselves with the right people and then maximize their team; and
    c. Understand their followers' needs.

Airfield Lighting

Developed by Robin Gardner, MPA, CM, ACE Operations

BACKGROUND

The primary goals of an airport operations team are the safety, security and efficiency of the airfield. Per 14 CFR Part 139, the airport certification manual contains instructions necessary to maintain the airport operating certificate. Airfield lighting, markings and signs per 14 CFR §139.311 are critical for pilot communication, airfield safety, and efficient movement of aircraft. Personnel performing self-inspections must ensure that all markings, signs and lights are operational for each runway and taxiway to remain open and operational. Many of these items are related to one another. For example, the runway edge lights, markings and signs are critical to identify the runway surface for landing and departing aircraft while mandatory hold signs, markings and runway guard lights are critical to prevent runway incursions. Additionally, if two consecutive runway edge lights are out of service, repairs need to be initiated and an accompanying NOTAM will need to be issued to communicate with users about the non-complying airfield condition.

MINIMUM REQUIREMENTS

Realizing the critical safety and efficiency requirements of airfield lighting, signs and markings and the aging electrical infrastructure on airfields, the FAA published three advisory circulars: AC 150/5340-18F, *Standard for Airport Sign Systems*; AC 150/5340-26B, *Maintenance of Airport Visual Aid Facilities*; and AC 150/5340-1K, *Standards for Airport Markings*.

These advisory circulars on lighting, signs, and markings recommend the minimum maintenance practices; daily, periodic and special inspections; as well as the need for an effective safety program. Additionally, the ACs recommend that airports utilize past experience to determine best practices. The problem is that often airfield lighting circuits are more than twenty years old and have cables directly buried in the ground that have not received regular inspections, upgrades, or preventative maintenance. AC 150/5340-26B, published in 2009, states that there is no ideal value for insulation resistance in a circuit, insulation resistance is expected to decline 10–20% per year, and past experience with a particular airfield are the best indicators of potential problems or failures. The AC also states that circuits with a 50% decline over one year or an individual circuit that has an insulation resistance of less than 1 megohm are destined for rapid failure.

FUNDING

Emergency airport repairs are generally funded by the airport with the FAA possibly providing compensation after the fact. NPIAS airports' projects are funded by the FAA through the Airport Capital Improvement Program (ACIP). ACIP is based on the FAA's five-year forecasted and approved airport projects. The FAA then provides airports with ACIP funding based on a priority listing starting with airports with the largest number of annual passenger enplanements. To receive FAA ACIP funding, airports must first provide 10–20% of the total projected budget as a cash contribution to the project. However, none of the ACIP funding handles emergency repairs.

LOCATION

At this airport, there are 2 intersecting runways, RWY 9/27 and RWY 18/36, with parallel taxiways (see Figure A-4). Taxiways A and E on the south side of RWY 9/27 and west side of RWY 18/36 are 150 feet wide designed for air carrier and air cargo use. Taxiways F and G on the east side of RWY 18/36 are 75 feet wide designed for general aviation use. The airport normally lands RWY 9 and departs RWY 18. Between the hours of 1800 and 2200 the airport has approximately 48 air carrier and 4 large air cargo operations. All airport electricians work from 0630 to 1600.

BASIC SCENARIO

On this day, at 1700, the FAA air traffic control tower contacts you, the on-duty airport operations supervisor, stating TWY A lights will not turn on. What do you do next?

Solution

TWYs A and E are the only taxiways rated wide enough for air carrier and air cargo operations. It is a pilot's discretion to use a taxiway with no lights, but if TWY A lights are the only lights out of service there should be no impact to operations. Airport operation's priorities are: safety, security, and efficiency. Below are steps airport operations will take:

1. Request ATCT to turn on all airfield lights. Inspect the airfield, noting operational conditions and issuing NOTAMs regarding operational conditions.
2. Contact the airport maintenance lead electrician requesting immediate assistance and personnel recall.
3. Contact airlines and tenants regarding TWY lights and provide additional information if necessary.

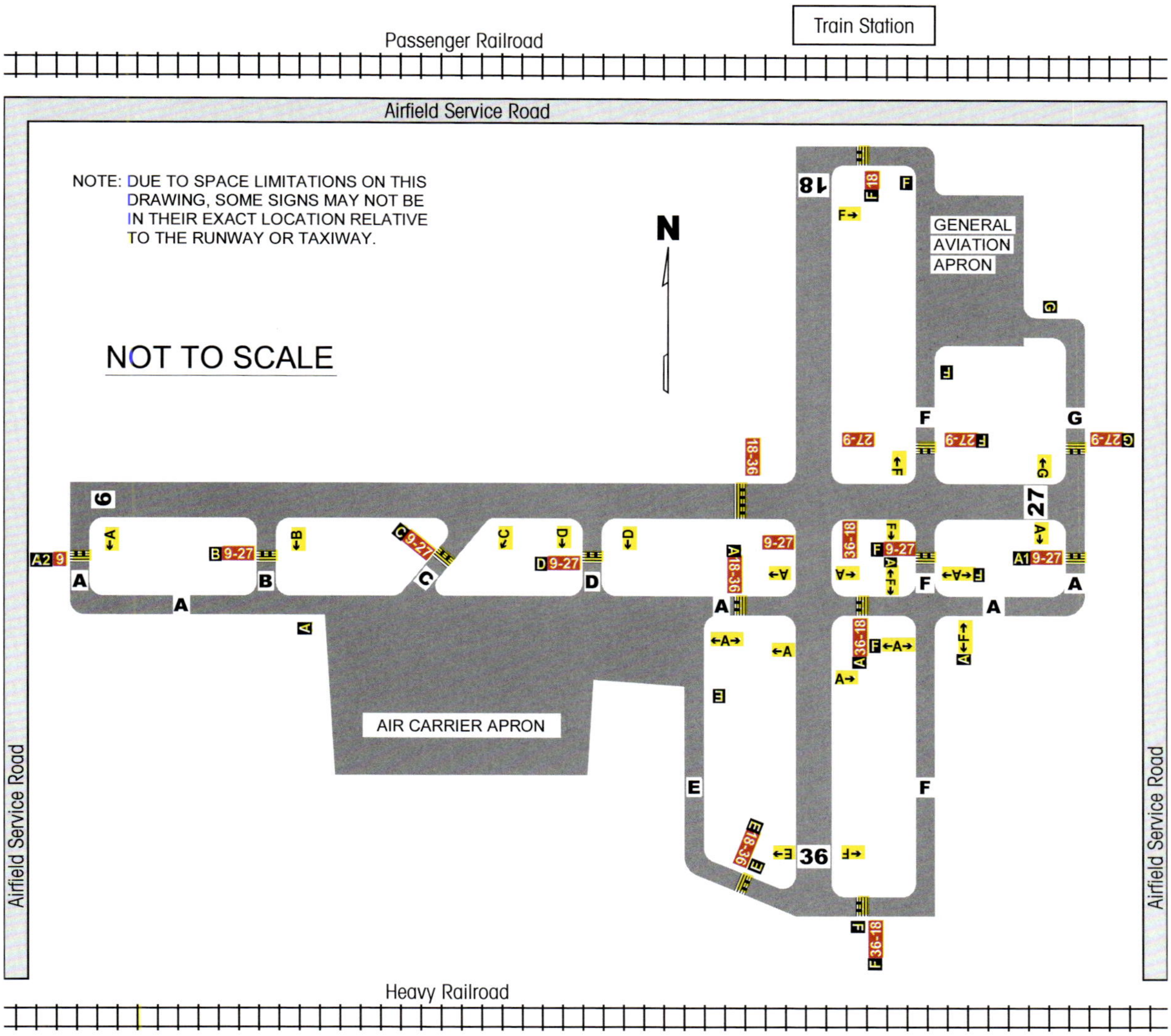

Figure A-4. Airport with intersecting runways from FAA Advisory Circular 150/5340-18F published August, 2010.

(FAA)

4. Contact senior airport management staff via emergency notification regarding situation.
5. Maintain contact with maintenance and offer assistance—i.e., an escort onto the airfield, plane spotting for workers, or an extra set of hands on the airfield. The maintenance department determines if and when to contact a third-party electrical contractor for assistance. Best management practice would be to contact a third-party expert within 4–6 hours after the situation begins if no reason for the outage has been determined and/or airport maintenance is unable to resolve it without additional experts.

ADVANCED SCENARIO

At 1700 hours, the FAA air traffic control tower contacts you, the on-duty airport operations supervisor, stating RWY 9 lights will not turn on. What do you do next?

Solution

RWY 9 is the normal departure runway based on wind-flow for air carrier and air cargo operations. To conduct reverse flow operations, the local FAA ATCT must coordinate with and receive approval from the Regional ATCT Approach and Departure TRACON. It is pilot discretion to use a runway with no lights, but seldom will an airline's dispatch allow them to operate on an unlighted runway. Thus, this situation will result in substantial impact to operations. Airport operation's priorities are: safety, security, and efficiency. Below are steps airport operations will take:

1. Follow the steps outlined in the solution to the basic scenario above, as well as other steps noted below.
2. Start an Incident Command System event, establish an Airport Disaster Emergency Operational Center (D-EOC), and request management staff to open all positions, finance, logistics, planning, operations and media. As the on-duty operations supervisor, you are the Incident Commander until a more senior manager arrives.
3. Contact the airlines and air cargo carriers to identify and maintain a log of the number of flights and passengers who are at the airport and will not depart or will divert to another airport due to the runway lighting issue.
4. Contact concessions and transportation entities to notify them of the situation and request additional services during the event.
5. Contact the FAA, FSDO and ADO manager and airport certification inspector to provide information regarding the situation and estimated time of fix.
6. Consider alternate runway(s) available, emergency generator, etc.

RESOURCES

14 CFR Part 139, Subpart D:

- Section 327—self-inspection
- Section 311—marking, signs, and lighting
- Section 325—airport emergency plan, with specific reference to the hazard section on power failure
- Section 339—NOTAMs
- Section 341—construction

FAA Advisory Circular 150/5340-26B, *Maintenance of Airport Visual Aid Facilities.*

American Association of Airport Executives (AAAE), ACE Maintenance Modules.

ADDITIONAL QUESTIONS

1. Describe the competing interests between airport management's priorities and the operations department's priorities. How do you balance these interests? Management's priorities are to limit revenue loss and manage airport authority, tenant, and media expectations. Operation's priorities are safety, security, and efficiency.
2. Describe the different D-EOC positions and tasks for each position.
3. Discuss preventative measures. What are the critical items that a new airport manager should know about an airport's airfield lighting system? (FAA AC 150/5340-26B, Chapter 5 lists inspections and minimum megohm rating for each circuit.)

Aircraft Laser Strike

Developed by Robin Gardner, MPA, CM, ACE Operations

BACKGROUND

Nationwide, laser strike incidents involving aircraft increased from 283 in 2005 to 3,591 in 2011, according to the FAA's Laser Safety Initiative. Most incidents occur on short landing or takeoff during early evening when the crew's eyes are more susceptible to bright lights. Pointing a laser aimed at an aircraft is a federal crime resulting in fines up to $250,000 and up to five years in federal prison for the offender. According to the FAA, any laser strike incident poses a serious safety risk to aircraft, crew and passengers. As of this publication, no aircraft accidents have been linked to laser strike incidents.

TERRORISM AND SABOTAGE

The history of terrorism incidents is such that no report or rumor, however vague, can be ignored. Each case must be thoroughly investigated in a manner that will safeguard the public and minimize damage if sabotage has occurred (or has the potential to occur). Sabotage is a deliberate action aimed at weakening a vehicle or aircraft from its intended purpose and course through subversion, obstruction, disruption, or destruction. An aircraft laser strike is considered an act of terrorism and/or sabotage.

14 CFR §139.325—AIRPORT EMERGENCY PLAN

The purpose of the airport emergency plan (AEP), per 14 CFR §139.325 and Advisory Circular 150/5200-31C, is to set forth procedures that ensure prompt response to all emergencies and other unusual conditions in order to minimize the possibility and extent of personal injury and property damage at an airport. The AEP also provides guidelines for maintaining and restoring airport operations as efficiently and effectively as possible. The three stages of airport emergency are response, investigation, recovery. These three stages can occur both concurrently and consecutively.

LOCATION

At this airport, there are two intersecting runways (Runway 9/27 and Runway 18/36), with parallel taxiways (see Figure A-4). Taxiways A and E on the south side of RWY 9/27 and west side of RWY 18/36 are 150 feet wide designed for air carrier and air cargo use. Taxiways F and G on the east side of RWY 18/36 are 75 feet wide designed for general aviation use. The airport normally lands RWY 18 and departs RWY 9. RWY 18/36 is bordered by train tracks while RWY 9/27 is bordered by city streets. There is a passenger train station on the approach end of RWY 18. There is an airport service road that follows the airport perimeter but is outside the secure airport operating area.

SCENARIO

The pilots of Flight 123, an air carrier aircraft, while on short final for Runway 18, experience temporary flash blindness caused by laser lights originating from a person on the ground at the train station.

The pilots' temporary flash blindness results in a hard landing on Runway 18. The hard landing damages both the left main wheel gear and the engine's right reverse thrust mechanism. After Flight 123 crosses both Runways 9/27 and Taxiway A at a high rate of speed, the damaged left wheel gear locks and the aircraft departs to the east off of the runway through the grassy safety area, crosses Taxiway F, and then penetrates the airport operating area perimeter fence line, finally stopping on an airport service road. The aircraft strikes multiple vehicles on the service road. The impact causes extensive damage to the aircraft and results in a fuel fire. As a result, ATCT issues an Alert III for this aircraft with 69 souls on board. Airport Fire, Police and Operations as well as the local city fire and police departments respond to Airport Bravo. The crash results in multiple fatalities on the aircraft and on the service road.

65 passengers on board
2 pilots
2 flight attendants
2,500 lbs. fuel on board
5 maintenance personnel on service road
3 cars on service road

You are the on-duty airport operations supervisor. What do you do next?

Solution

Airport operation's priorities are safety, security, and efficiency. Below are steps airport operations will take:

1. As the on-duty operations supervisor, you are the Incident Commander until a more senior manager arrives.
2. Stage at the approach end of RWY 18.
3. After ARFF and police exit the movement area, CLOSE the airport.
4. Inspect the airfield, noting operational conditions and issuing NOTAMs regarding operational conditions of the airport movement area.
5. Start an Incident Command System event, establish an Airport Disaster Emergency Operational Center (D-EOC), and request management staff

to open all positions, finance, logistics, planning, operations and media. D-EOC determines when to begin personnel recall. Best management practice for personnel recall is within the first 6 to 8 hours of a disaster. All personnel then work 12 hours on/12 hours off until the D-EOC demobilizes the event.

6. Contact airport engineering to inspect the movement area for any structural damage to runways and taxiways caused by the aircraft accident. Engineering is to provide the inspection report to you as Incident Commander.
7. Contact senior airport management staff via emergency notification regarding the scenario.
8. Contact airport police requesting they secure the airport perimeter and aircraft accident site. Verify that other security mutual aid agencies, TSA and FBI have been notified, as appropriate.
9. Contact maintenance requesting immediate assistance to replace the airport security fence, replace any affected signs and lighting, backfill the safety area between RWY 18 and TWY F, and restore the airfield to normal operating conditions as quickly as possible. Operations must inspect any work that maintenance considers complete before requesting the NTSB to restore airport operations.
10. Contact NTSB to provide information regarding airport conditions based on operation's and engineering's inspections. Request that normal air carrier operations are restored to the unaffected areas of the airport.
11. Contact the airline of Flight 123 and provide Friends & Family mutual assistance and verify locations of the Family Assistance Center.
12. Contact airlines and tenants regarding the airport closure pending NTSB approval to reopen unaffected parts of the airport. Identify and maintain a log of the number of flights and passengers who are at the airport and will not depart or will divert to another airport due to the aircraft accident. Provide additional information if necessary.
13. Maintain contact with maintenance and offer assistance—i.e., an escort onto the airfield, plane spotting for workers, or an extra set of hands on the airfield. The maintenance department determines if and when to contact a third-party contractor for assistance.
14. Contact concessions and transportation entities to notify them of the situation and request additional services during the event.
15. Contact FAA, FSDO and ADO manager and the airport certification inspector to provide information regarding the situation.

RESOURCES

14 CFR Part 139, Subpart D:

- Section 327—self-inspection
- Section 311—marking, signs, and lighting
- Section 325—airport emergency plan hazard section aircraft accidents
- Section 339—NOTAMs
- Section 341—construction

FAA Advisory Circular 150/5200-31C, *Airport Emergency Plan*

American Association of Airport Executives (AAAE), ACE Operations Modules

ADDITIONAL QUESTIONS

1. Describe the competing interests between airport management's priorities and the operations department's priorities. How do you balance these interests? Management's priorities are to limit revenue loss and manage airport authority, tenant, and media expectations. Operation's priorities are safety, security, and efficiency of the airport.
2. Describe the different D-EOC positions and tasks for each position.
3. Discuss FAA requirements for AEP drills, tabletops, and full-scale exercises. What should a new airport manager know about an airport's emergency plan? (FAA AC 150/5200-31C)

Airport Noise

Developed by Robin Gardner, MPA, CM, ACE Operations

BACKGROUND

Most airport mission statements include the contradictory elements of increasing economic development and sufficiency while providing environmental stewardship. Airports that are underutilized by passenger air carriers may utilize air cargo carriers to provide a self-sustaining revenue stream, as well as increase the airport's and community's economic development. Air cargo carriers operate primarily during nighttime hours, enabling an airport to increase operations without constraining the airspace or limiting passenger air carrier service. Unfortunately, these air cargo operations (especially during nighttime hours) can generate noise in the surrounding area, resulting in the community arguing and often litigating that the airport is not providing adequate environmental stewardship. If an airport's response to the community includes open, transparent, educated two-way communication, it may be possible for the community to become an advocate of the airport's economic development and active participants in the airport's environmental stewardship of the community.

NOISE REGULATIONS

Airport environmental stewardship begins with the Environmental Protection Act and Aviation Safety and Noise Abatement Act (ANCA) of 1979. These laws provided airports with the original guidance on how to measure aircraft noise and how to identify land uses compatible with various noise exposures. In response to ANCA, the Secretary of Transportation and the FAA developed the Aviation Noise Abatement Policy in 1976 delineating the responsibilities of the FAA, air carriers, airport operators, and local communities to reduce airport noise. The FAA also established 14 CFR Part 36 establishing noise certification standards for aircraft, as well as 14 CFR Part 150 and Advisory Circular 150/5020-1, *Noise Control and Compatibility Planning for Airports,* to provide additional requirements and guidance for noise control and land use compatibility planning. The FAA also developed 14 CFR Part 161 to provide additional mitigation for aircraft noise exposure, but severely limited restricting aircraft operations for noise purposes. The most common airport response is to proceed with a Part 150 study, which includes two distinct but complimentary sections: the airport noise exposure map and the airport noise compatibility plan.

NOISE EXPOSURE MAP (NEM)

ANCA and Part 150 codify the importance of accurately calculating and representing a community's annual aircraft noise exposure. The yearly day-night average sound level (DNL) is the cumulative exposure of individuals to aircraft noise using a 24-hour average sound level, in decibels, for the 24-hour time period with a ten decibel penalty added to the sound levels between the hours of 10:00 p.m. and 7:00 a.m., which is then averaged over a 365-day year. An airport's noise exposure map depicts a scaled geographic map connecting the noise exposure points to represent the 65, 70, and 75 DNL noise contours in relation to the airport and the surrounding community. Further, the FAA determined that residents in single-family homes within an airport's NEM 65 DNL noise contour are not compatible land uses with the airport. The airport then develops a noise compatibility plan in order to guide and coordinate the airport and community's efforts to achieve the maximum degree of compatible land uses within the airport's NEM 65 DNL noise contour.

NOISE COMPATIBILITY PLAN (NCP)

To date, over 190 airport noise compatibility plans have been approved by the FAA and over $1.9 billion in funding has been provided by the FAA to airports for noise mitigation. The NCP measures what an airport operator has done to reduce and/or prevent noncompatible land uses within the area covered by an airport's NEM. The NCP includes the requirements of the national aviation system to not impact or impede interstate or foreign commerce, affected local jurisdictions, governments, airport users and the citizens impacted by the noise or the solutions. Each suggested alternative in an NCP must achieve the goal of reducing or mitigating the impact of noncompatible land uses around the airport.

FUNDING

Implementation of the NCP depends on FAA approval of the NCP, the local jurisdiction's enacting and implementing noise compatibility actions, and the funds necessary to implement the NCP. Currently, 34% of the Airport Improvement Program discretionary funds are used for airport NCP implementation. The FAA matches airport funds at a rate of 75–90% share for implementing an airport's approved Part 150 NCP.

LOCATION

This airport has 2 intersecting runways, RWY 9/27 and RWY 18/36, with parallel taxiways (see Figure A-4). Taxiways A and E on the south side of RWY 9/27 and west side of RWY 18/36 are 150 feet wide designed for air carrier and air cargo use. Taxiways F and G on the east side of RWY 18/36 is 75 feet wide designed for general aviation use. The airport normally lands RWY 9 and departs RWY 18. Between the hours 0700 and 2200 the airport has approximately 30 air carrier operations.

SCENARIO

During the past five years, the city in which this airport is located has had most of the factories close, unemployment rates soar to 15%, and home foreclosure rates increase to 25%. Last month the airport, owned by the city, signed a 25-year lease with two air cargo carriers. The air cargo carriers intend to open distribution centers in three months that will employ 5,000 people in the first year, with employment increasing 10% each subsequent year. The cargo carriers will operate primarily between the hours of 2200 and 0700, with the airport having approximately 10 large air cargo carrier operations during this time period. You are the newly appointed airport manager.

Solution

Below are steps the airport manager could take:

1. Meet with the city mayor and council members to discuss the economic development and request guidance on how to educate the citizens about the air cargo news.
2. Request that the council appoint community advocates and business/airport-friendly citizens to an airport citizen's advisory board.
3. Meet with the city's public relations team and develop a full PR campaign.
4. Contact other airports that have both air cargo carrier operations and noise compatibility plans.
5. Contact the FAA Airport District Office manager and discuss funding for a Part 150 study. The FAA generally will not distribute funds for a Part 150 study until an airport has a full 365 days of increased aircraft operations. Best management practice would be to provide the FAA ADO Office manager with as much information about future airport funding needs as possible.
6. Contact the airlines and tenants regarding cargo operations and provide additional information if necessary.

RESOURCES

14 CFR Part 150

14 CFR Part 161

14 CFR Part 36

FAA Advisory Circular 150/5020-1, *Noise Control and Compatibility Planning for Airports*

Louisville International Airport Noise Compatibility Program
http://www.flylouisville.com/about-the-airport/noise-compatibility-program/

Tampa International Airport Noise Abatement Program
http://www.tampaairport.com/noise-abatement

ADDITIONAL QUESTIONS

1. Describe the competing interests between airport and city management priorities of increased economic development versus the citizen's priorities of a quiet community and environmental stewardship. How do you balance these interests?
2. Discuss NCP measures. What are the critical items that a new airport manager should know about NEM and FAA's approval of NCP measures? (14 CFR Part 150 and Part 161, FAA AC 150/5020-1)

Appendix B

Grant Assurances

FAA
Airports

March 2014

ASSURANCES

Airport Sponsors

A. General.

1. These assurances shall be complied with in the performance of grant agreements for airport development, airport planning, and noise compatibility program grants for airport sponsors.
2. These assurances are required to be submitted as part of the project application by sponsors requesting funds under the provisions of Title 49, U.S.C., subtitle VII, as amended. As used herein, the term "public agency sponsor" means a public agency with control of a public-use airport; the term "private sponsor" means a private owner of a public-use airport; and the term "sponsor" includes both public agency sponsors and private sponsors.
3. Upon acceptance of this grant offer by the sponsor, these assurances are incorporated in and become part of this grant agreement.

B. Duration and Applicability.

1. **Airport development or Noise Compatibility Program Projects Undertaken by a Public Agency Sponsor.**

   The terms, conditions and assurances of this grant agreement shall remain in full force and effect throughout the useful life of the facilities developed or equipment acquired for an airport development or noise compatibility program project, or throughout the useful life of the project items installed within a facility under a noise compatibility program project, but in any event not to exceed twenty (20) years from the date of acceptance of a grant offer of Federal funds for the project. However, there shall be no limit on the duration of the assurances regarding Exclusive Rights and Airport Revenue so long as the airport is used as an airport. There shall be no limit on the duration of the terms, conditions, and assurances with respect to real property acquired with federal funds. Furthermore, the duration of the Civil Rights assurance shall be specified in the assurances.

2. **Airport Development or Noise Compatibility Projects Undertaken by a Private Sponsor.**

   The preceding paragraph 1 also applies to a private sponsor except that the useful life of project items installed within a facility or the useful life of the facilities developed or equipment acquired under an airport development or noise compatibility program project shall be no less than ten (10) years from the date of acceptance of Federal aid for the project.

3. **Airport Planning Undertaken by a Sponsor.**

Unless otherwise specified in this grant agreement, only Assurances 1, 2, 3, 5, 6, 13, 18, 25, 30, 32, 33, and 34 in Section C apply to planning projects. The terms, conditions, and assurances of this grant agreement shall remain in full force and effect during the life of the project; there shall be no limit on the duration of the assurances regarding Airport Revenue so long as the airport is used as an airport.

C. Sponsor Certification.

The sponsor hereby assures and certifies, with respect to this grant that:

1. **General Federal Requirements.**

It will comply with all applicable Federal laws, regulations, executive orders, policies, guidelines, and requirements as they relate to the application, acceptance and use of Federal funds for this project including but not limited to the following:

Federal Legislation

a. Title 49, U.S.C., subtitle VII, as amended.
b. Davis-Bacon Act - 40 U.S.C. 276(a), et seq.[1]
c. Federal Fair Labor Standards Act - 29 U.S.C. 201, et seq.
d. Hatch Act – 5 U.S.C. 1501, et seq.[2]
e. Uniform Relocation Assistance and Real Property Acquisition Policies Act of 1970 Title 42 U.S.C. 4601, et seq.[1 2]
f. National Historic Preservation Act of 1966 - Section 106 - 16 U.S.C. 470(f).[1]
g. Archeological and Historic Preservation Act of 1974 - 16 U.S.C. 469 through 469c.[1]
h. Native Americans Grave Repatriation Act - 25 U.S.C. Section 3001, et seq.
i. Clean Air Act, P.L. 90-148, as amended.
j. Coastal Zone Management Act, P.L. 93-205, as amended.
k. Flood Disaster Protection Act of 1973 - Section 102(a) - 42 U.S.C. 4012a.[1]
l. Title 49, U.S.C., Section 303, (formerly known as Section 4(f))
m. Rehabilitation Act of 1973 - 29 U.S.C. 794.
n. Title VI of the Civil Rights Act of 1964 (42 U.S.C. § 2000d et seq., 78 stat. 252) (prohibits discrimination on the basis of race, color, national origin);
o. Americans with Disabilities Act of 1990, as amended, (42 U.S.C. § 12101 et seq.), prohibits discrimination on the basis of disability).
p. Age Discrimination Act of 1975 - 42 U.S.C. 6101, et seq.
q. American Indian Religious Freedom Act, P.L. 95-341, as amended.
r. Architectural Barriers Act of 1968 -42 U.S.C. 4151, et seq.[1]
s. Power plant and Industrial Fuel Use Act of 1978 - Section 403- 2 U.S.C. 8373.[1]
t. Contract Work Hours and Safety Standards Act - 40 U.S.C. 327, et seq.[1]
u. Copeland Anti-kickback Act - 18 U.S.C. 874.1
v. National Environmental Policy Act of 1969 - 42 U.S.C. 4321, et seq.[1]
w. Wild and Scenic Rivers Act, P.L. 90-542, as amended.
x. Single Audit Act of 1984 - 31 U.S.C. 7501, et seq.[2]
y. Drug-Free Workplace Act of 1988 - 41 U.S.C. 702 through 706.

z. The Federal Funding Accountability and Transparency Act of 2006, as amended (Pub. L. 109-282, as amended by section 6202 of Pub. L. 110-252).

Executive Orders

a. Executive Order 11246 - Equal Employment Opportunity[1]
b. Executive Order 11990 - Protection of Wetlands
c. Executive Order 11998 – Flood Plain Management
d. Executive Order 12372 - Intergovernmental Review of Federal Programs
e. Executive Order 12699 - Seismic Safety of Federal and Federally Assisted New Building Construction[1]
f. Executive Order 12898 - Environmental Justice

Federal Regulations

a. 2 CFR Part 180 - OMB Guidelines to Agencies on Governmentwide Debarment and Suspension (Nonprocurement).
b. 2 CFR Part 200, Uniform Administrative Requirements, Cost Principles, and Audit Requirements for Federal Awards. [OMB Circular A-87 Cost Principles Applicable to Grants and Contracts with State and Local Governments, and OMB Circular A-133 - Audits of States, Local Governments, and Non-Profit Organizations].[4, 5, 6]
c. 2 CFR Part 1200 – Nonprocurement Suspension and Debarment
d. 14 CFR Part 13 - Investigative and Enforcement Procedures14 CFR Part 16 - Rules of Practice For Federally Assisted Airport Enforcement Proceedings.
e. 14 CFR Part 150 - Airport noise compatibility planning.
f. 28 CFR Part 35- Discrimination on the Basis of Disability in State and Local Government Services.
g. 28 CFR § 50.3 - U.S. Department of Justice Guidelines for Enforcement of Title VI of the Civil Rights Act of 1964.
h. 29 CFR Part 1 - Procedures for predetermination of wage rates.[1]
i. 29 CFR Part 3 - Contractors and subcontractors on public building or public work financed in whole or part by loans or grants from the United States.[1]
j. 29 CFR Part 5 - Labor standards provisions applicable to contracts covering federally financed and assisted construction (also labor standards provisions applicable to non-construction contracts subject to the Contract Work Hours and Safety Standards Act).[1]
k. 41 CFR Part 60 - Office of Federal Contract Compliance Programs, Equal Employment Opportunity, Department of Labor (Federal and federally assisted contracting requirements).[1]
l. 49 CFR Part 18 - Uniform administrative requirements for grants and cooperative agreements to state and local governments.[3]
m. 49 CFR Part 20 - New restrictions on lobbying.
n. 49 CFR Part 21 – Nondiscrimination in federally-assisted programs of the Department of Transportation - effectuation of Title VI of the Civil Rights Act of 1964.
o. 49 CFR Part 23 - Participation by Disadvantage Business Enterprise in Airport Concessions.

p. 49 CFR Part 24 – Uniform Relocation Assistance and Real Property Acquisition for Federal and Federally Assisted Programs.[1 2]
q. 49 CFR Part 26 – Participation by Disadvantaged Business Enterprises in Department of Transportation Programs.
r. 49 CFR Part 27 – Nondiscrimination on the Basis of Handicap in Programs and Activities Receiving or Benefiting from Federal Financial Assistance.[1]
s. 49 CFR Part 28 – Enforcement of Nondiscrimination on the Basis of Handicap in Programs or Activities conducted by the Department of Transportation.
t. 49 CFR Part 30 - Denial of public works contracts to suppliers of goods and services of countries that deny procurement market access to U.S. contractors.
u. 49 CFR Part 32 – Governmentwide Requirements for Drug-Free Workplace (Financial Assistance)
v. 49 CFR Part 37 – Transportation Services for Individuals with Disabilities (ADA).
w. 49 CFR Part 41 - Seismic safety of Federal and federally assisted or regulated new building construction.

Specific Assurances

Specific assurances required to be included in grant agreements by any of the above laws, regulations or circulars are incorporated by reference in this grant agreement.

Footnotes to Assurance C.1.

[1] These laws do not apply to airport planning sponsors.

[2] These laws do not apply to private sponsors.

[3] 49 CFR Part 18 and 2 CFR Part 200 contain requirements for State and Local Governments receiving Federal assistance. Any requirement levied upon State and Local Governments by this regulation and circular shall also be applicable to private sponsors receiving Federal assistance under Title 49, United States Code.

[4] On December 26, 2013 at 78 FR 78590, the Office of Management and Budget (OMB) issued the Uniform Administrative Requirements, Cost Principles, and Audit Requirements for Federal Awards in 2 CFR Part 200. 2 CFR Part 200 replaces and combines the former Uniform Administrative Requirements for Grants (OMB Circular A-102 and Circular A-110 or 2 CFR Part 215 or Circular) as well as the Cost Principles (Circulars A-21 or 2 CFR part 220; Circular A-87 or 2 CFR part 225; and A-122, 2 CFR part 230). Additionally it replaces Circular A-133 guidance on the Single Annual Audit. In accordance with 2 CFR section 200.110, the standards set forth in Part 200 which affect administration of Federal awards issued by Federal agencies become effective once implemented by Federal agencies or when any future amendment to this Part becomes final. Federal agencies, including the Department of Transportation, must implement the policies and procedures applicable to Federal awards by promulgating a regulation to be effective by December 26, 2014 unless different provisions are required by statute or approved by OMB.

[5] Cost principles established in 2 CFR part 200 subpart E must be used as guidelines for determining the eligibility of specific types of expenses.

[6] Audit requirements established in 2 CFR part 200 subpart F are the guidelines for audits.

2. **Responsibility and Authority of the Sponsor.**

   a. Public Agency Sponsor:

   It has legal authority to apply for this grant, and to finance and carry out the proposed project; that a resolution, motion or similar action has been duly adopted or passed as an official act of the applicant's governing body authorizing the filing of the application, including all understandings and assurances contained therein, and directing and authorizing the person identified as the official representative of the applicant to act in connection with the application and to provide such additional information as may be required.

   b. Private Sponsor:

   It has legal authority to apply for this grant and to finance and carry out the proposed project and comply with all terms, conditions, and assurances of this grant agreement. It shall designate an official representative and shall in writing direct and authorize that person to file this application, including all understandings and assurances contained therein; to act in connection with this application; and to provide such additional information as may be required.

3. **Sponsor Fund Availability.**

   It has sufficient funds available for that portion of the project costs which are not to be paid by the United States. It has sufficient funds available to assure operation and maintenance of items funded under this grant agreement which it will own or control.

4. **Good Title.**

   a. It, a public agency or the Federal government, holds good title, satisfactory to the Secretary, to the landing area of the airport or site thereof, or will give assurance satisfactory to the Secretary that good title will be acquired.

   b. For noise compatibility program projects to be carried out on the property of the sponsor, it holds good title satisfactory to the Secretary to that portion of the property upon which Federal funds will be expended or will give assurance to the Secretary that good title will be obtained.

5. **Preserving Rights and Powers.**

   a. It will not take or permit any action which would operate to deprive it of any of the rights and powers necessary to perform any or all of the terms, conditions, and assurances in this grant agreement without the written approval of the Secretary, and will act promptly to acquire, extinguish or modify any outstanding rights or claims of right of others which would interfere with such performance by the sponsor. This shall be done in a manner acceptable to the Secretary.

b. It will not sell, lease, encumber, or otherwise transfer or dispose of any part of its title or other interests in the property shown on Exhibit A to this application or, for a noise compatibility program project, that portion of the property upon which Federal funds have been expended, for the duration of the terms, conditions, and assurances in this grant agreement without approval by the Secretary. If the transferee is found by the Secretary to be eligible under Title 49, United States Code, to assume the obligations of this grant agreement and to have the power, authority, and financial resources to carry out all such obligations, the sponsor shall insert in the contract or document transferring or disposing of the sponsor's interest, and make binding upon the transferee all of the terms, conditions, and assurances contained in this grant agreement.

c. For all noise compatibility program projects which are to be carried out by another unit of local government or are on property owned by a unit of local government other than the sponsor, it will enter into an agreement with that government. Except as otherwise specified by the Secretary, that agreement shall obligate that government to the same terms, conditions, and assurances that would be applicable to it if it applied directly to the FAA for a grant to undertake the noise compatibility program project. That agreement and changes thereto must be satisfactory to the Secretary. It will take steps to enforce this agreement against the local government if there is substantial non-compliance with the terms of the agreement.

d. For noise compatibility program projects to be carried out on privately owned property, it will enter into an agreement with the owner of that property which includes provisions specified by the Secretary. It will take steps to enforce this agreement against the property owner whenever there is substantial non-compliance with the terms of the agreement.

e. If the sponsor is a private sponsor, it will take steps satisfactory to the Secretary to ensure that the airport will continue to function as a public-use airport in accordance with these assurances for the duration of these assurances.

f. If an arrangement is made for management and operation of the airport by any agency or person other than the sponsor or an employee of the sponsor, the sponsor will reserve sufficient rights and authority to insure that the airport will be operated and maintained in accordance Title 49, United States Code, the regulations and the terms, conditions and assurances in this grant agreement and shall insure that such arrangement also requires compliance therewith.

g. Sponsors of commercial service airports will not permit or enter into any arrangement that results in permission for the owner or tenant of a property used as a residence, or zoned for residential use, to taxi an aircraft between that property and any location on airport. Sponsors of general aviation airports entering into any arrangement that results in permission for the owner of residential real property adjacent to or near the airport must comply with the requirements of Sec. 136 of Public Law 112-95 and the sponsor assurances.

6. **Consistency with Local Plans.**

   The project is reasonably consistent with plans (existing at the time of submission of this application) of public agencies that are authorized by the State in which the project is located to plan for the development of the area surrounding the airport.

7. **Consideration of Local Interest.**

   It has given fair consideration to the interest of communities in or near where the project may be located.

8. **Consultation with Users.**

   In making a decision to undertake any airport development project under Title 49, United States Code, it has undertaken reasonable consultations with affected parties using the airport at which project is proposed.

9. **Public Hearings.**

   In projects involving the location of an airport, an airport runway, or a major runway extension, it has afforded the opportunity for public hearings for the purpose of considering the economic, social, and environmental effects of the airport or runway location and its consistency with goals and objectives of such planning as has been carried out by the community and it shall, when requested by the Secretary, submit a copy of the transcript of such hearings to the Secretary. Further, for such projects, it has on its management board either voting representation from the communities where the project is located or has advised the communities that they have the right to petition the Secretary concerning a proposed project.

10. **Metropolitan Planning Organization.**

    In projects involving the location of an airport, an airport runway, or a major runway extension at a medium or large hub airport, the sponsor has made available to and has provided upon request to the metropolitan planning organization in the area in which the airport is located, if any, a copy of the proposed amendment to the airport layout plan to depict the project and a copy of any airport master plan in which the project is described or depicted.

11. **Pavement Preventive Maintenance.**

    With respect to a project approved after January 1, 1995, for the replacement or reconstruction of pavement at the airport, it assures or certifies that it has implemented an effective airport pavement maintenance-management program and it assures that it will use such program for the useful life of any pavement constructed, reconstructed or repaired with Federal financial assistance at the airport. It will provide such reports on pavement condition and pavement management programs as the Secretary determines may be useful.

12. **Terminal Development Prerequisites.**

    For projects which include terminal development at a public use airport, as defined in Title 49, it has, on the date of submittal of the project grant application, all the safety equipment required for certification of such airport under section 44706 of Title 49, United States Code, and all the security equipment required by rule or regulation, and has provided for access to the passenger enplaning and deplaning area of such airport to passengers enplaning and deplaning from aircraft other than air carrier aircraft.

13. **Accounting System, Audit, and Record Keeping Requirements.**
    a. It shall keep all project accounts and records which fully disclose the amount and disposition by the recipient of the proceeds of this grant, the total cost of the project in connection with which this grant is given or used, and the amount or nature of that portion of the cost of the project supplied by other sources, and such other financial records pertinent to the project. The accounts and records shall be kept in accordance with an accounting system that will facilitate an effective audit in accordance with the Single Audit Act of 1984.
    b. It shall make available to the Secretary and the Comptroller General of the United States, or any of their duly authorized representatives, for the purpose of audit and examination, any books, documents, papers, and records of the recipient that are pertinent to this grant. The Secretary may require that an appropriate audit be conducted by a recipient. In any case in which an independent audit is made of the accounts of a sponsor relating to the disposition of the proceeds of a grant or relating to the project in connection with which this grant was given or used, it shall file a certified copy of such audit with the Comptroller General of the United States not later than six (6) months following the close of the fiscal year for which the audit was made.
14. **Minimum Wage Rates.**

    It shall include, in all contracts in excess of $2,000 for work on any projects funded under this grant agreement which involve labor, provisions establishing minimum rates of wages, to be predetermined by the Secretary of Labor, in accordance with the Davis-Bacon Act, as amended (40 U.S.C. 276a-276a-5), which contractors shall pay to skilled and unskilled labor, and such minimum rates shall be stated in the invitation for bids and shall be included in proposals or bids for the work.
15. **Veteran's Preference.**

    It shall include in all contracts for work on any project funded under this grant agreement which involve labor, such provisions as are necessary to insure that, in the employment of labor (except in executive, administrative, and supervisory positions), preference shall be given to Vietnam era veterans, Persian Gulf veterans, Afghanistan-Iraq war veterans, disabled veterans, and small business concerns owned and controlled by disabled veterans as defined in Section 47112 of Title 49, United States Code. However, this preference shall apply only where the individuals are available and qualified to perform the work to which the employment relates.
16. **Conformity to Plans and Specifications.**

    It will execute the project subject to plans, specifications, and schedules approved by the Secretary. Such plans, specifications, and schedules shall be submitted to the Secretary prior to commencement of site preparation, construction, or other performance under this grant agreement, and, upon approval of the Secretary, shall be incorporated into this grant agreement.

Any modification to the approved plans, specifications, and schedules shall also be subject to approval of the Secretary, and incorporated into this grant agreement.

17. **Construction Inspection and Approval.**

    It will provide and maintain competent technical supervision at the construction site throughout the project to assure that the work conforms to the plans, specifications, and schedules approved by the Secretary for the project. It shall subject the construction work on any project contained in an approved project application to inspection and approval by the Secretary and such work shall be in accordance with regulations and procedures prescribed by the Secretary. Such regulations and procedures shall require such cost and progress reporting by the sponsor or sponsors of such project as the Secretary shall deem necessary.

18. **Planning Projects.**

    In carrying out planning projects:

    a. It will execute the project in accordance with the approved program narrative contained in the project application or with the modifications similarly approved.
    b. It will furnish the Secretary with such periodic reports as required pertaining to the planning project and planning work activities.
    c. It will include in all published material prepared in connection with the planning project a notice that the material was prepared under a grant provided by the United States.
    d. It will make such material available for examination by the public, and agrees that no material prepared with funds under this project shall be subject to copyright in the United States or any other country.
    e. It will give the Secretary unrestricted authority to publish, disclose, distribute, and otherwise use any of the material prepared in connection with this grant.
    f. It will grant the Secretary the right to disapprove the sponsor's employment of specific consultants and their subcontractors to do all or any part of this project as well as the right to disapprove the proposed scope and cost of professional services.
    g. It will grant the Secretary the right to disapprove the use of the sponsor's employees to do all or any part of the project.
    h. It understands and agrees that the Secretary's approval of this project grant or the Secretary's approval of any planning material developed as part of this grant does not constitute or imply any assurance or commitment on the part of the Secretary to approve any pending or future application for a Federal airport grant.

19. **Operation and Maintenance.**

    a. The airport and all facilities which are necessary to serve the aeronautical users of the airport, other than facilities owned or controlled by the United States, shall be operated at all times in a safe and serviceable condition and in accordance with the minimum standards as may be required or prescribed by applicable Federal, state and local agencies for maintenance and operation. It will not cause or permit any activity or action thereon which would interfere with its use for airport purposes. It will suitably operate and maintain the airport and all facilities thereon or connected therewith, with due regard to climatic and flood conditions. Any proposal to temporarily close the airport for non-aeronautical purposes must first be approved by the Secretary. In furtherance of this assurance, the sponsor will have in effect arrangements for-

1) Operating the airport's aeronautical facilities whenever required;
2) Promptly marking and lighting hazards resulting from airport conditions, including temporary conditions; and
3) Promptly notifying airmen of any condition affecting aeronautical use of the airport. Nothing contained herein shall be construed to require that the airport be operated for aeronautical use during temporary periods when snow, flood or other climatic conditions interfere with such operation and maintenance. Further, nothing herein shall be construed as requiring the maintenance, repair, restoration, or replacement of any structure or facility which is substantially damaged or destroyed due to an act of God or other condition or circumstance beyond the control of the sponsor.

b. It will suitably operate and maintain noise compatibility program items that it owns or controls upon which Federal funds have been expended.

20. **Hazard Removal and Mitigation.**

It will take appropriate action to assure that such terminal airspace as is required to protect instrument and visual operations to the airport (including established minimum flight altitudes) will be adequately cleared and protected by removing, lowering, relocating, marking, or lighting or otherwise mitigating existing airport hazards and by preventing the establishment or creation of future airport hazards.

21. **Compatible Land Use.**

It will take appropriate action, to the extent reasonable, including the adoption of zoning laws, to restrict the use of land adjacent to or in the immediate vicinity of the airport to activities and purposes compatible with normal airport operations, including landing and takeoff of aircraft. In addition, if the project is for noise compatibility program implementation, it will not cause or permit any change in land use, within its jurisdiction, that will reduce its compatibility, with respect to the airport, of the noise compatibility program measures upon which Federal funds have been expended.

22. **Economic Nondiscrimination.**

a. It will make the airport available as an airport for public use on reasonable terms and without unjust discrimination to all types, kinds and classes of aeronautical activities, including commercial aeronautical activities offering services to the public at the airport.

b. In any agreement, contract, lease, or other arrangement under which a right or privilege at the airport is granted to any person, firm, or corporation to conduct or to engage in any aeronautical activity for furnishing services to the public at the airport, the sponsor will insert and enforce provisions requiring the contractor to-

1) furnish said services on a reasonable, and not unjustly discriminatory, basis to all users thereof, and
2) charge reasonable, and not unjustly discriminatory, prices for each unit or service, provided that the contractor may be allowed to make reasonable and nondiscriminatory discounts, rebates, or other similar types of price reductions to volume purchasers.

c. Each fixed-based operator at the airport shall be subject to the same rates, fees, rentals, and other charges as are uniformly applicable to all other fixed-based operators making the same or similar uses of such airport and utilizing the same or similar facilities.

d. Each air carrier using such airport shall have the right to service itself or to use any fixed-based operator that is authorized or permitted by the airport to serve any air carrier at such airport.

e. Each air carrier using such airport (whether as a tenant, non-tenant, or subtenant of another air carrier tenant) shall be subject to such nondiscriminatory and substantially comparable rules, regulations, conditions, rates, fees, rentals, and other charges with respect to facilities directly and substantially related to providing air transportation as are applicable to all such air carriers which make similar use of such airport and utilize similar facilities, subject to reasonable classifications such as tenants or non-tenants and signatory carriers and non-signatory carriers. Classification or status as tenant or signatory shall not be unreasonably withheld by any airport provided an air carrier assumes obligations substantially similar to those already imposed on air carriers in such classification or status.

f. It will not exercise or grant any right or privilege which operates to prevent any person, firm, or corporation operating aircraft on the airport from performing any services on its own aircraft with its own employees [including, but not limited to maintenance, repair, and fueling] that it may choose to perform.

g. In the event the sponsor itself exercises any of the rights and privileges referred to in this assurance, the services involved will be provided on the same conditions as would apply to the furnishing of such services by commercial aeronautical service providers authorized by the sponsor under these provisions.

h. The sponsor may establish such reasonable, and not unjustly discriminatory, conditions to be met by all users of the airport as may be necessary for the safe and efficient operation of the airport.

i. The sponsor may prohibit or limit any given type, kind or class of aeronautical use of the airport if such action is necessary for the safe operation of the airport or necessary to serve the civil aviation needs of the public.

23. **Exclusive Rights.**

    It will permit no exclusive right for the use of the airport by any person providing, or intending to provide, aeronautical services to the public. For purposes of this paragraph, the providing of the services at an airport by a single fixed-based operator shall not be construed as an exclusive right if both of the following apply:

    a. It would be unreasonably costly, burdensome, or impractical for more than one fixed-based operator to provide such services, and

    b. If allowing more than one fixed-based operator to provide such services would require the reduction of space leased pursuant to an existing agreement between such single fixed-based operator and such airport. It further agrees that it will not, either directly or indirectly, grant or permit any person, firm, or corporation, the exclusive right at the airport to conduct any aeronautical activities, including, but not limited to charter flights, pilot training, aircraft rental and sightseeing, aerial photography, crop dusting, aerial advertising and surveying, air carrier operations, aircraft sales and services, sale of aviation petroleum products whether or not conducted in conjunction with other aeronautical activity, repair and maintenance of aircraft, sale of aircraft parts, and any other activities which because of their direct relationship to the operation of aircraft can be regarded as an aeronautical activity, and that it will terminate any exclusive right to conduct an aeronautical activity now existing at such an airport before the grant of any assistance under Title 49, United States Code.

24. **Fee and Rental Structure.**

    It will maintain a fee and rental structure for the facilities and services at the airport which will make the airport as self-sustaining as possible under the circumstances existing at the particular airport, taking into account such factors as the volume of traffic and economy of collection. No part of the Federal share of an airport development, airport planning or noise compatibility project for which a grant is made under Title 49, United States Code, the Airport and Airway Improvement Act of 1982, the Federal Airport Act or the Airport and Airway Development Act of 1970 shall be included in the rate basis in establishing fees, rates, and charges for users of that airport.

25. **Airport Revenues.**

    a. All revenues generated by the airport and any local taxes on aviation fuel established after December 30, 1987, will be expended by it for the capital or operating costs of the airport; the local airport system; or other local facilities which are owned or operated by the owner or operator of the airport and which are directly and substantially related to the actual air transportation of passengers or property; or for noise mitigation purposes on or off the airport. The following exceptions apply to this paragraph:

        1) If covenants or assurances in debt obligations issued before September 3, 1982, by the owner or operator of the airport, or provisions enacted before September 3, 1982, in governing statutes controlling the owner or operator's financing, provide for the use of the revenues from any of the airport owner or operator's facilities, including the airport, to

support not only the airport but also the airport owner or operator's general debt obligations or other facilities, then this limitation on the use of all revenues generated by the airport (and, in the case of a public airport, local taxes on aviation fuel) shall not apply.

2) If the Secretary approves the sale of a privately owned airport to a public sponsor and provides funding for any portion of the public sponsor's acquisition of land, this limitation on the use of all revenues generated by the sale shall not apply to certain proceeds from the sale. This is conditioned on repayment to the Secretary by the private owner of an amount equal to the remaining unamortized portion (amortized over a 20-year period) of any airport improvement grant made to the private owner for any purpose other than land acquisition on or after October 1, 1996, plus an amount equal to the federal share of the current fair market value of any land acquired with an airport improvement grant made to that airport on or after October 1, 1996.

3) Certain revenue derived from or generated by mineral extraction, production, lease, or other means at a general aviation airport (as defined at Section 47102 of title 49 United States Code), if the FAA determines the airport sponsor meets the requirements set forth in Sec. 813 of Public Law 112-95.

b. As part of the annual audit required under the Single Audit Act of 1984, the sponsor will direct that the audit will review, and the resulting audit report will provide an opinion concerning, the use of airport revenue and taxes in paragraph (a), and indicating whether funds paid or transferred to the owner or operator are paid or transferred in a manner consistent with Title 49, United States Code and any other applicable provision of law, including any regulation promulgated by the Secretary or Administrator.

c. Any civil penalties or other sanctions will be imposed for violation of this assurance in accordance with the provisions of Section 47107 of Title 49, United States Code.

26. **Reports and Inspections.**

It will:

a. submit to the Secretary such annual or special financial and operations reports as the Secretary may reasonably request and make such reports available to the public; make available to the public at reasonable times and places a report of the airport budget in a format prescribed by the Secretary;

b. for airport development projects, make the airport and all airport records and documents affecting the airport, including deeds, leases, operation and use agreements, regulations and other instruments, available for inspection by any duly authorized agent of the Secretary upon reasonable request;

c. for noise compatibility program projects, make records and documents relating to the project and continued compliance with the terms, conditions, and assurances of this grant agreement including deeds, leases, agreements, regulations, and other instruments, available for inspection by any duly authorized agent of the Secretary upon reasonable request; and

d. in a format and time prescribed by the Secretary, provide to the Secretary and make available to the public following each of its fiscal years, an annual report listing in detail:

   1) all amounts paid by the airport to any other unit of government and the purposes for which each such payment was made; and

   2) all services and property provided by the airport to other units of government and the amount of compensation received for provision of each such service and property.

27. **Use by Government Aircraft.**

It will make available all of the facilities of the airport developed with Federal financial assistance and all those usable for landing and takeoff of aircraft to the United States for use by Government aircraft in common with other aircraft at all times without charge, except, if the use by Government aircraft is substantial, charge may be made for a reasonable share, proportional to such use, for the cost of operating and maintaining the facilities used. Unless otherwise determined by the Secretary, or otherwise agreed to by the sponsor and the using agency, substantial use of an airport by Government aircraft will be considered to exist when operations of such aircraft are in excess of those which, in the opinion of the Secretary, would unduly interfere with use of the landing areas by other authorized aircraft, or during any calendar month that –

a. Five (5) or more Government aircraft are regularly based at the airport or on land adjacent thereto; or

b. The total number of movements (counting each landing as a movement) of Government aircraft is 300 or more, or the gross accumulative weight of Government aircraft using the airport (the total movement of Government aircraft multiplied by gross weights of such aircraft) is in excess of five million pounds.

28. **Land for Federal Facilities.**

It will furnish without cost to the Federal Government for use in connection with any air traffic control or air navigation activities, or weather-reporting and communication activities related to air traffic control, any areas of land or water, or estate therein, or rights in buildings of the sponsor as the Secretary considers necessary or desirable for construction, operation, and maintenance at Federal expense of space or facilities for such purposes. Such areas or any portion thereof will be made available as provided herein within four months after receipt of a written request from the Secretary.

29. **Airport Layout Plan.**

a. It will keep up to date at all times an airport layout plan of the airport showing

   1) boundaries of the airport and all proposed additions thereto, together with the boundaries of all offsite areas owned or controlled by the sponsor for airport purposes and proposed additions thereto;

   2) the location and nature of all existing and proposed airport facilities and structures (such as runways, taxiways, aprons, terminal buildings, hangars and facilities;

3) the location of all existing and proposed nonaviation areas and of all existing improvements thereon; and

4) all proposed and existing access points used to taxi aircraft across the airport's property boundary. Such airport layout plans and each amendment, revision, or modification thereof, shall be subject to the approval of the Secretary which approval shall be evidenced by the signature of a duly authorized representative of the Secretary on the face of the airport layout plan. The sponsor will not make or permit any changes or alterations in the airport or any of its facilities which are not in conformity with the airport layout plan as approved by the Secretary and which might, in the opinion of the Secretary, adversely affect the safety, utility or efficiency of the airport.

b. If a change or alteration in the airport or the facilities is made which the Secretary determines adversely affects the safety, utility, or efficiency of any federally owned, leased, or funded property on or off the airport and which is not in conformity with the airport layout plan as approved by the Secretary, the owner or operator will, if requested, by the Secretary (1) eliminate such adverse effect in a manner approved by the Secretary; or (2) bear all costs of relocating such property (or replacement thereof) to a site acceptable to the Secretary and all costs of restoring such property (or replacement thereof) to the level of safety, utility, efficiency, and cost of operation existing before the unapproved change in the airport or its facilities except in the case of a relocation or replacement of an existing airport facility due to a change in the Secretary's design standards beyond the control of the airport sponsor.

30. **Civil Rights.**

It will promptly take any measures necessary to ensure that no person in the United States shall, on the grounds of race, creed, color, national origin, sex, age, or disability be excluded from participation in, be denied the benefits of, or be otherwise subjected to discrimination in any activity conducted with, or benefiting from, funds received from this grant.

a. Using the definitions of activity, facility and program as found and defined in §§21.23 (b) and 21.23 (e) of 49 CFR § 21, the sponsor will facilitate all programs, operate all facilities, or conduct all programs in compliance with all non- discrimination requirements imposed by, or pursuant to these assurances.

b. Applicability

1) Programs and Activities. If the sponsor has received a grant (or other federal assistance) for any of the sponsor's program or activities, these requirements extend to all of the sponsor's programs and activities.

2) Facilities. Where it receives a grant or other federal financial assistance to construct, expand, renovate, remodel, alter or acquire a facility, or part of a facility, the assurance extends to the entire facility and facilities operated in connection therewith.

3) Real Property. Where the sponsor receives a grant or other Federal financial assistance in the form of, or for the acquisition of real property or an interest in real property, the assurance will extend to rights to space on, over, or under such property.

c. Duration.

The sponsor agrees that it is obligated to this assurance for the period during which Federal financial assistance is extended to the program, except where the Federal financial assistance is to provide, or is in the form of, personal property, or real property, or interest therein, or structures or improvements thereon, in which case the assurance obligates the sponsor, or any transferee for the longer of the following periods:

1) So long as the airport is used as an airport, or for another purpose involving the provision of similar services or benefits; or

2) So long as the sponsor retains ownership or possession of the property.

d. Required Solicitation Language. It will include the following notification in all solicitations for bids, Requests For Proposals for work, or material under this grant agreement and in all proposals for agreements, including airport concessions, regardless of funding source:

"The **(Name of Sponsor)**, in accordance with the provisions of Title VI of the Civil Rights Act of 1964 (78 Stat. 252, 42 U.S.C. §§ 2000d to 2000d-4) and the Regulations, hereby notifies all bidders that it will affirmatively ensure that any contract entered into pursuant to this advertisement, disadvantaged business enterprises and airport concession disadvantaged business enterprises will be afforded full and fair opportunity to submit bids in response to this invitation and will not be discriminated against on the grounds of race, color, or national origin in consideration for an award."

e. Required Contract Provisions.

1) It will insert the non-discrimination contract clauses requiring compliance with the acts and regulations relative to non-discrimination in Federally-assisted programs of the DOT, and incorporating the acts and regulations into the contracts by reference in every contract or agreement subject to the non-discrimination in Federally-assisted programs of the DOT acts and regulations.

2) It will include a list of the pertinent non-discrimination authorities in every contract that is subject to the non-discrimination acts and regulations.

3) It will insert non-discrimination contract clauses as a covenant running with the land, in any deed from the United States effecting or recording a transfer of real property, structures, use, or improvements thereon or interest therein to a sponsor.

4) It will insert non-discrimination contract clauses prohibiting discrimination on the basis of race, color, national origin, creed, sex, age, or handicap as a covenant running with the land, in any future deeds, leases, license, permits, or similar instruments entered into by the sponsor with other parties:

a) For the subsequent transfer of real property acquired or improved under the applicable activity, project, or program; and

b) For the construction or use of, or access to, space on, over, or under real property acquired or improved under the applicable activity, project, or program.

f. It will provide for such methods of administration for the program as are found by the Secretary to give reasonable guarantee that it, other recipients, sub-recipients, sub-grantees, contractors, subcontractors, consultants, transferees, successors in interest, and other participants of Federal financial assistance under such program will comply with all requirements imposed or pursuant to the acts, the regulations, and this assurance.

g. It agrees that the United States has a right to seek judicial enforcement with regard to any matter arising under the acts, the regulations, and this assurance.

31. **Disposal of Land.**

a. For land purchased under a grant for airport noise compatibility purposes, including land serving as a noise buffer, it will dispose of the land, when the land is no longer needed for such purposes, at fair market value, at the earliest practicable time. That portion of the proceeds of such disposition which is proportionate to the United States' share of acquisition of such land will be, at the discretion of the Secretary, (1) reinvested in another project at the airport, or (2) transferred to another eligible airport as prescribed by the Secretary. The Secretary shall give preference to the following, in descending order, (1) reinvestment in an approved noise compatibility project, (2) reinvestment in an approved project that is eligible for grant funding under Section 47117(e) of title 49 United States Code, (3) reinvestment in an approved airport development project that is eligible for grant funding under Sections 47114, 47115, or 47117 of title 49 United States Code, (4) transferred to an eligible sponsor of another public airport to be reinvested in an approved noise compatibility project at that airport, and (5) paid to the Secretary for deposit in the Airport and Airway Trust Fund. If land acquired under a grant for noise compatibility purposes is leased at fair market value and consistent with noise buffering purposes, the lease will not be considered a disposal of the land. Revenues derived from such a lease may be used for an approved airport development project that would otherwise be eligible for grant funding or any permitted use of airport revenue.

b. For land purchased under a grant for airport development purposes (other than noise compatibility), it will, when the land is no longer needed for airport purposes, dispose of such land at fair market value or make available to the Secretary an amount equal to the United States' proportionate share of the fair market value of the land. That portion of the proceeds of such disposition which is proportionate to the United States' share of the cost of acquisition of such land will, (1) upon application to the Secretary, be reinvested or transferred to another eligible airport as prescribed by the Secretary. The Secretary shall give preference to the following, in descending order: (1) reinvestment in an approved noise compatibility project, (2) reinvestment in an approved project that is eligible for grant funding under Section 47117(e) of title 49 United States Code, (3) reinvestment in an approved airport development project that is eligible for grant funding under Sections 47114, 47115, or 47117 of title 49 United States Code, (4) transferred to an eligible sponsor of another public airport to be reinvested in an approved noise compatibility project at that airport, and (5) paid to the Secretary for deposit in the Airport and Airway Trust Fund.

c. Land shall be considered to be needed for airport purposes under this assurance if (1) it may be needed for aeronautical purposes (including runway protection zones) or serve as noise buffer land, and (2) the revenue from interim uses of such land contributes to the financial self-sufficiency of the airport. Further, land purchased with a grant received by an airport operator or owner before December 31, 1987, will be considered to be needed for airport purposes if the Secretary or Federal agency making such grant before December 31, 1987, was notified by the operator or owner of the uses of such land, did not object to such use, and the land continues to be used for that purpose, such use having commenced no later than December 15, 1989.

d. Disposition of such land under (a) (b) or (c) will be subject to the retention or reservation of any interest or right therein necessary to ensure that such land will only be used for purposes which are compatible with noise levels associated with operation of the airport.

32. **Engineering and Design Services.**

It will award each contract, or sub-contract for program management, construction management, planning studies, feasibility studies, architectural services, preliminary engineering, design, engineering, surveying, mapping or related services with respect to the project in the same manner as a contract for architectural and engineering services is negotiated under Title IX of the Federal Property and Administrative Services Act of 1949 or an equivalent qualifications-based requirement prescribed for or by the sponsor of the airport.

33. **Foreign Market Restrictions.**

It will not allow funds provided under this grant to be used to fund any project which uses any product or service of a foreign country during the period in which such foreign country is listed by the United States Trade Representative as denying fair and equitable market opportunities for products and suppliers of the United States in procurement and construction.

34. **Policies, Standards, and Specifications.**

It will carry out the project in accordance with policies, standards, and specifications approved by the Secretary including but not limited to the advisory circulars listed in the Current FAA Advisory Circulars for AIP projects, dated ________ (the latest approved version as of this grant offer) and included in this grant, and in accordance with applicable state policies, standards, and specifications approved by the Secretary.

35. **Relocation and Real Property Acquisition.**

    a. It will be guided in acquiring real property, to the greatest extent practicable under State law, by the land acquisition policies in Subpart B of 49 CFR Part 24 and will pay or reimburse property owners for necessary expenses as specified in Subpart B.

    b. It will provide a relocation assistance program offering the services described in Subpart C and fair and reasonable relocation payments and assistance to displaced persons as required in Subpart D and E of 49 CFR Part 24.

    c. It will make available within a reasonable period of time prior to displacement, comparable replacement dwellings to displaced persons in accordance with Subpart E of 49 CFR Part 24.

36. **Access By Intercity Buses.**

    The airport owner or operator will permit, to the maximum extent practicable, intercity buses or other modes of transportation to have access to the airport; however, it has no obligation to fund special facilities for intercity buses or for other modes of transportation.

37. **Disadvantaged Business Enterprises.**

    The sponsor shall not discriminate on the basis of race, color, national origin or sex in the award and performance of any DOT-assisted contract covered by 49 CFR Part 26, or in the award and performance of any concession activity contract covered by 49 CFR Part 23. In addition, the sponsor shall not discriminate on the basis of race, color, national origin or sex in the administration of its DBE and ACDBE programs or the requirements of 49 CFR Parts 23 and 26. The sponsor shall take all necessary and reasonable steps under 49 CFR Parts 23 and 26 to ensure nondiscrimination in the award and administration of DOT-assisted contracts, and/or concession contracts. The sponsor's DBE and ACDBE programs, as required by 49 CFR Parts 26 and 23, and as approved by DOT, are incorporated by reference in this agreement. Implementation of these programs is a legal obligation and failure to carry out its terms shall be treated as a violation of this agreement. Upon notification to the sponsor of its failure to carry out its approved program, the Department may impose sanctions as provided for under Parts 26 and 23 and may, in appropriate cases, refer the matter for enforcement under 18 U.S.C. 1001 and/or the Program Fraud Civil Remedies Act of 1936 (31 U.S.C. 3801).

38. **Hangar Construction.**

    If the airport owner or operator and a person who owns an aircraft agree that a hangar is to be constructed at the airport for the aircraft at the aircraft owner's expense, the airport owner or operator will grant to the aircraft owner for the hangar a long term lease that is subject to such terms and conditions on the hangar as the airport owner or operator may impose.

39. **Competitive Access.**

a. If the airport owner or operator of a medium or large hub airport (as defined in section 47102 of title 49, U.S.C.) has been unable to accommodate one or more requests by an air carrier for access to gates or other facilities at that airport in order to allow the air carrier to provide service to the airport or to expand service at the airport, the airport owner or operator shall transmit a report to the Secretary that-

   1) Describes the requests;

   2) Provides an explanation as to why the requests could not be accommodated; and

   3) Provides a time frame within which, if any, the airport will be able to accommodate the requests.

b. Such report shall be due on either February 1 or August 1 of each year if the airport has been unable to accommodate the request(s) in the six month period prior to the applicable due date.

Wikimedia Commons Credits

For those image files that were downloaded from Wikimedia for use as figures in this textbook, the following list gives the attribution information for each (by figure number). All these images are either in the public domain, or under one or more type of "Wikimedia Creative Commons" license ("Attribution 2.0," or "CC BY 2.0," among others), which allow for commercial usage for the material licensed in this manner. For more information about Creative Commons licenses, see http://creativecommons.org/licenses/.

Figure 1-3: John T. Daniels / Wikimedia Commons / Public Domain

Figure 1-4: Florida Photographic Collection / Wikimedia Commons / Public Domain

Figure 1-7: US Post Office / Wikimedia Commons / Public Domain

Figure 1-10: ©Barcex (http://commons.wikimedia.org/wiki/File:Boeing_747-475_-_Aerol%C3%ADneas_Argentinas_-_LV-ALJ_-_LEMD_%281%29.jpg) / Wikimedia Commons (http://commons.wikimedia.org) / CC BY-SA 2.5 (http://creativecommons.org/licenses/by-sa/2.5/) / Aerolíneas Argentinas.

Figure 1-11: Adrian Pingstone (http://commons.wikimedia.org/wiki/File:Fedex.a310-200.n420fe.arp.jpg) / Wikimedia Commons / Public Domain.

Figure 1-13: © RHL Images (http://www.flickr.com/photos/levien66/5096710118/) / Wikimedia Commons (http://commons.wikimedia.org) / CC BY-SA 2.0 (http://creativecommons.org/licenses/by-sa/2.0/) / People Express B747 - London Gatwick

Figure 1-15: © UpstateNYer (http://commons.wikimedia.org/wiki/File:September_11_Photo_Montage.jpg) / Wikimedia Commons (http://commons.wikimedia.org) / CC BY-SA 3.0 (http://creativecommons.org/licenses/by-sa/3.0/) / September 11 Photo Montage

Figure 3-4: ©2006 Mintaka10 (http://commons.wikimedia.org/wiki/File:Nkr1.jpg) / Wikimedia Commons (http://commons.wikimedia.org) / CC BY-SA 3.0 (http://creativecommons.org/licenses/by-sa/3.0/) / Antenna tower of NDB NKR at Ochsenbach, Leimen, Germany.

Figure 3-6: Wikimedia Commons / Public Domain.

Figure 3-7: NASA (http://commons.wikimedia.org/wiki/File:GPS_Satellite_NASA_art-iif.jpg) / Wikimedia Commons / Public Domain.

Figure 3-12: © John Murphy (http://commons.wikimedia.org/wiki/File:ATL_TWY_B_-_RWY_Crossing_%2813534655025%29.jpg) / Wikimedia Commons (http://commons.wikimedia.org) / CC BY-SA 2.0 (http://creativecommons.org/licenses/by-sa/2.0/) / RWY Crossing, looking west on a misty night.

Figure 3-53: © Simon_sees (http://commons.wikimedia.org/wiki/File:Changi_Airport_traffic_jam_%285621408218%29.jpg) / Wikimedia Commons (http://commons.wikimedia.org) / CC BY 2.0 (http://creativecommons.org/licenses/by/2.0/) / Changi Airport traffic jam.

Figure 5-2: © 2008 John Murphy (http://www.flickr.com/photos/kingair42/6814677692/) / Wikimedia Commons (http://commons.wikimedia.org) / CC BY-SA 2.0 (http://creativecommons.org/licenses/by-sa/2.0/) / Long Beach Airport Ramp Construction.

Figure 6-5: Jim Pickerell / Wikimedia Commons / Public Domain.

Figure 6-6: U.S Air Force photo by U.S Air Force Staff Sgt. Jessica Briney / Wikimedia Commons / Public Domain.

Figure 6-7: Wikimedia Commons / Public Domain.

Figure 6-10: Navy photo by Photographer's Mate 2nd Class Timothy Smith / Wikimedia Commons / Public Domain.

Figure 7-2: © 2006 Loty (http://commons.wikimedia.org/wiki/File:College_Math_Papers.jpg) / Wikimedia Commons (http://commons.wikimedia.org) / CC BY 2.0 (http://creativecommons.org/licenses/by/2.0/) / College Math Papers.

Figure 7-25: ©2007 Plenumchamber (http://commons.wikimedia.org/wiki/File:JT8D_Engine_after_Bird_Strike.jpg) / Wikimedia Commons (http://commons.wikimedia.org) / CC BY-SA 3.0 (http://creativecommons.org/licenses/by-sa/3.0/) / Engine after bird strike.

Figure 11-3: ©2009 M.O. Stevens (http://commons.wikimedia.org/wiki/File:Portland_International_Airport_security_check.jpg) / Wikimedia Commons (http://commons.wikimedia.org) / CC BY 3.0 (http://creativecommons.org/licenses/by/3.0/) / Portland International Airport security check.

Figure 15-2: ©2006 Patriarca12 (http://commons.wikimedia.org/wiki/File:Skybus_Airlines_billboard_along_Interstate_75_south_of_Dalton,_Georgia.jpg) / Wikimedia Commons (http://commons.wikimedia.org) / CC BY-SA 3.0 (http://creativecommons.org/licenses/by-sa/3.0/) / Skybus Airlines billboard along Interstate 75 south of Dalton, Georgia.

Index

9/11 attacks *33, 34*
response to *33–40*
14 CFR Part 77 *163, 164, 211, 221–225, 301, 351, 361*
14 CFR Part 139, Certification of Airports *38, 84, 197, 277–306, 314, 349, 350, 352, 356, 359, 362, 363, 364*

A

active control *309–311*
activity-based budgeting *497*
acute-angled exit taxiway *207*
adjournment (Robert's Rules of Order) *431*
advertising *87, 401, 403–405, 406, 414, 415, 506–507, 566*
airport vacancies *90–91*
advisory boards *72, 429*
advisory circular *82, 121, 432–436*
aeronautical lease agreement *463, 472–478*
aeronautical revenues *498–500*
Aerospace Industries Association (AIA) *447*
agenda *430*
agreements *463–478*
AIP Temporary Extension Act *32*
Air Cargo Deregulation Act of 1976 *24*
Air Commerce Act of 1926 *17–18, 21, 101, 438*
aircraft accidents *17, 18, 22, 31, 33, 292, 296, 363–365, 368, 440*
aircraft approach category (AAC) *201, 202, 208, 562*
aircraft operator security coordinator (AOSC) *378*
Aircraft Owners and Pilots Association (AOPA) *40, 448*
Airport Watch Program *383*
aircraft rescue and firefighting (ARFF)
See also ARFF Index
communication with *130, 308, 364*
equipment *205, 206, 228, 290–291, 292, 295, 337, 433, 509, 511*
extinguishing agents *290–291*
operational requirements *38, 291–295*
personnel *85, 294, 356*
records *281, 294*
response time *292*
safety during construction *195, 197*
standby areas *365*
stations *266, 434*
training *293–294, 363, 433, 434*
airfield delay *143–145*
Airline Deregulation Act of 1978 *24–25, 413*
airline lease agreement *465, 472–478*
airline operating agreement *463–465*
Airlines for America (A4A) *446, 447, 543*
airmail *15–16*
air operations area (AOA) *132–133, 310, 476*
safety in *351, 356–357*
security *373*
airplane design group (ADG) *201, 202, 204, 562*
airport access plans *165, 476*
airport access problem *216*
airport airspace drawing *163, 168*
Airport and Airway Development Act of 1970 *22, 28*
Airport and Airway Improvement Act of 1982 *28–29, 260*
Airport and Airway Revenue Act of 1970 *22, 544*
Airport and Airway Safety and Capacity Expansion Act of 1987 *29*
Airport and Airway Safety, Capacity, Noise Improvement, and Intermodal Transportation Act of 1992 *32, 245*
Airport and Airway Trust Fund *23, 28, 544, 564*
airport authorities *69–72, 306, 465, 480*
Airport Capital Improvement Plan (ACIP) *158, 590*
airport certification manual (ACM) *38, 278–281, 282, 303, 356, 436*
Airport Development Aid Program (ADAP) *23, 28*
airport emergency plan (AEP) *296–298, 297, 362–363, 366, 434*
Airport/Facility Directory (A/FD) *105, 116, 291–292*
Airport Improvement Program (AIP) *28–33, 35, 36, 39, 41, 53, 60, 74, 158, 225, 249, 427, 432, 434, 435, 508, 537, 542–543, 544–548, 564, 599*
grants *65, 72, 88*
airport layout plan (ALP) *82, 162, 163, 166, 170, 174, 225, 252, 546*
airport lighting, requirements *286–287*
airport markings, requirements *286–287*
airport master plan *161–171, 176, 435, 479, 563*
airport operating certificate (AOC) *278–279*
Airport Privatization Pilot Program *72–75*
airport property map *164, 169*
Airports Council International (ACI) *89, 90, 445*
Airports Council International—North America (ACI-NA) *437, 445*
airport security coordinator (ASC) *84, 373, 377*
airport security program (ASP) *84, 373, 377*
airport signs, requirements *286–287*
airport surface detection equipment (ASDE) *132*
airport surveillance radar (ASR) *132*
air quality *259–260*

air service development (ASD) *78, 412–417*
See also Small Community Air Service Development Program
department of *78*
air traffic control (ATC) *18, 19, 21, 101–120, 138, 142, 144, 282, 299, 301, 439*
Air Traffic Control System Command Center *103, 145*
Airways Modernization Act *21*
alert area *104, 106*
Alert I *307, 364*
Alert II *307, 364*
Alert III *297, 298, 307, 364*
alternative minimum tax (AMT) *542*
amendment (Robert's Rules of Order) *430*
American Association of Airport Executives (AAAE) *29, 89–90, 431, 437, 444–445, 446*
Americans with Disabilities Act of 1990 *32*
annual report *87, 519–520*
AP-4 agreement *65*
approach lighting system *118–119*
approach lights *107, 109, 113, 119, 286*
approach surface *223–225*
appropriation *544*
aqueous film forming foam (AFFF) *290–291, 353, 354*
ARFF Index *289, 290–291, 292*
assets *509–523*
audits *80, 240*
energy *267*
environmental compliance *240*
financial *519, 547*
of development projects *83*
safety *361*
authorization *544*
automatic direction finder (ADF) *110*
automatic terminal information service (ATIS) *351*
available landing distance (ALD) *116*
aviation activity forecasts *176–182*
Aviation and Transportation Security Act (ATSA) of 2001 *33, 36, 368, 372, 375, 379, 441*
Aviation Investment and Reform Act for the 21st Century (AIR-21) *33, 146, 543*
Aviation Safety and Capacity Expansion Act of 1990 *29–31, 542*
Aviation Safety and Noise Abatement Act (ANCA) of 1979 *28, 598*
Aviation Security Improvement Act of 1990 *32*

B

balance sheet *509–512, 516, 518, 519*
bankruptcies *549–551, 561–562*
benchmarking *80, 551–552*
best management practices (BMPs) *256*
best practices *80*
bid *83, 228, 240*
biochemical oxygen demand (BOD) *258*
bond indenture *538*
bonding *295, 352, 355*
bond rating *539, 539–540, 552*
bonds *512, 522, 537, 538–542*
See also revenue bonds
boundary signs *122*
budget *493*
See also capital budget; operating budget
development of *493–497*
marketing department *173, 398, 405*
monitoring *495–496*
preparation *496*
techniques *497*
Bureau of Air Commerce *18*
Bureau of Transportation Statistics (BTS) *61*
business plan *175*

C

capacity, airfield *137–143*
capital budget *65, 466, 495*
capital development funding *563–564*
sources of *537–548*
capital expenditures *464, 493, 508, 509, 521*
capital improvement plan (CIP) *182, 495, 509*
careers *90–92*
cargo revenue ton miles *9*
CAT I ILS *109, 115, 118*
CAT II ILS *109, 115, 118, 121*
CAT III ILS *109, 115, 118, 121*
challenge procedures *350, 374*
change order *83, 199*
Chapter 7 bankruptcy *550*
Chapter 11 bankruptcy *550*
chevron markings *126*
Civil Aeronautics Act of 1938 *19, 438*
Civil Aeronautics Administration (CAA) *13, 19, 20, 102–103, 438*
Civil Aeronautics Authority (CAA) *13, 19, 370, 438*
Civil Aeronautics Board (CAB) *19, 21, 22, 24, 438, 439*
Civil Aviation Security Field Unit (CASFU) *368, 371, 441*
Civil Works Administration (CWA) *18*
Class A airspace *104–105, 141*
Class A fires *352–354*
Class B airspace *59, 104–105, 141*
Class B fires *353–354*
Class C airspace *59, 104–105, 141*
Class C fires *353, 354*
Class D airspace *104–105, 141*
Class D fires *353–355*
Class E airspace *104–105, 141*
Class G airspace *106, 141*
Class I *278, 279, 280, 286, 297*
Class II *278, 279, 280, 286*
Class III *278, 279, 280, 286, 289*
Class IV *278, 279, 280, 286*
Clean Air Act *32, 260*
clearance bars *116*
clearance delivery *131*
clearway *205*
cockpit over centerline steering *206–207*

commercial aviation *16, 17, 53*
commercial development *479–482*
commercial self-service *475–476*
commercial service airports *23, 28, 53, 54–59, 60, 62, 63, 64, 74, 368, 425, 561, 565*
airline agreements at *463*
airside congestion at *568*
design and construction *191, 211, 216, 220*
federal regulation applying to
See 14 CFR Part 139
financial management *88, 496, 500*
funding *541, 542, 545*
maintenance at *331, 340*
marketing *396–397, 405, 407*
operations *84*
planning *159, 163, 164, 175, 177*
common traffic advisory frequency (CTAF) *130, 282, 292, 351, 356*
common-use *217–220*
common-use terminal equipment (CUTE) *218, 219*
communication *410*
airport *282, 288, 299, 306–308, 351, 356–357*
emergency *263, 292, 293, 296, 307, 362*
with airport boards, municipal officials *429*
community relations *80, 239, 307, 366, 448–450*
compatible land use *246, 251–252, 253, 437, 547*
compensatory rate-making methodology *464, 466*
computer-aided design (CAD) *170*
concession agreement *466–467, 472–478*
concessionaires *80, 466, 504*
Conditionally Exempt Small Quantity Generators (CESQGs) *263*
congestion, airside *103, 136, 137, 144, 159, 160, 568–569*
congestion pricing *146, 148*
conical surface *223, 224*
consolidated rental car facilities (CONRAC) *503*
construction department *83*
construction phase *198*
construction safety and phasing plan (CSPP) *193–196, 197, 350*
construction standards *191–200*
consumers *393, 409*
contact approach *107*
continuing resolution *39, 40*
continuous friction measuring equipment (CFME) *328*
Contract Air Mail Act of 1925 *16*
Contract Air Mail (CAM) routes *16, 17*
controllable variables *408*
controlled firing area *104, 106*
cost leadership goal *396*
cost of sales *513*
cost per enplaned passenger (CPE) *80, 401, 495, 552, 561*
Criminal History Records Check (CHRC) *373, 375–377, 378, 379, 380, 444*
crossbar lights *119*
current assets *510, 511, 520, 522*
current liabilities *510, 512, 520, 522*
current ratio *520–521*
customer service *171, 172, 265, 397, 451, 566–567*
department of *88–89*
Customs and Border Protection (CBP) *371, 443*

D

day-night sound level (DNL) *164, 244–247, 252, 599*
debt service safety margin *522–523*
debt-to-asset ratio *522*
decelerometer (DEC) *328*
declared capacity *139*
deicing *84, 257, 257–258*
delegation *410*
demand management *145–148*
Department of Homeland Security (DHS) *35, 36, 371, 441–442*
Department of Transportation Act of 1966 *21*
deplaned passengers *54*
depreciation *511, 513–517, 522*
deregulation *24*
period after *24–33*
period before *21–23*
design aircraft *191, 201*
design phase *198*
design standards *200–220*
destination signs *122*
Development of Landing Areas for National Defense (DLAND) *19*
direct economic impacts *549*
direction signs *122*
Disadvantaged Business Enterprise (DBE) *29, 467, 483, 547*
discretionary funds *545*
dividends *512, 518*

E

easements *253–254*
econometric model forecasting *179, 181*
economic impact analysis *549*
economic impact study *402, 549*
emergency preparedness *262, 362–366*
Emergency Relief Appropriation Act of 1935 *18*
emergency training, requirements *363*
end-around taxiway *208*
engineered materials arresting system (EMAS) *126, 220, 221, 435*
enplaned passengers *9, 53, 54*
See also costs per enplaned passenger
entitlements *545, 546*
environmental assessment (EA) *242*
environmental impact statement (EAS) *243*
environmental management system (EMS) *239–240*
Environmental Protection Agency (EPA) *254, 257, 259–260, 262, 263*
environmental scanning *408*
Essential Air Service (EAS) program *25, 59, 413*
exclusive rights *435, 469, 475, 477–478, 481, 547*

exclusive use *217, 219*
exit taxiway *207*
expenses *494–496, 498, 508–509, 513–518*
See also fixed expenses; variable expenses
Experimental Aircraft Association (EAA) *446, 448*

F

FAA order *432*
facilities layout plan *163, 167*
facility response plan *255*
FBO agreement *467–471, 472–478, 500*
Federal Aid to Airports Program *20, 23*
Federal Airport Act of 1946 *20, 22, 65*
Federal Aviation Act of 1958 *21, 370, 439*
Federal Aviation Administration Authorization Act of 1994 *32*
Federal Aviation Administration (FAA) *22, 23, 28, 32, 38, 371, 439, 483*
regulations *409*
training programs *89*
Federal Aviation Agency *21–22, 370–371, 439*
Federal Aviation Reauthorization Act of 1996 *32*
Federal Contract Tower Program *134*
Federal Emergency Management Agency (FEMA) *363, 371*
Federal Emergency Relief Administration (FERA) *18*
federally obligated *63, 71, 170, 415, 475–489, 477*
Federal Register *73, 431–432*
Federal Water Pollution Control Act *32*
fees, rates, and charges *85, 412, 464, 524–526*
finance department *88*
financial management *490–528*
financial plan *493*
financial ratios *520–523*
financial statements *509–523*
relationships among *518*
financing activities *516–518*
finding of no significant impact (FONSI) *243*
finger pier terminal *212*
fire tetrahedron *353*
fire triangle *291, 352–353*
fiscal year *493, 496*
Five Ps *400–408*
fixed assets *511, 522*
fixed base operator (FBO) *64, 65, 66, 80, 192, 447, 464, 467–471, 475, 478, 481*
fixed expenses *496*
flexible pavements *209, 329, 333–336*
flight information monitoring system *82*
Flight Standards District Office (FSDO) *426, 440*
food and beverage (F&B) concessions *74, 211, 466, 481, 504–505, 507*
forecasts. *See* aviation activity forecasts; terminal area forecast
foreign object debris (FOD) *195, 310, 325–327, 333, 433, 434*
fuel flowage fees *80, 415, 468, 499–500*
fueling *295, 352–356, 500*
See also self-fueling
fuel spills *261, 355, 356*

G

general aviation (GA) *53, 56–57, 59, 306, 445, 447, 448*
See also general aviation (GA) airports
accidents *440*
performance indicators *552*
revenues *499–500, 513–514, 544*
general aviation (GA) airports *9, 37, 39, 60–61, 74, 427, 438, 477*
community relations *448*
financial management *497*
funding *548*
marketing *86, 396–398*
organizational structure *76, 84, 88*
planning *163, 164, 176, 177*
public protection at *349*
security *380–383*
training at *89*
General Aviation Manufacturers Association (GAMA) *447*
general obligation bonds *540*
geographic information systems (GIS) *87, 170, 251*
geographic position marking *128, 129*
global positioning system (GPS) *112, 136*
goals *396–399*
governmental affairs department *79*
governmental relations *425–443*
gradient *208*
grant assurances *72, 414, 432, 473, 474, 546–548*
grants *36, 330, 494, 541, 542, 544–548, 564*
See also Planning Grant Program; State Block Grant Program; Airport Improvement Program; grant assurances
gross profit *513*
ground access *216–217*
ground-based augmentation system (GBAS) *113*
ground control *131*
ground security coordinator (GSC) *378*
ground vehicle, requirements *194, 299–300, 351, 436*

H

habitat management *309–310*
hazardous materials (HAZMAT) *195, 293, 295, 296*
requirements *295*
hazardous waste *261–265*
hazard risk matrix *360*
heating, ventilation, and air conditioning (HVAC) *323, 339*
high-intensity runway lights (HIRL) *114*
holding position markings *126–127*
Homeland Security Act of 2002 *35, 371, 441*
horizontal surface *223, 224*

hot mix asphalt (HMA) *209–210, 336, 436*
hub and spoke *25, 26, 55*
human resources *174, 413, 552*
  department *78–79*
hydrant fuel system fee *499*

I

imaginary surfaces *163, 221, 223, 224*
Implementing Recommendations of the 9/11 Commission Act of 2007 *36, 379*
incentives *74, 415–416, 562*
Incident Command System (ICS) *362–363*
income statement *513–516, 518, 519*
income tax *514*
incompatible land use *246–248, 252, 253*
incumbent carriers *78, 415*
indemnification *467, 526*
indirect economic impacts *549*
induced economic impacts *549*
industry relations *444–448*
industry trade associations *444–447*
informal runway use program *82, 143, 472*
information circular *377*
information signs *123*
information systems *483*
information technology department *87*
inner portion of the approach surface drawing *163, 164, 168*
inspections
  See also self-inspection program, requirements
  construction *191, 195, 197–199*
  environmental *240*
  maintenance *323*
  Part 139 *285, 293, 429*
  property *463, 474*
  records *281, 299, 324*
  safety *436*
  security *378*
  self- *84, 281, 285, 287, 299, 301, 323, 436*
instrument approach *107, 111, 112, 204, 226*
instrument landing system (ILS) *107–111, 121, 286*
instrument meteorological conditions (IMC) *107*
insurance *228, 240, 465, 467, 468, 471, 474, 526–528*
Integrated Noise Model (INM) *251*
interest *538*
interest expense *513*
interest groups *409, 449–459*
interest income *513, 521*
International Air Transport Association (IATA) *146, 446*
International Civil Aviation Organization (ICAO) *229, 440, 442–443*
international commerce *78*
International Organization for Standardization (ISO) *239*
investing activities *516, 517, 518*
itinerant operations *59, 60*

J

joint-use airport *61, 62*
judgmental oversteering *206–207*

K

Kelly Act *16*
  See also Contract Air Mail Act of 1925

L

land and hold short lighting *113, 116, 117*
land and hold short operations (LAHSO) *116*
landing fees *147, 148, 247, 414, 415, 463, 464, 466, 498–499, 561*
land lease *465, 468, 471–478, 480, 482, 500, 507*
large hubs *28, 30, 33, 55–56, 77, 543*
Large Quantity Generators (LQGs) *263*
law enforcement officers (LEO) *37, 377, 378*
law resources *436–438*
Leadership in Energy and Environmental Design (LEED) *266, 267, 568*
leakage *74, 409, 412, 565–566*
leaking underground storage tanks (LUSTs) *263*
legal affairs department *79*
Legal Research Digests (LRD) *437*
letter of agreement (LOA) *85, 472*
letter of intent (LOI) *29, 541–542*
liabilities *509, 510, 512*
liability *526*
line-item budgeting *497*
line units *76*
load factors *26, 401, 498*
localizer directional aid (LDA) *110*
localizer (LOC) *107–110*
location signs *121*
long-term liabilities *512*
low-cost airlines *26, 27*
low-intensity runway lights (LIRL) *114*
lump sum budgeting *497*

M

maintenance *320–340*
  airside *325–336*
  department *86*
  equipment *324*
  landside *337*
  pavement *329–337*
  records *324–325*
  runway *326–328*
majority-in-interest (MII) *464*
mandatory instruction signs *121*
market expansion goal *396*
market focus goal *396*
marketing *390–417, 479, 519*
  department *86–87*
  expenses *513*

marketing mix *396, 399–408*
marketing plan *86, 173, 174, 395–408, 412*
characteristics of *411*
implementation *410–411*
market segmentation *399*
market share forecasting *179, 181*
mass marketing *400*
matching funds *537*
material safety data sheet (MSDS) *262, 443*
maximum takeoff weight (MTOW) *140, 245*
maximum throughput capacity *138–139*
media relations *366, 450*
medium hubs *28, 30, 33, 56–57, 537, 543*
medium-intensity runway lights (MIRL) *114*
memorandum of understanding (MOU) *85, 472*
mergers *561–562*
metropolitan aviation system plan *160*
microwave landing system (MLS) *111, 112*
midfield passenger terminal *213–214*
Military Airport Program (MAP) *31, 32, 545*
military operations areas (MOA) *104, 106*
minimum standards *23, 437, 469–471, 474*
minutes (Robert's Rules of Order) *430–431*
modification to standards *202, 563*
motion (Robert's Rules of Order) *430*
motivation *410*
movement areas *132–133, 133, 350*
driving on *356–357*
movement area training (MAT) *133, 282, 350, 356*
multiple target market approach *399*
multi-use airport *62*

N

National Airport Plan *20, 28*
National Airspace System Plan *103*
National Air Transportation Association (NATA) *447*
National Business Aviation Association (NBAA) *446*
National Civil Aviation Review Commission *32*
National Commission on Terrorist Attacks Upon the United States *35*
National Incident Management System (NIMS) *362*
National Plan of Integrated Airport Systems (NPIAS) *28, 53, 54, 60, 63, 157–159, 176, 178, 495, 544*
National Pollution Discharge Elimination System (NPDES) *254, 256*
National Response Center (NRC) *263*
National Transportation Safety Board (NTSB) *22, 439–441*
Go Team *440–441*
navigational aids (NAVAIDs) *107–113, 194, 196, 325*
protection of *301*
net profit *513, 514, 520*
net take-down ratio *521*
networking *91, 401, 405, 407, 444*
new business (Robert's Rules of Order) *430*
new large aircraft (NLA) *312–313, 562–563*
Next Generation (NextGen) *135–136, 142, 425*
noise compatibility plan (NCP) *242, 245–249, 545, 599*
noise compatibility program *28, 82, 249, 548*
noise exposure map (NEM) *242, 245–247, 251, 599*
non-aeronautical revenues *501–507, 562*
noncurrent assets *510, 511*
non-directional beacon (NDB) *110*
nonhub primary *57–58*
non-movement area boundary marking *128, 130*
non-movement areas *133–134*
non-operating revenues *507, 514, 521*
non-precision instrument approach *107, 224*
nonprimary commercial service *30, 58, 427*
non-signatory airline *464, 499*
notice of intent (NOI) *243*
notice of proposed rulemaking (NPRM) *431–432*
Notice to Airmen (NOTAM) *84, 195, 197, 292, 299, 304–305, 307, 434*
notice to proceed *192, 197, 200*

O

objectives *80, 172, 173, 239, 265, 396–399, 411, 412*
obstacle free zone (OFZ) *121, 122, 196, 204–205*
obstruction lights *117, 210, 325, 435, 468*
obstructions *117, 163, 203, 221, 223, 225, 286, 301, 437, 469*
Occupational Safety and Health Administration (OSHA) *443*
O&D *55, 503*
off-airport land use drawing *164*
old business (Robert's Rules of Order) *430*
oligopolistic *26*
omnibus spending bill *39*
on-airport land use drawing *164, 169*
operating activities *516, 517, 518*
operating budget *65, 494–495, 495*
operating expenses *71, 513, 513–515, 521, 522, 548*
operating ratio *521*
operations *274–314*
operations and maintenance (O&M) *88, 362, 508*
operations department *84*
organizational structure *75–77*
other transaction agreements (OTAs) *542*
owner's equity *509, 512*

P

parking *74, 211, 216, 325, 351, 501–503, 507, 552*
passenger facility charge (PFC) *29–30, 33, 40–41, 74, 162, 416, 446, 463, 508*
as source of capital development funding *537, 541, 542–543, 564*
assurances *432*
in financial statements *510, 511, 515, 517*
passenger retention *565*
paved areas, requirements *283–284*

pavement
See also flexible pavements; rigid pavements; *See also under* maintenance
design *209–210*
distress *331–336*
overlays *210*
pavement management program (PMP) *329–330*
pedestrian, requirements *194, 299–300, 351*
peer benchmarking *552*
performance-based budgeting *497*
performance management *80, 551–552*
personal protective equipment (PPE) *264, 265, 443*
personnel, requirements *282*
PFC-backed bond *541*
planning and development, department of *81–83*
Planning Grant Program (PGP) *23*
Portland cement concrete (PCC) *12, 209–210, 336, 435*
practical hourly capacity (PHCAP) *138*
prebid conference *192, 194, 227, 434*
precision approach path indicator (PAPI) *107, 119, 120, 433*
precision instrument approach *107, 224*
precision lightning warning system (PLWS) *366–367*
preconstruction conference *192, 194, 434*
predesign conference *192, 194, 434*
press kit *402–403*
press release *366, 403, 404, 407, 450*
preventive maintenance (PM) *323–324*
primary commercial service airport *54*
primary surface *223–224*
principal *538*
Private Charter Standard Security Program (PCSSP) *379*
private-use *40, 63*
privatization *72–75*
privilege fee *466, 503, 504, 507*
professional engineer *81, 255*
program plan budgeting *497*
prohibited areas *104, 106*
promotional mix *401, 405–407*
properties department *85*
public information department *80*
public-private partnership *64*
public protection, requirements *302, 349*
public relations (PR) *173, 366, 401–403, 448–452*
public-use *40, 53, 63, 66, 158, 222, 277, 425, 428, 476, 477*

Q

quality goal *397*

R

radio communications *130–133*
radio detection and ranging (RADAR) *102–103*
ramp control *131–133*
ramp control markings *128*
Record of Decision *74*
records, requirements *281–282*
Regional Airline Association (RAA) *447*
regional aviation system plan *159, 160*
regression analysis *162, 179*
regulatory agencies *438–443*
relievers *29, 59, 60, 427, 545*
rental cars *503, 507*
request for proposal (RFP) *83, 227*
request for qualifications (RFQ) *83, 227*
residual cost rate-making methodology *464, 466*
restricted areas *104, 106*
retail concessions *74, 481, 504*
return on assets ratio *520*
revenue bonds *63, 71, 523, 541*
revenue/cost-centered budgeting *497*
revenue diversion *71, 72, 414, 415, 437*
revenue passenger miles *9*
revenues *414, 482, 494–507*
rigid pavements *209, 329, 331–333, 336*
risk management *526–528*
Robert's Rules of Order *429–431*
rotating beacon *117, 339*
rules and regulations *350, 426, 465, 474–476, 478–479*
runway aiming point marking *124, 125*
runway and taxiway closure markings *129, 130*
runway blast pads *205*
runway bridge *210*
runway centerline lighting *115*
runway centerline marking *124–125*
runway departure surface drawing *164*
runway design code (RDC) *202, 562*
runway displaced threshold marking *124–125*
runway distance remaining signs *123*
runway edge marking *124–125*
runway end identifier lights (REIL) *119*
runway end lights *114*
runway guard lights (RGL) *115–116*
runway landing designator marking *124–125*
runway layouts *203*
runway markings *124–126*
runway object free area (ROFA) *196, 205*
runway occupancy time (ROT) *142, 207*
runway rubber removal *326–328*
runway safety area (RSA) *122, 126, 196, 204, 205, 208, 220*
runway shoulder *126, 205*
runway shoulder marking *126*
runway threshold marking *124–125*
runway touchdown zone marking *124–125*
runway visual range (RVR) *109, 202*

S

safety *17, 19, 349–366, 426*
  public *85*
safety areas, requirements *285, 350*
safety assurance *358, 359, 361*
safety management system (SMS) *357–361, 437, 443*
safety plan compliance document (SPCD) *194–198, 351*
safety promotion *358, 359, 361*
safety risk management (SRM) *194, 358–361, 437, 552*
safety training *85, 197, 359, 361*
satellite passenger terminal *213*
scheduled operations *38, 278*
security *367–383*
security directive *84, 374, 377, 442*
Security Guidelines for General Aviation Airports *39, 380*
Security Identification Display Area (SIDA) *282, 350, 356, 373–375*
  badge *374, 375*
self-benchmarking *552*
self-fueling *437, 473, 475–476*
self-inspection program, requirements *298–299*
sensitive security information (SSI) *372, 373, 380*
sequence flashing lights *118, 119*
shareholder's equity *509, 512*
signatory airline *464, 465, 499, 503*
simple linear terminal *211–212*
simplified directional facility (SDF) *111*
simulation modeling *180*
single target market approach *399*
slot *139, 145–148*
Small Community Air Service Development Program *405, 416*
small hubs *28, 30, 57, 77*
Small Quantity Generators (SQGs) *263*
snow and ice control plan (SICP) *287*
snow and ice control, requirements *287–289*
social media *86, 87, 399, 406, 452*
special use airspace *106*
spending bill *39*
Spill Prevention, Control and Countermeasure (SPCC) *255*
staff units *76–77*
stakeholders *162, 394, 397–399, 413*
state aviation systems plans *159*
State Block Grant Program *32, 33, 427–428, 537*
statement of cash flows *516–518*
statement of changes in equity *518*
statement of net assets. *See* balance sheet
statements of revenues, expenses, and changes in net assets. *See* income statement
stop bars *115*
stopway *126, 205*
stopway edge lights *114*
stormwater pollution prevention plan (SWPPP) *256*
strategic business plan *82, 175, 397, 399*
strategic plan *171–175*
subsidies *16, 24, 25, 413–415*
surface painted apron entrance point sign *128*
surface painted gate destination sign *128*
surface painted holding position sign *127*
surface painted taxiway direction sign *128–129*
surface painted taxiway location sign *128–129*
sustainability *265–266, 567–568*
sustained capacity *138*
SWOT analysis *171, 172, 174, 396, 398–399*

T

tactical air navigation (TACAN) *111*
target-based budgeting *497*
target markets *396, 399–400*
tax-exempt bonds *71, 542*
taxiway bridge *210*
taxiway centerline lights *115, 116, 210*
taxiway centerline markings *126–127*
taxiway design group (TDG) *202, 206*
taxiway edge lights *113, 114, 210*
taxiway edge marking *126–127*
taxiway edge reflectors *114–115*
taxiway ending marker *122*
taxiway layouts *206–208*
taxiway markings *126–128*
taxiway shoulder marking *127*
tenants, interacting with *478–479*
terminal area forecast (TAF) *162, 176, 178*
terminal area plan *163, 167*
Terminal Instrument Procedures (TERPS) *226*
terms and conditions *465, 471, 473–474*
T-hangars *64*
threshold end lights *114*
through-the-fence operations *476–477*
time series model forecasting *180–181*
total passengers *54*
total suspended solids (TSS) *258*
touchdown zone lights *115*
traditional budgeting *497*
traffic indicators, requirements *296*
training *89–90, 282, 303, 363*
  See also under aircraft rescue and firefighting; *See also* movement area training; safety training
  emergency preparedness *363*
  of fueling personnel *295, 352, 355*
  records *281, 294, 295, 299, 300, 324*
  requirements *255, 299*
  SIDA *350*
transfer passengers *55, 215*
transitional surface *223*
Transportation Security Administration (TSA) *33–35, 37, 41, 368, 371–373, 377, 441*
  baggage screening *378, 542*
  passenger screening *369–370, 378*
  security guidelines for GA airports *380*
transporter *215*
turret *291, 433*

U

uncontrollable variables *408*
underground storage tanks (USTs) *255, 263–264*
underwriter *538*
unfunded mandates *40, 564–565*
unmanned aircraft system (UAS) *569–570*
unpaved areas, requirements *284*
unscheduled operations *38, 278*
utility drawing *165*

V

variable expenses *496*
variance report *495, 496*
vehicle roadway markings *128–129*
vehicle roadway signs *123*
very high frequency omnidirectional range (VOR) *111, 128*
Vision 100—Century of Aviation Reauthorization Act of 2003 *35, 537, 544*
visual approach *107*
visual approach slope indicator (VASI) *107, 119, 120*
visual meteorological conditions (VMC) *107, 140*
vote (Robert's Rules of Order) *430*

W

warning area *104, 106*
water quality *254–258*
Wide Area Augmentation System (WAAS) *112*
wildlife attractant *309, 482*
wildlife hazard management *308–312*
wildlife strike *298, 302, 311–312*
wind direction indicators, requirements *296*
Works Progress Administration (WPA) *13, 18*
World War I *14*
World War II *19*
Wright brothers *10–11, 13*

Z

zero-based budgeting *497*
zoning *164, 252–253*